Lord Hope's Diaries

House of Lords
1996–2009

Other titles in this series

Senior Counsel 1978–1986 (2017)
Dean of Faculty 1986–1989 (2018)
Lord President 1989–1996 (2018)

Forthcoming title in this series

UK Supreme Court 2009–2013

Lord Hope's Diaries

House of Lords
1996–2009

by
Lord Hope of Craighead

Avizandum Publishing Ltd
Edinburgh
2018

Published by
Avizandum Publishing Ltd
25 Candlemaker Row
Edinburgh EH1 2QG

First published 2018
Reprinted 2019

© Lord Hope of Craighead 2018

ISBN 978-1-904968-96-2

British Library Cataloguing in Publication Data
A catalogue entry for this book is available from the British Library

All rights reserved. No part of this publication may be reproduced, stored in a retrieval system, or transmitted in any form or by any means, electronic, mechanical, photocopying, recording or otherwise, without the written permission of the copyright holder. Application for the copyright owner's permission to reproduce any part of this publication should be addressed to the publisher.

Typeset by Hewer Text UK Ltd, Edinburgh
Printed and bound by Martins the Printers, Berwick-upon-Tweed

Preface to the London Diaries

For many years I had been keeping a diary to record what my wife and I, with our growing family, had been doing during our holidays. I had not thought it worth extending this to record my activities as an advocate while I was in practice at the Junior Bar. But when I took silk in July 1976 I decided, without any clear idea of where this might lead, to keep a working-time diary. I knew that taking silk was bound to lead to a change in my career, and I thought that I would be likely to have more time for keeping a diary than I had had in my latter days as a busy junior. So I began to write, in manuscript of course, in an 8 by 5 inch, 140-page, all-weather cover Aldwych notebook. I used a fountain pen throughout, as the pen ran more easily over the page and was more suited to the quite narrow lining of this series of notebooks. This was no hardship, as my practice was to use a fountain pen when writing my opinions and when taking notes in court. Electronic means were not available, and by the time they were it was too late for me to change my ways. So I stuck to handwriting, although I had begun by the mid-1990s to use a PC for most of my written work including judgments. In the end, by the time of my retirement, my handwritten diary entries occupied thirteen of these notebooks. All the various stages of my career from 1976 to 2013, when I reached my judicial retirement age, are recorded in these pages.

It was never my intention to make an entry in my notebook every day. I wrote only when there was something worth writing about, as I looked back over the events of the past week or immediately after some happening that compelled me to write about it. The entries varied in length according to the time available and the subject matter. Sometimes there was simply too much else to do, so there are from time to time some quite long gaps before I was able to record what had happened. But I tried not to miss anything out, and the overall effect is to provide the reader with an unfolding narrative as one event leads on to another. As I was writing only for myself, with no idea that what I was writing would ever be published, there are moments of despair here as well as moments of triumph or elation. There were times when it was a struggle to keep going, as the pressures of work bore down upon me. Writing frankly and self-critically about these moments came as a relief to me. On these occasions resorting to the diary was not only a habit. It became a kind of confessional. There were other times when the extreme good fortune that has blessed my career prompted me to record the more extraordinary events in which I have been involved in as much detail as possible so that I could relive these moments again in the future. This has produced a contemporary record of unrepeatable moments in a world that was, in so many respects, very different from that in which we now live. I could never have recaptured them had I been relying only upon my memory.

The work on which I was involved, first as an advocate and then as a judge, brought me into contact with many people. Many of my contemporaries at the Scottish Bar and on the Court of Session Bench are mentioned in the earlier volumes of my diary. Then, as the focus of attention moved to my life in London, I found myself in the company of some of the finest judges of our time who were sitting with me as Law Lords. References to them by name, with character descriptions from time to time, are an essential part of the narrative. As the entries show, there were happy and amusing times which it was a privilege to share with them, and there were times of disagreement and tension too. My various descriptions of them fall into that pattern. This will, I hope, add colour to what was seen in public and can be detected from their published judgments. I have done my best to edit out those passages that should be kept private and to delete things that are best forgotten, of which in the event there were very few. That apart, what one finds in these pages is an account of the life which I shared with them, reproduced almost exactly as I wrote about it at the time.

From time to time national and international events seemed to me to be worth recording too. It was not my intention to maintain a complete record. I was not writing as a historian but as someone who had many other things on his mind. So what one finds in these records are no more than glimpses of what was happening. But they do provide a background to the life that I was leading as events unfolded around me. As bird-watching has been one of my greatest pleasures, I also found time to include a few notes about birds seen in my garden or in the streets which I thought were of particular interest. These notes may prove to be more interesting than I had anticipated, as changes in our climate lead to the disappearance of some species from the places where I saw them during my time.

Family life does not feature much in these diaries. This was a record of my working life, not life at home or while we were on holiday. I kept a separate dairy for our holidays together, which are packed with all the fun and sense of adventure that we shared when at our cottage at Craighead and when travelling abroad. My wife Mary, to whom I owe so much, and our children William, James and Lucy, do make appearances in these pages from time to time. But I have omitted from this published version my descriptions of some of the more intimate events, both happy and sad, that we have shared together as our lives have unfolded. The time I spent writing my diary was time, it could perhaps be said, which I ought to have been sharing with the family. On the other hand most of these entries were written late in the evening in my study before bedtime or in spare moments when I might otherwise have been working.

The idea of publishing these diaries came to me quite late, after my retirement from the UK Supreme Court. It had occurred to me, on looking back, that my handwritten text might be worth converting into something that others could read more easily. Then I was invited by Kenneth Pritchard, the Chairman of the Clark Foundation, to deliver a series of three lectures in Edinburgh to follow the Foundation's sponsorship of the outstanding series of lectures on aspects of the Disruption of 1843 which had given by Lord Rodger of Earlsferry at Aberdeen University in May 2007. In search of a subject, I decided to base my Jean Clark Memorial Lectures which were given at Edinburgh University in November 2013 on some of the material in my diaries. There were three lectures, about my time as Dean of the Faculty of Advocates, as Lord President of the Court of Session and as a Lord of Appeal in Ordinary in London. Bringing the existence of the diaries out into the open in this way brought me into contact with Professor Kenneth Reid of Edinburgh University, who encouraged me to take the idea of their publication seriously.

The first step, of course, was to prepare a transcript. For that I needed the help of an audio-typist, a person not easily found in the modern digital age. Mrs Jackie Batten, who had been Kenneth Pritchard's secretary and audio typist when he was Secretary to the Law Society of Scotland, agreed to undertake this work. It turned out to be a very time-consuming business both for her and for me. Starting in July 2014, I read out what was in the diaries onto tapes which I then sent to her for typing. She converted what I read into a series of electronically produced texts which she returned to me by email. It took us to December 2016 to complete the task. I owe an immense debt of gratitude to her for undertaking this work so faithfully over so many months, and to the Trustees of the Clark Foundation for meeting the cost of her doing so.

These books could not have been published without the encouragement and support of both Kenneth Reid and Kenneth Pritchard, to whom I wish to express my profound gratitude. I am most grateful to the publishers, Avizandum, for agreeing to publish what for them has been a project that lay outside their normal run of work. I am most grateful too for all the sustained and infinitely painstaking work that Margaret Cherry has done on their behalf to bring these books forward to publication. And I must, above all, express my thanks to my family who have lived with me through all the ups and downs in my career and have supported me so generously all the way.

David Hope
October 2018

The House of Lords

Under the system which still existed when I moved to London from Edinburgh the court of final appeal for all three jurisdictions in the United Kingdom was the Appellate Committee of the House of Lords. It was composed of 12 Lords of Appeal in Ordinary. They received life peerages under the Appellate Jurisdiction Act 1876 on their appointment if they were not already members of the House of Lords. There had always been at least one Law Lord from Scotland since the commencement of that Act. In 1913 the number was raised to two, and it had remained at that number by convention ever since then. Two vacancies were created by the retirements in 1996 of Lord Keith of Kinkel and Lord Jauncey of Tullichettle. As they were both from Scotland Lord Clyde and I were invited to take their places. There had been no judge from Northern Ireland since 1994.

For a judge from Scotland or from Northern Ireland accepting an appointment to sit as a member of the Appellate Committee of the House of Lords had quite profound consequences. In the first place I had to decide where I was to live. Some of my predecessors, such as Lord Reid and Lord Keith of Kinkel, had left Scotland on their appointment and moved their residences to England, although Lord Keith kept a holiday cottage in Scotland. Others, such as Lord Guest, Lord Fraser of Tullybelton and Lord Jauncey of Tullichettle, travelled to London each week from their homes in Scotland. For me and my family there was only one option. My home was in Scotland, so I decided to travel. In my case this meant leaving home late afternoon on Sunday and returning home late on Thursday evening. It also meant finding and paying for a place to live during the week while I was in London. Then there was the fact that I had to adjust myself to working with a legal system with which I was unfamiliar. The same was, of course, true for my English colleagues when they were asked to sit on an appeal from Scotland. But by far the greater volume of appeals to the House of Lords was from the Court of Appeal of England and Wales, and appeals to the Judicial Committee of the Privy Council, of which I was to become a member too, were from jurisdictions whose systems of law were based on English common law. I was, however, joining a group of lawyers each of whom came from different backgrounds and had different skills. We drew strength from the fact that we were expected to work as a team, playing to the expertise which we could each bring to bear on the cases we were dealing with.

I was conscious of the responsibility which rested on the Scottish Law Lords to ensure so far as possible that Scottish cases were decided according to the principles and practices of Scots law. I hoped that retaining my home in Scotland and returning there each weekend would help me to keep in touch with those principles and practices and with public opinion in Scotland. I also looked forward to taking advantage of any opportunities there might be for the cross-fertilisation of ideas to and from the legal systems on either side of the border.

1996 – October to December

5 October 1996

This is the end of the first week in my new job as a Lord of Appeal in Ordinary.

Last Monday I attended a Law Society of Scotland conference in Edinburgh on 'Crime and Punishment'. The topic was Michael Forsyth's White Paper of that name in which many of the so-called reforms of criminal justice in Scotland were, without discussion or consultation, taken as read. Only a few details were put out for views. James Douglas-Hamilton, the Minister of State, put up a typically stoical defence of his intransigent leader, but nobody was much impressed. My contribution – my last speech as Lord President before, as I put it, 'slipping quietly across the border' to take up my new appointment – was inevitably critical.[1] It drew what *The Herald* described next day as 'thunderous applause' from the audience. John McCluskey delivered an amusing speech, supporting the same general line. How odd, after for so long feeling uneasy at his public utterances, that I should find myself at the end of my career so much in sympathy with his views. Such is the nature of Michael Forsyth's method of government, heavily tinged by red-toothed politics. The press loved it.

That evening Mary and I were collected by a government car, for the last time as I will no longer have access to the Government Car Service when I move south, from our home in India Street and taken to the airport for our 8pm Shuttle to London. Paul Cullen, the Solicitor General for Scotland, was on the same flight and Bruce Kerr passed us in the lounge on his way home from London. So we were not moving south unobserved. We spent the night as usual in the Caledonian Club to which we have been so often allocated.[2] Next day, 1 October, was the day of the Opening of the Legal Year and the Lord Chancellor's Breakfast. James Clyde was there for the first time, and it was surely James Mackay's last time as Lord Chancellor. We were both in Westminster Abbey for the annual service for the judges. After the Breakfast, which seemed very full even in the space of Westminster Hall, I took James Clyde up to the Law Lords' Corridor which is on the second floor of the west front of the Palace of Westminster. There he met various people who were new to him. Everything in the Palace is in a state of unreadiness, not to say near chaos, as so much work of repair and conversion is being undertaken during the last weeks of the recess. James's room is not ready, and my room at the end of the Corridor – referred to as the *forum non conveniens*, as it is so remote from the other rooms – was only just habitable. It had been Lord Slynn's room until the end of last July and is full of empty bookshelves with no wall space at all. It will take some time and effort to make it habitable. There was a meeting in the

---

1 See fns 17–19 below.
2 As Lord President I had been granted honorary membership of the Club.

afternoon chaired by the new Senior Lord of Appeal, Lord Goff,[3] at which we discussed various administrative details. It transpired that Gordon Slynn is seriously ill. We are in any event one man short, as no replacement has yet been chosen for Lord Woolf.[4] It is clear that we are in for a very busy time.

Next day, Wednesday, we began our hearings with an appeal from Northern Ireland called *O'Hara v Chief Constable of the RUC*[5] which, as Parliament is still in recess, we heard in the Chamber. It was an interesting mixture of formality and informality. The mace was carried in and laid on the Woolsack. Then we, the five Law Lords who were to sit together, had prayers said for us and the clerk at the table by a bishop in an otherwise empty Chamber. For the first time the Princess of Wales was omitted from the list of members of the Royal Family following her divorce from the Prince of Wales. After prayers we went to small tables close to the Bar and counsel, the Queen's Counsel among whom were wearing long wigs, were called in. The hearing was completed in one day, and we discussed it in Robert Goff's room afterwards. It was a short point about the test for reasonable grounds for suspicion in the context of police powers of arrest. I was not surprised when I was asked to write the judgment, as it was in my field and a good one with which to start. As a result I was able to change my travel plans and take the 3pm BA Shuttle home to Edinburgh on the Thursday instead of the 8pm. 'Shuttle' is the name that BA have given to this service, which is modelled on that provided by US airlines between New York and Washington – an hourly timetable, with no pre-booking required and a stand-by aircraft available should every seat on the assigned aircraft be taken.

The morning of Thursday was spent in a meeting about one of last summer's Privy Council cases which had been causing us difficulty. Then I had a long session with my secretary Marilyn Byatt, whom I am to share with Gordon Slynn. I tried to sort out the library I have been given a little bit, but it is a huge and very dusty task. After a quick lunch in the staff canteen just off Westminster Hall I departed for Heathrow by Underground. I got there just in time, only five minutes before the flight was called. I was home by 4.45pm. I settled down to revise a pile of Criminal Appeal Court draft *ex tempore* opinions which are the residue of my last week's work in Edinburgh as Lord Justice General and was fully occupied until bedtime. So what amounted to the weekend for me began on the Friday, when the Law Lords do not sit but was always a working day for my court in Edinburgh. I devoted that day to finishing my work as Lord Justice General. Today, Saturday, I have spent writing my speech in *O'Hara*, with which I am far from satisfied. I felt disorientated, stateless in

---

3 His predecessor as Senior Law Lord had been Lord Keith, who had retired on 30 September after holding that position for ten years. The fact that a Law Lord from Scotland had held it for so long, as this was determined only by the seniority of the individual's appointment to the House of Lords as was the case for any other committee, was said not to have been welcomed by the English Law Lords. It was felt that Lord Goff's assumption of this position was long overdue.
4 Lord Woolf had retired as a Lord of Appeal in Ordinary on his appointment as Master of the Rolls.
5 [1997] AC 286.

a sense. The Lord President is now Alan Rodger, and time has moved on so rapidly that I am already a thing of the past in Edinburgh. 'The King is dead – long live the King', said Mary, who had attended Alan's installation as Lord President earlier in the week and Bill Nimmo Smith's installation as a Senator of the College of Justice the next day. Yet I am very content in London – relaxed and happy. How lucky I am that I at least have a job to do after my retirement as Lord President.

11 October 1996

The case for the week was an interesting but really very simple one about a salvage contract which provided for remuneration in the event of success in preventing or minimising danger to the environment. It all turned on the effect of the words 'a fair rate' of remuneration in an international salvage Convention which had been incorporated into the contract. *Semco v Lancer Navigation*[6] is the name of the case. The argument took two and a half days. As was the case last week, it was heard in the Chamber as the House is for all other purposes still in recess. What would usually have been a hearing by the Appellate Committee in a committee room upstairs was therefore convened as a hearing in the Chamber by the House itself, with a mace on the Woolsack and prayers said by a bishop before we sat. As the Lord Chancellor was presiding, each day began with his arrival fully robed and wigged, preceded by the mace. Prayers were then said, after which he removed his robes and wig and proceeded with the rest of us to the tables at the Bar of the House. Unlike us, he was dressed in court jacket, bands. breeches, tights and buckled shoes. The rest of us – Lords Goff, Mustill, Lloyd and myself – were in suits as usual.

It was a formidable experience sitting with James Mackay in charge. He made no concessions for me as his former pupil, nor did he give any sign of recognition that this might be treated as a special occasion. I suspect that he felt happier to be at a distance in view of the press treatment of my dispute with Michael Forsyth.[7] So it was a professional, dispassionate encounter. I felt that I held my own in the questions which I put, and that I had an answer quite early on to most of the issues in dispute. I took some time over my summing up in the end, speaking first as was required of me as the junior member of the team. Tony Lloyd said that it was a superb job, but how genuinely he meant this remark I cannot say. No one gives any tuition in these things. One has to find one's own level and one's own methods. We are all agreed about the result. James seemed rather nonchalant at the end about who was to write the judgment[8] until he was reminded about this by Robert Goff. It was his task, as the presider, to decide whom to choose for this task. Michael Mustill, who has had much to do in salvage cases, volunteered.

---

6 *Semco Salvage and Marine Pte Ltd v Lancer Navigation Co Ltd* [1997] AC 455.
7 About mandatory life sentences: see fns 17 and 18 below.
8 The convention was that this was a matter for decision by the presider.

I had a rather frustrating time with Marilyn Byatt, my charming and dutiful but hard-pressed secretary. I had given her my judgment in *O'Hara* to type first thing on Monday. But nothing appeared that day or by lunchtime on Tuesday, despite very little else from me. So I asked her to circulate an unrevised draft at the end of the day. She achieved this, but I felt that I was treading on her toes. Johan Steyn, and perhaps also Michael Mustill, will have points to raise so I thought that my draft should go out quickly. But here again there is little tuition about what to do. Part of the problem may be due to the fact that Marilyn is Gordon Slynn's secretary too, and he has hardly ever written a judgment. Almost all of his work for her, which is voluminous and takes up almost all of her time, seems to be extra-judicial. She was remarkably nervous about doing the draft for me, perhaps because it was so out of the ordinary for her.

On Wednesday afternoon at 4.30pm the Lords of Appeal in Ordinary went to the Lord Chancellor's magnificent room beside the river at his invitation to discuss the choice of successor to Harry Woolf. Tom Bingham, the Lord Chief Justice, and Harry Woolf himself, as the Master of the Rolls, were there also, as was Tom Legg, the Lord Chancellor's Permanent Secretary. When asked for his view first, Tom Bingham was unequivocal. He had only one name and, to my delight, it was that of Brian Hutton who has been Lord Chief Justice of Northern Ireland since 1988. Harry Woolf agreed, and a number of the English Lords spoke to the same effect. But the tone of the discussion changed when Tony Lloyd said that Brian was not of the required standard and hinted that others in Northern Ireland might be. This opened up the field, and various English names were suggested, Peter Millett, Robin Auld, Mark Saville and Nicholas Phillips LJJ being the main contenders. Two other names were suggested. They were not thought to be strong candidates, but much praise was given to the achievements and calibre of the other four. It was a frank discussion, and rather awesome. When asked at the end for my view, I suggested that time was not on Brian Hutton's side in view of his age and I offered general support to his appointment. As we left Michael Nolan and I reflected on the fact that our names must have gone through the same process.

It seems very likely that when James minutes the Prime Minister he will recommend Brian Hutton. I am very pleased. I appreciate Tony Lloyd's point about standards, although I did not say so. But the fact is that Brian has held office as Lord Chief Justice for quite long enough, and at 65 he clearly deserves the appointment and we need someone from Northern Ireland. I have to say that the fact that I have been given preferment over him has been troubling me for some time. I would find it much easier to see my own career in perspective if he were to be elevated now.

I went to Gray's Inn, of which I have been an Honorary Bencher since I became Lord President, on Thursday morning. I met the Treasurer, Conrad Deyn, for 30 minutes to discuss an initiative which the Inn is taking with the French Bar's education scheme. I then went with Mr Lush, the estate surveyor, to view the flat at 7 Gray's Inn Square for which I have applied. It is on the top floor, and quite small. It has one bedroom, a sitting room, a bathroom and kitchen. I have no great hopes of being successful, and I tried not to allow myself to be too hopeful or too impressed. It was bright – white and magnolia are the colours, and the views are open and attractive on both sides over gardens, north and south. It is however entirely unfurnished, and clearly a lot of work would be required to make it habitable. At lunch I sat next to Martin Collins QC and opposite Mark Waller, just promoted to the Court of Appeal. Peter Cresswell, a former Chairman of the Bar, came in as I was about to leave. I fear that I may have been too abrupt in getting up to greet him and exchange a few words. My fears were enhanced when I saw from *Who's Who* that Martin Collins is chairman of the Management Committee which deals with the allocation of flats when they become vacant. It is so difficult to move without hazard in a world to which I am so new.

I did, however, receive a most charming welcome to the Law Lords' Corridor from Lord Wilberforce, now long retired but still a frequent visitor. He has always been remarkably kind to me – remarking once long ago to James Mackay that I would go far. He clasped my hand most warmly and said how very pleased he was to see me in my new position. It was so good of him to take such trouble to say what he did and to offer me his support.

19 October 1996

It has been a difficult week, as I had a sore throat and a cough which hung around me and gradually cleared only to return again this weekend. But the business was interesting and enjoyable. We had a three-day appeal on the question of whether there was a remedy of damages at common law, independent of the fixed sums payable under the Warsaw Convention of 1929, for British Airways passengers who were claiming compensation for losses due to the fact that they had been landed at Kuwait Airport at the start of the Gulf War and detained there by the Iraqi forces who had taken over the airport before they could get away. There were two cases – *Abnett* from Scotland and *Sidhu* from England.[9] We sat in armchairs in Committee Room 1 as Parliament had resumed. For us it was very comfortable. As the junior member, my view was towards the river. On the slightly curved table around which we sat we were provided with notebooks, some writing materials and a glass of water on top of which a card had been placed, presumably to keep out any dust. We each had a trolley beside us in which were several volumes of law reports to which reference was expected to be made during the argument. Colin McEachran and Derek Emslie appeared in the Scots case. I was asked by Nicolas Browne-Wilkinson to write the judgment when it was over. This will be quite a task, especially as there is no unanimity about the reasons for our unanimous view that the appeals should be dismissed. No other Supreme Court has grappled with this issue, so it will be an important judgment and it will take some time

---

9 *Abnett v British Airways plc, Sidhu v British Airways plc* [1997] AC 430, 1997 SC (HL) 26.

to produce. On Thursday we had a hopeless appeal in the Judicial Committee of the Privy Council from Mauritius. It was over by midday. So I was able to get the 4pm Shuttle home.

James Clyde was made a Privy Counsellor on Tuesday, and he was introduced to the House of Lords on Wednesday. I was able to watch his introduction as we took time off from sitting in the *Abnett* case so that all the Lords of Appeal could attend. James chose Harry Woolf and Lennie Hoffmann to be his supporters, a nice choice, but interesting also that he was clearly not inclined to follow the Scottish tradition of choosing Scots as supporters. There is a strong independent streak in his make-up, which makes it rather unlikely that we shall be close to each other. He plans to travel by rail. I go by air. He wants to live out of the Inns, while I am still hopeful that Gray's Inn will give me a place in which to live. But he took the oath of allegiance in a very loud, firm voice and looked very fine indeed. The patent which was read out in his case was interesting, as it differs quite significantly from those used for everyone else except the Lords Spiritual which was given to me when I was appointed a life peer in 1995. His patent declared that he had been appointed as a Lord of Appeal under the Appellate Jurisdiction Act 1874 'so long as he behave himself', and that he had the right to a salary. He was appointed to fill the vacancy created by Harry Keith's retiral. I was invited to join him and Ann for tea at the Lord Chancellor's office so that we could receive our patents from him together. But unfortunately we were locked into our discussion in *Abnett* in our committee room at the critical time, from which I could not escape.

There was a dinner for me and Alan Rodger in the New Club back in Edinburgh yesterday evening which was given by the Scottish industrial appeal tribunal chairmen. This was an informal and very pleasant occasion. Today, Saturday, I attended a seminar at Edinburgh University, hosted by the Scottish Law Commission, on constructive trusts. This is a very topical subject, as *Sharp v Thomson*[10] is to be heard in the Lords next week. I cannot sit on that appeal, of course, as I dealt with the case as Lord President. There is much nervousness in Scotland about what the Lords will do, as there is unlikely to be more than one Scot on the Appellate Committee and I am not sure how dedicated James Clyde is to the principles on which our decision in the Inner House was based. There were many friends present, judicial, academic and from the Bar. It was fun to be in circulation again in such company.

27 October 1996

We had an interesting case about nuisance, arising out of the building of the Canary Wharf Tower which has interfered with television reception in the area.[11] Robert Goff was in the chair and Tony Lloyd, Lennie Hoffmann and Robin Cooke were the other members of the Committee. Lennie was in his

---

10 1997 SC (HL) 66.
11 *Hunter v Canary Wharf Ltd* [1997] AC 655.

element – property law is clearly one of his favourite subjects, and Robert was most impressive, searching in his gentle but uncompromising way for the appropriate guidance in principle. Tony was quiet and so was Robin, except near the end when he began to warm to ideas which quite clearly were out of tune with the other members of the Committee. In our summing-up I was the second to speak as Robin was sitting as the junior member, so I had to disagree with him on almost every point. But I knew that Lennie was with me, and so broadly speaking were the other two. Robert will write what I know will be a superb and most interesting judgment.

Proceedings were interrupted for a day by the State Opening of Parliament. As I had not booked a set of robes, which I would have had to do to be allowed to sit in the Chamber, I was free to wander around and look at what was happening elsewhere. The Grenadier Guards in greatcoats set up a guard of honour across the street from our windows, and with Lennie and James Clyde I then had the fun of watching the arrival of the State Procession – a Sovereign's escort of the Blues and Royals, and Her Majesty and the Prince of Wales[12] in the State Coach. The horses were magnificent, and they remained drawn up just below my window after the arrival until the ceremony itself was over and it was time for Her Majesty to return to Buckingham Palace. Meantime James and I went down to the Peers' Lobby, where there were no restrictions on where we could go. We had a splendid view of Black Rod marching down from the House of Lords to the Commons and returning with Madam Speaker, Betty Boothroyd, followed by the Cabinet and Shadow Cabinet and a large number of MPs. There was no room for them all at the Bar of the House, so many remained in the Lobby where we watched the Queen's Speech on television. At 12.15pm, when it was all over and various wealthy peers were settling down to expensive lunches, James and I went to the River Room where we were guests at a reception given by the Lord Chancellor, with the other Law Lords and their spouses and others connected with the law. They included the High Court and Court of Appeal judges who had been at the Opening and some friends of the Mackays who had watched the Opening as his guests. It was a very enjoyable reception. I met Lord Wilberforce again, who told me that it was he who had insisted on the practice of conferring at the table when hearings before the Appellate Committee were concluded. He said that up to then all that happened was that they stood in the Corridor for no more than the length of time it took for Lord Reid, his predecessor as Senior Law Lord, to smoke a cigarette. I said how impressed I was by the valuable practice, and how seriously it was taken by us all. In the evening I was a guest at a reception at the Scottish Office in Dover House to launch the Scottish Poppy Appeal. Admiral Livesay, known to us of old when he was at Rosyth as FOSNI,[13] was the President. Michael and Susan Forsyth were our hosts – a somewhat uncertain relationship, as I had had to protest so much about his sentencing policy when I was

---

12 The Duke of Edinburgh was absent that year due to illness.
13 Flag Officer for Scotland and Northern Ireland.

Lord President. George Robertson MP, Jim Wallace MP and Charles Robertson were there also, and a mixture of other Scottish personalities – Sheena McDonald of ITV, the Earl of Mar and Kellie, Russell Hillhouse and others. It was nice to be back in Dover House.

In my absence from Edinburgh the placards of *The Evening News* that evening proclaimed 'Top Judge in Gay Award'. I had apparently been nominated as one of the five candidates for an award for services to the gay community because of an opinion which I wrote in the summer as Lord President in support of an application for the adoption of a disabled child by a gay man who was living with another man in a stable relationship.[14] The article in *The Evening News*, which was accompanied by a photograph of me showing me in my criminal robes as Lord Justice General and not in my civil robes as Lord President, was sympathetic. It commented on the value of the opinion and the significance of a Scot being nominated for the award: the Michael Rhodes Award. It is, of course, out of the question for me to accept it. But I shall have to be tactful, as it would not be wise or fair to give offence. I do not want to be used for that kind of publicity. But I do not want, either, to be thought to be insincere in the views which I expressed in my opinion in that case.

On Friday I was delighted to hear from David Machin, the under-treasurer at Gray's Inn, that the Management Committee had decided to make the flat at 7 Gray's Inn Square available to me. This is a great step forward. I have been suppressing all my sense of expectation so heavily that it is still taking time for this news to sink in. Mary was marvellously enthusiastic. She is to travel down to London on Monday next week and, as I have leave of absence for this for the following two weeks, we shall spend much of our time trying to set it up for me to live in. It is completely unfurnished. It will be worth making the place really comfortable.

5 November 1996

Last week was taken up with two cases in the Appellate Committee. One was about whether the owners were entitled to compensation for the refusal of listed building consent for the removal of chimney breasts from a corner site in Piccadilly.[15] It was largely dependent upon the proper application of the statutory definitions of 'building' and 'listed building'. I suggested early on a solution to the case which had not surfaced in the Court of Appeal, whose decision seemed odd and very technical. Robin Cooke was again out on a limb, but Tony Lloyd and Nico Browne-Wilkinson agreed with me. 'I am a David Hope man', proclaimed Nico at the end of the discussion after the argument. As a result I am to write the leading judgment. The other case was about local authority funding for the assessment of a child and its unmarried parents for residential

---

14 See *T, Petitioner* 1997 SLT 724.
15 *Shimizu (UK) Ltd v Westminster City Council* [1997] 1 WLR 168.

care, and the powers of the court to order the assessment.[16] It was my first introduction to the Children Act 1989, whose principles are similar to the recently enacted Children (Scotland) Act 1995 but whose court-based structure is very different. Statutory interpretation was at the heart of this case also. I was the junior member of the Committee this time. I based my summing-up on the principle that welfare of the child was the first consideration and supported the decision of the judge who ordered the assessment. Donald Nicholls then said that he agreed with almost everything I had said – at which Tony Lloyd, sitting next to me, hissed 'well done' in my ear.

I had a hurried getaway from the hearing, as I had a dinner to attend in Edinburgh. To make the dinner, which was to be given by the BBC at the New Club for the new Chairman of the Governors, Sir Christopher Bland – the successor to Marmaduke Hussey – I had to get the 6pm Shuttle. For a time it looked as if I would be lucky to get the 7pm, and might even miss that one too. But I did get the 6pm, and walked through the door to join the party precisely at 8pm. The dinner itself was most enjoyable. I was placed next to Sir Christopher, who was impressive in the discussion afterwards – very calm, thoughtful, well-informed and articulate. Many familiar faces were there. Jim Naughtie, the BBC Today programme presenter from north-east Scotland, was on my left. He was cheerful but self-contained and not easy to penetrate.

Meantime, during the week, Mary paid a day visit to 7 Gray's Inn Square. She travelled south by the 6am train and took the 12 noon train home the next day. To my relief and delight she was charmed by the flat. She met Mr Lush and the contractor, and in her typically open and enthusiastic manner clearly struck up a very good relationship with them. She is determined to make a family home there, which is a marvellous contribution to our future together in this new life.

I spent yesterday in Edinburgh at a Family Mediation Service conference at which I acted all day as the conference chairman. And I spent today, as I had done last Sunday, writing a lecture which I am to deliver for the Howard League Scotland at the end of this month. So these have been busy days. There will be much to do in the flat during the next two weeks, and I have yet to start writing my judgment in the listed building consent case.

16 November 1996

We made excellent progress with the flat at 7 Gray's Inn Square. On our first visit last week we met the contractor, Mr Randall, and discussed various installations which he is to arrange for us. This time we went shopping and also made arrangements for the much-needed supply of electricity. Then it was time for us to return to Scotland. We had planned to go home by train, but I was persuaded to appear on Kirsty Wark's televised discussion programme *Words with Wark* at Clydebank about the Government's sentencing policy for Scotland. She

---

16 *In re C (A Minor) (Interim Care Order: Residential Assessment)* [1997] AC 489.

provided a car to take us to Heathrow and Shuttle tickets to Glasgow, as well as a car to go home. In the event it was a trouble-strewn journey. We made it all right to Heathrow, and boarded the Boeing 737 Shuttle at 5.15pm for Glasgow on time. But, on being pushed out from the stand, the pilot discovered that one of the engines was not working properly so we moved onto the Belfast stand to await repairs. It looked as though we would not make it to Glasgow in time for the programme.

I would not have pressed myself forward. But Mary insisted that, as I owed an obligation to the BBC to get to Glasgow as soon as possible, I should make my position known to the crew. By a stroke of good fortune a Glasgow lawyer, Michael Walker of Maclay Murray & Spens who recognised me, had his seat next to me. He offered me use of his mobile telephone, as I had none, to inform Kirsty Wark's producer of our predicament. There was a delay of about 20 minutes and then Mary and I – fortunately with hand baggage only – were ushered off the plane by a flight attendant for the last two seats on the 6.15pm Shuttle. As we were leaving a Pakistani gentleman who had become quite obstreperous asked Michael Walker who we were. 'I don't know' was his tactful reply. But the 6.15pm Shuttle was also half-an-hour late on take-off. It was the larger Boeing 757 aircraft, much more comfortable, but as we were stuck in the back row of the plane we were aware that we would find it very slow to get off. Again Mary pressed me to make myself known to the crew, with a plea to move as far forward as possible for the landing so that we could get off early. After some delay they found two places for us in the forward cabin, so we were able to get off quite quickly. It was a long walk to the car and a long drive to Clydebank from the airport. We reached Clydebank town hall just three minutes before my slot in the programme was due to begin – just in time for a bit of make-up powder and a sip of water before I was on the stage.

I was with Phil Gallie, the Conservative MP for Ayr, a lady from SACRO which works for the rehabilitation of offenders, and a police officer. The first question was directed at me by Kirsty Wark – who was very quick, positive and good to work with – and so was the last. So I had a reasonable opportunity to say my bit about my concerns as to the proposal that there should be a mandatory life sentence for a second conviction for a violent or sexual offence[17]– which is due I believe largely to Phil Gallie's lobbying following a notorious murder in his constituency which had been committed by a twice-convicted rapist.[18] The small audience of 30–35 people all had varying entrenched views and the discussion, whilst lively, was not very encouraging to those who believe in a fair system of justice. However, I did not let myself down, and it was

---

17 Referred to colloquially as 'two strikes and you're out'. The proposal was enacted as section 1 of the Crime and Punishment Act 1997, under the heading 'imprisonment for life on further conviction for certain offences.' The Act received the Royal Assent on 31 March 1997, shortly before the May 1997 General Election. Section 1 was among a number of its provisions which were not brought into force, as the Conservatives lost the election.
18 The case was that of Gavin Maguire, who was twice convicted of rape before being finally convicted of rape and murder following an incident in Kilmarnock in December 1995.

interesting and good fun to take part in something I could never have done as Lord President.

This week we returned to London. I went by the 6am train, and Mary and our son William drove down with our car full of luggage. They reached the Inn just after 7pm after a very long drive. It had taken them two hours to enter and get through London. We unpacked the car and then drove it to Westminster where I used my passes to park in the Lords' car park. We looked rather disreputable as at 8pm we went through the Peers' Entrance, clutching pictures and other things for my room on the Law Lords' Corridor. But my pass works wonders, and a suspicious attendant at once became very friendly indeed. We met Marilyn, who was working very late, in the Corridor on our way to my room.

It is becoming clear that I am making myself very unpopular with the Lord President and the Law Officers, and the Lord Chancellor too, as a result of my appearance on television and expression in public of my critical views about mandatory life sentences. James Mackay talked to me about this on the telephone – indicating, in the gentlest way, that I should be careful (a) not to offend the English,[19] and (b) not to create difficulty for the new Lord President. And at a reception in Parliament Hall for the Diplomatic Corps the Lord Advocate and the Lord President very pointedly gave me the cold shoulder. Things had not been helped by the publication in the Law Society Journal of my outspoken address on 30 September.[20]

I had already taken the opportunity last week of asking the Lord President to come to see me at India Street to discuss the issue. Having already spoken to Tom Bingham on the telephone to check his position – we are on almost precisely the same wavelength about mandatory life sentences – I was sorry, but not all that surprised, to find that Alan Rodger is far from being critical of the Government. He seems to see nothing wrong with the proposal and was not to be reasoned with on the issue. He said that it was all very difficult, and he did not want to have a public disagreement about it. The truth is – though I did not say so – that he would be far more damaged by this than I would, because it would just confirm the widely-held belief that he was put in my place as Lord President as a supporter of the Government. All his actions since his appointment have tended to show that, far from being independent, he is behaving almost as if he is still a Law Officer. That is not healthy for the system, but perhaps with a change of government he will get over it. Meantime, however, I am in a bit of a quandary. I would love to speak out in support of him, as I have so much more trust than he has in the Scottish media and have so many contacts with them. But, if he is to support the Government, he and I are at

19 The proposals which Michael Forsyth had adopted followed those which were enacted for England and Wales by the Crime (Sentences) Act 1997 which had been promoted by Michael Howard. They too were not proceeded with after the election.
20 Journal of the Law Society of Scotland, November 1997, p 433; see also the annotation to section 1 of the 1997 Act in *Current Law Statutes*. Among the points I made was that Scottish practice and procedure differed fundamentally from that in England and Wales where the idea originated, and that insufficient account had been taken of that fact.

loggerheads. All this has created very real problems for me in knowing what I dare say at the Howard League Lecture. I have already spent far too much time worrying about this. Today I wrote my third draft of it, to try to be less provocative. It would be so nice if I could do what the Bishop of Edinburgh[21] advised me to do at last night's reception, with a warm twinkle in his eye. 'Give way to temptation', he said. But I cannot responsibly do so – not all the way, anyway.

8 December 1996

The last two weeks have been spent in the Privy Council. There was a four-day case about Maori fishing rights from New Zealand, a two-day case about insurance from Hong Kong, a one-day commercial case from New Zealand and a day of petitions for leave to appeal. The Maori case was, at the same time, both frustrating and fascinating. It provided us with a most interesting problem about the conflict between the traditional Maori and their Iwi, or tribes, and the urban Maori – probably now two-thirds or three-quarters of all Maori in New Zealand are urban – about the distribution of money paid by the government as compensation for the imposition of quotas to preserve fish stocks. There were 15 counsel, several of them Maori, who gave us greetings in the Maori language, and there were many Maori spectators. It was a lively debate, but the frustration lay in the fact that the Court of Appeal decision, one of Robin Cooke's last and written probably after he had left office as President, was poorly expressed and unsupportable. We could do nothing but send the case back for further hearing. The cases in the following week were simple and rather quiet by comparison. I was given the judgment in the commercial lease case to write – *Melanesian Mission Trust Board v Australian Mutual Provident*, my first in the Privy Council.[22] The diet of petitions for leave to appeal was presided over by Michael Mustill. He was not the ideal chairman, as he dominates so much. But he was brisk, and we were through by lunchtime.

I attended a Grand Night dinner as a guest at Lincoln's Inn, where Peter Gibson is Treasurer, and a Dinner Night at Middle Temple as Robbie Lowry's guest.[23] Anna Ford and Moira Stuart, the television news presenters, were there also, tall and glamorous. Last week Tony and Jane Lloyd very kindly asked us to supper at their lovely riverside house at Chiswick where Donald and Jenny Nicholls and Sydney Kentridge QC and his wife were the other guests. It was a most enjoyable, if rather formidable, evening. Back in Edinburgh I went to a dinner given by the SSC Society, preceded by the Society's Biennial lecture given by Judge Stephen Tumim, formerly of the Prison Inspectorate. He is no friend of Michael Howard, the Home Secretary, in view of the latter's new, harsh policies. Next day, 23 November, the Faculty of Advocates gave a dinner

---

21 The Rt Rev Richard Holloway.
22 *Melanesian Mission Trust Board v Australian Mutual Provident Society (New Zealand)* [1996] UKPC 53.
23 Lord Lowry, from Northern Ireland where he was Lord Chief Justice, was a former Lord of Appeal in Ordinary.

in my honour at the Balmoral Hotel, while the judges' and Faculty officers' wives entertained Mary in the Advocates' Reading Room. Neither of us was looking forward to this very much, but in the end all went well. I particularly, and rather to my surprise, enjoyed being back with the Faculty where I received a very friendly welcome and managed to produce a reasonable speech without getting into trouble for being too stiff or too formal. Then last week, on Friday 29 November, I delivered the Howard League lecture which I had been worrying so much about. I decided to play safe and deliver the third, most restrained version, which some of the audience said later seemed remarkably unemotional – as indeed it was, most deliberately so. Fortunately the press coverage next day was quite modest, so no doubt I got the balance just about right.

That day, 30 November, Mary and I went to St Giles' Cathedral in Edinburgh for a special service to welcome the return of the Stone of Destiny to Scotland. This was a rather curious event, presided over by Michael Forsyth who said that his younger daughter had given him the idea of having it brought back here after spending 700 years at Westminster. There is a certain amount of scepticism about his motives, and some doubt about the significance of the event. But the service itself was well thought out and rather touching, especially when a group of schoolchildren read a litany which Gilleasbuig Macmillan[24] had written, in response to verses sung by the choir. We are no longer important enough to have front seats, so we did not actually see the Stone itself, and we were not asked to Edinburgh Castle where it was formally handed over to the Commissioners of the Regalia by Prince Andrew, The Duke of York. But we did go to a most enjoyable reception in Parliament Hall where there was a buffet lunch, and we could watch the ceremony later on television. In the afternoon I was a judge at a client counselling competition in the Law Faculty at Edinburgh University. These weekends home in Edinburgh are a very pleasant contrast to the weekdays in London. There is just long enough in each place not to feel rushed or travel-worn, and just short enough not to get too out of touch with the other place.

This weekend I have spent much of my time writing in my study – the Privy Council judgment, and some revisals to my House of Lords judgment in *Shimizu v Westminster County Council* where I hope to persuade Lord Griffiths to agree with me. I already have Lord Browne-Wilkinson and Lord Lloyd, but Robin Cooke is bound to dissent as, rather awkwardly, he always seems to do. But it would be good to bring Hugh Griffiths into line with me also.

21 December 1996

The term ended last Thursday 19 December, but James Vallance White[25] is always careful not to fill up the last two days before the end of term to allow for emergencies. In the result I did a two-day social security appeal on Monday and

---

24 The Rt Rev Gilleasbuig Macmillan, Dean of the Thistle, the Minister of St Giles.
25 James Vallance White CB, Clerk of the Judicial Office of the House of Lords 1983–2002.

Tuesday,[26] petitions in the Appellate Committee for leave to appeal for which oral hearings are almost always required on the Wednesday, and I was back in Edinburgh that evening with three-and-a-half-weeks' holiday ahead of me. This is a quite unprecedented span of holiday for this time of year in my entire career. But such is the Parliamentary timetable.

These last one and a half weeks have been most interesting. There was a criminal appeal about whether stabbing a pregnant woman causing her to give birth to the baby which died because of its consequent prematurity was murder;[27] a Scots appeal in a family case about an unmarried father's application for access to his child and whether this was in the child's best interests;[28] and a social security case about allowances for a young woman who is profoundly deaf and an elderly lady who is incontinent.[29] Robert Goff was in the chair and James Clyde was with us for all three cases, as were Michael Mustill and Gordon Slynn. It was a pleasant, thoughtful team – but then so are all the Committees at this level, which are such a pleasure to work with. I agreed to write about the Scots appeal, and I did it over the weekend as it was straightforward. The other two were delegated to Lords Mustill and Slynn, but brief contributions from the rest of us will be in order and I might write something during the holiday. My judgments in *O'Hara* and *Abnett* were delivered last week. They duly appeared together on the law reports page of *The Times*, creating the illusion that I have been working very hard.

Nothing has happened to the flat, apart from the delivery of a few more pieces of furniture. The kitchen will not be fitted until January. But it is very comfortable and peaceful nevertheless, and I have settled into an easy routine. I leave at about 8.15am, to arrive in my room in the Law Lords' Corridor at about 8.50am, where I change into my better suit whilst listening to Radio 3 if the annunciator which we all have in our rooms has been switched on.[30] In the evening I do not leave my room before 6pm, and often not before 8.30pm when I am having supper in the House. As there are no cooking facilities in the flat at present, there is no point in arriving home early. There are only three evening meals to arrange, as on Sunday I am fed by British Airways on the Shuttle,[31] and on Thursday I am back in Edinburgh.

Travelling has proved to be quite tolerable. I am small enough not to feel uncomfortable on the Shuttle, and the Boeing 757 in which we usually travel is a reasonably spacious aircraft. The BA Executive Lounge is available to me, as I am now a frequent flyer. This is a great help on Sunday evenings, as I can

26 *Cockburn v Chief Adjudicator* [1997] 1 WLR 799.
27 *Attorney-General's Reference (No 3 of 1994)* [1998] AC 245.
28 *Sanderson v McManus* 1997 SC (HL) 55.
29 See fn 26.
30 We were all provided with television screens in our rooms which showed the day's business in both Houses and had a link to the usual channels on radio and television.
31 This was the effect of competition from British Midland (Bmi). British Airways provided a simple complementary two-course meal, with roll and butter, and a bar service to all of its Shuttle passengers on its evening flights between Scotland and Heathrow.

sit and read my papers in peace and comfort before the flight. The discomfort arises on the Piccadilly line. It takes about 50 minutes to one hour to reach Holborn, my nearest station, from Heathrow. The space in between trains is erratic and, when it is long, it results in overcrowding and standing all the way. I am not particularly downhearted by this and there is some interest in the variety of the passengers, many of whom speak to each other in languages which I cannot recognise. My room on the Law Lords' Corridor is small and not very attractive. The bookcases overpower it, and the heating is not good at the end of the Corridor. I am getting used to it, however, and with a change of clothing and a pullover I find I can work there reasonably efficiently, especially in the evenings when I have petitions to read up.

Yesterday evening in Edinburgh Mary and I were at a drinks' party given by Paul and Joyce Cullen. They had very kindly asked all the Faculty officers of their day – me as Dean, Alastair Cameron as Vice-Dean, Alan Johnston as Treasurer and Brian Gill as Keeper of the Library. The Lord President and the Lord Advocate were there also. I heard that Hugh Foley, the Principal Clerk, is to take early retirement and I heard also from Mrs Small yesterday when she hinted very darkly that Donald Ross, the Lord Justice Clerk, is about to go as well. 'So many changes', she said.

It is odd to go to such a gathering without the aura of high office – a Lord of Appeal is so far away, and he has no patronage or responsibility in Edinburgh. So one is not looked on with the same eyes as are the Dean, the Lord Advocate and the Lord President. Any views I may have are now irrelevant, and they are not sought. It is so important therefore not to look back or to feel troubled by change – in personnel, policy or indeed in the case law, especially in the Criminal Appeal Court, all of which is now in other hands. As Mary says, we have moved on, and in a sense, grown up. The world in which we live now is so much wider, and so much more interesting, as a result. The decisions which we have to take, and the reasons to be given for them, are of far greater significance. One does not have to be in London long to realise that Scotland is quite a small jurisdiction as seen internationally, and that the unique features of its law – and of its legal language, of which we are so proud – are a kind of barrier to its case law being of much interest anywhere else. It is not so in the House of Lords. Our decisions are on the internet on the day they are delivered, and the Privy Council, although not so computerised, has a major influence on those parts of the world where it still has jurisdiction. Also the work is far from easy. I am still relatively tongue-tied and stilted in my judgment writing, compared to the fluency, authority and even a touch of mild arrogance which I felt I could bring to bear on the many opinions I was delivering each week as Lord President and Lord Justice General, which are still filling the last few issues of this year's *Scots Law Times*. It is probably a very good thing that I have time so much on my side, as I settle in to this very enjoyable, relaxed and satisfying new job.

1997 – January to March

7 January 1997

The term begins today in the Court of Session, but I still have one more week before work starts again in London. I said goodbye today to the set of *Scottish Criminal Case Reports* which have been such a feature of my life as Lord Justice General over the last seven years. They have sat with me throughout, at my left hand in my revolving bookcase beside my desk in my study. But it is clear that I no longer have any use for them – and in any case they were on loan to me from the Judges' Library which is no longer providing me with the monthly parts as they are issued. So one more link with the past must be broken. I calculated, as I removed the set from my shelves, that during these seven years I delivered 860 opinions which were either published in the *Scottish Criminal Case Reports* – there are 454 of them – or were reserved judgments in civil cases, of which there were 406. Most of the civil cases are reported somewhere. There were many more *ex tempore* opinions in criminal cases which did not justify reporting.

Donald Ross retires today as Lord Justice Clerk and is succeeded by Douglas Cullen. For Donald, after 12 years in that office, the process of adjustment will be very great. He has worked with prodigious energy throughout and kept on top of his job in a way which will be hard for his successor to live up to. As so many entries in my diary will have shown, I did not find him an easy man to work with. I suspect that Alan Rodger may have had less trouble, but for him the situation was easier as Donald had already resolved to go and there were no issues of importance to be dealt with. In my case it was very different. The gay judges' scandal, when we had such different views about how to deal with it and about which he offered me no real support or sympathy, produced a sense of mistrust between us which it was hard to repair. However, he has much good to look back on. Neither of the two Divisions was well staffed during our time in the two chairs. It was hardly surprising therefore, that he, like me, adopted the practice of doing almost all the leading opinions himself. In this way he upheld the work of the Second Division to a degree which would otherwise not have been possible. That was a fine achievement, which will find its place in history. Douglas Cullen will be a very different Lord Justice Clerk. He is reserved and careful, where Donald was frank and determined. He will not be as forceful a character, but he is very well organised. I am sad not to have had the chance of working with him for a year or two.

What changes there are in the court! Both chairs are now held by very different men, and the composition of both Divisions has changed. Only Lord McCluskey and Lord Sutherland are left from the Inner House judges at the start of last year. The Principal Clerk retires this year, as does Mrs Small. The tides have closed very fast behind me after my departure for the south, and once the General Election due this spring is over there will almost certainly be a new Dean of Faculty and a new Lord Advocate. The team with whom I worked will all have evaporated, and the scene will be almost unrecognisable. It is time now to concentrate on building a new life for myself on the Law Lords' Corridor.

17 January 1997

We returned to work in the House of Lords this week. I travelled south on the 7pm Shuttle, but fog at Heathrow produced an unexpected hazard because of the prospect of serious delay. In the event we reached Heathrow at 9.45pm in light fog, to find it almost deserted. There was only one other aircraft parked in the bays serving the Shuttle services and there were no waiting passengers. I reached the entrance to the Underground at 10.15pm, which was 45 minutes before the last train for Central London. The Pakistani superstore in Holborn, which is now open 24 hours a day and is my only source of supply on Sunday evenings, was able to supply bread and milk. So I was not greatly inconvenienced.

The case for the week was *Herd v Clyde Helicopters Ltd*,[32] another Scots appeal about carriage by air and the application of the Warsaw Convention to a claim for damages. The Lord Chancellor had decided to preside, so we had three Scots – Lords Mackay, Hope and Clyde. It was a very interesting and well-presented appeal. James Mackay was on very good form, and we had a most enjoyable debate over which he presided with skill and charm. At the end I found myself, somewhat at odds with the others, favouring an international approach to the jurisprudence to which we were referred. I shall no doubt find a way to bring myself into line, but my note of dissent made for an interesting and lengthy discussion at the end of the hearing.

Mary came down to London for two days, taking the 6am train from Edinburgh on the Wednesday and returning on the 5pm train on the Thursday. It was a very timely and useful visit, as there was a great deal to discuss with Mr Randall and the carpenter. Next day she joined me for a late lunch in the canteen in the House of Lords before we did some more shopping. We parted at 4pm, so that she could catch her train at King's Cross. Before setting out for Heathrow I returned to Westminster, where I spent a few moments in a crowded Chamber listening to a tense debate on the Firearms (Amendment) Bill, which was a response to the tragedy on 13 March 1996 when a handgun which was held legitimately was used to kill 16 children and their teacher in Dunblane Primary School. I was back in Edinburgh in time to collect Mary at Waverley Station on my way back home by car from the airport to India Street.

8 February 1997

A busy week, followed by a busy weekend – indeed my time seems now to be fully occupied. There are now so many extra-judicial matters to attend to, as well as the time spent reading myself into and considering the cases which I have been hearing in Committee.

32 [1997] AC 534, 1997 SC (HL) 86.

I have three addresses to give in a few weeks' time which now must be prepared – to the Judicial Studies Board at a conference in Northampton on 20 February, to students at Aberdeen University on 21 February and at the Annual Conference of the Law Society of Scotland at Gleneagles on 16 March. The Aberdeen engagement, set up for me by Douglas Cusine, is of long standing. I had been booked for this when I was Lord President, but now I can speak about my work in London. The JSB engagement is the result of an invitation from Lord Justice Judge – Igor Judge, the lively Chairman of the Board.[33] I am glad to have an opportunity of visiting this institution, which is gaining an increasing importance in the life of the judiciary. The Gleneagles engagement came out of the blue last weekend when we were at a supper party at the Law Society. This was a farewell party for Kenneth Pritchard, now retired as Secretary of the Society, who has served them so well and been such a good friend. So I have had a lot of writing to do. Mrs Small, who has been asked to stay on for another six months in the Lord President's Private Office, very kindly offered to help me out with the typing, which I am reluctant to entrust to Marilyn as she is so busy.

Above all this there are the Crime (Sentences) Bill and the Crime and Punishment (Scotland) Bill. The former had its second reading on 27 January. There was a full turnout of senior judges – Tom Bingham, Harry Woolf, Desmond Ackner, John Donaldson and Peter Oliver all spoke. So also did I, about some Scottish aspects which the Home Office Minister, Lady Blatch, described as 'kilting' the Bill. The hostility to the proposal for mandatory life sentences in the Crime (Sentences) Bill expressed by the English judges got a very bad press, on the whole. This was in sharp contrast to what I could have expected from the Scottish press, but the political situation in Scotland is very different. Unlike my English colleagues I tried to be constructive, which elicited a polite and helpful response from the admirably calm and efficient Lady Blatch and some kind inquiries from Lord McIntosh of Haringey on the Labour Front Bench and from Lord Sewel and Baroness Carnegie of Lour. This week it is to be our turn, when I shall be speaking at the Second Reading of the Crime and Punishment (Scotland) Bill. I shall try to be constructive here also, but I cannot avoid more overt criticisms in view of the weight of objection from so many informed quarters to much of what is proposed. These Parliamentary occasions add interest and enjoyment to my most absorbing and challenging work as a Lord of Appeal in Ordinary.

I have been much taken up over the last two weeks with developing my skills on the computer and with the installation at home of a fax machine. I have been driven into this by the marked difference in the secretarial support which I received in London compared with that which I had as Lord President where I had my own secretary to whom I could provide all my drafts for audio-typing. Also, living part of my life at home in Edinburgh remote from the office in London makes it essential for me to become skilled in the use of technology. Fortunately, thanks to our son Will, it is all on my doorstep – or upstairs in the

---

33 Later Lord Judge, the Lord Chief Justice of England and Wales.

computer room on the top floor of our house, to be more accurate. We invested in this equipment two years ago, and the children have all made extensive use of it while I ignored it entirely. Now I have discovered the huge advantages which it has to offer me in the preparation of correspondence, which I cannot now respectably conduct in my own handwriting except with close friends. I have also used the machine to type out my speeches for the Second Reading debates, which is a great advantage as I have been able to complete these tasks without delay within a weekend. There have been computer courses for me at Westminster, and next week a machine is to be installed in my room. I shall find it difficult to devote much time to it, but no doubt its uses will become more obvious as the weeks go by. The fax machine is proving difficult to reconcile with the BT 'call minder' service, which diverts calls to BT and interrupts the fax signal. But no doubt some solution can be found when its use is required.

Little has happened at 7 Gray's Inn, except that last week I cooked my first meal for myself without too much difficulty in the microwave. A proper cooker has still to be installed. Mary will be with me again next week to do further work on the curtains. We are settling into a very comfortable and peaceful existence there.

On the judicial front the Bulger case – a challenge to the Secretary of State's decision to increase the minimum period of detention of the two 11-year-old child killers, Venables and Thompson,[34] by five years over that recommended by the Lord Chief Justice – has proved to be very challenging. With Robert Goff and Nico Browne-Wilkinson pursuing rather different lines we have had some long and very spirited discussions. This is the Committee procedure at its best, I think. I do hope that we can fashion some worthwhile judgments as a result.

8 March 1997

Mary and I had a lovely visit to Craighead, arriving at 10pm on Saturday evening with skies clearing after rain to a jewel-studded night sky enlivened by the Comet Hale-Bopp, lower than it will be later in the month, to the north over the Hill of Craighead. Then today it was a brilliant cloudless day of unbroken sunshine until we left at 4pm. Buzzard, peregrine and blackcock were all seen. The oystercatchers are returning to the hills, and robins, linnets, skylarks and pied wagtails are singing. I did some very useful digging in preparation for planting my Nadine potatoes, weather permitting, at Easter.

I was much depressed two weeks ago by a decision of five judges to overrule decisions of mine in the Criminal Appeal Court about distress as corroboration in cases of indecent assault in cases where there was no evidence other than that of the complainer.[35] I had developed this by a series of decisions, building

---

34 *R v Secretary of State for the Home Department, ex parte Venables* [1998] AC 407.
35 *Smith v Lees* 1997 JC 73. I might have avoided this result if I had spotted in time a passage in Alison's *Principles of the Criminal Law of Scotland* (1832), p 247 where, when dealing with the

on dicta of Lord President Emslie and Lord Justice Clerk Ross. It was a pragmatic approach to a difficult problem, how to find sufficient evidence when the complainer is alone with the perpetrator, there is no injury and no one else who could corroborate on the *Moorov* doctrine. The strict approach to corroboration, which has now ruled out distress as sufficient for this purpose on the ground that distress is not evidence of what actually happened, thus rendering these crimes incapable of prosecution in Scotland, is no doubt logical. But it is a pity that the judges fell into this mould instead of supporting my own feeling that we should treat this as a question of fact for the jury. It opens up a rather unsatisfactory chasm in our law which is now incurable without a more drastic revision of the law of corroboration by legislation than is desirable.[36]

Then I was depressed by the decision of the House of Lords to overturn the First Division in *Sharp v Thomson*: see 17 April 1995.[37] This came as no surprise, as Nico Browne-Wilkinson had remarked to me before the hearing of the appeal began that he saw the Lords' function as being to 'restore order'. Unfortunately Scots property law does not lend itself readily to such an approach. But Lords Keith and Jauncey were no protection against the force of the English desire to rationalise the law of floating charges along their lines. Lord Steyn was with Nico. James Clyde was much more aware of what was going on, but he was unable to stem the tide. He wrote a careful and well-designed speech, which struck a very narrow line and would not have troubled me. Charles Jauncey wrote a much less cautious speech, which in some respects seemed to set our property law back to a state of confusion from which I had hoped we had managed to emerge. The other three gave no speeches but agreed with both Charles Jauncey and James Clyde, whose approaches were really quite different. However, an exchange of letters with Professor Kenneth Reid, for whom I have great respect and whose learning has inspired my own opinion, has cheered us both up. He has written a splendid article 'Jam Today – *Sharp* in the House of Lords',[38] which does much to set the decision in its context. A solution which may just satisfy everybody but does nothing for property law as a subject in its own right creates problems for the future and is full of inconsistencies. The decision is, like that in *Heritable Reversionary Trust* 100 years ago,[39] a clear demonstration of the risk of misguided decisions by the House of Lords on matters of Scots law which can be so difficult to put right.

Last week in the Privy Counsel, however, was enjoyable – one of the last really satisfying cases from Hong Kong before the Colony reverts to China in July.

---

problem of finding sufficient evidence for the prosecution of highway robbers who generally select the most lonely and unfrequented spots for robbing unattended defenceless people, he said that in such a case the evidence of a single witness was deemed sufficient if the witness was of unexceptionable character.

36 As I predicted, the Scottish Government came up with proposals for dealing with the problem by legislation. Their plan was to abolish corroboration altogether, but this proposal raised so many objections that it has not yet been proceeded with.
37 1997 SC (HL) 66, reversing the judgment of the First Division at 1995 SC 455.
38 1997 SLT (News) 79.
39 *Heritable Reversionary Co Ltd v Millar* (1891) 18 R 1166.

8 March 1997

This one, *Canon Kabushka Kaisha v Green Cartridge Co*,[40] was all about copyright in a cartridge for replenishing laser printers with toner and in various other replacement parts. Lennie Hoffmann was far ahead of us as usual, and, again as usual in these cases, will write the judgment. He is a fascinating man, with an electric speed of thought and a massively retentive memory. He is also very well organised and fast to move into print. He takes almost no notes yet manages to produce most attractively written judgments. It is difficult to keep up with him. Perhaps I should not attempt to do so. But he does present a challenge and is amusing to work with also.

On Thursday evening I was a guest at the Lent term dinner of the Navy Board at Admiralty House. This was the result of a very kind invitation by the First Sea Lord, Admiral Sir Jock Slater, who was at school with me at the Edinburgh Academy before, at the age of 13, he went to Sedbergh and I went to Rugby. We met at a Grand Day dinner at Lincoln's Inn last November, and he kept his promise to ask me to dinner. We were received in the Admiralty Board Room, a splendid wooden-panelled room with large portraits of Lord Nelson and William IV at either end, and a handsome fireplace with Grinling Gibbons carvings and a large weather-vane above it set in the middle of a map of Western Europe in the early 19th century. The large table in the room, leather-surfaced, had brass place labels for the First Sea Lord, Second Sea Lord, Controller of the Navy, etc. And all the present incumbents were there, dressed in evening finery: three Admirals, one Vice-Admiral and two Rear-Admirals, together with the Second Permanent Under-Secretary of State. Among the other guests were Sir Patrick Mayhew, Secretary of State for Northern Ireland, and Sir Robert Fellowes, the Queen's Private Secretary. The dinner was preceded by a group photograph. Jock was kind enough to put me in the front row on his left, and I sat there at dinner with the Garter King at Arms, Peter Gwynne-Jones, on my left. Jock was in splendid form. Our grace was a marvellous invocation ending with the words 'For what we are about to receive, thank God and the Royal Navy'. He made a relaxed, informal speech after the Loyal Toast, to which Patrick Mayhew replied in his charmingly urbane, relaxed manner. After our excellent dinner we adjourned to the drawing room, where there was much talk of the need for an urgent decision, despite the impending election, on the new frigate resulting from the Horizon project on which Mary's brother Robin Kerr has been much engaged while serving with the Royal Navy. Clearly these dinners have a function in 'networking' of the kind I tried to do as Lord President in my dinners at Bute House.

It is extraordinary how, as one gets older, all these great offices – First Sea Lord, Lord President, Lord of Appeal in Ordinary, etc – seem so accessible, occupied by people who are, in the end, really quite approachable. It becomes increasingly hard to recall how remote and awesome they appeared when I was on the threshold of my career. And, as I travel back and forth on the Piccadilly line to

---

40 [1997] AC 728.

and from Heathrow each week, it seems that with increasing seniority I have indeed become more and more ordinary myself.

24 March 1997

We are now in Holy Week, and the Hilary term – as I ought now to call it– is about to end. The practice is to avoid listing cases for this week, so I have been able to remain in Edinburgh for in effect two weeks' holiday as next week, Easter Week, really is a week off. It is time for administration, shopping and tidying up the garden ready for spring and summer.

Last weekend Mary and I were at Gleneagles for the Law Society of Scotland's Annual Conference. We had not expected to be asked, as I am no longer the Lord President. But Grant McCulloch, the President, approached me a few weeks ago with an urgent plea that I should be this year's Distinguished Speaker as their pre-arranged speaker had withdrawn. I agreed, and we were glad to be back among friends. Indeed we were in luck also, as this is the last Gleneagles weekend for some time. There has been some unrest about holding this event in such luxurious surroundings. To assuage criticisms next year's annual conference is to be in Glasgow and the year after, the 50th, is to be in Edinburgh. The Pritchards were absent as Kenneth is no longer Secretary, and there was no Sunday service so there were subtle changes in the atmosphere. But all-in-all, as usual, it was a very pleasant experience. Rather to our relief Alan Rodger, the Lord President, was not there either. He is keeping a very low profile, as indeed is Douglas Cullen also. The new Secretary, Douglas Mill from Paisley, said rather wistfully that he did not think that relationships between the Lord President and the Law Society were going to be as close as they had been in my day. Sadly, I think that he is probably right about this. Alan's rather brisk manner, and perhaps his shyness also, does not make for an easy relationship. It is a pity. I like Douglas Mill very much, and it would have been nice to have settled in with him for a while before I left office.

Now Hugh Foley, the Principal Clerk, is to take early retirement this week. Mrs Small said to Mary when they met in Jenners the other day that life is very quiet in the office and that she doubts whether, when she goes, she will be replaced as there is almost nothing for her to do. The withering away of the Lord President's Private Office is rather sad. It is hard to see how the independence of the Court can be sustained. The new Principal Clerk, who is coming from a regional sheriff clerk's post at the same salary as in his previous job, is unlikely to have the same enthusiasm as his energetic predecessor for the separate identity of the Court of Session from the rest of the court service.

Our term finished with some interesting cases but with no fresh opinions for me to write. There are still several on the stocks however, including the Bulger case which continues for us all to be troublesome. When we return it will be to an almost deserted Westminster, as Parliament was prorogued last week for a General Election on 1 May. It will not be until 16 May, when there is to be the

State Opening, that we shall have all systems working again. We shall, of course, carry on with the Appellate Committee as the statute requires us to do – with sittings in the Chamber instead of the Committee Room. But this will be without prayers, as there is no bishop available when Parliament has been prorogued.

It seems almost certain that the Conservatives will lose the election. Eighteen years in office is a long time. It is time for a change. Labour has moved much closer to the middle ground in order to attract the electorate. The prospect of a Labour Government is much less alarming than it was even five years ago. The party is so far ahead in the opinion polls that the election is now really theirs to lose – the Conservatives cannot win. In Scotland the SNP are a very strong force and, as 'new Labour' is not nearly so popular here, there may be a different result; perhaps fewer Labour members. That will set the scene for constitutional debates, which will no doubt take up much time in the years to come.

1997 – April to July

11 April 1997

We resumed for the Easter term this week, starting on the Tuesday. As the House was not sitting, I found myself in the Chamber with Brian Hutton, James Clyde, Gordon Slynn and Robert Goff in an English criminal appeal arising from the prosecutor's failure to disclose information to the defence and as to the safety of the conviction that followed.[41] It was a strange area for a Scots lawyer, as our law about corroboration would have provided an instant solution in favour of the appellant in one case, and the Lord Advocate's discretion would have provided an easy answer to the other. But English criminal law lacks both, and a series of miscarriage of justice cases have opened up a hornets' nest which recent legislation seems unlikely to cover up. It was an enjoyable case nevertheless, presented by very experienced counsel including Michael Mansfield QC, who has been involved in so many of the miscarriage of justice appeals during the past ten years.

Prayers were said for us by a bishop on the first morning, but Parliament was dissolved at 2pm that day and the mace was removed. Thereafter we sat, without bishops, prayers or mace, by virtue of a Warrant from Her Majesty. It was all very peaceful, as Westminster is almost deserted. Many places are shut and even the lunch places that are open shut at 2pm. So we had no lunch on Thursday as we were in discussion until 2pm. Then it was time to head off for a hurried 24-hour visit home to Edinburgh, before returning this evening for a wedding in London which Mary and I are to attend. Now that we have a flat to go to, all things are possible.

---

41 *R v Mills* [1998] AC 382.

4 May 1997

The General Election has come and gone, to the relief of many, after a six-week long campaign and some irritating disruptions to travel by road, rail and air by the IRA in order to impose their presence on the electorate. The result was astonishing – far beyond the expectation of a respectable victory for the Labour Party. It was a landslide victory, and every single Conservative MP in Scotland (and in Wales) lost his seat. It was a meltdown for the Conservative Party on a grand scale. The overall swing to Labour was 10%, but the remarkable thing was that only 44% of the popular vote gave over 60% of the seats to Labour – a majority of over 175, with only 165 Conservatives against over 400 Labour. In Scotland the Tories with 17.5% of the popular vote have no seats at all, the SNP with 20% have six seats and the Liberal Democrats with only 12.5% of the popular votes have ten seats. This is a bizarre and troublesome picture. The only party which has opposed devolution has been wiped out, although about 30% of the population in Scotland have misgivings about devolution. Malcolm Rifkind, Michael Forsyth and Ian Lang have all lost their seats – ex-Secretaries of State all of them. So too have James Douglas-Hamilton, Phil Gallie and Bill Walker. Paul Cullen,[42] who was selected for the 'safest' constituency in Scotland, at Eastwood after Alan Stewart resigned following allegations about his private life, was defeated in a 14% swing by over 3,000 votes. He must be shocked but was lucky as it would have been no life at all for him to have been the only Tory MP left in Scotland.

There is, of course, much acclaim for 'new Labour'. Tony Blair and his wife Cherie lack gravitas, and they have a lot to learn about discreet behaviour in public. The Labour Party will soon run itself into difficulties as the dissents, which have been kept under the table, begin to appear. But the majority is so large, and the Tories are in such disarray, that Labour will be able to do whatever the Cabinet wants it to do.

I have no sense of alarm or disappointment. I was already much out of sympathy with the Tory Government due to the antics of Michael Howard and Michael Forsyth about criminal law and punishment. There was much arrogance, and I felt uneasy about the attitude of both James Mackay and Donald Mackay, the Lord Advocate, who had clearly lost touch with Scottish public opinion. It is not good for democracy, however, that the Tory Party should have now become exclusively an English party and that the official Opposition has no place in Scotland. Unexpectedly, devolution and proportional representation in the Scottish Parliament is the only way back. But finding suitable candidates for them and for Westminster will not be easy.

This has been a busy weekend, as was the last, with judgment writing. I am still well below par on this front, lacking inspiration and confidence. Things are not helped by continuing problems in getting them typed in London. Marilyn is very well disposed, and tries hard to fit me in to the deluge of work which comes

---

42 He had been Solicitor General for Scotland since 1995. He was appointed a Senator of the College of Justice in 2008 with the judicial title of Lord Pentland.

from Gordon Slynn. But I cannot get things back as quickly as I would like. I have tried using our computer with some success. But this is still very time-consuming, so I have tried some dictation this week.

Last weekend the judges gave a farewell party for Donald and Dorothy Ross in Parliament Hall. Mary and I felt strangely apart. The absence of a position in that company was clear. No longer do I have powers of appointment or direction, and nobody needs to be nice to me any more. They were friendly but taken up with themselves. It was very hard indeed to believe that I was for seven years the Lord President.

10 May 1997

It has been a fascinating week at Westminster as life begins to return to Parliament.

The House is unable to sit for two weeks while the new Government settles in, so our week has been in the Privy Council. We cannot return to our Appellate Committee work in the House until after the State Opening when the Committees, including our own, will be re-appointed. But for the time being the Privy Council's premises at 9 Downing Street was the place to be. From the window of our retiring room which looks up the street to No 11 we were able to see various signs of the transfer of power, so sudden and so absolute in our democracy. There were ranks of press photographers and reporters in the stand opposite No 10. A Volvo estate drew up, packed with belongings. Cherie Blair alighted from the passenger seat, a woman friend from the driver's side. Bags were carried into No 10 as a group of willing young men appeared to give help. A large white van drove up and parked between the car and the cameras to provide a tiny bit of privacy. A large blue van with more inside was not far behind. Later various people who were being offered jobs in the new Government began to appear. John McFall was striding away with a confident look on his face, having been appointed a Government Whip. That was some consolation for not being on the Scottish team, for which he was a Shadow for most of the last ten years. Others were not so lucky. Andrew McIntosh, Lord McIntosh of Haringey, who was a powerful Opposition front bench spokesman in the Lords and had expected the Home Office brief – so much so that he had gone to inspect the office he was expecting to occupy – was passed over. He was deeply hurt and arrived as we were leaving for work one lunchtime looking crumpled and dishevelled as if he had not slept and had been out all night in the street.

The Blair family have moved into No 11 from their house at Islington – hence the removal activities. To get the family around there is now a smart new Ford Galaxy people carrier which has usurped the parking space for the Privy Council Daimler limousine that conveys us between the House of Lords and Downing Street. David Owen,[43] our Registrar, went out with a paint brush to mark out

---

43 David Harold Owen OBE, Registrar of the Privy Council, 1983–98.

our parking space – or so he told us. In the Lords I arrived on Tuesday morning after the Bank Holiday to find the corridor on the Principal Floor in the House of Lords full of boxes and bags of waste paper. The Government offices here too are being vacated by the Conservatives. By next day labels had been put up naming the rooms for the new occupants. Outside the workmen were removing bollards and keep left signs in the street to make the way clear for The Queen's carriage for the State Opening. The awnings are going up around the Peers' Entrance. Sniffer dogs – mostly very attractive spaniels – were much in evidence. The Royal Gallery was being lined with stands for seating, for the second time in 12 months as the last State Opening was in November.

On Wednesday swearing-in began. Each peer has received a writ of summons, which he or she must present at the Clerk's table and then swear or affirm allegiance before signing the Roll and shaking hands with the new Lord Chancellor, Lord Irvine of Lairg – for whom this procedure must be rather tedious. Two afternoons were set aside for this ritual. Without completing it a peer cannot vote or sit in the House. I managed to find a time when the queue was not too long. Derry Irvine gave me a very friendly greeting when I reached him, which was kind. We met each other two years ago at Gleneagles. He is a hugely successful silk and a man with strong views – 'a political thug', said Angus Grossart when I told him that we had met. That may be unfair, but he will clearly be a heavyweight in a Government made up of people with a long background of political ideology and friendship. He is one of the Glasgow University group which has produced so many eminent parliamentarians, was a longstanding friend of the late John Smith and is Donald Dewar's first wife's husband. It was no surprise to anyone that he has become Lord Chancellor.

On Thursday I took James Clyde to my first guest night at Gray's Inn. It was great fun for us both. To my surprise Charles Falconer QC, who was beside me at dessert, is the new Labour Solicitor General for England and Wales. I had not met him before and did not realise who he was until we spoke. Then he revealed that he is the son of Leslie Falconer WS, who gave me many instructions in my early days at the Bar. He shared a flat with Tony Blair in their early days. It is a small world. He is another example of a government being created from friends and personal contacts. But he is a charming and able man and will get great enjoyment from his peerage – as indeed will Andrew Hardie, who became Lord Advocate and gives up the position of Dean of Faculty. Colin Boyd is his Solicitor General – a very good choice. Lynda Clark QC has replaced Malcolm Rifkind as MP for Edinburgh Pentlands.

At the weekend I have a batch of interesting speeches to complete: after many drafts and a discussion which I won with Michael Mustill, *Attorney General's Reference (No 3 of 1994)*; *Launder*,[44] which is a case about an extradition to Hong Kong; and *Pierson*,[45] in which I am agreeing with Johan Steyn in a case

---

44 R v Secretary of State for the Home Department, ex parte Launder [1997] 1 WLR 839.
45 R v Secretary of State for the Home Department, ex parte Pierson [1998] AC 539.

where the lawfulness of the Secretary of State's decision to increase the penal element for a mandatory life sentence is under challenge. The computer at home is such a help in producing a final version which is legible and can be transported on a floppy disc and in hard copy on my way back to London.

14 June 1997

The Whitsun week has come and gone, and we are now into the summer term – or the Trinity term, as it is called in England. The return to London was not unwelcome, as there is so much of interest there and the flat at Gray's Inn is such a delightful haven of peace and comfort.

In the first week I was in the Privy Council, during which we heard the last criminal appeal from Hong Kong before the handover on 1 July. I have developed a special interest in this event, as we heard an interesting and difficult extradition case, *ex parte Launder* in which the applicant was resisting his return to Hong Kong to stand trial there on corruption charges. This was on the ground that, as his trial would take place under the new regime after the handover to China, he would suffer an invasion of his human rights. I was asked to write what turned out to be a long judgment, which we delivered just before the vacation, refusing his application for judicial review of the Secretary of State's decision that he should be extradited. No doubt he will seek further delay by going to the European Court of Human Rights. I suspect that he is playing the system at every level, which he can afford to do because of the wealth he has amassed by the transactions which are said to have been corrupt. By doing as Ernest Saunders did in the Guinness case when accused of manipulating its share price to assist it in its takeover bid for the Distillers Group, Launder is making the process of prosecution as difficult as possible. This is his right, of course. But it does have the atmosphere of one law for the rich and one for the poor, which is distasteful.

This week, at long last, we delivered our judgment in the Bulger case, *ex parte Venables and Thompson*. We were split 3–2 on each of the two main issues, with a different grouping on each. Johan Steyn and I were the only two who were in full agreement with each other. Robert Goff was with us on one point and Nico Browne-Wilkinson on the other, but they disagreed with each other on both points which was a pity. Nico and Tony Lloyd supported Michael Howard, the ex-Home Secretary, on all points. While it was unfortunate that we were divided, thus giving Michael Howard and his supporters the opportunity of drawing attention to the division of opinion in his favour, it is the decision which matters. Public reaction has been mixed, as one would expect. But there have been encouraging signs, such as 73% in favour of our majority view on the BBC's *Question Time* and three speeches out of four in our favour on the BBC's *Any Questions* – that Johan Steyn and I are right on the points which matter; that it was wrong for the Home Secretary to subject the children to the same tariff system as for adults, and that it was wrong for him to be swayed by public opinion in the disposal of this particular case. I am so glad that Johan Steyn, for whom I have much affection and admiration, was of that view which I believe very strongly is the right one. We are together in expressing views to a similar effect in an adult mandatory life sentence case, *ex parte Pierson*, in which Robert Goff and Nico Browne-Wilkinson are still undecided. I do hope that at least one of them comes onto our side. If so, that will be a further move towards a fair and rational approach to life sentences, which, I fear, have in England become encrusted with much political decision-taking which is quite alien to one who is used to the Scottish system.

We, as the Law Lords, had our first meeting with the new Lord Chancellor this week to discuss the question of Michael Mustill's successor. Contrary to what I had expected, perhaps rather unfairly, it was a very well-conducted meeting. We were all there, together with Tom Bingham and Harry Woolf and Tom Legg. There was a discussion, in a very orderly fashion, as to whether there should be a successor at all – as to which there was unanimity that there should be – and if so, what type of expertise or specialism was required. There is no doubt that Mark Saville and Nicholas Phillips, probably in that order, are the front runners from the Chancery side but we have several very fine Chancery lawyers already – Browne-Wilkinson, Nicholls and Hoffmann – and the need really is for a criminal/common lawyer. If, as I expect, Derry Irvine takes that view Robin Auld seems likely to get the appointment.

Later in the day I was asked to go and see the Lord Chancellor on my own. I had no idea why – perhaps about my request to visit South Africa in the autumn? As it turned out, he wanted to seek my advice on what he might say when he is awarded an Honorary Degree at Glasgow University later this month. I gave him some ideas about the place for Scots law in the UK, and the visit turned into a friendly chat about various things. He was extremely pleasant and relaxed, which I appreciated. He is clearly extremely busy also, as there is so much to catch up with after a period of limbo during the very long election campaign and he has four major Cabinet committees to chair. I do not think that it will be long however before he has mastered the job. The impression is of a somewhat ungainly figure, but a man of great powers of concentration and determination.

Later in the week I attended a reception given by the BBC to introduce a new TV series of court trials, this time in England. This is not a documentary of actual trials – the heads of the Judiciary in England are still firmly against the idea – but an unobjectionable documentary of a 'mock' trial in as real conditions as possible lasting three days, with random jurors, a mixture of actors and professionals as witnesses, a recently retired judge and practising barristers and solicitors. It is to go out over three evenings next week. It was good of the BBC to ask me. My old acquaintances Nick Catliff and Elizabeth Clough, with whom I worked in a Scottish series of documentaries, were there. It is clear that without the experience of that series behind them they would not have got this one off the ground. It will be interesting to watch the reaction this time. I notice that a much more low-key, tactful approach is being adopted.

I have suffered renewed depression this weekend about the five-judge case of *Smith v Lees*,[46] about which I wrote on 8 March 1997. The case has now been reported in the *Scots Law Times*. I had read press reports previously, but I had not realised until I read the opinions how wholly and utterly I had been discredited – and there are hints of more demolitions of my opinion in another case still to come. It is humiliating, only such a short time after leaving office, to be subjected by each of the five judges to such devastating criticism on grounds of what they saw as confused thinking, muddling essential principles and lack of logic. Of course, they were looking at the problem of distress as corroboration from an entirely different viewpoint. I was trying to rationalise it as best I could, to preserve what I saw as essential for there to be sufficient evidence to secure convictions in cases of sexual abuse conducted in private without violence where corroboration of the complainer's evidence of what was done to her would otherwise be impossible to find. It was, in retrospect, seeking to rationalise what could not really be defended on traditional grounds. But the result which has been overlooked by everybody, except in a brief passage by Lord Sutherland, is to leave an area of criminal activity which will be beyond prosecution in Scotland in almost every case. So my heart was in the right place I think, although I have exposed myself to severe criticism as a result. Added to this, I have been reversed again by my colleagues in the House of Lords in *Smith v Bank of Scotland*,[47] although this time on grounds that are much more respectable. And I felt out of my depth this week in a four-day appeal in which we ranged over areas of admiralty practice which were quite new to me.[48] Morale and self-respect are very low.

19 June 1997

I recovered my composure during a pleasant week in the Privy Council, when I heard my last two appeals from Hong Kong before our jurisdiction is brought to an end. These were typical Hong Kong cases. One was an appeal in *Real Honest Investment Ltd*[49] – a wonderful name, which only a Chinese enterprise would dare to use. Both were involved in various ways with the system of Crown leases, which is the basis of landholding in the Colony. One dealt with height restrictions in a condition of the lease and its possible waiver. The other dealt with a resumption of possession for public purposes on payment of compensation but without any public inquiry. I wonder how all of this will fare after the handover when the Governor will be replaced by the Chief Executive.

I find myself for the second time differing from my colleagues in a case about English criminal law. Last time it was in *Attorney General's Reference (No 3 of 1994)*[50] with Lord Mustill, who has very generously accepted that I am right on

---

46 See fn 35.
47 1997 SC (HL) 111.
48 *Semco Salvage and Marine Pte Ltd v Lancer Navigation Co Ltd* [1997] AC 455.
49 *Real Honest Investment Ltd v Attorney General (Hong Kong)* [1997] UKPC 34.
50 See fn 27.

the question of manslaughter. This time it is with Lord Slynn in *R v Myers*,[51] a case about hearsay evidence and the confessions of a co-defendant. I have yet to find out whether he will concede – this may be difficult and embarrassing for him – and what the others will do. I do not wish to cause trouble, but the points are important and must be got right.

This weekend I go to Regensburg in Germany for a seminar which I am to conduct there at the University at the invitation of Professor Reinhard Zimmermann. It will be my first visit to Germany for many years. The participants will all be of the highest calibre. It should be an exciting and fascinating experience.

13 July 1997

A very busy period has left little time to write about a most enjoyable visit to Regensburg, a day at Henley Royal Regatta and the end-of-term party for the Court of Session judges in Edinburgh to which Alan Rodger and Douglas Cullen very kindly invited us. The weekends have been much occupied as a result, and the days in London have been busy with sitting days fully occupied. We are nearing the end of our term – two and a half weeks still to do, but there is still a busy programme ahead.

Regensburg went very well. Professor Zimmermann was an attentive host and the seminar was well attended by about 24 very bright students. It was a three-hour affair, but I was able to maintain interest with the 'right to die' and surrogacy/adoption cases, and I enjoyed the discussion very much. It was a delight to visit Bavaria again after some 30 years. I travelled by Lufthansa via a very bright, new and efficient airport at Munich. I was taken out to lunch and supper at various delightful locations. There was time to explore the old town, despite the crowded streets as it celebrated its annual festival.

The judges' party was most enjoyable. I am still beset from time to time with feelings of lack of worth – no longer buoyed up by the pressure and aura of office as Lord President, and beset instead with the problem of making a sensible and effective contribution in London. This was such a weekend, following a day of almost impenetrable English law in the Appellate Committee and doubts about an opinion I wrote in a Scottish planning case, *City of Edinburgh Council v Secretary of State for Scotland*.[52] But a very friendly atmosphere at the party for both Mary and myself did something to restore morale before I went up to Craighead to try to restore order in the garden after five weeks of growth, rain and absence.

51 [1998] AC 124.
52 1998 SC (HL) 33.

26 July 1997

There is an end-of-term feeling in the air. This last week in London has been a round of parties and a delivery of judgments to clear the decks. There were four days of sitting in the House of Lords for me, but the Tuesday and the Thursday did not require us to sit long into the day and I had no writing to do in either of the two cases. I managed to complete a long draft speech in *Girvan v Inverness Farmers Dairy*,[53] in which a jury's award of damages was said to be excessive, last weekend. So, with almost all my work completed for the year, I felt that I could relax and enjoy myself.

On Tuesday evening Mary and I went to the dinner given annually for Her Majesty's judges by the Lord Mayor. This was a white tie occasion. Mary came down, again by the 6am train to make the most of the day. Much washing had been done by her by the time I reached the flat on a hot sunny evening at 6pm. At 6.45pm we set off in our fine clothes by taxi to the Mansion House. Five minutes later we were there, but the doors were not to open until 7.15pm, so we strolled around in the evening sunshine among the tourists outside the Bank of England. At 7.15pm we made our way into the dinner, expecting to know nobody. We soon found ourselves surrounded by familiar faces: the Cookes from New Zealand, the Huttons and the Carswells from Northern Ireland and the Gibsons from England among others. We went upstairs in a throng of guests to be received by the Lord Mayor in a large upper hall lined with magnificently dressed gentlemen-at-arms carrying pikes and with wonderfully coloured headgear. We spoke to a newly-appointed Old Bailey judge and his wife, admiring his court dress and the lace and buckled shoes which they are expected to wear. Other handsomely dressed liverymen were in the company also. Then to dinner where we together with the other Lords of Appeal who had decided to go – not all do, but Goff, Slynn, Lloyd, Nicholls, Hutton and myself were there – were at the top table. It was a very grand affair with some 350 guests, music, fanfares and speeches. Our host was Lord Mayor Cork, whose menu had a huge cork on the cover. Tom Bingham was there as Lord Chief Justice. He seemed very tense, but when he spoke was as ever neat and erudite. Derry Irvine made his first speech to this gathering as Lord Chancellor. Not surprisingly, it was very political. Our companions at dinner included, in Mary's case, a former Lord Mayor and, in my case, a former Lord Mayor's wife. So we were well briefed as to what was expected of us. Then, after the loving cup had been passed round, we rose from dinner, paid our respects to the Law Officers and the Lord Mayor in the upper hall and returned with the luxury of a lift in a government car to Gray's Inn.

Next day was the day of the Royal Garden Party at Buckingham Palace. We were fortunate with the weather. The previous day had been very hot, and about an hour after the party was over a storm of rain arrived. For us it was pleasantly bright and cool enough to feel comfortable. Mary came to my room

---

53 1998 SC (HL) 1.

in the Corridor and we then took a taxi to the Palace where we joined the queue in Buckingham Palace Road. Fortunately, as peers, we had the privilege of access to the side entrance used by diplomats, so we were able to divert into the building before too long. We walked along some rather dingy corridors into the wide central area and then out through the open bow windows onto the steps and into the garden. There was a large gathering on the lawn, but there was lots of space to walk around the most attractively contoured and landscaped gardens. There was a fine collection of roses, there were some interesting trees and there was a pond with ornamental wild fowl. The noise of traffic was not far away but not oppressive. It felt almost like Kew Gardens, only more intimate and more attractively laid out. There were some familiar faces: Alan Clark MP, David Hope the Archbishop of York, and others. At tea we suddenly saw Gordon and Winifred Coutts from Edinburgh. Later there were the Gibsons with Michael Wheeler-Booth, the recently retired Clerk of the Parliaments, and later still, Lord and Lady Templeton. It was relaxed, friendly and most enjoyable. We left through the spacious bow-windowed room and reception hall which I remembered from my day when I went to be sworn in as a Privy Counsellor. We walked back to the Lords where I changed and collected a copy of the Government's White Paper on Devolution for Scotland before we returned to Gray's Inn.

There is still a week to go into the long recess. Somehow James Vallance White manages to have no business in the last week in the House of Lords. But we had eight judgments to deliver on the Thursday morning. I was in seven of them, among which I had speeches in six and gave the leading judgment in four. This was the product of months of work, not a rush of effort in the summer term. Perhaps it reflects badly on our rate of turnover, as we really should try to restore the old regime of 6–8 weeks between the hearing and delivering judgment. Some of the cases – *Pierson* about the punishment period in a mandatory life sentence case,[54] and *Attorney General's Reference (No 3)* as to whether a pre-birth assault on a mother which resulted in the death of her child after its birth was manslaughter[55] – were quite significant. That evening I was shown on television as one of the majority for allowing the appeal against the Secretary of State's decision on the punishment period in the *Pierson* case – my words seem to have been easier for the media to pick up. Next day there was a portrait of the 12 Law Lords in *The Independent*. We were all listed with our ages, liberal, conservative or centre as our inclinations on human rights, together with our very nice recently taken photographs. I was pleased to be listed as liberal, and even more so as being 59 – still two years younger than anyone else, and the only one under 60. After some despondent weekends, it has been a very enjoyable happy week and I really do feel at ease with myself in a much better position than I was still occupying last year. How very fortunate I have been to have moved through the ranks without obvious mishap to where I am now and to

54 See fn 45.
55 See fn 27.

have, all being well, a reasonable amount of time to settle in to this difficult but not arduous job.

1997 – August to September

31 August 1997

We woke this morning to the dreadful news that Diana, Princess of Wales, had been killed in a car accident in Paris. The car in which she was travelling was being driven at high speed, apparently being pursued by photographers on motor-cycles. The driver lost control of it on entering a tunnel in an expressway beside the Seine in the centre of the city. There was an awful inevitability about this end to her short and, at times, tragic life. Yet her loss will be very deeply felt. She had a unique ability, due in part to the complex nature of her relations with the Royal Family but much more so to her own beauty, charm and ability, to reach out to people of all kinds in all circumstances. This was so attractive and had made her into an icon of the modern world. She was able to generate interest in causes which were unpopular or intractable such as landmines and AIDS, and to spread feelings of compassion and understanding for such causes across the world. All of this is irreplaceable. There is no one else who has such instant appeal and is in a position of such influence to take her place. The photographers, and the press who ply for their products, have – if the facts turn out to be so – destroyed their own most precious possession. They have robbed the rest of us of a force for good in the world which should have remained with us for many years. What a tragic waste.

6 September 1997

It has been a remarkable week, ending today with Princess Diana's funeral. There has been an expression of loss and sorrow by the public on a scale which no one could have imagined. Huge quantities of flowers have been laid at the Royal Palaces in London and at city and village centres almost everywhere else. Books of condolence especially in London have attracted immense queues, taking eight to ten hours on occasion. The press and television perhaps added to the scale of the expression of grief, as publicity made so many aware of what was going on and led to a desire to be part of the event. But it was really a genuine and spontaneous display of a sense of loss and affection. I know that I felt a sense of deep distress all week at the immensity of the tragedy and the scale of what we have lost. But it was not a hysterical reaction. The crowds were mostly silent, immaculately well-behaved and patient. So many were aware that a person who had the power, because of her unique and ultimately fatal attraction to the media, to do so much good for the disadvantaged has gone with no prospect of anyone to take her place.

The Royal Family, whose relationship with her has always been uneasy and at times almost impossible, has been caught completely off-balance by the event. A kind of revolution has taken place – 'people power' has, to a large extent, dictated the official response. Buckingham Palace has had to adjust time and again to public pressure expressed through people's voices in the crowds and in the press. The length of the funeral procession was trebled to give more people the chance to see it. The Queen came back from Balmoral a day earlier than planned to London, and she made a live broadcast – almost at the last moment – in praise of Diana. The Union flag was allowed for the first time to fly at half-mast from Buckingham Palace during and after the service, in response to public dismay at an empty mast which was the practice when the Queen was not in residence. This was a bad mistake. Symbolism is everything, and this and the Queen's absence at Balmoral, although in truth needed to comfort the two young Princes, were widely seen as showing a lack of interest in and concern for what was going on. There was much talk of the Monarchy being in danger. No one doubts that Diana was a true Princess, or that Prince William is someone who one day should be King. Perhaps Charles, the Prince of Wales, is in most danger. Yet again he has been overshadowed and outplayed by Diana and her public. He has been correct, well-behaved and concerned for his sons. But love and emotion have been elsewhere, in the public mind. I wrote a letter of condolence, through his Private Secretary, especially to him. He needs so much sympathy and understanding, even although the marriage did not last and she was, presumably with his consent, almost an outcast from the Royal Family after the divorce. It will not be easy to adjust. But something will have been learned from the week's events. The result may well be a softer, gentler, less formal and less private kind of Monarchy.

The referendum for a Scottish Parliament is now only four days away. All campaigning ceased for the week of public mourning. It will be difficult for the politicians to whip up much public enthusiasm, as we have all been drawn so close by this week's events.

12 September 1997

The result of the referendum, on a turnout of just over 60% overall, was a resounding vote in favour of a Scottish Parliament with tax-raising powers. 74% and 63% were in favour of the two questions asked. It was a much more ringing endorsement for the proposal than had been expected, as everything had been conducted in such a low key since Princess Diana's death. All the local authority areas were in favour of a Scottish Parliament, and all but two – Dumfries and Galloway and Orkney – in favour of tax-varying powers. There can no longer be any room for doubt about the will of the Scottish people. Whether it is a wise decision remains to be seen. The debate was rather brutal at times against those who dared to point out the difficulties and dangers. A tide of emotion rather than the exercise of careful and considered judgment has carried the day. Yet in truth any other result would have been a great misfortune. A weak vote or a

Parliament without tax-varying powers would have been a sign of such indecision as would have put the whole idea on the shelf for decades, while giving added fire to the undercurrent of discontent and nationalism. As it is, the victory has been won by democratic process with much goodwill and co-operation between all the political parties except the Conservatives. It now gives Scotland a chance to take real control over its own affairs and concentrate attention on what is decided in Edinburgh instead of what is done in London. I have found it difficult to know what is best, but I am happy to go along with this at the end of the day and will do my best to help it work. Attitudes towards the Scots in London are unlikely to change, but this will become increasingly irrelevant. And, as Mary and I have found all over the world, there is much goodwill for our country elsewhere.

We are off to Paris this weekend for a two-day seminar with the Conseil d'Etat. I am to be the leader of the British delegation, which is rather a large responsibility. Robin Auld, Richard Buxton, Robert Carnwath, David Keene and Janet Smith, all LJJ, are the other members, along with Tom Legg. Mary and I have invested a huge amount of time and effort in our preparation. We have been taking French lessons at Berlitz since May – in my case at least with only moderate success, under the tuition of a nice young man called Marc who has patiently conversed with us separately for many hours. I had my last lesson today, and I have spent about three days trying to understand voluminous French papers. I hope all this trouble will prove to have been worthwhile. I confess to feeling anxious and inadequate. I am sure that I shall be outshone by the English, who know so much more about judicial review and will no doubt speak and understand French much better than I do. A week later, however, I am to spend two days with the Conseil Constitutionnel in Paris, this time as the UK representative at a gathering of all the EU States. That will be an easier ride for me and, as it happens, a much more intelligible one also as a result of what I expect to have gleaned from the Conseil d'Etat. It was a happy coincidence that Lord Goff, who was originally invited, was unable to go because of a previous commitment to a seminar with a German delegation at Oxford, and that he chose me to represent the House of Lords in his place. The two visits, so close together, should make me much better informed.

18 September 1997

We were met on our arrival at Paris by Conseiller Roger Errera, who escorted us to the Hôtel Lutetia at the Boulevard Raspail on the Left Bank. We had stayed there four years ago on the last Exchange, and it was good to be back. Errera, an enthusiast for these Exchanges and virtually bi-legal as well as bilingual, was very friendly. He tactfully left us alone when we reached the hotel. There was time for us to walk to the Seine and the Tuileries Gardens before our team gathered for dinner in the evening. We were already in good form when the French arrived. My opposite number President Jean Massot said a few words of welcome to start the dinner, and I said a few words of thanks at the end to finish off. But it was all very informal. We spoke a mixture of French and English, but mainly English as those present seemed fairly fluent in our language.

Our working session began the next morning at 9.30am. We spent our time discussing 'Les Juges et la Loi', judicial review of legislation, and in the afternoon extradition. Both sessions were lively and full of interest, especially the first. At the end of our day we were joined by the spouses for the bus ride back to the hotel. After a brief tidy-up we were taken by bus to the Place Vendôme – still with eerie memories of Princess Diana's last visit there only two weeks' earlier – for a reception given by the Minister of Justice, Mme Elisabeth Guigou, at the Chancellery. As we were walking from the bus the Secretary General of the Conseil d'Etat told me that the Minister was expected to make a speech and he suggested that I should make a speech in reply, in French. Had I not had the benefit of foresight and laid my plans long in advance, I would have been caught off-balance – not to say greatly alarmed – by this request. But I had been carrying in my pocket for 24 hours a short speech which I had typed out in Edinburgh two weeks' earlier and had had translated through the offices of the Lord Chancellor's Department by the British Embassy. It was far from clear from the programme when it would have been appropriate for me to speak, if at all. But all the essentials for a speech for any occasion were there. So fortunately I was able to reassure the Secretary General that I would do my duty, and I remained calm.

When the Minister of Justice – La Ministre, as she likes to be called – arrived to join what had become quite a large gathering of legal dignitaries, it was clear that she was a much-respected figure. This was mainly by virtue of her office, because as Garde des Sceaux, she is the equivalent of the Keeper of the Great Seal and the Lord Chancellor. Her appointment recently by the new Socialist Prime Minister, Lionel Jospin, is controversial as she has no legal experience. But she is a determined and powerful character by all accounts. Quite slight and quiet, fair-haired and slim, she looked a little vulnerable as I followed her about introducing her to members of the British team – or them to her, rather – as she circulated before arriving at the podium where there was a microphone. She duly produced a typewritten speech which she proceeded to read in a serious, quiet voice beginning with some kind words of sympathy over Princess Diana's death. It was short and formal, the perfect setting for my almost equally short reply. I had included a brief mention of Diana's death also, saying how it had affected both countries in equal measure. I had been uncertain as to whether I should say anything about this, but in the event it was the perfect response to Mme Guigou's kind words. I included a few light-hearted remarks also and ended with a few words in English in more direct response to what she had said about the purpose of the colloquium. Mary said that there were murmurs of approval from the British team around her. I was relieved that I had done what was expected, satisfied everyone and not let the British team down.

Next day our subject was judicial review of administration. A very substantial paper by a French Conseillor provided the framework, and Robert Carnwath, presenting David Keene's paper, did a fine job setting out the British position. At the start of the afternoon session I presented the Vice-President of the Conseil d'Etat, Renaud Denoix de Saint Marc, with a copy of the latest edition of Woolf's Judicial Review, in English, about 1,000 pages, which he looked at quizzically as he speaks only French. It was a signed copy nevertheless for the Conseil's library. Then it was back to the hotel for another quick change before our bus took us to a reception at the British Embassy. The Ambassador, Michael Jay, was a familiar figure from recent coverage of the events two weeks ago. The guests were the British team and a few senior figures from the Conseil d'Etat. At 8pm prompt we left the British Embassy to be taken by bus back to our hotel. I arranged for the bus to stop just a bit short of the hotel for us all to have supper together in a delightful small restaurant to complete the occasion of our visit.

28 September 1997

I returned yesterday morning from my second visit to Paris in two weeks, this time to the Conseil Constitutionnel. The occasion was a seminar organised by Roland Dumas, the President of the Conseil. It was designed to bring together representatives of all the Constitutional Courts in the EU, or their equivalents, to discuss topics of mutual interest with representatives of the European Court of Justice. It was difficult for us to see, in advance, how the UK – the House of Lords being the obvious representative – might fit in to such a gathering. We have, of course, no written constitution and no constitutional court. In that respect, among many others, we are unique among all the Member States. However, I contributed a written response to a questionnaire which had been circulated in advance to all the 15 Member States, and I spent a day in preparation beforehand reading up the responses of the others in order to try to equip myself for the discussion.

The following day we gathered in beautiful sunshine in the sparkling surroundings of the Palais Royale for our first meeting. It was a big gathering. Some of the Member States had three representatives, others two and all nine members of the Conseil Constitutionnel were there also. I was in a corner at one end between Greece and Austria, with a Union Jack on the table in front of me. About us were various officials from the French side, and at one end the translators. The majority of the contributions were in French. Only the Scandinavian countries, the British Isles and Germany stuck resolutely to English. After the end of the morning session we were taken by bus to luncheon with the Minister of European Affairs at the Quai d'Orsay – the Foreign Office. This is a small palace, set in beautiful grounds beside the River Seine. There was a reception in huge gilded and tapestried rooms. Then we went in to lunch where, after some long formal speeches, we were given a superb meal with most excellent wines – light, interesting and delicious food, and three different soft, kind wines which included champagne with dessert to end it. The lunch was so light and delicious that we were quite able to settle down to two hours more of discussion afterwards. We were then taken by bus for a reception at the residence of the

Prime Minister, Lionel Jospin, at the Hôtel de Matignon in the rue de Varenne. A black redstart was singing from a building overlooking the large garden as we arrived, several times in full rich song. We were received by the Prime Minister with some handshakes – I was one of the lucky ones – and he then made a speech of welcome to which President Dumas replied. He had a fine, firm voice and spoke well. But his rather crumpled appearance in a grey suit seemed a bit out of keeping, except to make the point that he is after all a socialist.

The following day we continued our discussions in the morning. This time lunch was at the Hôtel de Lassay, the residence of the President of the National Assembly, Monsieur Laurent Fabius, second in Government only to the Prime Minister. He stood on the steps, flanked by a guard of honour, to receive us, very smartly dressed and debonair. Once again we had speeches before luncheon, including the inevitable reply by President Dumas. And once again the meal was quite breathtaking in its quality. We concluded our sessions after an hour in the afternoon. There was a little time for walking about on another lovely day of sunshine before the final event at the Chancellery in the Place Vendôme where Mme Elisabeth Guigou made a final speech to which, of course, President Dumas replied. People then drifted away from what had been a somewhat downbeat end to a magnificent round of receptions and entertainments.

On my return to London I was required to write a brief report on my visit for the Lord Chancellor's Department in exchange for their contribution towards my travelling expenses. I made the point that it was essential for the UK to be represented, despite our unique status as a country without a constitution and with no constitutional court. The main achievement of the conference was to raise general awareness of what each Member State is up to, and of the need to respect the ECJ as a unifying force despite the various constitutional differences.

1997 – October to December

4 October 1997

This year the Opening of the Legal Year was on a Wednesday. So no judicial business was set down for that week, apart from some petitions for leave in the Privy Council in which I was not involved. I spent much useful time clearing up in my room ready for the new term. On the Thursday morning I was interviewed by Sally Hardcastle for John Forsyth's programme for BBC Radio Scotland called *Lawful Business* about the work of the House of Lords as it affects Scotland. She was a mature, relaxed interviewer. I hope all goes well when it appears on air and when she writes a covering article for *The Sunday Times* on 12 October. I do not want to be controversial. But I do value the opportunity to communicate to a wider public about our work. The new Lord President, Alan Rodger, remains aloof from the media, as does Douglas Cullen, the Lord Justice Clerk. It is quite a different atmosphere from a year or so ago when Donald Ross and I were almost household names. Now there is nothing for the press to catch onto. It is a deliberate difference of approach, of course. How wise it is for my successors to remain under cover we shall have to wait and see.

7 November 1997

Mary and I returned last Sunday from Cape Town, where we had been attending a conference of the Commonwealth Magistrates' and Judges' Association (CMJA). The theme of the conference was human rights. This was a very topical and appropriate subject, as South Africa has emerged only so very recently from the shadow of apartheid. The holding of a conference of this kind in Cape Town ten years ago – perhaps even five years ago – would have been unthinkable. As it was, there was a huge attendance of over 500 people, with all the African countries very well represented, including Mozambique, which although never a British colony, has recently been admitted to the Commonwealth. There was genuine warmth and interest on all sides. We were welcomed at the Opening Ceremony in the South African Parliament building by the new Chief Justice, Ismail Mohamed, and by the Minister of Justice, Doctor Dullah Omar. Both made powerful speeches about the significance of constitutional change in their country which helped put the whole occasion into perspective. Most people in authority in the Government seem now to be black or Cape Coloured. But the policy is to respect all races, and the whites seem relatively calm and relaxed about what has taken place. Among those present at the conference was Tom Bingham, who was with us for 48 hours. He and I were to speak and then chair seminars. I was worried about what I might say. But in the event inspiration came when it was needed, and I filled my 15-minute slot with some fresh thoughts to add to a previously circulated paper. There was an afternoon spent on discussing asylum law, which is a dreadfully depressing subject just now in Southern Africa. The numbers of displaced persons are so large, the delays in dealing with them are so great and, for the most part, their conditions are so desperate.

Following our return to London I reported the following day at 8.30am for duty in my room. The week was one of two Scots appeals, one about equal pay with Browne-Wilkinson in the chair,[56] and the other about additional damages in copyright with Robert Goff.[57] All went reasonably well, and we had a pleasant time listening to the equal pay appeal for a day and a bit until my time came to contribute to the debate on summing-up. James Clyde did a neat job on his contribution, which was listened to as usual in silence by everybody. Then Browne-Wilkinson asked me to make mine, which I began to do. Then suddenly I found myself stumbling out an inept reply, which left me feeling rather isolated

---

56 *Strathclyde Regional Council v Wallace* 1998 SC (HL) 72.
57 *Redrow Homes Ltd v Bett Brothers plc* 1998 SC (HL) 64.

and ashamed at my incompetence. For the rest of the week I felt rather dejected and useless at having let myself down in this way.

16 November 1997

A much better week, I am glad to say. There were four days of relatively easy work in the Privy Council with Robert Goff which helped to restore morale. In one of them, *Daley v The Queen*,[58] we were able to set aside a conviction for capital murder, for which the death sentence is mandatory, and substitute a conviction for non-capital murder for which the death sentence is discretionary. We treat these mandatory death sentence cases with the greatest possible care, as that penalty is so objectionable. I was asked to write the judgment in that case, so I feel that I am back on the rails again.

31 December 1997

The rest of the term was spent in the Privy Council, except for two days off which I was given to write the judgment in a case from the Cayman Islands, *Detective Inspector Gibbs v Rae*.[59] This was an interesting, relaxed and enjoyable period, save for the fact that in *Gibbs v Rae* Brian Hutton, who had been with Robert Goff and myself in our discussion, decided to change his mind after I had written the draft judgment. In the result I had to spend the first three weeks of the Christmas break writing a dissenting judgment instead. The case is an important one about the consequences of a search warrant which was alleged to have been procured maliciously. This is a novel action, as there is no reported example of a successful claim for damages on such a ground where there was, as in this case, no arrest. Drugs legislation was the basis for the warrant sought by the detective inspector. The plaintiff had been sacked by the Amsterdam Bank for whom he was working in the Cayman Islands. He claimed that this was because of the execution of a search warrant. The trial judge was sceptical and dismissed the claim, but the Court of Appeal allowed the appeal and awarded aggravated damages. Robert Goff and I were not impressed by the plaintiff's claim. But Johan Steyn and Tom Gault[60] were, especially as the detective inspector did not give evidence to say what the basis was for his suspicion that the plaintiff had been engaged in drug trafficking as to which, in the event, no evidence was revealed. It was surprising that Brian Hutton should have favoured the plaintiff, with his background of similar problems for the police about disclosure of sources in Northern Ireland. His reasons did not seem to me to be very clear, and Robert and I remained convinced that there was no basis at all in the evidence for a finding that the detective inspector acted maliciously.

---

58 [1998] 1 WLR 494.
59 [1998] AC 786.
60 Gault J, a judge of the Court of Appeal of New Zealand, who was sitting with us as a Privy Counsellor.

31 December 1997

Travel to and from London, which had been beset by delays earlier in the term, settled down until the weekend at the start of the month when there was a fire at Heathrow about which I heard when I was getting up on Friday morning ready to fly home. I was able to revert to the train and get the 9am from King's Cross to Edinburgh instead. But here again there were delays, as the trains in both directions were more than an hour late. One just has to be patient.

On 5 December I delivered the David Hume Lecture in Edinburgh. I chose devolution and judicial aspects of it as my subject and spent a lot of time during successive weekends setting it up on the computer and revising it. Publication was expected, so I had to be thorough. As the Scotland Bill had not yet been published I had to base my comments on the White Paper and, latterly, on the Government of Wales Bill which came out first. I drew attention to the major impact which human rights legislation will have on the competency of the Scottish Parliament and the judicial role, and to the curiosities resulting from the choice of the Privy Council in place of the House of Lords as the court of last resort on devolution questions. The lecture was quite well attended and people were quite kind about it. To my relief there was no publicity about it in the press.

The lecture business is not over, unfortunately. I had to agree, after years of putting it off, to deliver the James Wood Lecture in Glasgow at the end of February. So I shall have to start work on that early in the New Year. But before I can settle down to that task I shall have to do my revisals to the Arbitration title in the *Stair Memorial Encyclopaedia* which I wrote when I was Dean of Faculty and is now in need of some updating. I had agreed to do this a year ago but had not been able to do anything about it until about a week ago.

Alan Rodger still shows no inclination to communicate with the public through the press, nor does Douglas Cullen hit the headlines even in his criminal sentencing role. It is all very different from the days when Donald Ross and I were in the papers with a major story almost every week. Devolution and all its various aspects absorb the media in Scotland at present. The law has no clear focus in this exciting new era of development. It is not my place to try to fill the vacuum, even if I could.

To my surprise I was asked last October by John Arbuthnott, the Principal and Vice-Chancellor of the University of Strathclyde, whether I would be willing to be nominated as the next Chancellor of the University when the post falls vacant next year on the retiral of Lord Tombs. I had not expected such an honour and was rather uncertain about it. But with Mary's encouragement, and after consulting Robert Goff, David Wilson[61] (Chancellor of Aberdeen) and James Mackay (Chancellor of Heriot-Watt), I agreed. I paid a visit to the Principal's residence to discuss the matter, calling in on the new Glasgow High Court extension in the Salt Market on the way. The Principal Clerk, Hugh Foley, kindly arranged this for me, and as the University provided me with a car

---

61 Lord Wilson of Tillyorn, a former Governor of Hong Kong.

I was also able to come and go in the style to which I am no longer accustomed. Now we must wait for the election of the Chancellor at the end of January, but it seems unlikely that anyone else will be nominated. I am the University Court's sole nominee. If I am elected the ceremony will be at the end of April when I will be installed. I have nominated my former devil Neil MacGregor, who has made such a success of his position as Director of the National Gallery, Angus Grossart and Bruce Pattullo[62] as my honorary graduands to share the day with me and Mary.

As the months slip by since I left Parliament House I find it harder and harder to believe that for ten years I was at the centre of events there, as Dean and then as Lord President. In some ways the huge excitement and responsibility for those offices appears to have diminished with time and distance. In others the experience is one which I find more and more daunting in retrospect, because my new job has so little to offer by way of ceremony and elevated circumstance. I move around in quite shabby clothes, without a car or a driver or a secretary of my own. And yet the work is much more demanding intellectually and the horizons seem so very wide, as does the range of people with whom I am now in contact. It is a remarkable thing to have experienced such fortunes before reaching the age of 60, which I fall to do next year.

1998 – January to April

1 February 1998

The Christmas and New Year holiday was much taken up with editing work on the Arbitration title of the *Stair Memorial Encyclopaedia*. I had undertaken to do this revision work, of a title which I wrote myself about eight years ago, in a fit of enthusiasm about 15 months previously. Time went by and nothing was done. The deadline was approaching, so I had to commit myself. In fact it was, although time-consuming, not too arduous. Use of the computer was a great help in presenting the publishers with a text which was presentable, in both hard copy and on disc. That task done, I then had two lectures to prepare. I had delivered the Hume Lecture on 5 December. Then I was asked to give the James Wood Lecture in Glasgow on 28 February, and the Faculty invited me to give one on 30 January on the Judicial Committee of the Privy Council. These take time, but it is becoming quite an industry for me as Kenneth Pritchard has asked me to give the inaugural lecture in his new series on 20 March. I have also been invited by the Reform Club in London to give the Atkin Lecture for them in October. In addition I have to give one in a law teachers' conference in Glasgow in April and another at an arbitration conference in May. Fortunately the number of judgments I am being asked to write in the House of Lords is not many. Browne-Wilkinson has not asked me to do one since the

---

62 Sir Bruce Pattullo, the Governor of the Bank of Scotland 1991–98.

summer, and I have had only one or two in the Privy Council from Robert Goff since October. I am content to go on the lecture circuit instead.

Last week I was elected to be Chancellor of the University of Strathclyde. As already mentioned, this came as a surprise to me when John Arbuthnott asked me whether I would be willing to be considered for the post. It is still difficult for me to comprehend what the job will involve apart, obviously, from presiding at graduation ceremonies. The process of learning has now begun. Last week I was given a fitting of the Chancellor's robe, bedecked with much gold braid and very heavy in consequence. Next Friday there is to be an interview for *The Herald*, and at the end of the month Mary and I are to visit the University. Mary is being a great support, and it is largely due to her encouragement that I decided to accept the offer.

Last week was, apart from the announcement of the Chancellorship, another rather depressing one for me. Yet another of my decisions in the High Court has been reversed by a court of five judges in the High Court of Justiciary.[63] It was done in quite a brutal fashion, prompting a *Herald* headline that I bungled the previous case. Colleagues in London who met me at the Scottish Peers' Association dinner were surprised and sympathetic. But, given such blunt and unfeeling criticism, I found it hard to be uplifted by their concern. I thought that my decision was carefully researched and well expressed, in an area of the law on corroboration which required clarification. To say that it was bungled gave quite the wrong impression. So it was with trepidation that I went to give my lecture to the Faculty, as I felt that I had been disgraced. In the event I was received very kindly by the Dean, Nigel Emslie, and the audience were friendly and attentive. I felt among friends. Then today, on a *Lawful Business* programme on BBC Radio Scotland, Gordon Jackson QC said that he was troubled by the five-judge decision as he had thought that my decision – concurred in by Lords Cowie and Allanbridge – was a good one. There was more than a suggestion that what was really happening was a consequence of a change of personnel – although Jackson said that he could not possibly comment on the remark, said to be current now in Parliament House, that the judges are searching out for decisions by Lord Hope. To me that is indeed what it feels like. The two cases on corroboration which had been overturned, taken together, made up a coherent and logical whole to prevent sexual abuse cases going unpunished where there were no eye witnesses or injuries while avoiding the risk of unfairness or injustice. Now the regime will find it easier to secure convictions across the board, while leaving those sexual abuse cases in a limbo of their own. That does not fit with my philosophy. I was glad that, although *The Herald* had missed the point, some others are starting to notice what is going on.

---

63 *Fox v HM Advocate* 1998 JC 94, disapproving *Mackie v HM Advocate* 1994 JC 132.

11 February 1998

Yesterday the Criminal Appeal Court sitting in Edinburgh delivered its judgment in the ice cream wars case of *Campbell and Steele*.[64] After serving a turbulent 12 years in custody of their life sentences for murder by fire-raising – a period punctuated by hunger strikes, dirty protests, prison escapes and other demonstrations to draw attention to their claims that they were innocent – the two men were released on bail in December 1996 by a court presided over by Donald Ross. Their cases had been referred back to the Appeal Court on the ground of fresh evidence, and in the light of the proposals for amending the law about appeals on this ground in the Sutherland Committee's Report. During their 12 months on bail they presented themselves to the press as civilised men who could live in society without causing trouble. Campbell in particular had grown visibly younger as he discarded his long beard and haggard appearance in favour of clean-shaven good looks, and he had had a baby by his girlfriend. As in the case of *Beattie*,[65] over which I presided some years ago, there was a general expectation, especially on this occasion as the appellants were on bail, that they would be freed.

In the event, after three hours delivering judgment, the court under Douglas Cullen refused the appeal. The two men are now back in custody to face several more years in prison and the consequent separation from the families which they had re-joined. This in itself is a difficult result for the public to accept, but the situation was made much worse by the fact that the court was not unanimous. John McCluskey wanted the case to proceed to the next stage, for the hearing of the additional evidence. But Ranald Sutherland, as tough as a brick in such matters as I discovered in *Beattie*, would have none of this. Douglas Cullen was of the same view.

The basic problem appears to have been that the additional evidence was that of a Crown witness at the trial who claimed that he had given perjured evidence as a result of pressure from the police. But the amendments made by the 1997 Act, while allowing changes in the evidence at the trial where there was a reasonable explanation for this, requires that there must be some independent evidence supporting the reasonableness of the explanation. There was no corroboration of the allegation of police pressure. But there never will be, will there? John McCluskey seems to have seen through this impasse. I was not there and did not hear the argument, so I am in no position to say who was right. But I wonder whether Douglas Cullen, seeing that there was a dissent and assuming that he could not secure unanimity, should not perhaps have given the appellants the benefit of the doubt and sided with McCluskey at least to the extent of allowing the additional evidence to be heard. The court would still have been divided, but at least the appearance of a miscarriage of justice would have been avoided. As it is, the disagreement will be seen as a signal that the law is in disarray and must be changed again.

---

64 Reported as *Campbell v HM Advocate* 1998 JC 130.
65 *Beattie v HM Advocate* 1995 JC 33.

15 February 1998

There has been much press criticism of the court about the ice cream wars case. It has been described as having damaged public confidence in the Scottish criminal justice system and the perceived fairness of the courts. The judicial system, it is said, has appeared to contradict itself, allowing the two men bail so that they could rebuild their lives and then, at a stroke, destroying all of that without hearing the evidence. I feel sad and frustrated. The *Mackie* case in 1994, so recently overruled by a court of five judges,[66] was said to have restored confidence in the justice system. The *Church* case,[67] in which I was also overruled by five judges, was also hailed as a breakthrough and as a sign of a new more liberal approach to miscarriage of justice cases. There is no one, except perhaps Lord McCluskey, who is prepared to take the lead for which I tried so hard to lay a basis. I am sad and frustrated because there is nothing I can do about it. I must, of course, remain silent. Writing about it here in the privacy of my diary is the only way in which I can give vent to my frustration.

A very enjoyable week in the House of Lords has restored my spirits. We sat as Goff, Lloyd, Nolan, Hoffmann and myself – a very pleasant team. We had two interesting and enjoyable cases. One about gaming machines and a charge of unlawful gaming, the question being whether teddy bears were 'tokens' and thus non-monetary prizes in which, Hoffmann dissenting, Robert Goff asked me to write the judgment.[68] One of the teddy bears had been brought along for the hearing, much to Tony Lloyd's delight. The other case was about interim certificates in building contracts, which we may all wish to write about.[69] So my days of inertia are over and I feel useful again. Next week it is back to the Privy Council for much of the rest of the term. But I have one really interesting case in the House of Lords in the week after next about restitution into which, for some reason unknown to me, I have been brought as a late member of the team.[70]

This weekend saw me deliver another lecture in my series of five lectures which have occupied much of my time since Christmas. This was the James Wood Lecture in Glasgow, under the chairmanship of Professor Joe Thomson. I took advantage of the journey to Glasgow to pay my first visit as Chancellor to the University of Strathclyde. The Secretary, Peter West, laid on a very efficient and interesting programme for me as an introduction to the structure of the University. Mary was given a programme of her own, which was a visit to Ross Priory by Loch Lomond. She joined me for the lecture and dinner at Glasgow University afterwards, where we were joined also by John Arbuthnott, Strathclyde's Principal. Mary was marvellous. She really entered into the spirit

---

66 See fn 63.
67 *Church v HM Advocate* 1995 SLT 604, overruled by *Elliott v HM Advocate* 1995 JC 95.
68 *R v Burt & Adams Ltd* [1999] AC 247.
69 *Beaufort Developments (NI) Ltd v Gilbert-Ash NI Ltd* [1999] 1 AC 266.
70 See fn 71.

of the thing. She will give, and is already giving, much pleasure to all she meets and much support to me as well.

14 March 1998

I went to Arniston House near Gorebridge yesterday to attend a seminar for the Court of Session judges on human rights. It being Friday, the court was closed for the day so that all the judges could attend. Jim McGhie from the Land Court was there also, as was James Clyde. Paul Kennedy from the English Judicial Studies Board and Anthony Campbell from the JSB Northern Ireland came too. We had a good day, with a talk from the Lord Advocate and lectures from Professor Christopher Gane and a senior legal assistant from the European Court of Human Rights in Strasbourg. There was time also for questions and discussion. The setting was lovely, in a fine Adam mansion in parkland with wood fires in the panelled room where we met and a buffet luncheon in the main hall. There was a relaxed and friendly atmosphere. But there were very real concerns about the problems which the courts will face when the human rights legislation takes effect.

Back in London we had sat all week on a most important case about restitution, the question being whether the remedy of unjust enrichment was available under the common law: *Kleinwort Benson Ltd v Lincoln City Council and Others*.[71] The panel was Goff, Browne-Wilkinson, Lloyd, Hoffmann and myself. The case has not yet finished. So we will have to sit early on Monday to finish it off by lunchtime, after which I begin a four-day appeal in the Privy Council.

The problem in the case is whether we should reconsider the bar on recovery on the ground of unjust enrichment where the error is one of law, which I dealt with under the law of Scotland when sitting as Lord President in *Morgan Guaranty* in 1994.[72] Then there are questions about the safeguards to be set in place, as errors of law may have much wider repercussions than errors of fact. The transactions with which we are concerned are complicated – 'closed swaps', as they are called. So there is a question as to whether it would be right to undo these transactions now. There is a large amount of English law to consider, almost all of it unfamiliar. I have the added problem that my Scots law background is of a civilian restitution system, not that of the common law. After remaining completely silent for two days, Lennie Hoffmann came out with one of his remarks which changed the whole character of the debate saying that – as both parties were agreed as to what they were doing and the law was at that time what they thought it was – there was no mistake. Nicolas Browne-Wilkinson too has seized on this approach, as I fear has Robert Goff also. I am baffled. How can you say there was no mistake in the case of an enrichment because the law, as we now know it to be, was not what they thought it to be at the time when they made the payment? I began to feel rather

---

71 [1999] 2 AC 349.
72 *Morgan Guaranty Trust Co of New York v Lothian Regional Council* 1995 SC 151.

alone, with my simple Scots law structure in mind. The lightning speed with which my colleagues mustered the authorities, while impressive, is also worrying to a newcomer. Various pennies dropped into my mind on the Shuttle home. At 2.30am, having been woken by our pet dog Rosie and our pet cat Sacha, I composed a note expressing my thoughts to Robert which I typed up and faxed to him last night. I have no idea what will come of this. If he does not agree, I shall have an interesting speech to compose.

21 March 1998

Robert Goff very kindly sent me a five-page fax on Saturday, which explained his thinking and reassured me that he saw the importance of my point. He accepts that the question whether or not there was a mistake will require very careful analysis. We resumed the hearing on Monday, to find ourselves presented with a masterly written reply by Robert Southwell QC which helped to resolve a lot of the problems and to confine the areas of difficulty to the mistake point. In our discussions next day both Nicolas Browne-Wilkinson and Lennie Hoffmann, both chancery lawyers, stuck to their point that there had been no mistake. Tony Lloyd was quite undecided, and Robert Goff also rather cautious about expressing a final view. I said that there was a mistake, but my reasoning will also require a good deal of careful refinement and study. Where the case will end up may depend on how Tony Lloyd's mind will work. I do hope that he agrees with Robert.

We had an interesting case in the Privy Council about the extradition of an alleged fraudulent businessman from The Bahamas to Switzerland, in which Johan Steyn took the lead.[73] Robert Goff seemed to be dreadfully bored. No doubt he was wishing that he was still discussing unjustified enrichment. On Thursday afternoon after we got back from the Privy Council Mr Marat Baglai, the Chairman of the Russian Constitutional Court, came to visit me at the request of the Foreign Office. He was a rather reserved, almost self-effacing man. But he is clearly astute and politically very aware – a Yeltsin supporter and a survivor. He asked me to explain how the House of Lords was a Supreme Court. This was not easy to do, in a short space of time through an interpreter. Then we were interrupted by Frances Rice, who came to me with an urgent change in the programme which she had to agree with me at Robert Goff's request. Next week the House of Lords is to hear a five-judge case on repetitive strain injury.[74] There will be some difficult law, but even more difficult facts. Apparently Robert had thought that his Committee – I was to be in the Privy Council – needed to be strengthened and had asked for me to be switched in place of Brian Hutton. This was rather a nice compliment, which Frances understandably was anxious to conceal from Brian. So I went home feeling unusually cheerful after a demanding week.

---

73 *Rey v Government of Switzerland* [1999] 1 AC 54.
74 See fn 76.

Yesterday evening Mary and I went by government car to Glasgow for Kenneth Pritchard's inaugural lecture. About 120 Glasgow lawyers came to listen to me speak about the practice of law under Scotland's Parliament. Then we were entertained to a delicious dinner in the Yes Restaurant in West Nile Street. So it was a happy occasion – so nice to see so many old friends.

11 April 1998

Easter weekend – Easter Sunday tomorrow, followed by a week at Craighead which looks likely to be very cold and unsettled. A strong Arctic air stream has been with us for almost a week, with heavy snow at the start. It fractured one of the wires leading from the generator in the steading, which supplies us with our electricity as there is no public supply, to the house at Craighead. This was very kindly reported to us by Andrew Mitchell and has now been repaired.

I have spent almost the whole of Holy Week doing three judgments. The first was short. It was a brief expression of regret in a concurring judgment in *Total Gas Marketing Ltd v Arco British Ltd*.[75] Then there was a large one in March about *Pickford v ICI*,[76] in which I have the judgment to do. Slynn and Steyn are dissenting, so care is needed. It is a case in which we are reversing the Court of Appeal's decision to overrule the trial judge and award the plaintiff damages for an alleged repetitive strain type injury while employed as a secretary. The third was *Kleinwort Benson* on which I spent three or four days. It continues to be a most interesting case. I am an outsider, as I see the case so differently from my English colleagues. I shall have to read what I have written in a week's time to see whether it still makes sense.

Our son Will has persuaded me to invest in a new laser printer for our computer. This has already within 24 hours of use proved itself to be a great improvement. It is so much easier to use. It is able to print off a 35-page judgment unsupervised – and also to do envelopes!

1998 – May to July

3 May 1998

A lovely day at Craighead, where Mary and I went yesterday after a fascinating week during which I was installed as Chancellor of the University of Strathclyde. I had asked to be released from judicial duties for the Tuesday to Thursday to allow me to get home on Tuesday and spend the next three days in the University. I was given the Monday off as well, but I thought that this was overdoing it. So I asked to be put into the Privy Council for the one-day case fixed for that day. Our resources are becoming very stretched, as Donald

---

75 [1998] 2 Lloyds Rep 209.
76 *Pickford v Imperial Chemical Industries plc* [1998] ICR 673.

Nicholls has been off for four months with a viral problem, Mark Saville is seconded to the Bloody Sunday Inquiry in Northern Ireland and Robert Goff is also ill with severe sinus trouble. Nico Browne-Wilkinson was also ill with a streptococcal infection in his leg, but he was able to sit on this case. I saw as soon as I received the papers that the single day allocated to the case – a tax appeal from New Zealand – was likely to be inadequate. So I spent much of Sunday packing to have enough ready for a quick getaway on the Tuesday. In the event I had to change my flight from Monday evening to Tuesday 3pm and fly instead to Glasgow, where Mary met me, having been taken there together with my suitcase by Kath, one of the Strathclyde drivers.

We were based with the Arbuthnotts in the Principal's residence at University House on the Jordanhill Campus. This was very peaceful, although somewhat austere with a rather awkward shower and no bath. On the Tuesday evening there was a dinner, black tie, in the Barony Hall to welcome me and the honorary graduands – Rector Josef Mayer of Łodz in Poland and my own three nominees, Neil MacGregor, Bruce Pattullo and Angus Grossart. The Chairman of the University Court, Roy Johnson, made a charming speech about me, much helped by Mary, to which I made a rather inadequate reply. Next day was the Installation Day. We gathered in George Square, from where we walked behind a pipe band to the Barony Hall, close to the Cathedral, after a buffet lunch in the Trades' House. Then there was all the colour of the ceremony itself, at the end of which I delivered my five-minute installation address. In the evening there was a promenade-style concert in the Barony, which gave us a chance to circulate as the students played some excellent music. Thursday was a day of visits by me to Jordanhill, Ross Priory, the Students' Union, where there was another buffet lunch, and various parts of the Anderson Campus. In the evening the Royal Scottish National Orchestra gave a concert of opera music in the Barony with student singers of very high calibre singing the vocal parts. This was followed by another buffet meal. Friday was the University Court and the annual Convocation. There was a lunch in between, which was very welcome after so little sustenance since Tuesday. After that I returned to Edinburgh via the airport where I collected my car. In the evening we went to the Society of the Writers to the Signet Ball, where Mary's brother Andrew Kerr, who is Clerk to the Society, had put together a delightful family party.

Mary and I were captivated by the reception which we received at Strathclyde. There was much kindness and goodwill wherever we went. The position is purely honorary, of course, but we were made at once to feel part of the Strathclyde family. It became clear that there was much that we could contribute to morale and a sense of well-being by taking an interest in all we saw and everyone we met. Mary is a marvellous asset on these occasions. Both John Arbuthnott and Roy Johnson have been charmed by her, and this reflects on me. Our comparative youth and our place in Scottish life are assets which help to set us on our difficult task of succeeding Lord and Lady Tombs who have preceded us. For us, public life of this kind is quite easy to handle after my time as Dean of Faculty and Lord President. But this is a much bigger affair altogether than being Dean and we are much more surrounded with goodwill than I ever felt when I was Lord President. The University is a very large business indeed, with an income and expenditure of about £132 million per annum and assets of £55 million. There are some 50,000 students overall, including many part-time, and there is a huge research activity. It is very efficiently run. We ended the week with a deep sense of privilege at having been asked to play a part in the life of this remarkable university.

24 May 1998

The Whitsun break has arrived, and we are at Craighead again. The sycamores are out in their bright green leaves, the leaves on the ash trees are still emerging and the air is cool and clear and very peaceful. The grass is cut, the potatoes are trenched, the peas and beans are well on and protected by nets. Several days of peace lie ahead.

The last case of the short Easter term was a Scots appeal: *Dollar Land v CIN*.[77] It was an interesting case in which the appellants seek compensation under the law of unjust enrichment for the financial gains, which were very substantial, which had been obtained by the landlord at their expense as a result of the exercise of an irritancy. The case had come before an Extra Division during my last year as Lord President. Ranald Sutherland presided with Douglas Cullen, and I remember arranging with the Keeper of the Rolls that Alan Rodger, newly-appointed to the Bench, should sit also as the law of unjustified enrichment is one of his special interests. In the event he dissented, but I think that Dollar Land would have appealed anyway as they are determined litigants.

Matthew Clarke appeared with David Johnston for Dollar Land. Nigel Emslie, Dean of Faculty, with John Wright was for CIN. Charles Jauncey sat with us, with Lords Browne-Wilkinson, Nolan and Hoffmann. James Clyde was not included, but I think that he had asked for one of the days off for other reasons. Matthew made the best of a difficult job but, at Nico's suggestion and as there was no answer to it, we did not call on the other side. I asked the four members of Faculty and James Clyde to a drink in my flat at Gray's Inn afterwards, which was a real pleasure for me. There was much amusing talk in our cool sitting room after a hot sunny day at Westminster. I was asked to write the judgment. I decided to say a bit about the structure of the law of unjustified enrichment, and the relationship between it and the various remedies. Various academics, especially Robin Evans-Jones of Aberdeen, have got very excited about this, so whatever I say will attract interest. He described what I said in *Morgan Guaranty* as 'chaos', which I thought was a bit overdone. I hope that I may get a better reception this time.

Robert Goff, now fortunately fully recovered, has produced a marvellous draft speech in the *Kleinwort Benson* case which, to my relief, has reached the same

---

77 *Dollar Land (Cumbernauld) Ltd v CIN Properties Ltd* 1998 SC (HL) 90.

view on all points as I have done. If Tony Lloyd agrees, it will not matter what Nico and Lennie say. They were taking a line in our discussions which I would have found very difficult. I spent some time before coming to Craighead tidying up my draft. But, apart from excising some pages on the idea of a simpler structure of English law which was unnecessary and rather too provocative, there was not much to do.

I was asked by Iain Noble – Sir Iain of Noble Grossart – to have supper with him and some others to discuss devolution issues. Having no excuse, I said yes. David Steel[78] and his wife Judy were there, and Brian Ivory of Highland Distillers and his wife. When I turned up Iain seemed surprised to see me. My acceptance did not appear to have got through to him via his secretary. He then said that he thought that he had invited Mary also, which he had not done. It all seemed a bit disorganised. It was difficult for me to say anything useful, as Brian Ivory was very loquacious and self-confident. He was the typical wealthy businessman. Iain Noble's ideas about things the Scottish Parliament might do, and how the banking and business community might be integrated in it as a kind of Senate, struck me as completely unrealistic. The Parliament will be far too busy with politics, and will be far more concerned with the demands and needs of their electorate, to be likely to do what these unelected businessmen will want it to do. And the English at Westminster will be jealous of giving our Parliament more scope to compete in the business world than it is able to do already. David Steel, however, seemed very well balanced and has a good grasp of the situation. His influence – and I do hope that he will have influence – will definitely be a force for good. That at least was something of value to take away from a very strange dinner party, where I felt very much the odd one out.

31 May 1998

I met a fulmar flying over Albyn Place towards me as I went to church this morning. There was a very strong easterly wind which has been with us for several days. It was odd to see this handsome seabird in the middle of the New Town, but they do tend to wander about from their nesting sites at this time of year. I saw one flying over Royal Circus from my window in India Street on 21 May 1992.

14 June 1998

It was a busy week both in London and in Edinburgh. There was a full programme of sittings. On Monday we sat on an extra day to complete the hearing in Re L about the Mental Health Act's provisions in regard to an autistic man who was detained in a mental hospital to which he had been admitted informally.[79] The question was, was he detained unlawfully and thus entitled to

---

78 Lord Steel of Aikwood KT.
79 R v Bournewood Community and Mental Health NHS Trust, ex parte L [1999] 1 AC 458.

damages for false imprisonment? Then we had three days about the animal rights protestors' attempts to prevent the export of live sheep and cattle through Shoreham Dock, in which the question was about the actions of the Sussex Police Chief Constable who had reduced the level of protection for the live animal exporters.[80] They were both very absorbing and interesting cases. Lord Goff presided in one and Lord Slynn in the other, each of them in their own way excellent chairmen. But the main interests of the week lay elsewhere.

There are to be three vacancies in our number over the next six months. Robert Goff and Michael Nolan are to go at the end of July, and Tony Lloyd will retire at the end of December. So the Lord Chancellor, Derry Irvine, convened a meeting on Wednesday afternoon to discuss the replacement. We had a preliminary meeting among ourselves on the Tuesday. It was an unnerving business, as the English members of our team got to work and sorted out the sheep from the goats – or the swans from the geese – among their colleagues in the Court of Appeal. The problem for James Clyde, Brian Hutton and myself is that we scarcely know any of them, whereas most of the others know most of them very well. Also the standard of expertise, brain-power and compatibility is set very high indeed, making me at least feel very much a second XI player whose place in the first team is very doubtful and will probably be untenable once the high-powered replacements arrive. There was pretty close agreement upon whom they should be: Robin Auld, Nicholas Phillips and Richard Scott, with Peter Millett as a fourth alternative. Johan Steyn put in a strong plea for Christopher Rose, but there was not much support for this elsewhere. The fear was that Derry, whose plans were already the subject of strong rumour, does not favour Nicholas Phillips at this stage and that he proposes to appoint John Hobhouse who was reputed to be a loner and very difficult to get on with. Several expressed strong resistance to him, but this was not unanimous.

When we met Derry next day he conducted a very efficient meeting. It was the day of the opening match of the World Cup for football in Paris, Scotland v Brazil, which was already in progress and on view on a large screen in the office as we went in for an hour or so of discussion. At Robert Goff's request he started at the junior end, and Mark Saville made a good job of recommending Auld, Phillips and Scott. Brian and I were duly reticent, and James Clyde was absent. Johan did not after all mention Rose, but he did mention his concern about Hobhouse on the ground that he was too much a man for black-letter law. So it went on up the ranks with little dissent. Tony Lloyd spoke favourably about Hobhouse, but Nico and Robert both stressed the importance of getting on with each other and with the staff. Robert ended our discussions about personalities and quality by saying that what was really needed on the Corridor was *brains*. Derry was receptive to advice about Phillips and said, to wide approval, that the fact that he is at present on a year-long inquiry[81] was no obstacle. Millett and Hobhouse appeared to be his preference, with unanimous support

80 R v Chief Constable of Sussex, ex parte International Trader's Ferry Ltd [1999] 2 AC 418.
81 The BSE Inquiry 1998–2000.

for Auld. Later Nico said that he believed the choice would go the other way. We shall have to see.

I suppose the truth is that, as in Scotland, the good people select themselves. But the standard is very high. I doubt very much whether, were it not for the need for two Scots and a kind thought for Northern Ireland too, James, Brian and I would make the grade. It was, as I have said, unnerving and disturbing, but it was also a unifying experience. We all felt closer and more sympathetic to each other afterwards and for some time, having had a really good frank discussion with each other about what matters to us all so much.

On Tuesday evening I was the host for a dinner in the House of Lords for the east London magistrates. Their leader, John Williams, had twisted my arm about this when we were in Cape Town. It was quite a trouble to set up, but my secretary Marilyn was most helpful – invaluable in fact. In the event 28 people came. They bought many things in the shop, and then had a very good dinner in the Attlee Room. I spoke afterwards and was questioned at length by an attentive audience, mainly women of middle class and a certain age.

On Thursday David Armati of the CMJA came to lunch. He is, as its President, on a visit from Australia to try to stir things into action after six months of slumber following the Cape Town conference. He is very direct, but I like and respect him very much. On Thursday evening, as Chancellor of Strathclyde University, I was host at a dinner in the Barry Room for an American professor, Professor Burton Clark and his wife Adele; the University's Principal, John Arbuthnott; and the Secretary, Peter West. The renowned educational reformer Lord Dearing joined us for dinner. Professor Clark was being rewarded for writing a book about modern entrepreneurial universities, among which the Scottish one which was listed was Strathclyde. He was very approachable and we had a delightful evening. His wife thought that the Chamber, which we visited briefly during a lively debate late in the evening, was quite 'awesome'. I felt so pleased to be able to help the University in this way. It is so easy for me, yet impressive for our visitors.

The catering staff in the House of Lords, on both occasions, were quite excellent. They brought home to me the immense privilege which one enjoys through membership of this amazing institution. Entertaining, on almost any scale, is made to feel quite effortless. The staff make it quite clear at all times that the peer – 'My Lord' – is the most important person. This does no harm to one's image in the eyes of one's guests.

I had to remain in London on the Thursday night. I came north on the British Midland flight from Heathrow to ensure an earlier arrival in Edinburgh as the Bmi flight is timed to arrive 20 minutes ahead of BA. This was because I had been invited to attend a family law seminar at which the Faculty's Family Law Group was being visited on a fact-finding mission by an English Family Law Working Party headed by Sir Stephen Browne, President, and Mathew Thorpe LJ, which included barristers, solicitors, academics and civil servants. There was little time to turn around, and I went up to Parliament House to meet them within one hour of arriving home. I spent the rest of the day with them, and returned home for a cup of tea. I then accompanied Mary to the Portuguese Consulate for drinks, before returning to join the seminar for dinner in the Stac Polly restaurant. On the Saturday morning I had to go back to the seminar. Today, as the London Underground goes on strike for two days this evening, I have to take a mid-afternoon flight back so that I can get into Central London before the strike starts. All very busy, but enjoyable.

The discussion in the seminar was concentrated on the provisions of the Family Law (Scotland) Act 1985 about financial provisions on divorce. Most of the cases were those for the opinions in which as Lord President I was responsible – *Little*, *Wallis* and *Geddes* in particular.[82] But it was the legislation rather than the cases to which the reluctant and suspicious English directed their questions, as Derry is said to be intending to introduce legislation on the Scottish model for England. The conversations were very lively. For us Anne Smith, Morag Wyse and Charles McNair, with Eric Clive and Joe Thomson – the architects of the legislation and professors of family law at the time when the 1985 Act was being put in place – put up a very good show, in the face of some very spirited and lively cross-examination from the English. Their culture and their methods are so different that it was not possible to find common ground. But that was not the point of the exercise.

28 June 1998

I met a common gull, an adult bird on its own, flying towards me in Gloucester Place this afternoon. It was a day of sun and showers, and there was a stiff westerly breeze. This was not as surprising as last month's fulmar. But common gulls are normally birds of the autumn and winter here in Edinburgh.

12 July 1998

A very busy period. I had been sitting most of the time in the Appellate Committee as a member of a very pleasant team: Goff, Lloyd, Nolan and Hoffmann with me. There was one visit to the Privy Council, however, for a one-day hearing presided over by the Lord Chancellor, Lord Irvine. It was rather chaotic, due to his impetuous and blustering chairmanship. Whether this was due to nervousness – this was his first such visit to the Privy Council – lack of judicial experience or his imperious nature, it is hard to say. Whatever the reason, we were in danger by lunchtime, as I remarked on our way through to the retiring room, of having counsel sacked and replaced by his own client, who had presented his own case in the court below. Fortunately, perhaps after receiving some guidance from his friend Lennie Hoffmann, Derry was largely silent when we returned after lunch. Things calmed down and we were able to

---

82 1990 SLT 785; 1992 SC 455 and 1993 SLT 494.

finish the case. The impression which was given was of a very unjudicial body, which was rather unfortunate.

At the end of the week we had a party in the Privy Council Chamber to say goodbye to our Registrar, David Owen. It is with real regret that we see him go, as he reaches the retirement age. His bright, alert, friendly Welsh countryman's manner under a splendid head of white hair has done much to set everyone at ease, and to reassure all around him that the system over which he presided was working at the peak of benign efficiency. His successor John Watherston[83] – whom I know from his days at the Foreign Desk in the Lord Chancellor's Department – is just as able, but he does not have quite the same outgoing and engaging personality.

Much of my time and energy have been taken up with Strathclyde University, as I had three days of attendance there as Chancellor at degree ceremonies. On the first day, a Wednesday, I was there because the Principal, John Arbuthnott, was receiving his well-merited KB from The Queen at Holyrood. As I had two days off from London, I spent the next day touring the campus and had a lunch for the media with David Penman of *The Daily Record* and John Arbuthnott. Then it was back for another congregation for degrees on the Friday. And this week I was there again for Friday ceremonies, which were preceded by a private ceremony to award a degree posthumously to Alan Forbes, a student who was killed when run over outside his house six months ago. His parents very bravely were there to receive the degree. On each day there was a very pleasant divine service in the anti-chapel for those graduands and parents who wished to attend. Liz Lochhead, poet and playwright, Roy Johnson, Chairman of the Court, and Ian Robinson, the Chairman and Managing Director of Scottish Power plc, received honorary degrees. Mary came with me for each of the three ceremonies, smartly dressed under a large hat. We were driven there and back by Kath in the University car.

These visits were all most enjoyable and the atmosphere was very friendly. I have had to conduct many ceremonies during my time as Dean of Faculty and Lord President, but these ones were bigger affairs than before. There are large gatherings in the Barony Hall with some 250 students to cap and shake hands with as they cross the platform, and a formal speech to make amounting to 10 minutes or so before the congregation ends with a procession to a reception. Each day involves two such ceremonies. Physically it is quite hard work, and there is some tension involved also, for fear that something – on such an important occasion – might go wrong. But there is much to enjoy also. There is the colour and movement of the ceremony, the smiles on the faces of the graduands as I try to catch their eyes and smile at them when they start to cross the platform, and the words quietly spoken as we shake hands. 'Cheers' is the usual greeting from them, as I say 'congratulations'. Then there are conversations with the graduates and their families afterwards, as Mary and I circulate at the

---

83 John Watherston CBE, Registrar of the Privy Council 1998–2005.

reception to find out where they are from, what they have done and what they plan to do. The academic staff tend to speak to themselves at the reception. But Mary and I are still so close to being parents of students ourselves that we are completely at ease as we move about and talk to people. From time to time photographs are taken of us by families, especially for those from south-east Asia, as many students come from there. Mary has entered into the spirit of things marvellously, and we both feel that we have had an introduction into a whole new world full of interest and friendship – such good fortune.

There are still three weeks to go until term ends. A busy time, but full of interest as the Scottish devolution legislation has just started its Committee Stage in the House.

31 July 1998

The term has ended, and Robert Goff and Michael Nolan have now retired. They are two of the nicest men one could ever wish to meet, who have contributed so much to the calm, measured atmosphere of the Law Lords' Corridor and – in Robert's case – to the sense of academic study of the problems which confront us. John Hobhouse, newly appointed, came in to explore his new surroundings. He is white-haired and elderly in appearance, in sharp contrast to the very youthful septuagenarians who are leaving us.

Much of my time in these last two weeks has been divided between hearings in the Privy Council – capital murder cases mostly – and the Committee Stage of the Scotland Bill in the Chamber of the House. The Privy Council cases were interesting. In one, *Stafford*,[84] we were dealing with a serious problem which has arisen in Trinidad and Tobago due to the abolition of the felony/murder rule by *Moses*[85] in 1996. The retrospective nature of the change – in fact putting right a failure by the Trinidad and Tobago judges to apply a change enacted by legislation 16 years previously – has thrown up a series of appeals against convictions under the old regime. We were presented with an amazingly biased judgment by the Court of Appeal, clearly very irritated by what had happened and determined to hang on to the convictions at all costs. It was not possible to follow their lead that far, but we were able to justify the substitutions of convictions for manslaughter in place of those of murder for which the death penalty is mandatory. This will no doubt attract very long sentences for imprisonment with hard labour in its place when the case goes back to the Court of Appeal.

The other case, *Fisher*,[86] has produced a division of opinion. It is a constitutional case, dealing with the question whether the Bahamian Government can now execute the appellant following his conviction for murder. The problem is that he has an outstanding petition to the Inter-American Human Rights

---

84 *Stafford v The State* [1999] 1 WLR 2026.
85 *Moses v The State* [1997] AC 53.
86 *Fisher v Minister of Public Safety and Immigration (No 2)* [2000] AC 434.

31 July 1998 59

Commission which is due to consider his case in October. The timetable has still nine months to run until the expiry of the five-year period when, according to the decision in *Pratt v Morgan*,[87] he can no longer be executed. To me the human rights case for staying the execution seems to be unanswerable, and Gordon Slynn is broadly of the same view. Tony Lloyd, as ever it seems, is on the side of the Government and Lennie Hoffmann, for reasons of politics and with a chancery approach to the case, is of the same view. Brian Hutton has been his usual self, rather tied up in detail and unclear as to which side to back. In the end he has come up with support for the Government. So I have written a brief dissenting opinion with which Gordon has agreed.

The Scotland Bill has spent eight days so far in Committee. Some of these days have been very short, it has to be said, due to a clutter of other business to do before the recess. I have been able to spend several evenings there, and I have contributed some points from time to time. The atmosphere is pleasant, as we have settled down to a hard core of about 30 to 40 peers, almost all of them Scots, who are taking a real interest in what is going on. I combined these evenings with supper in the Grill Room, which has been very enjoyable. We are not, of course, there to enjoy ourselves. This is very serious business, and there is much to discuss as part of our revising function. But there is no getting away from the fact that the House of Lords is a remarkably good debating club. The atmosphere of order and politeness rarely gives way to serious quarrels, and never to the rowdyism which drowns out so much real discussions in the other place. The Scottish element in our legislative business seems likely largely to disappear after devolution, which is sad. Perhaps it is because of this that so many are making a real effort to participate usefully in this debate.

Yesterday, Thursday, I was in Bristol at an international conference on comparative law. I travelled there and back by train. This was much less comfortable than the Shuttle, where one is so well looked after in peace and quiet in a seat and in a vehicle which is not being bumped about – not often anyway – along the way. The organisation was pretty shambolic, but there were compensations. I met again Professor François Crépeau of McGill University who taught us civil law in 1962 at Edinburgh University when Tom Smith[88] was away. He was very friendly and dapper, although now over 80, and very much recognisable. Madame Justice Claire L'Hereux-Dubé of the Supreme Court of Canada was there. She sought me out especially to pass on her greetings, as did two academics from Stellenbosch University who had entertained me there when I was in Cape Town. This was a pleasant surprise, and the session on gentlemen's agreements which I chaired was brilliantly presented by Professor Bernard Rudden of Oxford.

So there are now nine weeks off! There are no conferences to go to this year, as we are dropping off the list for these things. It is a relief on balance to have

---

87 Reported as *Pratt v Attorney-General for Jamaica* [1994] 2 AC 1.
88 Professor Sir Thomas Broun Smith, QC, FBA, FRSE, Professor of Scots Law at Aberdeen University 1949–58; Professor of Civil Law at Edinburgh University 1958–72.

the summer to ourselves. I end a happy year convinced that I have the best job of the lot of the range of positions in the law which might have been open to me.

1998 – August to September

20 September 1998

We returned from a walking holiday in Spain three days ago. It is time to start gearing up for the new session. There are two lectures to prepare. One, now finished, is for the Statute Law Society conference on 10 October on the task of the judges under the Human Rights Act. The other, now a third done, is the Atkin lecture for the Reform Club on 26 October. There are some judgments to check over, the remains of the last few weeks of the last term. They include the much-delayed *Kleinwort Benson* case[89] in which Robert Goff and I seem likely, sadly, to be in the minority. Otherwise there is correspondence to do, with the help of Will's computer, and some visits to Strathclyde University to fit in.

Robert Reed has been appointed a Senator of the College of Justice. Despite his conspicuous ability and charm, this is a surprise as he is still only 42 and took silk only three years ago. I am sorry also, as I felt that he had much to give as a member of the Senior Bar and was a possible Dean of Faculty or a Law Officer. He will miss all the fun and the rewards of successful practice at the Senior Bar, which seems a very real and unnecessary hardship. He will of course go far as a judge – a future Lord President, I should think, and a future Lord of Appeal in Ordinary. But he would have reached these offices anyway, even if he had waited for another five years. Had I been Lord President I should have tried to deflect the Lord Advocate from appointing him so soon. But no doubt Alan Rodger has other views. Also Robert Reed has been closer to government. He had been suggested as the new Advocate General when the Scotland Act comes into force next year and was on the shortlist for the UK judge on the European Court of Human Rights. So there may be much more in this than meets the eye. Several people more senior to him at the Bar must now feel very uneasy about their prospects.

28 September 1998

I was invited to a meeting at the Lord President's office with officials from the Scottish Office to discuss amendments to the Scotland Bill. The intention was that James Clyde should be there also, but nobody knows where he is so he could not be contacted. There were only four people at our meeting – Alan

---

[89] See fn 71. Happily it turned out that Lord Hoffmann changed his mind during the recess, so we were in the majority after all.

Rodger, myself, Iain Jamieson, who is the real architect of the Scotland Bill, and an assistant from the Scottish Office.

I had expected this would be an opportunity to discuss the wording of the clauses about the legislative competence of the Scottish Parliament. Some of the wording is obscure and, given a free hand, one would certainly wish to offer to effect some improvements to it. But it soon became clear that what Iain Jamieson – a very able man, who studied law with me at Edinburgh University – wanted was to conduct a seminar in order to explain the thinking behind each of the provisions which we were there to scrutinise. So Alan and I listened to what he had to say, and we were remarkably unsuccessful in suggesting that changes ought to be made. It was clear that most of the more obscure passages were the result of prolonged and somewhat dogged arguments between the officials and the parliamentary draftsmen. In the result there was no discernible room for manoeuvre. It would require a very strong mind on the part of a Minister to overrule the result of these deliberations, and no such mind is in evidence. In the long run it will be for the judges to say what the provisions mean. I am not confident that they will find the same meaning in the words as Iain Jamieson thinks they have, but it may be that we shall have good advocates who will be able to explain it all to us when the time comes. Iain Jamieson's belief that everything will in practice be sorted out in the Scottish Office seems to overlook the capacity for disaffected party litigants to dig up trouble where none is expected.

The Scotland Bill has its final Committee Day in the House of Lords next week. Then the Report Stage and the Third Reading have to be gone through before it returns to the Commons for consideration of the Lords' amendments. No controversial changes have been made so far. So, although the timetable is tight in order to get the Bill through before dissolution prior to the State Opening at the end of November, it should make the deadline and be on the statute book before Christmas.

It was surprisingly pleasant to sit within Parliament House again. I had been shy of doing so, but this was a Monday and not many people were about. Such people as there were seemed friendly enough. I handed in to the Faculty Office a pair of black breeches which Manson had tailored for me when I became Dean of Faculty. They were suitably small, and it seems unlikely that anyone else will need to wear them. On the other hand they are of no further use to me, as I have no prospect now of having to wear formal court dress. I did so as Dean of Faculty on visits to Paris for rentrées and in London for the Opening of the Legal Year, for my installation as Lord President and for the State visit of the King of Norway. Such delights are behind me, though Mary reminded me that Harry Woolf disposed of all his gear when he was appointed a Lord of Appeal in Ordinary only to find himself needing to buy it all back again four years later on being appointed Master of the Rolls.

Tomorrow, after lunch at Strathclyde, I return to London for a conference with judges of the European Court of Justice, a dinner for them at Lancaster House and the Opening of the Legal Year. We do not start sitting until next week, however, so there will be time to sort things out.

1998 – October to December

2 October 1998

An enjoyable two days in London. On Wednesday 30 September we had an afternoon meeting in the Large Pension Room at Gray's Inn with the ECJ judges. There were ten of them, including President Rodriguez Iglesias, David Edward and Francis Jacob, the UK's Advocate General. We had five from the House of Lords: Browne-Wilkinson, Slynn, Steyn, Hoffmann and myself, together with the Lord Chancellor, Tom Bingham,[90] Paul Kennedy and John Laws LJJ and Morison J. There were 28 in all round the long table, but we managed to have a good discussion during our two hours. The Finnish judge introduced the subject for our discussion, which was about references to the ECJ, and we had a frank exchange about the problems of delay and of a too-strict application of the *acte clair* rule. I sat next to the Greek judge who, rather naughtily, kept asking me questions about who was who and passing comments as the discussion was in progress.

In the evening we were at Lancaster House – fine surroundings, good wine but only passable although attractive food. Mary was beside Richard Scott and the Finnish judge and had a most enjoyable time. I was beside Odile Slynn and Francis Jacob's wife, who were also excellent company. The Lord Chancellor made an odd chairman. There was no toast to The Queen, perhaps just as well because the Greek judge insisted on smoking despite warnings not to do so before The Queen was drunk. He drank his own toast to her in jest, to make his point. There was then a speech about our guests, but there was no toast to them either. President Iglesias proposed a toast to the Lord Chancellor in reply.

Next day 1 October was the Abbey service, with the ten ECJ judges robed and in procession with us out of the Abbey afterwards. Derry Irvine had proposed to hold the service on 29 September so that he could attend the Labour Party Conference. Tom Bingham told him that this was quite unacceptable and – under warning that a very poor attendance might result – Derry backed down. It was a good solution to have the ECJ judges with us instead. The service was as brief, but as impressive, as ever. The National Anthem was reduced to one verse. This was probably a good idea, as no one seems to know the second verse and its wording is very odd. The Breakfast in the Westminster Hall was as well attended as I can remember, indeed more so. And the food was even better, when one could find it. The heated breakfast consisted of miniature bacon and sausage, scrambled egg on hearts of toast, kidneys and mushroom and a tiny cheese soufflé. There were many friends to see, from all levels of the judiciary

---

90 Then the Lord Chief Justice of England and Wales.

and the legal profession in general: Nigel Emslie, Dean of Faculty; Philip Dry, President of the Law Society of Scotland; and Edward Adams, formerly Tom Bingham's assistant, now in charge of the Judicial Studies Board. Much of the fruit on an attractive barrow was untouched as I left, although Tony Lloyd had managed to get away with a large bunch of grapes wrapped in a paper handkerchief.

Then back to my room for a meeting with Marilyn to sort out diary dates and a summer's correspondence, before leaving with Mary for the 7pm Shuttle back to Edinburgh.

6 November 1998

We are already five weeks into our term. It has been busy. I have sat most of the time in the House of Lords on two Scots appeals raising problems under the Mental Health (Scotland) Act 1984 among other cases. One of these is about the problem of detaining psychopathic killers in the State Hospital.[91] Most psychiatrists say that their condition is not treatable. If so, an absolute discharge with none of the safeguards of a life sentence under the prison system would be the only option. I have tried to suggest a more liberal interpretation of the word 'treatment', but this is a very difficult area where civil liberty groups may object to anything which might suggest that it is permissible to resort to detention in the State Hospital purely to confine the patient. I have had several useful discussions on the subject with Brian Hutton. He has a curiously inflexible mind but a good brain. He can see most of the pitfalls but has little inspiration as to how to get over them.

Another case of interest has been one about whether the public has the right to assemble on the public highway, arising from an incident at Stonehenge which led to a prosecution under the Public Order Act as amended by the Criminal Justice and Public Order Act 1994.[92] We were presided over by the Lord Chancellor, despite warnings from the two Senior Law Lords that he should not sit on the case. I think that he should have heeded that advice. Unfortunately, the criminal process conceals a most important issue of private law as to the extent of public rights of way over private land. I found myself in the rather lonely position of trying to stand up for the unrepresented private landlord in the face of Derry Irvine's desire to be seen as a champion of the freedom of assembly. Gordon Slynn is broadly in agreement with me. To my dismay James Clyde and Brian Hutton seemed to want to find a solution to the case on the lines favoured by Derry. His remark that it would be 'embarrassing' for us to decide against the participants in the assembly is disturbing. It would be embarrassing for him, politically, no doubt. But that is why indeed he should not have been on the case.

---

[91] *R v Secretary of State for Scotland* 1999 SC (HL) 17; the other case was *K v Craig* 1999 SC (HL) 1.
[92] *Director of Public Prosecutions v Jones* [1999] 2 AC 240.

Suddenly, at the beginning of last week, our schedule was thrown into confusion by the arrival of an urgent appeal by General Pinochet, a former President of Chile, against his arrest when in hospital in London at the request of a Spanish prosecutor for offences committed by him in Chile when he was Head of State.[93] It was decided that the Law Lords who were to hear the appeal should be the senior of those who were available. Nico was to be abroad at the opening of the new European Human Rights Court in Strasbourg. So Gordon Slynn was to preside, and I missed the cut by one. This had the odd result that I was required to take the chair in the Privy Council for the first time in an appeal from Trinidad and Tobago last week, and I am to take the chair in the Appellate Committee next week in a rather complex English employment law case. Such promotion is indeed remarkable, as only a week before I was a junior boy in an insurance case with Browne-Wilkinson, Jauncey, Lloyd, Steyn and myself. My team in the Privy Council and the House of Lords is myself, Cooke of Thorndon from New Zealand, Clyde, Hutton and Hobhouse. John Hobhouse is not slow to criticise if one says something silly, and his presence is a mixed blessing. The other three are pleasant to be with. We dealt in a day with the Privy Council case in which Hobhouse was in the minority. The House of Lords case will be more extended. I hope that he will be able to do the judgment, as it is not something that I would wish to entrust to the other three or, if avoidable, to handle myself.

The Scotland Bill has taken up much time in Committee and on a four-day Report Stage. I have spoken quite a few times and sat on to about 11pm several times. On one occasion during the Committee Stage I was on my feet at 2.30am. We have the Third Reading next Monday. It has been a good series of debates, among people who know each other very well. I feel that I have made a useful contribution from time to time. John McCluskey proposed, and I seconded, an important amendment to set out a procedure for fact-finding where there was a question as to whether a judge of the Court of Session should be removed on the ground of disability. We won the vote by a good margin – 144 to 108, I think. I hope that the Government will now, although too late for comfort, accept that the independence of the judges must be protected in this way. Sub-committee E of the Committee of the European Union, on Law and Institutions, to which I was appointed to be chairman at the beginning of this year,[94] has also begun to eat into my time. I have chaired two sessions taking evidence on the subject of comitology.[95] I barely understand what the issues are, but so far things have gone quite well. My problem is in finding time for the preparation. It is a very big commitment.

University work has also been prominent. There was a visit last weekend for 24 hours to Aberdeen for a seminar on good faith in the law of contract organised

---

93 See fn 100.
94 It was the practice for this sub-committee to be chaired by a Lord of Appeal in Ordinary. My predecessor was Lord Hoffmann, and my successor Lord Scott of Foscote.
95 A process by which the European Commission consults committees on which every EU country is represented when making proposals for the implementation of EU law.

by Angelo Forte. Then I chaired a lecture at UCL given by Professor Ewan McKendrick on breach of contract and measure of damages. I attended and presided over congregations to award degrees at Strathclyde University today. Then I will chair a working party on choice of jurisdiction clauses at the British Institute of International and Comparative Law next Tuesday. I am keen to maintain these contacts, and it is nice to be invited to take part in them. Keith and Jauncey do not participate, nor does James Clyde. So it is quite a compliment to me that the academics in London are showing an interest in me. Our decision in the great restitution case of *Kleinwort Benson* – Goff, Hoffmann and myself in the majority (Hoffmann having unexpectedly changed sides at the end of the summer, to Robert Goff's delight) – was given just before my visit to Aberdeen. I have yet to learn how it has been received. But at least what I have said will be read widely both north and south of the border.

There have been social events also in this busy period. I gave the Atkin Lecture at the Reform Club on 26 October. A week later I was at a dinner in the Athenaeum as a guest of King's College, London on the occasion of a lecture by Noëlle Lenoir, a lively and much-admired member of the Conseil d'Etat in Paris. It is a busy but very interesting and enriching life.

13 November 1998

A case on which I was sitting in the Privy Council from Brunei, *Prince Jefri v KPMG*,[96] overran from the two days allotted to it to the start of the next week. So I never got to the case which I was to chair which was *Mann v Secretary of State for Employment*.[97] It was put off until next term, when I may be assigned to something else. I was relieved. The pressure of work, especially with Sub-committee E to cope with as well, was too great for comfort. Instead we spent the whole of the third day, Wednesday, on the rest of the hearing in *Prince Jefri* about the efficacy of Chinese walls. We discussed the case on the Thursday morning. Peter Millett was with us for the first time. He is a very good chancery lawyer and brought a useful and pleasant mind to the hearing. Nico was, as always, the dominant personality. James Clyde and Brian Hutton were also on the Committee. I was uncertain as to how I could present my summing-up as the fourth to speak. In the event I managed to set out a structure for the approach which Peter Millett was kind enough to say that he found helpful. He is to write the judgment, which I am sure will be well done.

There was much excitement in the House as we are nearing the end of the session and two Bills are in the throes of serious disagreement between the Lords and the Commons. They are the European Parliamentary Elections Bill and the Scotland Bill. Yesterday evening the Lords rejected a Commons amendment for the third time, relating to the so-called closed list system for the Euro-elections. Next week we are to consider a not unrelated point in the Scotland Bill, where it is proposed

---

96 The case later settled.
97 [1999] 1 ICR 898.

that the number of Scottish Parliament seats should be tied to those in the Parliament at Westminster. The Government is trying to control the system by insisting on closed lists for the proportional representation element, which keeps the choice of members in the hands of the party. It is also insisting on common boundaries for the UK and Scottish Parliaments, with the result that any reduction in the number of Scots MPs would have to be matched by a reduction in the membership of the Scottish Parliament. There are serious issues of democracy here. The extent to which the Lords will assert their independence – the Liberal Democrats are divided, and even some Labour peers are against the Government – is the key to the dispute. Peers in the Lords are free, within reason, to make up their own minds. Inevitably resistance by the Lords is declared in the Commons as being the work of the hereditary peers, and it is linked to cries for urgent reform of the Lords. The coming week will be very interesting.

11 December 1998

A great deal has happened since I last wrote.

The House of Lords insisted on its position on the European Parliamentary Elections Bill, defeating the Government by a large majority. Some Labour peers, a few Liberal Democrats, some bishops and numerous Crossbenchers voted with the Conservatives. The Government decided to drop the Bill, declaring its intention to introduce it at the next session and to invoke the Parliament Act. This vote drew the teeth out of the resistance on the Scotland Bill, especially as the Liberal Democrats' front bench voted with the Government on the Elections Bill. So the Tories refused to join them on their stand against the Government on the Scotland Bill, with the result that the Bill was passed. Thank goodness, as it would have been a disaster for that Bill to have to start again. Parliament was prorogued in a ceremony which I attended, at which the six or so Bills to pass received the Royal Assent. The words 'La Reine le veult' were pronounced by the Clerk of the Parliaments after the words 'The Scotland Act' were read out. It was a splendid moment, after so many hours spent on the scrutiny and debate.

That weekend I was at Peebles, as chairman of the annual conference of the Scottish Association for the Study of Delinquency. I found myself among many friends there. It is a great meeting-place for all those in the Scottish justice system. We were addressed by Henry McLeish MP, the Home Affairs Minister at the Scottish Office, by Professor Robert Black of Edinburgh University, and by Patrick Chalmers from the media,[98] among others. The theme was the Scottish Parliament, and it went very well.

I returned to London for a day in the Privy Council followed by, on the Tuesday, the State Opening. The dark November day made a strange setting for the ceremonies in the street, but it was fun to watch from my window.

---

98 Head of BBC Television, Scotland 1979–82; Controller BBC Scotland 1983–92.

Then I went down to the Peers' Lobby, as I did last time, to watch the Commons arrive before the Queen's Speech. When she mentioned a Bill to remove the voting rights of hereditary peers there was an unseemly cheer from the Commons gathered in the Peers' Lobby which was heard in the Chamber. This was responded to by murmurs of 'shame' from their Lordships. This was interpreted by some of the press as a rebuke to Her Majesty's speech rather than to the Commons for their misbehaviour. Instead of moving backwards down the steps as his predecessors had done, the Lord Chancellor turned his back on the Queen on presenting her with her speech and taking it from her afterwards. This was a rather clumsy demonstration of so-called modernisation. He was a generous host, however, at the reception in the River Room afterwards, where there were many friends. The décor there, which I was seeing for the first time since the saga of his expenditure on wallpaper,[99] was not as bad as we had been led to believe, although it was dark and rococo in comparison with the warmth of the Mackays' charming drawing room when they were in residence during his time as Lord Chancellor. The staircase leading down to the office was a delight, however. It had been lined with prints on loan from the Royal Scottish Academy – etchings I suppose – of Raeburns and Allan Ramsays, many very familiar, including the portrait of my ancestor the Rt Hon Charles Hope as Lord Advocate, all very well mounted and beautifully presented on a warm rose-coloured wall. I went back to the Privy Council for the rest of the week.

Meantime the House of Lords had been completing its hearing of the appeal in the case of General Pinochet on the question of whether he was entitled to immunity against prosecution in the UK for crimes committed in Chile during his years as Head of State there, while presiding over a dictatorship.[100] He had come to London for medical treatment, as he had done on a number of previous occasions. The Labour Government, in pursuit of an ethical foreign policy under Robin Cook, did not warn him that he would not be acceded the diplomatic protection which he had had previously. So when a Spanish prosecutor presented an application for him to be extradited to Spain to face prosecution there for crimes against humanity, he was allowed to be arrested. The affair caused a diplomatic and legal nightmare – huge disruption in Chile's internal democracy, and the prospect of a long legal process before Pinochet could be released to Spain or returned to Chile. There were signs of a split of views as the hearing wore on. Indeed before it began Gordon Slynn said to me outside Lennie Hoffmann's room 'God, I wish *you* were sitting', nodding in exasperation at Lennie's door. Gordon did not reveal to me then the reason for his feelings which, in the light of later events, was perhaps a very great pity.

---

99 The residence had been redecorated by Lord and Lady Havers in the style of a family home before the Mackays moved in when Lord Mackay was appointed Lord Chancellor on the resignation of Lord Havers due to ill-health. Lord Irvine insisted on redecorating the residence with wallpaper in the Pugin style, which transformed its appearance and was controversial because of the expense.
100 *R v Bow Street Metropolitan Stipendiary Magistrate, ex parte Pinochet Ugarte* [2000] 1 AC 61.

The result of the Pinochet case, which was announced in the Chamber just before Parliament was prorogued in advance of the Queen's Speech, was dramatic. It was a vote by 3:2 in favour of the Spanish prosecutor. Steyn and Hoffmann were in his favour and against Pinochet. This was no surprise. 'That's two down for a start', Tom Bingham is said to have remarked when told that they were sitting on the appeal.[101] Lloyd and Slynn were in favour of giving immunity to him as a former Head of State. So the decisive factor was Donald Nicholls' vote, which was in favour of the Spanish prosecutor. The event was shown on television, as the speeches were announced in order of seniority. It was rather like a penalty shoot-out, as one commentator remarked. The first two votes – Slynn and Lloyd – were for Pinochet. The next two – Nicholls and Steyn – were against. So it was, apparently, all down to Hoffmann. There were gasps from the Gallery as he announced that he was against Pinochet. A large group of anti-Pinochet demonstrators, who had been outside St Margaret's Church opposite the St Stephen's entrance for the duration since the hearing began, burst into cheering and dancing with celebration. There was almost universal acclaim for what was widely seen as a bold, inspired move in favour of human rights and against dictatorships. Only a few voices – only a few press comments – expressed concern at what might lie ahead. Letters of congratulation came in, to the delight of Lennie and Johan. A woman who dared to suggest that Lennie might have been influenced by the fact that his wife Gillian worked for Amnesty International, which has campaigned against Pinochet and had made submissions against him in the course of the hearing, was derided on television by the daughter of President Allende whose regime Pinochet had displaced.

The Corridor, which had suffered greatly from the disruption caused by the case – huge quantities of material on the fax machine from Chile and elsewhere and repeated telephone calls from belligerent members of the press – began to calm down. There were a number of hearings in the House of Lords and the Privy Council on which I sat with Peter Millett and John Hobhouse, and I began to enjoy their company. Peter is very outgoing and talkative. John is reserved and dry. But both are impressive lawyers, and they are excellent additions to the team. I joined the Select Committee on European Affairs for the first time in my capacity as chairman of its Sub-Committee E, under the excellent chairmanship of Geoffrey Tordoff. It is a real pleasure to be involved with yet more members of the House, familiar faces only until now. This experience helped me to feel a little bit more at ease in my own chairmanship of Sub-Committee E as we reached the last of our witnesses on the very difficult issue of comitology. Joyce Quinn MP, the Minister of State at the Foreign Office, was our last witness.

But two dramatic events then took place, which were to transform the atmosphere in this last week of the term. One was in the House itself. The other was in regard to the case of General Pinochet.

---

101 He had presided over the Divisional Court which on 28 October 1998 quashed the warrants issued under the Extradition Act on the ground that Pinochet, as a former Head of State, had immunity.

11 December 1998

Behind the scenes discussions had been going on about how to deal with the issue of removing the hereditary peers, which had been moved to the top of the Government's priorities by the defeat of the European Parliamentary Elections Bill.[102] The official position of the Government had been that no concessions were to be made. All the hereditary peers were to be removed as stage one of the reform of the House of Lords, with a Royal Commission to consider what was to be done in stage two. But Bernard Weatherill, the Convenor of the Crossbench Peers,[103] began to make progress in extracting some movement towards allowing some of the more useful hereditaries to remain, in exchange for giving a fair wind to Government business which was otherwise under the threat of disruption. Then Robert Cranborne, the Leader of the House under the Tory Government and now Shadow Leader, began to be involved also. A deal appeared to be done, in return for an arrangement which would allow 92 hereditary peers to remain.[104] But this was done without, it seems, the authority of the Leader of the Opposition, William Hague. He was caught off-balance when the issue was raised at Prime Minister's Question Time. Within a few hours he had sacked Robert Cranborne, lost three more front bench spokesmen in the Lords including Peter Fraser[105] who resigned in protest, and dismayed the entire Tory Party in the Upper House. The atmosphere in the corridors around the Chamber was electric. I had seen Cranborne stalking back to his room, no doubt after the initial confrontation, and the Labour front bench were astonished and delighted by what was happening. It was, I think, inevitable, once Cranborne had acted as he did, for Hague to sack him. But that is all the more unfortunate. Tom Strathclyde has taken over as Shadow Leader, but all the morale which was building up to a bruising period of opposition has evaporated. I do hope that the arrangement which will keep 92 hereditaries in the House can be held. Probably it will be, as there is so much crossbench support for it.

Meantime, the advisors of General Pinochet were planning their next move. Questions began to be asked through the Judicial Office about Lord Hoffmann's involvement with Amnesty International. James Vallance White had confided in me one evening in the Law Lords' Corridor, and I looked up some references for him. Gordon Slynn, who had been concerned about this all along and had tried without success to persuade Lennie not to sit – Lennie was determined to do so, no doubt so that he could play his part in securing the prosecution of General Pinochet – turned as white as a sheet, so James said to me, when the news was broken to him that these questions were being raised.

At first the probing did not come to very much. Then *The Guardian* reported that the Pinochet lawyers had submitted to Jack Straw, the Home Secretary, that he should treat the House of Lords' decision as a nullity in deciding whether or not to authorise extradition proceedings. There was no chance of

---

102 See 13 November 1998.
103 Lord Weatherill was Speaker of the House of Commons from 1983 to 1992.
104 There were to be 90 'working' hereditaries and, as these two positions are held by hereditary peers, the Earl Marshall and the Lord Chamberlain *ex officio*.
105 Lord Fraser of Carmyllie QC.

his doing so, of course. Derry Irvine was said to be unconcerned about the allegations against Lord Hoffmann. He called Gordon Slynn in for discussions. Gordon told me that the Lord Chancellor did not see that there was a problem, but Gordon's instincts told him that there was – as indeed he had suspected from the very start. Meantime Lennie Hoffmann has departed for sittings in the Court of Final Appeal in Hong Kong where he is one of the non-permanent judges, and will not be back until January.

Things came to a head when Jack Straw announced that he had decided to authorise the extradition proceedings. A petition has now been lodged asking the House to set aside the decision on the ground of Lennie's involvement as a director and chairperson of Amnesty International Charity Limited, which funds and undertakes the charitable activities of Amnesty International. Now, at last, Nico is in charge. I am glad to say that he is showing signs of leadership and initiative – and now, not before time as Nico said to me, Derry is becoming worried. Clearly a differently constituted Committee must sit on this petition, and it will have to deal with an issue without precedent in the House of Lords' appellate history. The case is to be put out for next Tuesday and Wednesday, the last week before Christmas. Nico is to preside, with Goff and Nolan, myself and Hutton. The presence of Goff and especially Nolan – previously in charge of the Committee on Standards in Public Life – will add real weight to the proceedings. There will be none of the clash of interests and predispositions which marked the previous hearing. At least, I do not think so.

My own feeling – and I suspect Nico's also – is that we must be tough on this issue and not give in to any instinct there may be to protect Lennie Hoffmann. I have no inhibitions about setting the decision aside, if we can be persuaded it is competent for us to do so. Lennie was foolish not to accept Gordon Slynn's advice. His view that he was not biased because of his wife's employment with Amnesty International was not unreasonable, but his silence on the fact that he is a director of its fund-raising arm simply does not begin to meet the well-established principle that when he is performing a judicial duty a judge must be seen to be impartial. The huge human rights campaign against Pinochet has tended to obscure the fact that he has his human rights also, and I do not see how we – as the final court – can blind ourselves to this or cover up a defect in the decision. Had the matter been the other way around, it would have been regarded as an outrage to human rights of those who had suffered during the dictatorship.

Where this will lead is yet to be revealed. If we do set the decision aside, there will be more and more demonstrations and adverse publicity. And another hearing on the merits will have to be held. It was a relief when I was omitted from the first hearing. Now I am being involved in something much more difficult, and with consequences which are likely to be far more momentous and unpredictable. I shall set off for London on Sunday evening with more apprehension at the week's business than I have felt at any stage in my career as a Lord of Appeal in Ordinary. Indeed, I cannot recall feeling as deeply uneasy about a case which is to be heard in the next week at any time since I went onto the Bench.

31 December 1998

I returned from London on the British Midland flight on Thursday evening 17 December in time for a late supper at home. But there has been some delay in my recording last week's events in London.

Nico, Brian and I did Appeal Committee work on petitions for leave to appeal on the Monday morning. We refused three out of four appeals after all the oral hearings, which was an unusual balance of view as cases which get that far are more often than not allowed. Then on Monday afternoon we met under Nico's leadership to discuss how to handle the Pinochet hearing, which was to start on the Tuesday morning.[106] One issue was whether to allow Amnesty International to be heard. They had been allowed to intervene and to present oral arguments in the appeal, after a committee decision by Slynn, Nicholls and Steyn. Most of us agreed that this was a mistake, as there was no proper locus for Amnesty International to intervene at all – although it had campaigned for a long time to bring Pinochet to justice. This was because the relevant arguments were in perfectly capable hands elsewhere. But I said that it would be unwise for us not to hear Amnesty International in the motion to set aside as, having been heard and incurred expenses as they had, they had an interest to see that the decision was upheld. There had been a good deal of anger on their part when James Vallance White told them, on Nico's instructions, that they were not going to be allowed to be heard. My arguments that it would be unfair not to hear them, and a source of more bad publicity against us if we were to set the decision aside, carried weight with the others. Fortunately Nico agreed to change the instruction.

Next day we began the two-day hearing, in the large Committee Room 4 on the opposite side of the Committee Corridor from our usual Committee Room 1, to allow the large number of members of the public and the media to attend. The anti-Pinochet demonstrators were back in their usual place outside the Palace opposite the St Stephen's entrance. Many of the faces in the audience in the Committee Room were from the affected countries – Spain and Chile, judging by dark hair, brown skins and shape of face. At our end of the long room however it was a very British affair. There were many barristers and their solicitors, a shorthand writer on our side of the Bar and then ourselves, our attendants and James Vallance White. The petition to be set aside was presented by Clare Montgomery QC. Her leader, Colin Nichols QC, wisely decided to leave it to her. She is neat, polite, precise and very intelligent. Nico's early attempts to confine her argument were tactfully countered, and she pursued her own line with marvellous economy and determination. The factual situation

---

106 *R v Bow Street Metropolitan Stipendiary Magistrate, ex parte Pinochet Ugarte (No 2)* [2000] 1 AC 119.

which she presented, about Lord Hoffmann's undeclared links with Amnesty International Charity Limited and about Amnesty International's publications about Chile and Senator Pinochet, were rather shocking. We had not known any of this detail before, and by lunchtime it was clear that, in moving us to set the decision aside, she was pushing at an open door. The main problem for us, in upholding her argument, was likely to be to find a way of expressing the test which is to be applied in as tactful a way as possible. Most unfortunately, in a recent House of Lords case called *R v Gough* in 1993,[107] Robert Goff and Harry Woolf rejected the 'reasonable suspicion of bias' test which Scotland uses[108] and most other common law countries prefer, in favour of a 'real danger of bias' test. 'Danger' seems far too emotive a word for use in this context. Inevitably, however, Miss Montgomery's use of the approved phrase attracted headlines next morning in the newspapers.

We were then addressed by Alun Jones QC for the Spanish Government and the Bow Street magistrate whose warrant was in question, and by counsel for Amnesty International, Ian Brownlie QC. The argument took place until 4pm on the Wednesday. I had a problem because of commitments at 4.15pm to the EU Select Committee on the Tuesday and to Sub-committee E on the Wednesday. So I was unable to take part in the conversations after each day's hearing. Brian Hutton kept me briefed about them. We met on the Thursday at 9am for a full discussion, with a deadline to meet for our own decision. We were to sit at 10.30am in the Chamber that day to announce it. This was our last chance before the Christmas recess, and an early decision was clearly necessary.

There was never any doubt in our minds about the result once we had heard the facts. Our discussion was concentrated on a brief three-page summary which Nico proposed to read out, as our appearance in the Chamber was bound to be broadcast on radio and television. We went over it with a fine-tooth comb, to preserve as much room for our detailed reasons as possible. Things were not made easier for us by the arrival from the Lord Chancellor of a letter to Nico, to which he was demanding an instant reply so that both could be released to the media when the decision was announced. In his letter Derry Irvine was demanding that steps be taken by our chairmen to prevent such a thing happening again, by requiring the Appellate Committee to meet before each hearing to discuss possible conflicts of interest and take action on them. Robert Goff became extremely angry when the letter was read out, seeing it as quite unjustified political interference. Nico was exasperated by it as well, and I commented on the fact that Derry had already rejected advice from the Law Lords not to sit on a case which had been seen to raise issues which were political.[109] Double standards were being applied. Time was too short for a reply anyway. So the letter went unanswered.

107 [1993] AC 646.
108 *Bradford v McLeod* 1986 SLT 244.
109 This was the Stonehenge case, mentioned above.

31 December 1998

We made our way down to the Chamber, which was already filling up with the lay peers who were interested in the case. Prayers were said, counsel and parties came in and Nico read out his prepared speech, to which we in turn expressed our agreement. It was a unique decision, for the House to set aside one of its previous judgments. But no sounds were heard in protest. Outside the crowd of anti-Pinochet demonstrators lingered for a while, then melted away. The Houses of Parliament were already in the process of winding down for Christmas. After clearing up for the recess, I set off on the usual journey home via Heathrow.

Publicity for what we had done was dampened, rather to our advantage, by two more exciting events. The first was the decision by the United States and the UK – Clinton and Blair – to attack Saddam Hussein's Iraq with missiles and aircraft to eliminate his air defences and destroy as much of his arsenal of weapons of mass destruction as possible. Saddam Hussein had been playing cat and mouse with the allies since the end of the Gulf War, which was brought to an end for political reasons 48 hours too soon for the allied forces to reach Baghdad. So pictures of Baghdad under air attack and extensive reporting on this event from London, Baghdad and Washington were on the front pages. Then, just as the four-day assault was ending with the beginning of Ramadan, there was a crisis in the Government. Peter Mandelson, whose spin-doctoring had done so much to win the General Election for New Labour and had only recently taken over as a Cabinet Minister – as President of the Board of Trade – was forced to reveal that he had received a loan on favourable terms from Geoffrey Robinson, another Cabinet Minister, before the election to buy a luxurious town house which was otherwise well beyond his means. This undeclared favour was derided as an example of the very kind of 'sleaze' which New Labour had used to discredit the Tory Party and said that it would cleanse from government. The signs were that both Mandelson and Blair had tried to resist the pressure for resignation, but it became too great. Of course, it was a much more exciting story than our own. Lord Renton of Mount Harry, writing to *The Times*, did however draw the obvious comparison. It was between Mandelson and Hoffmann, as two very intelligent men so convinced by their own intellectual supremacies to be unable to see how others would view their conduct. The phrase 'justice must be seen to be done' was frequently referred to. How irritating it is that English law no longer uses that test.[110]

The atmosphere is of the lull before the storm. It is accepted by everyone that further comment must now be reserved until our reasons have been given. That will not happen until mid-January, just before we start to re-hear the case. Meantime Lennie Hoffmann, who has been absent in Hong Kong sitting with the Court of Final Appeal, is now away in South Africa on holiday. There have been suggestions that resignation from his position as a Lord of Appeal in Ordinary must now follow. But that also is something that must now wait.

---

110 I was able to reverse this situation later by setting out the definitive test for apparent bias in *Porter v Magill* [2002] 2 AC 357, para 103.

There is no doubt in my mind that Lennie has brought our system into disrepute. I also suspect that he knew perfectly well that, if he did not sit, the chances of the case going in favour of Pinochet would be increased.[111] That is a result which now, in the event, seems more likely as the two most anti-Pinochet judges – Steyn and Hoffmann – have now been used up. I would resent his staying on if he were not to be frank and honest about his mistake. On the other hand the principle of independence means that he cannot be forced out, nor is the decision for anyone else but him. There are other factors. He is a valuable member of our team, at his best in those difficult chancery cases that most of us are baffled by. I like and admire him greatly and suspect and hope that he will survive. But his survival will prolong the strain and suspicion which his actions have attracted. In the longer term our own future as the final court of appeal seems to be even more insecure than ever. If we have attracted ridicule and suspicion, we will have few friends when decisions are taken against us as part of the programme of Lords reform.

Tony Lloyd retires over the recess. So I am now promoted to the top half of our team of 12 – sixth in seniority. If Lennie resigns I shall be fifth. This is rather unwelcome, as Sub-Committee E is taking up so much time and I still have two and a half years to do before my period in this important role is ended. By the end of that period I shall have moved up even further, and the burden of chairmanship of appellate panels – which I accepted as Lord President as one of the pleasures of that office – will be mine to assume much more often.

On the whole, however, it has been a good year. I have a comfortable, settled routine. Parliamentary work on the Scotland Bill, and now on the European Select Committee and in Sub-Committee E, has been most enjoyable and I now have a wide circle of acquaintances. Peter Millett is a good addition to the team. He is friendly, lively and very industrious. As expected, John Hobhouse is much less of a team player, although of very great ability. Together they have added some much-needed weight at the bottom end. Work continues to be hard and very interesting, without being arduous or stressful. My contacts with the London universities are interesting, which adds an extra dimension to my life. On balance, the London job remains better than the one which I left behind me in Edinburgh.

1999 – January to April

15 January 1999

The affair of General Pinochet still hangs heavily upon us in the Law Lords' Corridor.

My only sitting engagement for the week was on an Appeal Committee with Lords Browne-Wilkinson and Millett to hear applications from Amnesty

---

111 As the Law Lord next in seniority to him, I would have taken his place.

International, Human Rights Watch and the Government of Chile to intervene in the proceedings next week and to present oral argument. This was fixed for the Wednesday, so neither Peter Millett nor I were free to do anything else – a good thing in my case, as I was moving rooms along the Corridor from the *forum non conveniens* at the far end to Tony Lloyd's room, which is much brighter and more comfortable and where the bookcases do not occupy all the walls. So I can at last put some pictures up.

The hearing did not take very long. We completed it within two hours. Amnesty International had a strong case, as they had been heard orally last time. I was relieved to find that my colleagues were agreed that they should be allowed to be heard again. The Government of Chile had a strong case also, as they can claim that the immunity which is in issue is their own State's immunity. Their problem is that they did not ask to be heard last time when they could have. But their right to be heard overcame that matter. The case for Human Rights Watch was weak, and we restricted them to written submissions only. I think this is a good thing as Edward Fitzgerald QC, who is their counsel, tends to be long-winded and to speak in paragraphs rather than sentences. He is full of enthusiasm, but I find his submissions difficult to take in, and even more so to intervene in by questioning.

Much more difficult was the finalising of our reasons for setting aside the previous decision that General Pinochet had no immunity because of the connections which Lord Hoffmann did not disclose. Nico sent his first draft by fax the previous Friday. We met on Tuesday evening to discuss it. My own and Brian's drafts have also been circulated. Robert Goff was at our meeting. Michael Nolan was in France on holiday. Robert was at first hostile to the idea that there should be more than one speech. Brian and I felt that appearances would suffer if that were to be the case, and that we both had something to add which would give weight to the judgment. Robert was quite sharp when I said, gently, that I disagreed with him about this. 'That is my view', he said. He also questioned Nico's use of the word 'interest' to describe Lennie's connection with the case. After a long discussion we went away to re-draft. On Thursday, however, a further meeting was much more constructive and good humoured. Robert had come round completely on both points. He had started to devise a brief speech of his own, and had accepted that the word 'interest' was appropriate. We spent the last two hours of the day with Frances Rice[112] sorting out the mechanics for communicating our reasons today – no easy task as email, copying, proof-reading and maintaining contact with Michael Nolan presented us with practical difficulties. Poor Frances has had a tough time trying to keep pace with this nightmare.

This morning, back in Edinburgh, the fax machine produced the final drafts for me to revise. I had two brief conversations on the telephone about details with Nico Browne-Wilkinson who has been very good to deal with throughout. In

---

112 Frances Rice MBE was the principal secretary to the Law Lords.

the event, despite all the rush and worry over detail, his leadership has produced a good team for a sad and potentially very damaging case. As I write the early evening news, armed with the judgment, is saying that the Law Lords 'have severely criticised Lord Hoffmann'. Let us hope that some of the dust will have settled by next Monday.

As for Lennie himself, he was sitting in the Appellate Committee with Nicholls, Jauncey, Goff and Lloyd. He was at a meeting of all the Law Lords on Monday evening to discuss our response to the letter from the Lord Chancellor, but remained silent. I spoke to him on Tuesday evening, and he came to sit beside me in the Chamber when Nicholas Phillips was introduced to the House of Lords as Lord Phillips of Worth Matravers. We spoke about Sub-Committee E, of which he had been a previous chairman, and a related debate scheduled for that evening. He had seemed very detached on Monday, but was more relaxed on Tuesday. It is a tense time for him. There will be those who think he should go. Others will urge him to stay. I am sure that he will not be asked to go by the Lord Chancellor. I should not like him to be forced out by politicians, as judicial independence must never be compromised.

Meantime we had a good meeting of Sub-Committee E to discuss the comitology report, and I have had a useful follow-up meeting with our clerk, Dr Christopher Kerse, yesterday. This evening I am off to Strathclyde University for a dinner with officials from the Scottish Office to discuss the effects of devolution on the affairs of the University. There is no shortage of things to do.

5 February 1999

Yesterday we completed the hearing – the re-hearing, indeed – in the Pinochet case.[113] It took 12 days, twice the time given to the original hearing of the appeal, spread over three weeks. We sat as a committee of seven – Browne-Wilkinson, Goff, Hope, Hutton, Millett, Saville and Phillips. Once again we were in the enlarged Committee Room 4. There was a full attendance almost every day, much of it by foreigners – I assume mainly from Chile. Peers were able to come and go, and other visitors including Mary and William, escorted by Marilyn, were able to get in also. There were 21 counsel in all. We were treated to some excellent speeches by some real experts in the field – Professor Christopher Greenwood, Professor Ian Brownlie, Lawrence Collins and David Lloyd-Jones, who was the *amicus curiae*. Clare Montgomery did an outstanding job for General Pinochet. Alun Jones QC for the DPP and Peter Duffy QC for Amnesty International were competent but in a different league. The result was a far more comprehensive argument on both sides of the case than it had been possible to put together for the original hearing, which began only seven days after the decision in the Divisional Court.

---

113 *R v Bow Street Metropolitan Stipendiary Magistrate, ex parte Pinochet Ugarte (No 3)* [2000] 1 AC 147.

5 February 1999

As a committee we work together very well. Browne-Wilkinson did not dominate the discussion, although intellectually he seemed several fences ahead of the rest of us. The rest of us asked questions from time to time, but nobody took over the case as was said to have happened last time with Hoffmann. It would be interesting to know how it appeared from the other side of the Bar. Each day we had tea together in the Conference Room, which helped to keep us in touch with each other.

Yesterday we had a more intense discussion before breaking up for the weekend. As I had expected from a fairly early stage, there was a division of opinion. Peter Millett was an anti-Pinochet man from the start, on the view that torture could never be a function from which a Head of State could have immunity from prosecution as it is an international crime, wherever he could be found even after he had left office. Mark Saville on the other hand was almost equally and firmly of the opposite opinion, as was Robert Goff. I was of the same view. Brian Hutton, in typical fashion, was very hard to pin down, at first taking points and working them out in his own time. I had hoped he might join us three, but he has ended up on Millett's side and there seems to be little prospect of a change there. Nicholas Phillips was difficult to identify until the end of our discussion, when he and Nico Browne-Wilkinson favoured immunity for Pinochet until the Torture Convention 1988 was ratified by the UK, when it was lost. So we had three different positions for the time being: three for immunity, two for no immunity and two for immunity for the whole period in office except the last 18 months. This is obviously in need of some tidying up, and minds can change including my own. Much will depend on Nico, who really has a casting vote. He showed signs of unease – rightly, I think – about the position which he has taken and had been signalling from the start of the discussion.

If the decision goes against Pinochet in whole or in part, there will be some very messy odds and ends to deal with as well. The range of charges which have been levelled against him is so wide and varied as to give rise to all sorts of problems about retrospective effect and extra-territoriality. A decision that he has immunity would enable us to leave these alone. A decision that he is caught only by the Torture Convention would require us to cut back many of the charges, and it would probably leave him facing only one charge of torture – which would throw the political aspect of the case into a very different focus.

We are to discuss the case formally next Tuesday. I do not think that Goff or Saville will have changed, nor any of the others except possibly Browne-Wilkinson. I shall have to speak first and leave early, as I have to go to deliver a talk in Oxford. This is most unsatisfactory if there are going to be compromises. But, despite the tensions at this stage, it has been a fascinating and very well-conducted debate in which it has been a privilege to take part.

I had to present my Sub-Committee's report on comitology to the main EU Committee on Tuesday and to start the next inquiry by Sub-Committee E into

Corpus Iuris on Wednesday. This was hard and tiring work after a full day on Pinochet. But it all went well and, despite the burdens, I find myself enjoying this aspect of my work.

I was lucky to get a place, at short notice, at the Scottish Peers' Association dinner. Barbara Kelly, Jack Shaw and Lord Marnoch were among the guests. It was, as ever, a most friendly, convivial occasion which was well run once again by Flora Saltoun. Sadly, as hereditary peers are on their way out, this may be the last. That would be a sad loss. Flora herself will probably be retiring anyway as her husband is now very infirm. I do hope that something can be done to keep the Scots peers together, as we shall need to keep in touch even more once devolution comes.

21 February 1999

When we met 10 days ago to discuss the Pinochet case again minds had indeed changed. It became clear that Nico had decided that he would say that, as a former Head of State, the Senator has no immunity from allegations of torture contrary to the Torture Convention. He has Nicholas Phillips with him and, for different reasons but reaching the same result, Brian Hutton and Peter Millett. Robert Goff remains resolutely of the opposite opinion and is deeply troubled by the line the others are taking. But Mark Saville is looking for ways to go with the majority and so am I. As far as I am concerned, I can now see my way to agreeing with Nico on the narrower and, I think, less damaging basis that he is suggesting. That is that the scale of the conspiracy to torture of which Senator Pinochet is being accused was such that his conduct amounted to an international crime, to which special considerations apply. I would still resist the idea that a single act of torture within the meaning of the Torture Convention committed in Chile, if that was all, would be enough on its own to deprive him of his immunity from prosecution for that crime in this country. Robert Goff was sympathetic to my ideas, but he may still hold out as a total dissenter.

I prepared a 32-page draft this weekend. Much of it is devoted to an analysis of the charges in the light of our decision, which may well be unanimous, that the definition of 'extradition crime' requires the crimes to have been punishable here when they were committed and not just at the present time – a point about retrospectivity that I raised early on, which has proved to be a good one. The result is devastating, quite without regard to the question of immunity itself. About 90% of the charges go out on this ground. There are only a very few charges of torture and conspiracy to torture left on which he could be extradited. But, on the view I take, that is enough.

We still have a week or two to go before our opinions are finalised and the judgment can be delivered. The press and the BBC are angling for information to leak out and our desk-top computers are vulnerable. I hope that we can keep things secure until the last moment, as was done last time.

It has been good to get back to ordinary work at last. Two interesting cases about the refugee status of Pakistani women under the Asylum Convention[114] and an application for adoption which was said to infringe immigration rules[115] were not far away from the subject of extradition, but they were simple issue cases nevertheless. More complex was a case about the Lloyds Names litigation,[116] which was presided over by Nico. At times he allowed his patience, or lack of it, to get the better of him. Before we had really been consulted he announced that the appellants' appeal was dismissed and that we were only interested in the cross-appeal. That was true, but the speed of his delivery was rather too rapid for comfort. Next week he is, wisely, taking time off to complete his Pinochet judgment. The strain was telling on him.

20 March 1999

We completed the Pinochet judgments this week and they will be delivered next Wednesday. By the end my draft had extended to 52.5 pages. It is the longest in a collection of long speeches which will give much to ponder over for those who take the trouble to read them. My analysis has secured the agreement of all except Robert Goff, which is a relief after all the work I have had to do over the last four weekends. This was very arduous, as there is much detail and it was so important to get it right. Robert is alone in saying that Senator Pinochet, as a former Head of State, has complete immunity. Nico, Mark and I are together in saying, for various reasons, that he lost his immunity on 8 December 1988 when the UK ratified the Torture Convention. Brian, Peter and Nicholas say that he lost it on 29 September 1988 when the UK brought its statute about torture, giving it extra-territorial jurisdiction, into effect. But the majority on the question of dates lies with Nico's group, as Robert gives the Senator immunity at least until 8 December 1988.

What will be the reaction? No one will have predicted such a result. The expectation is either a clear yes for extradition to Spain or a clear return ticket to Chile. Our decision will – as I said in my speech, and others have followed me – require the Secretary of State to think again. Politics will come into the case once more, but the weight will surely now lie with those who say that we should send him back to Chile. As only a very few incidents of torture in pursuance of a conspiracy to torture could be dealt with in Spain and, as I shall say, only Chile can deal with the full range of offences alleged against him, it would be ridiculous for him to be kept here with possibly 18 months to two years more of litigation to go and massive expenses to incur.

I suppose it is because the case has taken a lot out of me that I feel depressed again this weekend. During the week I felt overwhelmed by the brilliance of

---

114 *R v Immigration Appeal Tribunal, ex parte Shah* [1999] 2 AC 629.
115 *In re B (A Minor) (Adoption Order: Nationality)* [1999] 2 AC 136.
116 *Society of Lloyds v Robinson, on appeal from Lord Napier and Ettrick v R F Kershaw Ltd* [1999] 1 WLR 756.

my colleagues – Nico, Johan, Lennie and Peter – in a case about tracing from a trust into the proceeds of an insurance policy.[117] Mild criticism of my approach to the analysis of the charges in Pinochet by Robert Goff also depressed me. There is nothing I can do about that. He is disappointed in me, as we agreed on almost everything else. Then someone criticised a tribute that I wrote about Lord Reid for a Gray's Inn magazine, because I said that he thought much and spoke little, whereas it appears that he actually spoke rather a lot. And today I have been at Ross Priory as Chancellor at a meeting of the Court of Strathclyde University. I felt very small, inarticulate and inadequate, as I know so little about how the University is really run. It will take a day or so for me to recover, in time for a week's holiday at the end of next week as we enter Holy Week.

4 April 1999

Easter Day. There is time to write up the events of the last few weeks.

There was an unfortunate leak of the Pinochet judgment in *The Times* on Monday, with an even more well-informed piece on the Wednesday. Protests were received from Human Rights Watch and from Lord Lamont of Lerwick. It was suggested that the leak had been a deliberate one, on the pattern of Government 'leaks'. This is, of course, absurd. Nevertheless it is an embarrassment, and there is to be an inquiry. Whoever gave out the information was well informed but not wholly accurate. Frances Rice, who worked so hard to maintain secrecy, is upset. She suspects someone in the Judicial Office who had access to the draft speeches. The truth may be impossible to discover.

We gathered for the delivery of the judgment to find the Chamber full of peers, on both sides of the House. There were two bishops there also. After prayers the galleries filled to capacity, as did the places before the Bar. It was an impressive scene. Nico had prepared us well for it. Each of us had set out a two or three sentence reasoning to state as our turn came up, keeping this stage as simple as possible. Then he had a summary of the effect of the judgment, which he proposed to read out before putting the report of the Appellate Committee to the vote. As we each said our piece the scatter of different conclusions became obvious to each of us, and it was just as well that Nico was in a position to sum up. Mild laughter greeted his opening remark about the impenetrable nature of the reasons so far announced. The summing-up was listened to in silence. But as soon as it was over there was a sound of scrambling in the galleries as people tried to get out to spread the news of the result. It was 6:1 against Pinochet, but on a vastly reduced range of charges. Our task over, we withdrew and the peers who had come to observe the proceedings were issued with copies of the 122-page judgment. My old friend from Cambridge, Rob Napier – Lord Napier of Magdala – came up to me and asked for me to autograph his copy. Outside on the street the demonstrators on both

---

117 *Foskett v McKeown* [2001] 1 AC 102.

sides had greeted the judgment with acclaim. That indeed seemed to be the general view – that both sides had secured a victory. As the *Evening Standard* put it, the Law Lords had, with characteristic finesse, found a way of dealing with the problem which had returned it to where it belonged – with the Home Secretary, Jack Straw.

Both Nico and Robert thought that the odds were now in favour of a decision in Pinochet's favour by the Home Secretary. The huge expense and diplomatic fall-out with Chile of holding him on so few charges seemed to be out of all proportion to what could be gained. But even as we spoke a war was breaking out in Kosovo.

I had remarked a day or two earlier that we need not worry about press reaction to our judgment as we would be overtaken by bombing in the Balkans. A long-running diplomatic effort to try to persuade President Milosovic of Yugoslavia to stop his programme of ethnic cleansing in Kosovo – removing the Albanians to make the place available for Serbs – was running out of time. NATO had set a deadline under threat of bombs and cruise missiles, and it was becoming clear that its bluff was close to being called. By Wednesday morning the moment of military sanctions was close, and by Wednesday evening the first wave of air strikes was on its way. So the Thursday press was largely taken up with this much more significant crisis. On the whole the press was content with the general line which we had taken in our judgment. It was recognised that we had done an acceptable job of legal analysis, and that it is really now all up to the Home Secretary. William Rees-Mogg, writing a day or two later in *The Times*, was astute enough to point out, under reference to Lord Millett's rather extreme judgment, that its effect, while no doubt the law, was to make the world a much more uncertain and more dangerous place. I do so agree, but Peter Millett was not expressing a view which had the support of the majority. For more informed analysis we shall have to await the academics.

My own contribution attracted some attention, especially because I had examined the allegations in greater detail. It was described as 'Lord Hope's Key Judgment' by Geoffrey Robinson QC. This was because I put the few remaining charges into the context of a systematic campaign of official torture, which was essential to the line that I was taking to the law.

As for Kosovo, 10 days later the crisis seems infinitely worse than when it began. Milosovic's ruthless brutality has taken NATO completely by surprise. His troops and secret police have been driving thousands – tens of thousands – of Kosovo Albanians from their homes, slaughtering men of military age and burning their towns and villages, destroying all records of their identity to try to make it impossible for them to return. Huge columns of refugees have been arriving in a state of exhaustion and abject misery at the borders of Albania and Macedonia, where the resources are quite incapable of housing or feeding them. Left to gather in the open, in cold and in the rain, without food, shelter or sanitation, hundreds seem to be doomed to die. Many have died already. The air campaign has been quite unable to prevent this tragedy. A general war is wholly beyond the capacity of NATO, even if its members were willing to commit their troops to this.

It is a deeply disappointing situation. Right is on NATO's side. The more evil Milosovic perpetrates against the Kosovo Albanians, the more he demonstrates this fact. We could not have turned our backs on his determination to commit ethnic cleansing – or ethnic dumping, as it has now become. But there is much less certainty about the methods which have been used. At present Milosovic has won the propaganda war and has not been stopped from doing what he wants to do. It is said that, if the exodus continues at its present rate, Kosovo will be emptied of its Albanians in 10 days' time. If so, what then? Their return can only be achieved if Kosovo is occupied by ground troops. But Milosovic will never agree to this. He is not a man with whom NATO can now negotiate, and Russia is waiting in the wings not disposed to support NATO and sympathetic as ever to its Serbian soulmates. We are in a situation of some danger, which will require a steady nerve and steely resolve on the part of our political leadership.

11 April 1999

When walking home from Randolph Cliff to India Street I saw a cormorant flying over the West End from the south west towards the Forth. This is a new bird for me in the city centre. It must have been feeding on one of the city's reservoirs.

16 April 1999

Jack Straw decided yesterday that, despite the reduced charges, Senator Pinochet must still be extradited to Spain. The Kosovo affair, if nothing else, made this decision inevitable. It would have been to invite criticism of double standards to do otherwise, when we are at war with Milosovic for crimes against humanity and genocide. As it is, amid all the usual disasters, pain and destruction which goes with armed conflict, the Pinochet matter has attracted little attention. Several years of legal dispute still lie ahead.

23 April 1999

There was a treecreeper singing today in Heriot Row Gardens. It is remarkable how this tiny bird manages to eke out an existence in the city centre despite fumes from more and more traffic, the loss of our elm trees and other ecological difficulties.

28 April 1999

It was the University Day congregation at Strathclyde today. Yesterday afternoon Mary and I were collected from India Street in the University's car and taken to University House on the Jordanhill Campus, where we were to stay overnight with John and Elinor Arbuthnott. A quick change into black tie, and then on to Ross Priory where a dinner party was held for the four honorary graduands – Janet Morgan (Lady Balfour of Burleigh), Lord Dearing, Sir Philip Cohen and John McCormick. It was a lovely spring evening, warm and still, in sharp contrast to a haar-ridden Edinburgh where I had landed late the previous evening in thick fog at the airport. We had drinks on the lawn overlooking Loch Lomond before going into dinner. There were about 40 of us at the dinner: the Deans, presenters, University officers and the graduands making up, with spouses, most of the company. I made a speech at the dinner which spoke of the graduands' pastimes which was intended to be amusing, as an introduction to them before the next day's orations.

Today, again in lovely spring weather, I began with meetings and then went into the Barony Hall for photographs and brief rehearsals. There was then a buffet lunch in the Lord Todd Building before the congregation at 2pm. It was a much less crowded and hectic affair than the summer graduations – enjoyable though these things are. There were only the Strathclyder of the Year, the Alumnus of the Year and the four honorary degrees to present, in addition to some formal presentations, a musical interlude and an address by Lord Dearing. My task was to introduce each item and to present the awards. This was not entirely easy, as there was nowhere convenient for me to put my written instructions. As usual, it required quite a lot of concentration and ingenuity on my part to say the right thing at the right time. However, all went well in the end, and we retired to the Lord Todd for a reception before being driven home to Edinburgh. Tomorrow I am to return to Strathclyde University for a programme of visits and a lunch in the Hotel School.

I was given three days off work from London to attend to my duties as Chancellor. I found the adjustment from my weekly routine rather hard to accept. An uneasy feeling of truancy has been present with me for most of the time, but it was coupled with a glow of pleasure and enjoyment of friendly and stimulating company. I still find it hard to believe the width of my horizons and the variety of my activity since I left office as Lord President. That job now seems light years away and strangely diminished in importance from the remarkable position I now enjoy.

9 May 1999

Several days of east winds, rain, haar and low cloud coincided with the first elections for the Scottish Parliament. There was some rich song from the birds in our garden, nevertheless – robin, blackbird and chaffinch. And there was a blackcap in song at the St Cuthbert's entrance to Princes Street Gardens.

1999 – May to July

6 June 1999

The Whitsun break is over, and I returned this evening to London. Mary and I were at Craighead in a spell of lovely late May weather until rain came on the last day. It was a real pleasure to have time there to enjoy the birds, flowers and animals of late springtime.

I left London before the break in a state of some disarray. Nico Browne-Wilkinson appears to have suffered from some kind of breakdown. It has been obvious for some weeks that he has not been producing his judgments. One rather important one from last July is still outstanding, attracting some adverse comment from the press. He has been told to take time off work until October, which is no doubt wise advice. But it is somewhat of a blow to the rest of us, as we need our senior Lord of Appeal in Ordinary. He is a curious mixture of a man: affable, debonair, but impetuous and even rather disorganised. It is said of him that he was not a good administrator when he was Vice-Chancellor, and it seems that we may be in the same difficulty now. Then poor Brian Hutton has had to be given time off as his wife Mary is very, and perhaps terminally, ill. He is such a brave uncomplaining man in the face of adversity. He will have at least two weeks off at the start of the Trinity term and may need more.

So we are now down to eight permanent Law Lords, as Lords Saville and Phillips who are still engaged on their long-running Inquiries are unavailable. This is a sign of bad management somewhere, probably by the Lord Chancellor. He was chancing his arm in appointing Nicholas Phillips when he still had at least six months to go of his BSE Inquiry, now at least six more to go it seems. And Mark Saville looks like having to spend several more years on the Bloody Sunday Inquiry, so his space is really lost to us. Fortunately Robin Cooke, who is eligible to sit with us as a peer who has held high judicial office, is back for the summer from New Zealand, and Charles Jauncey and Robert Goff who have not yet reached the age when they become ineligible are still prepared to sit quite frequently. So we are covering the ground with their help. Gordon Slynn, charming and delightful as he is, now has a huge backlog of cases to write up. It is a pity that he is now the *de facto* Senior Law Lord, as he always wants to write the leading judgment and can never find time to do so.

There has been much talk recently of moving us out of the House of Lords as part of its reform programme and setting up a new Supreme Court, or perhaps a new Constitutional Court. My view is that this will not be feasible without much more research and much more money. It is unlikely to do much to improve things, given the inevitable problems which one finds in any team of judges, however bright, and the need for senior judges to be involved in other things.

Just before the end of the term a committee on which I was sitting in the Privy Council had an urgent petition for special leave to appeal from nine prisoners in Trinidad and Tobago.[118] They had lost their appeals against conviction and were facing the death sentence by hanging. The purpose of the application was to persuade us that execution by hanging was unconstitutional as a cruel and unusual punishment. We stayed the executions for a few days so that we could hear a full day's argument on the point, but in the end we had no alternative but to refuse leave. The Constitution of Trinidad and Tobago has a clause in it which preserves the existing laws from human rights challenges, and it is clear that death by hanging was sanctioned by the existing law which it inherited from the UK before independence. So it could not be said to be unconstitutional. Indeed, as matters stand, it is the only legal method of carrying out the mandatory death sentence in that country until the State's legislature, by the required majority, decides otherwise. There has been some adverse press comment, but it is ill-advised. The Judicial Committee cannot exercise a prerogative of mercy, nor can it alter the Constitution of Trinidad and Tobago. Under the Constitution that is a matter for the State's own legislature. I wrote a letter to Professor Alan Mills of the Scottish Human Rights Group pointing this out to him, in view of such comments attributed to him by *The Scotsman*. I have not yet had a reply. Later a very sensible reply did come in. He was most sympathetic, and is looking for more instances such as seminars on human rights where we can be in contact.

27 June 1999

A comparatively relaxed weekend, with few engagements other than the Faculty's Biennial Celebration Weekend for which I went to a lunch for delegates on the Friday, and for Lord Prosser's lecture on the Saturday. Neither were very well attended, so I felt that I was making a contribution by being there. The next two weekends are packed with public engagements. There are to be the Strathclyde graduation ceremonies and the Law Society conference which, amongst other things, will occupy all Friday, all Saturday and both evenings each weekend. This is too demanding really, as I need space at weekends due to the pressure of committee business and the absence of days off as we are so short-staffed in London.

But London is not all work and no play. I was invited, with Mary, to attend a State Banquet at the Guildhall for Arpád Göncz, the President of Hungary, and his wife. Why we were selected was not made clear. Perhaps it was because of Sub-Committee E. Or perhaps it was because I was there as a token Law Lord, although Gordon Slynn was there also. Whatever the reason, it was a truly splendid occasion presided over by Lord Levene, this year's Lord Mayor. We were in very good places on a central leg close to the top table. The robes and other accoutrements of the Aldermen and other officers were very fine. Two lines of State trumpeters at either end of the fine Hall, who introduced each important step in the evening's programme with a fanfare, were superb. Lights

---

118 *Boodram v Baptiste* [1999] 1 WLR 1709.

were dimmed, spotlights were on them and then one fanfare at one end of the Hall was replied to with a fanfare from the other end. The food was quite modest, but the wines were excellent and we experienced no hangovers afterwards. A government car made the transportation to and from Gray's Inn very easy; otherwise it would have been very difficult. We had preceded the evening by attending a party in Gray's Inn Hall given by Sir Iain Glidewell to mark his retirement. There were many friends there, who were very nice to Mary. She was in sparkling form, and very brave amongst such unfamiliar company.

What a contrast to the coming week's opening of the Scottish Parliament where the aim – if there is one at all – is to be as downbeat and politically correct as possible. Any attempt at pomp and ceremony is being minimised, and such as there is that remains after the process of censorship is being criticised. The new politicians have yet to learn the value of ceremony as a means of adding status and earning respect for their institution. But the democratic influence is for the lowest common denominator. Magnus Linklater gave his opinion in an article in *The Times*. 'It is a small world in Edinburgh – the Scottish Parliament is setting new standards in tedium'.

3 July 1999

The weather was kind on 1 July in Edinburgh. It rained at Wimbledon, but it was dry, warm and sunny in Scotland. So the festivities for the opening of the Parliament took place in the best possible atmosphere. There was, wholly contrary to the gloomy predictions, a very happy mixture of tradition and modernity, with some surprises to add to the emotion and excitement. Her Majesty did her part superbly, wearing a magnificent suit of purple and green with a similarly coloured, feathered hat which was so obviously based on the thistle and showed her determination to play her role as Sovereign. She looked as though she enjoyed every minute of the occasion, from the drive up in an open carriage from Holyrood and the ceremony in the Assembly Hall to the public processions and fly-past by Concorde and the Red Arrows at the end. I saw it later on television when I returned at 10pm from my day in London, having listened to a recording of the day's events on BBC Radio Scotland on my way in, in my car, from the airport. Nobody could find a word of criticism. There was much warmth and emotion. Some people did not want to be part of it – the Scottish Socialist Party MSP Tommy Sheridan and the Independent Labour MSP Dennis Canavan, for example. But this made it all the more obvious that those who were there went to enjoy themselves in the spirit of celebration and of friendship.

Friday 2 July saw Mary and myself back at Strathclyde University for the first of the two summer graduation days I am to do this year. After getting home at 10pm the previous evening, an 8.15am start for the full-day away in Glasgow was a bit of an ordeal, especially as I always feel nervous about these public appearances and how I will perform. All went well, but I did not feel able to relax at all during the day. I returned to Edinburgh at 5.40pm, only to have to go out to dinner almost at once for the opening of Dynamic Earth's new museum at Holyrood. This turned out to be rather enjoyable – no responsibilities and much to enjoy. There were a few familiar faces among the 500 or so guests. Many of them had been involved in fund-raising and designing the project, and there were a few patrons such as Lord McFarlane of Bearsden, Norman Irons, David Steel, Gerald Elliot and Lewis Robertson. Most of us were without our spouses, as there was no room for them on the guest list. There were several speeches at the start and a tour of the exhibits at the end. But the most spectacular thing of all was the building itself, a wonderfully designed open space under its unusual canopy with superb views of the east end of Edinburgh – Calton Hill, Salisbury Crags and Holyrood. It was light until after 10pm, and then as it got dark the building itself began to glow with its own lighting schemes.

31 July 1999

The term ended a week early, as the Law Lords were evicted from their Corridor so that a programme of rewiring and refurbishment could be put in hand during the summer. During the penultimate week of July Frances and all the rest of the staff were moved into the Conference Room. This was an ordeal for them as the weather became very hot and muggy and conditions there were very cramped. We were left in our rooms for the rest of the week, but on Thursday evening it was time to go. I spent two hours sorting things out into various crates: one lot for store, and another for easy access during the summer. Earlier I moved my pictures out and various other things had found their way to Gray's Inn. I returned to London for a day this week to find all our staff in Committee Room 2 with a table for each of us and our computer equipment, where appropriate, duly installed. The staff were next door in Committee Room 1, where there is a bit more space than in our Conference Room – but not much. There will be easier conditions for them once they go into the recess routine. There will be two members of staff only in at any one time.

The extra week's recess was a relief. A succession of very busy weekends and a series of quite heavy cases had left me with a backlog of four judgments to do – *Reynolds*,[119] *McFarlane*,[120] *Kebilene*[121] and *Factortame (No 5)*.[122] We were all writing in each of them, about newspaper defamation and qualified privilege; a failed sterilisation resulting in an unexpected but healthy child; compatibility of terrorist legislation with Article 6(2) of the European Convention on Human Rights (the ECHR); and the right to damages for loss due to UK

---

119 *Reynolds v Times Newspapers Ltd* [2001] 1 AC 127.
120 *McFarlane v Tayside Health Board* [2000] 2 AC 59, 2000 SC (HL) 1.
121 *R v Director of Public Prosecutions, ex parte Kebilene* [2000] 2 AC 326. This case gave me a chance to say something about the way we should approach disputes about Convention rights between individuals and the executive. My colleagues had not really got round to thinking about this as the Human Rights Act 1998 was not yet in force. But I was very much alive to the issue, as the Convention rights were already in place in Scotland under the Scotland Act 1998.
122 *R v Secretary of State for Transport, ex parte Factortame Ltd (No 5)* [2000] 1 AC 524.

legislation in breach of EU law. I had done a fifth judgment in *Coventry Waste*[123] the previous weekend. I was able to complete *Reynolds* and *McFarlane* and take my discs south with me on the Monday evening Shuttle. The aircraft was surprisingly empty, in comparison with Sundays when every seat is always taken.

Tuesday 27 July was spent in London. I had to give evidence to the Royal Commission on House of Lords Reform, and there was a meeting of the EU Select Committee. I cleared my flat of perishables and closed it up for the summer. Then I went to Westminster. The Underground station there is still, after two years, in a rather shambolic state as work on installing the Jubilee line, much delayed, continues. I hope that it will be in proper shape by October when I start using it again. Then I made my way up to the Committee Corridor. I was first in, but James Clyde, John Hobhouse and later Gordon Slynn with his wife Odile, as ever in close attendance, and Lennie Hoffmann appeared. We are so used to working alone in our rooms that it was disturbing, even slightly embarrassing, to be in the same room on top of each other. Plainly this was not an environment in which to do any real work. I suspect that the place will not be much used during the summer.

After lunch I went to Church House for the meeting of the Royal Commission. I had not expected to have to give evidence when I wrote two letters earlier in the summer on two points of fact which I thought should not go unnoticed, and which due to Nico's indisposition would otherwise have gone unobserved – and even he might not have wanted to pick them up: the confusion with 'Law Lords' involvement in legislation, what the Lords of Appeal in Ordinary do, devolution and a new Supreme Court. When I got the invitation, however, I did not think it right to refuse it. I think that their policy is to call everyone who writes anything of substance to give evidence in public, which is an admirable policy. I was surprised to find a large audience of about 250–300 people. I was one of several witnesses for the mid-afternoon session. There were to be two minutes of introduction and 20 minutes or so of questioning.

The Royal Commission is an interesting and well-designed body. Lord Wakeham is its chairman, and other members are Lord Hurd, Professor Dawn Oliver, Bill Morris (TGWU), the Bishop of Oxford (Richard Harries), Lord Butler (former Head of the Civil Service), Gerald Kaufman QC, MP, Michael Davies' predecessor as Clerk of the Parliaments Sir Michael Wheeler-Booth, Kenneth Munro from Edinburgh and Baroness Dean of Thornton-Le-Fylde. The atmosphere was polite and open. I was questioned in quite a lively manner by the Bishop, Michael Wheeler-Booth and Dawn Oliver. It was all over very quickly but quite enjoyable. I returned to find the House of Lords packed out with hereditary peers on yet another motion to delay the House of Lords Bill. This time it was to refer the issue as to whether it was effective to deal with the writs of summons which all peers receive to the Committee for Privileges. Our

---

123 *Coventry and Solihull Waste Disposal Co Ltd v Russell* [1999] 1 WLR 2093.

31 July 1999

meeting of the Select Committee was disrupted by two divisions, both of which took a long time as so many were voting: over 500 in one and about 450 in the next. This was a pity, as there were two rather interesting reports to discuss. Also we began to run rather over time which, unusually, was a matter of concern to me as I had to get out to Heathrow to get the flight home at 8pm. I was also anxious to be there in time to meet our son Will, on his way to Canada, as he passed through the airport. I managed to persuade our chairman, Lord Tordoff, to move a small item of mine up the agenda and left before the end of the meeting – feeling a bit of a fool, I have to confess. I should have had more courage. I reached Heathrow via the District line to Embankment, the Bakerloo line to Paddington and the Heathrow Express in just under an hour by 7pm which was ample time. However, I did manage to see Will as he was passing though the Underground station, in very good form after an excellent flight south on the Shuttle on a lovely clear smooth day.

Later I heard that the House had voted by a large majority to refer two matters arising out of the House of Lords Bill to the Committee for Privileges. Four Law Lords – not named – are members, and it is usual for three to sit. Gordon Slynn asked me to join him and Donald Nicholls when the Committee sits in October. This proved a bit awkward, because the first day is a day when Sub-Committee E was due to visit Luxembourg for a meeting with the ECJ. But I felt that this was too good and too important an offer to refuse, so I had had to spend some time re-organising our ECJ meeting for later this year. The alternative was to allow James Clyde to take my place, but I was reluctant to give way. He is taking my place already for a visit to the Conseil Constitutionnel in September and, in the longer term, as I shall be in the Lords for longer than James who is planning to retire at the end of next year, it is better that I should find out how the Committee for Privileges works.

So ends my third year as a Lord of Appeal in Ordinary, my tenth on the Bench and 34 years since I entered the profession. It has been a very busy year indeed, much enlivened by the Pinochet affair but also by Sub-Committee E, which is very rewarding despite the hard work on top of the heavy workload on the short-staffed Law Lords' Corridor. This is a remarkably interesting job, so much more wide-ranging and rewarding than being Lord President and Lord Justice General, which seems such a narrow, hermit-like daily grind by way of comparison. It is by no means a holiday. There is so much work to do, and I find that there is much less free time at weekends than I was used to when in Edinburgh. It is due perhaps to time spent travelling on Sunday evenings, when I was previously able to take time off. The informality – no uniform, no pretence at putting ourselves on a pedestal of any importance – is relaxing, as is the absence of responsibility for what others do which comes with being just one of a team, rather than being in charge of the entire court. The Court of Session now seems very small and very remote. There is almost no contact with its judges. This is sad, but I do not feel that it is for me to try to open up contacts when none are being offered to me. The Law Society of Scotland remains my best friend in the Scottish legal system.

1999 – August to September

1 September 1999

The Scottish Parliament sat today for its first meeting of the 1999–2000 Session. They are in their temporary accommodation in the General Assembly of the Church of Scotland premises on The Mound. This is convenient for the many tourists and other passers-by in and around the High Street and George IV Bridge. There is a visitors' centre in the Old Midlothian County Council buildings adjacent to Parliament Square. But the entrance to the public galleries in the Parliament Building is on the Lawnmarket, just up from Milne's Close. I went there out of curiosity this afternoon.

It was a surprisingly quick and simple matter, when compared with the distances one must cover at Westminster, to enter the premises there. As I went in, without having to queue, and after going through the electronic scrutiny, I met David Wilson, Lord Wilson of Tillyorn, coming out. He was in a white open-neck shirt and white trousers, completely relaxed and off duty. It was a very warm day. We exchanged amused comments about each other's interest in what was going on. Once inside I found a comfortable seat in the ample gallery space, looking down onto the chamber in which a debate was going on about the nation's health.

Initial comparisons, with what such a debate would have been like if it had been taking place at Westminster, were favourable. The layout is quite different. There is a semi-circle row of seats with tables in front for spreading papers. In front is the mace, behind which sat two clerks with a computer and behind them the Deputy Presiding Officer with two assistants. The seats were about a third full, spread right round the circle – SNP, Labour and Liberal Democrat, Conservative. Some men had their jackets off, but ties were being worn. A response was being made by Kay Ullrich SNP to the opening speech by Susan Deacon, the Health Minister. There were a few interventions, but not many. Her speech ended with applause from her own party, hand-clapping, not 'Hear, hear'. There were then four-minute speeches by various interested parties, closely timed by the Deputy Presiding Officer who called each speaker in turn, presumably from a previously prepared list. These speeches were well delivered and constructive. Having desks to write on and on which to lay out papers is obviously a help here. Christian names were used by some when referring to those in the other parties who sought to intervene. I left after about three-quarters of an hour, rather encouraged by what I had seen. Magnus Linklater was in the press gallery, no doubt taking notes for his column in tomorrow's *Times*.[124]

---

[124] 'MSPs Behaving Rather Well' was the headline to his article in *The Times* on 2 September 1999.

3 September 1999

The sweetness and light indicated by the previous entry disintegrated somewhat yesterday as the Scottish Executive came under fire from the opposition parties over its handling of the affairs of a psychopath who was released from Carstairs State Hospital by Sheriff Douglas Allan in the light of evidence from the psychiatrists that he was not amenable to treatment and accordingly that there were no grounds for continuing to detain him under the statute for treatment in the hospital. Jim Wallace, the Liberal Democrats' Deputy First Minister, and Andrew Hardie, the Lord Advocate, were particularly vigorously criticised, for different reasons: Wallace for procrastination and incompetence, and Hardie for engaging in politics. Of the two, the more deserving of criticism was Hardie, whose remarks in the Chamber sparked off calls for his resignation.

The real problem is a change in the approach to psychopathic disorders by psychiatrists. The House of Lords had to consider a similar problem in *Reid v Secretary of State for Scotland*.[125] In that case the sheriff accepted evidence that Reid was treatable, although several of the witnesses were of the other view. In this case the evidence seems to have been all to the effect that the patient, Ruddle, was not treatable. If that was so, his claim to be released was under the present legislation unanswerable. The solution now desired is to put through emergency legislation which will enable sheriffs in future cases to take public safety into account.[126] This is contentious, and it may be objectionable on human rights grounds. For now, however, it is enough for the Executive to be seen to be doing something, and the Bill has cross-party support. Jim Wallace was probably doing the best that could be expected, supported by some very able civil servants such as Niall Campbell who will have gone into the whole matter very carefully.

Andrew Hardie's position as Lord Advocate and a member of the Cabinet has looked odd from the outset. He is, of course, a member of the Executive and is to that extent a political office-bearer. But he allowed himself to criticise the conduct of the opposition parties in the course of his winding-up speech, rather than deal strictly and solely with the legal issues. The line is no doubt not easily drawn, but he will have to be much more careful in future if his position and that of his office is not to become hopelessly compromised. The role is a very different one from that which he was used to playing in the House of Lords on the Government front bench.

---

125 1999 SC (HL) 17.
126 The result was the Mental Health (Public Safety and Appeals) (Scotland) Act 1999 (asp 1) which was the first enactment passed by the Scottish Parliament. It survived a challenge by three restricted patients on the ground that their continued detention which was authorised under the Act was incompatible with their Convention rights: *A v Scottish Ministers* 2002 SC (PC) 63.

25 September 1999

I returned yesterday from a brief visit to Singapore as a council member of the CMJA and as Chancellor of Strathclyde University. The occasions were the CMJA's Annual Council Meeting and, taking advantage of my presence there on other business, reinforcing Strathclyde's relationships with academic institutions in Singapore. Among the people I met was the Chief Justice of Singapore, Yong Pung How – 'CJ Yong' in the vernacular. He is the force behind the remarkable transformation of the court system in Singapore since 1990, from massive backlogs to the forefront of information technology. He was a prominent and very successful businessman before he was appointed to the Bench in 1989, one year before becoming Chief Justice. He has close friends in very high places, especially the former Prime Minister Lee Kuan Yew, the architect of independent Singapore. 'We have been very lucky with money' he said. He has indeed, with access to funds on request such as the $19m he has been able to spend on information technology. This is about £7.3m for a country with a legal system about two-thirds as large as that of Scotland. As for procedures, he said he had modelled them on those of Australia with the help of Anthony Mason CJ and Murray Gleeson CJ. He has been a hard taskmaster, insisting on maximum effort and faultless time-keeping by everyone including the judiciary. He was not particularly interested in me and my companions, more so in telling us about his achievements.

I have just prepared a report on my visit for the Lord Chancellor's Department, which funded most of my travelling expenses. I ended it with these words:

> 'Overall the impression was of a well-managed, well-funded and effective court system which is in a position, due to a series of energetic reforms, to make the best use of the many benefits which flow from the comprehensive use of information technology. Considerable attention has been paid to meeting the needs of the public by improving access to information about the court process, minimising the time spent in court and facilitating the resolution of disputes by mediation wherever possible. I believe that our legal systems could benefit from a more detailed study by officials of the use of information technology in Singapore with a view to its wider and more effective use in the courts of this country at all levels.'

29 September 1999

To Strathclyde University for the launch of the University's Malawi Millennium Project. HRH The Princess Royal very kindly came from London to attend the event, and the High Commissioner for Malawi was also present. My function was to act as master of ceremonies. John Arbuthnott, the Principal, and Peter West, the Secretary, also spoke and there was a presentation by Professor Alan McGowan. It was a dark wet day in Glasgow. As the Princess Royal remarked, she would have liked to be able to take some of that rain with her when she visits Malawi later, as President of the Save the Children Fund.

Her matter-of-fact, committed and well-informed style was impressive as ever. She knows a great deal about local conditions in that country and cares deeply about the problems there. They are enormous, after years of neglect during the latter part of the rule of Hastings Banda, whose autocratic system was made all the more damaging as he descended into senility. Now much has been done to repair, improve and modernise. The Strathclyde ethic of useful learning fits well into this process, and much practical good can be done through the various educational, environmental, library and engineering schemes which are being set up under a five-year programme.

1999 – October to December

15 October 1999

We returned to work last week, with two cases in the Chamber presided over by Nico Browne-Wilkinson. He seemed to be once again in robust good health after three months' rest. He had lost none of his sharpness, nor his habit of dominating the discussion. In the first case, about the practice of transferring people accused of a serious crime in Ireland from England by the backing of warrant scheme, it was possible for me to contribute a bit to the debate.[127] But when the discussion time came Nico ignored both James Clyde and myself, and indeed Robin Cooke too, and asked Johan Steyn to explain his views and write the judgment. And in the next case, a dispute between Neil Hamilton, ex-MP, and Mohamed Al-Fayed, the notorious Egyptian businessman who owns Harrods, as to Hamilton's libel action and its interaction with Parliamentary privilege,[128] Nico did almost all the speaking in the course of Michael Beloff's address for the appellant Al-Fayed, and he brought proceedings to an abrupt end when Beloff sat down. It was a brisk start to the session, in a chilly Chamber as the House had not yet resumed and the weather outside was cold.

The Law Lords' Corridor meantime was scarcely habitable. We had been allowed back on Friday 1 October when the move from the committee rooms was taking place. But most things were still in crates. I was very fortunate as my bookcases and cupboards had all been put back in the same place. On Monday 4 October I found my books back on my shelves and was able to unpack everything during the week. Most others had no bookcases at all, and they may have to wait for up to six weeks for them to be fitted. On the plus side I have, at last, a decent telephone with some modern facilities, a television monitor which has a full range of programmes on radio and TV as well as access to both Chambers, and the promise of a much better service on the computer.

This week has been quite unusual. On Sunday afternoon, having travelled south the previous day, I went by Finnair to Helsinki with Lords Tordoff and

---

127 *R v Governor of Belmarsh Prison, ex parte Gilligan* [2001] 1 AC 84.
128 *Hamilton v Al-Fayed* [2001] 1 AC 395.

Grenfell to attend a meeting of COSAC[129] on behalf of the House of Lords. I returned from this on Tuesday evening. On Thursday I sat for the first day of a four-day hearing for the Committee for Privileges on two questions referred to it by the House on the House of Lords Bill, where Gordon Slynn, Donald Nicholls and I were sitting as the Law Lords with eight lay peers in the Moses Room.

The COSAC meeting was in essence a meeting of parliamentarians of the EU preparatory to a special Heads of Government under the Finnish Presidency at Tampere at the end of this week and the traditional Heads of Government meeting in November towards the end of the Presidency. All the 15 EU Member States were present and represented. In addition there were the applicant countries from Eastern Europe: the three Baltic States and the Central Europeans – Poland, Hungary, the Czech Republic, Slovakia, Slovenia, Romania and Bulgaria – plus Malta and Cyprus. This was an astonishing gathering, even more so as the chosen language for all the applicant countries, for whom translation in their own language was not available, was English. That is apart from one member of the Polish delegation who spoke German with a pronounced East German accent, despite expressing some very friendly thoughts about what membership of the EU would mean to his country. As most of the other countries, apart from Spain, Italy, Germany and France, were quite willing to break into English as well it was an extraordinary demonstration of how Europe has changed. Those great imperialists Nazi Germany and the Soviet Union have quite vanished, the influence of the English language is everywhere, thanks to the Americans and email. It is now the common language of Eastern Europe as well as of so much else of the world. For them it is a language of choice, not imposition.

Our delegation consisted of Jimmy Hood, Tom Dougan and Bill Cash from the House of Commons with Elizabeth Flood their clerk, and Geoffrey Tordoff, Julian Grenfell and myself from the House of Lords with our clerk Tom Mohan. The others were all politicians: three Labour, one Liberal Democrat, one Conservative. I was labelled as 'Crossbencher and Law Lord'. My precise role in the parliamentary gathering was a source of some puzzlement to, in particular, the Irish delegation who were very friendly and of course easy to communicate with. The event was run with great efficiency by the Finnish Government. It is their first Presidency, and a good deal of planning and effort has been put into it. The emphasis, to the relief and pleasure of the other Northern Europeans, was on making practical progress with established policy rather than grandiose ideas. The main focus of our discussions was on the so-called common European area of freedom, security and justice. This means increased co-operation on cross-border crime and asylum, rather than the harmonisation of everything which some such as the French prefer. There was also discussion of whether the European Commission should endorse the European Charter of Human Rights.

---

129 The Conference of Parliamentary Committees for Union Affairs of the Parliaments of the European Union.

This is a troublesome idea. It is favoured by the Germans and some others, but opposed by the French, the Dutch and ourselves in view of the risk of confusion with the European Convention on Human Rights which is well entrenched already throughout Europe. I was asked to speak for the UK on these issues. As I had only four minutes to do this, there was little scope for me to say much. We sat for the whole of Monday and the morning of Tuesday in a large room in a conference centre beside the ferry terminal. Huge ten-storey ferries arrived from Sweden and Tallinn in the course of the morning and parked just outside our windows. The atmosphere in the room was congenial and mainly friendly, except when the Spanish and the French tried to wreck a new set of rules for COSAC which had been hammered out at a previous meeting from which they were absent. Some deft work by the excellent chairman saved the entire process from collapse. He also disposed very well with objections to a draft communique at the end of the meeting, to which lots of people including the French had proposed numerous amendments. He declared that there would be no communique, just a statement by the President in his own name.

I was impressed by the Finns. They were efficient, friendly and practical. I saw almost nothing of Finland, of course. There were forests of handsome trees as we flew in – tall silver birches, leaves turned to gold, among the dark pines and broad motorways with not much traffic. This seemed to be a well laid-out, spacious city not exactly heaving with people. Indeed the streets seemed remarkably empty. Above all there was the Baltic with no tide, all around the peninsula where we were. The water, and yellow and white painted classical buildings under a northern sky – the latitude of Shetland – made me think of Lerwick, and of St Petersburg too. On the first evening I kept my promise to Mary and went to the Parliament Buildings sauna. This was an astonishing, breath-taking experience, like an oven, as I sat among a group of about eight naked men whom I could hardly see in the steam and semi-darkness. It was almost frighteningly hot, but after a cold shower was most refreshing.

Back in London, after a day to recover and read up to prepare, I was in the Moses Room for a hearing by the Committee for Privileges. We have two questions to consider, arising out of challenges to the very brusquely drafted House of Lords Bill. One is as to whether it affects sitting hereditary peers who have returned their writs of summons for this Parliament.[130] The other is whether the removal of all the Scots hereditaries is a breach of the Treaty of Union between England and Scotland.[131] The arguments on the first point are being presented by Michael Beloff QC and Lord Williams of Mostyn, the Attorney General. On the Scottish point we are to have Richard Keen QC of the Scottish Bar and Lynda Clarke QC, the Advocate General. The fact that I am the only Scottish Law Lord prompted Lord Strathclyde, on the suggestion of Lords Mackay of Ardbrecknish and Drumadoon, to ask for a second Scot. When Nico raised this with me, on the proposal that Donald Nicholls should switch with James Clyde

---

130 *Lord Mayhew of Twysden's Motion* [2002] 1 AC 109.
131 *Lord Gray's Motion* [2002] 1 AC 124, 2000 SC (HL) 46.

for the second question, I advised against it. This was for two reasons. First, it is undesirable that we should be thought of as representing our countries. One Scot is enough to advise the Committee on Scots law. Second, tactically it was unwise. At first there seems to be quite a lot to be said for the argument that the Bill does breach the Treaty of Union. It would be a pity to raise doubts about the motives behind the decision by increasing the number of Scots. Also, there were various practical considerations, such as a certain element of common ground between the two questions. So I am the only Scot.

The first question is turning out to be quite easy. The Bill achieves what the Government has all along said it was intended to achieve. It will extend to all sitting hereditaries at the end of this session, irrespective of when they returned their writs of summons, apart from 90 so-called 'Weatherill hereditaries' who are to be the subject of elections within the next two weeks. I was prepared to keep a more open mind on this than some others, as the Bill could certainly have been more explicit. But the arguments in favour of the Government view are irresistible. I shall have the task of giving my reasons orally to the Committee as soon as the hearing ends on Monday so that we can report that evening to the House. Then we will return to the Treaty of Union question, which is much more interesting and where the result may go the other way. This would present the Government with a political choice – whether to drop the Bill from this session out of respect for the Treaty of Union, which they are most unlikely to want to do, or to press on regardless of the Treaty which they are quite likely to do. There is no prospect of a sense of outrage in Scotland that on this issue, which is of no interest to the general public, the Treaty of Union is at risk of being breached.

7 November 1999

After four days of interesting debate in the Committee for Privileges we decided unanimously that the Bill did not breach the Treaty of Union and that the writ of summons issue had been correctly addressed. There was, in the end, really no doubt on either issue although counsel – Michael Beloff for Lord Mayhew on the latter point and Richard Keen of the Scottish Bar on the former – did their best. Gordon Slynn, who presided very skilfully and with good humour, wrote the leading judgment on the writ of summons issue and I did the same on the Treaty of Union. Donald Nicholls, a rather grumpy colleague as he tends to be when on unfamiliar territory, wrote brief concurring opinions. The results were published on 4 November. Lord Gray, who is a charming elderly Scottish aristocrat, had been deeply hurt when Lady Jay of Paddington, who was ruthless in her pursuit of the hereditaries, said that his question was frivolous. He phoned me shortly after I left for home this evening and very graciously thanked me for the care I had taken over my judgment. As with so many other hereditaries who are to go at the end of this week when Parliament is prorogued, he will be a loss to the House. He was a faithful, regular attender who had contributed much over the years for no payment except his daily allowance and travelling expenses. Most people accept that the hereditary element must go, subject to the 90 who are to stay following this week's elections under the Weatherill amendment. But, when it comes down to individuals and not the issues of principle, it is a sad moment which is being handled with merciless determination by a thankless Government.

In the election Lord Gray was, as he expected, unsuccessful. So also was Rob Napier of Magdala, my St John's College, Cambridge and Lady Margaret Boat Club friend. But most of the leading hereditaries, former Ministers, front bench spokesmen, chairmen of committees and so on were elected. Several leading Scots are on the list. They include the Earl of Dundee, the Duke of Montrose, Lady Saltoun of Abernethy and others. It could have been much worse.

To my great pleasure both Douglas Cullen and Alan Rodger made contact with me this week in response to letters which I wrote to them following Douglas's appointment to take the Ladbroke Road, or Paddington Rail Crash, Inquiry. Douglas, who is now working two days a week in London with his own office in Marsham Street, came to lunch in the House of Lords. He seemed relaxed and in good form. Problems at home were left behind, and he had the interest of a new job to do in new surroundings. I hope that I can offer some support as the going gets tougher next year and he settles in for a long haul. Then Alan Rodger asked to come round to see me at home on the Saturday morning for a general chat about the present state of play at Parliament House. The problems caused by Lockerbie and Paddington are immense.

There is of course the matter of man-management, which so often beset me. The most reliable men in the Inner House – Douglas Cullen and Ranald Sutherland – have been posted elsewhere, Douglas to Paddington, Ranald to Lockerbie. Philip Caplan and John McCluskey are about to retire. John Cameron, Lord Coulsfield, is off to Lockerbie too. New appointments to the Inner House will be needed to fill the gaps left by the two retirements. But who in the Outer House can do the job? The problems, as narrated to me by Alan, do not stop there. The Scottish Executive, he says, is not up to the job. Jim Wallace, supposed to be the Minister for Home Affairs and Justice, seems to be uncontactable, does not reply to letters, appears not able to grasp what needs to be done in the growing crisis facing the Bench. A challenge to the legality, on human rights grounds, of temporary sheriffs will be the subject of a judgment next week. The Government has stopped using them, as everyone expects the judgment to go against them. So temporary judges from the sheriff court are no longer available in the Court of Session, and civil business there is grinding to a halt. Donald Mackay ought on so many grounds to be offered one of the five new appointments to the Bench or one of the two appointments to replace retirements. But Andrew Hardie has passed him by. This seems likely to create a political storm, especially as a surge of seven new judges early next year will close off the supply for further appointments for years. This, Alan thinks, will make it impossible for Hardie to appoint himself. But that would side-line him also and cut off the attraction for able people of appointment as a Law Officer for the future. The office of Lord Advocate is no longer what it was.

These are difficult times for the Court of Session. I am so glad that facing up to all these problems is not my responsibility. If, as seems likely, James Clyde retires from the House of Lords next autumn Alan will get some relief soon, as he is the obvious replacement there. But replacing him will be a real problem.

11 November 1999

I was in the Chamber yesterday afternoon for the closing stages of the House of Lords Bill. It was a rather sad, confused session attended by a packed house. The Bill had returned from the Commons with the Weatherill amendment intact, but some of the Lords' amendments had been reversed. There was little that could be done about this. The Tories had decided not to insist, and the House as a whole wanted to get the thing over. All the battles were not well buried in the past, however. One or two diehards tried to make their point, but they had no support as the amendments were whistled through at such speed that everyone became confused as to which of them were under discussion. Several hereditaries who were about to leave forever were there – Rob Napier, who had failed to be elected by the crossbenchers, as had been Lord Kintore. Some, such as the Earl of Mar and Kellie, a Liberal Democrat, will be hard-hit by the loss of income and of status which as a relatively young social worker by background he clearly valued very much. They were all regular attenders, and the last two among many others will be much missed. Outside the Chamber after we rose warm and emotional goodbyes were being said by the doorkeepers. And there was the poignant sight of several teenage heirs to hereditary titles sitting for perhaps the first and certainly the last time on the steps of the Throne. All that said, there will be relief that some of the older people like the Earl of Dartmouth are to be leaving us, as they were using the House for political campaigns of little value elsewhere. Later the House was prorogued. Sir Hayden Phillips[132] declared the House of Lords Act as the last of the group of statutes to receive the Royal Assent.

I returned to Edinburgh, where the High Court of Justiciary had just released its judgment in *Starrs v Procurator Fiscal, Linlithgow*.[133] It has held that the use of temporary sheriffs in criminal trials is in breach of Article 6 of the ECHR. This was the judgment which everyone had been expecting. But it came nevertheless as a shock to the system, which had made almost no preparations for it. Much will follow from this, and the process of revolution will continue. The stark reality of the steps taken to subject the devolution process to the Human Rights Convention is upon us. This was irresistible and entirely logical, but

---

132 Sir Hayden Phillips GCB, the Clerk of Chancery.
133 2000 JC 208. Although the Human Rights Act 1998 was not yet in force, the Lord Advocate and those prosecuting under his authority were required to act compatibly with the Convention rights by section 54 of the Scotland Act 1998.

nevertheless we seem ill-prepared to deal in the face of its remorseless, penetrating gaze into the very roots of our legal system.

31 December 1999

We are within six hours of the end of this Millennium and the start of the next. It is unclear whether the centuries will change at midnight. The purists say that this will not happen until 2000 becomes 2001. But it has been quite impossible to stop the growing surge of excitement around the world, which has treated the change from 1999 to 2000 as the critical event.

So the city centres of both Edinburgh and London are emptying of traffic and filling up with people for huge street parties, to be set alight at midnight by spectacular displays of fireworks. This has already happened in Auckland, Sydney and Hong Kong, as we have seen on television. Now darkness has set in all over Europe as the sun rises over the Pacific and the final countdown has begun.

Last night Mary and I were at Holyrood Palace as guests of Prince Charles, the Duke of Rothesay. It was not at all clear why we were asked, as this was not the normal State Banquet for the great and the good. Had it been, we would probably not have been there anyway, as the days of our being on that list as Lord President are past. It was a gathering from the arts and culture life of Scotland – media, arts and journalists with sport and religion as well. The BBC was well represented with John McCormick, Kirsty Wark and Carol Smillie. There were Dougie Donnelly, the sports commentator, and Craig Brown, the Scotland football team's coach, the Bishop of Edinburgh, the Linklaters, the Tom Farmers, the James Millers, the Arbuthnotts, Andrew Cubie who has recently reported on student fees, John Houston and Elizabeth Blackadder and Jane and Timothy Clifford. There were many others, amounting to about 80 to 100 guests in all. Hazel and John Cosgrove were the only other legal people, much to my surprise. Perhaps I was there as Chancellor of Strathclyde, or perhaps because of my contacts with the media when I was Lord President. Anyway, it was a huge privilege and immensely enjoyable. As an end to, for us, a quite remarkable decade.

The evening began with a reception in the Palace, which was empty and cold as we waited in our overcoats to go out into the forecourt to view a parade of 1,000 pipers. This was the whisky-maker Dewar's Beating of the Retreat for the 20th century. Prince Charles went out onto the stand on the forecourt with the Lord Provost, Eric Milligan. The pipers came in five groups or bands down the High Street from the Castle, in an evening of magical darkness and light. They were brought from all over the country, all ages, shapes and sizes. There were some fine military figures with familiar Highland regimental cap badges. Others were almost too small to march, tiny children really. One was so small that his father was with him holding his drum. It took half-an-hour for the whole procession to pass. Then we went in for another reception at which Prince

Charles circulated in a very relaxed way among the guests, and we circulated too to meet many old friends. After this we went into the Banqueting Hall for dinner, to a wonderful scene as if from *The Nutcracker*. There was an immensely long table set with cotton wool with fairy lights like snow, in a lovely array of decorations for Christmas touched with silver spray and lit by candles. We ate loch salmon, organic chicken and pear with ice-cream, and there were delicious wines. I spotted Camilla Parker-Bowles among the guests, discreetly separated from Prince Charles. This was a very interesting, touching little glimpse into his private life, as The Queen would probably not have had her at one of her dinners. As Prince Charles' lover and close companion, they have to choose their public appearances with great care. Perhaps the calculation is that the Scots will be more relaxed and sympathetic than the English. A retired Royal Detective to whom I spoke said that His Royal Highness was spending his Hogmanay and New Year in Scotland and not going to the Dome in Greenwich, where the Queen is to be this evening with the Prime Minister Tony Blair and her two grandsons William and Harry. As we left we met Kirsty Wark who said that she had sat next to Prince Charles and argued with him about architecture. He had made a delightful little speech, at Tom Farmer's insistence he said, in which he said that love hath no greater thing to offer than that a father should carry his son's drum.

This celebration was a good boost to my morale, which was somewhat dented by an exchange with Nigel Emslie, the Dean of the Faculty of Advocates, about rights of audience in the House of Lords. It all goes back to Alan Johnston's Dean's ruling of June 1993 which prohibits members of Faculty from appearing in court with solicitor advocates: the so-called 'mixed doubles' rule. It had been prompted by the Faculty's wish to protect itself against competition from solicitor advocates, who now have the same rights of audience in the higher courts, including the House of Lords, as members of the Faculty. At the time when I was Lord President I had misgivings about the rule, but in the face of criticism and complaint by the Law Society I defended the Faculty's right to make it.

The issue came up in London when a solicitor advocate, Joseph d'Inverno, wrote to the Judicial Office asking whether he could instruct a member of Faculty who was also a member of the English Bar to appear with him in that capacity in a Scots appeal in the House of Lords. It was an interesting question, asked in what appeared to me to be good faith by the solicitor advocate. James Vallance White asked me for advice and I consulted James Clyde. James said that we should consult the Dean of Faculty. I reacted instinctively against this, with the comment that we would run into trouble if we were to try to negotiate with him. His uncompromising approach to his duties had already been clear to me in my attempt to secure his help on a previous occasion, so James and I discussed the matter between ourselves. There was the obvious possibility that this was a device to get round the Dean's ruling. But there could be no doubt that both the advocate and the solicitor advocate, having been admitted to practice as such, had a right of audience before us under our own rules in the House of Lords. So I drafted a minute, which James revised, saying that both had a right of audience before us, but that on the issue of professional practice the advocate must consult the Dean of Faculty. I signed the minute and passed it to James Vallance White with a suggestion that he should send a copy to the solicitor advocate. I was concerned that a verbal instruction to James Vallance White might result in a garbled version of a rather important ruling on a matter which might come up again. So consistency and accuracy were needed, as was a written record of our advice.

I then changed my mind about informing the Dean. It seemed to me that he ought to be told, in advance, of the issue which was likely to be raised with him. So I wrote a letter to him, in confidence, about the issue with which I enclosed a copy of my minute. This was I thought a friendly letter which as between two Deans and as a former devil-master to his former devil he would appreciate.

When I was in Helsinki a telephone call came to the Law Lords' Corridor asking for the letter to the solicitor advocate to be stopped. This was too late, as it had been sent out. On my return, and seeing a note to telephone the Dean as a matter of urgency, I rang his secretary Mrs Lawler who was clearly in a state of some distress and embarrassment. She said that the urgency had gone and that a letter was in the post. When the letter arrived I was shocked to find that it was highly critical of me and James Clyde for associating ourselves with 'a transparent device' to get round the Dean's ruling. James Clyde and James Vallance White were both astonished by this accusation, but the real culprit of course at whom the finger was pointed was myself. I wrote back a letter explaining our position in more detail, and saying there had been a misunderstanding about this on the Dean's part. Far from associating ourselves with any device – and it not being for us to say whether or not it was such – we had been doing our best to protect the interests of the Faculty.

To my dismay I received a reply just before Christmas from the Dean accepting that he had no locus to comment on the rights of audience issue, but maintaining his accusation that I had associated myself with a transparent device, or that I could be perceived as having done so. I had been hurt and angered by this, quite unreasonably so no doubt. But I found it impossible to get it out of my mind, as the accusation is a grave one for a Dean to make of a former Dean. It is unreasonable too, because the position we took was of strict neutrality on this issue. It was not for us to say that this was a device. That was for the Dean to decide as the guardian of professional practice. Matters of discipline according to the Faculty's rules were for him to deal with, and not for us. It was for him to say whether the ruling that the course proposed was prohibited should stand, and in this way resolve the whole issue. We had made all the facts known to the Dean and made it clear to the solicitor advocate that the Dean must be consulted before any appearance before us. Nothing that we did was at all underhand or improper. I shall write a final letter of explanation to clear my conscience.

This mishap apart, it has been a good ending to the year. We had a series of short cases in the Lords which kept us very busy in the last two weeks, together with a pile of petitions for leave. I secured agreement for two judgments which I had written. One was a case about certificates of alternative development,[134] where I seem to have had a greater understanding of the issues than my colleagues including Nico Browne-Wilkinson. The other was a real victory because it was about the use of a Scottish search warrant in England: *R v Manchester Stipendiary Magistrate, ex parte Granada Television Ltd*.[135] The Court of Appeal had held that the warrant was invalid, and the arguments by English counsel on both sides were rather inadequate, so much so that the Court of Appeal's decision might well have stood if I had not started to probe the issues more deeply in the light of my knowledge of Scottish practice. In the end the result that endorsement by a circuit judge was all that was needed for the execution of the Scottish warrant in England was obvious to all except Peter Millett who very kindly did not stand out against the majority, and the appeal was allowed. I felt that I had made a small but important contribution in the service of Scots law.

2000 – January to April

20 January 2000

Mary tells me that this afternoon she saw a magnificent male sparrowhawk in our garden catch and then consume an unfortunate blackbird. This seems a rather large item for the male of this species, although not for the larger female. All that remained was a withered clump of vegetation in our flowerbed where the incident had taken place. It seems that the blackbird was too big to carry away, so it had to be plucked and consumed there on the ground.

22 January 2000

I spent my weekend in reading up *Three Rivers v Bank of England*.[136] This is a large and important case about misfeasance in public office arising out of the BCCI collapse ten years ago, into which I have been brought at short notice. So too has Brian Hutton, following the objections to Lord Mackay of Clashfern and Lord Hoffmann which we felt it unwise to resist.

30 January 2000

The blackbirds are having a hard time. There were signs of another blackbird kill on the lawn under one of our apple trees. This time the complete absence of primary and tail feathers suggests that the prey was removed to be eaten somewhere else.

---

134 *Fletcher Estates (Harlescott) Ltd v Secretary of State for the Environment* [2000] 2 AC 307.
135 [2001] 1 AC 300.
136 *Three Rivers District Council v Governor and Company of the Bank of England (No 3)* [2003] 2 AC 1. In the event speeches were delivered by everyone who sat on the case.

11 February 2000

The last two weekends have been devoted to writing up my judgment on the Community law aspects of the *Three Rivers* case as to whether the First Council Banking Co-ordination Directive of 1977 gave rights to depositors against the Bank of England as the regulatory body, which is a matter on which we are all agreed. It amounted to 40 pages in all, which was quite an effort as it has all had to be done by myself on the computers here and in London and in such spare time as I can find. Johan Steyn asked me to do this bit. Thanks to my chairmanship of Sub-Committee E of the House's EU Select Committee, I seemed more at ease with EU law than anyone else. The other bit relates to the English common law on misfeasance in public office, about which Johan is writing the leading speech. We are less obviously at one here, but his clear desire is to get a single view on this subject as we have a second round of this case to consider whether there is an arguable case on the pleadings. Last week he proposed, in a note, that we should have a single speech on the whole case 'to which we have all contributed'. I am not at all keen on this, partly because I do not want to surrender my 40-page text to go out under his name. Also – a point he himself has made more than once – I do not think that it helps the development of the law to restrict freedom of speech in this way. I hope that he does not press this issue, as I shall have to resist.

On Monday and Tuesday we had a Scots appeal, called *Faulds*,[137] in a case about a fireman's claim for industrial injury benefit for traumatic stress disorder following his attendance at a series of fatal accident inquiries. On paper it looked very uninteresting. But some very good and attractive advocacy by Matthew Clarke and Gerry Moynihan transformed it into a fascinating debate which we all enjoyed very much. There were three Scots: Mackay, Hope and Clyde with Hutton and Browne-Wilkinson. I was responsible for putting forward the solution to dispose of the case during the argument, which in the end we all agreed on. Matthew's relaxed and charming approach to the case was much admired. On returning home yesterday I found a note in *The Scotsman* reporting that he has been appointed a Court of Session judge. This is excellent news both for him and the Bench. He was seriously considered for a place on the Court of First Instance at Luxembourg, but this has been given to an Englishman. He will be better off in the long run in Edinburgh, where his academic discipline and wide knowledge will be a great help to the Bench. He is the second of my devils to be appointed in as many months. Two weeks ago Ann Paton was installed as Scotland's second lady Court of Session judge. Other appointments, in what is going to be a huge round due to two retirements (McCluskey and Caplan) and replacements for the Lockerbie judges next month, are Lord Wheatley, who was formerly Sheriff Principal John Wheatley, and Lord Carloway, formerly Colin Sutherland QC. John McInnes has been appointed Sheriff Principal in Airdrie – at long last, he will say to himself I should think, as he has seen others junior to himself such as Douglas Risk, Ted Bowen and Bruce Kerr, being promoted to these positions. The Lord Advocate is clearly

---

137 *Chief Adjudication Officer v Faulds* [2000] 1 WLR 1035, 2000 SC (HL) 116.

very busy. There is no hint of criticism of these appointments. But if he were to appoint himself to the Bench there certainly would be, in today's atmosphere. There are also now two vacancies in the Inner House. Douglas Cullen, whom I entertained to dinner at Gray's Inn last week, suggested that there are disputes among the Inner House judges as to how these places should be filled. Alan Rodger, not surprisingly, is looking for quality but others favour seniority. Perhaps, with two places to fill, there is room for both.

Out of the blue came an invitation to accept an Honorary Fellowship of the American College of Trial Lawyers. This is a much-admired professional body which includes only the most senior or most outstanding judges on its list. They include, from the UK, Gordon Slynn, Nico Browne-Wilkinson, Nigel Bridge, Tom Bingham, Harry Woolf and Lord Chancellors Mackay and Irvine. There are Canadian and US Supreme Court judges too. I am rather out of my depth, I fear. I suspect that it was our participation in the Anglo-American Exchange which made the place for me, and kind thoughts by Bob Clare who is the doyen of this organisation. The exciting aspect to this honour is that Mary and I have been invited to receive the award at the March spring meeting of the College which is to be held in Hawaii – 10 time zones away! The journey will take about 24 hours and the journey back will involve two night flights in succession all in one week. This will be quite an adventure. I shall have to make a speech, which will be quite an ordeal, into the bargain.

Another heavy week lies ahead. We have a very heavy Scots appeal, *Dingley*,[138] about whether a neck injury in a minor road accident caused symptomatic multiple sclerosis. The Lord Ordinary, Lord Dawson, made no proper decision after a long and very technical proof. In the First Division Lord Rodger re-did the whole thing, writing in great detail but coming to quite different conclusions. A request for 14 days for the hearing has been squeezed back to three. I suppose that I shall have to write the judgment if we agree on the result, which will be no easy task. Also we have the EU Select Committee on Tuesday, when I have to present Sub-Committee E's Report on Reforming Competition Law. Then there is a meeting of the Sub-Committee itself on Wednesday, when we start on our new inquiry into the EU Charter of Fundamental Rights. It is all good stimulating stuff but very time-consuming.

15 March 2000

This morning, at 6.15am, we left 34 India Street to begin our journey to Hawaii. We have three flights to Honolulu today and one to the island of Maui, where the conference is to be held, the next day. Three days later we reverse the process. This time next week I shall be back at work in the Law Lords' Corridor.

But I must mention that, in the newspapers as we left home, was the news of two more appointments to the Bench to complete the huge and unprecedented

---

138 *Dingley v Chief Constable of Strathclyde Police* 2000 SC (HL) 77.

elevations of six to make the number of judges up to 32. The Lord Advocate did appoint himself two weeks ago, together with Matthew Clarke. There was huge publicity for the fact that Donald Mackay had been left out, plus a lot of unfortunate, and perhaps unfair, publicity about how Andrew Hardie was getting out of the Lockerbie trial before it had even begun. But today comes the very welcome news that Colin Boyd, Andrew Hardie's successor as Lord Advocate, has appointed Donald Mackay at last together with Robin McEwan, who has served as a temporary judge for eight years since I appointed him to that post with Hazel Cosgrove. So the last of the current round is complete. It is now clear that a different system for appointments will be in place by the time the next vacancy comes along. This has been discussed as a desirable change in the system for well over ten years. When I was in office as Lord President I was not looking forward to that change, but appointments like Lord Dawson's showed that it was desirable to move to a committee system. Now Andrew Hardie's handling of his responsibility, plus devolution and its effects, have made the need for change much more pressing. Those who are through the net and onto the Bench must feel a sense of relief. I ponder on my own position, as Peter Fraser had the power to promote me from the Bar to Lord President. But would a judicial appointments committee, especially one with several serving judges on it, have seen their way towards doing so? I rather doubt it. Had I not been promoted I most certainly would not have been here with Mary, setting out for Hawaii this afternoon.

18 April 2000

A magpie raided a blackbird's nest in our neighbour's garden this morning. It had been chasing the adults when they were feeding their young. I fear that the combination of magpies and sparrowhawks is robbing central Edinburgh of its thrushes and blackbirds. It may be the cold spring, but there is very little singing from them just now – just robins, chaffinches, greenfinches, wrens and tits, nice though they are.

21 April 2000

Easter is late this year, the latest for 57 years they say. Today is Good Friday. It has been a very long term since 10 January. But this has been a week at home as it is Holy Week, and I have had a lot of catching up to do. Fridays seem to have been in short supply this term, with several Strathclyde engagements including a most enjoyable moot final in the new High Court building where I was the judge. There was a backlog of draft judgments to do: *Berezovsky*,[139] a defamation claim by a Russian businessman in which I am dissenting in part with Lennie Hoffmann; *ex parte Evans*,[140] a case about damages for false imprisonment; the tidying up of my draft in *Faulds*; and finalising *Foskett* which was

---

139 *Berezovsky v Michaels* [2000] 1 WLR 1004.
140 *R v Governors of Brockhill Prison, ex parte Evans (No 2)* [2001] 2 AC 19.

heard 13 months ago[141] but has been so much delayed because Nico Browne-Wilkinson could not get down to writing the speech which he has now at last produced. I also had to prepare a paper for a devolution seminar in May, and there was a lot of correspondence.

There are big changes afoot in London. While I was away in Hawaii the Lord Chancellor summoned the Law Lords to announce that when Nico retires on 6 June his successor will be the Lord Chief Justice, Lord Bingham. We were also told that Tom Bingham's successor as Lord Chief Justice will be Lord Woolf, the Master of the Rolls; that the Master of the Rolls' successor will be Lord Phillips of Worth Matravers; and that Lord Phillips's place will be taken by Richard Scott, the Vice-Chancellor. It is a remarkable piece of re-shuffling. Tom, Dick and Harry all moving and changing places, as it were, with each other.

Of these moves, Tom Bingham's to be the Senior Law Lord is excellent news. We were in a bit of a jam, as Gordon Slynn, already 70, is not really suited to do the job as he is so engrossed in his many other activities. Neither Donald Nicholls nor Johan Steyn were really suitable either, then there is Lennie Hoffmann and then me. Tom will give us much needed organisation and stability and leadership. Press suggestions of a US-style Supreme Court are really wide of the mark, as we cannot avoid sitting in committees rather than en banc to get round all the work in the House of Lords and the Privy Council. Richard Scott's move to the House of Lords is as expected, and he will be a lively addition to the team. Harry Woolf has got the short straw. He would have loved to come back as Senior Lord of Appeal in Ordinary, I am sure. Now he has to work to retirement in a very tough but extremely prestigious job. Marguerite will be a most attractive consort for him on special occasions. The oddest move is Nicholas Phillips, who has spent most of his judicial career chairing big inquiries. He has been in the House of Lords for almost 18 months but sat with us only once in *Pinochet (No 3)*. His career in the Court of Appeal was almost as brief. There must be a few noses out of joint in the English establishment. There is certainly no hint here of an appointments commission to sort these things out, as is almost certainly now to be the case in Scotland.

2000 – May to July

5 May 2000

On Monday evening I returned to London with my bag full of papers that I had been working on during the Easter break. But it was a very brief visit, as after a one-day hearing in the House of Lords I had to fly up to Glasgow to fulfil a series of engagements as Chancellor of Strathclyde. The time spent in London was very fully occupied as I was not to return there for a couple of days. There were amendments to judgments to organise, correspondence to sort out and a day's

---

141 See fn 117.

hearing to attend. This was in a case called *Burke*,[142] which finished by lunchtime, as the point was a short one about the application of the extradition treaty with the United States to a convicted person who had not completed his sentence there as, although the custodial term had ended, there was still a term of supervised release to be served. I was asked to write the judgment to the effect that he remained liable to extradition, which I had hoped to avoid but could not refuse as I was about to have two days off. The afternoon was taken up with going over an important draft report from Sub-Committee E with Dr Chris Kerse on the EU Charter of Fundamental Rights. But I was able to leave in good time for Heathrow to catch the 6.15pm Shuttle to Glasgow, taking with me information received that afternoon from Glasgow by fax to brief me for a speech which I was to deliver at Ross Priory that evening.

The occasion was the dinner for three honorary graduands – a black tie affair, in the lovely surroundings beside Loch Lomond. The graduands were Dr Bakili Muluzi, the President of Malawi; Sir David Steel, the Presiding Officer of the Scottish Parliament; and Professor Amartya Sen, Master of Trinity College, Cambridge and a world figure in the economics of poverty and famine. Mary was collected from India Street as I travelled out to Heathrow trying to make up my speech. She had a suitcase with my dinner jacket, shirt and black tie to change into. I reached Glasgow Airport at 7.30pm just as the dinner began. I was collected by the Strathclyde driver who took me to Ross Priory. I had been able to read the fax in the executive lounge at Heathrow, so I wrote out some ideas onto envelopes while I was on the aeroplane. I changed on my arrival at Ross Priory and joined the party at 8.25pm just in time for the end of the second course. The company was already in very good form, and when it was my time to speak all went well. I told a story about Sherlock Holmes and Dr Watson, and then developed a theme to link all three graduands together which seemed to go quite well. Mary had been making friends with President Muluzi's wife Patricia. He himself was very friendly and indeed clearly delighted with his reception. My speech was recorded for showing on Malawi television. I had built in some nice remarks about the President himself, which was just as well.

On the Wednesday there was a presentation of the Malawi Millennium Project in the Barony Hall for the President and his retinue. There was then a long and rather disorganised series of photographs. A buffet lunch followed which gave me a chance to talk to Professor Sen, who was as sharp as nails and just as articulate. He can go anywhere and speak to anyone. He is a nobel laureate, a man who speaks to the Pope and to President Clinton. He is an Indian by birth and the first non-British Master of Trinity, where he was already a Fellow in 1957 while I was still doing my National Service over 40 years ago. Then we began the ceremonies. I had the usual, nerve-stretching task of acting as master of ceremonies without a script and with no lectern in front of me. It all had to be done from memory, helped by the occasional glance at a scrap of paper by my

---

142   *In re Burke* [2000] 1 AC 422.

feet on the floor. However, it all passed off without any serious mishaps. The Malawi contingent were very excited when the President was awarded his degree and 'ululated' as the others clapped. The same performance greeted his speech on behalf of the graduates. He was then serenaded as he and his entourage were driven away under police escort when the ceremony was over.

That evening Mary and I were guests of the First Minister, Donald Dewar, at Edinburgh Castle for a dinner in honour of the President. It was quite a small gathering: Donald Dewar, Jim Wallace his Deputy, James Douglas-Hamilton, Winnie Ewing, the Lord and Lady Provost, ourselves, the UK High Commissioner to Malawi and his wife and the Malawi party, including Bright Msaka, the High Commissioner for Malawi in London, and his wife Primrose. Mary, who had been working very hard throughout, was now on very friendly terms with Patricia Muluzi and Primrose Msaka. They were clearly delighted to see her again at the Castle. I was seated beside the Minister for Commerce and Industry who, like the President himself, had spent some time at risk of imprisonment, including some short spells when he was actually in prison, under Dr Hastings Banda – the old dictator – before democracy was restored to Malawi under Muluzi in 1994. After dinner we went to admire the superb view from the battlements under a glorious, clear, late-evening sky and then to view the Crown Jewels before our departure.

Muluzi has an immensely difficult task in bringing his country back to democracy and a sound economy. But there is no lack of enthusiasm on his part. He clearly delights in all the trappings of his office. He had with him a retinue of 43, including his press corps, ministers, an aide de camp who was a full colonel, and his wife and her lady-in-waiting. Yet he is warm-hearted and friendly and humorous. With luck he will adhere to the democratic ideal when the time comes, in about four years, for him to pass on his office as President to someone else. The greatest problem of all is the epidemic of AIDS, which affects about 35% of the population in his country and has reduced those over the age of 35 to only 3% of their total. A huge programme of education is his priority, so a university visit is valuable to him. We must all wish him well in his task.

14 May 2000

I was in the chair for the first time last week in the Appellate Committee in Committee Room 1 in the House of Lords. The senior team was dealing with a death row case in the Privy Council, and Nico is no longer sitting so that he can clear his desk by the end of this short term. So I was with Robin Cooke, James Clyde, John Hobhouse and Peter Millett. It was all very relaxed and enjoyable. But it was quite a thrill, in a quiet way, to find myself in the seat which had been occupied by so many distinguished men in the past – Reid, Wilberforce, Fraser, Keith. There were two cases, each for two days. One was about an engineering sub-contract and a tripartite arbitration,[143] which is a

---

143 *Lafarge Redland Aggregates Ltd v Shephard Hill Civil Engineering Ltd* [2000] 1 WLR 1621.

subject familiar to me and about which I felt ahead of the others as to what to do. The other was about State immunity for an alleged defamation by an official at the US Base at Lakenheath, which was much more puzzling and we are still uncertain as to the result. Next week, as Gordon Slynn is away – is he put out at being overtaken by Tom Bingham? – I am to preside again. This time James Mackay will be there and Brian Hutton, with James Clyde and Robin Cooke: three Scots, one from Northern Ireland and one from New Zealand. We will be sitting in an English appeal, needless to say!

2000 – August to September

19 September 2000

As the dates show it has been quite impossible for me to find time to put pen to paper to record what has been going on. This is not to say that nothing much has happened. Quite the reverse. I have been too busy, even during the first six weeks of the recess. In the Law Lords' Corridor important changes have been taking place. Nico Browne-Wilkinson left us at the end of the Easter term, just before the Whitsun recess. There was a long list of outstanding judgments from him to complete, most of which have now trickled in. I have to confess to a sense of relief that he has retired. He was not an easy man to get on with or understand, despite his affable and relaxed manner. All that was on the surface. Underneath was a very fast-moving, restless mind which encompassed thoughts which were difficult to detect. He was also highly disorganised, and this led to situations of confusion and difficulty which people of lesser intellectual brilliance might have avoided. He talked a great deal in committee and tended to dominate discussions, which was not always desirable. But his leadership during the *Pinochet* affair was an outstanding achievement. It did so much to carry us through that very difficult period.

Into his place has come Tom Bingham. He is probably just a little bit less brilliant intellectually, but by contrast is both reticent and highly organised. He has taken care to assess his surroundings and to find out how things work – or do not work – before attempting to assert himself. He was surprisingly lost when he arrived both geographically and procedurally. But he has never sat with us before, so this may not be so very surprising after all. Some guidance was needed, which I tried to provide from time to time when I thought it was required. To begin with he was for the most time hidden from sight in his room, as he had much to clear up after leaving his previous job as Lord Chief Justice. He did not sit for a while, and when he did sit with us he was quiet, polite and thoughtful which created a very pleasant atmosphere. In the administrative field things began to swing into action after months of uncertainty. Memos began to pass around, including a splendid one listing all the outstanding judgments with a sort of defaulters' parade of those whose contributions were awaited – mostly Nico and John Hobhouse.

It was rumoured some time ago that Lennie Hoffmann had suggested to the Lord Chancellor that Tom should succeed Nico. Gordon Slynn was visibly unhappy when the succession took this form, but he is now over 70, has many other interests and must in the long run see the sense in what has happened. As for Harry Woolf, he has settled quickly and easily into his new role. Mary and I saw him to his best advantage at the Lord Mayor's Dinner for HM Judges in the Mansion House where, as Lord Chief Justice, he had to give one of the traditional speeches. He spoke very well indeed, was received with very obvious goodwill and affection. Mary, to her delight and surprise, was placed next to him at the top table. This was quite a privilege, as she is by no means the Senior Law Lord's lady. Some must have wondered who this charming, lively, youthful person was who was seated beside the great man! They had much to say to each other. Harry told her about his time when he kept a horse when he was a schoolboy at Fettes.

Harry was also one of those on the stage in the Royal Gallery when the Lord Chancellor presented the American Bar Association with a facsimile of Magna Carta during their conference in London in July. This had been forecast as a huge event, but various factors such as the strength of the pound against the dollar reduced numbers considerably. The Royal Gallery presentation was a day off for us, but it was not well attended and was a curiously stilted occasion. One saw groups of American lawyers on the streets, around Trafalgar Square for example. But they were not much in evidence elsewhere to ordinary people like me who were not invited to the various lectures and receptions.

At work, I found myself in the chair quite often with a run of cases in the Privy Council on appeals from the Medical and Dental Councils. Two other cases in particular stand out. One was in the House of Lords about advocates' immunity from suit for negligence: *Arthur Hall v Simons*.[144] The other was the first devolution case in the Privy Council: *Montgomery and Coulter v HM Advocate*.[145] The *Arthur Hall* case was, I felt, set up from the start to abolish the immunity. The case was about the liability for negligence of solicitors in the conduct of various settlements outside the courtroom. The solicitors were trying to extend the advocate's core immunity beyond the clear limits in the existing case law, and it would have been quite possible to decide the case by clarifying the boundaries of that immunity. But it was put down – I suspect because of a deal with Nico – as a seven-judge case and both Johan Steyn and Lennie Hoffmann went into it with their minds made up that the immunity must be ended, looking for every crumb they could find to support their views. It ended up with a 3:3 split, with three experienced criminal lawyers (myself, Brian Hutton and John Hobhouse) in favour of preserving the immunity in criminal cases, and three commercial and chancery lawyers (Steyn, Hoffmann and Peter Millett) in favour of abolition right across the board. Although Johan Steyn tried to put together a case to answer on the criminal aspects, the truth is that this was a

---

144 *Arthur J S Hall & Co v Simons* [2002] 1 AC 615.
145 *Montgomery v HM Advocate* [2003] 1 AC 641, 2001 SC (PC) 1.

pure afterthought on his part. Peter Millett, having never sat on a criminal case ever, was in no position to form a judgment. Lennie wrote about 'plaintiffs' in criminal cases, which rather gave the game away in his case. Nico, who was in the chair, decided to follow the commercial and chancery line, which was hardly a surprise. He too had no criminal experience behind him. It was a frustrating case. There has been no published comment so far. No doubt the decision will be held as a forward-looking and popular one, but an Australian judge whom I met the other day said that he thought that in that country my position would carry more weight. We shall see.

The devolution case from Scotland nearly came off the rails when Lennie Hoffmann said that he thought that the issue raised was not a devolution issue at all. His agenda was to keep these cases away from the Privy Council, which is quite understandable but not what the legislation provides for. Unfortunately James Clyde was inclined to follow his argument, as was Donald Nicholls. Gordon Slynn was also at risk of being swayed by it. I was completely unpersuaded, especially as no one in the High Court of Justiciary at either level had suggested otherwise and the Court of Appeal in Edinburgh had given leave on the basis that there was a devolution issue with which the Law Officers agreed. I fear that my hackles were being raised, and I became rather too outspoken in the course of the discussion than I would have liked. But the issue at stake is most important. It is typical of the English judges that they like to see every issue in terms of the English common law. Lennie Hoffmann was using English terminology like 'stay' and 'demurrer' without having made any effort to understand the Scottish criminal law procedural context. We decided the case on its merits after a long and uncomfortable argument. Indeed the issue in the case, which was about prejudicial pre-trial publicity and its effect on fair trial, was never in doubt. But the question about the devolution issue remains an open one which will have to be dealt with in the judgments. I had to spend several days in the recess writing mine, which runs to about 90 pages on the Privy Council draft layout. I do hope that I have not been too entrenched or insular to find myself alone and without support. But some things needed to be said, as clearly as could be.

Much of my time during the summer and almost all of it during the frenetic last three to four weeks has been taken up with the 12th Triennial Conference of the Commonwealth Magistrates' and Judges' Association: CMJA Edinburgh 2000, as it came to be called. At the Conference in Cape Town three years ago it was agreed that the next conference should, if possible, be in the UK and that Edinburgh would be the best place. I was co-opted onto the Council with this in mind. Graham Cox, then Sheriff Principal of South Strathclyde, was already one of the elected Council members. On our return to Scotland I wrote to Hamish Hamill of the then Scottish Court Administration and through him secured the necessary financial commitment from the governments, both in London and in Edinburgh, to enable us to put forward a firm invitation for the CMJA to accept. There was then a slack period. Two Council meetings followed, according to the usual practice of holding one each year between the Triennial Conferences. One was in October 1998 in Cyprus which was a bad time for me and I did not attend it. The other was in September 1999, which I did attend as it was clearly necessary for me to do so in order to set the ball rolling in earnest for our own conference.

On our return to Scotland Graham and I put together a local organising committee, while we became members of the steering committee which met in London. Michael Lambert, the Executive Vice-President, and Dr Karen Brewer, the Director-General of the CMJA, were in overall charge. The steering committee consisted of them, Graham and myself, Keith Hollis, the Director of Education, and Graeme Garden, the other UK Council member. We met in a most uncomfortable, noisy room in Uganda House at the top of the Mall in Trafalgar Square on Mondays from 5.30 to 8pm or 8.30pm every six months or so. The local organising committee was under the joint chairmanship of Graham and myself. The other members were Sheriffs Brian Lockhart, Douglas Allan from the Sheriffs' Association, David Stewart from what had now become the Scottish Executive Justice Department, and Mary, who was chairman of the committee in charge of the companions' programme, having been persuaded to do this by Graham Cox. We met increasingly often in my study at 34 India Street, which was a relief to me and Mary. Later we were joined by Iona Ritchie of the Law Society of Scotland and later still by Mary's brother Andrew Kerr. Also involved, but to a much lesser extent and at a greater distance, was David Armati, the CMJA's President who lives in Sydney, Australia. He had to be consulted, usually through Michael Lambert, about the main details of the conference over which he was to preside.

The main problem which confronted us from the start, and which was to haunt us for much of the planning period, is that the CMJA has no money. It cannot, as it is a judges' association, attract commercial sponsorship for such events, and it exists mainly to serve the smaller and poorer jurisdictions of the Commonwealth. So we had to be careful to trim every aspect of the programme to what we could afford to pay out of delegates' subscriptions to the conference. We had first to find a conference centre and then venues for three receptions in the evenings and for a day out at prices which were within our limited budget. It soon became clear that we would have to use the Edinburgh International Conference Centre, newly developed just in time for devolution in 1999. It was very expensive, and a large number of delegates were needed to pay for it. Without sponsorship our evening receptions were not things we could afford to pay for as well. But the Law Society of Scotland, through Douglas Mill, and the Scottish Executive, through David Stewart, came to our aid. Receptions at the National Gallery and in the WS Library were set up, as was an opening reception in Parliament House which Alan Rodger agreed to give, saving us from a much less satisfactory one in the City Chambers. Johan Finlay, through a personal contact, set up arrangements for the day out at Blair Castle, which she and Mary went to explore and investigate routes there and back. We agreed to have home hosting for the fourth evening, although I warned that this was likely to be a massive and uncertain exercise and that we might not have enough hosts if large numbers were to attend.

There was then a decision to be taken about a venue for the Gala Dinner. I had been a Patron of Dynamic Earth, which opened its exhibition with a spectacular dinner in the autumn of 1999. I felt that this was the ideal location, but it soon became clear that it would be very expensive. My efforts to cling onto this idea were then overtaken by Graham Cox's initiative in going to a 'Taste of Scotland' evening in the stable marquee at Prestonfield House Hotel. He soon established that they could accommodate our largest predictable numbers at a cost which was within our budget. So the decision, with Michael Lambert's support for it, was taken. Graham Cox, David Stewart and Mary made various visits to endure the 'Taste of Scotland' programme in its full and awful detail as presented to tourist bus parties, with Harry Lauder-like caricatures of Scottish dance, song and music-hall jesting, with a view to seeing how the programme might be adapted to our requirements. The reports they brought back with them to the local organising committee meetings, lurid in their description of what they had endured, suggested that this event was likely to prove highly embarrassing. But the dye was cast. The Opening Ceremony required a presentation from some organisation equipped to carry in the 64 Commonwealth flags and to add colour and music to the occasion. This was our responsibility. I had admired the way it had been done by schoolchildren in Cape Town, and suggested that we approach George Watson's College as they still wear school uniforms, have a primary as well as a secondary department, both with boys and girls, and an orchestra and a pipe band. I wrote to the Principal, Frank Gerstenberg, and received an enthusiastic reply.

So bit by bit, and with much help from various friends with whom Mary and I had built up and maintained contact, everything began to fall into place. Brian Lockhart assumed responsibility for transport, using Lothian Regional Transport as his contractor. Douglas Allan assumed responsibility for home hosting. Graham Cox agreed to deal with Prestonfield House and with George Watson's in regard to the arrangements with them. Mary, with much help from Wendy Wilkinson and Mrs Lockhart and Helen Allan and Jean Cox also, put together a most attractive companions' programme. There was to be a city tour on Monday, a visit to Stirling Castle and Bannockburn on Tuesday, a visit to HMY *Britannia* at Leith on Thursday and to the Botanical Gardens on Friday, with transport and lunches to organise also.

For a while the numbers of delegates were alarmingly low. There were only 130 by April, 175 by May and 210 by July. We had fears of a large flop due to a lack of attendance. But suddenly as the last few weeks ticked by, we were deluged by late applications. Numbers rose to 450, then to 500, causing another embarrassment as we wondered whether our venues could cope with such an increase.

Meantime, Michael Lambert indicated that we should hold a meeting of Chief Justices to discuss the Latimer House Guidelines. I was able to put together venues for this without too much trouble. The Advocates Reading Room for the meeting, the Commissioner's Room in the WS Library for the lunch and our own house for an evening supper party. But here again numbers were alarmingly low. None of the large jurisdictions, not even England and Wales, Scotland and Northern Ireland, wanted to be there. Sandra Oxner's influence in favour of her own breakaway organisation secured many absentees from other countries. Chief Justice Dennis Byron from the Caribbean hedged and hedged about coming and then withdrew. Fortunately Chief Justice Richard Banda from Malawi, the next CMJA President, agreed to take his place as chairman. A fortnight before the event was due to start it seemed as if he might be the only person present. I emphasised that, as I was no longer Lord President, I was no longer eligible. However, due to much hard work by Karen Brewer, numbers increased and in the end we had 14 Chief Justices on our list.

Then suddenly the whole thing was upon us. I spent a day on shuttling to and fro between Edinburgh Airport and the city centre meeting our Chief Justices, greatly helped by the Government Car Service which, with David Stewart's help, I had enlisted free of charge. Then there was the Chief Justices' meeting the next day, the Saturday. We had a bus laid on to collect our Chief Justices from the various hotels. I acted as courier, guide and clerk to the meeting which was attended by Chief Justices from the Bahamas, Bermuda, Cyprus, Guyana, Botswana, Gibraltar, Nigeria, Sierra Leone, Papua New Guinea, Turks and Caicos, Swaziland and Malawi. The meeting was useful and friendly, but required some initiative by Derek Schofield of Gibraltar to get the result for which Michael Lambert had been looking – a suitably worded declaration of support for the Latimer House Guidelines. In the evening we had a dinner party for the Chief Justices at home.

I went early next day, Sunday, to the Conference Centre to watch George Watson's rehearsal of the Opening Ceremony. Graham Cox was already there with his joiner, arranging a contraption at the edge of the platform to hold the flags of all the members of the Commonwealth. All around were excited children and their teachers, the music master and the Deputy Principal. Somehow they made sense of their plans and, without revealing how it would all work out, they left as Mary and I set about working out and marking up a seating plan for the most important guests and delegates. There then followed a final Steering Group meeting to finalise arrangements and a Council meeting before we dispersed. The evening was taken up with the Parliament Hall reception, where Mary and I arrived early to introduce the Armatis to the Lord President. We were greeted at the door by Charles Mkandawire of Malawi who said to us 'I saw you on TV in Malawi – I said "I know that man"'. This was the TV programme of the President's visit to Strathclyde University in May. He told me later that in a quiz programme on Malawi television one of the questions was 'What is the name of the Chancellor of Strathclyde University?' To this the answer came 'Lord Hope of Greyhead'. The reception itself turned out to be very crowded and the Faculty officer, Mr Manson, was greatly put out when a Nigerian criticised his white wine. 'This is the worst evening I have ever had – never seen such bad manners', he said. As a gathering, however, it served its purpose. There was plenty to eat and drink and an opportunity for people to meet each other.

Next day, Monday, was the day of the Opening Ceremony. It turned out to be very wet, and many delegates arrived crouching under umbrellas or soaked by rain. However, the whole occasion was brought to life by Watson's. There was a jazz band in the foyer and then the orchestra was on stage as the platform party took their seats. We stood up and two pipers led a procession of the 64 Commonwealth flags down the aisles. Primary 7 who were carrying the flags did very well, putting all but one of them in place. And the one that was left out was quickly rescued. Well drilled and very smart, they turned to face the audience as the National Anthem was played. Then the whole thing came to life when the school's pipe major came on stage and a piece for bagpipe and string orchestra was played. This was most exciting and out of the ordinary and was warmly received. Then to everyone's amazement the entire pipe band came down the aisles and onto the stage as the orchestra left, and we were treated to a fine demonstration of pipe music beginning, to my delight, with 'Cabar Feidh', which was the regimental march of the Seaforth Highlanders. There was also a display of drumming which must have impressed our African visitors. They departed to the familiar tune 'We're No Awa' Tae Bide Awa'. The platform party then went onto the stage where four short but impressive speeches were delivered.

As we adjourned for coffee I heaved a huge sigh of relief. The whole ceremony had been superbly well executed, with dignity and precision worthy of the event. The next day, Tuesday, was an educational programme day. There was then a day out at Blair Castle, to which the delegates had to be taken by bus. A fuel crisis had broken out as lorry and tractor drivers campaigning for lower oil prices picketed Grangemouth and other oil refineries. This cut off supplies of fuel to every user of petrol and diesel oil. Fortunately for us Lothian Region had just enough fuel to secure our buses for the day. On the Friday I had to deliver a keynote speech on the principles of judicial conduct which fortunately I had been able to prepare before the conference began. This was followed by a Closing Ceremony then the Gala Dinner at Prestonfield House. As a touch of tartan this was somewhat over-the-top but far from embarrassing. The dancers were really quite good, the violin player and accordionist quite presentable and the music hall/pantomime acts not too excruciating. Once actions such as arm swinging to music and dancing began the exuberance of the African delegates really took over. We ended in a riot of fun and games before emerging to a farewell display of piping performed with great dignity by Watson's Pipe Band before retreating into the trees and darkness from the floodlit lawns around Prestonfield House.

The huge effort of these last three weeks has left me feeling quite exhausted. But it was all so much better than it might have been. On the whole I think a most impressive series of events was laid on for our visitors. Much was contributed to the success of the event by Sheriff Brian Lockhart, who had a well-drilled army of sheriffs ('Be on time, and do what you are told', was his instruction on the first day), and by all the bus drivers who served us so well throughout the whole programme.

Now it is time to get to work on two lectures which I have to get ready for delivery next term.

2000 – October to December

2 October 2000

The Human Rights Act came into force today. Many of us have been speaking and writing about what this may mean for quite some time. My first contribution, 'The Human Rights Act 1998 – the Task for the Judges', was in a lecture which I gave in October 1998.[146] The Act received the Royal Assent in November 1998. The Government has spent the past two years getting its own house in order to minimise the risk of successful challenges. We will now at last see what the Act's effect is to be when the new system is put into practice.

15 October 2000

The whole of Scotland was much shaken by the sudden death of Donald Dewar, the First Minister, last week. He had had a serious heart operation in May, just after we had had dinner with him in Edinburgh Castle where he had been a most entertaining and kindly host. He had given no sign of the concern which he must have felt about his forthcoming operation. His return to work in September was, perhaps, too soon. But such an industrious and dedicated person would not have wished it otherwise. A brain haemorrhage was not capable of being stopped due to the drugs he was taking, and within hours he was dead.

He was so far ahead of anybody else in Scottish politics, and so much a master of the devolution system that he did so much to formulate and bring to reality, that it is a statement of the obvious to say that he is irreplaceable. A replacement will have to be found, of course, as the Scotland Act requires the post of First Minister to be filled within 28 days. But the vision, dignity, political skills and fine commanding presence which earned him such respect from all sections of the Parliament and the public – integrity, honesty, commitment, all these things – will be hard to find in such measure in anyone else. I imagine that Henry McLeish will replace him, but not without controversy. I felt much sympathy for Muir Russell, the Permanent Secretary in the Scottish Office, who was devoted to Donald Dewar and will be bereft without him, and for Menzies and Elspeth Campbell who were among his closest friends.

---

146 (1999) 20 Statute Law Review 185.

25 October 2000

Mary and I were invited to attend the 50th Annual Meeting of the American College of Trial Lawyers in Washington DC this week – as honorary members. This was a very generous invitation, and I said yes. Almost by return our air tickets arrived which were non-refundable, so we could not change the dates except at our own expense or with much embarrassment as this would increase the cost to the College. So, having consulted Nico during the summer and Andrew Leggatt from the Court of Appeal who knows the College well, I resigned myself to the fact that we would be away from duty from today Wednesday 25 October to Monday 30 October inclusive. This means taking three days out of sitting duties, which is not very creditable. Tom Bingham, having taken over from Nico, does not believe in taking days off. He insisted that he would be away only from Friday to Sunday, so that there would be no loss of sitting days. Gordon Slynn has accepted everything that is on offer. I suppose that Tom has sufficient seniority to do what he pleases. I felt that we could not pull rank.

Among the events which we attended there was a superb one-hour long discussion between Chief Justice Rehnquist of the US Supreme Court, Chief Justice Beverley McLachlin of the Supreme Court of Canada and Lord Woolf, Chief Justice of England and Wales, about current issues in their respective courts. It was moderated by a senior member of the College with great skill and presentation. This was a piece of pure theatre. The four sat in armchairs with tables set with table lamps, water jugs and jars of sweeties beside each of them, under bright lights as if on stage. Harry Woolf did us proud, I thought, with his charming manner and skilful and succinct answers. That evening there was a dinner in honour of the US Supreme Court, which was black tie in the National Building Museum. This was a massive location, with over 1,300 people at dinner in a huge hall of enormous height. Tom Bingham remarked, at the start of his short speech to toast the Supreme Court, that it reminded him of Dr Johnson's remark on visiting Inverary: 'They spared no expense'. Before dinner there were a trumpet fanfare, toasts to the President and to the Queen (which had to be taken with water) and then Tom's toast to the Court. He delivered a measured speech, with two good jokes. One was about age, deafness and stupidity, and the other was about a man of 25 applying for a licence to run a pub.

We returned on 30 October to a state of chaos all over southern England after a night of torrential rain and hurricane force winds. Very few planes had got into Heathrow before us. All domestic services were at a standstill, and both the Heathrow Express and the Piccadilly line were out of action. The road system was at a standstill. Many travellers were very seriously inconvenienced. We thought of all those, including Tom Bingham on the earlier flight which might well have been able to land and had been diverted elsewhere. For us, however, there was only about an hour's delay before we were able to fly north from Heathrow to a peaceful sunny Edinburgh.

30 December 2000

Christmas has come and gone, and now the family is gathering at 34 India Street for this evening's annual family party.

In London I was able to leave with a clear desk. My main interests this last term have been in the devolution case of *Brown v Stott*,[147] where I tried to set out the scheme of Article 6 of the ECHR about the right to a fair trial in a way that would offer guidance. Whether anyone will bother to refer to my speech, coming third after Lord Bingham and Lord Steyn, remains to be seen. I also wrote in *Snell v Beadle*,[148] which was a case from Jersey raising a fascinating piece of Roman law which the island has inherited from the customary law of Normandy. Much of the law to which we were introduced was Norman French. The point at issue was the application to a grant for value of a right of servitude of the Roman law doctrine of *laesio enormis* where a sale of land takes place for less than half of the just price. Peter Millett and Sir Ivor Richardson, President of the Court of Appeal of New Zealand, agreed with me – I was in the chair – as to the result. Robin Cooke, who holds eccentric views on many issues, decided to dissent, as did Brian Hutton for reasons of sympathy with Mrs Beadle which did not appear to me to be entirely compatible with the strict Roman law rule. Much of the rather heavy opinion which I wrote consists of quotations from the French without translation, as the practice is in Jersey. It will look rather odd when published in the Law Reports. The work of producing the text on my computer complete with all the right accents was quite arduous, but it was enlivened by some research which I was able to do into Roman law and early Scots authority.

Our team of 12 Law Lords continues to operate under strength. Mark Saville is hardly ever seen, as his Bloody Sunday Inquiry continues in Londonderry with no end in sight for perhaps two more years. Gordon Slynn has had to make adjustments to his working pattern due to ill-health, with the result that he sits no more than two days a week at best. Bravely, he continues to be as active as possible. He could retire, as he is now over 70 and has more than earned his pension. That is plainly not what he intends to do, as he relies so much on the support services which he commands as a Law Lord, more than his fair share to be frank. So we face increasing absences with no permanent replacement for him until eventually he is unable to carry on. We continue, at Derry Irvine's request, to send a Law Lord to Hong Kong for a month several times a year. Tom Bingham is, as expected, very energetic, and the wisdom of bringing him in as Senior Law Lord is all the more obvious in view of Gordon's illness. There are limits to what he can do, however, apart from keeping a very close eye on delays in producing judgments. Richard Scott has replaced Nicholas Phillips, who sat with us only once due to the BSE Inquiry and is now Master of the Rolls. This is not something that Nicholas much enjoys, as far as one can tell.

---

147 [2003] 1 AC 681, 2001 SC (PC) 43.
148 [2001] UKPC 5, [2001] 2 AC 304.

It was an odd choice, but perhaps he will be regarded as Tom's successor as Senior Law Lord when he has served his time there. As for Richard, he is a most congenial companion, although he had a tremendous set-to with Lennie Hoffmann over a copyright case[149] last October when, as we were all agreed as to the result, he was asked by Tom to write the leading judgment. His reasoning met with fierce objection from Lennie who, as he tends to do, lobbied for support for his point of view amongst the rest of us. Richard stubbornly refused to give ground. How much personalities were at work here was hard for Scots like myself and James Clyde to judge. Whatever the result, Tom had to come to the rescue by writing a short judgment with which we could all agree.

As for the retired Law Lords, Charles Jauncey who was such a stalwart is now over age. This is a shame, as he is still fit and well. Robert Goff, sadly, shows signs of senility although he is still under 75 and Tom has said that he should not sit. Mustill and Lloyd show no enthusiasm for contributing. James Mackay, happily, still does when he is available, but he has only 18 months to go. Nico Browne-Wilkinson has taken six months off following his retirement. How much he will be able to contribute remains to be seen. We are really near the edge of being able to cover our full-timers when they are ill or absent.

Our four judicial assistants, Patrick Robinson, Deok Joo Rhee, Henry Warwick and Aysha Ahmad, have settled in well. This is a delightful team of really able, nice people. How much they can really do for us when we have to insist that they do not write our own judgments is open to review. I am anxious that they should not become a burden on us, as we try to fill their time. As it is, petitions for leave keep them busy. And the four senior Law Lords – Bingham, Slynn, Nicholls and Steyn – seem on the whole to find increasing research items to vary their assistants' diet.

My time with Sub-Committee E, which has proved to be so interesting and rewarding, is nearing its close. When the General Election comes my three sessions will be up and I shall have to demit office. Finding a successor for three years will not be easy. The ideal would have been James Clyde, but rumour suggests – as does his age – that he will want to retire in the next year or so. That would bring in Alan Rodger, who most certainly could fit the bill and be a suitable chairman. So a stop-gap appointment until he comes in might be the solution.

In the Court of Session there are signs of unease. Douglas Cullen's absence at the Ladbroke Grove Inquiry seems likely to continue until at least September next year. This leaves a huge hole. Alan Rodger's policy of mixing Outer House judges even more in the Inner House business does make the whole structure of the court seem somewhat ragged. Ranald MacLean, whom I met in Waterstone's bookshop two days ago, says that the timetabling of business is in a state of shambles. True or not, the pressures of trying to hold the organisation together must be very great. I am so glad that I am in a comparatively relaxed and

---

149 *Designers Guild Ltd v Russell Williams (Textiles) Ltd* [2000] 1 WLR 2416.

intellectually satisfying job in London, which I have now had for four and a half years. It is a very pleasant way of life, although there is remarkably little free time except when we are in recess. Even as Lord President I could go to Craighead once a month for a night. Now that is almost impossible. There are so many lectures to give and other engagements to fulfil, not to mention the extra time I must give to Strathclyde University. For compensation I have what is undoubtedly the most fulfilling and interesting judicial position that is available, and such an increasingly wide circle of friends and acquaintances in London whose company I enjoy. I would not have it otherwise.

2001 – January to April

11 January 2001

This evening I went to a reception in my capacity as one of the Bute House Trustees, whose responsibility it is to see that Bute House, on the north side of Charlotte Square in Edinburgh, is preserved as the official residence for Scotland's First Minister. It was in Wemyss House, on the other side of Charlotte Square, the Head Office of the National Trust for Scotland. The occasion was the making of a presentation to the First Minister, Henry McLeish, on his taking occupancy of Bute House. He was presented with two table lamps, needed for his Cabinet room, and a nicely bound book of Edinburgh prints. There were several people I knew quite well: the Countess of Dunmore who is Chairman of the Bute House Trustees, Angus Grossart, Lord Airlie, Brian Ivory and of course Henry McLeish himself and his Permanent Secretary, Muir Russell. McLeish has had two very bruising days in the press and in the Parliament, for reasons I need not go into. The sad thing is that the Parliament and the Scottish Executive are so young, volatile and open to criticism and ridicule. There is no *gravitas* or poise about the thing at all. I had a quite sensible discussion with him about the use to which he wishes to put Bute House. This was encouragingly constructive I thought, whereas Donald Dewar had little interest in the place. When he came to make his speech of thanks McLeish let his irritation, and perhaps his pain, at the criticisms he has been receiving show just a bit too much, I thought. This is the politician's way, I suppose. The statesman would have risen above it, rather as James Mackay always did with such dignity when he was in trouble.

20 January 2001

A cold spell brought redwings into the New Town gardens. Among a small party foraging in our garden was a handsome semi-albino. It had pure white primaries and tail feathers, and areas of its primary coverts and flanks were also white. Its head and back were unaffected. It appeared to be in very good health. There was no sign that this strikingly odd plumage made it unacceptable to its companions.

25 February 2001

After several very busy weeks and weekends much occupied with preparing draft judgments in the *Three Rivers District Council* case arising from the BCCI collapse (71 pages in the draft circulated at the end of last week) and in a New Zealand appeal *Harley v McDonald*[150] (also quite lengthy) – care required here, as it relates to the practice of finding barristers liable in costs in New Zealand, in which we are differing from a five-judge New Zealand Court of Appeal. We had Dame Sian Elias CJ with us from New Zealand, which was a great help. As I was presiding over the Committee I felt that I should write the judgment, which I wanted to do anyway with my background as Dean and Lord President. The others with us were James Clyde, John Hobhouse and Richard Scott – who was to Sian Elias's concern, inclined to view the exercise as an English 'wasted costs' case. At least being a Scot, I can take on the case with an impartial eye. I emailed my draft to Sian Elias last week for her views before I circulated it to others.

Last week itself was taken up in the relatively humble, but time-consuming, occupation of hearing a medical appeal and petitions for leave in the Privy Council and the House of Lords, all chaired by Tom Bingham. The medical case was a pretty hopeless one, as usual – an Indian doctor who had got into trouble for falsifying his records. But he has a plausible case that he was unwell and confused when he pled guilty on the day of the tribunal, so Philip Otton and I persuaded Tom to put the case back for a re-hearing. The case was memorable from the response which Tom got when he called upon the doctor, who had presented his case with hesitation and economy, with the words 'How are you today?' The doctor's face burst into a wide smile, and we were given a 15-minute account of how well he was now, what his medication was etc, etc. Other presiders might have interrupted him. But that is not Tom's style.

Thursday's case, back in the Privy Council, was a petition for special leave in the devolution case: *Follen v HM Advocate*.[151] We decided to order an oral hearing as the High Court of Justiciary had not given any reasons for dismissing the appeal to it and then refusing leave to appeal to the Privy Council. So the facts were obscure, as was the point in the case. The petitioner was represented by Michael McSherry. He is one of the most disorganised of the Scottish solicitor advocates, to whom Tom listened with great patience but scarcely concealed amazement that the argument that he was presenting was so bad. He is, however, the first solicitor advocate to make it to the Privy Council. Bit by bit – he was highly nervous – it emerged that he had no devolution issue to raise at all as Niall Davidson, the Solicitor General for Scotland, crisply pointed out in his reply. Tom agreed that I should write a brief judgment. As he put it, 'If I write it, you will have to put it into Scots.' I have added a paragraph suggesting that reasons should be given if permission to appeal is refused, and that, had

---

150 [2001] UKPC 18, [2001] 2 AC 678.
151 [2001] UKPC D2, 2001 SC (PC) 105.

they been given, the cost and inconvenience of this hearing almost certainly would have been avoided. The chairman of the court in Edinburgh was William Prosser. I suspect that he was so exasperated with McSherry that he brushed the case aside as not worth the paper it was written on. How true, but one cannot be too careful.

I have been much saddened by the death from a heart attack this week of John Mackay, Lord Mackay of Ardbrecknish. He was one of the trio of Mackays, with Clashfern and Drumadoon, that were on the Government front bench at the end of the Conservative Government. He stayed on as Chief Whip on the Opposition side, and was a robust, humorous and most effective spokesman on many issues. Last December he was elected Deputy Speaker, which for the first time – at 62 – gave him a decent salary and a position he could enjoy until retirement. He was ideal for the job and was settling in to it very well. He was looking forward to more time to enjoy his hobby of fishing and seeing more of his family. I went to a reception in his honour given by the Lord Chancellor in the River Room on Tuesday evening. I said goodbye to him at 8.30pm as I left, thanking him for the excuse for a good party. He was in excellent form. Within 12 hours he was dead. It is such a shame.

2 March 2001

Another cold spell – very much so, with heavy snow earlier in the week and very low temperatures. To my surprise, a redshank was feeding in Inverleith Park, now almost free from snow. It was close to a footpath, unperturbed by the passage of people and dogs. It procured a good-sized worm as I watched it from about 20 yards away. I do not get as close as that to these birds on the seashore.

16 April 2001

Mary and I are in the King David Lounge at Heathrow waiting for a flight later today with El-Al to Jerusalem/Tel Aviv airport. This extraordinary state of affairs has come about because I was invited last December to give this year's Lionel Cohen Lecture at the Hebrew University. This is quite an honour, as there is a long line of distinguished speakers stretching back to 1954. The system is to have an academic one year and a judge or senior practising lawyer the next. I was a bit cautious about accepting, as the security implications are not negligible. There was a breakdown of the peace process at the turn of the year as President Clinton's second term as President came to an end. President Bush shows no interest in resuming the efforts of the Clinton era. Sporadic violence in the West Bank and the Gaza Strip has been the result, and the Foreign Office's website advice was to keep away from those areas and to visit Jerusalem only if necessary. The latter part of this advice was relaxed a bit as an election in Israel resulted in a change of government from Prime Minister Ehud Barak to Prime Minister Ariel Sharon – a move to the right. But as we sit here, having decided to go and having got our tickets and all the other arrangements in place, we hear that last night Israeli jets bombed radar installations in Syria and that both Syria and the Lebanon are threatening Israel with war. Mary has overcome initial misgivings to come with me. I felt that I really had no good reason not to go. Of course, for both of us to go into a potential war zone has implications for our children.

Our hosts have, however, laid on a marvellous programme for us with our own car and driver and visits to Masada and to the Dead Sea tomorrow, and to Galilee and the Golan Heights at the end of the week after the lecture. In between we have tours of Jerusalem and official business to do. Beside commitments at the Hebrew University including the lecture we are to be the guests of President Aaron Barak, President of the Supreme Court of Israel, at the official wreath-laying ceremony at Vad Yashem on National Holocaust Memorial Day. Meantime this year's Anglo-Israeli Exchange is taking place during the same week, led by Johan Steyn. We are to be in the same hotel as the British team. Apart from an evening visit to a musical display on Tuesday evening, we have separate programmes. Ours seems much more interesting.

This all comes in the second half of the Easter break. There was quite a lot to do, and I have scarcely had time to draw breath. I was able to complete an important judgment in *R v A*,[152] a case about the new statutory evidential rules in rape cases – limiting questions to the complainant about other sexual behaviour – and their compatibility with Article 6 of the ECHR. Johan Steyn was from the start locked into the view that they were incompatible, modifying this only to the extent of 'reading down' rather than a declaration of incompatibility. My own view is that there is no overall incompatibility, and that it will be for a decision in each case whether the trial was unfair. A lot hangs on this decision. The women's groups will protest if the provisions are said to be incompatible. But other human rights activists will protest if they are not.

I was left with quite a lot of work to do on the Lionel Cohen Lecture, much helped by a recently published book on mixed systems worldwide[153] which includes material on Israel. I had decided on this subject in December without appreciating that it has particular resonance in that country. So I seem to have been fortunate, especially as I cannot deal with the kind of common law topics that had been the subject of previous lectures. Then I had to prepare a keynote speech for a Divisional Court conference in May, material for speeches at Strathclyde University Day and work on a chapter on the structure of Scots law for the next edition of *Gloag & Henderson* at Professor Hector MacQueen's invitation.

On Holocaust Memorial Day itself we were very kindly invited by President Barak to be his special guests at the ceremony. We were given a brief tour of the

---

152 *R v A (No 2)* [2001] UKHL 25, [2002] 1 AC 45.
153 V V Palmer, *Mixed Jurisdictions Worldwide, The Third Legal Family* (Cambridge University Press, 2001). Scotland is listed as one of the mixed systems, as is Israel. They are 'mixed' in the sense that common law and civil law co-exist as the basic material of their legal order.

Supreme Court, which is close to the Knesset on a beautifully landscaped hill in West Jerusalem. The building is probably one of the finest new buildings in the city, full of symbolism, with clean lines and fine open spaces. We were shown to comfortable courtrooms and then taken to the judges' quarters, which, by our standards, are sumptuous. Each judge has, of course, his or her own room, outside which are rooms for the secretary and eagle-eyed assistants. All sit along a corridor leading to the President's rather larger chambers. Aaron Barak and his wife were there to greet us, and we were invited to sit at a table laden with fruit and sweet-meats which we did not dare to touch. But we did have tea and coffee. Then we left for the ceremony at Yad Vashem. Barak was eager to speak to me and he invited me to travel in his armoured Volvo with his security guard. We arrived amid heavy security at Yad Vashem where trees lined the avenue, each with a name beside it of a person who had helped to save Jews during the Holocaust. We were ushered to seats in the front row of an open-air auditorium in front of the Memorial stone. An honour guard of paratroops arrived, with no great emphasis on drill and no music. Then the Mayor of Jerusalem and the Prime Minister Ariel Sharon arrived and they joined us in the front row. There was a brief introduction in Hebrew and then the sirens sounded for two minutes' silence throughout Israel. This was an eerie sound, like the wartime air-raid warnings. The sirens sounded continuously throughout the two minutes, during which the sound of small arms gunfire could be heard from the direction of Bethlehem, a Palestinian town, just a short distance away. Then the wreaths were laid, by the President of Israel, the Prime Minister, the Mayor, Aaron Barak and then various service and Holocaust survivor organisations. Then, without any more speeches or ceremony, it was all over. The President, the Prime Minister and the Mayor came along the row and shook hands with us as special guests. There seemed to be no others, so it was quite an honour for us. We were then driven back to the Supreme Court where we said goodbye and returned to our hotel to change for some sightseeing.

Later that day there followed the event for which we had come to Israel: the lecture. This was held in a small house, Beit Shalom, with an upstairs room with about 70 seats in it. I had had no idea of the size of my audience or its level of experience beforehand. As people began to arrive and join a sumptuous reception downstairs, it became clear that my audience was to be almost entirely Supreme Court judges and senior academics. The organisation of the event was delighted with the numbers. I seem to have attracted as large an audience as the room could hold. Some were standing at the back. The Dean introduced me briefly and then, with Mary in the front row, I addressed my audience. The lecture took just about an hour. Some nodded approval as I spoke. Others fell asleep – usual for such an occasion, especially after such a sumptuous reception – much to Mary's amusement as the wall behind me was a mirror which showed her what was happening. At the end the Dean invited questions. As there were none, he asked one of his own: a very well-directed question about the Scottish approach to limitation and prescription. 'Which did you adopt?' he asked – common-law limitation or civil law prescription. The answer I was able to give was to refer to the Prescription and Limitation (Scotland) Act, which typically adopted the solution of a mixed system. Then one of the academics beside whom I had sat at lunch asked about the division of matrimonial property. I gave fairly full answers to these questions. Honour and politeness had been satisfied. But as the formal session ended various people crowded round to ask further questions, including one man with a strong Glasgow accent who clearly disapproved of the 'not proven' verdict. I wondered how my accent and my lecture had gone down with him. Afterwards there was a dinner party attended by some of the senior judges, including Barak himself. Dorit Beinisch, who was expected to be the next Chief Justice, sat next to me so that we could talk about television in the courts. The conversation was continuous and animated and very enjoyable. We said our goodbyes. I promised to communicate with Barak and Beinisch about law reports and television, and then we walked home in the warm night air.

It was hard to know whether the event was a success. But both the organiser and the Dean were pleased, and it was a good excuse for an enjoyable party. At least part of the purpose behind these lectures, however, is to introduce the speaker to Israel, to spread a greater understanding of its culture, problems and character. In that respect at any rate the visit was proving to be a success.

22 April 2001

We are now on the El-Al flight on our way home, somewhere over Austria. What a privilege and what an adventure this visit to Israel has been. We began with great misgivings, feeling sympathy for the Palestinians, disapproval of the Israelis and some concern (Mary's mostly) about our safety. All of this has now been put into perspective. We feel at ease with the Israelis, sympathetic to their predicament and understanding of the struggle they must keep up if their country is to survive. That is, I think, what the Lionel Cohen lectureship is all about. But one must not forget the predicament of the Palestinians, to whom our hosts referred throughout as 'Arabs', too. Tension between the two sides was quite low during our visit. There appeared to be freedom of movement for Palestinians who wished to visit or had work in Jerusalem. How long this will last is impossible to predict.

25 April 2001

Derry Irvine, the Lord Chancellor, telephoned me in my room in the House of Lords just after 9am this morning. 'I expect you have been at work for quite a time' he said – he is reputed to start at about 6.30am. I was able to say 'Quite a time', as I am always in my room shortly after 8.15am – the third to come in after Tom Bingham and Johan Steyn. A recent article by Joshua Rozenberg in *The Daily Telegraph* about legal assistants had noted that Tom and I were in while journalists like him were thinking of having a second piece of toast. He asked me to come and see him. 'I will be with you in 10 minutes', I said, giving myself time to change into my suit from the slacks and pullover that I wear when I am working in my room.

'I expect you know what this is about' he said when I arrived. I did not, as he broke the news – not unexpected, but new to me – that James Clyde had given him notice that he proposes to retire on 30 September. There is no question that Alan Rodger is the obvious successor. What Derry wanted to discuss was the correct procedure. So I told him about the meeting I had attended when I was Lord President in that very room when James Mackay was Lord Chancellor. Lord Mackay of Drumadoon, the Lord Advocate, and Michael Forsyth, the Secretary of State for Scotland, were also present. I also explained how I had put forward three names in addition to that of James Clyde when we were discussing the successor to Lords Keith and Jauncey, how I had not really thought of putting my own name forward and how I only did so when these three names were rejected. We agreed that, although he was the likely successor, Alan Rodger should attend as also should Colin Boyd, the Lord Advocate, and Helen Liddell, the Secretary of State. Fortunately the appointment of Lords of Appeal from Scotland is a reserved matter, and that is for the Lord Chancellor to handle. If it had been devolved the position – according to the new procedure – would have been for the post to be advertised and would have been for decision by the Scottish Judicial Appointments Commission. All that may come, but for the time being it is all quite simple. I asked Derry whether he wanted other names and told him that Douglas Cullen was really the only other alternative. But he said that it was not his practice to offer two names to the Prime Minister.

It will be a huge relief for Alan to come to the Law Lords' Corridor. Rumour has it that he is pretty fed up with being Lord President. The political situation in Edinburgh is far from his liking, and he has not gone out of his way – as I think Mary and I did – to make friends and influence people. We had very good relationships with the Law Society, and our official dinners at Bute House were a good way of staying in touch. I suspect that, following devolution, much of that would now have been denied to us. My real problems, which I know Alan does not share, were within the Court itself. In the Lords Alan will really come into his own, and he will surely develop his academic links now that he will be much closer to Oxford. Who will succeed him as Lord President is open to serious question. That job, certainly, will have to be advertised. I suspect that it may be difficult to have a successor in place by the time Alan leaves the Court. We shall see.

2001 – May to July

19 May 2001

The General Election campaign is underway. The House of Lords is almost deserted, as indeed is the whole of the Palace of Westminster. The 'late Parliament', as we refer to it when delivering judgments in a Chamber with no mace and no bishop, is no more. The Law Lords are the only members of either House with a right to remain, as we go about our normal business.

Reform of the House of Lords is not a major election issue, but there is some talk of further changes. 'I would gladly trade in my peerage for £5', said my colleague Lord Steyn. I suggested that this was rather cheap. 'I might be persuaded to go up to £20' he replied. This was a surprising concession, as he is a man of very fixed ideas and has no taste for any of our traditions in the House of Lords. Lord Slynn, who was out of the room at the time – we were in the retiring room of the Privy Council – has diametrically opposed ideas about such things. He loves his peerage and enjoys the House, formal dinners and all the rest.

We have had two more very important human rights cases, and a third about the planning system in *Alconbury* in which I was not involved. The two in which I am involved are *R v A*, about rape shield legislation, and *R v Lambert*,[154] about controlled drugs and retrospectivity. The team, Slynn, Steyn, myself, Clyde and Hutton, is the same in both. It is a pity that Tom Bingham is not with us to give sensible leadership. Gordon Slynn is as usual beset with many other things and largely unobtainable for serious out-of-court discussion. We suffer as a result, because his huge common sense would be so useful if it were available. Johan Steyn is suffering from a serious bout of the tunnel vision to which he is so prone. The rape case was one in which he was determined on a declaration of incompatibility from the start. He has been steered off that in favour of solving the problem by interpretation, but remains obstinately resolved against applying an open mind to a discussion of the detail. The result is, I fear, a very untidy attempt to 'read down' the relevant subsection in a way which I think is contrary to what was intended by Parliament. That being so, he would have been better to stick to a declaration of incompatibility and leave it to Parliament to sort the thing out under the special procedure. In *Lambert* he was all for retrospectivity, but fortunately Gordon Slynn has sided with me and James Clyde and we can be a bit more constructive.

Johan is such a fascinating and stimulating member of the team. No one is more constructive in his research or more impressive in his use of language. But he has the unmistakable approach to life of one's image of those from the community in South Africa where he grew up – determined and quite dogged in holding on to his ideas, yet surprisingly uninterested in things that lie outside his vision of how things are. I greatly value his judgement, but sometimes wish that there was more room for wider discussion. This was particularly so in *R v A* where I was alone in my approach to the problem and quite unable to influence him on how to word or frame his 'reading in' formula, which I suspect will now be much criticised.

I return to London tomorrow for the last week before Whitsun. Strangely I have a week out of court, but I have much to do nevertheless. I shall try to

154 [2001] UKHL 37, [2002] 2 AC 545.

shape up my judgment in *Lambert*, mostly complete now, to introduce ideas on the techniques we are having to develop as to how and when, and how and when not, to 'read down'.

17 June 2001

The General Election has come and gone, and at last after a long period when the Palace of Westminster seemed to be deserted – TV monitors were switched off, and most entrances and exits were closed long before I left the building – people have begun to return. To nobody's surprise new Labour was returned with a huge and almost unchanged majority. The Conservatives lost their leader, William Hague – never convincing as a future Prime Minister – and he resigned at once when the extent of his party's defeat was clear. Their only crumb of comfort was the gaining of one seat in Scotland where there were no Tories at all in the last Parliament. There was almost another, as the SNP won Perth & Kinross by only 40 votes. Malcolm Rifkind tried to recover Pentlands from Lynda Clark but failed, although he reduced her majority by two-thirds. His political career is surely now over.[155] It seems no longer worth it, as probably eight years at least will now go by until his party returns to power. He can hardly complain, as he was a Minister for most of the 18 years when Mrs Thatcher and John Major were in Downing Street.

What this will mean for all of us in the Law Lords' Corridor is unclear. Derry Irvine remains Lord Chancellor, but there are already signs that power and influence has been removed from him as the structure of government has been re-designed under the direction of other figures in Downing Street. Tom Bingham, with the Heads of the Divisions, was summoned to Downing Street last week for some kind of a showdown at which Derry was also present, the details of which have not been revealed to us. There will certainly be a strong law and order agenda, which is not likely to be compatible with what the great men in the English judiciary would regard as acceptable. David Blunkett has replaced Jack Straw as Home Secretary, who has replaced Robin Cook as Foreign Secretary. Peter Goldsmith QC, a new Labour peer, has replaced Gareth Williams as Attorney-General, while Gareth Williams has replaced Margaret Jay as Leader of the House of Lords. So far so good. I hope that there will not be too much of a revolution on the way in which the House works, but we shall not know more about that for a while. My concern of course is that the Law Lords should be allowed to remain where they are and not out-housed to some obscure building in the vicinity.

Judicial work continues apace in this very interesting year. We have had five cases on human rights so far in the Privy Council, with two to come before the end of July and three big ones in the House of Lords. The results are a little

---

155 It was not. He moved to England and was MP for Kensington and Chelsea from 2005 to 2010 and for Kensington from 2010 to 2015.

untidy, as everyone rightly wishes to say something and the details have yet to bed down. But on the whole the thing seems to be going better than might have been feared. Lectures have to be done too. This weekend has been shortened for me by a day spent partly in London chairing an international criminal law seminar and partly in Edinburgh delivering a big lecture to the Society for Computers and Law. In between I had a much delayed and anxious journey through bad weather (thunder at Heathrow, fog at Edinburgh). I am about to go south again for a week which will include the State Opening.

27 July 2001

The summer term has come to an end, and with it my fifth year as a Lord of Appeal and my twelfth as a judge. Ahead lie nine weeks of holiday. The process of unwinding has just begun.

It has been a very busy year, due especially to the impact of devolution cases in the Privy Council and human rights cases in the House of Lords. A year ago this new jurisprudence had hardly begun. Now we have eight devolution cases behind us and five or six human rights cases. Everybody still wants to write in most of them, so we have had fewer of the old-style judgments where only one writes. The developing law is on the whole assisted by this prolixity, but it is not easy to be consistent. Few divisions of principle have emerged between us, except in *R v A* where I felt that Johan Steyn's use of the interpretive obligation in the face of a clear indication of Parliament's policy was unwise and likely to cause real difficulty in practice. How far my attempt to redress the balance in *R v Lambert* will assist – or even be noticed – will have to await next term. We are on the edge of a very real problem if we just mangle the statutes, as I think he did in that case to avoid a declaration of incompatibility.

Tom Bingham has been a very good influence. He is careful, as he has put it in an interview, not to be 'a platoon commander'. But he is keen on getting things done, judgments out and using up spare time. Gordon Slynn is impossibly slow as always, although he has been much disabled by cancer behind his eye and he has been very brave and quite determined in sticking to his share of the work. There has been an increase in output. No judgments are really seriously out of time this summer. In my case all those in cases on which I wished to write are done. So I have a clear slate.

Changes are on the way. I was rotated off Sub-Committee E when the General Election came, and last Monday I made my last speech in the House in a debate on one of its reports. As there has been little committee work done between the election and the recess, and as the House has been back for only about four weeks I have not really missed it. I shall in time, because of the lack of contact with other peers that will result. But there has been a change of personnel on the Sub-Committee anyway, so it was really time to go. Also, as we are sitting in three committees on appeals (two House of Lords, one Privy Council) almost every week next term, I am well out of the extra work involved.

James Clyde's farewell party – a gathering in the Committee Room one evening, a party given by him and Ann at the Lansdowne Club and a dinner I gave for him and Ann at the Oxo Tower, which was the greatest fun – have come and gone without the announcement of a successor. Our lists for next term mark the successor as 'R' – suggesting that this is to be Lord Rodger. But maybe 'R' simply means 'replacement'. There is no hint of a change of Lord President in the Scottish press nor, on speaking about something else to Alan Johnston this evening, do I gather that any rumours of a change have yet caught on in Parliament House. I suspect that there are very real problems in negotiating a change in this office through the Scottish Executive. It is unclear how they will proceed. Will the post be advertised? Will there be interviews with the Judicial Appointments Commission? Will there be a delay? I should have thought that Alan Rodger must remain on as Lord President until a successor is found, especially as Douglas Cullen is still out of action writing his report on rail safety.[156] So there is a hint of real tension here. It will be interesting to see how it is resolved. It may, however, be that the successor will be chosen under the old system, as the announcement of the new procedure[157] does not mention the Lord President. If so, the Scottish Parliament may raise objections. This is not an easy situation for the First Minister to handle.

Alan Johnston suggests that it will be a good thing for the Court if Alan Rodger were to go – the sooner the better, he said. They do not get on, as Rodger is very much Johnston's opposite intellectually. He is almost a non-figure so far as the public is concerned, as he makes no effort to communicate with the public through the press or otherwise. His aim appears to have been to re-design large areas of the criminal law (overruling me in five-judge decisions several times in the process) and to set a new standard of academic input into his Court of Session judgments. On the whole I think that he has done this well, and he certainly has the respect and approval of the academic community. But he has run the Court in a very different way from me, and some think that it was a mistake to allow Douglas Cullen to do the Ladbroke Grove Rail Inquiry while retaining his office as Lord Justice Clerk. This appears to have caused a good deal of unrest and disorder in the running of the Court. There was no summer party for the judges this year. At least James Clyde and I were not invited. With the Lockerbie appeal still to come, the new Lord President will have a hard task on his hands.

Tom Bingham has raised again the idea of a new Supreme Court, responding to questions in a press interview. The Liberal Democrats, urged on by Lords Lester and Goodhart, are firmly in favour of it. There also are some discussions going on about our being moved out to a new building with more room. I am a sceptic on both counts and hope things remain as they are. Being outhoused in some other building in Whitehall or elsewhere would cut us off from so many interesting people and all the buzz of the Palace of Westminster, for which it has to

---

156 The Ladbroke Grove Rail Inquiry.
157 In 2001 SLT (News) 1017.

be said Tom has no affection. The setting-up of a Supreme Court is much less likely. Legislation would be needed, and also the co-operation of Scotland. It is almost certain that the method of appointments to that Court will be legislated for, which would open up a new can of worms. I am sure that Derry Irvine is right to be unenthusiastic, and there is also the question of money. Either alternative will clearly involve much investment in the new building and its staff if we are to have anywhere worthy of the name. I suspect, and hope, that the Government would rather hang on to the bargain it gets under the present arrangement. I am not convinced that our output, in terms of numbers and quality of our judgments, would be any better if we were to move.

Brian Hutton, bereaved last Christmas, has remarried with obvious happiness and success. It is good to see him so happy after the many months of strain and sadness before Mary died. The Law Lords' Corridor will miss James Clyde's merry laugh, but at least Brian is much more himself again. On the whole relationships between the Law Lords now are as good as I can recall at any time during the past five years. For this we have to thank Tom, who has been so good with all of us.

Lastly I should mention the judicial assistants. Our first batch – Patrick Robinson, Henry Warwick, Aysha Ahmad and Deok Joo Rhee – are leaving us after a most successful first year. I have a new team – Akash Nawbatt, Elizabeth Conaghan, Lydia Clapinska and Kay Taylor – who I hope will serve us just as well. The presence of these young, keen and lively people has done quite a bit to freshen up the atmosphere.

2001 – August to September

25 September 2001

We are nearing the end of the long recess and, as usual, things are beginning to click into gear again. There is, however, an air of unease over the whole process of moving back to life at Westminster. On Tuesday 11 September 2001, while Mary and I were on a walking holiday in Italy, there was a series of violent terrorist attacks in America which caused great loss of life, massive destruction and a huge dislocation to travel and the world economy. Four aircraft were hijacked while on internal flights in the USA, three from Boston and one from Washington National. Two were flown directly into one each of the Twin Towers of the World Trade Center in New York, the city's tallest skyscrapers extending up to 110 floors. The third crashed into one side of the Pentagon in Washington. A fourth crashed into a field in Pennsylvania after passengers sought to overcome the hijackers. It was thought to have been intended to crash into the Capitol in Washington. These events followed one another within a few minutes. An hour or two later the Twin Towers collapsed, resulting in more than 6,000 deaths – many of the bodies never to be recovered. Overall about 7,000 people died, about 350 of whom were British citizens. The second impact on the Towers resulted in a huge billow of fire and smoke from the effect of the exploding fuel tanks on the aircraft. This was shown all over the world, as were the collapse of the Towers and the huge volume of smoke and dust that enveloped Manhattan. Planes all over North America were instantly grounded, aircraft crossing the Atlantic were turned back and huge dislocation to travel resulted. The US Stock Market was closed for a week, and markets everywhere tumbled as an incipient recession loomed large. There was talk of further expected terrorist attacks in the USA and in London. Bush declared war on terrorism and was firmly supported by Tony Blair. As I write it seems likely that military operations will soon start in Afghanistan, where the prime suspect Osama Bin Laden is in hiding. Saddam Hussein in Baghdad is another possible target. A long campaign against Islamic extremists everywhere is in prospect. It seems unlikely that they will not try to hit back where it hurts most. The world has suddenly become a much more dangerous place.

In the meantime, having returned from Italy on 18 September by air, I set off again by air on 20 September for a conference in Germany. This was being held in Osnabrück under the auspices of Professor Dr Christian von Bar with whom Lord Goff has had close contacts. It was a joint meeting of British, Dutch and German judges and professors. I was asked to join the British team to represent Scotland, which was very kind of Robert Goff from whom the invitation came. Others on our team were Peter Millett, Nicholas Phillips, Robert Carswell (Lord Chief Justice of Northern Ireland), Konrad Schiemann, Lawrence Collins, Timothy Lloyd J, Professors Peter Birks and Hugh Beale, and Dr Mads Andenas. There were about 30 participants in all. English and German were spoken according to inclination and ability. The Dutch spoke in English. There was instantaneous translation also. The whole thing was easy to follow and very well organised.

The British team met at Heathrow, to which I travelled on an early flight from Edinburgh. Worries about being unable to transfer in time to our flight to Germany were quickly dispelled. Heathrow, with almost no transatlantic traffic, was very quiet. We flew to Hannover, where we were collected in minibuses and driven by autobahn to Osnabrück, where we met our hosts and changed into smarter clothes in our hotel.

The next day we were in conference in the Rathaus in Osnabrück from 9am to 1pm, talking mainly about unjustified enrichment and examining two cases from each jurisdiction. The following day we were in conference again in the Rathaus from 9am to 1pm, where we talked mainly about the proposals for a European Code of Principles of Contract Law which the academics are enthusiastic about but which Peter Millett, and perhaps others in the English team, were firmly opposed to on the ground that it would eclipse the common law. We then broke up and went our separate ways. There was much to savour and interest and enjoy. The confident, relaxed and friendly atmosphere was very marked. The Germans showed no inhibitions about speaking English. Our language appears to be widely used on signs in public places. There is a genuine

European feel to the place, which was most welcome. In our discussions I maintained a Scottish viewpoint when I could, in accordance with my remit. I was not sure that Robert Goff liked my contributions, although they did liven up some of the discussions. Typically, I was on the side of the civilian jurisdictions in their support for a statement of the principles of European contract law. There is nothing in the draft with which a Scots lawyer will feel in the least uncomfortable. Just as typical were the English protests that such a proposal was wholly unacceptable to the common lawyer. I wondered whether I had gone too far.

In *The Times*, on Thursday at Heathrow before leaving for Hannover, I read that Alan Rodger has indeed, as expected, been appointed to succeed James Clyde as a Lord of Appeal in Ordinary. More fascinating is the absence of any news as to who is to succeed him as Lord President. He has already left his office, so it is said, as he is on holiday in Italy and will then go to a Heads of Division Conference in Luxembourg. The whole thing is quite extraordinary. Bruce Kerr, who met Mary at an opening ceremony at the Glasgow Vet School in his capacity as Sheriff Principal, said quite rightly that such a gap in the appointments was unprecedented. This is one of the effects of devolution. The appointment of Law Lords is reserved to Westminster, while the appointment of the Lord President has been devolved. The new system for the making of judicial appointments in Scotland by way of a Judicial Appointments Commission is not geared up for this. No doubt someone is trying to sort the whole thing out behind the scenes, but there is almost certain to be a political repercussion somewhere once the appointment is made. Lords Gill, Hardie and perhaps Macfadyen are the most likely candidates, I suppose. It is not really for me to criticise, as the situation has changed since my day. But I do not think that I would have been prepared to leave my post as Lord President and Lord Justice General until the date when I was in a position to hand over to my successor – to introduce him to the work, brief him and ensure continuity. Perhaps I have misjudged Alan Rodger. It does seem quite extraordinary that he was willing to go south leaving this void back at home in Edinburgh, but perhaps he had no alternative.

27 September 2001

Today the Scottish Peers' Association broke new ground and paid a visit to the Scottish Parliament. In the past its meetings and the annual dinner have been in London and it has been difficult to find a focus for anything in Scotland. But this is a new opportunity, and under the leadership of Baroness Veronica Linklater and Lord David Wilson of Tillyorn arrangements were made for lunch in the Signet Library and a visit to the Parliament in its temporary home in the General Assembly premises in the afternoon. Andrew Kerr greeted our group of 17 peers in the Signet Library, where we had drinks and a brief talk from him followed by lunch in the Commissioners' Room. We then walked up the Lawnmarket and, in a remarkably informal crush of people at the tiny entrance, which included Henry McLeish, the First Minister, himself passing through, we made our way to the VIP Gallery where at meetings of the General Assembly of the Church of Scotland guests of the Palace sit. We remained there for an hour or so, listening to Questions and First Minister's Questions. Sir David Steel, the Presiding Officer – Lord Steel of Aikwood – who had had lunch with us and delivered a brief introduction over coffee, mentioned our presence in his opening remarks and there was a pleasant ripple of polite applause from the MSPs to welcome us. The orderly manner in which questions were taken and answered (not always giving much away, and not infrequently met with noises of scorn or amusement as one would expect) was quite noticeable. This was in contrast to Prime Minister's Questions in the Commons, which is a rowdy gladiatorial set-piece between the leaders of the two main parties. There was some jousting between Labour and the SNP, but things never got out of hand. Then we went to an office in Cannonball House for a talk by a senior official on procedure.

It was a friendly, informal and interesting occasion. There may well be room for further contacts, as the new Parliament adjusts itself to its business. I raised the question of scrutiny by the European committees, where the Scottish Parliament may be at risk of swamping itself from useful work by trying to do too much. Now that to my regret I have left Sub-Committee E, however, I have to leave that initiative to others. But my professional interest in the legislative work of the new Parliament remains. The Privy Council is not short of things to do in that regard.

2001 – October to December

6 October 2001

Back to the Law Lords' Corridor after the long summer recess. Mary and I drove down on the Sunday as usual with a crate or two of supplies, including my bags of potatoes from Craighead, to start the session off in Gray's Inn. Next day, Monday, was the Abbey Service and the Lord Chancellor's Breakfast in Westminster Hall. Security was very tight, following the terrorist attacks in New York and Washington on 11 September. The spectators were kept well over 300 yards away from the procession as we crossed the road to the St Stephen's entrance from the service in the Abbey, where there was a curious mixture of good and bad music, a Walton anthem, a well-read lesson of the prodigal son. I thanked Derry Irvine as we went through the usual routine of shaking hands, for inviting us to his Breakfast. But as ever my remark elicited no reply. Perhaps, by the time the Law Lords reach him after all the Court of Appeal and Queen's Bench judges, he has run out of conversation. Among those in the Hall were Sheriff Iain Macphail and his wife Rosslyn as, to his great credit, he has been appointed the Goodhart Professor at Cambridge University for the coming year.

6 October 2001

Back in the Corridor after the service I found Alan Rodger settling into his room. Contrary to what I had understood and wrote about in my last entry, he had returned to the Court of Session last week after visiting Luxembourg. He said that he had been surprised when I worked through my last two weeks as Lord President, but that in the end there were things that he had to do. As for his successor, there is still no news and no movement. Where the blame lies for the delay is unclear. *The Herald* had a leader on Thursday which was sharply critical of the situation and blamed the Government at Westminster, suggesting that it was time to end the Prime Minister's involvement in this appointment. I am not so sure. I strongly suspect that the delays are all due to lack of urgency and commitment in Edinburgh. Alan said that Douglas Cullen has been asked whether he would be willing to take the appointment, which strongly suggests that he will be the new Lord President. As ever he will be a safe pair of hands. But it will be an unprecedented thing for a Senator who has already been on the Bench for 15 years, is aged 65 and is older than both of his two immediate predecessors, to take this position. Alan also said that Douglas has made it clear that he would not favour Brian Gill as Lord Justice Clerk. It seems that Donald Macfadyen is well placed to follow him into that position. Alan also has said that Anne Smith would seem likely to be the new Senator to fill the vacancy caused by his move to London. When these various appointments will emerge however is anybody's guess.

It struck me that Alan was somewhat lost in his new environment. He has, of course, spent the last 12 years in a succession of important offices – Solicitor General for Scotland, Lord Advocate and Lord President, each with much staff around him, not to mention the advantages of a personal secretary and a government car. The sudden change to the quiet, unsupported individualism that we all enjoy on the Law Lords' Corridor (to say we are unsupported is, of course, quite wrong as Frances Rice and the secretaries we share are very good to us, but it is not the dedicated one-to-one service he had before) must be a surprise. He also confessed to me that he was sorry to leave office as Lord President, which I have to confess I was not. But I believe that I had a much tougher ride within the Court of Session than he has done, and I also did two years more in that office than he has. Nevertheless I am sure that it will not be very long before he gets the measure of the place and begins to shine through his judgments as one of our more intellectually gifted Law Lords for many years.

Our first appeal of the session was heard, as is quite often the case when the legislature is not sitting, in the Chamber: *Director General of Fair Trading v First National Bank*.[158] Tom Bingham was on the Woolsack and presided with his usual charm, precision and efficiency. Alan was understandably diffident, as he was sitting as a Law Lord for the first time. But he was thorough in his summing-up and won general approval for his contribution. We then discovered that James Clyde has had to go into hospital for an urgent stomach operation. This is most unfortunate, as he was just embarking on his semi-retirement period

---

158 [2001] UKHL 52, [2002] 1 AC 481.

and was looking forward to sitting with us for many days in the coming term. We were told by Frances that he has been told that it may be six months before he will be fit to return south. I do hope that it is nothing too serious, as he has much to contribute both north and south of the border despite his retirement from full-time duty with us.

As Tom is to write the main judgment in the *First National Bank* case, there is nothing for me to do about that case this weekend. But I did settle down to write a judgment in one of the cases we heard at the end of last term: *R v Sargent*.[159] The question was whether the use of an unlawfully obtained telephone intercept to obtain a confession at a police interview rendered the confession inadmissible. John Hobhouse prepared the leading judgment over the recess, but it seemed to me to be lacking in detail on the reasons. I felt that there was an opening for me to write a concurring judgment which covered the ground in more detail. I was relieved to find that I was able to get the thing onto the computer without too much difficulty. This was an enjoyable and not too arduous return to composing on the word processor, which is now so much part of my routine.

20 October 2001

Still no announcement as to who is to be the Lord President. Alan Rodger told me on Monday that Douglas Cullen is deeply disturbed by what is going on. It is not only the delay so far as his position is concerned. It seems very likely, he has said, that Brian Gill will be made Lord Justice Clerk. He said that his own views about the unsuitability of this appointment had been made clear, but apparently to no effect. Another storm is brewing over the appointment of Anne Smith as a Senator, as Lynda Clark maintains that she should have been consulted as Advocate General. Lynda Clark probably feels that she too is a candidate for the Bench. The fact that she is said to be threatening judicial review may be a sign of her irritation at not being selected. What a turmoil! Was it wise to alter the previous system of making these appointments?

11 November 2001

Armistice Day and Remembrance Sunday.

Last week, it being November, I was beset by dinner engagements, annual general meetings and lectures. I was in Aberdeen at the start of last weekend introducing a lecture by Alan Rodger in memory of that great Roman lawyer, Professor David Daube. Various members of the Daube family were there too. The lecture told us, inferentially, a good deal about how Daube's influence has moulded the character and interests of Lord Rodger himself. Back in London there was a lecture on the Monday by Chief Justice Anthony Gubbay of Zimbabwe – now very recently forced out of office. He had a lot to say and said

---

159 [2001] UKHL 54, [2003] 1 AC 347.

it very slowly, so the proceedings were very long. It took one hour and 20 minutes for him to deliver his lecture, which discomforted many. I had dinner that evening with Professor Barry Rider to brief me for a meeting of the Advisory Board of the Institute of Advanced Legal Studies, which I chair, the next day. That meeting lasted from 5.15pm to 6.35pm and went off well enough. I dined that evening in Gray's Inn, where it was mixed messes night, to keep in touch with its affairs and sat with interesting company in the centre of the hall. Next day, Wednesday, there was another lecture. This time it was by Mr Justice Collins[160] in a series in honour of F A Mann. He was lecturing on international law with great skill and some nice touches of humour. As it was the 25th lecture in the series, Herbert Smith who sponsor these series of lectures gave a splendid dinner for past lecturers and chairmen (I was the chairman last year) in 2 Temple Place – a remarkably attractive building, with carved woodwork inside to match the much-decorated stonework outside the building. I travelled home by Shuttle on the Thursday as usual. The next day was a graduation day at Strathclyde University, with ceremonies both morning and afternoon. I enjoy these occasions but, as I find myself saying so often, they are quite nerve-wracking and tiring as everything depends on me – the introduction, the capping and shaking hands with some 500 graduates and then two speeches. I returned home very tired. The next day, Saturday, was the Stair Society's AGM and lecture. This was the fourth lecture in eight days. This time it was by Professor Alan Watson, who like Alan Rodger had been taught by Daube. This was another tiring session for me, as I am the President of the Society and must preside.

Behind all this there has been much heavy work to do. Human rights reared its head again in *R v Kansal*[161] where the debate has centred on whether views expressed by the majority in *R v Lambert*[162] – Slynn, Clyde, Hutton – that retrospectivity under section 22(4) of the 1998 Act does not extend to appeals in the proceedings by a public authority is sound and must be followed. Lloyd and Steyn agree with me that it is plainly unsound, but Johan Steyn has refused to accept that we should consider departing from that decision. The position seems to me to be very unsatisfactory, so I have written a very long judgment in draft saying what I think and why I believe we should depart from the majority view in *Lambert*. Lloyd has suggested that the issue should go to a panel of seven Law Lords, but Steyn disagrees with this too. So that solution will not be followed in this case. I suspect that the issue will have to go to seven Law Lords sooner or later – hence the importance, for good or ill, that is likely to be attached to my judgment which I tidied up finally this weekend. As usual, Hutton and Slynn, both desperately slow and neither really engaged in human rights law, have yet to produce their drafts. There is a potential here for further embarrassment, as the Court of Appeal urgently needs to know what our judgment is. I fear that this result will not help very much.

---

160 Lawrence Collins, later Lord Collins of Mapesbury and a Lord of Appeal in Ordinary.
161 *R v Kansal (No 2)* [2001] UKHL 62, [2002] 2 AC 69.
162 See fn 154.

On the political front Henry McLeish was forced to resign after only a year as Scotland's First Minister this week. The cause was his mishandling of an expenses claim when he was a Westminster MP. This was for his constituency office, which he sub-let without telling the Westminster authorities. He was not able to give clear answers, and his credibility collapsed under pressure. I felt sorry for him, but it was clear that he lacked the personality and ability to do the job. So we will have our third First Minister in three years by mid-December. Devolution looks a distinctly second-rate affair as a result – inadequate, immature politicians presiding over what is virtually a one-party state. The inability to appoint a Lord President continues, although Douglas Cullen has told Alan Rodger that he has now received a letter of invitation from Downing Street. They will need to have a Lord President sometime soon, as only he can swear in a First Minister. There seems to be no change in the position that Brian Gill will be Lord Justice Clerk. But some really good news is that Colin Campbell QC,[163] very able and most likeable, has been elected Dean of Faculty.

20 December 2001

The weeks – and the weekends – have been so full that there has been no time to write until now. And today I have returned from London for the Christmas break with two judgments to do and much else besides. For once I feel really burdened with work in this job, and scarcely know where to start as all the pressures of Christmas suddenly bear down on me.

It has been a hard term because Tom decided that we should sit in three panels, with the assistance of our retired Law Lords, for most of it. This meant that all the serving Law Lords had to sit almost every day, so there has been almost no spare time. There have also been some demanding cases – *Kansal* already mentioned and *Pretty*,[164] as to whether the Director of Public Prosecutions could be required to give an undertaking not to prosecute a husband for assisting his wife to commit suicide stand out, as well as *Millar v Dickson*[165] in the Privy Council from Scotland. There was a visit to the Conseil d'Etat in Paris, which I had to lead once again. This was very demanding, as my French was once again so very rusty. And we ended the term with a week in the chair in the Privy Council for me, followed by a three-day hearing there in another Scottish devolution case called *Watson and Burrows*.[166] So almost alone among the Law Lords, I had no days to clear up. Hence the amount of uncleared work for me still to do.

Paris was a looming worry. I bought and read *Le Monde* for weeks in advance on my way home each Thursday as I tried to refresh my memory of key phrases. My team was Konrad Schiemann, Stephen Sedley, David Keene, Robert Carnwath

---

163 Later, as Senator of the College of Justice, the Rt Hon Lord Malcolm.
164 *R (Pretty) v Director of Public Prosecutions* [2001] UKHL 61, [2002] 1 AC 800.
165 [2001] UKPC D4, 2002 SC (PC) 30, [2002] 1 WLR 1615.
166 Reported as *Dyer v Watson* [2002] UKPC D1, 2002 SC (PC) 89, [2004] 1 AC 379.

and Robert Reed from Edinburgh. The latter was of great help to me and to the team generally, as he is a fluent French speaker and had just spent two weeks with the Cour de Cassation. I went along by Eurostar and was met at the Gare du Nord by Roger Errera, who has been so attentive and supportive on these occasions. He delivered me to the superbly art deco Hôtel Lutetia, where once again we were to be based. We had an evening reception there which, remarkably, was very well attended by the French team. Last time they were mostly absent. Renaud Denoix de Saint Marc, the Vice-President, made an impromptu speech at the buffet supper in his elegant light-hearted manner, to which I replied in impromptu ungrammatical French. I included a joke which I had rehearsed in my mind beforehand to the effect that we were so few (only six on our team) that we could not compete with them at rugby, football or cricket, but only at water-polo. Next day we spent in session at the Palais Royal with considerable success. There was a reception in the evening given by the Minister of Justice, at which fortunately no speech was needed unlike last time. Then we were taken through lovely streets glistening with the most elegant of Christmas decorations, especially in the Place Vendôme with neat pyramids of mock Christmas trees set about with white fairy lights, to the Palais de Luxembourg where we were entertained in his residence by the President of the Senate. Here a speech was needed, as he started the dinner with an address from a lectern to which I struggled to reply. I used an abridged version of a pre-planned speech which I had in my pocket. It was not very elegant but just enough to do the job. Next day we had a session all morning, but Saint Marc declared at lunchtime that, as it was such a nice day, he proposed that we should cancel the afternoon session and enjoy Paris instead. I said that we all agreed to his proposal with acclaim. That evening we were entertained to a reception in the British Embassy. This was somewhat spoiled by its being badly timed – 7.30 to 9.30pm. This was rather too late as no food of any substance was offered, and rather too long. I was interested to learn that the newly appointed Ambassador was just about as capable of speaking French as I was. However, we were able to say goodbye to our French hosts. We returned to our hotel for a late, light supper.

The appointment of the Lord President was resolved at last, and in the nick of time. This was because of the political crisis which I mentioned in my previous entry affecting the First Minister, Henry McLeish. His problem was due to oversight rather than dishonesty. But his attempt to explain himself was remarkably unconvincing. He made a disastrous appearance on BBC *Question Time* when, in front of the television cameras, he appeared more confused and evasive than ever. A few days later the inevitable happened. He resigned with tears of despair. It was a sudden and sad end to his career. Fortunately, his recommendation had gone south to London that Douglas Cullen should be the Lord President. So Douglas was installed in mid-November, just a few days before Jack McConnell appeared in the First Division courtroom to be sworn in by the Lord President. The statute provides that the Lord President is appointed on the recommendation of the Prime Minister on the nomination of the First

Minister. If Henry McLeish had gone before the nomination was made, the machinery set by section 91 of the Scotland Act 1998 would have broken down.

Douglas has undoubtedly earned this appointment. He now stands head and shoulders above the others in the Court of Session. He is greatly respected after all the public services he has performed in his three major inquiries – Piper Alpha, Dunblane, Paddington. It is a mark of the standing he has achieved, and his appointment was universally welcomed. The same cannot be said for Brian Gill who has succeeded him as Lord Justice Clerk, as the press were quick to appreciate that his appointment could be controversial. It was pointed out, correctly, that he is not an establishment figure, nor is he a team player. But he is a very able lawyer, and I do hope that the misgivings will be shown to have been wrong. Back in London I found the flow of human rights cases both frustrating and fascinating. A number of English criminal appeals, two more devolution cases in the Privy Council and two English civil appeals in the House of Lords have raised questions of great interest. The devolution cases have gone well, with Tom Bingham in charge. *Pretty* was a sad case involving a woman with motor neurone disease who wanted her husband's help to commit suicide. We had to hold that he would not be immune from prosecution under the Suicide Act 1961. *Porter v Magill*[167] was an appeal by the commissioner of audit against a successful appeal by Dame Shirley Porter, formerly of Westminster London Borough Council, who had been surcharged in the sum of £32m for loss caused by wilful misconduct.

Both *Pretty* and *McGill* were presided over by Tom Bingham. Here again the human rights issues were relatively straightforward. There was no possibility of upholding Mrs Pretty's request that her husband be permitted to commit the crime of assisting her to kill herself. But it was right that we should hear her appeal and give our detailed reasons in public on a matter of great social and moral interest. Mrs Pretty attended one of our sessions in her wheelchair, which added to the sense of tragedy which hung over the case. Dame Shirley Porter – a Mrs Thatcher character, only more so, and less wise – came to see us too. She glared at us as Tom conducted the hearing with uncharacteristic scorn and ferocity. It was hard not to feel that he had taken a strong dislike to the affair long ago, and that it was quite impossible for him to feel as neutral about it as I – an outsider – did. Richard Scott was in much the same position as Tom, and the case was not well handled by her counsel. Tom asked me to write about the human rights aspect of the case, which I duly did. As we were agreeing with the judges in the Divisional Court and the Court of Appeal on all issues, it did not seem too controversial a task. But my 40-page judgment was criticised by William Rees-Mogg in a centre-page article in *The Times* on the ground of its 'thinness'. In truth there was nothing much more that I could have said, especially as Tom brushed aside an offer for us to see a video of the auditor's public statements which had led to him being accused of apparent bias. For me,

---

167 [2001] UKHL 67, [2002] 2 AC 357.

however, the case provided an opportunity to close the gap at last between England and Scotland as to the test to be applied to apparent bias which I identified first in *Pinochet (No 2)*[168] and which the Court of Appeal in England have been working towards ever since. The English formula by Lord Goff in *R v Gough* – the 'real danger' test – was at odds with almost everyone else. I hoped that my formula, with which everyone else agreed, will now settle the issue.

Sadly, agreement has not been forthcoming on the retrospectivity issue. Section 22(4) of the Human Rights Act 1998 is neat but very obscure, and we have had great difficulty in making sense of it. Johan Steyn and I have been more 'engaged', as Johan puts it, in trying to work out a solution. Gordon Slynn, our chairman, has been much less so, and this was not helped by the long drawn-out time-scale to which he works and the impossibility of getting to grips with him as he is so distracted by his many extra-mural activities. In *Lambert* we were split 4–1 against Johan, but my reasons were different from the other three (Slynn, Clyde, Hutton). Apart from one point where I obviously went wrong, my approach seemed to win more approval from commentators than any of the other four. When *R v Kansal* came before us I tried to get support for my approach. Tony Lloyd and Johan Steyn agreed with me, but Slynn and Hutton stuck to their view that there was no retrospectivity for appeals. Then Steyn said that, the point having been decided against me by Slynn, Clyde and Hutton in *Lambert*, we could not now depart from it. Tony Lloyd's suggestion that we should go to a committee of seven, which I supported, fell apart when Johan, after a weekend to think about it, changed his mind and decided against it. Tony Lloyd departed on a world cruise for six months (he is now a retired judge) and Gordon, who really should have been showing leadership on an issue which will not go away, let the matter rest there. So rather oddly there is a long judgment by me in favour of retrospectivity with which Lloyd and Steyn agree, but a decision against me out of loyalty to a decision of the three in *Lambert* which disposes of the issue on a narrow basis in a very few paragraphs. I am sure that the point will have to be gone over again in 2002. As it is, it looks to have been badly handled and I appear to be swimming against the tide set by the others in the Committee.

Frustrating though *Kansal* has been, it has been an enjoyable session and the general atmosphere on the Corridor remains very pleasant and stimulating. I ended the year with a week presiding in the Privy Council over a judicial committee consisting of myself, Browne-Wilkinson, Nolan and the retired Lord Justices of Appeal, Slade and Leggatt. This was hard work, especially sitting with Browne-Wilkinson who is easily side-tracked and impatient despite his genial exterior. I ended up with the judgment in the important case that week, which was *Jaroo v Attorney General of Trinidad and Tobago*.[169] The appellant was seeking the return of a vehicle which had been retained by the police for use as evidence by means of a constitutional process, which we held he

---

168 See fn 106.
169 [2002] UKPC 5, [2002] 1 AC 871.

could not do as it was an abuse of that process. I am also at work on a lengthy judgment in a conjoined Warsaw Convention case about carriers' liability for psychological injury called *King* and *Morris*,[170] in which Johan Steyn and John Hobhouse are both courting me with irreconcilably opposed views about the nature of this kind of injury. Then our last week in the devolution case of *Watson* produced another judgment for me to work on over Christmas.

The House authorities are keen to get us to move out into new premises – just as much as Tom Bingham is to see us removed from the House of Lords altogether and to set up a UK Supreme Court. I am not in favour of either, for purely selfish reasons. I do not believe that we could have a better environment to work in than we have now, or as convenient or as enjoyable a setting in which to have our premises. The Supreme Court idea is a minefield if Scotland, whose attitude is ignored or at least misunderstood by Tom and the other English judges, is to be involved in it – and, if Scotland is not, how can it really be a UK Supreme Court? Fortunately Derry is against the idea, on the very sensible ground of cost with which there is, for the time being, no argument. Moving out is another matter, so far as the House authorities are concerned. We were asked to inspect Fielden House, which was recently purchased for about £7.5m and into which they urged us to agree to go as a place to sit as the Appellate Committee as well as to work in. I suggested that overlays should be prepared to illustrate how committee rooms could be fitted into the plans for such a confined building. It seemed to be agreed that this exercise was worth attempting, but then Tom – with Donald Nicholls's encouragement – decided to reject the suggestion without waiting for the result. I am uneasy about these tactics, as it would have been better to wait and show that the scheme was unworkable. As it is, we may have stirred up more hostility, which could be awkward in 2002. We shall see.

2002 – January to April

26 January 2002

Back to work on 14 January on a case in the Appellate Committee which has now taken seven days and will take two more. It is a complicated dispute, arising out of the seizure of ten aircraft belonging to Kuwait Airways Corporation at the start of the Gulf War by Iraq.[171] The panel consists of Nicholls, Steyn, Hoffmann, myself and Scott. Donald Nicholls's quiet manner is well suited to what was always going to be a long and rather arduous case. Lennie Hoffmann is at his best, taking no notes, relying on his prodigious memory and keen eye for the points that matter. Johan Steyn is thinking around the subject as he always does, and Richard Scott is as lively and unpredictable as ever. It is a

---

170 *King v Bristow Helicopters Ltd; Morris v KLM Royal Dutch Airlines* [2002] UKHL 7, 2002 SC (HL) 59, [2002] 2 AC 628.
171 *Kuwait Airways Corporation v Iraqi Airways Co (Nos 4 and 5)* [2003] UKHL 19, [2002] 2 AC 883.

pleasant team. I am not sure that I can contribute anything useful. But I have spent more time on the facts than anyone else and have been taking more notes. I do this partly to avoid carrying too much stuff home with me at weekends when I am going over the material to work out my approach to a decision.

Meantime we have been finalising judgments in two cases which I wrote about over the recess: the devolution case of *Dyer v Watson*[172] and the Warsaw Convention cases, *King v Bristow, Morris v KLM*. In the devolution case Tom Bingham, Alan Rodger and I are the leaders, with Brian Hutton and Peter Millett on the wings. They do not appear to have the same insight into devolution and human rights law and its general structure as us three, which is a bit worrying. Fortunately we three are a solid majority. Alan has really come into his own in this case, greatly impressing Tom with his knowledge of Scots practice and procedure. He is of great benefit to the system in the Privy Council, and I am finding him an excellent colleague. He is much more sure-footed than James Clyde, although not as open a personality. He is the academic rather than the advocate, one might say. His sources of material and his contacts with people who matter are voluminous, and he is able to grasp points with great speed and to build upon them. The other cases involved quite a contest between Steyn and Hobhouse, as indicated in the previous entry. But it seems as though Steyn and I – me having aligned myself with him – have a majority with James Mackay. Here there is quite a sharp difference of view, and Donald Nicholls has sided with Hobhouse. The result is a bit messy, but my judgment has carried the majority view.

House of Lords reform is being debated again without any reference to the future of the Law Lords. For the time being it seems to be accepted on all sides that we should remain as members of the House. No rancour has been expressed, so far, about our declining the offer of Fielden House.

The Lockerbie appeal began at Kamp Zeist in Holland this week, presided over by Douglas Cullen. He agreed to the proceedings being televised, and I was able to watch the start of the appeal on the TV monitor in my room. As one commentator said, it was innovative but dull. It did not take long for the coverage to cease, although it continues to be shown on the BBC's website. As was the case with earlier decisions about televising, the prospect of coverage was more exciting than the reality.

16 February 2002

The House has gone into recess for a week this weekend for a short eight-day February break. We, the Law Lords, carry on. Fortunately we stick to the judicial calendar of the English courts, which is more predictable than the political timetable. There was the annual Scottish Peers' Association dinner on

---

172 See fn 166.

Wednesday before the recess began. This was as warm-hearted, friendly and relaxed as ever. I was placed between Lord Mackie of Benshie and Lord Gordon, both good company. The event was presided over by David Wilson, Lord Wilson of Tillyorn, with his usual poise and charm. Veronica Linklater, Baroness Linklater, had organised it. About 40 members were present. The Welsh and the Irish do not do this sort of thing. I hope that, despite devolution and the loss of the hereditaries, we can keep these dinners going.

In the Scottish Parliament the anti-fox hunting Bill[173] was passed in an atmosphere of confusion and bigotry. The Committee for Rural Affairs had said that it would be unworkable, but the socialist majority were undeterred. The result, after a series of amendments, is said to be a shambles. Proposals for compensation for those put out of work were rejected. The result was widely condemned in the press. The police say that they do not have the resources to enforce it. Civil disobedience may follow, and there will be challenges in the courts which will no doubt eventually reach us in the Privy Council. The affair has done nothing for the reputation of the Scottish Parliament in the wider community, though no doubt the socialists will be pleased.

There was a dinner this evening in Parliament Hall given by the Court of Session judges to celebrate Alan Rodger's appointment as a Lord of Appeal. The fires were lit in Parliament Hall, which looked magnificent. Douglas Cullen presided with calm dignity, much helped by Rosamund who clearly loves her new position as the headmaster's wife. I sat between Donald Ross and Alan's sister Christine, who were both very good company, and Alan himself made a neat amusing speech. He used Lord Marnoch as the focus of his attention which was well judged, as it raised much laughter, including from Marnoch himself. In the end it was a good party. But, like going back to one's old school, Alan and I did not really feel that we belonged there anymore.

Alan sat with me in an appeal in the House of Lords about warrants for search and arrest in extradition proceedings.[174] The previous week I replaced him in *R v Shayler*,[175] which had some links to the Lockerbie Inquiry in which he was involved as Lord Advocate, and he felt he should not do. This resulted in another very interesting human rights judgment for me to do in parallel with Tom Bingham. In the warrant case Alan became quite excited and short-tempered, protesting under his breath at what he regarded as nonsensical arguments. He was right to regard them as such, but such is not my style. I found it a bit off-putting and tried, without success, to find a way of disagreeing with him. That was an instinctive and equally ill-judged reaction on my part. The others – Donald Nicholls, Lennie Hoffmann and Brian Hutton – were calm and studious by comparison.

---

173 Protection of Wild Animals (Scotland) Act 2002 (asp 6).
174 *R (Rottman) v Commissioner of Police for the Metropolis* [2002] UKHL 20, [2002] 2 AC 692.
175 [2002] UKHL 11, [2003] 1 AC 247.

24 February 2002

Remarkably I found myself this weekend for the first time this year, and for as long as I can remember, with no judgments to write or revise over the weekend, no lectures or speeches to prepare and no case of substance to read up for the coming week. This is due to a combination of things. For much of last autumn and early winter I was involved in a succession of cases in which we all wrote judgments and had several lectures to prepare and book work to do – *Gloag & Henderson*, the *Stair Memorial Encyclopaedia* section on the House of Lords and Privy Council procedure. Also there were almost no days off. Last week by contrast I was in the Privy Council for four days in a New Zealand case where there is to be only one judgment which Tom Bingham asked Johan Steyn to write, and next week there are two blank days for me in the Privy Council and only two short cases on the other two days. Also, I have no outstanding judgments. My draft in the *Shayler* case has been circulated, and I have a draft in *Kuwait Airways v Iraqi Airways* which is ready for circulation when Donald Nicholls, who is taking two weeks off for the purpose, comes up with his leading judgment in this very substantial case. So it has been a weekend for odds and ends. The weather is too cold and inhospitable for there to be any attraction in tidying up the garden, as we begin to emerge from a very mild winter and the birds start to sing again.

It was, however, a busy week in London and I was grateful for the lull in work at the end of it. The New Zealand case was an interesting one about that country's system of dealing with legal aid in the context of criminal appeals. They have been faced with the same problems as we have: too much criminal work and too much expenditure on legal aid. Their 1990 Bill of Rights required a fresh approach to the hearing of criminal appeals. Rather too rashly, it was decided to do away with the previous system of requiring leave to appeal, on the view that under the Bill of Rights everyone had a right to be heard. The European Court of Human Rights, which could not operate without a system of leave, has not taken that view in Europe. So too in Scotland we were able to reintroduce a system of leave in 1995, with legal aid following automatically for cases that got leave. In New Zealand legal aid applications are considered before decisions are taken on the appeal process, and they were treated by the judges virtually as if they were leave applications in themselves. This has led to all sorts of problems. The system is being reorganised as a response to the 12 cases which were before us. Nevertheless we have to be tactful in our criticisms, as the responsibility for the muddle which resulted does not lie with the current members of the Appeal Court. It is fairly obvious that, had it not been for the final right of appeal to the Privy Council, the system which never really adapted itself to the demands of natural justice and legality in modern human rights culture would have been unshakeable.

On the Wednesday evening Mary and I went to the Middle Temple, to a dinner in my honour as the Lionel Cohen lecturer, which was given by the Friends of the Hebrew University of Jerusalem. This was a fairly intimate affair, there being about 60–70 people in one of the smaller rooms in the Inn. But it was quite an important occasion, as those attending were fairly senior members of the Jewish legal community in London who contribute financially to the Hebrew University's links with the UK. It was clear that I would have to make a speech after dinner. Nothing much had come to mind by way of ideas in previous weeks, but as usual the pressure of the impending engagement helped to concentrate my mind last weekend. I spent much of Sunday searching for inspiration, and by the time I set off for London had a couple of good jokes and a theme worked out. I was able to commit much of it to memory, which I now try to do for all such occasions – although I had it written out on the backs of envelopes as well. In the event, all went well and the thing came out more or less as planned, with laughs in all the right places. This was a relief, as I really did not want to let our kind hosts down. They deserved an enjoyable evening. John Dyson, a Lord Justice of Appeal, was in the chair.

We returned to Edinburgh on the Friday morning. For Mary this was a return trip with British Midland. She had had a clockwork train trip south to King's Cross, with the system at its best, leaving on time and arriving just before time with her reaching Holborn by the Piccadilly line almost exactly four hours after leaving India Street. On our return however we encountered what I had met up with on my way south the previous Sunday: an unserviceable aircraft and a cancelled flight. On the whole my journeys back and forth by Bmi and BA are uneventful with small delays only. But there is always the odd one out, and I have had three such delays in my last six Bmi flights. This weekend I shall be back with British Airways. Ringing the changes helps to ease frustration and boredom.

17 March 2002

This has been a tough week. A series of four cases, all involving in one way or another issues as to contribution between wrong-doers under the Civil Liability (Contribution) Act 1978, were put out for hearing over a period of eight days. We heard one, *Royal Brompton*,[176] on its own in the second half of week one. Then there were two cases – *Heaton* and *Cape & Dalgleish*[177] – heard one after the other over the four days of the week just ended. And we have one still to go, *Co-operative Retail Services*,[178] over the first half of the week which begins tomorrow. It has been hard work sorting out the facts of each case, remembering them and yet keeping them apart for the consideration of each one as we went along. The two cases in the middle were made all the harder for me, as a decision in which I wrote the leading judgment – *Jameson v CEGB*[179] – was at

---

176 *Royal Brompton Hospital NHS Trust v Hammond* [2002] UKHL 14, [2002] 1 WLR 1397.
177 *Heaton v AXA Equity and Law Life Assurance Society plc* [2002] UKHL 15, [2002] 2 AC 329; *Cape & Dalgleish v Fitzgerald* [2002] UKHL16.
178 *Co-operative Retail Services Ltd v Taylor Young Partnership Ltd* [2002] UKHL 17, [2002] 1 WLR 1419.
179 [2000] 1 AC 455.

the heart of the argument. It was not an easy case, and there was a dissent from Tony Lloyd and a speech on different grounds by James Clyde. There was a suggestion, based more on what James had said than on my own speech, that its reasoning was mistaken. So I was a bit on edge, and even more so as we spotted a misprint which the reporter should have picked up.

However, things became really uncomfortable when Alan Rodger began to attack my speech and put bits of it, with no attempt to disguise his distaste for it, to counsel. I kept quiet, unable to keep up with the pace of the discussion and not wishing to be drawn into an argument about my own work. Then Johan Steyn showed signs of agreeing with Alan, so I felt really embarrassed and isolated. Others might have tried to be more tactful, but that is not Alan's style. In the end of the day, however, *Jameson* survived this scrutiny remarkably well and in the end Alan was alone in our discussion when he said that he was 'not a fan' of it. But he too accepted that the decision must stand and would not be departed from. My contribution to the discussion went reasonably well under the circumstances. But I was not at ease at any time. The coming week should be easier as the remaining case does not raise a *Jameson* point at all, thank goodness.

Meantime Douglas Cullen, whom I met at a Sheriffs' Association Conference at Peebles last weekend, produced the judgment of the Appeal Court in the Lockerbie case at Kamp Zeist refusing Megrahi's appeal. The 200-page judgment was available almost at once on the internet. I accessed it and found it full of impressive detail. It left no room for argument that I could see, except on the inevitable basis voiced by Libya that the whole exercise had been 'political'.

This weekend was the Strathclyde University Court residential weekend at Ross Priory. I went as usual to spend the Friday night, to have dinner there and attend the first session on the Saturday. It was cold, wet and very overcast outside, so the joys of spring were largely absent. But it was a pleasant enough occasion, and a valuable one too in the process of maintaining contact with the officers and other leading figures in the University. Once again I came away with huge admiration for the way the place is run, with a lightness of touch which matches well with scrupulous efficiency.

30 March 2002

William and I were idly watching television late this evening, Good Friday having come and gone and this evening being Low Saturday, when the screen went blank. After 30 seconds or so Peter Sissons, the BBC newscaster, came on as someone said that they had an important announcement to make. Then the news was given that Her Majesty Queen Elizabeth, The Queen Mother, had died at 3.15pm that afternoon. Both BBC and STV then went into an extended session of special programmes to respect this event. It was a well-judged mixture of news, interviews and flashbacks, giving a sense of what we had lost with the passing of this grand old lady in her 102nd year, a much-loved 'Queen Mum'.

There was no sense of shock or tragedy as in Princess Diana's case, and none of the risk of over-doing things as in the case of Princess Margaret. This time there is no question that a life of quite outstanding heart-warming public service has come to an end, and that the majority of the British public will wish to honour her memory.

My own thoughts were with The Queen, who spoke with great affection of 'my mamma' when I sat beside her at dinner at Holyrood Palace when I was Lord President, and with the Prince of Wales who has made no secret of his great love and admiration for his grandmother. For them this is a very sad loss. For the rest of us, realising that life cannot go on forever and that for most of this year she has been very frail, it is an occasion for looking back, for admiring the immense contribution which she has made to the Royal Family as an institution since her husband became King in 1937, and for giving thanks.

There is a suggestion that she will lie in state in Westminster Hall and that the funeral will be on Thursday 9 April. I shall be returning to London on Sunday 7 April at the end of the Easter break, so with luck I shall be able to pay my respects in Westminster Hall on Monday 8 April. I should like to do that, if I possibly can. I still remember her fine bearing and her lovely blue eyes when I was presented to her as a very junior advocate at a Faculty dinner which she attended in October 1965.

11 April 2002

I returned to London as planned on Sunday evening, 7 April, and was back in my room on the Law Lords' Corridor on Monday 8 April to a quite extraordinary atmosphere of silence. The police had established a quiet zone around Westminster, so the noise of traffic was greatly reduced. The emergency services vehicles, so ready to use their sirens when on the move, were being diverted elsewhere. There was a quiet hum of slow-moving cars and other light vehicles, nothing more. Inside the Palace, the place was almost deserted as almost nobody except essential staff had come in. Yet, on looking out of my window, I saw a huge column of people moving slowly along the pavement towards the St Stephen's entrance to view the lying-in-state, and later from the riverside windows I could see the same column stretching right along the Embankment on the other side of the river as it made its way up to turn and cross at Lambeth Bridge. In a remarkable tribute almost a quarter of a million people were to make this journey during the three and a half days of lying-in-state, some having to go as far down the river as Tower Bridge to start a wait of many hours. The weather was dry and cool and often sunny, but cold at night. Whatever the weather had been, they would not have been deterred.

In search of information I went to the Moses Room, where the Operation Headquarters had been placed. I was assured that there would be no problem in my going to Westminster Hall and taking guests there as I had planned. I was taken to see Black Rod, who has been superb in his handling of the whole affair with military precision and compassion mixed in equal quantities. He too was reassuring when I asked about attending the departure of the coffin the next day.

I busied myself with work, there being much to attend to after the vacation, until lunchtime. But before settling down to this I took the advice of the clerk in the Operations Room and walked through Westminster Hall and explored the route for peers and their visitors. I was beckoned by a policeman and inserted discreetly into the line of people entering the Hall from the south end. I had been told not to feel guilty at being so favoured over those who did have to queue. There was no sense of outrage from those whom I joined as we made our way down the steps and past the hugely impressive catafalque. The coffin was draped with the Queen Mother's personal Standard and was topped with her magnificently jewelled crown and a single wreath of white flowers on which was placed a message of love from the Queen. Four Irish Guards officers were standing guard at each corner, heads bowed, utterly motionless. There were hundreds of people in the Hall. Yet you could have heard a pin drop. Carpets had been laid to muffle footsteps, and no one talked. The ceiling of the Hall and the catafalque itself were beautifully lit by spotlights. The scene was breathtakingly lovely, and yet very simple and dignified. I returned with some guests at 3 o'clock that afternoon in time to see the guard changing. This time the Irish Guards had been replaced by the Royal Company of Archers. They were less precise and less motionless than the Guardsmen – a bit less tragic, one might say, as those completely still Guardsmen with bowed heads were utterly so. But it was quite remarkable to see the Archers on duty in Westminster Hall. Later that evening, after 6pm, I could not resist going back again to observe events from the Cloisters at Old Palace Yard. The Royal Princes had been standing on guard for 20 minutes, and they were about to leave. There were distant views of the senior Princes – the Prince of Wales and Prince Andrew – in their naval uniforms as they got into two huge Royal limousines. I then went back into the Star Chamber Yard where just in front of me, sorting themselves out into their various groups for transport, were the Princess Royal and Peter Phillips, Princes William and Harry and the Earl and Countess of Wessex. They were deep in private conversation and waved gently to each other as they moved off. The public way in which they have to sustain themselves in this period of great private sadness must be quite a strain, especially for the Prince of Wales.

I returned to my room on Tuesday, the day of the funeral, to find it quieter still. There was a traffic exclusion zone around the whole area. The procession had gone, as the lying-in-state had ended late the previous evening after an almost continual 24-hour-a-day process since it began. Gradually things began to happen, as guests for the funeral service started to arrive, some in coaches, others in official cars. The Abbey's minute bells, striking once every minute 101 times to mark Her Majesty's age, began to sound out. The television coverage, for which several large stands had been built during the weekend, came to life. I dressed in morning dress with black tie and black jacket, and at 10.15am

I went to Westminster Hall once again. There was already a gathering of peers and MPs with spouses at the south end of the Hall. I took up a place on the steps where I could get a good view. The Irish Guards were again in place, mounting their silent vigil. In front now, very still and very erect, was the unmistakable figure of James Mackay. He was intent on paying his own tribute to Her Majesty, whom he must have met many times when he was Lord Chancellor. We stood quietly and mainly in silence. Behind me Betty Boothroyd chatted to her predecessor as Speaker, Lord Weatherill, but after a while she too was silent. The Conservative Front Bench team arrived in procession to join the MPs. The guard changed, and after 20 minutes it changed again. It was hard to stand still for so long with nothing to lean on or against. Then, very gradually, people began to arrive at the north end: the Speaker, the Lord Chancellor, and Black Rod, who greeted members of the family who had come to accompany the coffin to the Abbey. Then there was the Royal party – Prince Philip, the three Royal Princes and the Princess Royal, who moved close to the catafalque as the Bearer party of eight Guardsmen, three NCOs and an officer moved into position. We watched as they performed the very delicate operation of removing the coffin from its resting place and then turning it to process slowly out of the Hall into the sunlight. We moved down the Hall behind the Royal party, and were able to hear the quiet words of command when the coffin was placed onto the gun carriage and the procession to the Abbey began.

I met Alan Rodger who had also been in the Hall. We went to my room to watch the final moments of arrival at the Abbey on television and the start of the service. Then, at my suggestion, we went out into the open to make our way through back streets across Victoria Street and down Cockpit Street into St James's Park. All the while the service was being broadcast on loudspeakers around us. We crossed the Park to stand about four rows back on the Mall opposite Clarence House to hear the rest of the service. And then, at last, to see the procession of cars on their way down the Mall – the hearse with a now very familiar coffin, Standard, Crown and wreath, some accompanying cars including the Prince of Wales. There was silence as they passed, except from above as two Spitfires and a Lancaster bomber flew low overhead in salute. Then as the Queen passed there was a ripple of applause for her, and then it was all over.

It was slow progress back through the crowds to the House as Parliament Square was cleared, the soldiers and bands left and the guests in their buses and cars. But the weather remained clear, dry and cool in sunlight and the crowds were as gentle and restrained as they had been throughout these remarkable few days. There were people of all ages, many families there for a day out, some tourists too wishing to share in such a unique occasion. It was very impressive in a quiet British way. The event was beautifully stage-managed from start to finish, and there was a genuine feeling of a wish to pay tribute to a much-loved and respected Queen. It was a moment in history which all present wanted to observe and to share. I was very glad, and much honoured, to have been able to take part in it.

30 April 2002

The Queen's Golden Jubilee celebrations began today with an Address to both Houses of Parliament in Westminster Hall. So once again we were back there for a Royal occasion. We had a day off as well, as it was thought too difficult for the Law Lords to set up a full hearing on the Committee Corridor until it was all over.

I went with Alan Rodger to prayers in the Lords' Chamber at 10am, where we sat in a row on the crossbenches with Lords Wilberforce, Templeman and Jauncey. After prayers the Leader of the House, Lord Williams of Mostyn, moved that we adjourn to Westminster Hall. This was agreed to, and we set off to take our places there. There was no seating plan, just Lords to one side and Commons to the other. There were some front row places reserved for the Party leaders. We found seats about a quarter of the way down the Hall on the east side which was well placed as the Hall was filling rapidly. A band of the Grenadier Guards was playing a selection of familiar British music – Holst, Vaughan Williams and Handel (he counts as British too). At about 10.45am the march 'Scipio' accompanied the arrival of the Yeomen of the Guard and the Gentlemen at Arms with ostrich-plumed helmets. They took up positions on either side of the steps at the south end and behind the seats for the Queen and the Duke of Edinburgh. Then the Speaker's procession and the Lord Chancellor's procession arrived from the north door as State trumpeters appeared as if by magic on a small gangway across the south window. Big Ben struck 11am. There was a silence. The Queen was late. But three minutes later the trumpeters moved their instruments and sounded a handsome salute as the Royal party arrived and took up their places and the maces from each of the two Houses were covered over, as is always done when the Monarch is present.

There then followed two humble Addresses, one by the Lord Chancellor, the other by the Speaker. It struck me as remarkable, and probably unique and unrepeatable, that both of these speakers were Scots – Derry Irvine and Michael Martin. Derry's rather ponderous voice has disguised his Scots accent, but the Speaker's is undisguised Glasgow – soft and attractive. Each of them went up to The Queen to hand their Address over after reading it and returned to their places. During the reading Her Majesty, in a rich blue jacket and skirt with a large hat of the same colour, was impassive – with scarcely an acknowledgement at the occasional attempt at humour. But she smiled very nicely at each Speaker as he came up to her. And then it was her turn.

It was most impressive. She stood up, and with complete confidence and absolute poise, went forward to the microphones to read her own speech which she held in front of her. There was no lectern. Unlike the State Opening speeches, this was her own creation – full of tact and genuine warmth. She ended with a triumphant sentence assuring us of her resolve to continue to serve us all to the best of her ability. There was no indication here of an intent to abdicate in favour of Prince Charles. It was faultlessly read, as always, in a clear firm voice. She sat down to prolonged applause. It lasted for well over a full minute which seemed to move her quite a bit. Then there was the National Anthem which, after some hesitation, we all sang. It was over by 11.30am.

The Royal party left the Hall by the south end to meet members of staff on their way to the Central Lobby. James Mackay, the sole surviving former Lord Chancellor, and former Speakers with their spouses followed them to be presented in the Lords' Library. The rest of us made our way to the Royal Gallery for a reception, where later The Queen and the Duke of Edinburgh joined us. It was a very relaxed gathering, with a mixture of Lords and Commons. Most spouses had to be left behind to avoid too big a crowd. I found myself next to Geoff Hoon, the Secretary of State for Defence, and his wife both of whom were very easy to talk to. James Vallance White, looking very fine in his uniform as Fourth Clerk at the Table, asked Geoff Hoon how the state of justice was in New Zealand. He had mistaken him for Andrew Tipping, a New Zealand judge, who had just arrived to sit with us in the Privy Council for three or four weeks. Later I warned Tipping J that he might be mistaken for the Secretary of State for Defence. He found this most amusing, and then asked me what he should say. Sir Edward Heath appeared beside us. I was now with Donald Nicholls and Michael Nolan. Sir Edward was beaming with unusual good humour and was delighted to be spoken to about his dinner the previous evening at 10 Downing Street, where the Queen and the Duke dined with the surviving Prime Ministers – Heath, Callaghan, Thatcher, Major and Blair. There were 14 in all at that dinner, with spouses or companions. He said that it had been a marvellous evening. Later I heard a much more jaundiced account of it by Baroness Jay, Lord Callaghan's daughter, who said to a friend as I was reading the paper in the Library that it had been dreadful. Perhaps meeting Baroness Thatcher and Edward Heath was too much for her. But she conceded that John Major had, as one would have expected, been all right.

Then the Queen came towards us, having had a series of animated conversations further away down the Hall. Michael Nolan had his back to her as she reached us. When he was tapped on the shoulder by Derry Irvine and turned round he was so astonished to see her standing beside him that he dropped his biscuit, or whatever he was eating, onto the floor in front of her, much to her amusement. Derry then introduced me, as the former Lord President of the Court of Session. This did not seem to register much with her, as I rather rashly thanked her for coming to see us and giving us a day off. There was no reply, as she was then introduced to Donald Nicholls who simply said 'Your Majesty' as he took her hand. But when Robin Cooke was introduced as a judge from New Zealand she said 'I hear that you are about to end your appeals to the Privy Council'. Robin replied that it would not affect him, as he was already over the magic retirement age of 75 and would no longer be able to sit. 'When was your birthday?' she said, as quick as a knife. When he said that it was in June, she exclaimed 'You are two months younger than I am!', and passed on to speak to the Duncan Smiths who were just behind him.

Looking back, I was struck by two things. One was how unsuccessful I have always been, on the three or four chances offered to me, in striking up a conversation with Her Majesty. There is a reserve there which is not easy to break through, and I always wonder whether I should help by speaking first, only to regret it. On the other hand what a wonderful exchange with Robin Cooke. It brought home to me what a superb master she is of her craft. At 75, as she now is, to do so much with such poise and stamina is quite astonishing – and the Duke of Edinburgh is 81. She was in sparkling form. Her eyes are less superbly blue than her mother's were, but close to she has a most attractive face. What a privilege to meet her again in this way.

Moments later I was in more of the same, in a sense. James Mackay appeared and over came Michael Martin the Speaker. He greeted James with genuine pleasure. 'I was looking for a friendly face when I came in, and I saw yours', he said. James introduced me, and the Speaker rested his hand on my arm as he recalled a public inquiry on which he had sat in Edinburgh which was said to be for two weeks but lasted for three and a half months. Andrew Hardie was a junior when it began, and a QC when it ended he said, with a chuckle. He struck me as a most engaging, friendly man. He is probably not the most elegant of Speakers. But one can see at once why he was chosen.

The previous weekend to all this excitement I had been in Germany for a seminar. I had been invited by Professor Ulrike Seif who is now at Passau but who had come to see me in the House of Lords when she was working on her pre-professorial thesis. The invitation was all the more attractive as the seminar was to be in Münster where I had spent a year in Oxford Barracks about 45 years ago when on National Service with the Seaforth Highlanders. The subject of the seminar was comparative law, with particular reference to the use of case law in the ECJ and the UK. The leaders were Professor Seif and Professor Reiner Schulze of the University of Münster. The participants were about 12 in number. David Edward was there, as were Konrad Schiemann and a professor from Cambridge. There were a number of other academics from Turin and Paris, as well as from elsewhere in Germany. We spoke in German, French or English. The German speakers all spoke excellent English, so in practice much of our discussion was in English. We were engaged all day Saturday and all morning on the Sunday in a very interesting and well-conducted discussion which drew attention to the value of comparative law in the EU. Full marks to the Germans for being so outward looking about this.

2002 – May to July

26 May 2002

The Queen is in Scotland this week as part of her Golden Jubilee celebrations, with seven days of events up and down the country. Mary and I had the good fortune to be invited to two delightful events, one in Glasgow and the other here in Edinburgh.

The first was the opening event of her Scottish tour. It was the service of celebration which was held in Glasgow Cathedral. I was chosen, much to my surprise, by the crossbench peers to represent them at this event. The convenor, Lord Craig of Radley, said that I was the obvious choice, but I am sure there were others who might have done just as well. However, we said we were willing to be invited, and then came the invitation. The service was on a Thursday, so I was given leave of absence by Frances Rice from my duties in the Lords. It had been a light week as it happened, so there was no real embarrassment.

The service was due to start at 2.30pm, but guests were to be seated by 1.30pm and the doors were to open at 12.45pm. So we set off from home in Edinburgh at about 11am in my car. I took advantage of my position as Chancellor of Strathclyde to secure a permit to park in the Cathedral Street car park beneath the University library, and to use the Hotel School in the same building as a place for us to wash and brush up before the service. These were huge advantages. There was very easy access to the car park, a very easy exit when it was over which avoided various bottlenecks and a very kind and friendly welcome with coffee and cakes from the Hotel School manager. We then walked in dry and windy but uncertain weather the short distance to the Cathedral. At the door Lord Nickson, in uniform as an officer of the Royal Company of Archers and Chancellor of Glasgow Caledonian University, greeted us most warmly. We had red tickets so we were special guests, he said. We were ushered up the Nave and beyond the screen into the Chancel where, at row 14, we took our seats beside the aisle so that Mary could have a good view. Gradually the place began to fill up. Most ladies were wearing summer hats, most men were in morning dress. There were many friends and people we recognised. It was almost like old times when as Lord President I was a regular attender at such functions. There were new friends also from the House of Lords, like Lady Ramsay of Cartvale in front of us, joined later by Andrew Hardie who said he had an invitation as a former Law Officer and member of the Scottish Executive. The Sheriffs Principal were not far away. Charlie Robertson,[180] on duty as a Clergyman of the Chapel Royal, greeted Mary with his usual warmth and affection. There were others: a former Chief Constable of Lothian & Borders Police and his wife; Lady Carnegie of Lour; Ian Lang; Michael and Susan Forsyth. Then the processions began as the officials came in. There were 12 Senators of the College of Justice in long wigs and Justiciary robes which made them look rather grim and serious, the Knights and Lady of the Order of the Thistle with Lords Wilson and Mackay full of friendly smiles, and an amazing number of clerics of all faiths. At 2.30pm the trumpets sounded and the Royal procession began, led by the Heralds including David Sellar, on parade for the first time as Bute Pursuivant, and Robin Blair as Lord Lyon King of Arms. They led Her Majesty and the Duke of Edinburgh to their places. She was in a handsome blue suit with a suitable hat. He was in the robes of a Knight of the Thistle.

---

180 The Rev Charles Robertson, Minister of Canongate Kirk, Edinburgh.

26 May 2002

The service itself was remarkable for its intimacy. There was a sermon by the outgoing Moderator, the Rt Rev Dr John Miller, which was delivered with beautiful clarity and touching simplicity. He took as his theme the rather puzzling parable of the talents in Matthew 25:14-29 and turned it into a tribute to the Queen's commitment to her vocation. There was a charming reading in Gaelic, to the music of the clarsach, of Psalm 136 by the Glasgow Islay Junior Gaelic Choir, sung to memory on the steps of the Choir to lovely lilting music and with smiles on every face. There were, of course, stirring hymns and there were prayers of blessing, thanks and re-dedication. The processions then led out of the church. The Queen smiled as we bowed and curtsied, and Robin Blair gave me a wink as he went by. It had all been great fun and it was a privilege to be there. We were also so glad not to be part of the Senators of the College of Justice group. We felt so much freer and out in the open in a much wider world.

On Saturday the Queen went to the Opening of the General Assembly of the Church of Scotland, there being this year no need of a Lord High Commissioner to represent her. At the last moment I discovered that the Household Cavalry was to be there too. So I hurried up to the top of The Mound to observe the goings on. She was already inside when I got there, as the Royal Standard was up on one of the towers beside the Saltire. And the Blues and Royals were at the foot of The Mound, with dust-carts ready in Hanover Street to clean up afterwards. I secured a place on the railings at the top of Playfair Steps where I could get a bit of a view over the heads of the crowd. The Highlanders, very smart indeed, were spaced out as a guard of honour along the street. The Scottish State carriage, small and simple, was on one side of the Assembly building with four rather restless white horses, and there were various army officers and other officials around the entrance. An English salesman wandered about trying to sell flags to the tourists. After about 30 minutes things began to move. Two huge lorries scattered more sand over the difficult camber in front of us. Then the Cavalry came up, with much glorious clatter and smells of leather and horses, to form up facing up-hill to where the carriage still stood. The Cavalry horses, all black and close together, seemed almost motionless as the white horses continued to toss their heads in restlessness. Then the Heralds appeared with two banners – the Saltire and the Royal Banner of Scotland, which were borne by their Hereditary Bearers. And then there was the Queen herself, just visible with a broad-brimmed hat of bright blue, and the Duke with a black top hat. The Cavalry set off with the Royal coach and an open landau behind, with Lady Airlie and other courtiers between them. The Duke of Edinburgh doffed his top hat to the Black Watch Memorial on The Mound as he passed it, and it was all over. But I lingered for a while to watch others emerge and depart. There was a procession of civil dignitaries, led by the city's Sword-Bearer with his huge broadsword who walked up the hill to the City Chambers. There were the Heralds and the Service Chiefs who swept down The Mound in official cars, and there were the Archers who marched stiffly up Bank Street leaning into the steep slope as they climbed up the hill in close order and out of sight. Finally the Highlanders were marched off. Another gem of ceremonial was over.

In the afternoon Mary and I went to Holyrood for the Royal Garden Party. It is six years since we were last there. The July parties are on weekdays when it is not possible for us to attend as my duties are in London. But this was a Saturday – a Jubilee Garden Party for 2,000 guests – so I put my name down for this one and we were invited. The atmosphere was quite different from the July parties – far less for the great and the good, far more for the really good, based on the General Assembly and various organisations associated with its youth work and social services. Far fewer morning coats, but many more kilts. The weather was quite different too: very heavy thundery showers and gusts as we arrived equipped with much-needed umbrellas. We had a quick tea as we arrived and then, braving showers, we moved from the shelter of the marquee to the open ground to watch a wonderful display by 24 pipers of great expertise: former army pipers with some civilians – the Royal Scottish Pipers' Society. The Queen arrived at 4pm, clad sensibly in a splendid rain-proof broad-brimmed hat and a poncho, as the clouds moved away and the sun came out. It was a wonderful change which warmed us up, dried us out and set just the right note for the rest of the party. We watched as the slow Royal progress took place, to gentle band music and quiet chatter behind us. Courtiers selected people to meet Her Majesty, and they stood about in small groups being put at their ease by the Captain General of the Royal Company before Her Majesty moved over to speak to them. This was done with a gentle sweet smile and an interested look on her face as she made quiet conversation with them, one by one. Meantime the Duke, in raincoat and grey top hat, looking very elegant was working his own way along his row. It was a slow progress too, but we all watched fascinated by the spectacle. Then the courtiers began to move to where we were standing. A visiting African clergyman, five young people from the Boys Brigade, a dancer in shirt and kilt and his mother, and a lady in a wheelchair were singled out from our group. A sparkling official and well-turned out lady-in-waiting said to the Boys Brigade people: 'If the opportunity arose, would you like to be introduced to Her Majesty?' They were hoping for such, as we knew from their conversation, and they certainly deserved it as did each of the well-chosen groups. So we watched the gentle progress as they were brought out into the open, the courtiers put them at their ease and the small motherly figure of Her Majesty approached to speak to them. They returned with exclamations of excitement, hands that they would not wash for days, shaky knees and all the other symptoms. Then the Duke approached as he made his way along our line. He asked me why I was there – was I involved in the General Assembly? It was a very good question to which I had to say no, that I just lived here in Edinburgh. But the Boys Brigade people were the real point of interest, as several of them were the holders of the Duke of Edinburgh's Gold Award which was pinned to their blazers. He asked each one whether they remembered the Award Ceremony and whether the others in their group were trying for gold too. He looked close to being quite elderly, but he was in sparkling form and was the last to go into the Royal Tea Tent for tea, having to be encouraged to go there by Lord Airlie. Then it was time for us to go. What a happy remarkable experience.

3 June 2002

Golden Jubilee weekend. Mary and William are in London, as Mary is doing an examination to qualify with British Dressage as a List 4 dressage judge. I am alone here in Edinburgh for three days, spending most of my time preparing a draft judgment in a case called *Clingham and McCann*[181] about anti-social behaviour orders. This has involved quite a lot of Strasbourg human rights law and is very interesting. But it took quite a struggle for me to get into the swing of the thing.

Much of the celebration is now centred in London. On Saturday evening 12,000 guests, chosen by ballot, were invited to a classical music concert in the gardens of Buckingham Palace. It was shown on television and broadcast around the surrounding streets and gardens. It was attended by many members of the Royal Family, of whom we had occasional views on television as they sat in the Royal box. The pleasure of the event was infectious, and the singing of 'Land of Hope and Glory' after a fine display of fireworks and two verses of the National Anthem after a Royal Marine fanfare was very emotional. The Queen and the Duke clearly enjoyed every moment of it, as did their many guests.

Yesterday was a day of church services, including an ecumenical one in the Chapel Royal at Windsor. But today has been a day of street parties. Rain cleared during the day to give way to brilliant sunshine for the afternoon, spreading across the country as the television broadcast of 'All you need is Love' was spread up and down the country by various groups singing in unison. It had been started by the Queen in Slough and moved up to Falkirk, where six pipers played a background tune to the Beatles' music in harmony. This evening 12,000 more guests are at the Palace for a pop concert which will end with fireworks and the lighting of beacons. Huge crowds are in the Mall and around the Palace in a quite extraordinary occasion. Tomorrow there will be a State Procession to St Paul's Cathedral, more processions in the afternoon and a flypast (weather permitting) which will include Concorde.

Almost everyone is caught up in this quite remarkable feeling of celebration, much of it hugely informal, happy and enjoyable. It feels like a great family party, which is passing off far better than anyone could have expected. Such celebrations in a Republic would be unthinkable. There is no politics in this at all. Our politicians are unseen. This is the Queen, celebrating with her people, with heart-breaking generosity to those lucky enough to be there. England now needs only to do a bit better in the World Cup. They secured only a draw with Sweden on Saturday, which was a bit of a let-down.

---

181 Reported as *R (McCann) v Crown Court at Manchester* [2002] UKHL 39, [2003] 1 AC 787.

16 June 2002

I was in Rome for 36 hours for a seminar organised by the Venice Commission for the Council of Europe on resolving conflicts between regional and central government. It was very hot, with brilliant sunshine and the temperature up to 30C in the shade. Two species of birds stand out in this brief visit: yellow-legged gulls and swifts. The yellow-legged gulls (previously known as yellow-legged herring gulls but now re-named as a separate species) were much in evidence, especially at night. They were circulating in the spotlights which illuminate the Victor Emmanuel Monument beside the Forum near to the River Tiber and I could hear their deep tenor calls, like those of the lesser black-backed gull, from my hotel bedroom. The swifts were a delight – thousands of them, screaming and chasing each other, especially in the early morning before the heat of the day. They woke me at 5.15am and were soon racing about in groups of 25 or more. The air was filled with their exuberant behaviour.

23 June 2002

Well, England went on to the quarter-finals in the World Cup, where they were knocked out by Brazil who look set to win the competition. It was fun while it lasted, at least for those in England. Huge interest was shown, despite the odd timing for television relays from Japan and South Korea. My secretary, Gail Munden, told me that the 5.30am train to Liverpool Street was packed so that last Friday people could get into their offices by 7.30am for the start of the Brazil match. England were good losers, unlike France and Italy who showed characteristic ill-grace and petulance. On the whole the team and many fans acquitted themselves well.

Meantime I sat in the Privy Council and the House of Lords doing two appeals from Scotland. They were *Mills v HM Advocate*[182] and *Robertson v Fife Council*.[183] These were the last appeals in which James Mackay can sit as he reaches the age of 75 in two weeks' time. Neither of them was argued at a high level, although the *Robertson* case which was about the provision of community care and the assessment of need for it was quite demanding intellectually. At the end of the *Robertson* case Andrew Hajducki QC – prompted by James Vallance White – said a few nice words as a tribute to the great man, to which Gordon Slynn as our chairman added his own contribution. It was a calm, serene end to the wonderful career that James Mackay has enjoyed as an advocate, judge, Law Officer, Lord of Appeal and Lord Chancellor. Alan Rodger, George Penrose and I had taken him out to dinner on the Wednesday evening at the Oxo Tower Restaurant as a means of saying thank you to him for all he had done for us. It was a lovely summer evening, with glorious views over London as the sun set and the evening came. James was in excellent form. We shall all miss him greatly. But, as he said in the Committee Room of the House of Lords before we

[182] [2002] UKPC D2, 2003 SC (PC) 1, [2004] 1 AC 441.
[183] [2002] UKHL 35, 2002 SC (HL) 145.

left on Thursday afternoon, he much preferred to go when the rules required it than end his career by not being invited because he was no longer welcome.

11 July 2002

I was in Glasgow today as Chancellor of Strathclyde University for the last graduation ceremony of the term. Last Friday I had two over which I had to preside. Today, as the University is about to close for the summer holidays and for the Glasgow fair, there was only one. Last week Elish Angiolini QC, Solicitor General for Scotland, was given the Alumnus of the Year award. Today the Very Rev Dr Finlay Macdonald, Moderator of the Church of Scotland and Clerk to the General Assembly, was made a Fellow of the University. Meeting these interesting people and having lunch with them in the Scottish Hotel School adds a special dimension to these occasions. Today was the last appearance as Convener of Court of Roy Johnson who, with his wife Heather, has made both Mary and me feel so very welcome. His successor is Archie Hunter, who is going to find Roy's rather severe but effective chairmanship quite a hard act to follow.

In London things are on the move too. Gordon Slynn has at last decided to retire, although he left it very late to set the wheels in motion. This has created a vacancy which needs to be filled. Francis Jacobs, the UK's Advocate-General at the ECJ, would be the ideal successor. But he is determined not to sit in the Court of Appeal, and without that experience he is not suitable for our team. So the front-runners are Lord Justice Robert Walker and Lady Justice Brenda Hale. We had a meeting on Tuesday morning with Derry Irvine to set out our views on possible candidates. He summoned us to his office at 8am, very much earlier than most of us are in the building except for Tom, Johan and myself. But there was a full turnout, and Harry Woolf and Nicholas Phillips were there too. We went round the table. Various names were mentioned, but the choice is probably between Brenda Hale, much tipped in the press as the first woman Law Lord, and Robert Walker who has been favoured by Derry Irvine in the past as a very interesting and thoughtful candidate. But we are losing Frances Rice, James Vallance White and Kate Ball his assistant – all in one fell swoop. This will remove much stability from the office team, and it is bound to make a difference of a kind which is hard to predict in these uncertain, reforming times. We also lose our delightful team of legal assistants; Akash Nawbatt, Lydia Clapinska, Kay Taylor and Elizabeth Conaghan. I selected a new team last week, who at first meeting seemed equally good: Thomas Brown, Diya Sen Gupta, Robin McCoubray and Emma Parker. As Gordon is leaving and Lennie Hoffmann does not want to participate in this scheme, I move up one and will have to take on an assistant myself. I hope I can live up to this without too much disruption. I felt that of the four Thomas Brown – a music graduate from Oxford – was best suited for Tom Bingham. I chose Emma Parker for myself, a formidable and very able young lady whom I shall try not to disappoint.

26 July 2002

Yesterday the term effectively came to an end. Officially it does not end until 31 July, which is next Wednesday. But no business has been allocated for next week which gives us all time to wind down.

My last substantial piece of work was the judgment in *Rodney District Council v Attorney-General*,[184] a New Zealand case on valuation for rating. We are all agreed as to the result, and I volunteered to write. It is an area of law which I know well, of course, from my practice as an advocate. New Zealand has some strange features which suggest that the fundamental principles which we have developed so well in Scotland have not been fully understood there. I found that I was quite a long way ahead of the others as a result, who have almost no experience of the law of valuation. This is where the breadth of practice at the Scottish Bar shows its value. I worked hard last week to complete my draft, and Tom made some useful comments before I sent it into the Privy Council office. Tom is admirable on these occasions. He really does take the trouble to read through one's drafts from start to finish, and he does so very promptly. With dear Gordon Slynn one might have to wait for many weeks.

I found myself doing petitions for leave on the Monday with Brian Hutton and Peter Millett, which was not too arduous. It is quite tricky being in the chair on these occasions, as all the hearings are short and to the point. That is good. But one has to be well up on the case to run the show, and in some specialist fields that can be quite difficult. This time, however, the cases were not too hard to grasp. Then on the Wednesday and Thursday I was in the Committee Room again for my only full hearing in the House of Lords this month. All the rest of the time I have been in the Privy Council. It was a case about asylum seekers from Sri Lanka[185] – Tamils, who had entered the EU first in Germany, been refused asylum there and come to the UK in the hope of a better result. The authorities, relying on the Dublin Convention, decided that they should be sent back to Germany, from whence they will very probably be returned to Sri Lanka. This is a very difficult area for the politicians, but the law is reasonably clear. It is said that the Germans are much less inclined to grant asylum in non-State persecution cases such as those involving Tamils, who are not persecuted by the State in Colombo to where they will be returned. But in practice they look at the facts much as we do. There are important consequences for future cases, and the judgment which Richard Scott is to write will require careful attention. I may write as well.

The week has, however, been characterised by parties. On the Monday evening I was invited to attend a dinner for the legal assistants for the last two years, with James Vallance White, Andrew Mackersie and Kate Ball. We just fitted into the Reid Room after a reception on the terrace. It was a very happy occasion. The team from last year were all there, and within minutes it was as if they

---

184 *Rodney District Council v Attorney-General (New Zealand)* [2002] UKPC 47.
185 *R (Yogothas) v Secretary of State for the Home Department* [2002] UKHL 36, [2003] 1 AC 920.

had never been away. They mixed well with this year's team as well. It would be hard to find a nicer group of young people. Then on Tuesday I entertained Mark Sheldon, formerly President of the Law Society, to a guest night at Gray's Inn. On Wednesday we had a party to say goodbye to Frances Rice. There were many people there, all packed into the Conference Room at lunchtime. Tom wisely did not attempt to engage in long speeches, and Frances was relieved by that. James Clyde, who has been so very ill with cancer this year and has made an excellent recovery, came to join us and was in excellent form. A month ago he had only begun to emerge into the public world. Now he is looking forward to sitting again with us, which is marvellous. Frances has begun handing over to Helen, who has only just been appointed to succeed her. What Helen's surname is and where she has come from have not been revealed to us, although no doubt Tom knows.[186] The whole thing has been organised internally by the House authorities. Helen shows every sign of being very capable. I hope that she will be as sensitive to everyone's needs and idiosyncrasies as Frances has been. That will come with time, no doubt.

On Thursday we wound up with a brief informal party for James Vallance White and the assistants in Tom's room after the end of our hearing in the asylum case. It was squeezed in after the end of our hearing at 5pm, before our departure for home. But there was enough time to say a very sincere word of thanks to all those who have served us so well throughout a very happy year.

2002 – August to September

19 September 2002

I made my first move towards a resumption of work after the summer holiday by joining a visit by the Scottish Peers' Association to the Scottish Executive and to the Scottish Parliament. This was partly a social occasion, but primarily educational. There were about 12 peers in our group, which was led by Lord Hogg of Cumbernauld and Baroness Veronica Linklater. We were received in St Andrew's House by Muir Russell, the Permanent Secretary, and a team of senior civil servants, several of whom I knew from pre-devolution days when I was Lord President. There was a discussion for one and a half hours, which covered a wide area and was really quite stimulating as they pointed out various respects in which effective communication between the Scottish Executive and Scots peers at Westminster was lacking or in need of improvement. After a buffet lunch we were taken by minibus to the Parliament, still in the General Assembly building, to watch Question Time. The first few minutes of general questions were well done, with a wide range of questions, perhaps twenty or so, responded to with reasonably well-constructed replies by a variety of Ministers. This was information-seeking for the most part, and there was not much overt

---

186 Her full name was Mrs Helen McMurdo.

political point-scoring. The depth of follow-up questions does not compare with the Lords at Question Time. But David Steel, the Presiding Officer, was clearly trying to cover the ground as widely as possible and I doubt whether the background and calibre of the Scots parliamentarians enables them to probe with quite as much wit, good humour and knowledge as is the case in London. Then there were 20 minutes of questions to the First Minister, which was a quite different matter. It was rabble-rousing and largely pointless, apart from an attack on the handling by Jack McConnell of a dispute within his own Cabinet due to Mike Watson's public disagreement with him on health issues. McConnell's abrasive, staccato method of delivery is not particularly attractive. But he was in command of his brief and stands out head and shoulders above the rest among the Labour benches. It looks as if he will be First Minister for quite a long time. We then made our way down the High Street for a brief meeting with David Steel in his office. John Swinney, the friendly leader of the SNP and our local MSP in Alyth, turned to me and spoke very kindly about the problems caused by a proposal for a wind farm on a hill called Drumderg just beside Craighead. He obviously knew of our concerns, although I had not raised them with him myself directly. The informality of the Parliament, when not in session, is one of its high points.

This was a good and useful meeting. It was fun to share it with colleagues from the Lords, and a privilege to be among them once again. I remain mystified as to why Alan Rodger cannot bring himself to take part in such activities. His skills and sympathies lie elsewhere, of course. But there is much to gain, nothing to lose, by taking part and making the most of these opportunities.

28 September 2002

I went to London this week, the last of the summer recess, to attend a conference organised by the CMJA and its annual Council meeting, as I am a co-opted member of the Council and a Director of the Company. Michael Lambert, the Executive Vice-President, has been hinting for months that I should make myself available for election as the CMJA's next President. He was working on the idea again as the Council meeting began. I had been very reluctant to commit myself, due to pressure of work, commitments to Strathclyde University and the prospect of having to spend large sums of money on travel as President which are unlikely to be subsidised. But it became increasingly clear that I was trapped, and things came to a head in the afternoon of the Council meeting when Joe Raulinga of South Africa said that the issue had to be settled and that he wished to propose me as President. Various others chimed in and I found myself faced with the unanimous request to agree to the proposal. I said that I was greatly honoured but that, as I was not my own master, I would have to ask Tom Bingham first before I would agree. 'Does that mean that, if he says yes, you will accept?' asked Claudia Taylor of Sierra Leone, to which there was only one answer. Of course Tom will not say that I must not do this. So I am effectively sewn into the job. It is touching that so many people of vastly different backgrounds have so much confidence in me. I am a reluctant candidate. I do hope that I will be able to repay their trust and not let them down. Mary, of course, is wholly committed to the idea and will be a tremendous support in every way, as she was when the CMJA had its last conference in Edinburgh in 2000.

5 October 2002

The legal year opened on 1 October, as usual, with the service in Westminster Abbey followed by the Lord Chancellor's Breakfast in Westminster Hall. Mary joined me in my room at 10.15am and we walked together across a traffic-free road. Much work is being done on the road to restrict the flow of traffic and increase pedestrian access. We met our new recruit, Robert Walker, on the way. He was very polite and careful, responding to our inquiry whether he was to join us for the service by saying that he was more concerned about settling into his new surroundings. At the Abbey we circulated in the Nave, delightfully free of seats, meeting various friends. I took Mary to her seat in the South Lantern and then went to the choir stalls where I found myself in the front row next to Sir Hayden Phillips, the Lord Chancellor's Permanent Secretary. The service began with the procession of judges and their clerks, followed by the County Court judges and then barristers and solicitors. The many foreign guests and others were already seated. The procession seemed longer than ever. What used to be about twenty barristers had become over a hundred. The standard of hospitality has increased in proportion. Then there was a good service, with a pleasantly spirited anthem by Gerald Finzi, and some moving hymns – 'To be a Pilgrim', etc – which, unlike last year, everyone could sing. The procession out seemed to be longer than ever too. Also, before it was our turn to go, Lennie Hoffmann was there beside me. He had sidled in late, in a suit, not morning dress, into a back row. I insisted that he should take the right place in the line with us. Fine autumn sunshine greeted us as we emerged. Such onlookers as there were were kept far away. Then into the Hall where, as usual, my words of thanks to Derry Irvine elicited no reply. He seems to say something to everyone else. Why not to me?

Once the festivities were over, I tried to settle down to work. One of the first tasks was to meet my new judicial assistant, Emma Parker, and discuss the week's case which was about a local authority tenant's right to buy property in the green belt. It is not going to be easy to find really useful things for her to do. But she is very able and was said to be thrilled to have been selected. So, with luck, I may be able to get onto a reasonable wavelength with her. The case itself, *O'Byrne v Secretary of State*,[187] was not too difficult. We heard it in the Chamber where, as the Second Senior Law Lord, I had the task of moving the adjournment at the appropriate stages while Tom Bingham retreated up the

---

187 *R (O'Byrne) v Secretary of State for the Environment, Transport and the Regions* [2002] UKHL 45, [2002] 1 WLR 3250.

Chamber to move the motions from the Woolsack. Our lack of drill as we tried to work out where to stand and when not to move caused amusement to those behind the Bar. The decision at the end of the case, on grounds which Alan Rodger and I had identified at the outset, was unanimous and Richard Scott agreed to write the judgment. So I have a weekend with no writing to do – an Indian summer surely, as before long I shall be composing things again on my computer.

10 November 2002

It is halfway through the Michaelmas term, and today is Remembrance Sunday. This week's work has been lightened somewhat as Monday's case – a passing-off action about whisky from the Court of Session, which raised an interesting point about acquiescence – has settled. Then on Wednesday it is the State Opening, which is a day off for us. Only a one-day case from Northern Ireland about sex discrimination in the Royal Ulster Constabulary (that was – now the Police Service of Northern Ireland)[188] will see us sitting again. So there is time to work over two outstanding draft judgments and to write about some events since the last entry.

The most anxious case during this period was *R v HM Advocate*,[189] which was a devolution case heard in the Privy Council. It raised the question as to the remedy to be given in a case of pre-trial delay contrary to Article 6 of the ECHR. The panel consisted of Lord Steyn, myself and Lords Clyde, Rodger and Walker. It was good to have James Clyde back with us, much restored in health, as a retired judge. His presence was to turn out to be critical to the result. Johan Steyn was, as so often, already committed to a view before the case began. He had gone too far in a case called *Darmalingam v The State*[190] from Mauritius, a post-conviction case, in saying that quashing the conviction was the only remedy. We had corrected this in another devolution case called *Mills (No 2) v HM Advocate*,[191] which was also about post-conviction delay. In the meantime, in a rather obscurely reasoned decision, the Court of Appeal in England had held that stopping the prosecution was not the appropriate remedy under section 6 of the Human Rights Act 1998, so Johan was determined to stand by that decision. To do otherwise, in England, would cause chaos, he said. He showed no inclination to face up to the different language of section 57(2) of the Scotland Act 1998 and its implications. The case itself was not particularly well argued. But what really mattered was our discussion afterwards.

Robert Walker indicated that, as a newcomer to this jurisprudence, he needed more time to think but that he tended to agree with Johan. Alan Rodger, on the other hand, was firmly of the view that there was no escape from holding

---

188 *Shamoon v Chief Constable of the Royal Ulster Constabulary* [2003] UKHL 11, [2003] ICR 337.
189 [2002] UKPC D3, 2003 SC (PC) 21.
190 [2001] 1 WLR 2303.
191 [2002] UKPC D2, 2003 SC (PC) 1, [2004] 1 AC 441.

that the Lord Advocate had no power to continue the prosecution and it had to be stopped. James Clyde then expressed the contrary view. I said that I would like to agree with Johan, but that it was very difficult not to agree with Alan. So we ended up with what looked like a majority for taking Johan's line and allowing the prosecution to proceed with remedies by way of reduction in sentence to be given afterwards. When I came to write a judgment, however, I found myself firmly in the same position as Alan Rodger. We regarded the likely result with increasing dismay and despair, as first Johan and then Robert produced judgments the other way. I wrote to James Clyde suggesting that he wait and see what Alan and I said before he committed himself. Then to my huge pleasure and relief, he telephoned to say that he had been persuaded, that his mind was changed and that he was about to issue a judgment agreeing with me and Alan. He then did so in a tactful draft, which avoided doing so in terms but it was the same as ours in its effect. What would have happened if he had not changed his mind, or we had had another English judge instead? I fear that, as Alan and I would not alter our view – with which Tom Bingham, as it seems, agrees – we would have been much embarrassed and the Scottish judges would have been too. The effect would have been to create a lot of uncertainty about other aspects of the devolution system. So it was a fortunate escape.

Lectures are one of the more difficult aspects of life as a Law Lord. Not everyone is called upon to deliver or chair them, but I have been quite frequently. I chaired a splendid lecture on International Law and Terrorism by Professor Christopher Greenwood QC in the current Legal Problems Series at UCL. It was attended by a huge audience, with standing room only to spare as we began. But a more serious event was the Personal Injuries Bar Association lecture in the Inner Temple Hall, which I undertook to do in April to be given on 23 October. This hung over me like a millstone, until I hit on the idea of going to Prestongrange and Prestonpans in East Lothian to research into the case of *McGhee v National Coal Board*,[192] which had recently played an important role in the House of Lords mesothelioma cases of *Fairchild*,[193] etc. From this start I managed to build up a lecture in which I had some confidence.[194] So it was with a feeling of relief rather than anxiety that I turned up with Mary, who had been invited to attend, and to an informal dinner afterwards to deliver it. The event was very well attended with many senior members of the profession and some judges. So it was not something to be trifled with. I was lucky that, in the event, I had something worthwhile to say. It all seemed to pass off well, and our hosts were very kind and generous. What I said owed quite a bit to Alan Rodger's example of how these things should be done, to Kemp Davidson's personal recollections of his appearance as counsel in *McGhee* and to his excellent notes of the hearing in the House of Lords.

---

192 1973 SC (HL) 37, [1973] 1 WLR 1.
193 *Fairchild v Glenhaven Funeral Services Ltd* [2002] UKHL 22, [2003] 1 AC 32.
194 'James McGhee – A Second Mrs Donoghue?' (2003) 62 Cambridge Law Journal 587.

At the end of the evening things took a bizarre turn. Although Mary and I would have much preferred to go back to Gray's Inn by Underground from Piccadilly where we were for dinner, our host's junior assistant insisted on getting us a mini-cab. The driver looked like somebody from Afghanistan and his car was not much better. The assistant told him to take us to Gray's Inn but did not pay for this in advance. Apparently it was for us to make the payment, although he might have made this clear beforehand. The driver thought he said Gravesend, which is about 15 miles away. This did not become clear to us until we found him proceeding down the Embankment past Blackfriars to the Tower of London. It took some persuasion to get him to turn round from this no doubt lucrative engagement to take us back to Gray's Inn. When we reached the street outside he rubbed his fingers together indicating, to our surprise, that he expected to be paid. He asked for £10 which was not too steep in the circumstances, but a metered black cab would have been less. I only had £20 notes in my possession. So rather ignominiously I had to get change in a 24-hour photocopy shop to get rid of him. But this was more amusing rather than anything else, as an end to an enjoyable evening.

A much more glamorous evening about two weeks later saw Mary and myself as guests of the City of London and its outgoing Lord Mayor, Michael Oliver, at a ceremony in the Guildhall to present the Freedom of the City of London jointly to the Duke and Duchess of Gloucester, with dinner afterwards. I was rather apprehensive, as no one else on the Law Lords' Corridor had been invited, and transport to and from the Guildhall even with a government car is not easy. But our driver turned up on time, and we soon found ourselves in the courtyard of the Guildhall where an Army detachment was gathering to welcome the Royal couple. We were ushered into the picture gallery where VIPs with pink tickets like ourselves were gathering. We then joined a procession of guests which was making its way to the library. There, rather to our consternation, the guests were being ushered in one by one or in couples by an announcer and were expected to walk up a corridor to applause to greet the Lord Mayor and the Lady Mayoress at the far end. We did what we were told. I was announced as a Lord of Appeal in Ordinary, which gave us some kind of an introduction to the audience. We were greeted very warmly by the Lord Mayor and his splendid wife Sally, who has made such a success of her time as Lady Mayoress. I last sat beside her at the Mansion House dinner and she seemed perhaps to recognise me. Then we were ushered to our seats in the VIP section. Mary's eyes nearly popped out of her head when she saw that we had been placed in a row of four seats the other two of which were already occupied by Baroness Thatcher and Sir Denis Thatcher. As we took our places he very politely rose to his feet and I think she said to me 'Good evening, David' – though how she knew my name I have no idea. It was not possible to make conversation with them. Sir Denis, who was beside me, seemed to be quite deaf and they are both now quite elderly. But there was so much to see and watch that this did not matter. Various other guests arrived whom we knew – the Slynns, the Woolfs and Nicholas Phillips MR. Others were well known in public life.

The ceremony began with the arrival of the Royal couple, outside and unseen. But then they all came into the library where we had fine views of the proceedings and presentations. The Duchess of Gloucester, whose Livery Company is the Fanmakers as she showed by carrying a large fan with her, made a charming and witty speech of thanks. Her Danish accent added a touch of class, and the thoughtful pose of the Duke – one of the better educated and more reserved and accomplished Royals – was a delightful backcloth to her speech as she gave us some insight into their down-to-earth and amusing family life. We then proceeded into dinner where we sat at the top table facing the most important guests. Enormous menus with the Royal couple's initials and a crown or coronet above them were at our places. I was beside Mrs Carey, the wife of the newly-retired Archbishop of Canterbury, who was very good company, and Lady Newall, the wife of the former Lord Mayor who was beside Mary. On her other side was Lord Brooke, the former Northern Ireland Secretary and brother of Henry Brooke LJ. It was, of course, a quite excellent dinner. Marvellous fanfares followed. The speeches – the Lord Mayor and the Duke of Gloucester – were short and quite witty too. So the evening ended, and our Government Car Service car appeared when called for in the courtyard without too much delay or difficulty. We both felt very privileged and had that strange feeling that one sometimes has after such occasions that there was no one to whom we could really describe it other than ourselves.

That was last Tuesday. On Wednesday there was a much more downbeat dinner for me in the Inner Temple Hall – the Society for Advanced Legal Studies. I sat next to Harry Woolf and Dame Sian Elias of New Zealand, at the centre of the top table, as I am chairman of the Advisory Council of the Institute. Professor Barry Rider for whose reappointment as Director I had to work quite hard with Graham Zellick, the Vice-Chancellor of London University, was in charge. He is an enthusiastic, if somewhat disorganised, person. His speech had the same characteristics as he brought the evening to an end.

Then on Friday, again with Mary, I was at Strathclyde University for the November graduations. These occasions mix ceremonial duties with pleasure and enjoyment as contact is made with the staff of the University and with the graduates at the receptions. We had a delicious lunch as usual in the Hotel School. The morning ceremony was so well attended that two of the front rows had to be occupied with graduands of the Graduate Business Studies School. We were taken to and from Strathclyde by our driver Wallace in the University car. Wallace is a former policeman and his ability to find shortcuts through Glasgow is deeply impressive. On our return home I felt completely worn out.

1 December 2002

The judgment in *R v HM Advocate* was issued this week. Not surprisingly, Johan Steyn's highly-charged remarks about the effect of the decision as he sees it caught the attention of the press in Scotland. 'English judges warn of trial chaos', proclaimed *The Herald*, which quoted extensively from his judgment and gave little space to what James Clyde, Alan Rodger and I have said. Johan's sweeping assertions, with no regard to the real meaning of the legislation in the Scotland Act and no attention to the realities of the Scottish legal system, are quite breath-taking. Alan Rodger, not blessed with the most patient and tolerant of dispositions, is scathing in his criticism – though more restrained in his judgment. 'As bad as McCluskey', he muttered to me as we sat together in a Jamaican murder case in which Johan was allowing his imagination to run riot in his usual campaign against the police. He is blind to his own shortcomings, is Johan. This may be why, when he is on the right track, he is such a superb colleague! He has just gone into hospital for a hip operation which will keep him out of action until late January. But his fertile mind will no doubt keep turning and Gail – the delightful secretary whom I share with him – is certainly not going to be idle.

Mary and I were at Parliament House yesterday evening for a reception to mark Kenny Cameron's retirement from the Bench. The main focus of the occasion was the presentation to the Dean of Faculty, Colin Campbell, of a piece of Scottish dance music – a hornpipe – called 'Her Majesty's Advocates'. This was something which Kenny, Peter Fraser, Alan Rodger and Donald Mackay of Drumadoon produced at a charity fair at Brechin Castle last summer. It was a good gathering of former and current Crown Office staff, advocates depute and Law Officers with their spouses. At the end we went to the Reading Room to look at the portraits which were unveiled yesterday of Kemp Davidson and Alan Johnston which were of particular interest to us. My portrait, as another former Dean of Faculty, is to be painted by Sandy Fraser in the New Year. Kemp was a particular challenge to the artist, as he suffers from multiple sclerosis and an accurate portrait could not entirely mask his disability. Alan Johnston's on the other hand is an excellent likeness. It conveys all the warmth and generosity of his character without the somewhat overweight and blustering manner which he displays on a bad day. It is a great honour for my own one to be in line now for adding to the collection. Like these two, I plan to be portrayed without a wig but dressed in court jacket and fall with a Court of Session robe somewhere in the background. Sandy Fraser is coming to India Street in January to plan the details, and will execute the work in an upstairs bedroom where it can rest in peace and quiet between sittings.

After this reception we were invited to Alan Rodger's spacious town house in Dublin Street for a buffet supper, to which many of the more senior people at Parliament House had been invited as well. Alan's dog Angus, a large black poodle, was on display also. He was big enough to hold his own in a crowd, and content to be among the guests after protesting at being shut in the study at the start. It was good to see James and Ann Clyde there with James restored to health, and Kemp and Mary Davidson there too. Alan is very good at keeping in touch with these Dublin Street neighbours, both of whom have been suffering so much through illness.

31 December 2002

The term ended with two pieces of work still in my mind, both of them about discrimination law in the field of employment. One of these, *Shamoon v Chief Constable of the RUC*,[195] is particularly troublesome. It is a sex discrimination case in which the central problem is about the choice of the comparator that is needed to test whether the woman police officer was being discriminated against. This is an area of law which is surprisingly lacking in authority. Such authority as there is is apt to mislead, as it is also in the related but quite distinct field of discrimination by victimisation. To begin with it all seemed quite simple, and it appeared that we were all agreed. Alan Rodger's summing up was clear and decisive, and I was asked to write the main judgment and did so. But then one after another the team began to have doubts, none more so than Alan who is so tenacious and relentless once he begins to worry about a problem. He departed from his previous line, and Brian Hutton and Richard Scott did too. This left me rather isolated and Donald Nicholls in a state of dismayed silence. I tried to hang on to what I had written, and went public in a series of redrafting efforts in the process. But Alan remained ominously unconvinced. I took no papers home with me, but worried about the case for the first few days of the Christmas break until – having studied the statutes and cases again – I realised that Alan was right and that his original position could not be defended. So I prepared yet another draft.

The other case, involving all three discrimination statutes in a question as to the position of ex-employees, is not nearly so difficult. But as it involves three statutes and three different sets of facts, it is quite a long judgment. I had not been able to complete it before the term ended, so in this case I did have to bring the papers back. Foolishly – and unusually – I left the vital floppy disk behind in my room on the Law Lords' Corridor. So I cannot complete my tidying up of the text until I can make contact with Gail next week by email.

The other item of work which I brought back with me is the initial work on a lecture which I have to give at King's College London in March. I have chosen the issue of judicial fallibility as my subject, but have not yet been able to get much done on it. I hope very much to be able to make some progress in the New Year. Otherwise I shall be in trouble, as it is almost impossible to create these things during term time. It is rather a thankless task, I fear. Organisers of lectures – in this case at King's College, London – like to fill their diaries and regard Law Lords as the ideal way of attracting audiences. But not all of our number participate. Those who do (Bingham, Steyn, Hoffmann and Rodger especially) set very high standards. So it is hard for me to live up to what is expected of me.

The year ended on a rather quiet note on the Corridor. Johan was off having the operation on his hip and Peter Millett was in Hong Kong to sit with the Court of Final Appeal there. Our new team have settled in, and there was no

---

195 See fn 188.

need for a Christmas party as no one is leaving our establishment to whom we must say farewell. Instead I asked Alan Rodger to join me in entertaining our four legal assistants to drinks in the Peers' Guest Room, which made up a very jolly party for all six of us. The general feeling is that this year's group, while good, are perhaps not quite as good as last year's. But this may just be a reflection of the annual cycle which brings in new people and ends with them at the peak of their experience. My impression, having spoken to each individually, is that morale is high, that they all get on well with each other and that they are still very enthusiastic about the job they are doing with us. I cannot ask much more than that.

Changes in the routine of the House, as part of a programme to 'modernise' Parliament, are affecting us. Business on Thursdays, when we usually deliver judgments, has started at 11am instead of 2.30pm since the new session began with the State Opening in November. This means that, prayers having already been said, we no longer have prayers before we give our judgments on that day of the week. Instead the proceedings start, the mace already being there, with the marching in of the Lord Chairman who bows to us when he reaches the Woolsack. Some time is saved by not having prayers, which always seemed a bit odd with only a few Law Lords present. But I shall miss seeing the bishops so much more closely on these occasions.

More changes are in the air too. There are earlier starts, earlier finishes, and more work to be taken in Grand Committee rather than in the Chamber to increase the capacity of the House to handle its business. All of these are matching changes in the House of Commons. And the pattern of the year is to alter, with the rise for all but the Law Lords in mid-July and a short two-week session for all but the Law Lords in September. This will be expensive and awkward for the staff and workmen during summer refurbishment, and the benefits from the change are not obvious. The only effect on us will be an empty building with workmen about at the end of July and, perhaps, the bishops as we are left to ourselves again during that period. But the change to the pattern of the evenings will remove much of the atmosphere of the place as people leave early, restaurants remain empty and the companionship which is so characteristic of both Houses when they sit late is disappearing. I fear that the modernisers are being beguiled by the undoubted logic of their argument into destroying something which will never be restored which lies at the heart of our democracy.

My journey to and from London follows a regular, familiar and on the whole quite comfortable pattern. I drive myself to Edinburgh Airport on Sunday at about 5.30pm, park in almost the same place each time in the relatively unfilled parking area and make my way to the lounge upstairs – BA or British Midland according to the choice of timetable – where I get my boarding card. Security checks present no problems, as I have learned to put all keys, cash, etc in my travel bag. There is then a period of quiet reading, with a drink of tomato juice before the flight is called. Flights south are usually more or less on time, especially with BA. I get a window seat in the forward area of the cabin which enables me to get off the plane more quickly at the other end. The flight south is about an hour, giving more time for quiet reading with a light evening meal during the flight as well. This consists of cold salad these days with BA but a hot meal with a hot towel with Bmi. On arrival at Heathrow I make the best speed to the Underground where I take the Piccadilly line to Holborn, which takes 50 minutes once the train has started off on its journey to its arrival there. Then I walk along High Holborn to a 24-hour shop run by a group of men of Middle Eastern appearance for my milk and other supplies. Door-to-door, on arrival at Gray's Inn, should take me between four and a quarter to four and a half hours, which certainly beats the Sunday train by quite a margin. The return journey starts usually at Westminster. I take the District line to Baron's Court, then the Piccadilly line to Heathrow where I make for the lounges according to my choice of airline. BA's lounge is best for views over the runways and for general atmosphere, but Bmi gives you a better tea. Until recently BA had the advantage over Bmi of an earlier flight at 8pm getting me home in time for supper at 10 o'clock, while Bmi's 8.40pm flight got me home at 10.45pm. But BA's time-keeping has been bad this autumn, with flights north being delayed by 45 minutes or more, which eliminates that advantage.

It is nice to have three weeks off from this routine over Christmas and New Year.

2003 – January to April

24 January 2003

Discrimination in the field of employment is still very much on the agenda. The judgments in *Shamoon* and *Rhys-Harper*,[196] difficult enough, are still incomplete and unsettled, although I had hoped to achieve a final draft in each of them. There was a refreshing interval for the first week of the term, when, sitting as number three to Tom Bingham and Lennie Hoffmann – very demanding, however stimulating this can be – I sat on two cases involving human rights, the argument in each case being that the provisions of the relevant statute were incompatible with the rights that were being claimed. They concerned a serviceman who was claiming damages in tort for an injury sustained during a period of service when such claims were barred by the Crown Proceedings Act,[197] and a homeless person who had rejected an offer of accommodation and was complaining about the fairness of the proceedings for the review of actions of the housing authority.[198] The judgments in this batch of cases are almost ready, such is the speed with which Tom and Lennie work, and I was able to contribute one too last weekend. But this week, again with Donald

---
196 *Rhys-Harper v Relaxion Group plc* [2003] UKHL 33, [2003] ICR 486.
197 *Matthews v Ministry of Defence* [2003] UKHL 4, [2003] 1 AC 1163.
198 *Runa Begum v Tower Hamlets London Borough Council* [2003] UKHL 5, [2003] 2 AC 430.

Nicholls and Alan Rodger plus Hobhouse and Scott, we are back in employment law. These are two cases, each of which raises the question whether sex discrimination law under the Sex Discrimination Act 1975 extends protection to those who were being dismissed on the grounds of homosexuality before the law that discriminated against them was changed. One of these cases is *MacDonald*[199] which concerns an officer in the Royal Air Force who was forced to resign following his declaration that he was a homosexual. The other is *Pearce*[200] which involves a lesbian schoolteacher who had been dismissed from her employment for the same reason. We are to hear these cases next week. In the first half of the week we had a case about whether a couple, who were obviously deeply committed to each other, could enter into a marriage. Their problem is that one of them, although living now as a man, is a transsexual female whereas the statute says that a marriage is void if it is not between a man and a woman.[201] The same team of Law Lords was chosen for all three cases. So we have become steeped in difficult problems about sex as well as employment. On the bright side Johan Steyn has returned to the Corridor after his hip operation looking very fit and well. He has avoided mishaps and lost quite a lot of weight, all of which is very good news.

My old sparring partner Michael Forsyth, formerly Secretary of State for Scotland, now Lord Forsyth of Drumlean, made a general reference to our disputes over fixed and mandatory minimum sentences when speaking in the House of Lords. He was vigorously in favour of them when he was Secretary of State, and I was just as vigorously against. In a speech about gun crime which I went to listen to in the Chamber he said very kindly that he was delighted to see me in my place and admitted that he had been wrong. He also admitted, in another speech on House of Lords reform, that he had become a convert from believing that the House had to be wholly elected to believing that it should be wholly appointed. There are powerful arguments against elected members – too many elections, not enough power in the House to attract good ambitious people, party-placed men, and the risk of instability if we were to have a hybrid House. Many of the speakers in a two-day debate were in favour of a wholly appointed House, and so am I. I shall vote for this if the votes take place at a time when I am free from other work and able to do so. The House of Commons will vote the other way, leaving the casting vote to the Government which now believes that an appointments system is right.

1 February 2003

Another week of sex discrimination and homosexuality was enlivened by the appearance of Cherie Booth QC, the wife of Prime Minister Tony Blair, for one of the parties to an appeal by the lesbian schoolteacher. She appeared for the

---

199 *MacDonald v Ministry of Defence* [2003] UKHL 34, [2003] ICR 937; reported as *Advocate General v MacDonald* 2003 SC (HL) 35.
200 *Pearce v Governing Body of Mayfield Secondary School* [2003] UKHL 34, [2003] ICR 937.
201 *Bellinger v Bellinger* [2003] UKHL 21, [2003] 2 AC 467.

school and put up a very competent performance in what was, of course, her speciality as an employment lawyer. As before, I was struck by her ability to detach herself – or so it seemed – from her turbulent and exciting life as the Prime Minister's consort. There was a burst of scandal over Christmas as the press found out that she had used the services of a dishonest businessman to buy two flats in Bristol where her son Euan now lives as a student. She was driven to making a television appearance to explain her innocence, which she did with great drama and skill but failed to convince anyone. However, memories are short, and much more pressing must be the crisis over Iraq where Tony Blair and George Bush are almost alone in urging military action against Saddam Hussein and war may be only six weeks away. None of that showed, however. But she did show a rich head of black hair under her wig, flowing over her ears. 'A seriously provocative hairstyle', muttered Donald Nicholls who was sitting beside me in the chair. I saw her whip her wig off the instant she got out into the Corridor when the case was over – not her favourite garment, obviously.

More dramatic, however, was my return journey from London at the end of the week. Snow and ice had been forecast, but it came to the London area with a vengeance in late afternoon on the Thursday. I left my room at 5.30pm for the 8.15pm BA flight home with flurries of light snow outside but nothing spectacular. So there was no sign of anything wrong. When I reached Westminster Tube station, however, the District line platform was packed with people and there were obviously delays as no trains were indicated on the arrivals board. So I went down to the Jubilee line, which was milling with people too. The indicator board showed that a train was due in one minute, but this soon changed to eight minutes and it did not alter for what seemed a very long time. At last a train came in, but it was not going where I needed to go. My plan was to get off at Green Park to change to the Piccadilly line, but just after I had fought my way onto the train the driver said that Green Park was closed due to overcrowding. I managed to get off just in time and joined a surge of people making their way up to the District line. The announcer was telling us that stations were closing and lines shutting down overground on all sides.

With luck on my side, however, I got a place on an Ealing Broadway District line train and, when I got to Baron's Court, a relatively less crowded Piccadilly line train was due in and I got onboard it. But then things began to seize up. Snow was lying, and the line to Rayner's Lane was closed. Then we were halted near Turnham Green due to a stalled train at South Ealing. We were held there for about 30 minutes – I was standing, as usual, as the train was full. I could hear the driver in his cab just feet away, as I was in the front car as usual, asking for permission to move and a voice telling him that trains were not going beyond Acton Town. By now it was after 7pm and I was becoming resigned to having to travel back to the flat instead of home. Twenty minutes later we drew into Acton Town and were told to get off the train. But almost as we did so staff were advising us to get on again as they were 'scraping' the line clear at South Ealing. We set off again after some further delay and made a hesitant journey into the snow-covered outskirts. It was an extraordinary experience, as the electric contacts with the centre line kept failing – due to ice, no doubt – with a constant array of blue sparks lighting up the signs of blizzard on bushes and trees on either side of our train. But the driver kept going. Eventually we reached the safety of tunnels and we arrived at Heathrow Terminals 1, 2 and 3 at 7.40pm. I sped through the airport to the lounge at Terminal 1 where I found that my flight to Edinburgh, BA1464, was one of the very few flights that had not been cancelled. Only it and a Glasgow flight were still going, and I had checked in already thanks to the website checking-in system. Back in the terminal there were huge columns of people trying to book onto other flights. Ours was indicated to be leaving on time, but soon we were delayed to 9.30pm and then to later still. Hardly anything was coming in or going out, although I saw Concorde land in the darkness in front of our lounge. The runways were clear but there was obviously a problem with ground staff who were in short supply because of travel problems and the air crew were in the wrong place. We were a select group of travellers in the lounge as the Manchester/Newcastle folk were all elsewhere. Some aircraft, having loaded up hours earlier – seven hours earlier in one case, it was said – were still on the ground. However, at 11pm we were bussed to a remote stand, loaded onto our Boeing 737 and told by the pilot that he proposed 'to get the hell out of here'. This he did. We landed in Edinburgh, nicely clear of snow and ice, at 1am. The air hostess bid us 'Good morning' as she welcomed us in. It was a grim experience for them too, being so long delayed. I was home shortly after 1.30am. But I was very, very lucky. The chances of getting another flight out for the next 24 hours were almost nil, and the train service would not have been much better. Some people were stuck for up to 13 hours in their cars on the M11. It was astonishing but, as someone said, our transport systems run on very narrow margins. If something goes wrong, it goes wrong very fast.

23 February 2003

The weather has improved, but the term remains very busy. *Shamoon*, at last, has been resolved and judgment will be given this week. The other employment- and sex-related cases are proving that much less troublesome. I have had some relief this weekend as we had a chancery case in the Privy Council on which Robert Walker will write, and then a day of hearing petitions for leave to appeal, for which I was in the chair, as these applications are disposed of without reasons. This week we are in the Privy Council on crime, with Tom Bingham in the chair, and he will no doubt want to write on this one. There will be time for me to tidy up my King's College Lecture on Fallibility for 4 March. Then I am back in the thick of it, in the House of Lords for two weeks, on cases raising human rights issues and the issue of retrospectivity, which are highly contentious and debatable.

My Saturdays have been taken up this month with two-hour sittings at home with Sandy Fraser who is painting my portrait for the Faculty of Advocates as a former Dean. He is very pleasant to deal with. He has a quiet sense of humour, is very painstaking and rather self-effacing. He is producing a rather splendid picture in which rich colours are being produced by my Court of Session robe as the background. Quite what he will make of my face is unclear at the moment, but it will certainly be recognisable. I sit on a raised platform in a chair which has flat arms and its back angled to the seat which came from my father's office and now lives by the desk in my study. I gaze out over the rooftop of 25 India Street on the other side of the street as we talk of this and that. He uses photographs a bit and works on the painting during the week. So the sittings are for checking up on detail. There is one sitting still to go, with possibly one final one if needed in reserve. I found the process really quite enjoyable.

9 March 2003

To Strathclyde University on Friday 7 March for the giving of an update on the Malawi Millennium Project to HRH The Princess Royal. The project is of increasing interest in view of our impending visit to Malawi in August. I was collected from India Street at 7.30am and was in the Barony Hall by 8.45am in time to wander round and speak to various people involved in our work there. Real progress is being made in nursing provision, civil engineering at a basic level, famine relief and water provision and purification, although no doubt this is just a drop in the ocean as the country is in a state of extreme poverty. The Lord Provost, Alex Mosson, arrived in time to receive HRH who arrived on time, driving herself in a very smart Range Rover. There were brief introductions and then she went to speak, as she does very well, to various fundraisers before sitting down to receive the presentation, with the Principal on one side and me on the other. The Principal and the Secretary, Peter West, conducted proceedings, and there was nothing for me to do except to take it all in. Afterwards I walked her back to the entrance. I asked her how many times she had been to Malawi – three times she said – and I told her that we were going in August, for which she wished us well. She added that Dr Hastings Banda, latterly too autocratic for most people's taste, had been unduly vilified as the country was well run in his day. It will be interesting to see the reality when we get there.

Meantime a very heavy term in London continues. I have spent a second weekend on a long Privy Council judgment in *Benedetto and Labrador v The Queen*.[202] It runs to 77 paragraphs, as there are so many topics in this appeal in a murder case from the British Virgin Islands that we must deal with. Last week we heard *Aston Cantlow Parish Council*,[203] and this week we are to hear *Wilson v First Country Trust*.[204] These two cases raise very significant questions under the Human Rights Act 1998. The first is about a lay rector's responsibility for the cost of carrying out repairs to the chancel of their parish church. The question

---

202 [2003] UKPC 27, [2003] 1 WLR 1545.
203 *Aston Cantlow Parochial Church Council v Wallbank* [2003] UKHL 37, [2004] 1 AC 546.
204 [2003] UKHL 40, [2004] 1 AC 816.

is whether the enforcement of that responsibility by the parish council, which arises under the ecclesiastical law of the Church of England, is a breach of the lay rector's Convention rights. The other is about a consumer credit agreement. Recovery of the amount of the loan was barred by the statute because the amount had not been correctly stated in the agreement. The question here is whether the statutory bar is compatible with the right to protection of property guaranteed by the Convention. They are not easy cases. The other team has gaps in its diary as cases in the Privy Council settle. There are no gaps for us. I am happy to be busy, however, and these cases are indeed fascinating, if very hard to work through and resolve.

Two other brief notes. My state pension papers came through this week, offering me a pension of £109 per week. I can hardly believe that I have reached this stage. There is, however, a much wider and more significant matter. The 'war' on Iraq, led by President Bush and Tony Blair, seems to be only days away. How they got themselves into this highly questionable position requires much more writing than I have time for just now.

17 March 2003

At the time of writing, Tony Blair, George Bush and the Spanish Prime Minister are meeting at a US Air Force base in the Azores to discuss whether to go to war this week with Iraq. Attempts to get a resolution through the Security Council of the United Nations have failed, largely due to a declaration by France that it will veto any resolution authorising the use of military force. Its position, which it shares with Germany and Russia, is that Iraq should be persuaded to disarm by negotiation. That was a sensible position to take before President Bush began to raise the stakes by threatening force some months ago and moving his forces into the Gulf. Tony Blair's attempts to restrain him from taking immediate action had some effect, but France has made any further attempts to persuade Saddam to disarm by the threat of force quite pointless. If the nations who sit on the Security Council cannot agree to the use of force as a last resort – and France which is, of course, one of the permanent members will not agree to this – the calls on him to disarm are without backing. So Saddam can ignore them, as he has been doing for the past 12 years since the last Gulf War. So it seems that there can be only one result from today's meeting. To withdraw from the use of force – with such a huge arsenal in Kuwait and in the Gulf all ready to go now – would be to give in to Saddam and make any further attempts to disarm him quite unattainable. France's principled stand comes too late. As for Bush, he has left himself no room to change his mind. Having marched his forces to the top of the hill, as it were, he cannot without huge damage to his credibility just march them down the hill again.

There is huge opposition to the use of force all over the world and the outcome, after a certain military victory, is quite unclear. Lord Goldsmith, who incidentally was appearing before us in the House of Lords in *Wilson v First Country*

Trust and was his usual calm, careful self, is said to have advised that, taking all the resolutions to date, to use force would not be in breach of international law but that it would be if the final resolution which Tony Blair was seeking were to be defeated in the Security Council. I think that this is right. But many Labour politicians and all Liberal Democrats seem to disagree. Cabinet resignations are in prospect. They include Robin Cook, probably, and perhaps Helen Liddell and Alistair Darling, who was looking very disconsolate and withdrawn when I travelled home on the same BA flight with him on Thursday evening. If – or when, I should say – the war starts it had better be over quickly. Otherwise a huge range of political uncertainties will emerge.

28 March 2003

A busy, remarkable and worrying week.

We are now days into the war with Iraq. There has been no quick end to it, despite what the Americans had predicted. The 'shock and awe' campaign which Donald Rumsfelt, the Defence Secretary, and General Tommy Franks proclaimed is looking increasingly absurd. The Americans, with a force of about only 100,000 men, have pressed rapidly up the banks of the Euphrates to within about 50 miles of Baghdad. But their supply lines have become stretched and the weather – severe dust storms and torrential rain – has slowed progress and made life for them very difficult. Attacks are being mounted against them along this route by irregular forces, causing much concern if not yet many casualties. The British – the Seventh Armoured Division and the Royal Marines – have been achieving better results in the south east around Basra, having re-opened the port at Umm Qasr to receive humanitarian supplies, secured the southern oil fields and destroyed a column of Iraqi tanks. But here too the weather has been grim, and there has been determined resistance from local militias which employ tactics that are difficult to deal with – operating in civilian clothes, terrorising and intimidating their own people, and so on. The expected welcome has not come, perhaps – probably – because of the stranglehold which the regime has over its people. At the same time a potential humanitarian disaster of lack of water and food in Basra is causing real concern. The troops dare not enter the city yet for fear of causing civilian casualties. In Basra there are many more casualties due to the pro-Saddam factions firing on their own people. In Baghdad there have already been two major incidents of rockets – from which side is unclear – falling on market areas, with loss of life for which the Americans have been blamed. There have been many Iraqis killed in fighting, while there have been very few casualties on the Coalition side. More of these are due to accidents and friendly fire than to enemy action. It is all very messy, rather dangerous and ominously out of keeping with what we had been led to expect. There remains much opposition to the venture at home, increasing ill-feeling in the Arab world and complete disintegration of the various international groupings to which we belong. No clear evidence of weapons of mass destruction – the *causus belli* – has been found. The regime of

Saddam is revealed as odious and callous, as was expected. But the justification for what has been done is hard to find.

On Tuesday, having a day out of court, I seized the chance and paid a visit to the Bloody Sunday Inquiry. It is at present hearing evidence in London from soldiers who cannot for reasons of personal safety be asked to travel to Northern Ireland, having moved temporarily from Londonderry where it has been going on for several years. It was day 312 of the Inquiry, which is not expected to end until next year and has already cost over £200m. The Chairman is Lord Saville, under whose leadership superb technology has been installed. It has been duplicated in London in the Central Hall, Westminster, so that it is just as it is in Londonderry. The entire documentary evidence is on disk and can be – and is – shown to everyone including the public on-screen as the witness is being questioned. The witness, just starting that day, was Lieutenant Colonel Wilford, the former OC 1 PARA, whose men were responsible for the deaths of 14 civilians that day. He was questioned with great skill, calmly and persistently, by Christopher Clarke QC, counsel to the Inquiry. He did not make a good impression. It was clear that he had gone in 'hard and fast' to deal with the demonstration, despising what he saw as the soft tactics of the local security forces. He was evasive and easily shown up, I thought. But we did not reach the critical stage before it was time for lunch and he left as, being unwell, he was fit only to give evidence in the morning. The afternoon was taken up with some much more straightforward evidence from a Coldstream guardsman who had been on a rooftop somewhere. One was struck how everyone involved had now reached middle age or more. The incident took place, after all, 31 years ago. As I sat listening to Colonel Wilford, who should come in and sit almost beside me but Gerry Adams and Martin McGuinness – Sinn Fein MPs who have refused to take their seats in Parliament but are strongly suspected of having been – and perhaps still being – in very senior positions in the IRA. These are senior figures, deeply implicated in acts of terrorism in the past. McGuinness is said to have been second-in-command in Londonderry at the time of the massacre. They were as cool as you could wish, very well groomed and very well dressed. The peace process owes a lot to them, of course. They have taken risks for it and are brave men, whom one must admire. But they are deeply committed to their cause nevertheless. At lunchtime I went to see Mark Saville and his two colleagues. One from Canada (Judge William Hoyt) and the other from Australia (Justice John Toohey) for a sandwich lunch and a general view of how things are looking behind the scenes. It has become Mark's life work, almost. He will probably have reached his statutory retirement age by the time it is all over.

On Wednesday I voted in a bizarre election, for the one vacancy which has emerged among the hereditary peers following the death of Lord Oxfuird. There were 81 candidates for one place. We could vote for them all, in order of preference. Like most people I chose five. I selected Lord Napier of Magdala, with whom I was at Cambridge and in the Lady Margaret Boat Club, and Lords Rowallan, Weir, Kintore and Gray – all Scots. None of them got very far. Lord Ullswater, an ex-Tory Minister, much respected, was the successful candidate.

Today, Friday, I was at a Human Rights Conference in Edinburgh. Among the speakers was Cherie Booth QC, Tony Blair's wife. 500 people turned up, as she is a great draw. It was a very well-run affair. There were six speakers, with 20 minutes each. I did the first half of the event as rapporteur, and Alan Rodger did the second. Then we had lunch, at which I sat next to Cherie herself. As always, I was struck by her ability to detach herself from the worries that would beset most wives of such stressed-out men as Tony Blair must be just now. She was friendly, wholly committed to what she was doing and thoroughly professional. Behind it all, of course, there is a fierce political drive. She was going to visit Labour Party members before returning to London, as the Scottish Parliament has just ended its first session and elections for the next session are only five weeks away.

I have been elected a Fellow of the Royal Society of Edinburgh. It is a very pleasant honour. It was suggested ages ago that I should be made a member of this body, but nothing came of it and I thought that I had been forgotten. There was no particular reason why I should now be remembered, although it is usual for a Lord President to be so honoured. Alan Rodger was honoured when he was Lord Advocate, though Lords Keith and Jauncey were not. Some kind friends in the universities seem to have revived interest in me, and so it has come about. It will not be easy to do much for the Society as I am so much in London. But there is a small conference near the end of April in which I can participate which will be nice.

5 April 2003

The US Forces are on the outskirts of Baghdad and are claimed to have secured Saddam International Airport. This news is denied by the Iraqi Minister of Information, who proclaims that the Republican Guard have secured a great victory, crushed the enemy and cleaned the whole of the airport entirely of Americans. This is a pathetic example of self-denial which can offer little comfort to anyone. There is no early end to the war in sight either there or in Basra, where the British Forces are taking their time to move closer into the city to avoid civilian casualties.

It has been a curious war so far, nevertheless. The Iraqis have completely failed to mount any organised opposition or create serious obstacles to the advance such as by blowing bridges over the Tigris or the Euphrates. A few attempts have been made to mount counter-attacks with disastrous consequences, and there have been several suicide bomb attacks which have created disproportionate problems for the US soldiers at checkpoints. But much of the rhetoric by the Iraqi Ministers has been unmatched by action on the ground, so far.

There has been no collapse of the regime, whose masters are hidden from view. They continue to broadcast to the world as before, with occasional views of Saddam himself on video. Whether this is himself, or one of his several doubles, is hard to tell. No clear evidence of weapons of mass destruction has yet been found. Opposition to what has been going on remains strong in the UK, if rather too often hysterical and ill-reasoned to be convincing to those like myself, who remain very uneasy but are reserving judgment until it is all over and the wisdom of what has been done can be assessed.

15 April 2003

Now, after only 27 days without any major battles having been fought and without the horrors of urban warfare we had all feared, the war is over. All the cities are in Coalition hands. There is no longer any military campaign to fight. The organised opposition has melted away.

There were amazing scenes a week ago as the US Marines drove into the centre of Baghdad. There had been an incursion the previous day on the west side of the river, which was filmed from the hotel on the other side of it which was being used to house the journalists – the Palestine Hotel. Iraqi soldiers were seen running away. The absurdly comical Minister of Information, in military uniform as always, assured us that it was the Americans who had run away and that the Iraqi Forces had had a famous victory. 'God will barbecue their bellies in hell' said Mohammed Saeed al-Sahhaf, who has become something of a cult figure as he is so shamelessly out of touch with what is really going on. This was to be almost his last appearance. The next day the Marines arrived in the central square on the east bank on the other side of the hotel, having driven in unopposed from the outskirts. A small crowd of Iraqis was there to welcome them. There was a huge bronze statue of Saddam Hussein, which had now become the focus of attention. Several young men climbed the plinth, tied a rope around the neck and tried to pull it down. But it was firmly fixed, and manual force was plainly inadequate and probably unsafe. Eventually one of the Americans' heavy-armoured vehicles was brought into service, by popular request. A wire rope was attached. A marine climbed up and put the Stars and Stripes over Saddam's head. But this was, wisely, ordered to be taken down and an Iraqi flag was substituted. But these were trivial insults compared with what happened next. The vehicle drew back, pulling the hawser tight. The statue shuddered a little and then bowed forward, hand out-stretched in an extraordinary gesture of submission, hesitated and then fell forward onto the ground, leaving only two stumps behind on the plinth. Iraqis leapt upon it, jumping up and down and bashing it and hitting it with their shoes – the ultimate gesture of contempt. *The Times*, portraying this moment on its front page, set out beneath it Shelley's epitaph for the fall of the then glorious tyrant Ozymandias which was inspired by the broken colossus of Pharaoh Rameses II in Egypt: 'I met a traveller from an antique land who said: "Two vast and trunkless legs of stone stand in the desert . . . Look on my works, ye mighty, and despair" '. At this moment the regime was indeed utterly destroyed. There can be no going back, which is why Saeed al-Sahhaf has now disappeared.

The conflict in other respects is, however, far from over. There were pockets of resistance, and widespread looting and civil disorder took over. The Coalition forces were not prepared for that, and were still having to deal with fanatics and others who could spring on them at any moment. Government buildings, hotels, museums and hospitals were ransacked in an orgy of reaction to what had happened after decades of repression and tyranny. A great deal of damage was done, and confidence in the aims of the Coalition has been much diminished as a result. Attempts to restore basic things like water and electricity, and to provide medical services and distribute food, are being hampered. And attempts today to convene a meeting of potential leaders to take over the running of the country were being vilified as attempts by the USA to dominate the agenda from now on. It is not at all clear what can be done to sort all this out and restore some kind of normality. The mood of the people is highly volatile, and there is very little goodwill towards the Coalition for removing what was there before. And there is still no sign of weapons of mass destruction, which was the *causus belli* in the first place.

Instead media coverage fuels public demand at home for instant results. The military campaign, so rapid and so decisive, has been like a long show in a cinema. There has been none of the grinding effort, loss of life and dysfunction on a huge scale that a real war extended over months or years would have brought. To expect equally quick results from the peace is too much. Mistakes are being made before our eyes in the peace, as in the war. But time is needed for it all to work out, if public opinion can hold out that long. For the present the reservations about the wisdom of what has been done remain. There is no feeling of any real victory. We are not allowed to be triumphant, nor indeed should we be. On any view it is sad that it had to come to this, and there is no certainty that it will work out for the best.

At home local elections and the Welsh and Scottish Assembly and Parliamentary elections are to be held on 1 May. There is a great deal of apathy, and not much to encourage any party. There is no Falklands factor for Labour. The anti-war Liberal Democrats are probably worse off, but not by much. The SNP were anti-war too. They could afford to be, as they have a stronger identity anyway. But there is no great surge in their favour either.

The Easter holidays have now arrived and with it a long spell of dry, lovely weather which makes any work during this interval rather unattractive.

2003 – May to July

9 May 2003

This has been my week at Strathclyde University as Chancellor. On Monday evening, it being a bank holiday, I went south to London. Normally this journey is done on a Sunday. I took with me a collection of draft judgments which I had been working on throughout the long weekend. These included *Aston Cantlow*, with revisals, and *Wilson v First Country Trust*. These are very important cases, but – along with the three employment law cases – they have become becalmed with a huge delay now looming. John Hobhouse seems to be incapable of getting his drafts out and Donald Nicholls, our chairman, seems to be almost equally lacking in enthusiasm too. It was hard to get my mind to work on my drafts, but I did.

Monday having come and gone in Edinburgh, I spent Tuesday in London getting my judgments tidied up and into the system through Gail Munden, my very efficient secretary. There was quite a lot of administration to do. I entertained a young student from Münster University to lunch on the Terrace and then sat in the Chamber for a while, before setting out for Heathrow en route to Glasgow for the dinner at Ross Priory for the Strathclyde honorary graduands. The dinner was 7pm for 7.30pm. Mary left Edinburgh at 4.15pm. She was collected by car driven by Wallace, the University chauffeur, taking with her two suitcases. One had my dinner jacket, etc for Ross Priory, the other had my suit, etc for changing into next day at University House where we were to stay overnight. I left Westminster at about the same time, but my flight was at 18.35 hours (20 minutes later than the previous years due to an altered timetable). So I had no chance of being at the dinner on time. By now I was busy working out my after-dinner speech in honour of the honorary graduands and getting it into my head so that I could speak without notes. Fortunately I have kept up the ability to do this, but it requires time and preparation. The BA flight was in a Boeing 757, as had been the flight on Monday morning. This is a rare privilege these days, as we are normally on an Airbus 319 which is smaller, less elegant and less comfortable. So that was a turn-up for the books, and things kept going well as the flight was precisely on time. There were almost no waiting aircraft to delay our take-off, and we arrived five minutes early. Wallace was at the airport to collect me, and at 8.45pm I made my entrance to the Ross Priory dining room as discreetly as possible. I had my speech sorted out by now, was able to enjoy the dinner from the main course onwards and say what I wanted to say when the time came.

Next day at University House Mary and I had breakfast with the Principal and his wife, Andrew and Suzanne Hamnett, and I then set about preparing myself for the next round. The University Day ceremony is presided over by the Chancellor, who takes centre stage and has to announce each item in a quite complex programme after a 3 to 4 minute impromptu introductory welcome. This is made more difficult than it sounds by the fact that I have no lectern or other surface onto which I can put papers to read from as I stand on the stage in front of my audience. It is really rather absurd, and it imposes quite a strain on me as I have to have everything stored in my memory. I can refresh it, just occasionally, when I am sitting down listening to presentations by others from the lectern as honorary graduands or others take their turn. But I have to concentrate on what I am doing very hard – names of presenters, of honorary graduands and the various degrees which are to be conferred on them all have to be remembered, and all in the right order. So there was quite some preparation to do. The morning was taken up, however, with coffee to meet – once again – the graduands we had seen the evening before at Ross Priory, and then join them for photographs outside the Barony Hall. Then there was a buffet lunch in the Lord Todd Building and, starting at 2pm, the ceremony itself.

The presentations this year were for Roy Johnson, just retired as Convener of Court, for Fellowship of the University, and five local people for honorary degrees: Alex Mosson, just retired as Lord Provost; Tom Shields the *Herald* journalist, with many years of experience behind him as a diarist; Mrs Hannah Stirling, an 86-year-old campaigner for the preservation of Loch Lomond; Professor David Hamblen, just retired as Chairman of the Greater Glasgow Health Board and Professor Edward Friel of the Greater Glasgow and Clyde Valley Tourist Board. This was a very happy group, celebrating Greater Glasgow from Loch Lomond to the Clyde, as I had said in my speech at Ross Priory. Alex Masson, an irrepressible character, was full of amiable Glasgow chatter. Tom Shields was strangely moved by the event. He had dropped out of his degree course at Strathclyde, but was allowed to complete it 30 years later, just four years before being awarded his Honorary Doctorate. Mrs Stirling was delighted by the award, and the two Professors were very cheerful and pleased by the occasion too. There were some very amusing presentations as well. I got everything in the right order and said almost everything right except my introduction to the musical interlude, where a whole collection of facts that I had to recite did not quite come out, apart from the mention of names, which, fortunately, I did get right. I was very tired that evening when we eventually got home at 5.30pm.

I spent the following Thursday at Strathclyde again on visits to various places to do with student affairs, including the Chaplaincy Centre, and was given presentations by John Martin, the Director, and Imelda Devlin who deals with the Goals Project attracting children from local authority schools to the University. We were entertained to lunch by Peter West in a rather good local restaurant, which was a nice reward to the two Directors for their hard work. Today I was back at Strathclyde again for three meetings. The first was as Convener of the Court nominations group which I chair, then there was the University Court and finally the General Convocation of which I am chairman. This meant a 7.30am start from India Street, but at least this was in daylight. The Court meeting was interesting, as ever, but in some places it was hard to stay awake. The Convocation lunch is fun, because there are many people in this body who come only once a year and are drawn from the wider community. Then we had the meeting itself from 2pm to 4pm with presentations by Graham Roddick on the developments on our Estate and by Andrew Hamnett, the Principal. Andrew spoke for almost an hour, which was about half an hour too long. He is prone to this, and I must try to remember to tell him to keep it short next year or we will lose our audience entirely.

So, this little ordeal is over for another year. It is mostly very enjoyable, as there are many friends and new graduands are interesting to meet also. The ordeal for me, as I had been saying, lies in the things I must say from memory. And the

Ross Priory speech is not all that easy either, as I have to work out something to say about the graduands which does not enter upon what the presenters will be saying about them at the ceremony the following day. I could not help reflecting today on what a remarkable transformation it is for me to find myself sitting in Glasgow on a Friday afternoon as Chancellor of this University when 15 years ago – and for 24 years previously – I spent my Fridays in a courtroom somewhere as a member of the Faculty of Advocates.

24 May 2003

Last week was the last of the Easter term. There were some unimportant cases in the Privy Council for me, with Lennie Hoffmann wasting no time as our chairman. It was, however, a memorable week for other reasons.

On Tuesday evening Mary and I were guests at a dinner at Admiralty House to say thank you to Andrew Tipping, a judge of the Court of Appeal of New Zealand, who has been sitting with us this month. Tom Bingham presided, and the Nichollses, the Hoffmanns and the Huttons were the others from the Law Lords' Corridor. John Watherston and his wife were our hosts, as the place is available – rather like Bute House was to me as Lord President – through the senior civil service. There was also the High Commissioner of New Zealand and her companion. It was a good evening, tinged slightly with sadness as the Bill to end the appeals to the Privy Council from New Zealand is well on its way in Wellington and the measure should be enacted by November at the latest.

On Wednesday one of the two items for debate in the House of Lords was 'Relationships between the judiciary, the legislature and the executive, and the judicial participation in public controversy'. I wondered over the weekend whether I should speak on the second part of this subject. I was feeling a bit guilty at having sat silently on the crossbenches for so long, as I am, unlike my colleagues, often in the Chamber. This is partly to earn my travelling expenses when I am sitting in the Privy Council, as that part of our work does not count as business in the House for this purpose, and partly out of a genuine interest as to what goes on there. I felt that I probably ought to try, but was uncertain as to whether I had enough to say to make it worthwhile. I was still uncertain on the Wednesday morning when I arrived in my room. But we had the day off because Lennie had moved things on at speed in the Privy Council, and there was time to try to put something together. I checked the list of speakers in the Whip's room as I came in. No other serving Law Lord had put his name down, but Lord Woolf, the Lord Chief Justice, had done so, as had Lords Lloyd and Ackner. I had until noon to add my name to the speakers' list. By 10am I had enough of a draft to make me decide to do so. Indeed, I felt that not to speak now would make me rather spineless and be sure to increase my concern that I was not pulling my weight. I thought that none of my colleagues would notice what I was doing.

In the event there was a clutch of Law Lords in the Chamber when Harry rose to speak second in the debate – Bingham, Hoffmann, Rodger and Scott were there, as well as Lloyd and Ackner and myself. Richard Scott said that he was very glad that I had decided to speak, which was nice of him. He added that Tom really ought to have put his name down too. But it is easier for me, as I could lean heavily on my experience as Lord President and detach myself a bit from the great problems that Harry is having at present with David Blunkett, the Home Secretary. Rather to our surprise almost all the politicians in the House who spoke were critical of David Blunkett and supportive of Harry Woolf. There was an outstanding speech by the Bishop of Worcester. Harry's speech was not particularly sparkling, and he was interrupted as he approached his tenth minute in a time-limited debate in which we each had only seven minutes, but at least he was there making his point. I followed Earl Russell. I had to speak very rapidly, using my draft speech to stick as closely as possible to my carefully structured text so that I could finish it within the time limit. I got almost all of it in, and felt content with what I had managed to say. Lord Goodhart for the Liberal Democrats went out of his way in his speech to say how glad he was that I had spoken, which was a relief. I felt that I had done my bit without causing anyone any embarrassment and a sense of pleasure that I had not run away from this opportunity.

This weekend concrete barriers have been put in place around the Palace of Westminster to protect it from bomb attacks by terrorists. There have been enough terrorist attacks – Al Qaeda originated, it is thought – since the end of the war in Iraq. These have been in Muslim countries, but there are threats to the US and to the UK. So we must take precautions, ugly though they are. I have a close interest in this development, as my room looks directly out on the area that is thought to be most vulnerable.

7 June 2003

A rare luxury in term time: a weekend with no draft opinions to revise or prepare. We went back to work on Tuesday for a two-day case on a point of insolvency law[205] which finished in a day, and Thursday's diet of Appeal Committee oral hearings did not materialise. I was able to draft something in Tuesday's case whilst still in London. Peter Millett will give the leading speech. Yesterday, Friday, was much taken up with administration, including sorting out my retirement pension papers with a view to taking advice about what to do with the various schemes that I have to make the most efficient use of them. I have reading for two cases next week to occupy me tomorrow before I head south again. I also have two lectures to prepare for January and February next year. It is hard to get worked up about either of them so long in advance of the event. But these things creep up on one if some work is not done in advance. So I shall have to try to do a bit on at least one of these lectures as well.

---

205 *In re Pantmaenog Timber Co Ltd* [2003] UKHL 49, [2004] 1 AC 158.

13 June 2003

There was a Cabinet reshuffle yesterday which has ended Derry Irvine's career as Lord Chancellor and put our own futures as Law Lords in doubt. The sudden and bruising way in which this has been conducted is breathtaking. But it is the result, one must be sure, of bitter arguments in the Cabinet which made Derry's position as a member of it untenable.

Rumours that Derry was to leave office as Lord Chancellor had been circulating in and out of the press since last weekend. The core of the argument was supposed to be about the division of responsibilities between the Lord Chancellor's Department and the Home Office presided over by David Blunkett. Unknown to us until the news broke yesterday afternoon, it has given rise to a much more deep-seated issue. The plan, as now revealed, is to terminate the office of Lord Chancellor, wind up his Department immediately, set up a new Department of Constitutional Affairs which is to take over the Scotland and Wales Offices, and to remove the Law Lords from the House of Lords. It is plain that Derry could not bring himself to push through such a programme. His attempts to preserve the existing structures have failed, and so he has had to go. Charlie Falconer, Lord Falconer of Thoroton, a much softer character, takes over as the Secretary of State for Constitutional Affairs. He is also the new Lord Chancellor, to fulfil the duties required by statute until that office is abolished. But it is already known that he has decided not to sit as a judge, and he probably will not try to sit as Lord Chancellor on the Woolsack either if the House will let him get away with that too.

As for the Law Lords, without warning or consultation[206] it has simply been announced that they will be removed from the House of Lords and that there will be a new Supreme Court. When, where and on what terms all this will happen has not been worked out, and there are no details. I suppose that we have a legitimate expectation that our judicial careers will not be terminated, but even that is unclear. A new Supreme Court will require new appointments, no doubt by an appointments board of some kind or another. There may be an age limit too. What the Scottish participation in a new court will be is unclear, and where it will sit is unclear too. The whole structure of personnel will have to be created from nothing, as in the House of Lords we depend entirely on personnel employed by the parliamentary authorities. Both Alan Rodger and I have been against this move for both practical and personal reasons. I doubt whether the accommodation and support will be anything like as good as we have at Westminster, and there will be huge personal loss in moving from these handsome and stimulating surroundings to some obscure building nearer Charing Cross. But there is nothing that we can do about all of that for now. Tom Bingham has been calling, from his lofty position, for a Supreme Court for years now, as has Johan Steyn. But I am sure that neither of them were consulted

---

[206] The first I knew of this was when seeing an evening TV news broadcast in a lounge at Heathrow while waiting for my flight home to Edinburgh on Thursday evening, 12 June.

about this announcement, and Tom could be forgiven if he felt demeaned by it. As it is, an enormous amount will now rest on his shoulders if, out of this wreck, something worthy of the name of the Supreme Court is to be created. Whether I shall be part of it all, who knows?

A week ago, as others who are faced with redundancy or career ends were attracting my sympathy, I was congratulating myself in having a secure future. Now all of this is in the air. My one consolation is that I shall have completed my 15 years on the Bench next summer before any of the reforms which affect us can be introduced. So at least I will be in a position to retire on a full pension. But the prospect of another five years or more in service now looks rather doubtful. The feeling is one of some anxiety and unease.

15 June 2003

Lord Williams of Mostyn, the Leader of the House and a committed and determined radical, was on the radio this lunchtime trying to justify the steps which had been taken by the Government. He enunciated the principle, which he would of course apply to the Supreme Court, that no judge should be a member of either House of Parliament. As the law stands, this would exclude me (and Alan Rodger and Tom Bingham, as it happens) from membership. I assume that all those who have peerages under the Appellate Jurisdiction Act are to be disqualified from membership, but what about Lords of Appeal in Ordinary who have retired? We three, on the other hand, all have life peerages under the Life Peerages Act 1958 which cannot be renounced – unlike hereditary peerages under the Peerage Act 1963. Does this mean that, as we cannot escape from being members of the House of Lords, we cannot be judges? If so we are in baulk, twice over. Perhaps this will all be sorted out, perhaps not. Perhaps we will be allowed to remain peers under a transitional arrangement until the House itself is reformed. Perhaps we will be told that we must give up our life peerages as a condition of Supreme Court membership. That would greatly diminish the attraction of London for me, and perhaps others from Scotland.

I leave for London in two hours' time in the rather forlorn hope that our future will be clearer by next weekend.

22 June 2003

A turbulent week. Alan Rodger and I had rather sleepless nights on Monday in London's heat and humidity. On Tuesday Tom Bingham saw Charlie Falconer and was assured by him that the plan is to move all the Law Lords 'sideways', so to speak, and that there is no question of our being deprived of our jobs. How reliable this assurance is, given the hostility of this Government to the judges and its brutality, remains to be seen. There is absolutely no sign that the Scottish position regarding House of Lords appeals is being considered or what will be done if these appeals are to be terminated. So I decided to try my luck with a little lobbying. I made contact with Frances Gibb of *The Times*. She telephoned me back, and I was able to explain to her that there were some features of the Scottish position that had never been mentioned by Tom Bingham, Johan Steyn and others who had been promoting the Supreme Court idea and which were absent from the current discussion about it. I then sent her an email with some of the details. I also wrote to Lord Strathclyde, the Leader of the Opposition in the Lords, in the hope that he might raise the issue with Lord Williams of Mostyn when he repeated a statement by the Prime Minister on the reshuffle on Wednesday. He duly did, and was ignored. On Thursday a brief piece by Frances Gibb about my views appeared in *The Times*. A larger version of it was on the front page of the Scottish edition of the newspaper which I saw when I got home. And next day a well-expressed and perceptive leader on the issue appeared in *The Scotsman*. So I have succeeded in bringing it out into the open. By chance I sat beside Tam Dalyell MP on the Bmi plane on the way home from London. He was deeply interested and critical of the Government. This inspired me to write brief notes to James Douglas-Hamilton MSP, to the SNP leader John Swinney and to Lord Goodhart, the Liberal Democrat peer, as well as a further note to Lord Strathclyde. I also wrote a letter to *The Times*, but the subject is already receding into the background as a row about gay bishops in the Church of England and a dispute about higher rate taxes in the Labour Party have taken over from the reshuffle. So there my efforts must come to an end for the time being.

There is a serious point to be considered. The basis of the Scots jurisdiction in the House of Lords is the 1689 Claim of Right to appeal to 'the King and Parliament'. Is this why Scots appeals have always come to the House as of right and do not require leave? Then there is Article XIX of the Treaty of Union 1707 which prohibits appeals to any of the English courts 'or any other of the like nature'. With a bit of care these oddities may be sorted out, and one or two other things too, in order to ensure that the new institution has constitutional legitimacy. What is missing is any hint that the Government is taking these points on board or is in the least interested in them. Overall the way in which the thing is being handled, given its importance, is, to be blunt, contemptible.

Mary and I were guests of the Faculty, along with other former Deans, at the Faculty's Biennial Dinner in the Signet Library. There seemed to be more guests than members of Faculty at this splendidly well-handled occasion. We were at a table with Douglas and Rosamund Cullen – Douglas is to be introduced in the House of Lords as Baron Cullen of Whitekirk on Tuesday this coming week – and the Vice-Dean, Roy Martin, and his wife together with the delightful chairmen of the Belfast and Dublin Bars and their wives. It was a most enjoyable party which helped to restore morale a little bit. Suddenly everything in Edinburgh seems so normal and stable in comparison with the revolution which is going on in London, to which I must now return.

5 July 2003

The Supreme Court issue moved forward apace during the last ten days. My piece in *The Times* bore further fruit when I was contacted by BBC Scotland seeking an interview with me. At first it was Reevel Alderson, a senior broadcaster in their news department. We arranged to meet with a view to a programme he wants to do in mid-July when the consultation paper is issued. Then Glenn Campbell, a relatively junior interviewer on BBC Scotland's political programme, asked for an interview on 27 June for broadcasting that evening. I agreed to do this, thinking that it would be a radio broadcast. He then turned up at 34 India Street with a TV cameraman. Fortunately I had just had my hair cut and had put on a shirt and tie. I changed to a smarter tie and put on a jacket to look more presentable. I was then subjected to a 15-minute interview. It was quite like old times, I suppose, as I was used to this as Dean and Lord President. I managed to get my sentences out in the right order, keep to the point and avoid political controversy. The BBC team left, with no need for any retakes. I was telephoned later with the information that they wanted to use part of it on the evening news programme and, just as I was leaving for a drinks party at Edinburgh University to mark the end of Hector MacQueen's term as Dean of the Law School, I heard a piece on BBC Radio Scotland which put my points over very sensibly with an extract from the interview. I missed the television news but was back in time to see the full programme at 9pm. At Hector's party Colin Boyd, the Lord Advocate, came over to tell me that he had heard about the interview and had been invited to comment on it as part of the programme which, rather against advice in his office, he had agreed to do. My bit came over as well as I could have wished for. Colin made his point under rather more cross-examination than I had been exposed to, and there were contributions by Margo MacDonald who was very complimentary about me as well as Gordon Jackson and a Tory MSP. Overall my point that the Scottish position had been overlooked and was in need of attention was being reinforced.

Then things started to move in London. Alan Rodger and I were asked to see Charlie Falconer, the new Secretary of State for Constitutional Affairs and Lord Chancellor. Colin Boyd, who was to see him too, asked to see us as well. These meetings took place on the Tuesday. The meeting with Falconer was at 8.30am in his office in Selborne House, Victoria Street – a characterless office block, which is a far remove from the Lord Chancellor's room in the House of Lords and, of course, far less convenient for us than just going downstairs and along a corridor. We were on time. He overran due to something else, and we were not seen until 8.45am. This caused problems for me, as I had agreed to do a meeting about petitions for leave at 9.15am. Once we got going it was an affable and quite constructive meeting. It was clear that my interventions had prompted it, and that he had done some homework. How much will come out of it we shall see, but at least the Scottish position is being appreciated. It is, I suppose, a slight advantage that Falconer is himself a Scot by birth, if not now by practice or residence. The meeting lasted for about 35 minutes. There was a secretary there to take notes.

Our meeting with Colin Boyd, Patrick Leyden and a senior civil servant from the Scottish Executive was much longer and more detailed. On the whole we were all in agreement about the general line to take: keep the existing system for civil appeals, leave the system for criminal appeals in Scotland alone, move the devolution system from the Judicial Committee of the Privy Council to the new court, insist on a separate institution for the UK in a neutral location, and ask for two Scots and one from Northern Ireland among its membership with an appointments system independent of those for each of the three jurisdictions. I had suggested that the new court should have its own budget and the administration of it, but this was more to make things difficult than to ease it into the present system of departmental responsibility. It looks as though the new court will be run and funded through the Department for Constitutional Affairs (DCA), as are the English courts. The shame is that our advocate in the person of the Lord Chancellor will be so much weaker, as Falconer has nothing like the same muscle power as did Derry Irvine.

Meantime a conversation with Tom Bingham revealed that he had been meeting Hayden Phillips, the Permanent Secretary. Clearly Tom is exercising a lot of influence behind the scenes. This is without consulting us, of course, as he has his own ideas. He has achieved one thing – the separation of the consultation paper on the Supreme Court from that on the new Judicial Appointments Commission for England and Wales. In the first draft, a copy of which Alan Rodger had obtained under the counter as a 'silent copy' from Douglas Cullen, the Supreme Court was tacked onto the end of the Judicial Appointments Commission, underlining my concern about Scotland. So now there will at least be separate papers. Tom has visions of us all being called no longer 'Lord' but 'Justice'. 'Oh God', said Alan Rodger when I passed on this bit of news: 'It gets worse and worse!'

Various people saw me on TV, including the young man in the airport at Edinburgh who gives me my exit ticket for the car park when I get home. He was there when I got to the airport on the Sunday evening and handed me my ticket from the machine. 'I seen you on TV' he said. 'It doesn't happen very often' was my reply.

To Strathclyde University on Friday for the first of the two summer graduation days that I do. Brian Gill, the Lord Justice Clerk, was awarded an Honorary LLD and I had the unusual experience of presenting it to him, as I had done earlier to Hazel Cosgrove. It was a glorious sunny day, the finest weather in the whole country. Then back to Edinburgh for an unusual party at the Scottish Poetry Library in the Canongate. The occasion was the unveiling of a preliminary statue of the Scots poet Robert Fergusson which has been created by David Annand and is to stand, once the full-size version has been completed, in the street outside the Canongate Kirk where he is buried.

13 July 2003

The main event last week was the Lord Mayor's Dinner for HM Judges at the Mansion House in London. This is always a splendid affair: white ties and, if desired, tiaras, music, State trumpeters, a loving cup to share and circulate and speeches by the Lord Mayor, the Lord Chief Justice and the Lord Chancellor. We were unsure as to whether Lord Falconer, the new and temporary Lord Chancellor, would agree to grace the occasion. But he was there, under the anxious and watchful eye of Sir Hayden Phillips, the Permanent Secretary.

When it came to the speeches, after the banquet and the music, the atmosphere was electric. The Lord Mayor, Gavyn Arthur, showed no inhibitions in his attack on the Government's lack of commitment to the funding of the commercial court, which operates (it is said – I have not been there) in thoroughly unsuitable and unprepossessing surroundings. 'Why spend money instead on a Supreme Court?' was the thinly veiled challenge to the Lord Chancellor. He also criticised the proposed ending of the award of silk, which seems to be almost certain now after the forthcoming review is over, on the ground that the kitemark of QC was a distinction that those in other jurisdictions would die for.

Then came Harry Woolf, sometimes hesitant and even diffident. He was on sparkling form this time, and he too showed no inhibitions. He launched into a powerful defence of the judges and a direct attack on many of the highly suspect policies which threaten their independence and the quality of the judiciary. Hayden Phillips looked more and more glum as almost every sentence was greeted with applause by the audience. Marguerite Woolf, who was sitting next to me as I was placed – unaccountably, as I was not the most senior Law Lord there – on the right of the Lady Mayoress, hissed 'There were phone calls all afternoon asking him to change this, but he refused to do so'.

It was inevitable that Lord Falconer's speech would be an anti-climax. He tried a few jokes to start with, including a bizarre reference to me as one of the children he had played with in Edinburgh when young – I was 13 when he was born. Then there was a political speech with its mix of warnings and platitudes, which was listened to in complete silence. At the end, after a toast, there were a few desultory hand claps. There can have been no doubt as to where sympathies lie as to his new radical policies.

The week ended with another graduation day at Strathclyde – anxious as I always am to do my best and to encourage and please my audience, I found the occasion exhausting but full of amusement and pleasure. Mary is a wonderful support. She helps so much to make us both feel part of the team. After it was over we had a meeting with Peter and Margaret West, Margaret Hastie and Professor McGowan to discuss and be briefed on our proposed trip to Malawi in August on behalf of the University: quite a complex exercise, not without its risks and dangers. But we will be doing quite a lot of good for Strathclyde, and their support and organisation is impressive and will make this visit a very real privilege.

19 July 2003

A terrible thing happened this week. The BBC and Downing Street have been at each other's throats for weeks about a report by a BBC reporter, Andrew Gilligan, that, based on information he had received from an unnamed source, the Government had 'sexed up' a Ministry of Defence report on how ready for use Saddam Hussein's weapons of mass destruction really were. Then an MoD civil servant, Dr David Kelly, was named as Andrew Gilligan's source for this report. This was vehemently denied by Downing Street. Dr Kelly was called before a House of Commons committee, where he was plainly ill-at-ease. He was bullied and humiliated. He said, among other things, that he was not the source of the BBC's story. Gilligan, who had earlier given evidence to the committee, was called back before it. He refused to name the source. The committee had suggested that Dr Kelly had been 'set up' by the MoD. That same afternoon Dr Kelly went for a walk in the countryside near his home in Oxford and committed suicide.

The horror of the event, coming as it does after such intense political in-fighting, is hard to describe. Dr Kelly was 59, a highly responsible and respected scientist. He was a member of the UN Weapons Inspection Team that had been active in Iraq, until Saddam Hussein ended their activities. He was highly effective and very well informed. To make matters worse, Parliament is in recess and the Prime Minister was on his way on a world tour from Washington, where he had addressed Congress and had received many standing ovations, to Tokyo. Euphoria turned to tragedy and a real sense of political crisis.

The Opposition had been calling for months for a judicial public inquiry into the so-called 'dodgy' dossier, and the reasons for going to war. Now there is to be a judicial inquiry into Dr Kelly's death and the circumstances surrounding it. Brian Hutton has been chosen to conduct it, and he is to report 'in weeks rather than in months'. It is not a task which any of us would have wished on ourselves. There will be great pressure on him to enlarge his remit beyond the narrow limits which the Government will certainly seek to put on it. There will be awkward decisions to be taken, and the press will fasten on every word and every action – as will the politicians in this fevered, highly dangerous atmosphere. Brian is a safe pair of hands. He will not rock the boat. He is not likely to seek to do any more than he is asked to do. The rest of us will have to plug the gap he leaves on the Law Lords' Corridor as best we can. If this inquiry fails to satisfy what is expected of it, who knows what will happen next?

27 July 2003

It was the Royal Garden Party at Buckingham Palace on Tuesday. Mary was in London already, having spent several days at dressage events during which she stayed for two nights with great enjoyment with Richard and Rima Scott at Foscote. One wonders whether the days of such privileges are numbered for us Law Lords. If we are moved elsewhere the ease of getting to Buckingham Palace from Westminster will be lost. We had a government car to take us to the diplomats' entrance, which meant that there was no queuing – a real privilege. It was a pleasant afternoon, neither too hot nor too windy. Among others we met James Dingemans QC[207] who has just been appointed as counsel to Brian Hutton's inquiry, which means that he will have to give up his summer holiday with his family. He was there in recognition of his having taken silk – another privilege that seems, under this administration, to be on its way out. Then Concorde flew over on its way into Heathrow, giving us a splendid view of this magnificent aircraft which, too, is about to go into history as BA are to end the service in the autumn of this year. Later we walked back to Westminster where Mary's car was parked, and she set off for another dressage engagement in Northumberland.

Brian Hutton seemed very relaxed when we met him on Monday. We – the Law Lords, the Master of the Rolls and the Lord Chief Justice – gathered in the Lord Chancellor's room on Monday to discuss with Lord Falconer who should succeed Lord Millett as a Law Lord when he retires at the end of this year. This was a new experience for Lord Falconer. I think that he may have been surprised by how detailed and informative our discussion was. This time Simon Brown LJ was the front-runner, but Brenda Hale LJ was also much favoured – not only on the ground that we must surely have a woman on the team. It appears that Simon Brown has the advantage. But I suspect that Falconer will jump at the chance and appoint Brenda Hale next time.

We had a delightful dinner party on the Wednesday for our judicial assistants, past and present. There were very few absentees. James Vallance White was there, as were Lords Bingham, Nicholls and Steyn. There were no speeches.

I took over a Privy Council judgment in a capital murder case from Jamaica which Brian had agreed to do but was obviously a burden to him in his present circumstances. That, plus a concurring but quite substantial judgment in a death in prison case called *Amin*[208] in which the issue was whether an independent public investigation was necessary to give effect to the State's duty to protect the lives of those in prison, and tidying up my judgment in a seven-judge case called *Rees*[209] about how to recompense a severely handicapped mother for the extra costs of her having given birth to a healthy child due to the failure of a negligently performed sterilisation operation kept me very busy over the weekend. Now it is back to London for the last week of the term, which promises again to be a busy one.

---

207 Later Mr Justice Dingemans.
208 *R (Amin) v Secretary of State for the Home Department* [2003] UKHL 51, [2004] 1 AC 653.
209 *Rees v Darlington Memorial Hospital NHS Trust* [2003] UKHL 52, [2004] 1 AC 309. The case was complicated by the fact that in *McFarlane v Tayside Health Board* [2000] 2 AC 59 the House had held that in such circumstances the costs which normal, healthy parents would incur were not recoverable. But in this case the mother had a severe visual handicap.

2003 – August to September

10 August 2003

The normal practice, before Brendan Keith became head of the Judicial Office, was for the last week in July to be a light, clearing-up week. This year we were on duty for all three full days. Nine of us were sitting in *Attorney General's Reference (No 2 of 2001)*,[210] and Robert Walker looked after medical appeals with two retired Lords Justices in the Privy Council. Then on Thursday, as most of the others melted away and the House became more and more uninhabitable – the recess for the ordinary peers started two weeks ago, and carpets are up everywhere and people almost nowhere – I sat with Tom Bingham and Lennie Hoffmann on an Appeal Committee in the Privy Council, for which two of the three cases were from Scotland.

The *Attorney General's Reference* case was put out before nine judges because of a potential, perhaps inevitable, conflict with *R v HM Advocate*: see 10 November and 1 December 2002. The case had previously been heard by five chancery/common law judges presided over by Donald Nicholls. They were 5–0 against *R*, hardly surprising as Peter Millett was part of the team and he had been very vocal in promoting his ideas about Article 6(1) of the ECHR and its analysis as regards the reasonable time guarantee. Brian Hutton, Alan Rodger and myself were brought in to give an added UK dimension to the thing, and Tom Bingham was to preside. In the event Brian had to be taken off as he has now to devote all his time to his Inquiry. So we had Richard Scott in his place.

We sat in the Moses Room, which proved to be very comfortable with lots of space and good lighting and acoustics, as it has been recently refurbished for use by Grand Committees on Public Bills not taken for their Committee Stage in the Chamber. We were ranged around a large U-shaped table which had three on each leg and three round the top – very well placed so that we could see each other and benefit from eye contact. I had the pleasure of being seated opposite the magnificent 'Judgment of Daniel' mural by John Rogers Herbert, which has a wonderful scene in the city of Babylon as Daniel confronts Susanna's accusers, full of depth and interest. Counsel were Ben Emmerson QC, David Perry and Hugo Keith. Our doorkeeper said that they were very nervous at having to appear before nine Law Lords. One tends to forget these things, as we are so used to each other and do not find anyone on our side of the Bar in the least formidable. We even have the measure of Lennie and Tom, as we know them so well.

As for the argument, it was largely dominated by Peter Millett. I tried to keep the other point of view in play, as occasionally did Alan Rodger. At the head of the table Donald, Tom and Johan Steyn were largely silent. When it came to summing-up Alan spoke for 30 minutes, setting out the case for consistency

---

210 [2003] UKHL 68, [2004] 2 AC 72.

with *R v HM Advocate* very well, but his thoughts fell on deaf ears. Peter Millett went on and on for three-quarters of an hour – so long and so repetitive that Alan hoped, as he told me later, that he had bored everyone so much that they would reject his views. That did not happen. Richard Scott, without much understanding of the issues, and John Hobhouse, with more concern and insight, were on Peter's side. At this point, as we made our way up the ladder of seniority, we began to run out of time. Rather than come back for more another day, we cut things short for the remainder. I was ten minutes, and Lennie much the same. The senior three were shorter still. Tom, I had hoped, would join Alan and me, but he did not do so. Donald urged him to write the main judgment for the majority. Alan said that he did not think that *R v HM Advocate* could survive, and that he proposed to say so. This is a matter of some importance, as section 103 of the Scotland Act says that in devolution matters Privy Council cases are binding in every court. Later, as Alan and I chewed over what had happened, we began to wonder whether a coherent opinion can be written to express the majority view, and whether *R* might still survive.

The issue really is very narrow. We are all agreed that the scope of the remedy for a breach of the reasonable time requirement under the Human Rights Act is wider than under the Scotland Act. The English are very anxious not to be driven into a corner and forced to say that there always has to be a stay in the prosecution where the requirement is breached. But there is no need for this. Section 8 of the Human Rights Act allows a choice of remedies, while section 57(2) of the Scotland Act does not. But the problem in the Scottish context is different, as cases which raise this issue, as compared with time issues under the Criminal Procedure (Scotland) Act 1995, are so rare. As I write Tom's draft opinion has just arrived in the post from London. He has not explored the Human Rights Act context at all, and there is the inevitable logical inconsistency of saying that to proceed to trial is not incompatible with Article 6(1) and then going on to discuss remedies which are only relevant if to do so is unlawful, and it can only be unlawful if it is incompatible. That is exactly what Alan and I had predicted.

The comfort of the Moses Room, and the ease of discussion which it promoted, meant that it was really a very harmonious and enjoyable case despite this major difference of viewpoint. It was a good way to end the term, all in each other's company.

A heatwave was beginning to affect London, so it was a relief to escape on Bmi's flight, the BD64, at 20.45hrs to Edinburgh with a clutch of papers for written work still to do – three judgments of no great length, including one of the Scottish cases in the Appeal Committee (*Scott Davidson v Scottish Ministers*[211]), and of course the papers in *Attorney General's Reference (No 2)*. I spent a rather intense weekend on my return home getting the other things out of the way before I could begin to contemplate the vacation.

---

211 *Davidson v Scottish Ministers (No 3)* 2005 SC (HL) 1.

Among other things to engage my thoughts, apart from getting ready for our visit to Malawi starting on 16 August, are two lectures as yet scarcely started and one almost ready due to be given next session: the Sir William Dale Lecture in October, the Essex/Clifford Chance Lecture in January and the Royal Aeronautical Society/Beaumont Lecture in February. To my relief the Dale Lecture which I had been working on since April was almost ready and I was able to complete it without too much difficulty. The Essex/Clifford Chance Lecture is on Torture; a gruesome subject which I chose to match my predecessor Tom Bingham's piece on Slavery last time. I found quite a lot of material at home, including some old Scots, about what was going on in Scotland during the latter part of the seventeenth century when torture had ceased to be used in England, to add to some other stuff I had been gathering. So this is now making good progress. The Beaumont Lecture, which I have already begun, can remain in the background for now. So I feel a bit more at ease and – in some really lovely weather – was able to relax during two very energetic days cutting grass and tidying up at Craighead ready for the holiday.

Time ticks by, of course. I have now completed seven years as a Law Lord in London – the same period as my time as Lord President. So I have done 14 years on the Bench. Life at the Bar seems increasingly remote and in the past. My library here at 34 India Street, which I have kept up, continues to serve me very well, however. The whole environment in which I work is very pleasant and enjoyable, with a pleasing air of informality which adds to the enjoyment.

I was fortunate enough to be included among guests at the opening of the Scottish National Gallery/Royal Scottish Academy refurbishment and the 2003 Monet Exhibition this week. Sir Timothy Clifford, the exuberant and colourful Director, was in charge on one side, and there was a clutch of thoughtful, more reserved academicians on the other. There were familiar faces from my past – Malcolm Rifkind, Ian Lang, David Steel and Jack Straw among others. The Prince of Wales opened the Exhibition in his typical disarming way. I was delighted to be there – and wondered why I had been so honoured.

16 August 2003

In two hours' time Mary and I set off for Malawi where we are to spend two weeks on business for Strathclyde University and the CMJA. The first week will involve four days of visits to clinics, orphanages, the University of Malawi and to the President himself – President Muluzi, who is one of Strathclyde's Honorary Graduates. Then we have two days off for a brief safari before going to the conference with the CMJA. I regard this trip with some apprehension as the risks of road accidents, diseases and other misfortunes are not inconsiderable. On the other hand to be welcomed into this lovely country as Chancellor of Strathclyde will be a real privilege, and we are bound to see some things that the ordinary visitor would not see. So we leave, with our luggage somewhat weighed down with certificates, US dollars and simple presents such as pens, notebooks, pencil sharpeners and rubbers to hand out during our visits.

2 September 2003

Somewhat to my surprise we returned unscathed from Malawi yesterday, having suffered from nothing more than slight tummy trouble on the way. It was a very busy, intense visit. We have learned a great deal about the country and have returned with many happy memories, some carvings and my appointment as President of the CMJA.

Yesterday evening, having just had time to unpack, I went to the Royal Society of Edinburgh to sign the Roll of Fellows. There was a ceremony, a lecture given by Professor Neil Hood and an informal dinner afterwards. There were one or two familiar figures – Sir Ian Robinson, an Honorary Graduate of Strathclyde, and Tam Dalyell. Strathclyde was well represented, with several of us there, including Neil Hood. Lord Robertson of Port Ellen was given an Honorary Fellowship. The lecture was relaxed and enjoyable, and so was the dinner with Lord Sutherland of Houndwood, the President, in charge. I doubt whether I shall be able to make much of my membership as meetings are mainly on Mondays when I am in London. But it is a very welcome privilege to have been made a member of this very fine Institution which has so many prominent Scots amongst its Fellowship.

26 September 2003

We returned today from Craighead, and are about to go to Madrid for a Spanish-British Judicial Exchange before the Michaelmas term begins next week. This is a turnaround which is rather too quick and complex for comfort. But the offer of a visit to Madrid seems too good to resist.

Meantime various things have happened. Our new team of judicial assistants – Anna Burne, Laura Johnston, David Blundell and Joanne Clement – has arrived and they have begun to settle in. The Hutton Inquiry, which has been going on throughout August and September, has just completed its public hearings. Brian has now retired to prepare his report. He has conducted the process with great politeness, restraint and dignity. As Magnus Linklater put it in today's *Times*, he has listened to the evidence gravely and courteously and has spoken very little. James Dingemans QC, as I expected, has proved to be impeccable as counsel to the Inquiry, a master of his brief. As he put it at the end of his speech, 'Somewhere along the way we have lost a summer. I hope we exchange it for understanding'. We shall not have Brian back with us until December at the least.

Very sadly Gareth Williams, Lord Williams of Mostyn, died suddenly last week of a heart attack. He was a former Attorney General and was currently the Leader of the House of Lords. This is a great loss. He was a brilliant spokesman for his Government, able to find many touches of wit and humour to spice up and add appeal to some stern positions he was adopting on the crucial questions of House of Lords reform and getting the Government's business through the House. I confess to having regarded him recently as a rather dangerous and sinister character. But that was because he was so effective. I suspect that in Cabinet he was just as effective as an advocate on behalf of the House of Lords, where he could reconcile his reforming zeal with what was constitutionally appropriate. To have lost both him and Derry Irvine in just a few months is a real blow. The door is open for David Blunkett – hugely hostile to the judges, especially – to force his views in upon us. Lord Falconer, the new (and temporary) Lord Chancellor, has already sold the pass to him. He takes a very low place at the Cabinet table and will carry very little weight.

Draft judgments in *Attorney General's Reference (No 2 of 2001)* have started to come in. As I predicted, Tom Bingham has found it difficult to produce a coherent argument to support the majority view which he does indeed support. It is a disappointing opinion. So far Lords Millett, Steyn and Scott have concurred. Alan Rodger and I produced lengthy dissenting opinions. I did mine early in August, and Alan wrote his early in September. We showed each other what we had written before circulation. We are, of course, in complete agreement. The Scottish problem has driven our approach as to how the issue is to be analysed. We believe that we are right and that the English, looking over their shoulders at the result rather than how to achieve it, are wrong. But I fear that there will be no recanting by the majority. The result will be a muddle, most unfortunate for a bench of nine judges. If ever there was a need for sound, careful analysis, it was here. Tom has failed to achieve this – or so I believe.

2003 – October to December

4 October 2003

Last weekend Mary and I went to Madrid as part of a British-Spanish judicial conference. In the event all went off very well. Our team leader was Jonathan Mance, who had led the British team last time when the Spanish came to London. The others were Richard Scott, Jonathan Parker LJ, Stephen Sedley LJ, Lord Carloway (Colin Sutherland) from Scotland and Michael Burton J. Wives came as well, except that Michael Burton who is a widower brought his daughter. We were all met as we arrived on different flights at the airport, were given special treatment and were accommodated in a very comfortable hotel in the centre of Madrid. It was once a palace and had the renowned footballer David Beckham and his wife as permanent guests. Rumour has it that she is not happy in Madrid. Jonathan Parker overheard an argument between them on the staircase which seemed to bear this out. Neither Mary nor I saw the great man.

Our meetings were with judges from the Spanish Supreme Court. Conversation in Spanish was possible only for Mance and Sedley, who had been learning the language. But we were greatly helped by the fact that Rima Scott and Jonathan Parker's wife, who is known as 'MB' and is Spanish, also speak the language and several of the Spanish judges spoke quite good English. Instantaneous translation was provided at the meetings, which was essential. There was too much reading of lectures and too little time for discussion to make much useful progress. But criminal justice, asylum and EC Directives provided good discussion points. It is clear that the judges in Spain are not held in very high esteem, and that the advocates are not bound to the same ethical standards as members of the professions in the UK. We saw an appeal hearing which seemed a waste of time and money, as the addresses were simply read out and there was no interplay between the Bar and the Bench in the form of questioning. In some respects, however, there was room for common ground. The Spanish had felt that they were very well treated in London, and they were most hospitable and generous. The visit ended with a visit to Toledo, where a huge number of serins were coming in to roost in mimosa trees in a square close to the Cathedral and a flock of storks had chosen the towers of a nearby monastery as their roosting place.

We returned to Heathrow together on Wednesday 1 October. I was too late to attend the Abbey service, which was Lord Falconer's first and probably his last as Lord Chancellor. He did not make a good impression. He did not wear a wig or robes, of course, being determined to show that he is not a judge. He read a short lesson too fast and had no feel for the language, said Alan Rodger who was there. At the end of the service, instead of leading a procession of judges, he scurried out of the back (says Alan) and I saw him arrive at the St Stephen's entrance by motor car to get into position to receive the judges for the Breakfast while Harry Woolf, the Lord Chief Justice, leading the judges' procession, had to stand waiting outside the Abbey.

Next day, Thursday, I was with Tom Bingham and Nico Browne-Wilkinson on petitions in the Privy Council. That evening I was a guest at the dinner of a Franco-British Judicial Colloquium in the Middle Temple. David Keene LJ was the organiser, and I was asked to attend as a senior judge and 'say a few words'. This was rather daunting, as my French has become rusty again. I had worked out a speech of a kind, but things were made more complicated by the fact that David Keene had persuaded the Lord Chancellor to attend and say a few words also. It was unclear how this was all to be done, but in the event the speeches were made from the top table as soon as the guests had sat down. Falconer made his brief, rather boring and repetitive speech of welcome. I then spoke partly in French and partly in English. I took as my theme 'Change', starting with the increase in average speed to over 70 km per hour in England which has now been achieved by Eurostar, the last weeks of flying over London by Concorde whose service is to end this month, and then moving to the constitutional changes in the UK. I thought it wise to cut out some of the things I was going to say in jest about the Lord Chancellor. Instead I diverted to congratulations for the choices for discussion at the meeting of matters on life and death. It was a reasonable presentation, to which Guy Canivet, Premier President of the Cour de Cassation, replied. I had the pleasure of sitting beside him and Mme Myriam Ezratty of the Paris Cour d'Appel and my old friend Roger Errera who was there too. Robert Reed, Anne Smith and Sheriff Noel McPartland were there from Scotland, as well at Peter Beaton who has retired from the Government service and moved instead to Turcan Connell as an international expert.

On Friday I spent an hour and a half listening to the opening of this conference which included addresses by Elizabeth Butler-Sloss and Roger Errera and a fine summing-up by Anne Smith. Then I had to get out to Heathrow for a lunchtime plane to Edinburgh as that evening I was to attend an RSE event for new fellows with Mary where I had to make yet another speech. That, however, is now all behind me. I can settle down to the business of reading, listening and writing and to the old, practised routine of moving between London and Edinburgh as we face the trials and tribulations of a new term beset by constitutional problems of various kinds.

24 October 2003

Concorde flew over London and Edinburgh for the last time today. This wonderful aircraft has lost its market, all as the consequences of a fatal accident in Paris about three years ago. And the events since 11 September 2001 have collapsed the demand for first-class air travel. Yesterday evening at Heathrow, as I was waiting for my flight home, I heard the long roar of it taking off for New York into the darkness. Today I caught a final sight of it as a last flight over the UK from Edinburgh to London and back again came in over the Forth to Edinburgh Airport – a glimpse, through a gap in Doune Terrace as I walked down into Moray Place. It has been so familiar in London over these last few years – passing over Westminster at about 5.30pm on its way in, with the familiar deep sound and then the sight of the thin body with long wheels lowered as it adjusted them for landing. And then at Heathrow in the evenings, sometimes seen magnificently from the BA Shuttle lounge as it raced down the runway and rose, with white heat shining from the afterburners in its engines, into the sky. Much of the magic of Heathrow, where there was always the possibility of that sighting, will go. To travel in Concorde, as Mary and I found once on a journey to Washington in 1995, was a wonderful experience. But seeing and hearing it was magnificent too.

Donald Nicholls and I met the Project Team to discuss the new Supreme Court building this week. Out of 200 possibles a shortlist of five has been selected – depressing in its low quality: apart from the west wing of Somerset House, two dreadful places in Holborn/Chancery Lane – Central Court and Bream's Buildings – and a place in Bloomsbury called Victoria House, all of which are to be ruled out as unsuitable, and 4 Matthew Parker Street, which is an office building down a back street behind the Methodist Central Hall at Westminster. The west wing of Somerset House is occupied by the Inland Revenue, who have not allowed the inside to be inspected, and is under the protection of English Heritage. The Project Team have little grasp of what we really need, which is why we were meeting them. But the real problem is the building. Either we have nowhere to go, in which event the whole sad exercise is a complete waste of time. Or we are to be shoved off into temporary accommodation, which would be a disaster.

Brenda Hale has, as I had expected, been appointed a Lord of Appeal in Ordinary. This raises the problem of address. Convention in the House is that all peers are addressed as 'My Lords' collectively, irrespective of whether ladies are present. But she will not like that. Tom, who has little feeling for the conventions of the House,[212] may feel that she should be accommodated in this somehow. Are counsel now to begin their speeches with 'My Lords and Lady'? The answer, surely, as we are the masters of our own procedure in the hearing of appeals, is that they must do so.

2 November 2003

Iain Duncan Smith, who had never looked convincing as leader of the Tory party and would clearly have lost the next General Election, was voted out of office by a vote of no confidence this week. His successor is Michael Howard, a much more astute, aggressive and presentable character – although there is, as the press have been reminding us ever since he emerged as the front runner, 'something of the night about him' as his fellow Conservative MP, Ann Widdecombe, famously said when he was Home Secretary in John Major's Government. He had professed to be a supporter of Iain Duncan Smith before the vote was taken. But I caught sight of him as I followed him and an assistant into lunch at Strangers before the vote, and it was absolutely obvious from his barely concealed excitement – glowing, one could say with the thrill of it – that he knew that it was all over for IDS and that his hour had come.

30 November 2003

This week there came before the House what some have said is the most important Scots appeal of the century: *Burnett's Trustee v Grainger*.[213] It raises the issue as to the rights of a permanent trustee in bankruptcy to heritable property belonging to the bankrupt which was the subject of a delivered, but as yet unrecorded, disposition in favour of purchasers in good faith and for value. The standard answer for over 100 years has been that the real right in the property remains with the seller until the purchaser records his disposition in the Register. So a permanent trustee who records his notice of title first takes an absolute right to the property, unaffected by the personal obligations owed by the bankrupt to the purchaser. Instability to this system was introduced by the decision of the House of Lords in *Sharp v Thomson*[214] in which Lords Jauncey

---

212 The convention is that in all meetings in the House, whether in the Chamber or in committees, peers are addressed collectively as 'My Lords', whatever their gender. It was agreed, however, that the phrase 'My Lords and Lady' was to be used by counsel when Lady Hale was present, as this was already the convention in the Court of Appeal.
213 [2004] UKHL 8, 2004 SC (HL) 19.
214 1997 SC (HL) 66.

and Clyde, for reasons not wholly consistent with each other, delivered speeches overruling the decision of the Inner House in that case in which I was sitting as Lord President. That case concerned a similar situation in the context of a floating charge. Here we were faced with a similar argument in the context of personal bankruptcy.

Our Committee consisted of Lords Bingham, Hoffmann, myself, Hobhouse and Rodger. Stuart Gale appeared for the appellant purchasers and Patrick Hodge for the trustee. Hodge was in *Sharp* also, and has been deeply involved in this argument from the beginning. Gale has been in this case from the start, but was not up to Hodge's standard in knowledge of detail and the quality of his advocacy. It ought to have been a fairly easy case to dispose of. Professors Kenneth Reid and David Carey Miller, steeped in the history and practice of Scots property law, came along to observe the hearing.

In the event it was far from easy, and I could see the professors becoming increasingly worried as the argument went on. Predictably Lennie Hoffmann began to open things up, expressing astonishment that the trustee could walk off with both the house and the price when the bankrupt herself could plainly not have done so. John Hobhouse prodded away at the idea of trusts as a solution – something which Scots law has always set its face against and which would cause great confusion among creditors. Then Alan Rodger opened up as well. He is no admirer of Kenneth Reid – in contrast to the view which I hold of him and of what he has done to explore and explain property law in a way that has never been done before with such clarity. But Alan is an academic himself, who takes nothing for granted. Also he is Glasgow – not, as Reid is, Edinburgh. It was Alan's sharp and rather querulous style of questioning when Patrick Hodge started his argument that gave rise to real alarm on Kenneth Reid's part. Some of the propositions which Alan put forward as he was testing the argument were very strange, and I could see Reid jerking his head in astonished bewilderment. At the end of the second day I felt that it was really all over and that I would be left alone in a minority of one.

Then the day of the State Opening intervened. We had to take a day off, as the House devoted itself to the ceremonial and the Appellate Committee could not sit. So I asked Kenneth Reid to observe the procession from my room. He loved this and was a model guest. No mention was made of the case until we were saying goodbye, when I remarked that I thought that he was in need of rest and recuperation. He admitted that he was feeling tense and uneasy about the case.

The interval helped Alan to do some more research of his own. He came to see me first thing next morning to say that he felt that the appeal could not succeed, and that it was plain we were – thank goodness – now of the same view. When we came to discuss the case Lennie Hoffmann and John Hobhouse said that they would allow the appeal for the reasons they had deployed in the argument. Alan and I said we would dismiss it, for detailed reasons which we both gave. Fortunately Tom Bingham, who had remained in the background during the hearing, said that he was not prepared to disagree with a unanimous Court of Session and the two Scots Law Lords on a point of Scots law. 'I do not wish to create alarm in the drawing rooms in Edinburgh', he said. So the day had been saved, and Alan and I can write in the knowledge that Tom will support us.

How fortunate we are that Tom was in the chair. Donald Nicholls might not have taken the same view, and Nico Browne-Wilkinson, who dominated the discussion in *Sharp* where he was the chairman, would almost certainly not have done so. On such slender threads does the purity of Scots law hang when appeals come to London.

6 December 2003

Most unusually a case we were due to hear this week in the House of Lords settled – a six-day case it was – leaving a gap which it was hard to fill with enthusiasm, so used is one to sitting during the week. I spent much of my time putting together a supporting speech in the *Grainger* case. But there were other distractions too. I had to chair two lectures – one at Kings on EU Law on Monday with Professor van Gerven, and the other at UCL on Genetically Modified Organisms on Thursday with Dr Joanne Scott. On Wednesday I went to another of Professor van Gerven's lectures on the EU draft constitution. On Tuesday I chaired the autumn meeting of the Council of the Institute of Advanced Legal Studies of which I am Chairman at which the Librarian, Jules Winterton, very ably stood in for Professor Barry Rider, the Director, who has been suspended pending an investigation for breach of contract. The remarkable thing is how smoothly the Institute is running without him. They could run just as well without me too, I suspect, but I am only a figurehead really. How things will be when a decision is taken on Barry Rider's future is hard to predict. Getting a new Director, if that is needed, will not be easy and trying to build things up again if he comes back will not be all that easy either. Perhaps I will have more of a role after all.

The most interesting event of the week was giving evidence to the House of Commons Constitutional Affairs Committee. The chairman was Alan Beith, a Liberal Democrat MP. Other members known to me were Keith Vaz and Ross Cranston. Other familiar names were Peter Bottomley and Clive Soley. The atmosphere was pleasant and the questions well-informed and politely put. I am not sure how effective I was or what sort of impression I made. Nor am I sure what influence, if any, this Committee has on what is going on. Rather too little, I suspect. I was asked about the Act of Union and possible challenges, which I tried to play down, and about risks for Scotland in the new arrangement, to which I responded more vigorously. There was a piece about my evidence next day in *The Herald*, and a second letter which was sympathetic to my complaint that there were important Scottish issues which the speed of the project seems likely to ignore. Joshua Rozenberg was there too, but there was not much in what I said that was of interest to *The Daily Telegraph*. The Committee took my evidence first. Then there was a witness from Northern

Ireland, Brice Dickson of the Human Rights Commission for Northern Ireland – ubiquitous on these occasions. He suggested that the Supreme Court should have a member from the Irish Republic when it is considering issues arising from the Good Friday Agreement. Then two witnesses from Wales recommended that there should be a Welsh Speaker on the Court and that hearings should be in Welsh when the Court is sitting in Cardiff. All this was rather entertaining. The reality is that it is hard to imagine a sufficient volume of cases coming our way to justify requiring that one of our number must speak Welsh and our sitting in Cardiff, however desirable that might be.

On Monday evening, after the lecture, I was a guest at one of Lord Falconer's judicial dinners. He is working his way through the judiciary, on a getting-to-meet-them exercise. This is very good of him although the Lord Chancellor's residence, in which he does not reside, is a shadow of the bright, homely and friendly place that it was when James and Bett Mackay were living there. He was, as ever, very affable and friendly. But he does not listen much – and there was, of course, no discussion of the really important issues.

Last week, I should have mentioned, Tom invited himself to my Gray's Inn flat after a lecture by Johan Steyn as he had to change for a dinner at Gray's Inn. He had met up with Derry Irvine, who invited himself for a drink with me as well. Fortunately I had a bottle of quite reasonable Vouvray which I had bought to offer drinks to the Faculty team who were appearing in the *Grainger* case along with Alan Rodger, at his suggestion. So, by happy chance, I was able to entertain Derry in the style to which he is accustomed. He is relaxing in his retirement, basking in the general chorus of approval for what he stood for as the protector of judicial independence and of disapproval of Charlie Falconer.

14 December 2003

I am about to set off for the last week of term before Christmas. A heavy week lies ahead. There will be a three-day constitutional case from Mauritius, in which I am the junior on the team so I will have to sum up, and a day of petitions in the Privy Council for which I am in the chair. There are engagements each evening and most lunchtimes too, as it is so near Christmas.

Last week saw two quite separate chasms appear in our treatment of human rights issues in relation to the mandatory death penalty in some of the Caribbean States, which leave me with a feeling of huge regret at our inability to get our minds to meet on these issues. To a large extent the fault lies with those whom the outside world might regard as most committed to human rights: Lords Bingham and Steyn. The problem is that they are campaigners for the abolition of the mandatory death penalty, not jurists, when it comes to these issues. They see the target ahead very clearly and bend everything in their endeavour to get there. Of course we all abhor the death penalty, and that for it to be mandatory is even more abhorrent. And we can all admire their desire for change. But this, surely, is not how a constitutional court should behave. There are plenty of statements in the books, some from these two themselves indeed, that make it plain that our duty is not to strive for values but to construe the constitution. To do otherwise is divination, as Sir Sydney Kentridge once famously said. Yet this advice is not being heeded. Lip service only, it would seem.

The worst offender is *Roodal v The State*,[215] a case from Trinidad and Tobago about the mandatory death penalty for murder. An attack was maintained against it on the ground that this penalty was unconstitutional. That would have been all very well, had it not been for the existing laws clause in the State's Constitution which preserves the laws that the new State inherited from the UK before the death penalty was abolished in this country. On a plain reading of it, the clause has preserved the mandatory penalty as part of the law of Trinidad from being held void by reference to the Constitution's human rights provisions, which prohibit cruel and unusual punishment, unless and until the law is changed by the required majority. Tom Bingham is so vehemently against the fact that the penalty is mandatory that he tried to get us all to sign up to a letter, to be written by us as judges of the Privy Council, to protest against an enactment in Barbados of 2002 which entrenched the mandatory death penalty there from any consideration by the judges. We refused to do this as it would compromise our independence, so he wrote to the Lord Chancellor about it privately instead. Needless to say, Johan Steyn's mind is already made up. Robert Walker, who had been a silent unknown quantity on the issue, went along with them. Peter Millett and Alan Rodger dissented in a long and vehement judgment, which Alan wrote, in an effort to expose the fallacies in Steyn's reasoning on behalf of the majority. Needless to say (again!) all his efforts had no effect. The majority were unmoved, and their judgment is unaltered. Now the flaws in the majority judgment have, within three weeks, been exposed in the hearing before a differently constituted tribunal in a case on the same point from Barbados. All the defects are there to see – the points skated over or not addressed, all under the guise of how constitutions are to be constituted 'in the law of today', as Johan puts it. And all the chaos and uncertainty which this ill-considered approach has created for Trinidad has been revealed too. That case (*Boyce v The Queen*) will now have to be reheard before seven judges in view of the conflict of authority.[216] On the present team are Steyn and Millett – but Hoffmann, Nicholls and I are all with Millett's approach, except that we feel that we cannot ignore *Roodal*. When *Boyce* will be reheard and before whom has yet to be determined.

Of course there is also *Attorney General's Reference (No 2 of 2001)*,[217] which disagreed with *R v HM Advocate* by 7–2 with Alan Rodger and myself in the minority. Here the shame is not nearly as great. It is a minor constitutional hiccup by comparison. But I still feel that, with a little more care and

---

215 [2003] UKPC 78, [2005] 1 AC 328.,
216 In the event, because of the importance of the case, the constitution of the Board was increased to nine: see 2 April 2004.
217 See fn 210. See also *Spiers v Ruddy* [2007] UKPC D2, 2009 SC (PC) 1, discussed in the entry for 9 November 2007.

willingness to discuss and try to agree on a mutually acceptable solution, this difference too could have been avoided. It all went wrong when Johan Steyn decided to dissent in R on grounds which were plainly directed at problems in the English criminal justice system which do not occur in Scotland because the regime on delay here is so different. Whether R can now survive is for another day. I fear that it will not, unless the English members of the team can bring themselves to see that Scots law is entitled to be different.

31 December 2003

The term ended with a week in the Privy Council. For three days I was in the now unusual position, for me, of being the junior member of the team, as Tom and Johan were joined by Gordon Slynn and Tony Lloyd for a case about the right to education under the Constitution of Mauritius. It was an interesting and enjoyable case, but hard work. We ended up divided 3–2 in the Mauritius case, with Tony and myself on one side, in favour of the argument presented by the Roman Catholic Church, and the others on the other. My presentation after the hearing was carefully prepared, but in the event rather short as we had to give a decision that afternoon and time was pressing. As Tony said to me afterwards, although we are in disagreement with the others, there is not much point in our putting our thoughts in writing. The case is not of the widest significance. It is a point of law relating only to the wording of the Constitution of Mauritius. Written dissents are not needed every time there is a difference of view on the Privy Council. There are too many of them as it is.

On the last day I was in the chair in the House of Lords' Appeal Committee for a round of petitions for special leave. I do not much enjoy them. Much preparation is needed, and pressure is required too, to keep each oral hearing short so as not to overrun the programme. But it was an uneventful day and I was free in good time to clear up and travel home by a BA flight which was at last on time.

On Wednesday at lunchtime we had a party to say goodbye to our three leavers: Brian Hutton, John Hobhouse and Peter Millett. They are all junior to me, so I remain fifth on our list. Brian retires due to long service and on grounds of age. He has been a judge since 1979 and he will be 73 next January. John sadly retires on grounds of ill-health, although he too is in his 70s. He will be 72 in January. He has dropsy and is in a quite serious condition which he has borne with much courage. Peter Millett retires to give all his attention to being Treasurer of Lincoln's Inn, which Ann Millett will enjoy to the full as much as he. But he too, although seemingly much younger, is in his 70s as he will be 72 in January. I shall miss all of them: Peter for his unfailing good humour, John for his steadiness and careful attention to detail and Brian for his friendship and support on so many occasions. A new team of Brenda Hale (Monday 12 January will be 'Hale Day', says Alan Rodger), Bob Carswell and Simon Brown will inject a different atmosphere into the Corridor. Work will be done faster I suspect. Brian and John were very slow to produce judgments, due to their painstaking and perhaps rather outdated working methods and a greater caution and conservatism than most of the rest of us possess. Of the three, Simon will keep up the spirit of good humour. Bob will drop neatly into Brian's shoes as our man from Northern Ireland, and Brenda will be a source of some anxiety until we adjust to the very different contribution that she will make. Above all this hangs the spectre of the Supreme Court, the Bill for which will emerge by the end of January.

2004 – January to April

6 January 2004

For once I had no judgments to prepare over the Christmas and New Year period. Instead I was faced with the arduous business of preparing two rather important lectures. One is for Essex University/Clifford Chance on 'Torture', the other for the Law Group of the Royal Aeronautical Society on 'Air Law'. The invitations to give these lectures, one on 28 January, the other on 25 February, came in ages ago. But as usual it was impossible to settle down to the task during term time. I gathered a great deal of material on both subjects with the help of first Emma Parker and then Joanne Clement, my admirable judicial assistants, and brought it home with me. I set about 'Air Law' first and managed to get it done just before Christmas. 'Torture' was rather interrupted by our New Year festivities with so many family commitments, but I finished that too yesterday. In the end some good ideas emerged, and the two pieces hang together reasonably well – each equipped liberally with footnotes, in case of publication afterwards. The sense of relief at having these great tasks, for in each case there will be an important and critical audience, behind me is very great.

Alan Rodger spent his time working on his judgment in *Burnett's Trustee v Grainger*: see 30 November 2003. It is, fortunately, in line with the draft which I prepared during a light week in December but hugely filled out with the products of his own researches in the Advocates Library. The result is perhaps too long and too detailed to be a masterpiece. But it will be even more difficult for the two English judges to dissent from what he and I, with Tom's reluctant support, have said about the case. Alan's restless determination to get to the bottom of every point and to question every proposition, however familiar and from whatever source, is quite remarkable. His piece is more in the character of an academic paper than a judicial opinion. He would be more at home, one suspects, as a Regius Professor in Oxford which he often visits. Nevertheless he is up there with the greatest judicial figures for the depth of his learning and scholarship.

24 January 2004

The most interesting event of the week, during which I sat for the first time with our new Law Lords Brenda Hale, Bob Carswell and Simon Brown, was a meeting about the proposed Supreme Court. It was with the members of a so-called OGC Group, three senior civil servants, who had been asked to assess the feasibility of the project as 'a high risk' project. On our side were Donald Nicholls, Richard Scott and myself. We answered various questions about how much, or how little, we had been told and explained why several of the buildings on the shortlist for the accommodation of the new court which they had prepared were wholly unsuitable for our purposes. But the most significant piece of information came from their side. We were told that the Treasury's position is that the expenses of running the Supreme Court (apart of course from our own salaries) will have to be met entirely out of our fees.

This is not surprising, as the Treasury has been arguing about this for years with court services up and down the country. But it is also quite devastating. Much of our present operation is subsidised because so many of our facilities are provided to us by Parliament – all the support services, the library, the doorkeepers, the rooms and their heating and maintenance, etc. There is a figure of about £250,000 which we provide to the House from what we charge litigants for the use of our services to defray some of the costs. But they are nothing like the costs we would have to face if we were on our own. At a rough guess the annual cost of doing this would be about £1.5m. This would represent an increase in our fees of 600%. Thus access to justice at our level would be denied to almost everyone.

I had always thought that the financing of the project would prove to be an obstacle. But I did not foresee it in quite this form in our case. But it serves to confirm the fears which have always lain below the surface in my opposition to the proposal – which the Government has locked itself into but not, of course, thought through. Sooner or later it was bound to happen, and better now that the issue should surface. Concerns that we should be given freedom to run our own budget will disappear if the consequence is to be that we are going to have to do it all ourselves without a subvention from Government. But all the promises we have been getting from Charlie Falconer about equipping the building to the highest standard suitable for a court of our position are quite worthless if he cannot – as he must know he cannot – deliver the money to finance this year after year into the future. In effect, by setting out to equip the court to this standard, he is leading us into a trap. We will be equipping ourselves to a level which, given the only source from which we can fund it, we cannot afford.

I have written letters to Sir Hayden Phillips, the Permanent Secretary of the DCA, and to Colin Boyd, the Lord Advocate, drawing attention to this development and, in Sir Hayden's case, seeking guidance about the excuse that I cannot give advice about the library provision which I have been asked to do until I know what we are to be able to afford. Donald Nicholls, whose silent reaction to these problems I find difficult to fathom, was so unresponsive to this information that I did not consult him before writing. But, as Richard Scott advised, I let him have a copy of my letter which has evoked no response either. Perhaps I was too forward. But I am angry at the naivety of those who have led us into this trap – Johan Steyn and Tom Bingham, who ought to have known better, among them – and the deceit which has been perpetrated by Government which is yet to tell the public that this is what the project will involve.

30 January 2004

At last Brian Hutton's report has been published, during a week of considerable drama in the political arena. The week began with two potential blows to Tony Blair's premiership. One was a rebellion in the Labour Party at Westminster against his policy for tuition fees in the English universities. It was suggested that the opposition to it was so strong that he would lose the vote on a Second Reading of the Bill, despite a massive Commons majority. A great deal of pressure was brought to bear, deals were done and concessions were made and in the event the vote was won by five votes. The relief on the faces of the Government Ministers in the Lords was massive – broad smiles and generous gestures. There was great disappointment, of course, among the Opposition. The Bill will still be very difficult to handle, but a vote which had become in effect a vote of confidence was won – and a win is a win, however thin the margin.

The focus of attention then passed to Lord Hutton. Much was expected of him, as he had conducted his Inquiry with great attention to detail, courtesy and dignity. In the event there was a huge feeling of disappointment. He levelled serious criticisms at the BBC, which was expected, but none, so it appears, at any of the organs of Government, which was not. It has been described as one-sided, as a whitewash. Blair has been seen gloating at the result, which was a complete victory for him over the BBC. It had accused him of lying over the claim by Andrew Gilligan that he knew there was no evidence to support the allegation that Saddam Hussein's weapons of mass destruction could be operated within 45 minutes. To describe him as gloating may be unfair – relief and delight were more possibly the emotions. But his former spin doctor Alistair Campbell, who too was exonerated, called for apologies and more from the BBC. Now the Director General, the Chairman of the Governors and Andrew Gilligan have all resigned and the BBC is in crisis. The public are unwilling to accept this result. Two-thirds, on a rough poll, think that the report has missed the point and that the result is wholly unfair.

All of this comes as no real surprise, although I confess to a feeling of great disappointment too. As I said at the start, Brian was a safe pair of hands. Charlie Falconer chose his judge well. His instincts were to stick precisely to as narrow a brief as possible in his investigations into the circumstances of Dr Kelly's death. He was instinctively prone to criticise journalists, and it was probably not too difficult for him to condemn the handling of the affair by the BBC. But the devious, almost sinister, workings of government have left him quite unmoved – again instinctively very cautious in criticising anything there. His report reads like his judgments. There is much quotation, no attempt to proclaim, declaim or dramatise. The sentences are long and precise and complex, rather than direct and immediate. All this tends to defuse all the more any hint of criticism in his report except where, as in the case of the BBC, he went out of his way to criticise. The Government knew what they were looking for in him, and he was absolutely true to character and did not let them down. This is not to suggest at all that he was anything other than scrupulously judicial and completely independent. But he was predictable and reliable, and so was the product at the end of it.

One other anxiety. I gave the second of this session's three lectures on Wednesday. This was the Essex University lecture, sponsored by Clifford Chance. It was entitled 'Torture'.[218] Much of it was historical. But I used it, in order to make it more interesting and immediate, to draw lessons from history about today, with mention of Pinochet's regime, Saudi Arabia, Israel's Supreme Court and Guantanamo Bay where the US are detaining many prisoners taken in Afghanistan without any civil rights at all. Johan Steyn delivered a very highly charged and provocative lecture on the 'Legal Black Hole' there last autumn, and it was inevitable that I would be drawn into the backwash of it by mentioning this topic. But I could hardly not do so, as it is the most pressing example of a situation where torture could be being perpetrated, unobserved and uncorrected. Two problems then emerged. One was press interest, as Clifford Chance's press officer wanted to brief the journalist on *The Independent* about it. I resisted, but eventually compromised on the basis that I could see him and correct his article, which I did. The other was how to distance myself, just a bit, from Johan. He had set out evidence, or at least allegations, of torture in his lecture – thereby, as I thought, inviting the conclusion that this was going on there without actually saying so. I said in my lecture that I was a little more cautious than he perhaps had been inclined to be in inviting my audience to draw their conclusion. Johan was in the audience, with a group of Israeli judges with whom he had been all week. He took it that I was saying that he had actually said that they had been tortured – and I was met by a letter next morning saying that I had misrepresented him. This is not so. I was equally careful in my choice of words. But Johan is as stubborn as they come and, having taken this view that he has been misrepresented – on an issue where he was, as he knows, sailing too close to the wind anyway – he will, I know, not be corrected. I suppose time will allow his resentment to subside. But press comment next week may inflame it. He is rather too self-righteous actually. He is fiercely critical of others in his judgments, attracting press comment for being so and then saying that he meant no such thing. Disingenuous, one might say. Yet I like, admire and value him greatly!

---

218 (2004) 53 ICLQ 807.

22 February 2004

Debate about the proposed Supreme Court rumbles on, and this week the Bill will be published. There was a full debate on this and the related proposal to abolish the Lord Chancellor on Thursday 12 February in the House in which I took part. Lords Nicholls and Hoffmann also spoke from the serving Law Lords. Lords Lloyd, Millett and Hobhouse spoke for those who have retired, and Lord Woolf and Lord Cullen – his maiden speech – spoke for the Chief Justices. There was much support for us from the Conservatives, Crossbenchers and some on the Labour and Liberal benches. But Lord Brennan spoke up for the Government, citing Lord Bingham in his support, which did not go down too well on our side as Tom and Johan are remaining silent now. All they have to offer is their lectures, delivered before the paucity of the arrangements on offer were realised. The Liberal-Democrat team of Lester and Goodhart stuck religiously to their script. But they too should be looking more carefully at the consequences. There is no suitable building to which we can go, and – in response to my protest about the original proposal – all our running costs are now to be met from a 1% levy on all court fees throughout the country. It was an anxious debate for me, as I wanted to get home on the 8.25pm BA flight and time ran on beyond expectations. But fortunately it ended at 6.50pm and I was able, after running in places until out of breath and making quick connections on the Tube, to reach the departure lounge ten minutes before boarding time.

This Friday evening Charlie Falconer came to Edinburgh to give a lecture on the subject to the WS Society in the Signet Library. I was invited. I was reluctant to go but decided to do so as it was a lecture in honour of his father, J Leslie Falconer WS, who was a long-standing friend of my father, of Mary's father too and myself. He did much to encourage me when I was starting at the Bar. There was nothing new in his lecture as far as I was concerned, but it was good of him to make the journey to his native city and explain the proposals here. Then there were questions. It had been expected that this would turn out to be a highly-charged affair, but the press were disappointed. Two very tame questions were asked and answered. There was silence, so I put up my hand. I said how much I appreciated the efforts he had made since the initial announcement to see that Scotland was properly attended to. I then put questions about the opportunity for detailed debate in the Scottish Parliament. He gave a reasonably clear answer and then, to fill the gap, I put a supplementary which he also answered. Then there was silence again and the proceedings ended. It was just as well that I was there. A rather pleasant dinner followed in the Commissioners' Room which gave an opportunity for some more informal contact. I think that he knows very well that the whole project is at risk of foundering for lack of suitable premises. But I would not care to bet on this. There will be plenty of room for debate and argument still when the Bill starts to go through Parliament.

14 March 2004

The Constitutional Reform Bill had its second reading this week in the House of Lords. But a cleverly designed motion by Lord Lloyd of Berwick, which attracted much crossbench support, was carried by a majority of 33 as it had the support also of the Conservatives who turned out in force with the aim of defeating the Government. It was for the Bill to be sent to a Select Committee for scrutiny before it goes any further. The Liberal Democrats and the Government are opposed to this, despite a recommendation to the like effect from the House of Commons Constitutional Affairs Committee, on the ground that it would make it impossible to complete this 'flagship' Bill this session. There is a new carry-over system which they conveniently forgot about or refused to accept, despite the Bill's constitutional importance. But it now looks as though they will have to carry it forward – or reintroduce the Bill in the Commons, which will have a disruptive effect on their programme. It is very likely that Tom Strathclyde, the Leader of the Tories in the House of Lords, devised this plan and persuaded Tony Lloyd to front it for him.

There was a list of about 45 speakers for the debate. I decided not to take part, and no other serving Law Lord did either. We said all we could a few weeks ago. But at the start, with Alan Rodger, Richard Scott, Simon Brown and Bob Carswell, I had been inclined to vote in support of Tony. Then the thing became very obviously highly political and Harry Woolf, who spoke in favour of the Government (Why? Had he been persuaded by some offer behind the scenes?) said he would not do so in the course of his speech. So we dropped the idea, which proved to be the right thing in the end. Unfortunately Lennie Hoffmann was not to be dissuaded, and he evoked much criticism by voting in favour of Tony's motion. I hope this will not rebound on the rest of us.

The result is good. We shall now have a chance to get into the detail on the issues such as how to protect the independence of Scots law and above all cost – and the absurd and unfair proposal that all civil litigants in the three UK jurisdictions should pay for the entire thing. It may be hoping too much that the whole bad idea of a Supreme Court will go away completely. But the delay can only work towards the advantage of those who wish to persuade the Government to think again.

This is the weekend of the Strathclyde University Court Residential Weekend at Ross Priory beside Loch Lomond. It is the very start of spring, with some thrushes in full song and the resident great-spotted woodpecker drumming on a suitable tree to proclaim its territory. This weekend is a very pleasant occasion. I have no particular function apart from saying grace at dinner at Archie Hunter, the Convener's, request. So I feel rather inadequate. But it is a good opportunity to mix and speak to people. I continue to be much impressed by the way this most friendly of universities is run.

2 April 2004

We spent six days last week and at the start of this one hearing three constitutional appeals in the Privy Council about Caribbean mandatory death sentences. This is a follow-on from my entry of 14 December 2003. The fallout of the majority decision in *Roodal v The State* made it necessary for an enlarged Board to sit. In the event it was decided that we should enlarge to nine, and that we should hear three appeals raising the same issue in the hope that we would be able to achieve some form of consistency. These were *Boyce and Another v The Queen* from Barbados[219] (a rehearing), *Lambert Watson v The Queen* from Jamaica[220] and a third case from Trinidad and Tobago.[221] We had to hear the cases in the Moses Room in the House of Lords, as the Privy Council hearing room cannot accommodate nine judges and the space there for so many counsel and solicitors was not large enough either. From our point of view this was, of course, much more convenient. I had the pleasure once again of sitting opposite the magnificent mural of the Judgment of Daniel which shows his confrontation of Susanna's accusers in the city of Babylon in all its depth and glory.

All the usual suspects among counsel were there: Edward Fitzgerald, Keir Starmer and Nicholas Blake on the appellants' side with many hangers-on and Peter Knox and Sir Godfray Le Quesne with many supporters for the Governments. It was, on the whole, an enjoyable and amicable hearing. Most of us kept fairly quiet, as is necessary when nine are sitting. From time to time Lennie Hoffmann, as is his way, came up with observations that went in their usual devastating way to the heart of the argument. Alan Rodger, who has been steeped in these mandatory death cases for the last two years and has struggled to get the others to see sense, made perceptive observations too. I am much less into the subject, so my contributions were exploratory rather than critical. The senior trio of Bingham, Nicholls and Steyn remained almost totally silent – ominously so, one felt. For them, of course, the mandatory death penalty is anathema and any obstacle to its removal is an obstacle to be brushed aside. The only question, as Donald was heard to remark to Tom, was how this could best be done – not whether, under the Constitutions which all had clauses protecting the law as it had existed immediately before independence, this was permissible.

Towards the end preferences were beginning to become clear. Tom, Donald and Johan kept apart, but it was clear where their minds were going. Alan and Lennie were firmly anti-*Roodal* and against the other three. Sir Edward Zacca from Jamaica could clearly be relied on to support them, as preferring the Constitution to abolition at all costs. Indeed Alan believes that Lennie persuaded Tom to have Edward Zacca on the team, for fear that Brenda Hale might have quite different ideas if she were to sit with us. Of the rest Richard Scott's line of questioning made it clear that on the whole he was with Lennie – as indeed I was, as it has always seemed to me that the majority judgment in

---

219 *Boyce v The Queen* [2004] UKPC 32, [2005] 1 AC 400.
220 *Watson v The Queen* [2004] UKPC 34, [2005] 1 AC 472.
221 *Matthew v State of Trinidad and Tobago* [2004] UKPC 33, [2005] 1 AC 433.

Roodal, which Johan wrote and Tom concurred in, was blind to all the difficulties it created and inexcusably bad. That left Robert Walker, careful, reserved and unwilling to commit himself until he had thought things through – so difficult to read, as he says so little during the argument. But with Richard on its side Lennie's team were in the majority – just, by one.

And so it turned out in discussion, though there were differences in each case. The Jamaican case of *Watson* and the Barbados case of *Boyce* were relatively easy, as the law in these States had been changed since independence and it was possible for all of us to agree that in their case, consequently, the mandatory death penalty was unconstitutional. The critical case, of course, was *Matthew* from Trinidad and Tobago, which made it necessary to decide whether or not to overrule *Roodal*.[222] As we worked up the seniority ladder the line-up was as expected. Robert Walker supported *Roodal* – he had been in the majority in that case anyway – but was willing to go the other way in the Barbados case. Then Richard, Alan, Lennie and I all spoke against *Roodal*. This left the senior three, who reacted with predictable scorn, anger and resentment at the result which left them in the minority. It was all most unfortunate. But the most regrettable thing is that Tom and Johan are so emotionally involved in the subject that they are incapable of deciding the case according to the law which the Constitutions have laid down for us. Never was it clearer that the duty of a constitutional court is to put aside personal inclinations and prejudices – a principle to which Tom subscribes on paper but cannot grasp. It is so easy to get carried away by a crusade for justice and human rights and by the idea that changing values should prevail over what the Constitution actually says. But, oh how dangerous this is in the wrong context! The existing law clauses in these Constitutions are as much part of the Constitution as the clauses which set out the fundamental rights and freedoms. To bend them to secure one right may have grave consequences elsewhere. The constitutional imperative has to be respected. The reversal of *Roodal* will be heavily criticised, of course. But the truth is that the minority in that case were right all along, and that to leave it as it stands would do more harm than good.

Tom delegated to Lennie the task of organising the majority judgments. I volunteered to do the Jamaican one where we were all agreed and will aim to do this over the weekend. The other two are in Lennie's capable hands, but I fear that the dissents – which will probably come – may be quite bitter and unpalatable.[223] It is sad to find our team, who usually work together so well, so deeply divided.

222 See fn 215.
223 Tom Bingham referred to this trilogy of cases in his third Hamlyn lecture of 2009: see *Widening Horizons* (Cambridge, 2010), pp 68–69. He pointed out that all members of the Board had accepted that the mandatory death penalty constituted inhumane or degrading punishment or treatment and that this had been accepted by Trinidad and Tobago while defending its constitutionality, but not by Barbados. He drew comfort from the fact that on 3 May 2009 the Deputy Prime Minister and Attorney General of Barbados announced that his Government would be moving to abolish the mandatory nature of the penalty, while preserving the penalty itself. Despite further such undertakings, however, section 2 of the Offences against the Person Act 1994, which provides that the death penalty is mandatory for all those convicted of murder, remains on the statute book.

The Select Committee on the Constitutional Reform Bill sat in public for the first time yesterday. I went, a loner among the Law Lords, as they all seem to be out of touch or so scornful of the public business of the House, to listen to Charlie Falconer giving evidence and being cross-examined by the Committee. It was an impressive performance, more on their side than his, it has to be said. There was a succession of penetrating questions, pursued to a much greater depth than is possible on the floor of the House. Geoffrey Howe in particular has some very interesting and useful thinking about funding and accountability. It looks, on this showing, as though something good will come out of this Committee. I am to give evidence before it on 29 April and will have to be well prepared if I am to stand up to this kind of questioning.

Meantime Donald joined me for two meetings with the Constitutional Unit's advisers. A Mr Hines came to see us about the building, which he says is to be the Middlesex Guildhall – but rumours to the contrary still circulate. As the present occupants will have to be rehoused and work cannot start until Royal Assent, the timescale is now for completion in mid-2007 at the earliest. The cost is going up to about £40m. Edward Adams came to see us about the Bill. As expected, he was willing to engage in useful discussions about it. Donald was disinclined to do likewise, but I have a much stronger personal interest in the subject as he will have retired long before we get going.

So I tried to get down to some points of detail. I hope that we can keep this dialogue going. But with Tom conducting all his discussions behind closed doors – and clearly not getting all he wants out of this – and Donald for obvious reasons being so lacking in enthusiasm, it is quite hard going.

At last, however, it is the Easter break and, apart from doing the Jamaican judgment, I have a two-week break.

2004 – May to July

1 May 2004

We had a light week this week in the Privy Council. There were two cases, each over within the day. There were important occasions to attend in connection with the proposed Supreme Court, however, which occupied my time and thoughts. On the Tuesday evening we paid an official visit to view the Middlesex Guildhall – 'official' in the sense that all the Law Lords who were available and wished to come (Lennie did not, and Johan was there for a short time only) were invited so that we could express a corporate view prior to the making of a recommendation within the next two weeks by the civil servants to the Minister. Tom was there, of course, as was Donald with whom I had viewed the place earlier. Donald and I found the place more gloomy and claustrophobic than on our first visit. A gathering thunderstorm did not help the atmosphere.

But we were not alone. As we went from courtroom to courtroom, the unsuitability of the layout and the heavy Victorian gothic furniture became more and more apparent to everyone. Attempts to suggest to us that a few cosmetic changes only would do were met with derision and disbelief. Tom's disgust was plain to see. There was little enthusiasm for a more general exploration of the other rooms which might be used as offices, sitting-rooms and a library. We gathered for a brief meeting with the architect and the senior civil servant who oversees the project. It was suggested that we might like to give our views there and then. Some questions followed. We were told, with great emphasis, that there was no alternative; this was the only place we could go. Somerset House, with its 400 civil servants, is not available. That was an end to Tom's ideal scenario – the grandeur of a fine building which would fit his image of an internationally respected Supreme Court. Even then the detail would have almost certainly let us down. But that is all out of the question now – and I am not sorry, as the location would have been all wrong. Then I asked whether the existing building on the Guildhall site might be pulled down. This, too, is out of the question. It is a World Heritage Site, and that would cost over £100m anyway. So it is Hobson's choice after all. The site itself, of course, could not be better. It is face to face with the Palace of Westminster, between the Treasury and Westminster Abbey. But some of the interior would need to be gutted to suit our purposes, and English Heritage will need a lot of persuading to let this happen.

For Tom, who said that he would rather write with our reactions than express them at the meeting, this must be deeply depressing. I cannot feel much sympathy, as so much of the blame attaches to him for getting this rash idea off the ground in the first place. Great man as he is, it probably never occurred to him that he would not get the place he wanted – and he wholly under-estimated the political minefield into which he has taken us. He has written a fierce letter to the Chairman of the Select Committee, condemning almost everything we saw. In a memo which she has circulated to us all Brenda Hale has pointed out that it is unclear what Tom's message is meant to be: (a) to stop the move altogether, (b) to stop the move to the Guildhall, (c) to get them to tear it down and rebuild on that site, or (d) to make the best of it. (b) is what Tom wants; (d) is what we will have to do; and (a) and (c) are ruled out on political and financial grounds.

Next day *The Guardian* carried a leaked report on our visit, with the pronouncement that this was to be our new home and a leader which said that it was the best site – the right site for the right reform. The Government will still not go public on this, as the Minister has yet to receive this advice from his project team.

On Thursday afternoon it was my turn to give evidence to the House of Lords Select Committee on the Bill. Tom and Donald, rather loftily I thought, have treated my part in these proceedings with complete indifference. Tom especially is so wrapped up in himself and his battle to salvage what he can from his project that he is probably incapable of grasping what I can and cannot contribute to the debate. They gave evidence to the Committee in the Joint Session a week ago. This was rather awkward for Donald, as Tom and he are opposed to each other. They were heard with more respect than enthusiasm I thought. Donald was, as was to be expected, overshadowed by Tom's forceful and firm declaration of his views. I entered into these proceedings with a good deal of unease – in case I was not articulate enough, or said something that would unduly irritate either Tom or Donald, or was pulled to pieces by the Committee whose members are now so well informed on almost every detail.

I was preceded by the Law Society of Scotland – Michael Clancy, Gerry Brown and Duncan Murray, whom I met for a discussion beforehand in the Royal Gallery. They were not very convincing, with some rather strange ideas. They suggested three Scots, a panel of 15 and various other proposals to strengthen the Scottish position. They were also at times hard to hear, and thus lost the attention of their audience. Then it was my turn. The pattern is about one hour per witness or group of witnesses. I was there for an hour and 20 minutes on my own.

I had put in a note of written evidence. I supplemented this with some more detailed points on Scots law and the Scottish issue. I was able to begin by saying, with no hint of dissemblance, that Charlie Falconer had done much to address the Scottish issues about which I had been making a nuisance of myself since the disastrous start which had ignored Scotland altogether. I also went over the bits with which I agreed, while emphasising my fundamental disagreement with the whole proposal – a maximum of 12 judges, with no entrenched number for Scots and merit as the sole criterion for appointment. As I pointed out, it would do the Scots no good if the people who came from Scotland were not up to the job and were there purely as placemen. We then moved into questioning. This was more friendly and lively than I had expected. To my surprise and relief, Lord Carter and Baroness Gibson of Market Rasen, a Labour Baroness (who had remained silent when Tom and Donald were there), asked me questions about my record in the House and what I thought I had derived from participation. They were not aggressive – appreciating, I thought, that I had made genuine efforts to interest myself in their work and contribute on points of practice and procedure, not policy. Lord Carter teased me a bit about the benefits that were available to peers who do not sit and take leave of absence. There was also general surprise that I am not entitled to claim a daily attendance allowance to offset the cost of rent and so on for my flat, to which I referred as a reason for my warning that my job was not always attractive to people from Scotland. As a salaried office-holder I am denied that benefit. All in all, I thought that I got a good hearing. I hope that I came over as friendly and genuine, not remote or arrogant as my colleagues are somewhat thought to be. The impression I got was that the various members of the Committee (five Labour, five Conservative, three Liberal Democrat and three Crossbench) are now settled into their positions on the Bill, and that only a few loose ends remain to be looked at before their detailed negotiation in private begins. I was able to raise some laughter when I said that I was not allowed to mention the identity of the proposed building ('We all know where it is', chuckled Lord Goodhart), and when I told them about my conversation with the President of Malawi, who said of the judiciary – 'You do what I want. I give you the money'. I emerged from this experience exhausted, but not as downcast as I feared I might have been.

20 May 2004

Mary and I were invited, out of the blue, and to our delight and surprise, to dinner at Holyrood as guests of Lord Steel of Aikwood, the Lord High Commissioner to the General Assembly of the Church of Scotland. This was on a Thursday, so I had to ask for time off to get a late afternoon flight home rather than the usual routine one at 8.50pm. This did not present a problem, as I was sitting in the Privy Council and there were one-day cases on the Wednesday and the Thursday. I sat on the Wednesday, on a case from the Turks and Caicos Islands where I was presiding over two former Chief Justices of Northern Ireland (Brian Hutton and Bob Carswell), the Chief Justice of New Zealand (Sian Elias) and a former Vice-Chancellor in England and Wales (Richard Scott). I never cease to marvel at the odd situations in which I find myself.

We drove to Holyrood Palace for the dinner to find that security was very tight. The previous day in London the Prime Minister was hit by purple flour thrown from a gallery in the House of Commons by guests of Baroness Golding who were members of the Fathers 4 Justice protest group. We were a bit early, so we were taken for a tour round the public rooms which were teeming with guests for an afternoon reception and Beating of Retreat. We were then ushered into the West Drawing Room where various guests for dinner were gathering. Eventually their Graces arrived, we were presented and shortly afterwards we went into dinner. It was a simple, undemanding but excellently-presented meal. His Grace was remarkably abstemious, a very well-mannered, attentive and approachable High Commissioner I should think. There was time for some reminiscences about Malawi and its President Muluzi before the piper came in to go round the table with a lovely presentation of airs and marches. Then back to the drawing room after the toasts and shortly it was time to go. It was a delightful, privileged interlude.

29 May 2004

The Whitsun holiday has arrived – such a delight. Last weekend was very arduous, as I spent the entire three days grinding out a judgment in a competition case from New Zealand, *Carter Holt v The Commerce Commission*.[224] It was

---

224 *Carter Holt Harvey Building Products Ltd v The Commerce Commission (New Zealand)* [2004] UKPC 37.

29 May 2004

complex on its facts and delicate to present as we – Bingham, myself and Carswell – are differing 3–2, with Hale and Scott in the minority, from an experienced competition judge in the New Zealand High Court and a unanimous New Zealand Court of Appeal in which Gault J, the acknowledged master of this branch of the law, wrote the judgment. This is one of the last cases to come from New Zealand to the Privy Council, as the door closed on 1 January and the new Supreme Court, chaired by Sian Elias as Chief Justice, is in being. I do not suppose that that court would have reached the decision we have done, in the circumstances. We were greatly aided by a more recent Australian judgment and a mistaken reliance on EU law which takes a different approach. Tom was kind enough to say that my draft was excellent when I circulated it promptly on Monday morning. I am sorry that the minority look like not being persuaded by it.

It took, as I say, three full days – in all 70 paragraphs, 35 pages. At first I was quite despondent as it seemed that it would not work out. Intuition plays a large part in the composition of these things, and it is hard at the start to imagine where the spirit will lead. I spent most of the first two days on routine stuff – setting out the facts, which required an extensive précis summarising the judgments below and identifying their weak spots and quoting from the important authorities. Then suddenly on Sunday morning, when I read through the draft, it came alive. There was a great sense of relief that it was not going to hang over me for another weekend.

This week we had two interesting cases in the House of Lords. One was about the 'loss of a chance', where a cancer patient was suing his GP who had failed to identify that there was a possible cancer with the result that months of delay ensued.[225] The other was a disability discrimination law case from Fife.[226] The latter is not one I need write about, as we are all agreed and Brenda Hale will write the judgment. The former is much more difficult, and I am glad that I have some time now to think about it.

On Wednesday evening we went to the Athenaeum for the Law Lords Dinner. Derry and Alison Irvine and Brian and Lindy Hutton were our guests. Charlie and Marianna Falconer were there too at Johan Steyn's insistence, and I agreed that they should be asked to join us. I think Charlie was rather thrilled to be there. He is quite junior and still new to the job, despite all the bravado and the destructive regime he is planning for us. We sat at a series of round tables. Mary was beside Derry, who is still disconsolate at having too little to do and not earning what he was accustomed to. I was beside Alison who, by contrast, was as well, happy and relaxed as I have ever seen her. We were well looked after by the Athenaeum. There was a good simple meal with good wines and an attentive, elderly butler. There are great divisions among us just now on several important issues, but none of this filtered through to what was a most enjoyable

---

[225] *Chester v Afshar* [2004] UKHL 41, [2005] 1 AC 134.
[226] *Archibald v Fife Council* [2004] UKHL 32. 2004 SC (HL) 117.

evening. It was good to meet Brenda Hale's other half – Julian Farrand – and for Mary to meet Brenda Hale, who is certainly much more lively than the now rather elderly wives of the more senior Law Lords.

6 June 2004

Today is the 60th anniversary of the landings in France on D-Day. There were many images in the newspapers and on television of that momentous and awful day, when so much was achieved to bring about the invasion to free Europe and so many young men lost their lives.

I am alone in my thoughts as I watch the ceremonies and services which are taking place in Normandy. No one else in the family is interested. For me, however, it is a surprisingly emotional time. I was only six at the time of the invasion, and only seven when the War ended. So I was not there. But 11 years later I was in the Army, and much of our clothing, equipment and tactics were the same as those poor, brave people had to endure as they faced the Germans on the beaches and in the orchards and villages of Normandy. National Service took me to Germany where many of the relics of war were still visible, and several members of my Battalion had very real memories of the campaign in Europe only just a decade earlier. We were training to face a threat from the Soviet Union, which fortunately never came to reality. But I do wonder how I would have stood up to what had been expected of us if it had – or if I had been a dozen years older and been with the Seaforth battalions that came ashore shortly after D-Day and went through the war in Europe. I fear that we never reached the level of training and tactical awareness which our predecessors did. There was no need for that. But above all I feel deeply humbled as I think of what they had to do, and what I so nearly had to face too.

2 July 2004

The main event for the week was the visit by the Law Lords to Somerset House, to see the premises which the Lord Chancellor is still considering as the home for the Supreme Court and which, for ages it seems, has been advocated by Tom Bingham. We went in two groups: most on Monday, and then myself, Mark Saville and Bob Carswell a day later. There was a reception party which consisted of the project team, architects and a senior officer of the present occupiers, the Inland Revenue, to show us round. The name 'Somerset House' conjures up images of grace, space and luxury. In reality what we are being offered is the so-called 'New Wing' – an add-on structure which is between the west wing of Somerset House proper and Lancaster Place, which carries all the traffic to and from Waterloo Bridge. It did not take long for us to discover that there are major, almost certainly incurable, disadvantages. The public access from Lancaster Place is almost impossible for motor vehicles – no parking or dropping-off space, despite a bay which leads off the road to the doorway, because its design is 100 years old and will not admit anything but the tiniest of vehicles. The two hearing rooms are beside the street, with noise, vibration and visual disturbance from all that heavy traffic. Much usable space is wasted by the presence of columns, which are load-bearing and cannot be moved, a quarter of the way in from each end. Security is almost non-existent, with the judges' access to and from the street particularly vulnerable. In addition the whole of the office area, with high ceilings, dirty windows and views across a rubbish-filled space to the wall of the west wing is deeply depressing and far bigger than we need. I wrote a note to all the Law Lords next morning, setting out my reactions and suggesting that all efforts should now be concentrated on the Middlesex Guildhall. To my surprise and delight Johan responded immediately by saying that he agreed with me, and notes from others agreeing with me followed thick and fast.

The situation is really quite ridiculous. Somerset House, I believe, is wholly unacceptable whatever steps may be attempted to try to sort things out. The Middlesex Guildhall is unacceptable in its present state, and it will require a major refit inside – which English Heritage resist – to make it usable by us. So what is the Lord Chancellor to do? Common sense suggests that, as there are no other options, the idea of a new Supreme Court should be dropped. But of course that will not happen. A final decision as to where we are to go is to be taken in September.

11 July 2004

I spent the last week on the first half of a two-week appeal in a patent action: *Kirin-Amgen v TKT*.[227] It is all about bio-engineering and nano-technology. The competing patents were about the production of erythropoietin by the use of DNA technology: amazing, fascinating stuff, for which we have been well prepared in private seminars by Professor Michael Yudkin of Oxford University. Lennie Hoffmann is in the chair with an invited team consisting of myself, Alan Rodger, Robert Walker and Simon Brown. The advocacy, especially of TKT's silk David Kitchen QC, is of a high level – accurate, painstaking, well informed and attractively presented. Lennie is in his element, of course. Thanks to the seminars, it has not been too difficult for the rest of us to keep in touch with what is going on. We have another week to look forward to.

Meantime extra-mural things commanded attention. The second July Friday of graduation ceremonies at Strathclyde, always quite arduous for me to maintain the high quality needed to set the right tone; a selection process for the new Director of the Institute of Advanced Legal Studies, which is to come to a head next Friday when we meet under the chairmanship of Graeme Davies, the University's Vice-Chancellor and Principal, to make our choice; and preparing my President's report for the CMJA's Council meeting in Jersey next September. It is a relief not to have a judgment to write this weekend – nor next, as Lennie will want to write the leading judgment in our patent case.

227 *Kirin-Amgen Inc v Hoechst Marion Roussel Ltd* [2004] UKHL 46, [2005] 1 All ER 667.

18 July 2004

We completed our patent case in sufficient time for a useful discussion on the Thursday afternoon. There were so many issues and the subject matter was so complex that we departed from the usual formalities and enjoyed a relatively relaxed and unstructured exchange of ideas under Lennie's gentle but amazingly well-informed leadership. We reached agreement on all the main points and left it to Lennie to write the judgment. We all hope that he does not fall off his bicycle on journeys to and from home, or during his summer holidays when he plans a marathon journey from London to Spain, before he completes it.

I stayed on in London overnight to sit on the selection panel for the new Director of the Institute of Advanced Legal Studies, of whose Advisory Council I am the Director. This took up the whole of Friday from 9.30am to 3.30pm. It was an interesting experience, as well as a duty. Graeme Davies, the Vice-Chancellor, was in the chair. He conducted the business with brisk efficiency and not too much formality. We were a panel of nine, and there were four candidates of whom two were clearly above the other two: Professor Hugh Collins and Professor Avron Sherr. Of these, Collins was by far the more distinguished legal scholar. But his diffident manner indicated that he would not be as good on public relations. So we decided on Sherr who is the Woolf Professor at the IALS, already well-versed in its affairs and a safe pair of hands.

Two events deserve mention on the political front. The House of Lords resumed consideration of the Constitutional Reform Bill last week. The Government were defeated on the first crucial vote, calling for the retention of the office of Lord Chancellor, by 32 votes. This was encouraging for those who wished to see it defeated on the Supreme Court issue too. But by the autumn, when that comes along, there will be several more new Labour peers. So the outcome is uncertain, and of course there will be pressure to reverse lost votes in the House of Commons to force the Lords to back down. The thing becomes a game of chance and political compromise in view of the impending General Election.

The other event was the publication of Lord Butler's report into the use of information by British Intelligence in the run-up to the Gulf War. This was an opportunity to redress the imbalance of the Hutton Report which laid all the blame for Dr Kelly's death on the BBC and none on the Government – a result which a sceptical public found hard to accept. The Butler Report has succeeded in avoiding laying the blame on anyone, although there were serious administrative failings and a breakdown in the proper handling of information by Government. 'Another whitewash', claimed *The Evening Standard*. Blair seemed to have escaped again. But I find it hard not to believe that he was so determined to go to war together with Bush that he was using the information to support a predetermined case, and that he was more concerned about its presentation than with its accuracy. He acted 'in good faith' his supporters proclaim. But what does this mean?

23 July 2004

This week it was the Lord Mayor's Banquet for HM Judges in the Mansion House. I was placed once again in the most senior position between the Lady Mayoress and Marguerite Woolf; with Mary close by between a senior Alderman and Peter Goldsmith, the Attorney General. The Lord Mayor made a charming speech. Harry Woolf's speech had, so Marguerite told me, been heavily censored to avoid causing offence to the Government, and Charlie Falconer (still the Lord Chancellor and still cheerful) made a speech which was almost entirely empty of anything except platitudes and rather too familiar references to 'Harry' when he should have called him the Lord Chief Justice. It was received with reasonable applause and patience by most except for Alan Rodger, next to Rima Scott, who worked himself up into an apoplexy of indignation at the offensiveness of it all – to her amusement, especially as he protested at people clapping, as she was in the process of doing at the time. He was still over-excited and red in the face with indignation as we shared a government car back to the Inn. The dinner itself, and the musicians, were as always excellent and the Lady Mayoress was very good company.

2004 – August to September

2 August 2004

The term came to an end last Thursday, 30 July. The House had risen a week before, so the contractors had moved in, carpets had been removed from all the main corridors and almost all the facilities closed down including the library. Two Appellate Committees of five sat for all four days. One, chaired by Richard Scott, dealt with an issue arising out of a bitterly contested contest between *Three Rivers District Council v Bank of England*[228] about an alleged misfeasance in public office – Gordon Pollock and Jonathan Sumption are the leading advocates. An application for the disclosure of documents had been met by a claim for legal advice privilege. I was on the other Committee chaired by Tom Bingham, in which we sat for three days on a medical negligence case and on a case about the introduction into evidence of material obtained by telephone intercept.[229] The weather had become hot, humid and sultry, and it was a relief to reach the end of the case on Thursday. I was left to take home with me the leading judgment in the medical negligence case (*Chester v Afshar*) in which we are divided 3–2, and a judgment much in need of revision in another medical case where we have still to reach some kind of an agreement (*Gregg v Scott*[230]). There are two lectures to put onto the building stocks: one for Strathclyde in December and another for the Judicial Studies Board in March. Then there is the CMJA Council meeting and seminar in September to attend.

---

228 [2004] UKHL 48, [2005] 1 AC 610.
229 *Attorney General's Reference (No 5 of 2002)* [2004] UKHL 43, [2005] 1 AC 167.
230 [2005] UKHL 2, [2005] 2 AC 176.

10 September 2004

The holiday is over, and for the past week I have been trying once again to get to grips with paperwork.

There were two judgments to attend to – one in *Chester v Afshar*, which I wrote before the holiday and needed tidying-up with references checked in the Advocates Library before sending off by email to London; the other a five-page concurring judgment in a case about the interception of communications where I thought I had something to contribute. Then my attention turned to lectures – a dreaded task, as these are so open-ended and hard to judge. I did four last year. This year I have at least two. We are also to go to The Bahamas in January, where I shall be expected to speak. Alan Paterson of Strathclyde University had asked me to give a keynote speech on a more prestigious lecture at the annual conference of the Society of Legal Scholars in Glasgow next September, in the first quarter of the month. With great feelings of guilt I turned this down, aware that preparing lectures in term time is almost impossible, and conscious of the need to be free to fulfil my obligations as President of the CMJA whose conference next year is on some as yet unspecified date in September – not to mention the family holiday, when I am completely and deliberately out of touch with paperwork. I spent three days on a paper headed 'A Phoenix from the Ashes? Designing a new Supreme Court'[231] for Strathclyde, and had a 20-page product at the end of it which will need some updating by December. It is otherwise quite serviceable. Whether the subject, so close to my heart, is right for them is another matter. But at least it is an opportunity to put some interesting details on record. The lecture for the Judicial Studies Board is to be on 'Writing Judgments', which is much more difficult. But I may be able to double up on this one for The Bahamas trip too, as the subject will be of interest there also. A paper by Alan Rodger, enormously researched and erudite, will be a great help. I discovered it in my bookshelves after I had hit on my own title. My audience will be different from his, as his was a lecture to the Society of Legal Scholars, not to judges.

Next week Mary and I go to Jersey for a week for the CMJA's Conference and Council meeting. There is a good deal of email traffic about this, and I shall have to prepare myself for various speeches. But there will be time for that next week.

I have been approached, as is now the current practice, by two members of Faculty asking me to provide references for them to support their applications to the Scottish Judicial Appointments Commission for appointment as a Senator to the College of Justice. There are currently two vacancies, as Douglas Cullen has secured approval for two additional appointments in view of over-use of temporary judges which is attracting much criticism. One of these is Patrick Hodge, who was standing counsel to the Inland Revenue before taking silk and has been for six years a part-time Commissioner in the Scottish Law

---

231 (2005) 121 LQR 253

Commission. He is also a Judge of the Courts of Appeal of Jersey and Guernsey, and is aged 51. He is a first-class advocate, extremely able and an obvious candidate who, under the old system, would certainly have been regarded as appropriate for an early appointment to the Bench by the Lord Advocate. It is rather a pity that he should have to go through the long drawn-out process of applying for the position and being submitted to an interview. The other candidate is much more unusual. Iain Macphail, for many years a sheriff, then a member of the Scottish Law Commission and since 2002 Sheriff Principal of Lothian & Borders, was – so he told me – approached out of the blue by Jim Gallagher, Head of the Scottish Executive Justice Department, and told that he should put his name forward for appointment as Senator. Iain, quite understandably, was taken aback by this. He is six months older than I am, already 66, and had every reason to think that he is now at the top of his tree. Jim Gallagher was adamant however that he was not too old, so Iain decided to accept his advice and telephoned me to ask if I would be a referee. He too, in his quiet rather diffident way, is a first-class lawyer. He might well have been a Senator had he not chosen a career on the Shrieval Bench in 1973 when he was still at the Junior Bar.

The approach by Jim Gallagher cannot have been a mere whim. Something is undoubtedly going on. I cannot believe the Scottish Executive is seeking to use Iain as an example of the opportunities that exist nowadays for promotion. My hunch is that Douglas Cullen, Lord President since 2001 and now 68, has told the Executive of his wish to retire next year, which he has already confided in me, and they are looking for a successor. There are two other possible candidates, one who is unpopular among the judges and another who is not favoured by the Executive. Iain Macphail could well be the compromise candidate and, I believe, would fill the position, even if only for a few years, admirably well until someone like Patrick Hodge is in a position to take over. We have come a long way since my own promotion to the office in 1989. But it would be interesting to see if this indeed is the way things work out.

26 September 2004

Mary and I returned yesterday from the CMJA's Council meeting which was held in Jersey. These annual gatherings are the life-blood of this organisation. The Council must meet each year under the Association's constitution, and it has become the practice to add on a few days educational programme. So it has become a mini version of the Triennial Conference – not so mini either, as a full week is now involved and there were about 150 delegates this year. I was elected to be the President last year in Malawi, so I had to be on hand all week and there was a good deal of preparation beforehand.

29 September 2004

I returned to London this evening for the start of the Legal Year. The Abbey service is on Friday this year. Today it is only Wednesday. But we are to start a nine-judge case on Monday, so I shall need two days this week in order to get myself organised again for the new term. We have a new team of judicial assistants – Alan Bates, John Hunter, Emma Waring and Melanie Tweedie.

I face this new term with some misgivings. There is the looming problem of the Supreme Court, for one thing. I have no idea yet of what has been going on during the summer. I cannot imagine that the project team has been idle. We have had some more information about the New Wing at Somerset House, which shows that the ceiling heights of the hearing rooms would be about half those of the committee rooms which we use in the Palace of Westminster. This is not the atmosphere that is needed for a Supreme Court. But I fear that, as the availability of Middlesex Guildhall has not yet been settled, we may be faced with no alternative.

More immediate are impending breakdowns in my travel arrangements which have worked like a well-oiled machine so far: open tickets for the Underground to and from Heathrow so that I do not have to queue for them, airline tickets linked into my frequent flyer service for telephone check-in and a British Airports Authority car park pass which gives me, as a member of the Houses of Parliament, free parking at Edinburgh Airport for my car which I use to get myself to and from India Street. This summer American Express, which ran the travel office at Westminster, had their contract terminated – whether at their own request or not is unclear. A new travel office no longer provides Underground tickets, so I am in a jam as to how to get round the queues at Heathrow when I arrive there on Sunday evenings. Then, when I tried to check in for my flight this evening by telephone, I was unable to do so as the details on my booking did not match. And to cap it all, BAA have been forced by objections from shareholders to terminate their free car-parking scheme for parliamentarians. The current pass will be allowed to run on until April 2006, which is some leeway. After that I may have to use the airport bus as to park for five days would be very expensive. The BAA car pass was, it has to be admitted, a rather unfair benefit, given only to parliamentarians as 'the company's bit for the country'. It could be said to have been a benefit of a kind that compromised their independence, hence the objection from some shareholders. I would have been denied it anyway on my removal to the Supreme Court. So I suppose that I have been lucky that this system was available to me for so long.

On 1 October I will have completed 15 years' service as a judge. This means that I will now be able to retire at any time of my own choice. There is no question of course of my retiring just yet. Mary is not at all in favour of this as she herself is so active, and I would find it hard to find enough to do at home to occupy my time. So I would be better to carry on despite the looming Supreme Court and all the travel problems.

I feel somewhat despondent as I look back on my judicial record. 'Have I achieved anything?' I ask myself. 'Not much' seems to be the answer. Most of the many judgments I issued as Lord President have vanished into the mists of time. Those that have not were overruled during Alan Rodger's purge when he was Lord Justice General. As for my record as Law Lord, I have lived under the shadows of Bingham, Nicholls, Steyn and Hoffmann for years – hugely able, productive and creative men, who show no sign of leaving for some time to come. My judgments are rarely referred to or quoted. I sometimes wonder what the point is of spending so much time writing them. On the other hand judgment writing is the most creative part of the job. Like the artist, one has to go on producing them to get the thoughts one has out of the system. So perhaps I should just soldier on, a foot soldier among the team of Führers above and below me, trying my best not to get into trouble or to let anyone down.

2004 – October to December

3 October 2004

The Abbey service was marked by several departures from practice prior to Lord Irvine's removal from the office of Lord Chancellor. They were present last year too, I suspect, but I was absent: (1) Lord Falconer, not robed, came into the Choir at the end of the procession of judges, not the head; (2) there was a sermon; and (3) due to Lord Falconer's decision to leave the Abbey by car to avoid leading the procession to Westminster Hall, there was a long delay before the huge queue of judges could get out. Things were made more bizarre by the fact that both Tom Legg and Hayden Phillips, who were in the front row of the stalls in front of the Lords of Appeal in Ordinary, were in front of us in the procession. Tom Bingham insisted on maintaining what he described as a 'cordon sanitaire' between us. Absentees from our group were Richard Scott, Robert Walker, Lennie Hoffmann and Simon Brown. On our arrival in the Hall Lord Falconer exchanged some polite words with me. As his predecessor never did, this too was another departure from old times!

Yesterday evening I was a guest at the 40th anniversary of the founding of the University of Strathclyde Law School. Kenneth Norrie, the current Head of the Law School, presided. Joe Thomson, Alan Paterson and Kenny Miller, stalwarts of this highly successful venture, were there. So were John Arbuthnott and Graham Hills, the two Principals still alive from earlier days. Elish Angiolini, the Solicitor General for Scotland, spoke with great wit and charm. It was a typical Strathclyde occasion – relaxed, informal and friendly. 40th anniversaries will crowd my thoughts in 2005: my engagement to Mary, my LLB degree and my admission to the Faculty of Advocates.

8 October 2004

We sat this week as nine in the Appellate Committee in the Moses Room in the case of A and Others v The Home Secretary.[232] The appellants are being detained indefinitely in Belmarsh Prison. They claim that the abrogation of their right to liberty under the Human Rights Act by means of a derogation order made by the Home Secretary was not justified by the situation of emergency which resulted from the attacks on 11 September 2001 in New York and Washington. It raises complex and difficult issues of balancing the public interest in national security against the right of the individual to liberty, which it is the Court's duty to safeguard. The appellants were all foreign nationals. The Home Secretary, David Blunkett, used the immigration route to detain them, knowing that there was no place of safety to which they could go if he were to try to extradite them. There are British nationals who are a threat to national security too, but no measures were taken to detain them. So there is a discrimination issue here as well.

We had four good days of debate, in the course of which Ben Emmerson QC, David Pannick QC and Peter Goldsmith QC, the Attorney General, addressed us – the leaders in this field. When the time came to discuss our conclusions the division of view was much narrower than we had expected. Tom Bingham, in the chair, kept the score in red pencil as we spoke in turn and in reverse order of seniority: Bob Carswell against the appellants; Brenda Hale for; Robert Walker against; Alan Rodger for; Richard Scott for; myself for; Lennie Hoffmann and Donald Nicholls both against. So Tom had the last say, as we were equally divided. His view had not changed from the outset, when it was clear to me that he was in favour of allowing the appeal. So by 5–4 we will set aside the derogation order[233] and make a declaration that section 23 of the Anti-Terrorism Act of 2001 is incompatible with the appellants' Convention rights. Many others have been saying the same thing. But the last word of all on the section 23 issue will rest, under the Human Rights Act, with Parliament. A majority of 6–3 would have been more influential – a unanimous view even more so. Perhaps such a narrow vote will carry little weight. But the declaration will have been made. It is now for the majority to come up with convincing reasons for their view.

31 October 2004

So far only three opinions have surfaced in the detainees' case – Robert Walker (minority) and myself and Alan Rodger (majority). Unusually Tom has not yet come up with his – too busy on other things, he says, and he proposes to write at length. So we are unlikely to have a judgment before mid-December. Meantime he and I, with Johan, Brenda and Bob, are engaged on another

---

232 A v Secretary of State for the Home Department [2005] 2 AC 68.
233 Made under Article 15 of the European Convention on Human Rights, on the ground that there was a state of emergency threatening the life of the nation.

complex case. This time the issue was whether the extra-territorial screening at Prague Airport of Roma seeking asylum from the Czech Republic in the UK was discriminatory and thus contrary to customary international law and international treaties, as well as their rights under the Race Relations Act.[234] There is a mass of authority once again, and detailed speeches have been made by Lord Lester, Guy Goodwin Gill (for UNHCR) and John Howell. We sat on it for four days last week and have one day to go next week. Then we are all into more cases with no let-up. It is quite difficult to keep up-to-date.

These are, however, extremely interesting and challenging cases – as indeed have been *Chester v Afswar* and *Gregg v Scott* on medical negligence, where we have a divided court once again and are pressing quite hard against the frontiers of the law to achieve a result for the patient which matches the scope of the duty of care.

Looking ahead there is a busy year once again with little spare time due to a plague of conferences. The Christmas/New Year holiday will be cut short because Mary and I are to go to The Bahamas for a week of official engagements, including a seminar on the influence of international treaties on national law. Fortunately the current case is on target for that subject. There is a lecture to give to the Judicial Studies Board in March, another lecture to give to the Scottish Law Commission's 40th Celebration in June and then during the summer holiday the CMJA Conference in Ghana. There will have to be some clearing-up time before we can go. Now I am being pressed to participate in the Commonwealth Law Conference in London starting four weeks after our return from Africa. If I do that, there will be only at best three weeks' holiday at Craighead. This is a bit too tight for comfort and a small return for all the trouble we take over that property.

28 November 2004

Three vignettes this week illustrate the character of some of my most enigmatic and intellectually powerful colleagues.

On Thursday afternoon, as we were summing up our conclusions in our discussion after counsel had left us after three days of argument (in *R (West) v Parole Board*[235]), Tom Bingham fell asleep. Three of us had spoken – Bob Carswell, Robert Walker and myself. Now it was the turn of Gordon Slynn, sitting with us as a retired Law Lord. Gordon, of course, was overtaken by Tom as Senior Law Lord. He is full of wisdom nevertheless, and a quite remarkable survivor. Perhaps it was lack of interest in what he was saying. Perhaps it was because of his soft voice and quite a long presentation. Perhaps it was just because we had

---

234 *R (European Roma Rights Centre) v Immigration Officer at Prague Airport* [2004] UKHL 55, [2005] 2 AC 1.
235 [2005] UKHL 1, [2005] 1 WLR 350. The question was whether the refusal by the Parole Board to recommend the re-release of a prisoner whose licence had been revoked engaged his right to liberty so as to entitle him to an oral hearing.

had a long day. Whatever it was, I watched Tom's pen stop writing, his head drop and his eyes close in more than just a bout of greater concentration. He was asleep. I fear that Gordon saw this. I hoped that he was not too dismayed. I wondered too whether Tom would wake up again. But he did. Then Alan Rodger spoke to me – earlier in the week in fact – about his exasperation at the way in which Brenda Hale claims anything to do with children as her own. They were in a case about the use of CCTV evidence in a case involving a child witness in a criminal case. Alan is, of course, as well equipped as anyone to prepare an opinion on this issue. But Brenda volunteered her services to Donald who was in the chair. Alan might not have cared, had he not run into a very thin patch of work with almost nothing of any substance all term. Nor would Brenda's claiming this opinion be all that remarkable were she not seriously behind in other work: no opinion yet in our ill-fated *Gregg v Scott*, heard last June, and with the rest of us in a state of disagreement; and no opinion yet in the Belmarsh detainees' case heard in the first week of this term.

Then Johan Steyn gave a lecture in Belfast. He seized the opportunity to speak his mind once again about Guantanamo Bay and to get his oar in on the detainees' case – on which he did not sit, fortunately, at his own suggestion. An email from my secretary Gail Munden on Friday about her being very busy because of his lecture with the press did not alert me fully to what had been going on until I saw in *The Daily Telegraph* on Friday the headline 'Lord Steyn Attacks Fellow Law Lord', with smiling faces of Johan and Lennie Hoffmann gazing out at me. It seems that, no sense of self-restraint, Johan had used some dicta of Lennie's to criticise judges for being too supine in the face of monstrous deeds by the Government. Lennie is, of course, still – so far as we know – a dissenter in the Belmarsh case. Perhaps Johan knows this. Lennie is far too clever and well-balanced to mind, but it was hurtful for the article by Joshua Rozenberg to say that he was best known for his failure to declare an interest in the Pinochet case. I suspect that Johan released a copy of his lecture to the press. Rather like John McCluskey, he loves – yet abhors – that kind of publicity.

Meantime Donald Nicholls has changed his mind on the Belmarsh detainees' case. The weight of Tom's opinion, backed up by Alan Rodger and myself, may have been too great for him to see an answer to. He is a very significant convert, however. Apart from changing the vote from 5–4, an unconvincing result, to 6–3 he may carry others with him. Bob Carswell was a dissenter too, but he is clearly waiting for a lead from Lennie as he has not written. I doubt whether he is up to writing a strong dissent in a case of this kind. Robert Walker too may change his mind, as his rather brief dissent looks rather isolated without Donald. Tom looked 10 years younger when I told him about Donald's opinion, which he had not yet seen. The prospect of leading a 5–4 majority which could so easily have been derided was not attractive. Now, with both of the Senior Law Lords at one over the issue, it will be much harder for the Government to ignore the decision.

5 December 2004

There was a kingfisher today in Edinburgh's Royal Botanical Gardens. It was in its usual place beside the pond. What was unusual was that the weather was mild and settled. So it was not a refugee from swollen or frozen waters elsewhere. I saw it drop from its perch and catch a small fish, so there was obviously some food there for it to take.

30 December 2004

The Belmarsh detainees' judgment was delivered on 16 December. There was a lot of publicity, and we made very brief statements for our televised audience instead of our usual formalities. Our 8–1 decision (Robert Walker did not change his view) was suitably emphatic, but it was the more eccentric and colourful judgments by Lennie Hoffmann and Richard Scott that caught the headlines and attracted the attention of the commentators. The Government was slow to react, as within a few hours of our judgment – before it, I should say – David Blunkett was forced into resignation by accusations of improper conduct over the speeding up of a visa application by the nanny of his former lover Beverley Quinn. Charles Clarke had just succeeded him when the judgment came out. Not surprisingly, the Government line is that the detainees must stay where they are as it reflects on the decision until the New Year.

At the start of the following week, when I was already home for Christmas in Edinburgh, the Constitutional Reform Bill had its Third Reading. Tony Lloyd marshalled such support as he could for his attempt to defeat the provisions for the setting-up of the Supreme Court. Donald Nicholls spoke in his support. Harry Woolf really has scuppered the campaign as a result of what seem to have been some dark deeds done behind our backs with Charlie Falconer, who had also managed to turn around to his side Viscount Bledisloe, a Crossbencher. Harry spoke against Tony, and at the end Tony Lloyd's amendments were defeated by 199 to 133. So we are set now for this most unwelcome change. When it will happen is still unclear. The Middlesex Guildhall is now the preferred choice of location: good location, bad building. But it will be the back end of 2008 before it will be ready for us. And there will very probably be slippage here if this choice is held. I would not put it past Tom Bingham to try to resurrect the Somerset House option, but the prospect of a greatly increased rent is so unpalatable for the Government that this option – bad location, unsatisfactory building – is really now out of the picture.

It is a relief, of a kind, to have the uncertainty and tension which this caused removed. We can now concentrate on the practical things. The prospect is of cost-cutting and compromise. English Heritage and the Westminster City Council planners are reluctant to permit changes to the interior of the Guildhall, which really needs to be completely redesigned if the quality to be expected of a Supreme Court is to be achieved.

Our new team of Brenda Hale, Bob Carswell and Simon Brown have settled in well. Bob is the steady, conservative Ulsterman one would expect from his background. He is not yet quite in tune with the thinking of the majority, but wisely did not insist on his dissent in the Belmarsh case. Simon is very much at home here. There is a genial manner on the surface, but beneath it he has much of real value to contribute to what we do. He has not had much of a chance to blossom yet as so many of our appeals have been from his decisions in the Court of Appeal, but his time will come. Brenda has, of course, proved to be much the most forward and free-thinking of the three. She irritates Alan Rodger, who finds a soulmate in Simon. Simon, indeed, thrives on the company of others. He keeps his door open, welcomes visitors and makes no secret of his love of golf and of the time he spends in his club, the Garrick. Brenda on the other hand is deeply absorbed in her work, with much emphasis on children's rights and family law where her vision and expertise is needed most. She is very much aware of herself as a woman and an academic. Having been badly treated early in her career, she is sensitive and easily upset. But she has a lot to give and is proving to be well worth her place on our team. No retirements appear to be in prospect in the coming year. Tom, Donald, Johan and Lenny, all above me and all over 70, show no signs of wanting to retire. This stability is good. We all know, respect and like each other so well. It makes for a very alert, active and happy court.

2005 – January to April

1 January 2005

About a hundred waxwings spent most of the morning in the nearest of the tall poplar trees close to our garden. The flock came and went in bits from time to time, but this was their base. Several birds appeared to be feeding on insects among the branches, hovering or reaching out to pick things off the bark. Others were just preening themselves. It was very windy, but this did not seem to trouble them at all as they hung onto the swaying branches. All the while there was a delightful trilling noise, which varied in loudness from time to time as members of the flock came and went.

3 January 2005

Dawn, at Heathrow Airport watching the sun rise. Mary and I are on our way to The Bahamas. This unlikely expedition has come our way as a result of an invitation from The Bahamas judiciary. Each year, for the past three or four years, they have invited a Law Lord and his spouse to spend a week with them to mark the start of the New Year. The Steyns, the Milletts and the Binghams have been. Now at Tom Bingham's kind suggestion, it is our turn . . .

We were escorted from the aircraft on our arrival to the VIP Lounge where we met Sir Burton Hall, the Chief Justice, and Indira Francis, the Deputy Registrar of the Court of Appeal. Our passports and baggage tags were taken from us to allow others to attend to these formalities. Then we set off in a small motorcade to the Sandals resort where we were to stay and which was to be our base for the week. We were greeted with much warmth and kindness.

5 January 2005

We are now two days into our programme of activities, which have been conducted against the somewhat unreal backdrop of our temporary home in the resort. Each day we dress in formal business wear – a suit, white shirt, collar and tie and black shoes for me and their equivalents for Mary – while everyone else ambles around the resort in beach-wear. But the programme itself has been both stimulating and interesting.

We began yesterday with a visit to Government House in Nassau to pay a courtesy visit to Dame Ivy Dumont, the Governor General. After that there was a luncheon engagement with the Bar Association. In the evening there was a reception at the British High Commissioner's residence. Today, 5 January, was spent in the Court of Appeal and with the court system generally. We were taken to Claughton House on Shirley Street, a small modern office block. The entrance was unimpressive, typical of such a building. But once transported by lift to the third floor it was quite different. The whole enterprise for the Court of Appeal is here – courtroom, judges' chambers, registrar's office, secretariat, registry, an accountant and the library. The President of the Court of Appeal, Dame Joan Sawyer, appeared already robed and wigged, to greet us. Then the other Justices – Churaman, Ganpatsingh and Osadebay – gathered with us for a group photograph before Mary was taken into the courtroom to her seat and we processed onto the Bench where a series of speeches was delivered, including one from myself. Then there was a reception in the court following which we were taken, by request, to see the Supreme Court premises nearby. Here the lack of money and investment to support the court system were very obvious. The Chief Justice has his chambers and courtroom in an annex to the Parliament complex. His room is cramped and his courtroom is open to the elements in some respects, as windows broken by hurricanes months ago have not been repaired. The noise of traffic is intrusive, and the room itself is no more than functional. If this was bad, the other courtrooms in the main building, which is shared with the Senate, are worse – although here there were no broken windows and the noise of traffic was less evident. The whole impression of the area was of faded grace and decay. We ended our tour with a brief visit to a local Magistrates' Juvenile Court. Here we met a charming Chief Magistrate who was operating in a small and almost bare courtroom. There was a hallway in which several sad, depressed unfortunates were sitting awaiting justice.

7 January 2005

Yesterday started with a visit to the Eugene Dupuch Law School, where I had been asked to give a lecture. When I met my audience I saw that they were all smartly dressed in suits and business clothes, not t-shirts. It turned out that they were all postgraduates of the University of the West Indies, doing their two-year postgraduate diploma course. I delivered my lecture, after which there were some three or four well-directed questions. They included the inevitable one about the Privy Council's attitude to the death penalty which most people here regard as an essential sanction in the public interests, however out of tune it may be with our conception of human rights. It is not easy to defend our position, and there are several very determined abolitionists among our number: Bingham, Steyn, Nicholls. As already mentioned, others (myself, Rodger, Hoffmann) believe in the Constitution and the democratic process, rather than solutions imposed from England. But this does not fit with Tom's and Johan's convictions, which to me seem to involve an unacceptable amount of legal imperialism – however much one may sympathise with the ideals. There was a brief reception and time for a quick lunch before our next event, which was a visit to the Prime Minister.

The Rt Hon Terry G Christie is a large man, full of self-confidence and self-assurance. He reminded me a bit of President Muluzi of Malawi, although he is much more in tune with the democratic process and far better educated. He did most of the talking, of course. Like so many senior politicians, listening is not his strong card. He gave us a most instructive verbal tour of the vast array of islands and shallow seas which make up this country, assisted by a large map, framed and held up for us by his secretary. He told us about his student days in England at Birmingham University in the time of the Wilson Government, when he had been studying law and became deeply involved in student politics. Jack Straw was President of the National Union of Students, and there were other names he mentioned of people in high places then or now that he had met. He spoke of the way women are taking over in The Bahamas, as so few men seem to be getting into the higher positions in law, business and government. 'Perhaps we should have separate schools for boys', he said. It is true that the court registrars, the President of the Court of Appeal and the Governor General are all women. But in the Law School it seemed to me that the balance was about equal, as at home. I thought that he was exaggerating the problem, which is more a product of a male-orientated culture than of a failure by men to compete with women who have been liberated and whose doors once closed are now open. He spoke of the death penalty too, which he fiercely supports, and of the new Caribbean Appeal Court which, for the time being, The Bahamas does not intend to join. He deplored the UK Government's recent decision to close the British High Commission in The Bahamas. But welcomed Virgin Atlantic's decision to open up flights to Nassau once they can get the facilities in their airport sorted out. He assured a rather startled Chief Justice, who was with me, that he was determined to provide him with the new court buildings he needs. I said that I had my fingers crossed for him as we left the

Prime Minister's office. The Chief Justice smiled broadly. He knows, I think, that it was an empty promise. The money is simply not there.

12 January 2005

Back home to stormy weather in Scotland – a complete contrast to our last few days in Nassau.

Looking back over our visit, we were struck by the dignity and the formality of the occasions we attended. Dark suits, white shirts and ties are expected of professionals. Dressing down in the American style has not yet reached The Bahamas. Fortunately we had prepared ourselves for this, and we were, we believe, appropriately dressed for all occasions. It was odd, looking at photographs of the Binghams' visit last year, to find pictures of Tom with no tie and an open-necked shirt and of him giving a lecture with his jacket off. The CMJA has taught us to beware of such informality. One other thing: the words 'Lord' and 'Lady' really do mean something there. We were treated with genuine and gracious respect because of these titles. Not so, we found, in Australia or even in Canada where indifference at best or derision at worse is the response. It was rather touching to find that the people actually liked calling us by these names. They did not want to use our first names as substitutes, even when invited to do so. The formality which they preferred was out of choice, not indifference. They felt, in an old-world way, more comfortable with this, as with the formality in their dress.

19 February 2005

The Supreme Court issue developed an unwelcome and potentially very serious aspect this week.

I was asked by Tom about a year ago to be a member of a sub-committee whose function was to discuss our accommodation requirements with the DCA's implementation team. Donald Nicholls and Richard Scott were the other members. Donald, who acted as chairman, told me last month that he had decided that it was pointless for him to continue, as he will retire before the new Court is set up. We have, in any case, completed the first phase of our work on the accommodation requirements. So he asked me to take over from him as chairman, and I asked Brenda Hale to fill the vacancy. A meeting of our sub-committee with the DCA implementation team has been arranged for this coming Monday 21 February. The papers for this meeting arrived three days ago. They contain material which goes far beyond a discussion of our accommodation and the architect's design work. The whole organisational structure of the Court is in the agenda for discussion, including the staff's organisation and responsibilities, human resources issues, the corporate design for the new Court, disciplinary procedures for the Justices and a memorandum of understanding between the Supreme Court and the DCA about funding arrangements and measures to ensure the full corporate independence of the

Court. It is clear that the civil service machine has been working itself up to create what, in comparison with our present arrangements, is an administrative nightmare. Deep in my heart, aware of the tensions that were never far below the surface in Edinburgh and of the huge burden of administration that fell on my shoulders as Lord President, I feared that this was precisely what the Supreme Court project would throw up. Now it has, and Tom Bingham – having started this hare, or at least acted as one of its most articulate champions – is quite unable to contain it. His image was that of a seamless transfer to a new location, with no symbols, badges, logos, robes or anything else that would spoil the understated but highly effective image that we have of ourselves at present. This, it seems, is far away from the image which the officials have of it, and it seems that it is now too late to do anything about this. If there is to be a Supreme Court, it has to be seen to be such. In their minds this means all sorts of things that Tom despises and will not have.

The problem deepens however when one appreciates, as one must, that Tom cannot now be the first President of the new Court. He will be 75 in October 2008, which is the earliest date it can now begin to function. Donald will of course retire before then, and so will Johan Steyn – and Lennie, due to reach 75 in April 2009, has made it clear that he will not join the new Court. I am next in line of seniority and will not be 75 until June 2013, so I will have nearly five years to go after October 2008. So, unless something else happens, it looks as though it will fall on me – one of the most vocal critics – to bring the new system into operation. But my position is by no means clear-cut. Tom Bingham was brought in as Senior Law Lord over the head of Gordon Slynn, who should have filled this post by seniority but was far too unreliable. The same thing could happen to me. Nicholas Phillips, currently Master of the Rolls but junior to me, could be given this job to move him on. So could Mark Saville, also junior to me, to reward him for his toils in the Bloody Sunday Inquiry. Others may appear more suitable than I am – a Scots lawyer after all, and by no means the most gifted member of our team on the Law Lords' Corridor.

Yet someone now has to take the initiative. The agenda we have been given is calling for some vitally important decisions which Tom is not cut out for – as he will not be there and is in denial about the effects of what he has done so much to bring about. We cannot meaningfully consult everybody before the decisions are taken, as over half the current Law Lords will not be there. Everything points to my having to get a grip of the situation myself. But do I have the authority to do this? Tom, to an extent, has told me to get on with it. And I had a useful discussion last Thursday with Brendan Keith, the Clerk in the Judicial Office, who is very troubled about his own position and those of his staff whose move sideways to the new Court is proving much less attractive than was assumed to be the case until now. The terms and conditions of service will be much less benign than they are in the Palace of Westminster. He needs support too, and his relationship with Tom on this issue is not an easy one either.

I propose to be much more pro-active therefore than Donald, in his quiet and self-effacing way, ever was. I shall ask Brenda to take the lead on our accommodation requirements. Alan Rodger will deal with the library and Mark Saville will deal with the IT. I shall assume responsibility for the administrative arrangements with, I hope, Brenda's approval. But I need to clarify my own position with Charlie Falconer as soon as possible. I can be an immense help to him if he will listen to me, although this will commit me to a project I would much rather had not been started in the first place. My background as Lord President and all I did for image-making then, including initiating television and working with the press, will be a useful one. I can see ceremonies being conducted on the Court of Session pattern which the image-makers can build on but Tom Bingham would no doubt abhor or at least find uncomfortable. But unless I can get some understanding as to where I stand – having no ambition whatsoever, but only a wish to do the best for the new system – it will be very difficult for me on my own to commit us to anything.

I went, as arranged through Brendan Keith, to see Charlie Falconer yesterday at 8.30am. Joe Wilson, the head of the implementation team, was there too – a comparatively junior civil servant. Also present were two senior people, Alex Allan the Permanent Secretary, and the Head of the Court Service whose name I did not catch. I went straight to the point, as I had a list of five things I needed to get over in quite a short time: the present state of play, status, image, timing and implementation. It was quite clear that Charlie's thinking had not progressed beyond the Bill and the choice of building. He listened carefully as I explained that there was much more to it than that, that important administrative decisions had to be taken, that we needed to know who was to be the Chief Executive and who was to be the first President at least 12 months prior to our assumed starting date of 1 October 2008 and that money had to be available for getting advice on image and for the proper handling of the handover before the new Court came into being. No decisions were taken of course, but he did say that the President was to be one step above the Lord Chief Justice of England and Wales in the order of precedence. What this will actually mean in practice is another matter, as the President will certainly not be Head of the Judiciary in any of the three jurisdictions. We shall have to wait and see what comes out of the meeting in other respects. But at least it is accepted that image is an important issue. I explained that this was necessary if we were to get across the point of principle on which the reform has been built – complete separation from Parliament. He seemed a bit surprised by this, but did seem to appreciate that we could not go on as if nothing had happened, that some lead would be expected from us and that, if there was no lead, we could have the image created for us by the media. We were with him for 45 minutes, which was a satisfactory amount of time.

Last Monday I spent the morning with the civil servants going over more details. They are quite keen to have guidance, and there was no sense of friction – quite the reverse. But there is an awful lot of detail in the new structure which seems to be pure bureaucracy – detail, rather detached from substance.

That afternoon I went as President of the CMJA to the Commonwealth Day Service in Westminster Abbey. I had not been before, so I was very pleased to have been given the opportunity. Perhaps because I am a Law Lord I was given a superb seat in the Sub-Dean's pew, first up on the lower side of the Choir just next to the Lantern. Much of the action took place just beside me, so I had a wonderful completely unimpeded view. Opposite were all the High Commissioners and their wives. On our side were various office-bearers of Commonwealth organisations. Behind us I saw Michael Ancram and Michael Howard – Leader of the Opposition – and Paul Boateng, just nominated as our High Commissioner in South Africa, and his wife. As I could not turn my head round that far I failed to notice until the end that immediately behind me was Tony Blair, the Prime Minister. The service itself was long and full of participation by young people from various ethnic and religious groups. It had been well rehearsed, and there was some fine singing by a soprano soloist and a Gospel choir. Kelly Holmes, the Olympic athlete and now a DBE for her two gold medals last summer in Athens, brought in the rather odd boomerang-like Commonwealth games symbol, the Queen's Baton, which was about to be taken away on its journey to Melbourne for the summer games in 2006. She was most elegant, calm and beautifully poised as she did so. The Queen and the Duke of Edinburgh were there, coming in up one aisle and going out down another so that everyone could see them. They sat in the two stalls at the west end of the Choir where the Lord Chief Justice sits at the judges' service in October. At the end the man behind me left his seat and brushed past me as if in a hurry to get out first. It was then that I realised that I had for the first, and probably the only, time brushed shoulders with Tony Blair. I did not see his face as he went past, but he was taller and broader in the shoulders than I had expected.

This evening I gave another lecture, the Judicial Studies Board annual lecture. I called it 'Writing Judgments'. It had been in preparation since September and was used in an earlier version for my visit to The Bahamas. A lot of detailed work had gone into it. I had been suffering from a bad, irritating cough and had been worried that it would interfere with my delivery. In the event I had only one episode of coughing which I just managed to control. Being rather less than well, I found the event rather exhausting. But the audience was friendly and appeared to be appreciative.

We sat as nine this week in Committee Rooms 3A and 3B for a Privy Council case from Jersey about the circumstances in which the defence of provocation to a charge of murder is available in English law.[236] This composition was needed because of a conflict of authority on this issue between the Privy Council (Lord Steyn dissenting) and the House of Lords (Lords Hobhouse and Millett dissenting) as to whether mental abnormality can be taken into account in this defence. Now that English law has accepted the Scottish doctrine of diminished responsibility, one would not have thought that this case was

---

236 *Attorney General for Jersey v Holley* [2005] UKHL 23, [2005] 2 AC 580.

necessary. One would have expected the test of whether the accused had reacted appropriately to the provocation offered to be an objective one, as it is in Scotland. But once again we were divided: 3–6 with Lords Bingham, Hoffmann and Carswell supporting the House of Lords decision and the rest of us led, surprisingly, by Lord Nicholls supporting the Privy Council. Our majority was composed of three Chancery judges – Nicholls, Scott and Walker – two Scots – myself and Alan – and Brenda Hale. We thought that Donald Nicholls should write the judgment to reply to Tom Bingham's dissent. I felt a bit guilty, as Donald – despite ample days off – has amassed quite a large backlog of judgments to write. Had I not been feeling rather unwell myself due to a prolonged cold and bronchitis I might have been more forceful in my initial offer to write. I hope that I do not have to do it anyway after a great delay because Donald cannot get round to it.

9 April 2005

It has been far from a normal week in the outside world. Various momentous events have occurred. On Sunday 2 April the Pope, John Paul II, died. On Tuesday 4 April, having delayed his expected announcement by a day because of the Pope's death, Tony Blair went to see the Queen for a dissolution of Parliament so that a General Election can be held on 5 May. On Friday 8 April a funeral service for the Pope was held in St Peter's Square in Rome. Today, having been delayed for a day because of the Pope's funeral, the Prince of Wales and Mrs Camilla Parker-Bowles were married in a register office in Windsor and blessed in a church service in Windsor Great Chapel afterwards. And today, having been delayed for 25 minutes because of the wedding, the Grand National was run (and won by the favourite, Hedge Hunter), Parliament has cleared up all its outstanding business and all the MPs have disappeared to their constituencies. The dissolution will take place in private on Monday, with no ceremony. For the next four weeks the Law Lords will have our end of the Palace to ourselves.

More of the Election later, no doubt. At present it seems fairly clear that, distrusted and unpopular though he is, Tony Blair will win a third term for Labour but with a substantially reduced majority. The funeral and the wedding deserve a little more comment.

Pope John Paul II, for all the drawbacks brought about by his implacable adherence to the right to life from conception to the last breath and his refusal to countenance any relaxation to meet the distressing effects of HIV in the Third World, has been an outstanding success as Pope. His emergence, during the period of the Cold War as the first from Poland – the first from outside Italy, indeed – gave him an unprecedented opportunity to broaden the appeal of the Papacy. His command of many languages, his capacity for travel – 142 countries visited, I think – and his great courage, during a long and debilitating illness, have earned him great respect and admiration, and love and admiration for him has extended well beyond the role and Catholic Church itself. It soon became clear that, in contrast to what happened when the previous Pope died 27 years ago, this was to be a world event. There was a procession of devout Catholics from Poland, more than a million it was said, to the Vatican. Possibly a million more came from elsewhere. It was an open-air service, held in front of the Basilica. Heads of State and Prime Ministers, including George Bush and Tony Blair, were there. So of course were all the Cardinals who must soon choose a new Pope and representatives from other churches and faiths, including the Archbishop of Canterbury. The funeral mass was beautifully executed, immensely colourful and listened to with rapt attention by the thousands, mainly Poles, in the Square. There were calls for John Paul II to be made a Saint '*subito*'. His remains were encased in a large, simple coffin made of cypress wood. So fitting for a simple, brave, godly man who gave so much to the world with complete dedication to the task which was thrust upon him so unexpectedly so many years ago.

The ceremonies at Windsor were in complete contrast. Members of the Royal Family, except for the Queen and Prince Philip, made the somewhat unlikely journey to the register office for the civil ceremony to cheers from a small crowd in the narrow streets. There then followed an elaborate service of blessing, presided over by the Archbishop of Canterbury, in Windsor Great Chapel which the Queen – Head of the Church of England – was, of course, able to attend. All the Royal Family were there, and many celebrity guests too. Kneeling before the Archbishop the Prince and the Duchess of Cornwall (as she now is) said their confessions in the words which begin the 1622 communion service – all the congregation joining in. This was an atonement for the adultery which had been committed on both sides. There was an absolution in the same 1622 language which is so familiar to me, but so out of fashion for all services other than the 8am communion. There was lovely music, of course, and some fine readings. Then it was over, and the couple – so very obviously happy and relaxed together, despite Camilla's nervousness and slight awkwardness in places which Charles with great kindness helped her to overcome – went out into the public eye and to whatever the future now holds for them. It has been a long, long, slow and careful process. Diana remains an icon whose glamour will not be forgotten. There are some who blame Charles for what happened to her, others who blame Camilla and maybe others who adopt studied indifference. But there is a growing and obviously justified awareness that this is a true love affair, which was best brought to a conclusion in this way so that Camilla can now play her full part in Charles's life. Unlike Diana she will not seek stardom. She will live only for him. This will be good for him and – with time still on their side – good for the Monarchy too. It was a low-key but very happy, honest occasion which showed the Royal Family at its best – a real family, coming together to forgive the past and look for good in the future. Now, as is their right, they are on honeymoon in Deeside. Like so many others I wish them well, and I am sure that they are immensely relieved and pleased that it all went off so well.

15 April 2005

Back to work – two fairly easy cases, both down for two days but finished in one, raising issues of statutory construction. I was with Donald, Johan, Lennie and Robert, which was a good team for this kind of problem. Nothing for me to write afterwards, which is a help as this weekend is curtailed by my having to travel south this evening, Friday, to be in London for an early start en route to Bahrain where Brendan Keith and I are to attend the opening of their new Constitutional Court. This improbable invitation was thought to be one that could not be turned down for diplomatic reasons. Neither Tom nor Donald wanted to go, so I was selected to represent us. This will mean two days travelling there and back, and two days there. I shall be in London for a two-day case on Wednesday and Thursday next week. I have no idea what to expect. Bahrain is not the most exciting place in the world to visit, but our hosts will undoubtedly be very friendly and hospitable. I am taking two books to read: Dickens's *Bleak House* and Buchan's *The Three Hostages* – selected at random from our library at home.

The Supreme Court affair is in suspense during the Election so far as the Government is concerned. But there have been developments. Charlie Falconer has written to us to say that he has appointed as additional architects for the Middlesex Guildhall project the Norman Foster Partnership, whose more noteworthy projects have included the Millennium Bridge and the Reichstag in Berlin. This will certainly help to inject some vision into the design, but it will not be easy to sell anything very radical to English Heritage or the planning authority. So it is good news, to be tempered by realism.

Tom has responded with typical vigour to a letter from Charlie, drafted by his officials no doubt, about the proposed system for disciplining the Justices. There were a number of quite sensible points raised, but Tom has reacted to them with ill-concealed disgust. He asked us for comments on his draft letter of reply. I spent over an hour working out something more tactful and constructive, only to have all my suggestions rejected out of hand. I suppose Tom thinks that he can get away with this. It is not my way, however, and I suspect that the officials – who know, surely, that Tom will not ever head the new Court – will be tempted to by-pass him. I would rather that he had laid a more closely and politely reasoned basis for his views which would resolve the matter by agreement.

As to who will head the Court, there was a piece in *The Daily Telegraph* commenting on the succession to Harry Woolf as Lord Chief Justice. Igor Judge, one would think, is the obvious successor. Peter Goldsmith has been mentioned too, and Nicholas Phillips, the Master of the Rolls. Nicholas is not a likely candidate really, as he has not had much to do with crime, though both his predecessors – Tom and Harry – moved up that way. But more convincing was the comment that he is unlikely to want the job as he wants to succeed Tom as the Senior Law Lord. He has been making a point of sitting with us quite frequently, and he is steeped in what Alan Rodger has described as political correctness – unlike me, with my habit of sitting in the Chamber and my opposition to the plans for the Supreme Court. It would not surprise me either if the English were behind him. Those who have done their calculations will know that he is junior to me on the list of Law Lords and only a few months older. So he would be taking what would otherwise be my place. I have to confess to having no particular enthusiasm for the job, as it will not be at all an easy thing to lead the new Court as it settles down once transfer takes place. There is so much room for distrust and disagreement, and any attempt at leadership is bound to upset more than it pleases. The whole business of the 'image of the court' is so much a matter of personal choice, and it will be almost impossible to get everyone to agree. So the new President may have to make important decisions without the benefit of unanimity. There however lies the real problem which I face.

Unless Nicholas Phillips is brought in over me, this will be my responsibility. I do not want to be seen to be assuming that the job is mine or to step in where it would be premature to do so. But Tom may delay his departure right up to the wire, leaving us all in a state of uncertainty. We could leave these decisions to him – but it will not be his Court, and the problems with his essentially negative approach to 'image' will not be his to solve when he is gone.

Succession problems are not confined to us. Douglas Cullen will retire as Lord President later this year. Brian Gill will no doubt see himself as the successor. Hazel Cosgrove has spoken to Alan Rodger of her dismay and alarm at the prospect. But Brian has been careful to cultivate those who matter.

24 April 2005

The visit to Bahrain was a mixture of moments of great interest, periods of prolonged boredom, a good deal of eating and the inevitable problem of trying to communicate with people with whom one does not share a common language. Our landing after the flight to Bahrain was very mysterious in the hazy gloom of a desert country after sunset. We were ushered rapidly off the aircraft by Protocol into a VIP lounge where there was a welcoming party. Delegates from France arrived shortly afterwards and delegates from Egypt were already there. The British and French Ambassadors were there too, as was the delightfully modest, English-speaking President of the Constitutional Court. When our bags and passports had been attended to we were ushered to our cars. Each of us had a black Mercedes with a driver in full Arab dress: white robes, white head-scarf. They were to be our individual means of transport throughout the visit. The British Ambassador, Robin Lamb, very kindly invited us to supper at the heavily fortified and guarded Embassy close to the Sheraton Hotel where we were to stay. He was very relaxed, friendly and informative.

Next day, Sunday 17 April, we were taken in our cars to visit what comes as close as is possible in this Monarchy to a Legislature. It comprised the Shura Council, appointed by the King, and the Council of Representatives, elected as individuals, as there is no party system as such. We were taken to a comfortable sitting-room where the Shura Council gathered to welcome us. There were 40 members, almost all in Arab dress. They included six women who were in western-style dress. The Chairman greeted us in Arabic to set the scene, with an appropriate English translation. Then began a debate about whether women should be given a quota in these assemblies. A delegate from Lebanon raised the issue, speaking in Arabic. Others from Arab States responded, and it became quite heated. The Lebanese view was that quotas were unconstitutional but others felt – with some justification – that without quotas women would not get into these Councils at all. When we Europeans were asked to comment I said a few things to fill the space but I was not confident that they were entirely relevant. We were served with chocolates and then, in mercifully tiny handleless cups, Arabic coffee. This was orange in colour, warm and heavily spiced to give it a taste which was as repellent at first encounter as it was surprising, poured from magnificent deep-spouted metal jugs, much ornamented. In the afternoon we were taken for a visit to the newly-built and well-presented National Museum. There were signs here of the British administration after 1917 when the civil service got to work, organised the country and introduced English as a second language which it very much still is. In the evening there was dinner in the hotel. The reception was in the Arab style, sitting down on sofas arranged around a large room. The meal itself was very generous, with many items turning up on each course as the waiters filled up any empty spaces on our plates. There were no speeches. Suddenly our hosts got up and it was time to go. I learned from one of our dinner companions that none of the varieties in their dress, differently coloured head-scarfs, differently coloured over-robes and gold linings – meant anything. It is all a matter of choice, of how 'Bedouin' an image you wished to create for yourself and, of course, how much you can afford.

Monday 18 April was the day of the Inauguration of the New Court. The building itself was heavily guarded for the event, but there was no trouble. A guard of honour was on duty, looking very much as a British guard of honour would do. Dressed in white, but in similar style uniform, identical drill and familiar rifles. We were ushered to seats in the large hearing room. I was in the second row behind a row of local dignitaries. This was the front row of our delegations, representing 'England' next to 'Egypt'. But I think it was more a mark of the importance given to the UK. His Majesty King Hamad Al Khalifa arrived with the Crown Prince. The National Anthem was played outside as the guard of honour presented arms. Then they came onto the Bench with the President. He made a speech which was responded to by the President, by an Arabic-speaking visitor on behalf of the Arab States and by Gianni Buquicchio of the Venice Commission on behalf of the rest of us. The King was very genial, thoughtful, attentive and completely convincing as the prime mover in this reform. When the speeches were over each of us, with me first, presented ourselves in greeting and shook hands. It was a solemn, well-conducted ceremony which made much of the presence of the many international guests. It was shown extensively that evening on television and much covered in the press, to which I and others gave interviews. Later, after a substantial lunch on the same pattern as dinner yesterday, we returned to the court to inspect the premises, and sign the visitors' book in which we each wrote appropriate complimentary messages. Those written in Arabic, which were many, were especially beautiful to see. They put my own handwriting to shame. We also delivered gifts. Ours was a fine print in colour of Westminster Bridge with the Palace of Westminster in the background. It was well received, and had the benefit of looking big and generous.

I found much to admire in the kindness and generosity of our hosts. But I despaired at the lack of my good French. This inhibited conversation with the French delegates including the ones from Turkey and North Africa, although I did manage a long talk in French with a man from Tunisia.

I left on Tuesday morning to get back to work in London. The President very kindly came to see me off and spent nearly half-an-hour with me in conversation, which was very thoughtful of him. Back home in London the wonderful news is that Tom Bingham has been made a Knight of the Garter. It is a mark of the enormous respect in which he is held that this is said to be the first occasion on which this award has been given to a serving judge.

2005 – May to July

7 May 2005

This has been my 'week' at Strathclyde University. It followed the usual pattern. Monday was the May Day holiday. I flew down to London that evening. Tuesday was spent in meetings about the Supreme Court project with the civil servants, Brendan Keith in attendance. This lasted from 9am to 1pm. Then I spent an hour after lunch with Kay Taylor and Lydia Clapinska, former judicial assistants, about how the image of that post could be improved. I then flew to Glasgow on the 5.30pm BA flight – earlier than usual, as I had not had to sit – to be at Ross Priory for the honorary graduands' dinner. There were heavy thunder showers around Glasgow and landings were delayed. Our circuits to use up time gave some quite lovely views of the lower Clyde and the hills around Loch Lomond in the crystal air between showers.

Then Wednesday was University Day. There were seven honorary graduands including Helen Liddell, former politician now to be the UK's High Commissioner in Australia; Alastair Campbell, now as a Senator of the College of Justice Lord Bracadale; and the much celebrated professional footballer Henrik Larsson – Swedish by birth, Celtic's hero by adoption and now with Barcelona. His award attracted a great deal of press attention and there were many admirers who followed him everywhere. He behaved impeccably, with great patience and dignity. His award was as much for his personality and the personal standards he set as for his footballing skills. The next day was a day of talks and visits in Strathclyde. There was a briefing by the Secretary to the University, Peter West, on our visit to Malawi in August, a visit to the students' residential village and a newly set up internet café and a visit to the Estates' Department for a briefing on works to be carried out to develop and improve the Estate. The following day was the Court meeting and the annual Convocation of the University which was much enlivened by a talk on the place which Strathclyde has in our economy and how it should be measured by Professor Iain McNicoll. It prompted many questions – so many that I could not take them all before handing over to Andrew Hamnett for his address as Principal.

22 May 2005

Mary and I have just returned from the Palace of Holyrood where we were the overnight guests of this year's Lord High Commissioner to the General Assembly of the Church of Scotland, the Lord Mackay of Clashfern KT. The routine for these occasions is well settled. Our luggage was whisked away as we were ushered into an upstairs drawing-room for tea. Later there was dinner in the State Dining Room along with the guests who had been invited to dinner. It ended with a fine pibroch played by one of the Royal Piping Society's pipers. There was then a musical interlude in the Throne Room which was provided by a very talented jazz quartet from George Heriot's School. On the following day we were taken to St Giles' Cathedral for the morning service. The sermon on the subject of Joy was preached with great enthusiasm by the new Moderator, Dr David Lacey. We left after lunch at 2.30pm to return to normality.

18 June 2005

Whitsun has come and gone. So far the work on the Law Lords' Corridor has been undemanding, although we had an interesting case about mussel farming from New Zealand. This was one of the last appeals from there that we shall ever have, sadly, as we are almost through the backlog since the new Supreme Court of New Zealand came into operation. I volunteered to write the judgment. Tom Bingham's mind was on other things, as the following Monday he spent the day at Windsor for his installation as a Knight of the Garter.

This week I had the arduous task of sitting on the selection board for next year's four judicial assistants. Philippa Tudor, the Head of Human Resources, was in charge again. She had altered last year's rather absurd policy of not allowing us to see the candidates' references. Brendan Keith was in good form, well organised and suitably critical in a way that I find it hard to be. There were 87 applications, far more than last year. Sifting them down to 12 to interview was quite a task. Then we had to find four to make up our team. There were some quite surprising and disappointing failures when people who had looked so good on paper proved to be either hopelessly inarticulate and ill-informed or far too garrulous and imprecise to be of use to us. At the end of the first day, having interviewed seven, we had four promising candidates with two outstandingly good. Things settled down by the end of the second day, with five more to see. The first three of the day were poor but we had a good final pair and we were able to agree on our four without any real difficulty: two men and two women – Richard Moules, Charles Banner, Rachel Avery and Catherine Tracey. Catherine is a Scots solicitor, and I will ask her to work with me. As usual, some of the achievements of these young people were most impressive – first-class degrees, hugely energetic and active careers so far, with scholarships, prizes and other awards along the line. The only problem for us is that one of our successful candidates is being very slow in responding to our offer due to problems in his chambers. This is unfair on our reserves, who cannot yet be told that they have been unsuccessful.

Tom Bingham asked Alan Rodger and myself to have a word with him on Thursday evening before we went home about the Supreme Court. His message was the unsurprising one that rumours are at work that the new premises are going to be very costly and that the blame for excessive costs is going to be laid at the doors of the Law Lords. We are, I think, well away from that kind of crisis as we are still in the planning stage and the costs of the project are still far from clear. But Tom was also suggesting that the Law Lords should call for a re-appraisal of the whole scheme, the suggestion being that if it was going to cost too much the project should be abandoned. This had huge appeal to Alan Rodger. But it is wholly unrealistic, in my opinion. We are now too far down the line to make it acceptable politically for the Government to withdraw. And the criteria for what is acceptable and what is not acceptable are so much matters of opinion. Brenda Hale, moreover, is giving me enthusiastic reports of how well the project is shaping up. This irritates Alan, who said 'Who put her in charge of these discussions?', waving his hands around. He knows very well that I did. It will be very hard for us to say that the result is not fit for purpose, although we may be sharply divided as to whether it is up to standard.

However, one very good thing which came out of this meeting was the reminder that section 148(5) of the Constitutional Reform Act 2005 requires the Lord Chancellor to consult the Law Lords before he gives his approval to the plans for the building. We require clarity as to when this stage will be reached and what the procedure is to be for securing our approval. I have been asked to have lunch with the Minister, Baroness Ashton of Upholland, next Tuesday, so I shall have an opportunity of exploring this issue then. All this activity is of course very odd, as it should be Tom Bingham who is taking these initiatives. But he is almost wholly disengaged from the project as far as one can tell. And Johan Steyn, who never was actively interested in it, has announced that he will retire at the end of September. His understanding of what our removal from the Lords, which he was advocating so powerfully, will mean is surprisingly incomplete. He does not seem to appreciate that members of our team will no longer be able to chair Sub-Committee E of the EU Committee as we now do, or to enjoy the other facilities in the House while in office and after our retirement except in the case, as to the latter, of those of us who are already peers.

It was announced yesterday that Nicholas Phillips is to be the next Lord Chief Justice, and that Lord Justice Clarke, whom I do not know, is to be the Master of the Rolls. Igor Judge, who has been waiting in the wings as a very possible Lord Chief Justice, has been appointed to be President of the Queen's Bench Division. The fact that Nicholas has been given the job of Lord Chief Justice clears the air a bit at our end, I suppose. It seems rather unlikely now, but not impossible, that he will be asked to succeed Tom as Senior Law Lord. On seniority grounds this still looks likely to be my fate, but one cannot rule out someone else emerging as more suitable. We are two years or so away from this event yet. Indeed, Tom can go on for three and a half years more if he remains until he is 75. So the position of his successor still remains open. This is not a very satisfactory state of affairs, as we so much need a committed leader as we get closer and closer to the setting-up of the Supreme Court.

7 July 2005

Two remarkable days in London – one of joy and triumph, the other of appalling carnage and confusion. The contrasts could not have been more extreme.

On Wednesday 6 July, at a meeting with the International Olympics Committee in Singapore, the 2012 Olympic Games were – against all the odds – awarded to London in preference to Paris. A large crowd had gathered in Trafalgar Square to watch the event on a huge television screen. We were in the Privy Council in Downing Street. The announcement that the Games had been awarded to London was at 12.46pm just as we were rising for lunch. There were distant sounds of cheering as we left for our lunch at Bellamy's and when we arrived there the staff told us what had happened. As we were having lunch the Red Arrows flew over Trafalgar Square trailing smoke in red, white and blue. Huge euphoria – and a remarkable achievement for Lord Coe and his bid team.

On Thursday 7 July, as I left for work, the news was still full of excitement about the Olympics and I picked up a copy of *Metro* in the Westminster Underground station after an uneventful journey from Temple on the District line because it was so colourful. The first signs of trouble were the absence of the bishop when at 9.45am we were in the House for the giving of judgments. Tom Bingham said prayers in his place. The bishop was said to have been stuck on the Underground as it had been closed down because of a power surge. When we got upstairs, however, Sky News was reporting an explosion on a bus near Russell Square, and then reports came in of explosions on Underground trains at Aldgate, Edgeware Road and between Russell Square and King's Cross. It rapidly became clear that this was a terrorist attack – co-ordinated, in the manner of an Al-Qaeda incident – of major proportions. The whole of central London was now without public transport, and trains on the surface lines were being held back as the main rail stations were closed also. A huge emergency services operation was underway. There were sirens everywhere, helicopters in the sky and streets empty.

Later it became even clearer that there had been dreadful casualties. Twelve people were killed on the bus, whose top had been blown off, and scores were killed on the Underground. The worst incident was on the packed train between King's Cross and Russell Square on my much-loved Piccadilly line: sheer horror, deep down in a narrow tunnel. I can see the usual group of fellow passengers, as I write – ordinary, mainly young, people getting to work as usual, suspecting nothing. From time to time I have wondered whether these were to be my own last companions – but what can one do? One has to use the deep lines to get around. There was, of course, no warning – no chance of escape.

By a lucky chance we were not sitting on Thursday as our case in the Privy Council finished in one day, so I was able to get out of London with the aid of a government car at 3pm. There were huge traffic jams on the approach to Heathrow and – with no public transport, and taxis refusing to go there by 5pm because of the congestion – I would not have made it otherwise. So I got home safely to Edinburgh to prepare for my duties next day awarding degrees at Strathclyde University.

The occasion for these attacks? The G8 were meeting – at great cost to our country, due to the need for massive security – at Gleneagles, under Tony Blair's chairmanship. Needless to say, the outrage in London completely overshadowed this event. Numerous protests had been taking place in Edinburgh, Stirling, Auchterarder and Glasgow. But they were mainly non-violent and, if at all violent, were mainly of the breach of the peace variety. The Summit could easily have eclipsed them. But not what happened in London. With typical skill and ruthlessness the group had chosen their targets and their timing well. No doubt within hours London will bounce back. The tragedy to so many innocents will be marked. But life has to go on.

17 July 2005

Mary was with me in London for the social highlights of the year – the Lord Mayor's Dinner for HM Judges in the Mansion House and the Buckingham Palace Garden Party with tea in the Royal Tea Tent. It was a busy week for me too: four full days in the House of Lords, on an appeal about the effects of an order made by the Director of Fishing of South Georgia and the South Sandwich Islands refusing a licence to a UK-registered vessel to fish for Patagonian toothfish on long lines[237] (which cause serious loss of life to that glorious bird, the black-browed albatross, which is attracted by the bait and gets caught on the hooks at the end of the lines). There was also another appeal arising from the

---

237 R (Quark Fishing Ltd) v Secretary of State for Foreign and Commonwealth Affairs [2005] UKHL 57, [2006] 1 AC 529.

Hunting Act 2004 which banned fox hunting in England,[238] the question being about the legality of the Parliament Act 1949 under the authority of which it was passed. That case was heard by a Committee of nine Law Lords.

There was, however, an understandable feeling of tension in London after last week's atrocities. The media were full of reports of the police investigation, which has proceeded at great speed. To everyone's horror it has emerged that the bombers were suicide bombers and that they were long-established British residents belonging to the Muslim community. The Muslim leaders have been quick to condemn the bombers' activities, as have their own families who professed complete ignorance that any such thing was being contemplated and asserted that they must have been brainwashed. That indeed – as visits to camps in Pakistan indicate – may be so. But if they were brainwashed, many others will have been too. The risks of further attacks have been stressed by the security services. Of course, there is almost nothing that we can do, short of staying away from London which is precisely what we must not do if life is to go on.

My journey to London on Sunday evening was not much disrupted. There were glorious views from the right-hand side of the Bmi Airbus 321 as we made our way south through amazingly clear air – Ben Nevis, Schiehallion, Cruachan, the Paps of Jura, Isla and Rathlin Island off Northern Ireland were all clearly visible. There was remarkable clarity too of the Isle of Man and Birkenhead as we made our way into England, with Anglesey also etched out beyond Great Orme's Head on our right. At Heathrow I used the Piccadilly line which was operating only as far as Hyde Park Corner, and changed at Hammersmith to the District line which now stops on Sundays at Temple, which is a welcome change. The journey took just under four hours door-to-door as we took off on time and had a clear run into Heathrow. Mary arrived by train at King's Cross at about 10.30am on Wednesday to find a taxi queue at least 300 yards long. Very sensibly she took a bus, which brought her to Gray's Inn in five minutes.

We had arranged to travel to the Mansion House dinner by government car which was to go first to Alan Rodger's flat in Pimlico. Confusion and delay ensued as Alan professed not to be able to find the car. Then, having been directed to it parked a short distance away from his flat, he went to the House of Lords where he had left his invitation card in his room, causing still further delay. The driver was unfamiliar with London, much to Alan's exasperation. He arrived hot and bothered and only partly dressed at 7.30pm which was the dinner start time. I was able to guide the driver to the Mansion House, where we arrived just in time to join the last of the guests moving into dinner. As in previous years I was seated between the Lady Mayoress and Lady Woolf, with Mary only a short distance away. It would have been very embarrassing to have come in late after the entry of the Lord Mayor and his top table guests. Speeches were far too long of course, but the food and wine were excellent. We extracted

---

238 R (Jackson) v Attorney General [2005] UKHL 56, [2006] 1 AC 262.

Alan Rodger from the crowd afterwards after he had swallowed – gulped down – a 'stirrup cup' and made our way home with a more accomplished driver without incident.

We sat right up to the wire on Thursday and just beyond it as the Attorney General, Lord Goldsmith, and Sir Sydney Kentridge made their closing remarks in the Hunting Act case. Tom postponed discussion of the case until next Tuesday. Mary was already in my room ready for the Garden Party when we got back to the Corridor. Alan was to come in our car to the Palace, but he then announced that he had left his trousers in his flat. Mary was amused and astonished by his rather chaotic life-style. We insisted on going to the Palace ourselves first. We were just in time for a quick inspection of the gardens before we were admitted to the tea tent. The Queen and Prince Philip mixed briefly with the guests but did not stay long. I thought that he looked very tired. They had left the garden well before 6pm.

I had decided to walk back through the park rather than to take a car, and Mary was enthusiastic about this too. I thought that it would be quicker, and we needed to be prompt to get out in time for our flight home from Heathrow. Alan was most critical of my putting Mary to this inconvenience. But in the event he joined us, and we walked back to the House through what appeared to be a completely solid traffic jam. After a quick change we were on our way by Underground, and we arrived in plenty of time at Heathrow for a comfortable flight north to fresh, cool air in Edinburgh.

23 July 2005

Forty years ago today I was admitted to the Faculty of Advocates and, with some trepidation, began my career at the Bar. I noted in my diary on that day that it was as if I was stepping off the high dive – and that there could be no going back. It was, of course, quite impossible to see into the future and the quite remarkable turns in my career after a very slow and nervous start. Lord Reid was the Senior Law Lord and Lord Wilberforce had just been appointed. There was an enormous gulf between where I was on that day and where they were then. The most remarkable thing, in retrospect, was that I had taken my LLB degree only two days earlier. Such leaps in my career – including my leap from Dean to Lord President – are unrepeatable in today's politically correct and overly bureaucratic world. I am not conscious of having been any less effective as an advocate or as an appellate judge because of this, however. And it is a sobering thought that Lord Reid, and perhaps Lord Wilberforce too, would not have got to where they were if the machinery for admissions and appointments then was what it is today.

We discussed the Hunting Act case last Tuesday. Bob Carswell came to see me on the Monday evening. He was in doubt but tended to favour allowing the appeal and declaring the Parliament Act 1949 invalid. That too had been my initial view, but it had dawned on me over the weekend – indeed since the end of the Attorney General's speech – that the acceptance of that measure by both major parties, as each of them have used the 1949 Act, and by both Houses as they have passed further Acts with the assent of both Houses amending Acts passed under it, would make it seem very ill-advised for us now to declare it invalid. So I cautioned him against the view he had in mind. Wisely, I think, he revised his view and, as is his way, had a new draft paper of his conclusions ready by the next day for circulating when his time came. This was just as well, because it turned out that in our discussion we were all of the view that the attack on the 1949 Act failed and that the appeal would have to be dismissed. Some expressed regret, and others were at least concerned that we should not depart from the arena altogether – better to lay down a marker for the future, in other words. Not so Tom Bingham who, as he sometimes does, revealed the fires burning so fiercely beneath his carefully composed exterior as he gave us a long and impassioned lecture on the Liberal Party's long campaign to remove the power of the Conservative-dominated Upper House. It was quite clear that he had aligned himself to the Liberal cause and saw the 1949 Act as part of the same campaign. It will be interesting to see what he makes of all of this when he puts pen to paper.

Thursday of this week was once again marked by bomb attacks on London transport and great disruption to movement as the police tried to control the situation. By the luckiest of chances none of the four bombs went off, although there is no doubt that they were intended to do so with great loss of life. The explosive material had, it seems, deteriorated so there was no reaction when the detonators detonated. I was lucky too. Our two-day case in the Privy Council had ended on the Wednesday and, because it was so hot and I had to continue my preparations for trips to Ghana and Malawi which start in a week's time, I had changed my evening flight to a mid-day one. I was back in Edinburgh as the news was breaking. But I must return to London for two more days next week. The chances of encountering a bomber are remote, of course. But travel days, if they continue like this, could make my way of life very difficult.

Yesterday it was announced that Jonathan Mance is to take Johan Steyn's place on the Law Lords' Corridor. He is 62, very energetic and self-confident. His ability as a commercial lawyer is very considerable, and he will fit into that part of Johan Steyn's contribution to our work admirably. He is less obviously the kind of campaigner for the rights of man than Johan is – perhaps more balanced and less dogmatic, which will be a good thing. He is married to Lady Justice Mary Arden, of course. It will be a first for us to have a Law Lord who is married to a member of the Court of Appeal. As a team they are already making a significant contribution to public life, and that is bound to become even more so as a result of this appointment. I am not quite sure what sort of relationship I shall have with him, as he is so much brighter and self-confident than I am. But he will add much strength to our team – a good appointment.

29 July 2005

Packing up for Ghana and Malawi has been the business of the day. Amidst all of that, this afternoon there was a meeting at 34 India Street of the panel that is to make recommendations to the First Minister for the successor to Douglas Cullen as Lord President. Gone are the days when this was the preserve of the Lord Advocate. Now it is done by an independent body with a substantial lay element. The chairman is Sir Neil McIntosh, Chairman of the Judicial Appointments Board for Scotland. David Edward and I have been invited to serve as the senior judicial members. We have a lay member, Barbara Duffner, a senior administrative officer in the Post Office, also of the Judicial Appointments Board. David Stewart of the Justice Department is our secretary – an old friend, very shrewd in these matters. Our meeting today, without Barbara Duffner, was to discuss procedure. Those interested are to be invited to express interest, in a deliberately informal way. The Dean, the Deputy Keeper of the Signet, the President of the Law Society and the Law Officers are to be written to in order to canvas interest as widely as possible. It seems a bit absurd, as the likely candidates are all already Senators on the Bench. But I was appointed direct from the Bar, so we cannot rule that out. As David Edward reminded us, however, solicitors are unlikely to be eligible unless they are Writers to the Signet: see Article XIX of the Act of Union. There will be a shortlist meeting on 30 September and interviews three weeks later with a view to putting three names to the First Minister. George Emslie would turn in his grave about this, but we have to live with the times. I can only reflect how improbable it would have been for me to have been selected under the new procedure – so too Alan Rodger for that matter, both of us aged 51. The likely candidates will, it seems, be chosen with a view to their being active for a few years but not too long. Mid-60s seems the likely age, as is the case with the Lord Chief Justice of England and Wales. Alan Rodger teases me by saying that everyone interested will be eyeing our every move until the choice is made. In the old days it was all over before anyone was any the wiser.

2005 – August to September

24 September 2005

The applications for the appointment to Lord President have come in. The list of applicants is highly confidential, of course. But I suppose that I can confide in my own diary who they are. There are six candidates and they include Brian Gill and Arthur Hamilton. There are a number of things that trouble me. The list itself – a response to invitations issued to the usual legal bodies, not a press advertisement – is disappointing. I can think of several other people who, in former times, might well have been thought of as suitable for appointment to this position. Hazel Cosgrove (but she has said that she wishes to retire next spring), Robert Reed, Anne Smith and Patrick Hodge, for example. Had we approached the task by consulting first with the Lord President, the Dean and the President of the Law Society for their suggestions and then invited applications from selected individuals our list would have been very different. Brian Gill and Arthur Hamilton would certainly have been on the list. The others probably would not. As it is, we seem to be short of the required three good names to recommend to the First Minister. Other things trouble me. We said that we would interview the candidates on Friday 21 October. But how do we do this without breaching confidentiality? The absence of judges from the Court of Session Bench is bound to be noticed, even if they can be released without disrupting the business of the court. And the slippage of time is worrying. Douglas Cullen says he is to retire in November: he is 70 on 18 November 2005. It seems highly unlikely that the appointment of his replacement will have been secured by that date if – as we must now (and I should have spotted the problem earlier) hold our interviews on a Saturday. The time it will take to make the appointment, and the way this will be done, contrasts rather badly with the old system. And it is already quite obvious that neither I nor Alan Rodger would have stood a chance under the system as it now exists, even if we had been rash enough to apply.

Douglas's departure in November will leave me as the oldest and longest serving member of the Scottish judiciary: and I am still only 67 and, all being well, will have at least five years still to go and could indeed go on for another eight. This is an odd situation to be in, and a highly fortunate one too. Clearly I could not, in the current climate, have continued as Lord President after the age of 70 assuming that I was still there, and I would probably have had to think of going now after 16 years on the Bench as so many of my contemporaries are doing around me. In London the situation is the reverse. I am still one of the youngest Law Lords: Alan Rodger, Brenda Hale and Jonathan Mance being the only ones who are below me in age. The tradition is to carry on until 72 or thereabouts, as Lord Steyn has done. The work remains stimulating and attractive and the way of life, though demanding, is well within my physical capabilities. Retirement now is out of the question for me, nor would I wish it as I have the luxury of being able to carry on in the best of all judicial roles.

2005 – October to December

1 October 2005

This year this significant date – the start of the Legal Year in England and Wales – falls on a Saturday. So here I am at 9.45am in my sunlit study in Edinburgh listening to Radio 3's absorbing Saturday morning programme, with no work to do.

Yesterday the group of which I am a member charged with the responsibility of recommending to the First Minister the person or persons he should consider for the appointment of Lord President met here in my room at 34 India Street to discuss our candidates and plan how to deal with them. We were joined this time by Barbara Duffner, the fourth member of our group. She is a nice friendly sensible woman with a sharp eye for the important details. Neil McIntosh chaired a meeting of the Panel. His rather soft diffident manner conceals a very able well-ordered mind. He ran the meeting well, encouraging each of us in turn to say what we thought of the candidates and varying the turns so that each of us had an opportunity to speak first or last. Our raw material was made up of the candidates' CVs and their papers on the challenges ahead and how to meet them which they had been asked to prepare for us. To this, which was all our two lay members had to work on, David Edward and I added our own personal knowledge and assessment of each candidate. The two most obvious candidates were Arthur Hamilton, clearly a most able lawyer and well fitted to follow in that tradition, and Brian Gill, whose paper was by far and away the best on offer and who had impressed our colleagues accordingly. Brian's personality is quite different from Arthur's, of course. Arthur's CV looks dull in comparison with Brian's, which sparkles with all his many overseas visits and extra-mural activities. We agreed to interview five of the six candidates. We are to give up a Friday afternoon and the whole of a Saturday, 21 and 22 October, to this exercise. It is a demanding one, but it is so important to get the thing right. We have been careful not to discuss our views privately outside the Panel meetings.

I said at the start that I was disappointed at the field on offer, and Barbara Duffner, as to be expected, joined me in lamenting, for example, the lack of a female candidate. But there is no going back now on the course we have been following. As Neil McIntosh pointed out, it was for Douglas Cullen, who had the opportunity, to ensure that those he thought worthy of the appointment put their names forward. Of course Douglas had the opportunity to do that. Whether he was willing to take that initiative is another matter. I suspect that he chose to remain silent for fear of causing trouble. His calm, stable manner promises much, but the general view seems to be that, while he was a safe pair of hands, he might perhaps have made more of the Presidency. The most fundamental problem that will face his successor is the way the Judiciary has become isolated from the Executive, the profession, the press and almost everyone in public life; and how to correct this. The drift began with Alan Rodger, who had no time for the press or the products of the devolution exercise. Douglas has not been able to restore the position as Harry Woolf has been able to do with such success in England. I hope that Douglas's successor will be able to face up to these challenges.

Tomorrow Mary and I will drive down to London, as the Abbey service is on Monday and our new session is about to swing into action. There is to be a dinner in Gray's Inn for Gordon Slynn on Monday, for which she will join me. There is to be another in the Royal Courts of Justice for Harry Woolf who retires today as Lord Chief Justice, and we will both be there too. Then, after all these excitements are over, it really will be back to work.

14 October 2005

We gave judgment in *Jackson*, about whether the Hunting Act 2004 had been validly passed under the Parliament Acts, yesterday. All nine of us were there, except for Donald Nicholls who was working at home. The gallery was full of hunting supporters who left in disappointment as we told them what they did not want to hear. The importance of the case for relations between the Judiciary and Parliament, and between the two Houses of Parliament, was much wider than their cases, however, and the human rights issue in their case remains to be determined.

The Supreme Court came to the fore during the week. I had a full morning meeting with the civil servants on the administrative issues, as a case had settled and I had a day free. The atmosphere was friendly, but it was disturbing to find that so much decision-taking is being delegated to the civil servants at a lower level. The reality is that the Lord Chancellor and the Permanent Secretary have moved on to other things, and they are more or less unreachable now on such delicate things as the question of whether, and if so to what extent, the appointments procedure in the Act for the Supreme Court should be introduced before the Court is set up and applied to the House of Lords. This is an issue which is never raised in debate but is capable of being achieved under the transitional arrangements, which the civil servants have studied carefully and are seeking to make use of. I found it hard to argue against this being done for new appointments, as these will so obviously have a major effect on the make-up of the new Court and it would be odd to have the old system used when everyone else is operating through Commissions or Boards and the Lord Chancellor is extracting himself more and more from the remnants of the judicial function.

But I did my best to resist it being applied to the two top posts – the Senior Law Lord and the Deputy Senior Law Lord. The need for continuity of knowledge and experience is crucial in that case, and it would be disrupted if, as could happen, recruits for both of these posts were being attracted from outside during this period. Of course, it is quite absurd to have to go through this rigmarole for the Deputy's post – having to apply for it and then no doubt to write an essay saying why one wants to do the job. Who would bother, given that there is no extra pay and there are no benefits attached to the post whatever?

On Wednesday afternoon we had a crucial plenary session with the architects Hugh Feilden and Spencer de Grey to decide which of the two options in play for the refurbishment of Middlesex Guildhall should be proceeded with. They did a good job presenting the alternatives to a fairly sceptical audience. Alan Rodger and Lennie Hoffmann, predictably, were suspicious and hostile – 'we voiced extreme objection', said Lennie himself afterwards – to either scheme, on the view that neither had anything to recommend it and the whole place was wholly unsuitable. But it is far too late for that. We have been boxed into a corner long ago and must make the best of what we have. I told Tom that his sub-committee (me, Brenda and Richard) supported option B – the library in the middle, a new court on the south side – and Robert Walker and Jonathan Mance, our new Lord, spoke to the same effect. That was what the architects themselves wish, of course, and so it has been decided. Brenda and Jonathan, who will be there longest, are quite enthusiastic. I am realistic, as is now Tom who said to me afterwards that it was too late to adopt Alan and Lennie's line. He clearly cannot now go back to Charlie Falconer and say that the Middlesex Guildhall will not do. That would get him nowhere, and politically we are in a dead-end now anyway. Colin Lyne, the civil servant in charge, told Richard Scott that there is no extra money: we have a fixed limit on the budget, and it can go no further. So much for the Treasury's interest in the idea. He too regards Lennie and Alan as best ignored, as nothing will change their minds and there is no point in trying to negotiate with them. No matter about Lennie, who will probably not be there. But I am sad about Alan, who would do better to relax and accept and work with the inevitable.

22 October 2005

Much of yesterday and most of today has been spent with the appointments panel interviewing candidates for appointment to the post of Lord President. We met in the Royal College of Physicians in Queen Street, a neutral venue far from prying eyes. Yesterday we interviewed two candidates. Today we saw three more and then discussed our assessments with great care and attention to detail for two and a half hours before reaching our conclusions. Although we had little difficulty in deciding that three of the candidates whom we interviewed could not be recommended as suitable for the post to the First Minister, our discussion with them was extremely useful as a means of setting the scene for the more obvious contenders today. The point was made very forcibly by them both that the Court is in serious difficulty due to poor decisions on resourcing by the Scottish Court Administration, especially by downgrading the Court of Session clerks below the level of those in the Sheriff Court and to a sense of isolation from the outside world which affects morale. The structure of the Court too is looking increasingly out of touch with the work it does, with the inevitable consequence that delays are building up where with a more modern structure they could be eliminated.

So we were left with Arthur Hamilton and Brian Gill as the only two acceptable candidates. Arthur Hamilton was fresh, enthusiastic and articulate, careful but positive, well informed and very obviously keen to do the job well and make a real success of the opportunity. Brian Gill, on the other hand, appeared surprisingly nervous and defensive. Of course his record of achievement is impressive, and Barbara Duffner was inclined to doubt Arthur Hamilton's ability to manage the Court to the same level. David Edward and I did not share the same doubt, but we were all agreed that Arthur showed more potential for growth in the job than Brian and a clearer sense of the way forward in the longer term. So, as between the two, we decided that we should provide the

First Minister with a recommendation, and that our advice should be to offer the post to Arthur Hamilton.

It has been a fascinating but exhausting two days. The discussion has been intense, penetrating and informative. We have all learned a great deal from it, and the selection process has never been more carefully handled. I am still uneasy about the gaps in our candidature, but I believe that the right person has emerged at the end of it. So this time round it has worked out for the best, and it will be thought to have done so too if our advice is accepted by the First Minister.

Of course, I have come away from this experience full of doubts about how I would have performed had I been exposed to a similar process when I was being considered for this appointment. Surely I would have been ruled out on grounds of lack of experience and James Clyde might well have been preferred. Politically no doubt I would have been seen as best suited to face up to the reforms being sought by the Thatcher Government. I had been an active and reforming Dean, and my practice at the Bar was of the required quality. But a team of independent adjudicators would have doubted my ability to step into the chair without any previous judicial exposure whatever. It was James Mackay's assurance that this was not necessary, and Alan Rodger's too, that helped Peter Fraser through this difficulty in pressing me to accept his nomination as one of the three candidates. So it is not that this point was not considered. But the current climate is different, and I cannot help wondering whether my Presidency of the Court really was a success after all.

20 November 2005

Several events to record briefly before I head off early this Sunday afternoon to try to get an earlier flight to Heathrow because of fog.

John McCluskey produced an article this week in *The Scotsman* which was highly critical of the selection process for the Lord President which, he says, is designed to divert attention from 'the obvious candidate' – by which I assume he means Brian Gill. Meantime, according to Alan Rodger's informants, Brian has been protesting about the situation in which he finds himself and insisting that he is consulted, as is his right, by the First Minister personally. Jack McConnell has apparently responded by asking to meet each of the six candidates himself.

Last Monday I was interviewed in Gray's Inn Hall by Joshua Rozenberg, the second in a series of three involving Tom Bingham and Bob Carswell as well as myself: all of us three former Chief Justices and all of us Masters of the Bench in Gray's Inn. It was an enjoyable experience, which gave me the opportunity to say some useful things about the Supreme Court. He produced a fair account of what I said in Thursday's *The Daily Telegraph*.

This weekend Mary and I paid a quick visit to Cyprus for the inauguration of the new building of their Supreme Court. It was a very worthwhile expedition despite its brevity. I had been invited as President of the CMJA, of which Cyprus is a very loyal member. We were very generously and warmly looked after by our hosts, along with equivalent judges and their spouses from about 15 other EU countries. The new building is very modern, in the Norman Foster style, with a wide impressive spacious entrance and various other fine features which work well. It was inaugurated by the President of the Republic, Tassos Papadopoulos, who had earlier welcomed us all to the Presidential Palace, the former Governor's residence, which has retained many of the original features including the Royal coat of arms over the main entrance. Much was made of the illegal occupation of Northern Cyprus by the Turkish Army which no one except Turkey has recognised and is, of course, an outrage. The UN has kept the peace, however, and there must be some hope that in the long run the problem can be resolved through the EU. It was nice to see Petros Artemis again and Christos Artemides, the President of the Court, both of whom had been to CMJA events.

Much trouble with Tom Bingham over his opinion in a case which we heard in October,[239] where he and I are in disagreement on the test to be applied by the Special Immigration Appeals Commission to the admissibility of evidence alleged to have been obtained by torture in a foreign state. Tom has paid far too little attention to this issue and it may be difficult for him, having gone one way which seems now to be acceptable to the majority, to adjust to my views on this issue which – all being well next week – will be accepted by them too. Alan and Simon agree with me. I hope that Bob will also.

25 November 2005

Yesterday, after much coming and going, it was at last announced that Arthur Hamilton is to be the Lord President. It is a relief that the First Minister, who may have been exposed to all sorts of pressures, has accepted his panel's unanimous recommendation. I spoke briefly this evening to Alan Johnston, who tells me that Brian is blaming Lord Mackay of Drumadoon for colluding with the First Minister because they both have houses on Arran. This is quite extraordinary, as Brian must know perfectly well why he has not been preferred. According to Alan the whole thing is highly improbable anyway, as Donald Mackay was apparently hoping – and perhaps expecting – to become Lord Justice Clerk. Arthur's understated but dignified and determined manner is so much more suited to what the job really requires.

Today, according to a 15-second slot on BBC Scotland television, there was a ceremony in Court 1, with the Whole Court sitting, in which tributes were paid to Douglas Cullen, to which he replied. No such thing was attempted in

---

239 A v *Secretary of State for the Home Department (No 2)* [2005] UKHL 71, [2006] 2 AC 221.

my day, fortunately. But Douglas is actually retiring from the Bench, not moving on. His retiral leaves me now as the longest-serving member of the Scottish judiciary.

Back in London, there was another arduous meeting of the Supreme Court sub-committee. Our logo, robes and how to address the Justices were all on the agenda – each one a highly sensitive subject, on which views are sharply divided up and down the Corridor. Some guidance was given to the civil servants, but sooner or later we will have to grapple with these issues and reach decisions ourselves. I am in a dilemma. I fear the result of any vote will be unattractive, so I am reluctant to press the issues. Also, as I am not the leader, I do not feel that it is my job to do so. I shall have to confront Tom about this in the next few weeks. As our views are so far apart, that is not an attractive proposition either.

On a happier note we had a very demanding case about corporation tax, advanced corporation tax, franked investment income and tax credits.[240] I spent a lot of time trying to understand it all, and by the time we started the hearing I had begun to get on top of it. So, in the event, it was quite fun – really good intellectual stuff. We divided 3–2 at the end: Scott, myself and Nicholls in the majority, but I suspect that Brown and Walker will be content to join with us. I feel that Simon Brown, delightful and diligent though he is, is really struggling to get the point, which is hardly surprising. I had the advantage of reliving a tax world that I used to inhabit when advising the Stenhouse Group about their tax affairs in the mid-1970s and early 1980s. That was a great help to me.

27 November 2005

Rosamond Cullen and her family gave a party yesterday evening to celebrate Douglas's 'freedom'. He was, as he put it in his speech to an audience in Court 1, which was shown for a few seconds on BBC Scotland television, 'dis-installed' on Friday. The whole Court sat in tribute and speeches were made by Lord Osborne, the Lord Advocate, the Dean of Faculty and the President of the Law Society of Scotland. It was a very happy select party.

On the way home Alan Rodger told me of one more twist in Brian Gill's approach to the appointments process. Jack McConnell telephoned Brian on Wednesday evening with the news that he had decided to accept the recommendation in favour of Arthur Hamilton, but stressed that he was doing so in confidence as the announcement was to be withheld until 11am the next day. Brian then broke the news immediately to Nigel Griffiths, one of the Edinburgh MPs, who was onto the First Minister by telephone within half an hour to tell him that he had made the wrong choice. In the meantime I had been asked to attend Arthur Hamilton's installation next Friday. I have declined. My instinct,

---

240 *Pirelli Cable Holdings NV v Inland Revenue Commissioners* [2006] UKHL 4, [2006] 1 WLR 400.

fortified by Rosamond Cullen's advice – she knows what has been going on – is that I am too close to this highly controversial appointments process, and that my presence would have been an embarrassment. I am far too shy to go on my own anyway.

22 December 2005

A blackbird was singing in East Princes Street Gardens amid all the noise and excitement of the Christmas festivities. It was perched in a large weeping ash tree above the ice-skating rink, shouting at the top of its voice to make itself heard above all the other noise. It was 4.30pm and dark, it being the shortest day.

26 December 2005

Boxing Day! The Christmas party is over. The weather is cold and damp and dark outside – all the greater pleasure to be indoors.

The term was fully occupied right up to the end of last Thursday, with a four-day seven-judge appeal. It was another human rights case, this time about the Article 8 ECHR right to respect for the home and its effect on actions for the recovery of the possession of local authority houses and other heritable property from persons with no legal right to be, or to remain, there.[241] Two cases were being heard together. So there were a lot of speeches to get through, most of them rather too long and some very boring. Tom Bingham presided, and we had Donald Nicholls, myself, Richard Scott, Robert Walker, Brenda Hale and Simon Brown to make up the seven. We were in the modernised, enlarged Committee Rooms 3A and 3B, which were comfortable and pleasant although cold on the first day. Meantime there were other distractions crowding in on our week: another dinner for Harry Woolf, this time white tie at Lancaster House. I was at a table with the Binghams – Tom resplendent in his KG sash, and two of the Woolf sons with their wives. A lunch for the judicial assistants in the Barry Room for Christmas, a 5pm party for Catherine Tracey, my judicial assistant who was getting married the next day, a long meeting about rules for the Supreme Court and a visit with Mary to Olympia for a dressage display and competition to music which had attracted most of Europe's finest exponents of this art.

At the end of our case, having discussed long after 4pm, we ended up with another split decision 4–3 with me leading the majority, and Tom supported by Donald and Robert. Things could change over Christmas. This is the third time, at least, that I have found myself in this position – one of these in a case called *Qazi* which was under review in the *Leeds* case. Tom's messianic and purist approach to this issue does not appeal to me. I am, on the other hand, from his point of view too easily diverted from decisions based on principle by

---

241 *Leeds City Council v Price and Others* [2006] UKHL 10, [2006] 2 AC 465.

thoughts about how our decisions will work out in practice. Perhaps I can claim to have common sense on my side, as well as the majority.

Then, on Thursday evening, it was back home with three judgments to do over the three-week break. One was the entertaining case about corporation tax, *Pirelli*, which I enjoyed writing about in a supporting opinion to that by Richard Scott. The other was a supporting opinion to Alan Rodger in three devolution cases about whether the appellants were barred by acquiescence from complaining that their convictions by temporary sheriffs were nullities, *Robertson and Others*,[242] which we heard in the Privy Council in the first week of December. There were two devolution cases that week in one of which, *Kearney v HM Advocate*,[243] Alan could not sit. This was because it was about whether a temporary judge, Roderick Macdonald, whom he had appointed when he was Lord Advocate, was to be regarded as an independent and impartial tribunal when presiding over a criminal trial. So I was the only Scot. The *Robertson* case delves deep into Scottish criminal procedure, about acquiescence in decisions which would have been set aside if challenged timeously. We were addressed by Colin Boyd, the Lord Advocate, and by Niall Davidson QC. Alan Rodger went home to do his own research and came up with a whole lot of very eclectic Scottish material which had not been cited to us and, as a result, produced a brilliant, highly-influential opinion on how the issues of waiver and acquiescence should be approached by the Scottish criminal courts. This is hardly a devolution issue, but as it was consequential on a devolution issue it was within the jurisdiction of the Privy Council to comment on it. This is strong stuff from the Privy Council, but it is only possible because we have someone of his intellectual strength on the Board. I hinted, in my brief opinion, at the troubles that would lie ahead for Scots criminal practice if the Privy Council were to venture into such areas without such expert guidance. Donald Nicholls, who is no respecter of the Scottish legal system and would apply his own carefully-reasoned thoughts to our problems without regard to where the border lies, is at the back of my mind. Fortunately one of Tom Bingham's many good points is that he does respect these boundaries and has done much to preserve them in the many devolution cases on which he has sat.

We delivered our judgment in the torture case on 8 December. This was another split decision 3–4, with me again leading the majority: *A v Home Secretary*.[244] Tom, rather naughtily, but knowing that the event would be televised, devised a form of words to express what he thought we were agreed about: not to admit evidence which 'had or may have been' obtained by torture. I had not been consulted or warned about this but, suspecting that he might try to go along this road, had a formula of my own in which I set out in a few words what I was in favour of and what I agreed to – which did not include that the evidence

---

242 Reported as *Ruddy and Others v Procurators fiscal of Perth and Aberdeen* [2006] UKPC D2, 2006 SC (PC) 22.
243 [2006] UKPC D1, 2006 SC (PC) 1.
244 See fn 232.

might have been obtained by torture, on the ground that in the real world it would set the barrier too high. My words got no publicity at first, of course. So a misleading and confusing version of our judgment, for which Tom was responsible, went out over the airwaves and into the headlines until the Home Secretary, Charles Clarke, began to put his points across quoting what I had written instead and saying that he accepted and respected the majority judgment. Simon Brown was rather taken aback by Tom's initiative. 'Were you expecting that?' he asked me, as we left the Chamber. I think that he thought that what Tom did was rather underhand. Simon is a very decent soul, who would never have done that without consultation. In retrospect I wondered whether I should have challenged Tom's version in the Chamber. Truth to be told, I did not spot the error as he spoke when he included words suggesting that torture had actually been used which was not the factual basis for our decision, as I was concentrating on my own formula which I was about to give. But it was better not to have a row in public, nor did I protest privately, on the view that Tom's mental block on the issue was so complete.

I reflected on this during the long hours in the Cathedral during the Christmas services. Great man though he is, Tom is on such sensitive issues, about which his admirable and deeply held convictions take complete control of him, a most awkward judge. He spent hours and hours writing extensively about the history of torture. This was wasted effort really – although he delights in expositions of history. He hardly touched on the real issue of great difficulty which neither he nor Donald Nicholls were willing to debate with the rest of us, which is what to do where the sources on which our intelligence depends cannot be exposed so as to reveal whether or not torture was indeed used. Blinded, as I would see it, by principle, Tom asserts that if there is simply a *risk* that torture might have been used the information cannot be relied on at all by the Commission (SIAC). That is all very well as a declaration of high moral values. But the reality is that much of the information that comes to the security services is at fourth or fifth hand, and that it comes from countries which are alleged to use torture sometimes, or even often, but who do not tell us what their methods or sources are so that we can check the facts for ourselves. To exclude information on Tom's approach as to what might have happened would cut us off from all of this information whatever the circumstances: too high a price to pay, in my view, which fortunately Alan Rodger, Simon Brown and Bob Carswell all share. We – the majority – also have article 15 of the Torture Convention and a German Appeal Court decision on our side, all of which Tom disparages and brushes aside. Much damage might have been done to our national security if Tom's view had carried the day, which is no doubt why Charles Clarke has made so much of my opinion which sets a standard which our system can respect and live with.

Judges like Tom and Johan Steyn too, now retired, attract huge praise and admiration for basing their decisions on high moral principle. But we have a wider responsibility, which is to secure the public interest too and not to impose on the public the consequences of our own view of morality. More and more we seem to be drawn into issues of this kind. There is such a narrow line between what we should do as judges and what we should not do. Tom is unreachable for discussion about this, unlike Alan, Simon and Bob. I regret this. I cannot help feeling that it would have been better if we could all engage in this debate.

So ends another fascinating and most enjoyable year. Visits to The Bahamas, Ghana, Malawi and Cyprus have added four more countries to my list – now beyond easy calculation. The Supreme Court issue has now settled down to planning for the future, and work is reasonably well in hand for this with several very important meetings to look forward to in January and February. There is a new Lord President in Edinburgh. I am now the longest-serving judge in the Scottish/UK judiciary. Our work in the House of Lords and the Privy Council has remained at a high level of intensity, with human rights issues still occupying much of our time. Scots appeals reached a remarkably high level this autumn. There were two major decisions – *Percy v The Church of Scotland*[245] and *Davidson v Scottish Ministers*[246] – which are likely to make a substantial impact, both of them reversing the Court of Session. Jonathan Mance has replaced Johan Steyn. The early signs are that he will not make such a remarkable impact as Johan has done, and that as he has many outside interests he may not be quite so dedicated to his work on the Law Lords' Corridor. There is no sign of Tom, Donald or Lennie retiring. So we may not have any changes in 2006. This will allow us to settle down with this new member of our team. Our four judicial assistants – Richard Moules, Charles Banner, Rachel Avery and Catherine Tracey – are delightful, contributing much to a relaxed happy atmosphere on the Law Lords' Corridor.

2006 – January to April

5 February 2006

The big gap since I last wrote is due to a lot of heavy work at weekends – a run of very interesting cases: a discrimination claim by a retained fireman (*Matthews*[247]), the possible abuse of police powers to deal with terrorism (*Gillan*[248]) and a week spent on financial provision on divorce (*Miller v Miller* and *McFarlane v McFarlane*[249]). A good start to the term to be followed by lighter work this week, as I am in the chair in the Privy Council on two cases about which I shall not have to write. Then, next weekend, I shall have very little time at home as I have to go to speak at the Winfield Society dinner on Saturday at St John's College Cambridge.

The Supreme Court project continues on its way. I spent a Friday in London on 13 January going over the plans with the professionals and the architects under

---

245 *Percy v Board of National Mission of the Church of Scotland* [2005] UKHL 73, 2006 SC (HL) 1.
246 [2005] UKHL 74, 2006 SC (HL) 41.
247 *Matthews v Kent and Medway Towns Fire Authority* [2006] UKHL 8, [2006] ICR 365.
248 *R (Gillan) v Commissioner of Police of the Metropolis* [2006] UKHL 12, [2006] 2 AC 307.
249 [2006] UKHL 24, [2006] 2 AC 618.

Brenda Hale's chairmanship. Tomorrow we have our final meeting with the architects and Alex Allan, the Permanent Secretary in the DCA, before the plans are put to the Law Lords as a whole for their approval. This weekend saw the start of this season's Six Nations Championship. England were dominant over Wales yesterday but today, to everyone's amazement and delight, Scotland beat France 20–16 at Murrayfield. What a start to the season.

18 February 2006

Last weekend I broke my usual routine and went to a Saturday evening dinner at St John's College, Cambridge. The occasion was the Law Faculty's Winfield Society dinner, named after the famous Johnian tort law academic, Sir Percy Winfield. I had been invited to speak as a Law Lord and as an Honorary Fellow of the College – an offer which, on the last count at least, I could not refuse. It was a bit of an ordeal getting there from Edinburgh, eating into much of a precious weekend. On arrival at the station I walked to the College to savour the sights and the atmosphere, surprised by the huge quantity of parked bicycles everywhere and the absence of college scarves which seem so completely out of fashion in these days of dressing down. I had invited myself to stay at the Master's Lodge, which is my privilege as an Honorary Fellow. The Master is Professor Richard Perham, a very fine and successful scientist who was a near contemporary of mine when I was at the College. He and his Canadian wife Nancy, herself a very distinguished academic, were very hospitable in the enormous mansion that is their lodge. I was shown to a large very comfortable bedroom with an ample bath and changed for dinner.

The dinner was in Hall, which was a delightful privilege. There were about 60 present, a mixture of students, academics and some practitioners and a retired High Court judge. The husband of my judicial assistant Catherine Tracey, Chester Brown, was there. He had done a Master's degree at John's a few years ago. Richard Perham's presence as Master added dignity to the occasion. The organisers, third year undergraduates, were on my left and right. When I spoke it was for about 15–20 minutes, about the transition from the House of Lords to the Supreme Court and the present state of play – an easy subject for me. There was not much follow-up, as I circulated among the Society members for an hour or so after the dinner was over. I suppose it was too much to expect them to question me about what I had been saying, some of it rather provocative, afterwards.

After a comfortable, rather late night I had breakfast with the Perhams and then went to the College chapel, where I had not been to a service for over 40 years. It is a huge, chilly, barn-like place but the choir is, of course, superb and so are the acoustics. There was some magnificent singing but it was a rather impersonal kind of service. There were only about 30 people there. I dare say that King's was packed out, but they undoubtedly have the higher profile.

I was in the chair for two short cases in the Privy Council on Monday and then in a two-day case in the Lords which shrunk into a single day. This was the last stage in the *Preston* part-time workers' litigation[250] which I began with as a junior Law Lord seven years ago. Bob Carswell and Jonathan Mance agreed to write the judgments in the Privy Council cases, and I undertook the House of Lords one which has occupied me for much of this weekend. Bob's was a criminal case where he was in his element and he quickly produced a very well-crafted and readable draft. Jonathan was as enthusiastic and quick in his draft in a case about banking regulations in The Bahamas. But his style is rather too dense to be read with ease or enjoyment, unfortunately. There is a real knack here. Johan Steyn was superb as a writer, and Simon Brown is too, with rather less rhetoric. I hope that Jonathan will develop a better style, as we need to set a high standard if we are to communicate properly with our audience.

My secretary Gail Munden came to see me as I was working on paperwork on Thursday afternoon. She was a bit downcast, as she had decided that the conditions for moving with us to the Supreme Court were so unattractive in her case that she could not accept them. This is hardly a surprise, but it is quite depressing for us all to have to face up to the reality. The terms and conditions of work in the civil service are much less generous than they are in the Houses of Parliament. A full five-day week is expected every week, and there are only six weeks' holiday. For Gail, who lives near Colchester, this would mean £1,000 more in travelling expenses, quite apart from the boredom and labour of having to put in extra time when we, the Justices, will be at home on Fridays or absent during our recesses. There are all the other perks that go with working in the Palace of Westminster, and a better salary scale too. She is one of our best secretaries and has been a great support to me. But she has to look to her own future, and pressure to take a decision and get out before the rush is forcing her to apply for yet another job straightaway. The glorious principle of independence which Tom and Johan have proclaimed from the rooftops, with no real thought for its consequences, is being shown up at every turn. The fact is that the independence which we enjoy within the Palace of Westminster – far from the civil service and from the Executive – is incapable of being replicated anywhere else. It is a precious jewel which will be lost forever when we move.

Arthur Hamilton came to see me today, at my suggestion, to discuss the Scottish Executive's proposals for modernising the judiciary in Scotland which are now out for consultation. This is a rather over-worked series of proposals for appointments, discipline and administration which will create a lot of extra bureaucracy for not much benefit, all in the name of 'inspiring confidence in the judiciary'. It is all part of the same game that has been getting increasingly out of hand at Westminster. Potential judges of real quality and ability are being turned away because they do not want to be locked into this process. The over-regulated system is in danger of being choked and made unworkable. Yet we have to go along with much of this, for that is the political reality. Arthur

---

250 *Preston v Wolverhampton Healthcare NHS Trust (No 3)* [2006] UKHL 134, [2006] ICR 606.

himself is finding the pressures of his new job rather close to intolerable. But I suspect that he will get used to this as he becomes more organised. I was lucky, I suppose, as I moved from my very high-pressured job as Dean of Faculty to a well-run machine that George Emslie had been in charge of for years. I had my problems, but a feeling of being over-worked was not among them. I was used to it and was on top of the routine quite quickly. The Lords Ordinary, however, of whom Arthur has been one for about eight years have a much easier time. So it must be a real effort to have to gear himself up to the much more demanding office of Lord President. The Scottish Executive's consultation paper will not help, of course.

25 February 2006

I was so disturbed by Gail's obvious distress at the pressure she is under because of the Supreme Court project that I decided to raise the whole issue of how our staff is being treated with Tom. He in his turn asked me to draft a letter about the issue for him to send to Charlie Falconer. As a result I was invited to go with him to see Charlie to raise the issue in discussion, and Brendan Keith provided me with a useful briefing note. The two key issues were the unfortunate terms and conditions of service that will follow from being transferred to the civil service, and the very low grading new staff will have for what we need in comparison with others in the service due to the tiny scale of our operation. These are huge and almost certainly intractable problems, but it was worth making a fuss about it. Charlie was on his own, without his senior civil servants. He was relaxed and sympathetic. But he dropped a small bombshell when he announced that he had been told by his architects that, due to delays over planning permission for the movement of the Crown Courts, the earliest date that the Middlesex Guildhall would be ready for our occupation was 1 January 2009. The fact that he seemed quite unperturbed by this was a great surprise, as we have been led to believe that the 1 October 2008 date was a political imperative. He was just as unperturbed when I said that we could not move our operation from the House of Lords to the Supreme Court over Christmas, and that this delay means that in practice the date would have to be put back one year to 1 October 2009.

This year's delay is of great significance to our staff. Delaying from two and a half to three and a half years for our move is a major change in the programme. On our own front, four Law Lords will reach the retirement age of 75 during that extra year: Lords Bingham, Hoffmann, Carswell and Scott. This will leave me as the senior man on the team, but not necessarily the Senior Law Lord – this may have to be a special appointment. I told Gail and Brendan as soon as I could. They were quite visibly taken aback, as was Helen McMurdo once I had clearance from Alex Allan to pass the message around the Law Lords. I am taken aback too. But for my initiative we might well have been left in ignorance for ages.

The revelation is timely, as on Monday we are to have the critical meeting to be 'consulted' about the plans for the refurbishment. Our approval, if we give them our approval, will mean that the plans will then go to the Lord Chancellor for his approval and then for planning permission and listed building approval. The fact that five of the Law Lords – Donald Nicholls too – will not be with us when we make the move will make this a rather odd meeting. I expect it to be a lively one too.

Scotland lost to Wales in Cardiff two weeks ago after Scott Murray was sent off after 20 minutes for reacting by kicking a Welsh player on the head, recklessly rather than deliberately, after a late tackle. They did not lose by much, and today they scored another famous victory at Murrayfield when they beat England 18–12 to win the Calcutta Cup.

19 March 2006

The championship of the Six Nations ended with a third victory for Scotland, away to Italy, and a thrilling try by Ireland to beat England in the last minute of the match at Twickenham. This left England in the bottom half of the table with only two wins and Scotland in third position with the Calcutta Cup, Ireland in second with the Triple Crown and France with the championship: a superb result.

I spoke briefly to Douglas Cullen today. He is very concerned about Arthur Hamilton. The pressures of the job have taken their toll and he is now on medical leave at his cottage, leaving his post unfilled. Douglas suspects that we may be faced soon with a resignation. This would give rise to all sorts of problems. I suspect, in retrospect, that the judicial appointments panel did not go about getting a suitable candidate in the right way. Head-hunting would have been the best route, although it was impossible to say that to the lay members. Perhaps next time it will be different.

1 April 2006

Not yet on holiday. Easter is later this year. That is just as well, as the cold spell which has gripped the country since January broke only last weekend and snow is still threatened for the northern Highlands. We have a busy week still to go in London.

Much to my regret my faithful secretary Gail Munden has given up her post with us in favour of a job which has become available in the office of the Clerk of Parliaments. This is all down to the Supreme Court. It was made clear to her that under the civil service rules a job there would compare very unfavourably, and there would be a risk of a lower rate of pay increases. She is as upset at having to move as I am at having to lose her. She looked quite woebegone when she came to tell me about this several weeks ago. This week she has been offered an even better job, as secretary to the Clerk of Parliaments himself. She was in tears in my room as she told me and asked me whether she should apply for that job as she was being urged to do. Then we had a farewell party. There is one week to go and then we will be without her. I have not dared to ask Helen McMurdo what replacement for this loss is to be given to me.

Mary and I were at a party given by Hazel Cosgrove this evening to celebrate her retirement as a Court of Session judge after 27 years of judicial service, ten of them in the Court of Session. There were many, many old friends. It was a privilege to have been asked, I thought – though, in truth, I did play a major role in her advancement, selecting her as a temporary judge and then presiding over her installation shortly before I stopped being Lord President. Among those present was Arthur Hamilton. He looked quite relaxed, though Christine was less so. He has still not returned to work after his sick leave, but it was reassuring to see him there. The best thing no doubt would be if he were able to settle down and do the job he has been appointed to do. Otherwise we face a very difficult period of finding a replacement. The next two or three weeks will be crucial, as things cannot go on as they are.

29 April 2006

The problem has now broken out into the press, but has been treated in a very low-key fashion so far. Arthur is expected to return to his duties next week. I hope that this can be achieved, as the longer this goes on the more unlikely a fast return to duty becomes.

Last Wednesday evening I was the principal guest at a dinner of the Worshipful Company of Distillers, given in Vintners' Hall, Upper Thames Street. David Grant, with whom I grew up in Edinburgh when we lived in Moray Place, is the Master of this livery company. Out of the blue – we had not met for over 40 years – he asked me to speak at his dinner. I felt that I could not refuse. I owe him everything, really. It was at his first engagement party in October 1962 that I first met Mary and, with remarkable insight into the future, knew that same evening that we would marry each other. For me it was love at first sight, although I was in a poor state as a penniless student in comparison with her secure position as a primary schoolteacher. Had we not met then, and she not met me, we might never have come together as we did. So I owe him 40 years and more of delight and happiness. Anyway I said that I would do him this favour. I spent a lot of time working up a speech: six minutes, light-hearted, I was told. It must have taken me a day. I injected some short jokes taken from long forgotten speech material collected when I was Lord President. I duly presented myself for the dinner, realising as I had expected that I knew no one there except David who was busy greeting his guests. No one showed any interest in me at the reception. 130–140 people sat down to an excellent dinner, liberally beset with wines and whiskies of which I could, of course, partake little. However, when my turn came to speak my plans worked out perfectly. It was short, as required, with short sentences. My jokes were met with gentle laughter to begin with, but as I went on full laughter burst out at almost every sentence. I had them eating out of my hand. It was all great fun, and when I sat down they all stood up to applaud me. David Grant abandoned his speech and we went off for some more whisky. And suddenly everyone was full of smiles for me and I was given a special visit to the Vintners' cellar as a reward. I had done my duty! It was a great relief not to have let David down, and have this particular ordeal behind me. Next week, for which I am now preparing myself, is University Day at Strathclyde: another speech, but at least this time it will be to people I know and in an environment which I understand.

2006 – May to July

20 May 2006

Strathclyde University Day and its associated events passed off smoothly enough. My flight up from Heathrow was timed rather better this year at 17.30hrs which meant that I was just in time for the start of the dinner instead of arriving at Ross Priory an hour late. The Moderator of the Church of Scotland, David Lacey, was one of the honorary graduands. I based my speech on the three Heavenly Graces 'hope, faith and charity' – adding 'joy' to accommodate our fourth graduand John Wallace, a trumpet player and Director of the Royal Scottish Academy of Music and Drama. The Da Vinci Code, very topical, as a High Court case about it had just recently gone to judgment and the film had its premiere this week, also featured. I am not sure that I can keep up such a high level of ingenuity. The visits on Thursday were to Jordanhill Campus, which is due to be sold off in a few years' time, following the move of the Faculty of Education to the John Anderson Campus. Friday was exceptionally busy. There was a 7.15am start; then the nominations group meeting; a short speech of welcome to a law conference in the Lord Hope Building; the meeting of the University Court; the Convocation; return for an hour or so to the law conference; and then the RSNO annual conference after which I returned home at about 11.15pm.

Two busy weeks in London have followed – sittings mainly in the Privy Council, but with visitors from St John's College, Cambridge to look after; a meeting in the Middlesex Guildhall with the Art Collection trustees; the usual half-yearly meeting of the Institute of Advanced Legal Studies; planning meetings for a forthcoming colloque with the Conseil d'Etat and the CMJA Conference in Toronto in September; and participation at a conference held by the Commonwealth Parliamentary Association. This last event was quite good fun. There was a reception and dinner on Tower Bridge on the Monday evening. This was a remarkable venue, rather like the inside of the Forth Railway Bridge, full of rivets and girders but with superb views up and down the Thames. The company, with delegates from 27 Commonwealth countries and a mixture of MPs and peers, was excellent. My contribution was a brief address on the role of the judiciary two days' later, in a session chaired by my old friend John McFall MP and joined by Edward Garnier QC, MP. This was followed by a question and answer session which concentrated, predictably, on undue leniency to criminals and the problems faced by asylum seekers as portrayed in the popular press. Time was too short to do more than skirt over the surface on these very sensitive issues. Then, on Thursday, the huge new airbus A380 flew over Westminster on its way to its first landing at Heathrow.

On Friday morning, back in Edinburgh, I had a meeting at 34 India Street with Sir Neil McIntosh, the chairman of the Judicial Appointments Board, and the excellent David Stewart of the Scottish Court Service. It had been prompted by more news about the Lord President, Arthur Hamilton. It had been expected that he would return to duty, after a long absence since February, at the beginning of June. This clearly cannot now happen. It looks as though his recovery will need much more time. This gives rise to a number of very considerable problems. There is, of course, much work to be done that requires the input of the Lord President. Even if Brian Gill had been willing to do all in his power to stand in for Arthur with a good grace (which by all accounts he has not – what an opportunity missed!), there are things only a Lord President can do. These include recommendations for the award of silk and a long-awaited judgment in a criminal human rights matter, for example.

The solution for which the officials are looking is that Arthur should resign. But he is not in a fit state to take such a decision at present, especially as resignation would have such an effect on him and his career and on his finances. He cannot be forced out of office, except perhaps on the production of medical certificates and a joint resolution of both Houses of Parliament. This is not an option. If he were to resign, the issue of his replacement would arise. That is where Sir Neil and I come in, as the senior members of the panel which appointed him – as David Stewart described us. My preference would be for a head-hunting process to begin, and for three or even two preferred candidates to be interviewed by a panel and then reported on to the First Minister. Anne Smith and Patrick Hodge come to mind as young, vigorous and attractive people who would have the personality and strength of character to take on this now very arduous job. But this solution is hardly possible given that our panel has already told the First Minister that Brian Gill was an acceptable candidate.

As to how the process is to be handled, it is obvious that Neil McIntosh is committed to the principle of open competition. That is the central rule on which his Board operates. There is no room there for a system that does not call for advertisement and a disclosed report on candidates. Head-hunting of the kind I favour is not something he can accept. If Brian were still to be in the frame we would have to re-run the system as before, but it would be impossible for us to say, based on facts known to all of us, that he was unsuitable when nine months ago we said that he was. My hunch is that the First Minister will find it politically unacceptable not to appoint Brian Gill without further reference to the panel. There was a big row, created by Brian himself when he was told of his appointment: see 27 November 2005 above. As David Stewart said, we do not know what commitments, if any, the First Minister gave to Nigel Griffiths. But he can expect more of the same, increased perhaps three-fold, if he passes over Brian Gill again.

The whole thing is a tragedy: for Arthur himself, of course, and for Christine. They should have been at Holyrood this weekend as guests of the High Commissioner to the General Assembly of the Church of Scotland, Lord Mackay of Clashfern. It is a tragedy for the Court of Session too and for the whole judicial system. But as much of a tragedy is the flaw that it has revealed at the heart of the new appointments' system: encrusted with all the encumbrances of political correctness at the cost of speed of delivery and common sense. Never until now has the system failed to deliver a Lord President who could last the course. It is ironic that the first such failure should occur at the outset of the new system and that the system is unable to take the urgent and positive action that is needed to correct it.

2 June 2006

Just back from Craighead after the Whitsun break. It is Friday evening, and I am clearing up ready for a weekend devoted to final preparation for a colloque with the Conseil d'Etat from Sunday to Tuesday.

Meantime the press have carried reports of Arthur Hamilton's admission to the Priory, and today emergency legislation is to be rushed through the Scottish Parliament to enable the Inner House judges to declare Arthur unfit and have him replaced temporarily by the Lord Justice Clerk as acting Lord President, who in his turn will be replaced by Lord Osborne as acting Lord Justice Clerk.[251] The Scottish Executive say that they are confident that Arthur will recover. Let us hope so. On this basis, if he does not, Brian Gill must surely be appointed Lord President. It would be quite unacceptable to do anything else.

Before Craighead I had two opinions to do and also the preliminary sifting of this year's round of applications for judicial assistant. There was a lot of dross in the 70 or so applications, but we have just enough promising material to go on. This year's team however is quite exceptionally good, and I wonder whether we will be able to keep up that standard.

Before I left London we had another meeting of our Supreme Court subcommittee to discuss the plans for the building, now getting down to detail. It is interesting and, in a way, enjoyable. But I think that once we get inside the place we will find it very claustrophobic compared with the open vistas and space that we have in the Palace of Westminster. One good thing, however. I have been issued with a special Palace of Westminster/House of Lords Visa card which enables me to pay for car parking at Edinburgh Airport and transmit this directly to my House of Lords account. This is a great relief, now that the free parking arrangements for parliamentarians provided by the British Airports Authority has been terminated.

---

251 Senior Judiciary (Vacancies and Incapacity) (Scotland) Act 2006 (asp 9).

10 June 2006

I returned to London a day early at the end of the Whitsun recess to chair the British team at this year's colloque between the Conseil d'Etat and La Chambre des Lords which was held in London. All too conscious of my lack of practice in French, I was very anxious about the whole affair, for which the excellent Wendy Howard of the DCA has borne almost the entire burden of organising at our end.

In the event it all passed off very well and, apart from a few fluffed lines when I tried to speak French, I felt content with what we had achieved. Our team was myself, Jonathan Mance, Stephen Sedley, George Newman (a member of SIAC, the Commission which deals with those suspected of terrorism), Philip Brodie from Scotland and Paul Girvan from Northern Ireland. Catherine Tracey, my judicial assistant, was on our team too and was very useful indeed. The French team was the Vice-President, Renaud Denoix de Saint Marc (whose last year this is in office), Bernard Stirn, Mme Josseline de Clausade, Marcel Pochard (with whom I had corresponded, each in our own languages, by email when making the arrangements), Mme Isabelle de Silva and Mattias Guyomar, to whom the Vice-President kept referring as 'mon jeune collègue'.

Wendy Howard and I met the delegation from France on their arrival at Waterloo by Eurostar on the Sunday afternoon. On Monday we spent the day in session in the Parliament Chamber of the Inner Temple, very well looked after and comfortable. Dinner that evening was at Lancaster House with Charlie Falconer, the Lord Chancellor, as host. Tuesday morning was occupied by a further session. We then had a very slow bus trip to the French Ambassador's residence in Kensington Gate, where we were entertained to a delightful late lunch by the Ambassador – a table in a lovely summery dining-room, with huge windows looking out over the trees and gardens, covered in rose petals. Then off to the British Museum where the Director, Neil MacGregor, in excellent French received our guests and we were taken round a fascinating and highly-organised exhibition of Middle Eastern art which was much influenced by the current troubles there. Then it was all over.

We discussed our respective countries' response to the problem of international terrorism. This was more interesting to us, I felt, than to them as we are so much more challenged by the extreme measures being taken by our Government. We also discussed urgent procedures in administrative laws, where discussions were very fruitful and interesting in view of their reforms which have introduced a much more rapid response as well as oral hearings by a single judge. We took our guests for a short visit to the House of Lords at their request on the Monday before our dinner. This was obviously much appreciated. The mystique which attaches to the House of Lords adds value to these exchanges. It will be hard to emulate that when we become just another Supreme Court.

1 July 2006

A very crowded week in London. There were meetings each day and an oral hearing at 9am as well as a full three-day libel case in which the issue was whether what had been published fell within the test of responsible journalism: *Jameel v Wall Street Journal Europe*.[252] Then it was home to Edinburgh on Wednesday evening for a day on an exchange with Indian judges. Our meeting with the judges was held in the Caledonian Hotel, starting at 10am, which gave me time to draw breath. I had met the Chief Justice of India, Justice Sabharwal, in London when he came to have lunch with the Law Lords together with his registrar and his personal secretary. The other members of the Indian team now appeared, including two justices from the Supreme Court, the Chief Justice of the Madras High Court together with Soli Sorabjee, an old friend and a senior advocate. On our side there was Lord Phillips, the Lord Chief Justice, and Lord Justice Anthony Campbell from Northern Ireland, Lady Justice Mary Arden, the Lord Advocate and the Dean of Faculty, later joined by Chief Justice Brian Kerr of Northern Ireland and Peter Goldsmith, the Attorney General for England and Wales. The Lord President, Arthur Hamilton, appeared too. He was in a relaxed and confident frame of mind, which was most welcome. I was very pleased to hear him contribute to the discussions, and he played a full part throughout the day. We discussed the separation of powers and the relationship between judges and the media. I missed the second day, when the environment and international terrorism was to be discussed, as I was at Strathclyde for my first round of the summer degree ceremonies.

But Mary and I attended two very enjoyable evening functions to entertain our guests. There was an informal dinner at Prestonfield House, and a more formal one in the Signet Library. The plan had obviously been to push the boat out for the Indians. This is good because, as one of the two fastest growing economies in the world with enormous potential but with a great loyalty to the English legal tradition, it is a relationship which must be nurtured and carefully kept in good repair. The Indian team were very articulate and friendly, and it was a most successful meeting. Arthur made a neat little speech of welcome as host in the Signet Library, and he brought the proceedings to an end with a 'Surprise' in Parliament Hall for which we went after the dinner was over. This was a brief but impressive Beating of Retreat in the Hall by the Edinburgh Police Pipe Band, excellently drilled and neatly dressed in indoors order.

This evening England's hopes in football were dashed when they were knocked out of the World Cup by Portugal in a penalty shoot-out in the quarter finals. But Scotland kept the flag flying at Wimbledon, as Andy Murray beat the third seed Andy Roddick in straight sets and moved into the fourth round to be played next Monday.

---

252 [2006] UKHL 44, [2007] AC 359.

21 July 2006

These last two weeks should have been occupied by an eight-day hearing of appeals from Pitcairn arising from prosecutions against several of the islanders in that remote and isolated community,[253] for what in our terms would be regarded as child sex abuse but – as they go back over 40 years, and were unchecked until police investigations were carried out by Kent police in 1996 – were, on the surface at least, apparently part of the life-style of the islanders' male population. Various points of interest were raised in the appeals, and a huge amount of effort had been put into the preparation of historical documents – over 4,000 pages of them. They were there for us to look at as we reviewed the decisions of the courts below as to the rights of the UK to legislate for Pitcairn and whether the laws made for the island had been properly promulgated, as well as issues of abuse of process on a variety of grounds. Flat screens had been installed for our benefit, and memory sticks produced with material stored on them. A DVD was to be created with a record, visually and in sound, of the entire proceedings to be shown on Pitcairn to the islanders and to interested parties in New Zealand.

To the great misfortune of counsel who had put such an effort into preparation our Board in the Privy Council was presided over by Lord Hoffmann. He expressed a total disinterest in Pitcairn, its culture and its history, and was determined to cut to the bone the scope for any argument. The other members of the Board were Harry Woolf, Johan Steyn – both retired – and myself and Bob Carswell on the wings. Lennie had reduced counsel, in a state of shock, to almost abject surrender and speechlessness within half an hour in a manner reminiscent of Lord Diplock. It did not help that – with the exception of David Perry, who had not yet got to his feet – they were all from New Zealand or New South Wales and unfamiliar with the ways of the Board. Nevertheless it was a devastating start to the proceedings, which resulted in the whole affair being over in under two days after the thinnest of arguments. I did my best to keep the thing alive, bearing in mind that our proceedings were to be on view by the islanders, and with some support from Harry Woolf. But the whole stuffing had gone out of the affair and Lennie had collapsed the whole event with his devastating ability to cut to the core issues and demonstrate that there was nothing of substance in any of them. He has just produced a draft judgment, which is just as terse. The novelty and difficulty of the issues is not apparent from what he has written.

I am in a quandary. I felt that there was much more in the case than he had given it credit for, and I am sure that if Tom or Donald had been in the chair the issues would have been debated in much greater depth. I feel that I must write something, even – unusually for the Privy Council – in a concurring speech. But it is going to be difficult to do so without breaking all the conventions that dictate that the Privy Council does not go in for separate opinions. I

---

253 *Christian v The Queen* [2007] 2 AC 400.

am sad for the teams on both sides of the case who had put so much effort into it. They deserved more, and were understandably dismayed by the reception they received after having expected to be heard in full over so much longer, on issues which could have been regarded as some of the most interesting to reach the Privy Council for decades.

In the result it looked as though I would have one and a half weeks off. But I was brought into a three-day case in week two in the House of Lords, in place of Lord Mance who has had to decline due to a prior involvement. And next week two empty days have become full as I have been brought into a difficult case about the recovery of tax paid under a mistake. This too will be presided over by Lord Hoffmann, but there is no way in which he will get away with slicing this one to pieces. It is a really good commercial/chancery type of case of the kind he relishes, and it will be a good debate conducted by very experienced English silks.

Meantime the weather, which was delightfully cool during the two days of the Pitcairn hearing, developed into a record-breaking heatwave. It was hot and dry, with easterly winds on Monday but became even hotter and more humid as the week wore on. On Tuesday 18 July Mary came down by air from Edinburgh for the Lord Mayor's Dinner for the Judges in the Mansion House – enduring the Piccadilly line from Heathrow on a day when *The Evening Standard* declared that the temperature on the Tube was 47 centigrade and, on the buses, up to 52 centigrade. This is twice the permitted heat, it was said, for transporting cattle. The committee rooms are air-conditioned and pleasant to work in, but our west-facing offices became so hot as to be almost unbearable. The dinner was in comfortable air-conditioning in the Mansion House, however, and was as ever a great pleasure. Once again I found myself placed next to the Lady Mayoress, but this time as Donald Nicholls was not there I was the senior Law Lord present. Nicholas Phillips, in his first speech as Lord Chief Justice, was conciliatory and supportive, as was Charlie Falconer in similar close harmony: both on the side of the judges against criticisms from the executive. The confrontational atmosphere of previous dinners was absent, for once.

On Wednesday, having finished my case, I took the afternoon off to escape from the heat of my room. Mary came to lunch on the terrace in the House of Commons, joining Simon Brown, Alan Rodger and Jonathan Mance for a pleasant, leisurely occasion in the brilliant sunshine. We then went to spend the afternoon in the shade at Kew where the dryer grasslands amongst the trees reminded us of scenes in Spain or in Malawi. Then we endured a journey back on the District line of such heat and humidity on the hottest day of the year that we were dripping as we sat in our seats as if in a Turkish bath. It was not quite so hot on Thursday, which was a blessing as it was the day of the Royal Garden Party at Buckingham Palace. When we arrived there we were just in time to watch the Queen and the Duke of Edinburgh arrive at the top of the steps of the Palace, to be greeted by the National Anthem and then applause. We then explored the garden keeping in the shade as much as possible, admiring some of the magnificent trees, the herbaceous border, the roses and the pond. We then made our way for tea – such a privilege – in the Royal Tea Tent, where we were bidden with special red cards for 4.45pm.

There we concentrated on meeting people rather than having tea. Some Commonwealth High Commissioners were guests there too, as well as Bishops, Law Lords, Black Rod and some other people in high places. We made our way to a group of Africans, the ladies beautifully attired in traditional dress. To our pleasure we found that we were speaking to the High Commissioner for Malawi, recently appointed, and his wife. There was much to talk about, especially as they had recently been to visit Strathclyde University. Beside them was the Ambassador, as he must be called, for Zimbabwe. He was delightfully modest, reserved and charming – most encouraging for the future, we thought. Then we found another group, from Senegal whose Ambassador told us how anxious that French-speaking former French colony is for closer links with the UK. Is this a possible new Commonwealth member, we wondered? Then the Duke of Kent, Princess Alexandra – so elegant and friendly – and Lady Airlie ended up in our group. 'Are you going cruising?' said the Princess to Lady Airlie – referring to the cruise which the Queen starts tomorrow on a chartered vessel from Islay through the Hebrides as an eightieth birthday present to herself and her family. Lady Airlie explained that she was not, as she was heading north that evening back to Angus for her own holiday. Then suddenly it was all over. The Royals left, and almost as suddenly so too did the diplomats and their families. Left behind, the three Law Lords and their spouses helped themselves to some of the raspberries, iced coffee and other delicacies that there had been hardly time to touch before it became indecent for us to remain any longer.

30 July 2006

The last week of the term was again almost unbearably hot and humid. There was less direct sunshine, more cloud. But this only served to increase the feeling of being inside a Turkish bath. At the end of the week – Thursday, that is – it all broke down into scattered but sometimes very intense thunderstorms. But it was heat and humidity everywhere, except in the air-conditioned Committee Room 1 where I sat on two cases to finish off the term.

One was a fairly simple case, on complex facts, about the ranking of insurers' costs of negotiating claims in asbestos-related cases where the company concerned was in administration. The case was very well argued by very experienced specialist counsel, and the two-day hearing was over in a day. Lennie, who presided, circulated his draft judgment the following afternoon – quite a tour de force, considering the working conditions. The other case was a much more interesting one about a taxpayer's right to recover tax paid under a mistake of law.[254] It revisited cases I was in during the 1990s about mistake and the

---

254 *Deutsche Morgan Grenfell Group plc v Inland Revenue Commissioners* [2006] UKHL 48, [2007] 1 AC 558.

restitutionary remedy. This is a product of those decisions, which were revisited with great care and attention to detail. It was a full-day case. We ended up with a more or less agreed result but a lot of work to do to explain how we got there.

In addition to these sitting days there was plenty to do each evening. On Monday we had the judicial assistants' photograph, followed in the evening by the judicial assistants' annual dinner. Richard Moules, Tom's assistant, most unfortunately could not be there as he was in hospital, having broken his leg in a bicycling accident and suffered from accumulated clots as his fracture was being reduced. So we had a spare seat in the photograph which he will be fitted into with the wonders of modern technology when he is back to work. Brenda Hale complained to me that she had not been included in the photograph. Our practice has been to have the four senior Law Lords only, with no awkward decisions to be made as to which of the others take their judicial assistants seriously enough to be fitted in. I am reluctant to change the practice just for her. Happily Alan Rodger, who has never complained, was in the photograph and at the dinner in place of Donald Nicholls who was absent for family reasons. The dinner was very well attended. Many old friends were there, including James Vallance White and Andrew Mackersie, as well as previous judicial assistants back to 2000, now developing their careers and having children. We will welcome a new team next October – Matthew Slater, John Summers, Sasha Blackmore and Zoe Christoforides.

Then on Tuesday there was a meeting in Uganda House of the organising committee of the CMJA for the Toronto 2006 Conference over which I must preside. Plans are falling into place pretty well except for anything that is to be done by the Canadians, where much of it is still in a state of uncertainty. It is a relief to be reaching the end of this long-drawn-out process. Then on Wednesday, in a very hot and stuffy conference room, we had our last meeting of the term of the Supreme Court sub-committee. It too had a heavy agenda – necessarily so, in view of the coming recess, and it was scarcely possible to cover all the ground in the two and a half hours from 4.30–7pm. The next step is the hearing of the applications for planning permission by Westminster Council on 7 September. Any delay in that process could have quite serious consequences. If permission is granted, however, contracts will be placed during December with a view to work starting in April next year. By that stage, surely, the process – unattractive though it is – will be irrevocable even by a Tory Government.

The journey home on Tuesday was hugely affected by a severe thunderstorm in and around Heathrow at about 5pm. We were told at Westminster Underground station that the Piccadilly line was suspended at Heathrow Central because of a signalling failure and were advised to go to Ealing Broadway where the Heathrow Connect service, which I had never taken before, would take us to Heathrow without extra charge. By the time we got to Ealing Broadway on the District line it was pouring with rain. Large numbers of people were on the platform waiting for a Heathrow train to come in. At last the train did come in and we all got on. The train made its way on to Heathrow through the storm which, unknown to me, was causing a landslide at Acton Town which blocked the reopened Piccadilly line. Meantime we were charged for our trip to Heathrow because the concession was said to have been lifted at 4pm. But this was a minor hiccup compared with the chaos at Heathrow due to the effects of the storm. Several flights were cancelled, including the Newcastle and Aberdeen flights, probably because these airports close down at about 11pm and could not be reached in time. All others were delayed for about two hours at least. Mine was three hours late and got me to Edinburgh at 00.45 hours. I was home just before 1.30am. All but one of my flights for the past month have been delayed by at least 40 minutes. It is a relief to have finished this term and not to have to go through these delays yet again this coming week.

Now I am left with three judgments. One, in *Fornah*,[255] about the 1951 Refugee Convention in which the question was whether the applicants were entitled to its protection as being members of a particular social group, I have just finished. Then I must write about the Pitcairn case which Lennie had treated almost with contempt, and then there is the mistake of law case from last week. This will occupy me for almost all the spare days until next weekend, when we go to Craighead for our holiday.

Thus ends my tenth year as a Lord of Appeal in Ordinary. I am astonished that I have been there so long. It has been such an absorbing and privileged position to enjoy, in such very good company. Ten happy years!

2006 – October to December

8 October 2006

Twenty years ago today I was introduced as the newly elected Dean of the Faculty of Advocates. What adventures Mary and I have enjoyed together since that date. How different our lives would have been had I not been successful in that election.

On Monday 2 October we went to Westminster Abbey for the judges' service to mark the opening of the New Legal Year. There was one significant change, to make up for – or rather eliminate – the delays we have experienced at the end of the service. The Lord Chief Justice and the Lord Chancellor/Secretary of State for Constitutional Affairs came in side by side, both read lessons and both left, side by side, by the east door. This was certainly an improvement, if a little odd. I wonder whether it will survive for long, especially when a non-lawyer in the House of Commons becomes Lord Chancellor. Tom Bingham was not there to observe and pass comment on this piece of symbolism. He stayed away from the service in protest. Quite why was not entirely clear. It is known, however, that he had been protesting at Lord Falconer's references to Lord

---

255 *Fornah v Secretary of State for the Home Department* [2006] UKHL 46, [2007] 1 AC 412.

Phillips, the Lord Chief Justice of England and Wales, as the Head of the Judiciary. Strictly speaking, Tom is right to believe that he – as Senior Law Lord – is the most senior judge of all. But the roles are very different, and of course each of the three UK jurisdictions have their own Heads. I do not see why Tom should feel diminished by these references. Another complaint is the way the Law Lords are treated at the service, grouped with retired Law Lords, retired Permanent Secretaries and the Heads of the Judiciary in Scotland and Northern Ireland. But the fact is that the Law Lords do not parade as members of a court and, if Tom and most others have their way, nor will the members of the Supreme Court as, according to his plans, they will have no robes or mace or uniform. We can hardly complain if we are grouped, in our rather splendid place in the Choir, with everyone else.

In Scotland things took a sudden turn when Colin Boyd, Lord Boyd of Duncansby, who has been under attack in the press on several issues recently, retired suddenly as Lord Advocate. There was no immediate crisis or cause, however. He has served for six and a half years, and it has not been an easy time. Nor is there, in the new order, the obvious reward or place to go. He has probably had enough of the job, and who can blame him? He says he will spend more time in the House of Lords. That could be interesting. The Advocate General, Lord Davidson of Glen Clova, is already there. Colin sat on the cross-benches as Lord Advocate, to everyone's surprise. If he moves to the government benches he may find himself head-hunted for something else.

Meantime Elish Angiolini, the Solicitor General, has been appointed Lord Advocate and John Beckett QC, from the Crown Office, has been appointed Solicitor General. Beckett is a member of the Labour Party and Elish is a career procurator fiscal. The appointments were made with great speed, in sharp contrast to the time it takes now to fill vacancies in the judiciary. Alan Rodger is, naturally, very critical. He doubts Elish's ability to give the kind of advice, across the board of civil and criminal law, that the most senior Law Officer can, and must be able to, give. He may be right. Elish's strengths have lain elsewhere as an administrator, and the qualities Alan and his predecessor showed are not hers. But the days of top-quality lawyers filling this post have long gone. The prestige and patronage which made it such a great office were lost amid the many revolutions brought about by Tony Blair's government – devolution, and the removal of so many functions as to the appointment of judges at all levels are the main mileposts. Elish is as good a choice as there could have been in the circumstances. I hope that she has the vision to adapt the job, as it now is, into something more obviously independent of the Scottish Executive and, in the course of doing so, stand up for the independence of the judiciary.

21 October 2006

A relatively light weekend. We were in the Privy Council last week and the judgment is to be written by Jonathan Mance. So there has been time to do two short notes on costs and to revise a judgment in the Privy Council which I have written about a disputed taxation of costs. Looking ahead, I have adapted my Strathclyde University congregation speeches – fortunately both on file in my computer, to be read for the November session in two weeks' time. I have also begun work on revising the text of a long-delayed publication which I prepared years ago and has drifted out of date, for the reissue of the *Stair Memorial Encyclopaedia* Procedure title. It is not easy to get to grips with this again after such an interval.

I had two meetings about the Supreme Court two weeks ago. The first was to go over room furnishings, in which Brenda Hale has taken a close interest and for which she effectively leads our sub-committee. It was encouraging. A good deal of work has been done to get the details of shelving, lighting and fabrics into a form that will be acceptable. Decisions are having to be made a little too early for comfort at our end, as our team of Justices is so far off being settled. Only six of the current Law Lords will still be in post in October 2009. But we in the sub-committee are all going to be there. So it seems reasonable that the decisions should be taken by us now.

On a more sombre note, however, was the subject of a meeting that I was asked to attend with Tom Bingham, Alex Allan and John Lyon – both of the DCA, of course. It was to discuss the Chief Executive, I was told. But in fact it was to discuss the future of Brendan Keith who, as the Clerk in the Judicial Office, has been so closely involved in all the plans to date and is our assurance of continuity of management at our end. The problem is that, on the one hand, there are promotion prospects within the next 15 months in the House of Lords and, on the other, there is a lack of equivalent prospects for him in the Supreme Court. The Clerk of Parliaments is to retire towards the end of next year. As Fourth Clerk at the Table Brendan, in all fairness, should be able to put his hat into the ring within the parliamentary clerkships – if not for that job for which the competition will be fierce, at least for a promotion somewhere. We cannot offer him anything like this in the Supreme Court. One of the great weaknesses of the project is the substitution of the civil service regime for the benign and happy regime in the House of Lords. So we now face the very real prospect of losing Brendan at a critical stage, when there will be about two years still to run and still no Chief Executive. And who, one wonders, will take over from Brendan – and on what terms? It will not be an attractive post if a condition of acceptance is having to transfer to the other place. This is a great obstacle to the continuity of effort that I was hoping for.

This revives thoughts about the leadership of the new Court that I mentioned in my entry of 15 April 2005. It has been suggested to me by Brendan that Charlie Falconer has asked for a meeting with Tom Bingham to discuss Tom's future. It would certainly help if Tom was to make his position clear. He might quite reasonably set a retirement date of 1 October 2008, two weeks before he has to go, so that plans can be made. Lennie Hoffmann could still be with us for another six months, but it would be better for it to be understood that a new Senior Law Lord will be in place from 1 October 2008 to head up the new

Court. He (or she) could then be consulted when the new Chief Executive is being selected in the spring of 2008. This would help to ease the problem which Brendan's promotion away from the Judicial Office will create.

I had a rather unhappy time this week at heading an Appeal Committee in the Privy Council with Alan Rodger and Jonathan Mance. There were, as usual, four petitions. Three went well enough and I got the business done with acceptable fairness and despatch. But the last, *Smith and Evans v The Queen* from The Bahamas, was a bit of a mess. Alan suggested to me that we should tell the appellants' counsel, James Guthrie QC and Anesta Weekes QC, at the start that we want to hear from the Crown through Peter Knox, who was to become a QC a few days later. This is the usual signal that the appeal is likely to be given leave. I adopted this tactic, with Jonathan's agreement, and told Guthrie at the start that we had read his case. 'Is there anything you would like to add?', I asked. He looked relieved and said 'No' – asking whether he could reply to Knox, to which I of course replied that he could. We then heard more fully from Anesta Weekes, who had a more difficult case. The discussion with Knox then followed, and we ran over into the lunch interval. Guthrie and Weekes replied when Knox had finished. Knox was, as so often, quite persuasive. In our private discussion Jonathan was marginally for dismissing the petitions, Alan marginally for granting them and I agreed with Jonathan. When I gave the result Guthrie protested, saying that, as I had led him to think that his petition would be granted, he did not develop his whole argument. I went home feeling depressed – having made two mistakes: by indicating that we were in favour of granting his petition at the outset and then by not supporting Alan in what was a marginal case, giving the benefit of the doubt to the petitioner in what was, after all, technically a capital punishment murder case, although as five years have gone by the petitioner will not be executed. The problem has however now been resolved, as I later suggested to Mary Macdonald, the Registrar, that it should be. At the petitioners' request the decision has been set aside in the interests of fairness and the two petitions will be re-heard by a different Committee. It is always a fine balance between allowing counsel to be too prolix and cutting them off too short. But the tactic I adopted was unwise unless I had been sure of the result, which I was not in this case.

4 November 2006

I was at Strathclyde University yesterday for the November graduations: Strathclyde Business School in the morning, the Faculty of Law, Arts and Social Sciences in the afternoon. The morning ceremony was given over almost entirely to MBAs in various forms, and the graduands were for the most part from overseas – India and China both very well represented. The audience was very quiet, possibly because most of them could not speak English, but the students were very lively and determined to enjoy themselves. One Japanese woman was beautifully dressed in a kimono and several Chinese and Indians were dressed in black tie and kilts. There was much cheering and laughter from these groups as their friends came forward for their degrees. I expected the afternoon to be a bit of a dampener by contrast. But here and there were several very happy and successful groups, particularly one for a Master's degree in IT law which had attracted students from Saudi Arabia, Jordan, Greece, Australia, Pakistan and Romania, all of whom were delighted by their year at Strathclyde. Meeting the students in the receptions afterwards is a real pleasure. There were many requests for photographs while I was still dressed in my gold and blue robe.

News from Archie Hunter, Convener of Court, of two important developments. Andrew Hamnett, the excellent Principal, is thinking of retiring in two years' time; and a major reorganisation of the variety of courses to be on offer is to be discussed at the residential weekend, leading probably to dropping a substantial number of unprofitable ones and consequent redundancies. Andrew will be a hard act to follow. He is astonishingly unfit, with an ever-enlarging girth. But intellectually and administratively he is a tower of strength, and he gives a very real leadership in a no-nonsense, good-humoured style. As for the reorganisation, financial crisis has been forestalled year after year by good management. But lack of government funding has the inevitable result. Universities are having to concentrate on what they do best and cut out the rest. I am out of all the responsibilities, of course, as the Chancellor is decorative, not executive. But I am there to be talked to by people who want to talk, and I must remain at my post for the next five years or so at least while these upheavals go on.

The Supreme Court project may be sliding into real problems over timetable. The reason is an unlikely one. There is a requirement for three disabled car-parking spaces. It had been assumed that they would be available in the Queen Elizabeth Conference Centre. This turns out not to be so, and it appears that there is nowhere else nearby that is acceptable. Until they are identified, the section 106 agreement which the developer is expected to enter into cannot be signed and planning permission will not be granted. There are only two months of slack in the programme, assuming that planning permission is issued in time for the contracts for the work to be entered into in December.

Today I spent the morning as President of the Stair Society for its AGM and annual lecture at the Surgeons' Hall in Edinburgh. This is a relatively relaxed occasion, but it does depend on preparation and once again much depends on my chairmanship. This time I had the pleasure of presenting Sheriff J Irvine Smith, now almost 80, with Honorary Membership with a certificate to record this, in recognition of his contribution to the Society for over 50 years. This was an occasion for speeches from me and from him. Then there was an enjoyable lecture from Professor Olivia Robinson, a Roman law scholar, and sherry afterwards before I left to regroup at home after these busy two days.

10 November 2006

I went back to London as usual by air on 5 November with British Midland, whose time-keeping just now is much better than British Airways. It was a beautiful clear evening, and the whole country from West Lothian to Heathrow was alive with fireworks – chrysanthemum shapes sailing into the sky as we set off down the runway at Edinburgh and came into land, and there were sparkles of coloured lights in an amazing profusion as we got further south over heavily populated England. It was an extraordinary celebration of Guy Fawkes – probably with not very much thought of what his attempt to blow up Parliament really meant.

Donald Nicholls told Tom this week that he is to retire on 10 January 2007. He will be greatly missed – quiet, thoughtful, careful, immensely painstaking and accurate and with remarkable insight into what our cases are really about. The procedure for finding his replacement will be a hybrid between the old and the new, at Tom's insistence, as Charlie Falconer will not be Lord Chancellor for ever and the chances now are that his successors will be from the House of Commons with no feel from the Judiciary: will it be Harriet Harman, Geoff Hoon or Jack Straw? So, we are to discuss the successor with Charlie in the usual way, but all those who must be involved under the statutory procedure for the Supreme Court are to be consulted as well. This will include each of the three appointments boards, the Lord President, the Lord Justice Clerk, the Lord Chief Justice of Northern Ireland, the Heads of Divisions in England and Wales and the Lord Chief Justice too. Tom was told that it will take six months to fill the vacancy under the new statutory procedure, which may well be true. We cannot wait that long, especially as Mark Saville is still away on the Bloody Sunday Inquiry. I am glad that Tom is still in a position to stamp his authority on the new procedure and try to set the pattern for the future.

There is to be a dinner at Parliament House this evening to mark Douglas Cullen's retirement as Lord President. It is hard to believe that I was starting my career as Lord President 17 years ago. There will be a lot of absentees. Alan Rodger has an engagement in London, Brian Gill is just absent and Alan Johnston has refused to go. Arthur Hamilton, who sat this week but is not sitting next week, will preside. It will be a venture back to strange, uncertain territory: such a contrast to our busy, committed, happy band on the Law Lords' Corridor.

25 November 2006

The dinner turned out to be relaxed and enjoyable. There were many retired judges – Cowie, Allanbridge, Cameron of Lochbroom, Sutherland, Weir, MacLean, Penrose with wives – and Kirkwood and Clyde. Fewer serving judges, but Ann Paton was there and sat next to me. Arthur made a short, unremarkable speech and Douglas responded in kind. Donald Ross was there too. We did not reminisce on our past or comment on how things are. I did not want to trespass on frayed nerves. Nicholas Phillips from England and Wales was there, as was Brian Kerr, with their wives which was a nice touch. Also there were James and Bett Mackay.

The Law Lords met Charlie Falconer to discuss Donald Nicholls's replacement last Tuesday. As we were considering a chancery candidate Jonathan Mance was omitted. But, as it happened, there was no suggestion that Mary Arden, his wife, was a candidate. There was almost complete unanimity on the two front-runners – John Mummery and David Neuberger. Tom put forward a strong bid for David Neuberger as a star suitable for the Supreme Court, which he wants to be inhabited by such people. David Neuberger is a genuine star, but he has been in the Court of Appeal for only three years and is only 57. Also Nicholas Phillips has identified him as his candidate for Chancellor – formerly Vice-Chancellor – to head the Chancery Division when Andrew Morritt goes. John Mummery is 67, so Tom does not favour him. But most of the rest of us do, as he is the obvious replacement for Donald on a wide range of subjects including employment law. A lot will depend on how much Charlie prefers Nicholas's wishes to those of Tom. It would be a pity, as I pointed out, to bring David Neuberger in to then lose him in two or three years' time when Andrew Morritt goes. It is possible that the options will be put to David Neuberger himself. This may be the last time that the candidate is selected in this way. It is hard to see how the new system will work. There is an absurdly long list of people to be consulted, such as the First Minister of Scotland who will have no idea of who the candidates are. But I suppose they can be persuaded that this is a matter best decided in London.

Mary came down for the Law Lords dinner in the Athenaeum the next day. She was placed between Richard Scott and Lennie Hoffmann: an excellent placing from everyone's point of view. I was between Robert Walker and Romayne Carswell, but Simon Brown and Rima Scott were the real sparks of amusement and entertainment at our table. There were no judicial guests this year as we have had no retirements. But Charlie and Marianna Falconer were there. Could this be their last time? Tony Blair goes next summer and it must be doubtful whether Gordon Brown, when Prime Minister, will want Charlie Falconer in his Cabinet.

2 December 2006

I went up to Parliament House yesterday evening for a reception in honour of Matt Weir, who has served four successive Lords President as the Clerk to the First Division of the Court of Session. It was timed for 4.45pm in Parliament Hall. I was unsure where I could hang my coat, but a telephone call to Alan Maxwell in the Lord President's Private Office established that I could go to the Judges' Robing Room where I would be expected. It is ten years since I had been there. Not much had changed. Judges' robes, wing collars and falls, all laid out neatly on a dark blue cloth-covered table; mirrors, of course; one or two notices. The Lord President's robe is in the main room, not in a place of its own along with the ermine robe of the Lord Justice General as it was in my day.

As I made my way back towards Parliament Hall Matt Weir himself emerged from the First Division courtroom. This was a very pleasant surprise for us both – time to catch up with each other before we met the crowds in the Hall. He reminded me that Mr Higgins was my clerk when I arrived in the First Division. Matt came in 1994 from other posts in various departments, and has served me, Alan Rodger, Douglas Cullen and Arthur Hamilton since then. He is to retire from his full-time post now, but to remain available for service part-time. 'Seeing how things are now', he said, 'I will probably be busy'. There is a real crisis of expertise and experience among the much downgraded and demoralised clerking system, which is a real tragedy when one compares what kept the Court's standards up when I was in practice. The devolved government has much to answer for.

In Parliament Hall there was a large gathering of Bench and Bar, solicitors and clerks and macers: a real family occasion, as Matt said in his reply to speeches by the Lord President and the Dean of Faculty, Roy Martin. He said, with touching frankness and regret at how things are, that the Court of Session had been his life and how much the family atmosphere had meant to him. Photographs were taken of all the judges serving and retired with Matt Weir under the great south window, and then of him with the four Lords President he has served, his wife and a bouquet of flowers.

I had been anxious about venturing back for such an occasion. But there were many familiar faces, and everyone was very friendly. The only exception, perhaps, was Brian Gill, the Lord Justice Clerk: a rather detached figure, I thought, who seemed to be less interested in mixing with others in the Hall – a brooding presence by the fireplace when I last saw him. Arthur Hamilton, on the other hand, seemed quite relaxed. Perhaps those of us who have left the Court of Session Bench find it easier to mix than senior serving judges. We are no longer conscious of the need to maintain authority.

It was a world tour in the Privy Council this week: an appeal from Jamaica on Monday; one from Mauritius on Wednesday – a member of the Mauritius Bar presented the appeal which, as usual, gave local flavour to it because of his accent and style of presentation; and on Thursday I presided over petitions for leave from Turks and Caicos and from Brunei. Richard Scott became quite difficult to deal with on the case from Brunei. It involves a dispute between Prince Jefri, the Sultan's son, and Brunei Investment Agency which is an alter ego for the Sultan. The Sultan is an absolute Monarch who rules the State like a Tudor or Stuart king. He can do no wrong. and passes laws to suit himself as he has presided over a state of emergency which gives him absolute authority since 1962. How can Prince Jefri get justice in such a situation, Richard asks, and why should we have anything to do with it? But there is a statutory basis both in Brunei and in the UK for our jurisdiction, and both sides have agreed expressly to abide by the advice which we give to the Sultan. Alan Rodger, like me, did not see what the fuss was about. We have a duty to perform, within the limits of our jurisdiction, as the highest tribunal of that State. In the end Richard agreed to proceed with his point noted – and we gave Prince Jefri special leave to appeal, so the case will come back to us next year. Remarkably, the Privy Council continues to attract work and is busy.

10 December 2006

I delivered a lecture to the Statute Law Society in the Middle Temple on Thursday evening. I called it 'Voices from the Past',[256] reflecting on the contribution that serving Law Lords had made to the legislative process at Westminster and on the circumstances which have already made it practically impossible for them to contribute even before our eviction on 1 October 2009 to the Supreme Court. It had taken months of working up, with much recourse to the pages of Hansard which are so easily accessed through the House of Lords library. I had had a very runny head cold with the usual fits of coughing all week, so giving the lecture under the residue of these afflictions was rather an ordeal. Fortunately my voice held up and I did not cough too much.

This was a prelude to a very busy weekend while I was trying to recuperate and only now, Sunday midday, getting back into order again. The Thursday lecture meant staying overnight in London, a morning flight on Friday back to Edinburgh, reaching home at 12.45pm, to go at once to a conference on alternatives to custody at the Royal Society's premises in George Street, where I was to chair a session next day. That evening we went to dinner at Gogarbank House as guests of Brigadier Euan Loudon and his wife Penny. He is GOC Scotland/Second Division and is about to retire to become the officer in charge of the Edinburgh Tattoo. Among the rather daunting list of guests were Michael O'Shea, formerly Press Secretary to the Royal Family, Dorothy Leeming our neighbour in India Street, and Sandy McCall Smith, the celebrated author. He spoke to me before dinner about the very real hardships he has to live with due to incessant travel and the constant demands on his time, all due to the status he has earned for himself all over the world because of his charming, idiosyncratic style of story-telling. He confessed to an inability to say 'No', due in part to a belief that the bubble of celebrity that surrounds him may collapse at any time. I thought that he looked very tired, but he was in his usual, most amusing and delightful form, full of stories and giggles of self-amusement. Dorothy teased him for not saying very much about India Street in his stories about Edinburgh. But he responded by saying that he had said things about Moray Place which had brought protests from its residents. He had said that Moray Place Gardens was the last place in Edinburgh to practise naturism.

Next morning I was back at the RSE to chair my session at the conference. My task was to introduce the Lord Chief Justice of England and Wales, Nicholas Phillips; the Chief Justice of Ireland, John Murray, who were to

---

256 (2007) 123 LQR 547.

deliver 30-minute speeches, and Baroness Vivienne Stern, who was to sum up. The audience was made up of specialists in the field from Ireland, Scotland and England – judges, sheriffs, barristers, criminologists, prison officers and many others including Andrew McLellan, the Chief Inspector of Prisons in Scotland; Bishop Richard Holloway; and Baroness Linklater. As I said of the Chief Justices, each brought a fresh mind to the subject, having had virtually nothing to do with criminal justice since their appointments in 2004 and 2005 respectively. Nicholas made a very good speech about alternatives to custody for children and projects to keep them out of trouble in England. John Murray's speech was more diffident, giving the impression that he had indeed still not really got to grips with the subject. Vivienne Stern summed up brilliantly, mentioning every speaker of note during the two-and-a-half-day conference.

31 December 2006

The year ended quietly, so far as work in London was concerned. A team of five went off to sit as the Judicial Committee of the Privy Council in Nassau in The Bahamas on Friday 15 December. It consisted of Tom Bingham, Richard Scott, Brenda Hale, Simon Brown and Bob Carswell. They had a week of work ahead of them while the rest of us were in recess, as no cases were due for that week in the House of Lords. I went home to prepare for Christmas, with only three relatively short speeches to prepare. The Bahamas trip is a first for the Privy Council. The burden it imposes on those who were chosen is not slight. For Bob Carswell, in particular, it meant getting his clothes together in London from Belfast and then making a journey back to Belfast on his return as a transit passenger through a crowded Heathrow, whose programme was severely disrupted by fog earlier in the week. I would have found that hard to take, in view of what is expected of me here at home at Christmas. I am uneasy about setting a precedent for sitting abroad in view of these burdens. No doubt Tom Bingham will take it all in his stride, but I wonder about the others. The hothouse atmosphere in Nassau, where the expectation will be that views will alter among their Lordships about the value or otherwise of the death penalty (some hope!) will add to the pressures, and there will be little freedom or time off. I will be very interested to hear how it all went when we meet next term.

Meantime back in London I prepared my room for the move of my things to Donald Nicholls's larger room next door. Jonathan Mance will take my room, and David Neuberger will take his. As our rooms are not all the same, a retirement such as Donald's has given us the opportunity to move up to better rooms according to our seniority.

2007 – January to April

2 February 2007

A quiet start to the year, most of it spent in the Privy Council with cases of no great interest or importance. But on the Law Lords' Corridor I have, as planned, moved next door into Donald Nicholls's room – larger by quite a degree and with a bay window. I was unhappy at leaving my old room with what I felt was the best view of the Abbey from my desk. But the room I now have, although with a less perfect view of the Abbey and less well positioned in relation to the other surroundings, has many benefits. There is a cupboard to hang clothes in, and much more space. This, curiously, is more restful and more comfortable than the smaller rather cramped space I used to occupy next door. David Neuberger has arrived, but only just as he has spent the last two weeks in Egypt on holiday. He will start sitting with us for the first time next week.

Two developments on the Supreme Court front to report. The first was in regard to Brendan Keith's future. His predecessor James Vallance White came to see me about this at his request, and I entertained him to tea in the Lords' dining room. He expressed much concern at the news that had reached him that Brendan was not being viewed as the right man for the equivalent job in the Supreme Court because he is not a lawyer – while I, for my part, was concerned that Brendan might want to leave us early to secure his own future in the Parliament network. It soon became clear that there were misunderstandings on both sides. Brendan wants to stay, and he is not being thought unsuitable because he is not a lawyer. But there was a real gap in making his future clear to him. Prompted by this conversation I made contact with Paul Hayter, the Clerk of Parliaments, to see whether he could clarify the issue on behalf of all of us. I had a useful meeting with him, arranged for me by my erstwhile secretary Gail Munden, one of the first casualties of the project who has landed the best job in her career ladder as a result. He then spoke to Alex Allan, and it appears that the only remaining hurdle is to settle the arrangements which will preserve Brendan in his salary scale when he moves over. So there, at least, is some real progress.

When the move over will be, however, is now again in doubt. The application for judicial review of the planning permission decision by Westminster Council, for some time expected, has now gone in, much to the dismay of the civil servants in the Project Team. They have worked out a best and worst case scenario for us, on assumptions as to the time it will take for the application to be disposed of, and assuming that in the end of the day it will nevertheless fail. This shows how precarious the 1 October 2009 date really is. Only three or four weeks of delay due to the application will mean that this date will become unattainable. We will not have our start date until January 2010, which in effect means that it will have to be deferred until October of that year. And there is a risk, if the application takes months and not weeks to resolve, that our start date will move to October 2011. But by then Lord Chancellor

Falconer and Tom Bingham will have gone and we may have a Conservative Government. The whole thing looks very uncertain – the product of thoroughly bad planning based on principle rather than practicalities and the lack of a real commitment by all who really matter in government. My feelings are mixed. I really do want to get on with it if, as remains more likely than not, it is to happen. But I would be greatly relieved if the project was stopped. I do not look forward to having to lead the way forward if, contrary to my expectations, I am asked to do so.

There was talk at lunch this week of Nicholas Phillips's plans to abolish the wearing of wigs in civil cases in England and introduce simpler dress for judges without wing collars and bands. Tom wants to do the same for counsel appearing in the House of Lords. He was not pleased when I said that this was a matter for the House itself, not for him. And he was uneasy when Lord Rodger pointed out that in Scotland we regard dress for counsel as a matter in the last resort for decision by the Faculty of Advocates.

10 February 2007

There was one judgment to deliver in the Chamber, and neither Tom nor Lennie wanted to preside over it. The case was *Beggs v The Scottish Ministers*,[257] a Scots appeal against a decision of the Inner House in a case arising from the breach of an undertaking not to interfere with a prisoner's correspondence with his legal advisers. So, all of a sudden there I was, as the third Senior Lord, taking my chair on the Woolsack – until recently the place taken by the Lord Chancellor and usually in our case by the Senior Law Lord.

The Bishop of London, the Rt Rev Richard Chartres, was there to say prayers. This was a rather special treat, as he is a very fine figure of a man, familiar on television in his capacity as Dean of the Chapels Royal conducting services at the Cenotaph on Remembrance Sunday. One of the pleasures of our being on the Woolsack is the opportunity of a few words with the Bishop, who is placed right beside it before the mace is brought in. He told me that he was standing in for another Bishop who was very unwell and cannot travel. The Bishops of London, Salisbury, Winchester and Durham, together with York and Canterbury, are in the House as of right, not elected. Then the mace arrived – a huge weight, which bounced on the other side of the Woolsack as the doorkeeper lowered it down. I knelt on an enormous maroon cushion with gold braid around it after the Bishop had begun prayers as usual with a psalm and we had bowed to each other. His voice beside me was very loud, and only Richard Scott and Alan Rodger were on the benches far away and, it seemed, out of earshot. So, as he left a gap at the end of each prayer for an 'amen' which he does not fill, I had to say 'amen' very loudly on behalf of us all. It was all beautifully read and inspiring. Then it was over, I stood up, the doorkeeper removed the enormous cushion and I turned to face the Chamber,

---

257 [2007] UKHL 3, 2007 SLT 235.

bowed to the Law Lords – as Jonathan came in late – and our case was called on.

As the door at the far end opened I had a view down the corridor to the Central Lobby. Then two wigged junior counsel appeared, came in and bowed and Brendan Keith, robed and wigged at the table, called the case in the name of Lord Nicholls of Birkenhead – Donald, now retired, had presided. I stood to the left of the Woolsack to introduce the motion, to approve the Committee's report (a ritual now extinct in ordinary sittings in the Chamber as the Lord Speaker, unlike the Lord Chancellor, does not move motions). I was a bit too quick in returning to the central position, but I did not suppose that anybody noticed. Then I had the questions to put: 'As many as are content will say content; the non-contents, not content'. The contents had it all the way through, of course. Then Richard Scott moved that 'The House do now adjourn during pleasure until 3 o'clock', which I put to the House and declared that the contents had it – and then it was all over. What a privilege! I was not sure that I would ever have the chance of doing this again before we left the House.

We were hearing a very interesting case in the Appellate Committee that day, well presented in argument, about the rights that a cohabiting couple who had lived together for about 28 years had in the family dwellinghouse, which had been taken in joint names.[258] English property and trust laws presented real challenges for me as I tried to understand the case. Daily discussions with Zoe Christoforides, my judicial assistant, were a great help. We finished the four-day case under Lennie Hoffmann's brisk chairmanship in three days: Robert Walker, Brenda Hale and David Neuberger, on his first case, were the others in a very congenial team. David is very bright, but he was helped in this case too by being on very familiar ground, as was Brenda. Lennie, anxious to get away for a planned week's holiday in South Africa, postponed our discussion of the case for ten days. Meantime Brenda too will be away in India. I will be in court every day next week, presiding at three appeals: one in the House of Lords (a Scots appeal), the other two in the Privy Council (appeals from The Bahamas).

Snow caused chaos in London on Thursday. 'The worst snowstorm of the century', said one London newspaper – no exaggeration, as the last significant fall was in 1999. However, it had all settled down by the late afternoon, and I was home at a reasonable time having been able to shift to the earlier evening Bmi flight. At the airport I presented a pre-booking voucher which I had obtained over the internet with my House of Lords credit card reducing the cost of parking my car from £71 to £45, which makes the expenditure (about the same as a taxi each way) a bit more respectable.

Mary and I went to Strathclyde University next morning. The Princess Royal was visiting a presentation of the Strathclyde Malawi Project as one of its joint patrons. Andrew Hamnett was on duty as a Deputy Lieutenant. Peter West had organised four demonstrations of work being carried on by the University in

258 *Stack v Dowden* [2007] UKHL 17, [2007] 2 AC 432.

Malawi: the David Livingstone clinic, with Professor Alan McGowan; environmental health at Chikwawa with Dr Tony Grimmerson; the Making Wonders Project for the blind with Norman Wagstaff; and the $100 Dollar House, an architectural project, with Dr Stirling Howieson. Mary and I and Suzanne Hamnett greeted Her Royal Highness at the entrance to the Winter Gardens. I then made a three-minute introduction, handing on to Peter for a bit more and then escorted HRH around the stands. She took a keen interest in almost everything, giving 15 minutes to all except Making Wonders, where she was perhaps rather too brief because time was running out. I had to stand just behind her in respectful silence as she listened and asked questions and gave advice. Much of it, I have to say, seemed to be just a bit too dogmatic and unrealistic given the poverty and lack of infrastructure in Malawi. She poured scorn on shipping surplus blankets there because they could be taught to make blankets themselves, and on the use of a bicycle ambulance for getting people from remote communities to the nearest clinic or hospital because they ought to have been using a motor-cycle. It was not altogether comfortable, I felt. She is not a very easy person to deal with, much as I admire her. It was all over by 12.15pm and we went home for a late lunch.

Today I was a guest at another occasion. This time at Edinburgh University at a special honorary degree ceremony to mark the tercentenary of the founding of the first chair in public law at Edinburgh. There were three Honorary Graduates: Mary McAleese, President of Ireland; Brian Gill, the Lord Justice Clerk; and Albie Sachs, a Justice of the Constitutional Court of South Africa. I joined the academic procession clad in a red gown as an Honorary LLD, together with James Clyde, David Edward and Alan Rodger. There were many old friends amongst the academic staff and others in the long procession into the magnificent but only partly-filled McEwan Hall. Sadly those of us in this procession were seated behind the speakers. Due to bad acoustics we found it almost impossible to hear what was being said, but I did catch snatches of tribute to the remarkable career of Mary McAleese, to the office of Lord Justice Clerk as well as to Brian Gill himself, and to the enormous personal courage of Albie Sachs who, despite 160 days in solitary confinement and the loss of an arm and an eye due to his work as a defence lawyer in apartheid South Africa, has risen to become one of the most celebrated of today's jurists. He had spoken to me earlier over coffee of his life-long friendship with Lennie Hoffmann. He made a very charming speech of acceptance, saying how an occasion he had expected to be rather mundane had turned out to be very emotional due to the friendship he had met with in Edinburgh. The South African National Anthem was sung as a tribute to him and to his country. The body of the hall was filled with many law graduates who had become Senators or other leading members of the legal profession in Scotland. We then made our way to the Playfair Library for a celebratory lunch which ended in time for us to arrive home in time to watch Scotland beat Wales 21–9, all penalty goals, at Murrayfield in sleet, rain and wind: not conditions for open rugby.

23 February 2007

A rather tiring week. I was in the chair all last week and for three days again this week. Last week's cases were well argued and pleasant to preside over. This week's were not – at least that which was before us on Tuesday and Wednesday. It was in the Privy Council, an appeal from Gibraltar about the loss of a chance in an action against a firm of solicitors for missing the deadline in an action of personal injury. It ought to have been easy to focus the points for us, but counsel were slow, diffuse and imprecise. I am easily cast down by this. I do not like to bully counsel – indeed, I am not able to do this – so I worry that I am letting my colleagues down by being soft. And I missed points that I should have noticed, which makes me wonder whether I am up to the job. Lennie and Tom, our leaders now, set such high standards.

There was, however, a splendid occasion on Tuesday. I had accepted an email round-robin invitation to attend an address by the Moderator of the Church of Scotland in Speakers' House at 7pm, to be followed by a reception. The Moderator this year is the Rt Rev Alan McDonald from St Andrews, who is to get an Honorary Degree from Strathclyde later this year as he is a Strathclyde LLB. We have met already, and as I am Vice-Chairman of the Scottish Peers' Association I thought I should go. This was a bit of tourism too, as peers do not often get asked to the splendid residence of the Speaker of the House of Commons just beside Big Ben and Westminster Bridge. The Barry touch is everywhere of course – and Pugin too. Magnificent portraits of recent Speakers, including Michael Martin, the genial Glaswegian who holds this office just now and is in his second term, adorn the equivalent of the Lord Chancellor's recently abandoned River Room. Those present were almost all MPs, who were to have dinner there afterwards. The Duke of Montrose and the former Bishop of Oxford, Lord Harries, were the other peers. As it was a Scottish event there were many Scots MPs whom I knew, which was a pleasure in itself.

One of the questions put to the Moderator was about the church's position on Trident, with particular reference to the Government's decision to renew the Trident nuclear deterrent which is serviced from the Faslane Naval Base. This is a very sensitive issue, as we are facing a Scottish Parliament election in May. Labour is tied into Government policy, but the SNP are seeking to make political capital by opposing it, as do the Greens and others. The churches see this as a question of morality – a weapon of mass destruction – and oppose it too. That is the Church of Scotland's position, and it seems to be the Scottish Episcopal Church's position too. Now I am in a real torment of conscience. I see the issue about Trident as a question of national security, to be answered on pragmatic grounds. It is there as a deterrent, not a weapon to be used unless in self-defence in the most extreme circumstances. The pragmatic answer is that it should be retained in a dangerous and unpredictable world. To disarm in the expectation that others will follow seems to be highly irresponsible. The present Trident force needs to be renewed soon, or it will become unusable. There is a genuine issue as to whether the option for a renewal needs to be addressed now. But that is not what the churches are on about.

The following evening I was at University College London acting as chairman and a speaker at a reception for the UCL's Legal Review. I spoke about the Pitcairn case,[259] off the cuff, for about 30 minutes, followed by Lord Carlile of Berriew, who did the same thing for 30 minutes on his work in connection with legislation on terrorism. There was a well-informed undergraduate audience. It was mature and enthusiastic, many of them from overseas. The reception during which I spoke to many of the students afterwards was like a graduation day at Strathclyde.

3 March 2007

I came across about a dozen excited magpies which had gathered in the trees beside the river on my way to the Botanical Gardens. What was causing such a fuss was unclear. I have never seen so many of these birds together in a flock before. As a young woman said to me as I was staring up at them, the well-known rhyme does not stretch that far. But *The Birds of the Western Paelearctic* indicates that it was probably provoked by an invasion of high-ranking birds into an established territory, the reaction to which had encouraged non-breeders to gather round as spectators. It was a very noisy group, and quite spectacular.

18 March 2007

I spent the last two weeks in the House of Lords in a team chaired by Lennie Hoffmann, with Robert Walker, Jonathan Mance and David Neuberger – the chancery team – as the others were engaged on mainly criminal business in the Privy Council. We disposed of three cases, two of them Scots appeals: *William Grant & Sons*,[260] about the treatment of depreciation for corporation tax; and *Melville Dundas v Wimpey*[261] about a set-off provision in the JCT 1998 Standard Form of Construction Contract. The Scots cases were on the whole well argued, especially by Colin Tyre and by Colin Campbell, now just elevated two days ago to the Court of Session Bench with the judicial title of Lord Malcolm. It was a great pleasure to sit with this excellent and very friendly team. I felt very much part of it, able to keep on top of the issues. From time to time I marvelled at my good fortune at the privilege of being a member of such a tribunal. Lennie was, of course, miles ahead of anyone else in seeing a way through the issues. But we did persuade him to change his mind on at least one major point as the argument went on.

---

259 See fn 253.
260 *Commissioners of Inland Revenue v William Grant & Sons Distillers Ltd* [2007] UKHL 15, 2007 SC (HL) 105, [2007] 1 WLR 1448.
261 *Melville Dundas Ltd v George Wimpey UK Ltd* [2007] UKHL 18, 2007 SC (HL) 116, [2007] 1 WLR 1136.

On Friday afternoon, back in Edinburgh, I attended the first meeting of the Judicial Council for Scotland in my capacity as the senior of the two Scots Law Lords. Arthur Hamilton presided and did so very well. We had a full representation from the various branches of the Scottish judiciary including Robin Wild who was there for the District Courts. It is early days yet, but this body has every prospect of being a very useful sounding board. Lord Justice Clerk Gill, who showed little interest in it at our original meeting, was absent. Later Arthur told me that there is a prospect of an impasse between him and Brian Gill about the next promotion to the Inner House. He said that he might need to have one of the Lords of Appeal in Ordinary brought in as an umpire if it materialises. But that would require an amendment of the statute.

3 April 2007

The term ended last Thursday. The only case of the week for me was a three-day hearing in the Privy Council in a Scottish devolution case: *Scott v HM Advocate*.[262] I was in the chair with Alan, Brenda, Bob and Simon. The issue was whether an amendment to the Criminal Procedure (Scotland) Act 1995 by the Scottish Parliament requiring the disclosure of the previous convictions of a person accused of a sexual offence, in cases where he wishes, and is allowed, to question or lead evidence about the complainer's behaviour to challenge her credibility or reliability, was within its power to legislate. The case was, as so often in criminal devolution cases, rather poorly argued. Mungo Bovey QC was for the appellant. His enthusiasm is not wholly matched by his powers of advocacy. The Advocate General, Lord Davidson of Glen Clova QC, had almost nothing to contribute, although he should have been able to do so had he troubled with some research and some homework. The advocate depute, Sean Murphy QC, was a pleasure to listen to in comparison. But his task was mainly defensive and was less helpful as a result. It was left to us, as so often is the case in these situations, to come up with the ideas. Alan and I benefit greatly from the contributions of our English and Northern Irish colleagues on such issues. This was a topic on which cross-fertilisation from other jurisdictions, of which Alan and I too have a good deal of experience, is beneficial. The absence of any thought having been given to this from north of the border is quite striking. I spent two and a half days over the weekend preparing a long and detailed judgment, some of which is unashamedly designed to introduce some useful and pertinent ideas from England into Scots law. I had almost finished it when Alan's draft arrived by post from London. So I drove myself on to finish mine so I could email it to London for circulation in time for tomorrow's post.

I had to remain in London overnight on Thursday as I had been invited to a ceremony to mark the end of the Crown Court sittings in Middlesex Guildhall on Friday 30 March. Tom Bingham, who is primarily responsible for the policy that has brought this situation about, had been invited but had departed for his

262 *DS v HM Advocate* [2007] UKPC 36, 2007 SC (PC) 1

home in Wales. So it was left to me, Brenda Hale, Jonathan Mance and Brendan Keith to represent the Law Lords and the Judicial Office. I had an hour's meeting with a DCA official about staffing in the Supreme Court before walking over to the Guildhall with Brenda and Brendan.

On arrival we were ushered upstairs to the Council Chamber where a large gathering of court staff, present and past; of barristers; magistrates past and present; members of Westminster Council; the Middlesex Regiment and others with connections to the institution were assembled. There was a delay of a quarter of an hour as Charlie Falconer, the Lord Chancellor, was late. Then, at last, the platform party came in, preceded by a loud bang on the Council Chamber door to bring us to order. It consisted of the Lord Chancellor; Sir Igor Judge as President of the Queen's Bench Division; Peter Gross and David Calvert-Smith JJ, the presiding judges of the south-eastern circuit; Councillor Alexander Nicoll, the Lord Mayor of Westminster; Jan Pethick, the High Sheriff of Greater London, and HHJ Roger Chapple, the resident judge. Igor Judge presided. He spoke first, followed by Miss Joanna Korner QC on behalf of the Bar, by the resident judge and then the Lord Chancellor. Igor Judge was quite short and relatively uncritical. But Joanna Korner made it clear how dismayed the Bar felt about dismantling what has been a very close-knit successful Crown Court in this building. The resident judge then delivered a masterly account of the great misfortune that had beset his court and all who had worked in it. On 29 March, he said, the jury that last sat here had been unable to agree. He gave a brief history, pointing out the main milestones: the 1913 opening of the building, with woodwork by Wylie-Lochhead who had supplied woodwork for the Titanic; 1965, the last sitting of Middlesex County Council; 1971, the commencement of the Crown Court; 1982–1988, a programme of refurbishment to suit the needs of the Crown Court. It had been a happy, extremely busy court, all now to be dismantled. He confessed that he had not enjoyed this experience: all that it had taken to make a court work, to see it then pulled to pieces. He spoke of the warmth and friendship of the staff, most of whom were being redeployed. Others had taken early retirement. Together they had given 380 years of service to the Crown Court. Its ending in this way was a sad reward for all they had done for it. Lord Falconer had a hard task to respond to this. 'I feel like Brutus at Caesar's banquet' he said. He spoke of the future, and did his best to reassure everyone that the new Supreme Court would be a worthy successor to the Crown Court in such a fine location.

Thereafter there was a reception. By chance I came across Catherine Wilmott, the office manager. I asked her about the Middlesex County flag that, according to what we were told about it in our programme, is flown on 16 May each year in remembrance of the battle of Albuhera when the Middlesex Regiment won its greatest battle honour. I assured her, a splendidly sparky Scots woman from Glasgow, that we would want to continue that tradition and wondered what we could do to ensure that the flag was passed on to us. At once she put me in touch with the security officer who arranged to have it ready in his office on the ground floor for me to collect and take back with me to the Law Lords' Corridor.

I then met two members of the Regiment who told me of their connections with the building. One said that his father had been a company sergeant major in 1st Battalion Seaforth Highlanders in Malaya at the end of the War. Thus, full of enthusiasm for the Regiment, I collected the flag, packed it in a huge plastic bag and carried it off with me to the Corridor. 'I have a trophy!' I said to Brendan and Helen. They decided to take it into their possession, to be cleaned and stored carefully for the day when we move into the building and can raise it from our own flagpole.

21 April 2007

Just back from 24 hours in Rome. Tom Bingham asked me to take his place in response to an invitation from the President of the Italian Constitutional Court, Franco Bile, to take part in a seminar to discuss the interface between constitutional law and EU law under their system. This was a wise decision, really, because I think that I have more to give on that subject – I am less cynical about it also than Tom is. So I was given Thursday off so that I could fly to Rome on the midday Alitalia flight from Heathrow. The weather has been fine over a large part of Europe for many days, under the influence of a wide and persistent anti-cyclone. So it was a fine flight in clear skies, with excellent views over France – of Paris with the Seine wiggling through the conurbation in a way only an aerial view could reveal; of myriads of fields of yellowing oil seed rape until we reached the Jura; of Geneva and the wide white area of the Alps. I was, rather to my surprise, met off the plane and whisked away by car across the tarmac to a VIP lounge where I was met by the Court's Director of Protocol, Dr Maria Biabella, and served with orange juice. A professor from Belgium joined us and we were driven into Rome to the Hotel Quirinale in the Via Nationale where I stayed on my last visit to the Court in 2002. A spacious elegant room overlooking the garden dominated by a cypress tree, in which a melodious warbler sang with remarkable vigour, and above which the air was filled with many swifts, screeching and tumbling about in the sunshine.

A large bundle of papers was delivered to my room, a sensible reminder that I was there to work. Wisely, as it turned out, I settled down there and then to work through them and write out notes for my oral intervention the next day, for which I was to be given nine minutes. We were then entertained to a welcome dinner in the hotel. I was anxious about this, as I do not speak Italian. But several of those present spoke English, some very well, and President Franco Bile had a woman interpreter with him. There was a lively Professor from Poland, Miroslaw Wyrzykowski, a judge of the Polish Constitutional Court, whose other language was English. There was a reception at which we sounded each other out and then the dinner itself. To my surprise I was summoned to sit beside the President, no doubt because he had an interpreter. On the other side was Professor Sabino Cassese, another judge of the Constitutional Court, who spoke English very well. In the result we all had a very lively enjoyable conversation during an excellent dinner.

21 April 2007

Woken by the melodious warbler, I was able to shave with my tiny travelling razor which had made it through the security machine at Heathrow. After breakfast we were driven to the Court on the Piazza Quirinale. Former President Oneda took me and the Polish judge in his car, and guided us into the President's suite from which we were taken on a brief tour of the magnificent establishment which this Court inhabits. I was met now by Mrs Fullwood of the Protocol Office, who is Scottish. She told me that she is a former pupil of St George's School in Edinburgh and that her mother lives in Balerno. Then to the Chamber for our meeting where 37 of us sat at tables forming a hollow square, with an audience at each end of another 30 or so people. I was glad that I had done my homework as we settled down to our seminar.

The contributions from those round the table were well controlled by the President. He had armed himself with an hourglass whose sand ran through from top to bottom in nine minutes. Most contributors, apart from the three opening speakers who were setting the scene, obeyed this rule. The President kept us hard at it, running beyond time from the start of coffee and lunch breaks and keeping the sessions going until 5pm. Almost everyone spoke in Italian, of course. There was an instantaneous translation into English and French. But this is an imperfect medium of communication. The translators did their best, but some of the depth of the discussion was lost and there were passages that were not translated. The concepts, taken from a very different legal system, were not easy to grasp either. But the main themes did emerge as repetitions by speaker after speaker returned to them. I was called upon for my nine minutes shortly before lunch. Fortunately my preparation paid off, and I was helped too by an earlier contributor, Professor Sergio Bartole from Trieste. He had spoken of his wish that the Constitutional Court would open up a simple 'motorway' for the dialogue between national and EU law. I explained that I came from a very different system, which could nevertheless be seen as a living example of such a 'motorway'. I drew laughter when I said that it was probably not quite the motorway that he had envisaged, because the British do other odd things like driving on the left-hand side of the road. 'Even worse at roundabouts!', chipped in the Professor, to general merriment after a rather intense morning. So I was listened to very kindly. I had also brought with me and circulated our House of Lords decision in *Dabas*[263] about the European arrest warrant in which I had written the main opinion drawing on ECJ case law, which several people said they read with much interest. The afternoon session was as intense as the morning had been. A contribution from Dr Ivana Janu of the Czech Constitutional Court fell a little flat because she read her text and ran out of time. But it was obvious that the professors and the judges were deeply interested in the subject, and that they had worked hard to develop ideas. As I said in my contribution, I left it to them to work out what help, if any, it offered to the discussion. I had the impression that our hosts were genuinely pleased that some member states other than Italy were represented.

---

263 *Dabas v High Court of Justice in Madrid, Spain* [2007] UKHL 6, [2007] 2 AC 31.

Needless to say, the coffee and lunch breaks were a delight. There was time to enjoy the lovely surroundings by going out onto a balcony from which there was a glorious view over the city below us. After the seminar I walked around as a tourist for an hour or so. But there was little time for this, as at 7pm I was driven back to the airport in a Constitutional Court car. I then found myself in the custody of the carabinieri, none of whom could speak a word of English but were polite, friendly and attentive until, with parting salutes, I was ushered onto the aircraft for the flight home. We passed once again over Paris, all lit up below us, shortly before we began to descend over the Channel towards England.

Tom Bingham has written a particularly trenchant letter to Charlie Falconer, insisting that, as he is to retire on 30 September 2008 before the Supreme Court is set up, the statutory procedure for the appointment of the President and the Justices must be used for the selection of his successor as Senior Law Lord and his replacement in the House of Lords as a Lord of Appeal – and for all such appointments from now on. Charlie is, apparently, reluctant to give up his function as Lord Chancellor in these matters. But the worry is that, once Tony Blair goes and the Home Office is split to create a new Ministry for Justice, the functions of the Lord Chancellor will soon pass into other less reliable, less knowledgeable, hands. So Tom's point is really unanswerable, and I wrote a brief concurring note to his circular to that effect. It is a can of worms, nevertheless. Tom expects to be in charge of the process, as the President (Senior Law Lord) chairs the selection commission under Schedule 8 to the Constitutional Reform Act 2005 unless the office of President is 'vacant'. Was it intended that the out-going President should do this, to choose his successor? Tom is, of course, determined and unapproachable on such matters. I am almost certain that he is looking to Nicholas Phillips to succeed him. Nicholas, after all, as Lord Chief Justice has a 'profile', and he is continuing to sit with us with rather sinister regularity to keep his toe in the door. What my position will be in all of this is obscure. If no such processes were insisted on I would gravitate to the top as the Senior Law Lord, and I have already much to do with planning the new Court. But Tom shows no interest in consulting me, which is a fairly obvious indication that he does not see me as his successor. Perhaps he is right.

2007 – May to July

6 May 2007

The Strathclyde University Day was last week. This weekend is extended, unusually after that event, by the Bank Holiday Monday. So there has been time to recover from an exhausting round of engagements.

Before I went north for the Ross Priory dinner on the Tuesday evening I had two interesting meetings in London. One was with Paul Hayter, the Clerk of the Parliaments, who had asked me to see him to brief him on Brendan Keith's performance for his annual report. I wondered why he chose me to do this rather than Tom or Lennie. But I was happy to give Brendan a warm endorsement, adding that he deserved special recognition for the work he is doing on top of everything else in connection with the Supreme Court. This will, I hope, be recognised by the small increment to his salary which is available in such cases.

The other meeting was with Charles McCall, the civil servant in the DCA, about plans for selection of the Supreme Court's Chief Executive. I had assumed that Tom Bingham was in charge of this, but the civil servants have quite rightly decided that the chairmanship of the selection panel for this post should be taken by the person who will be President when the Court opens, not Tom who is in charge now. This has interesting implications. Tom will not retire until 30 September 2008, but the Chief Executive will have to be selected well before that, not later than April 2008. This means that the process will have to begin in the autumn of 2007. The dates which were suggested were: advertisement in September 2007, shortlisting in October and interviews in November. This is to give time for the Chief Executive to detach himself or herself from his or her existing post with a view to starting in about February or March 2008. For all this to happen the President will have to have been identified no later than November 2007 – in six months' time, in other words. I do not think that this is what Tom had in mind when he wrote to Charlie Falconer.

The timing of this meeting enabled me to get to Ross Priory for the honorary graduands' dinner before the first course was ended. There were five of them, from very different backgrounds. I had to make my usual witty speech, designed to find a connection between them such as a word created from the initials of their surnames. In this case I found it, I hope without causing too much offence, in the word 'cheers'. The beds in University House where we have to spend the night are uncomfortable, despite my taking my own pillow, so I slept badly. This had an influence for the rest of the visit as I struggled to keep my eye on the ball, maintain enthusiasm and keep awake. The University Day itself was complicated by the insertion of addresses to mark the seventh extension of the collaboration between Strathclyde and the Technical University of Łodz in Poland. The organiser of the programme for the ceremony had this in one place in the instructions to myself and the Principal, and in a different place in the printed programme. I spotted this, but then failed to call the Strathclyder of the Year at the right place, which was an embarrassment. However, I did get the honorary graduands in the right order: Alan McDonald, this year's Moderator of the Church of Scotland; Frans van Vught, formerly of Twente University with which our University has connections; Elish Angiolini, the Lord Advocate, who may be on the verge of losing office as the result of elections to the Scottish Parliament; Ron Hamilton, a very successful entrepreneur; and Eddi Reader, a well-known singer whose song 'Perfect' was the theme for the day. She sang 'John Anderson my Joe' after her award, which had obviously thrilled her very much. My Thursday visits were to the University library and to a building called the SIBBS Building, both of which have undergone a transformation since my last visit. On Friday there was an early start from home as usual for the nominations group meeting, the Court meeting and the Convocation. I was content with the way things went. Andrew Hamnett is thinking of retiring in 2008/2009. Archie Hunter is handing over to Fraser Livingston as Convener of Court this summer, and Peter West will be 60 in 2009. I am becoming the elder statesman, with a collective memory that goes back nearly ten years. This may be useful in view of changes that lie ahead quite soon.

Meantime elections to the Scottish Parliament have been marked by the eclipse of Labour, the rise of the SNP as the majority party by one seat, and confusion and chaos at the ballot as about 100,000 ballot slips were rejected as invalid. Two legal challenges are being suggested, and there is no clarity as to where we are going. One of these challenges, if successful, could result in a reversal of the result giving Labour a one-seat lead over the SNP. Coalition arrangements with the SNP seem to be in difficulty, because they will not drop their insistence on a referendum on independence which is not supported by the Liberal Democrats. Doubts are in the air too as to who will take on the job of Presiding Officer, as each seat counts so much in making up coalitions or allowances: SNP 47, Labour 46, Conservatives 17, Liberal Democrats 16, Greens 2 and other (Margo MacDonald) 1. It was Alex Salmond's victory. He comes over as a far more astute politician than Jack McConnell. He also has the moral authority (like him or not) to try to form an administration. It seems more likely than not that this is what we are in for.

20 May 2007

Alex Salmond is settling into his time as First Minister. He is a welcome change from Jack McConnell, and his slimmed-down team looks a much brighter lot than the old Labour team which lost the election. As head of a minority government, Salmond is playing things soft and conciliatory. He did not rush into things, just settled into government. On Thursday he met Her Majesty at Holyrood, with due respect and a sense of mutual pleasure on both sides – judging by the photograph. The Queen is excellent in such circumstances – adaptable, experienced, respectful of democracy. Elish Angiolini retains her position as Lord Advocate, but with a diminished role as she is not to be in the Cabinet. This is a wise move, which should have been the position from the outset. John Beckett, whom I met at the Ceremony of the Keys at Holyrood to which I was kindly invited for the first time in ten years, told me that, as he is a well-known Labour member, he expected to lose his job as Solicitor General. So it has proved to be. Frank Mulholland QC, a much-respected procurator fiscal, is his successor. So the Faculty of Advocates, for the first time ever, no longer has a Law Officer. Alan Rodger is dismayed, but it is clear that these offices no longer have the pulling power they did as progress to the Court of Session Bench is, in practice, denied to them. Good for open government, one might say, as the Bench should be staffed on merit, not for reward. But the traditional standing of the Law Officers as lawyers of outstanding quality must suffer in consequence.

27 May 2007

Two weeks ago I was awarded a prize at the Scottish Academy of Merit. This is the David Kelbie Award, named after the late Sheriff David Kelbie who was a remarkably able free-thinking man who got into trouble with the Appeal Court from time to time but never held it against me as we met afterwards at various conferences. I felt that I hardly deserved this, as my life has been so sheltered in comparison with his spent constantly in the front line. I began my ten-minute address, delivered to a small audience in the award ceremony in the Roxburghe Hotel, with a tribute to him. His wife and daughter were there, which was a real pleasure. I was one of 12 recipients from various aspects of public life in Scotland. The affair was presided over by Kenneth Roy, the founder of the Institute of Contemporary Scotland which sponsored it.

Back in London the week ended with more discussions about the Supreme Court. We had a sub-committee meeting about IT which was helpful and constructive. The issue on Thursday was more difficult. I had been asked to join Tom for another meeting about Brendan's future with Paul Hayter, the Clerk of Parliaments. There were two new problems. One was a change of position by the civil servants in the former DCA, now the Ministry of Justice. It had been agreed, as we understood it, that Brendan would move over to the Supreme Court and serve out the rest of his career there on secondment from the Parliament. But unwelcome pressure is causing second thoughts – or at least fears that there will be pressure and discrimination/equal pay claims, should the arrangement be put into effect. This has been reported to us as a matter which was still under negotiation. This is bad news, as all the officials will accept is a six-month secondment for him which is, of course, far too short. I suggested that we should ask for 18 months, as a sufficient period for the job to settle down and give sensible time for recruitment.

The other problem was that someone, believed to be a Law Lord, had said to Brendan himself that he understood that he was not going to the Supreme Court after all. Brendan had reported this to Paul Hayter, and it was feared that the civil servants or the politicians were moving by devious means to talk him out of the job. But when Paul Hayter revealed who the Law Lord was – it was Simon Brown – Tom was able on talking to him to trace the matter back to a conversation which Simon had had with me. He had asked me why the President-elect was to be identified so soon, apparently ignoring Lennie Hoffmann's right to succeed as Senior Law Lord. I explained that it was to establish who was to chair the Chief Executive's selection panel, in response to which Simon protested that this was Brendan's job and that no selection was needed. I had difficulty in getting the points across, that Brendan was not going for the position of Chief Executive and that he would be there in effect as our registrar. There was obviously a misunderstanding – awkward, but not the sinister spin-doctoring we had feared.

Later the same day John Lyon, the senior civil servant in charge of the project, came to see me at my request. I explained to him that I needed to see him about the system for selecting a President, which I could not discuss with Charles McCall or with Tom who would be chairing the selection commission under Schedule 8 to the 2005 Act. He saw my point, and was grateful when I pointed out that the commission might decide to select Lennie Hoffmann as Tom's successor as Senior Law Lord for two terms only, leaving the problem of who was to chair the Chief Executive panel as the prospective President of the Supreme Court, which he cannot be because of his retirement date, unresolved. That would need a further commission to identify the replacement for Lennie as Senior Law Lord, who will be the prospective President. A commission was needed anyway for Lennie's replacement as Second Senior Law Lord – and for the two new Lords who are to replace Lennie and Tom. I do not think that he had grasped the complications, as, I am sure, Tom has almost certainly not either. I asked whether I could be kept informed if there were problems, as it was still my responsibility come what may to see that there was a selection panel for the Chief Executive in November as the appointment of that official must not be delayed. This was a very helpful meeting. I wondered whether I should have asked for it but, in the event, I was glad that I did,

Later still, I met Brendan to do our sift of candidates to interview for the posts of judicial assistant for next year. We made our choices, and then Brendan raised with me the problems that Paul Hayter had wanted to discuss. Our discussion had been relayed back to him, with the main emphasis on the misunderstanding by Simon Brown. He wondered whether we had grasped that his future to the Supreme Court was now in doubt. I assured him that we had, and we commiserated with each other as I said that my own future was in doubt too.

I must try not to be oppressed by the uncertainties as to who is to be our President. Robert Walker told me a few days ago that he was assuming that I would be asked to take this position, and Richard Scott said the same thing to Mary when she was staying at Foscote ten days ago. But I certainly cannot take this for granted. Nicholas Phillips has been sitting with us this week. His determination to keep in touch despite having so much to do as Lord Chief Justice suggests that eyes are on him. That will not be ideal, as there is so much to think of and organise from within our body before Tom goes and his post becomes vacant on 1 October 2008 – only three years after Nicholas became Chief Justice. I doubt whether I would have the enthusiasm to carry on as chairman of the sub-committee, marshalling ideas and thinking about how best to move things forward, if I am to be in effect replaced by him. Tom will no doubt have his own ideas and will do his very best to persuade his Commission to accept them. So it is an awkward situation, with six months more to go of uncertainty.

Geoffrey Howe said in a debate on the Government in the House last Thursday that it was clear that the Supreme Court would be much safer from external pressures if it were to remain in the hands of Parliament than it will be in the hands of the Executive. How right he is. That has been his position all along, and no one is listening to him. But I met Tom Strathclyde, the Shadow Leader of the House, in a corridor the same day. He asked how things were going. I told him that the project is still on time for 1 October 2009 but that, due to planning and judicial review delays, time was now very tight. He said that there were bound to be more delays and that, if they got the chance, the Tories would scrap the project. I said that too much money would have been spent. Tom brushed that aside, saying that they would use the Middlesex Guildhall as a Crown Court. So we may not go there after all. Maybe somebody is listening to Geoffrey Howe after all.

9 June 2007

There were a pair of house sparrows, male and female, at the east end of West Princes Street Gardens today, just beside the head gardener's house. I watched them from the steps leading up to the Floral Clock. This is worth recording, as this species has almost disappeared from urban central Edinburgh. They used to be well established in this part of the Gardens. It would be nice to think that they are coming back, but it is more likely that they were just visitors passing through.

17 June 2007

Sunday – at home for 24 hours after a very busy week. It involved three nights in Athens, but also the annual series of interviews with candidates for the post of judicial assistant for the coming year. Hence there were no sittings for me.

The field for judicial assistants was, at first sight, smaller than last year. There were about 40 applications rather than the previous 80, but the quality was much improved. We interviewed 13 over two days, ending up with seven distinctly acceptable candidates. We could have filled six places without embarrassment, but we have room for only four. Three were well above the rest however: an impressive solicitor and two barristers who between them covered much of our range of work – Nicholas Gibson, Victoria Ailes and Corrina Ferguson. Both of the barristers are already tenants in their chambers. They were easy to allocate to Tom, Alan and Brenda – a man and two women. For myself, with Supreme Court responsibilities, I wanted a solicitor. The other members of the panel were impressed by a rather lively woman who is a solicitor with an American law firm, glittering with achievements, but with a career far removed from the work we do. I chose instead Matthew Hancock, a Scot who was with McGrigor Donald, having trained with Maclays. He had done his degree at Edinburgh with an excellent first and a strong recommendation from Hector MacQueen. If he is as responsive and friendly as Catherine Tracey was, we should have a good year. The team overall is rather more mature than last year's selection, which has been a mixed success. My assistant, Zoe Christoforides, was the best of the group as it turned out, from the point of view of a satisfactory working relationship. The interviews were enjoyable but hard work – and it was, as so often, not until the end that the shape of the team for the year was established. Brendan Keith and Philippa Tudor were with me for, I think, the fifth time. We understood each other's position well and it all went as smoothly as one could have wished.

Then to Athens. I had been invited to take Johan Steyn's place in a plenary session of the Seventh World Congress of Constitutional Law organised by the International Association of Constitutional Law of which Professor Tony Bradley is a vice-president. This was rather a tall order. The subject for my group's discussion, in a three-and-a-half-hour slot in a week-long programme, was to be the internationalisation of constitutional law. I needed some guidance on what this meant, but with Tony Bradley's help and some useful research by Zoe I put a brief paper together which I proposed to use as a basis of my remarks. There was a much-delayed journey from London, as Olympic Airways had to substitute a chartered aircraft for the one that had been planned for. So I arrived at the vast new airport at Athens a good deal later than had been intended. I was met by a young lawyer as arranged, who had very kindly waited for me. He drove me into Athens by way of the impressive tolled motorway which now links the city to the airport – part of the rather too expensive infrastructure which was put in for the Olympics last year. I arrived in Athens too late for the evening function to which the conference members had been invited.

Next day I had breakfast with Tony Bradley and walked with him in fierce heat and strong sunshine to the Zappeion in which the conference was being held. I attended two excellent sessions. One was a plenary for three hours on religion, the State and society, and the other was a workshop on proportionality with lunch in between. This was a good preparation for the following day. The affair was truly a world event. Seventy-four nations were represented, including all the former Soviet Republics, China, Japan and South America as well as Europe, North America and North and Southern Africa. French was spoken almost as much as English. The quality was high, with senior academics and a sprinkling of senior judges, many of whom were professors as so often seems to be the case in civil law jurisdictions.

The session in which I spoke was presided over by Professor Eivind Smith from Norway, a future President of the IACL, who organised us very well. I spoke first for ten minutes, followed by a judge of the Constitutional Court of South Korea and a judge of the Constitutional Court of Columbia, both of them in their mid-40s. There were comments by three other members of our panel: Professor Brun-Otto Bryde of the Constitutional Court of Germany; Professor Vassilios Skouris, President of the ECJ; and Professor Christos Rozakis of the European Court of Human Rights, to which I was asked to reply. There were about a dozen very well-directed questions from the floor to which we, but mainly I, were also asked to reply. Then, after coffee, it was the turn of Bryde, Skouris and Rozakis, with follow-ups as in the previous part of the session. It went on from 9.30am to 1.30pm – a long but very interesting and enjoyable experience. Everyone seemed very pleased with what had been achieved.

Professor Cheryl Saunders, just leaving office as President, said to me how refreshing it had been to hear the views of serving judges. It is true that some of the ideas of the academics were rather detached from reality.

There was little free time. But I did climb up to the Acropolis to enjoy the view. Alpine swifts were twittering to each other as they scythed through the air around this marvellous granite outcrop. And a hoopoe flew past me as I walked up through the olive trees. Later it gave me 15 minutes' pleasure as it walked around the bushes about 30 yards away, pecking busily at things on the ground and raising its crest from time to time. It was a surprisingly modest-sized bird, in contrast to the impression it gives of a giant butterfly when in flight.

6 July 2007

After an extraordinary week I am unwinding from the stress of the Strathclyde graduation ceremonies. This was the second Friday of this summer's series: one congregation only this time, for those graduating as engineers. Last week there were two, for the Strathclyde Business School and the lawyers. As I have said so often before, I put a lot of physical effort into these occasions. I have to make an impromptu speech of welcome to a large audience in the Barony Hall to start with, concentrate on the faces of the 200–260 students who come across the stage, deliver a formal address from the lectern and then close the ceremony with another impromptu speech. The receptions afterwards, when I can meet the graduates, and the informal lunch in the Business School are most enjoyable. But at the ceremonies everything depends on me. It is right that I should be on edge and give of my best. But it is exhausting.

They were not what made the week extraordinary, however. In the afternoon of Saturday 30 June, without any warning, a dark green Cherokee 4x4 was driven at speed into the doorway of the international departures hall at Glasgow Airport by two men and set on fire. It was loaded with propane gas cylinders. For a moment it looked like an accident. But it was a terrorist attack. By good fortune there was no explosion, and the two men were apprehended. One was very severely burned. There was a localised fire at the entrance, but no worse. What could have led to huge loss of life in the airport full of families going away on holiday turned out, in the event, to be a major disruption but nothing more than that. The airport was evacuated, some people were held in their seats in departure aircraft for hours, and airports all over the country were put into a critical state of emergency as the police tried to work out what was going on. Two cars had been found in London the previous evening also packed with gas canisters, and a rich seam of clues led rapidly, via emails, mobile telephone calls, etc to the discovery that these incidents were linked, and to more arrests. By Tuesday the critical state of alert was reduced, as it had become clear that the entire plot had been uncovered and dealt with.

Meantime, I had to get back to London on Sunday evening. The flights were working more or less normally by then – Bmi was anyway – from Edinburgh.

But getting to the airport was a problem. I found out via the website that the car parks were all closed, so I had to use the bus instead. That was not bad in itself, but the city was being attacked by a prolonged thunderstorm as I set off on foot to get the bus. I got to Shandwick Place before the heavens really opened, but waiting for 15 minutes in the street for the packed bus to arrive was an ordeal despite some shelter in a doorway. Then at the exit from the A9 to the airport there was a complete traffic jam. The bus driver said that it would take 40 minutes for him to get to the airport. The alternative was a 20-minute walk in the thunderstorm. So I stayed on the bus for another 20 minutes, during which we hardly moved at all. Then I walked. The rain was easing, but I got pretty wet as did trails of people coming in the other direction returning from their holidays. A miserable sight, as the police grimly stopped all traffic. We were checked before entering the airport, but from thereon all was well and I was able to dry out a bit before taking the flight, more or less on time, south to London. I was worried about getting home again, especially in view of my duties at Strathclyde. But by Thursday things were back to normal, and Mary collected me from the airport.

Extraordinary too were various happenings during the week itself. On Monday evening James and Bett Mackay gave a dinner party in the Inner Temple for James's 80th birthday. This was a delightful family occasion, but it was a challenge for me too as he asked me to make the speech for the evening to which he would reply. This took a lot of preparation: whether to get some original material together or draw on my own memory of times past was the first problem. I took the latter course and typed out a six-page draft with a mixture of tributes and the light-hearted. The next thing was to memorise it, as I was sure that to read this out would be quite unsuitable for such an occasion. It had to appear to be spontaneous. Of course, I was not entirely sure of my audience either. I spent much of the previous few days going over it over and over again. On Monday itself I felt quite ill with fear that I might not remember my words, and then put my speech into half-page form just in case. In the event, thank goodness, all was well. There were fewer Law Lords than I had expected – fewer lawyers indeed – more family, and other older friends and colleagues and quite a few Scots. But the speech was light-hearted enough for them too. People laughed, once they realised that I was making jokes. There were cries of regret when I said that it was time to stop so that we could enjoy James's birthday cake. Afterwards all sorts of people went out of their way to congratulate me. And very kindly Tom Bingham, an exacting critic, wrote me a note saying that it was exactly what was wanted. What a relief! I did not let them down.

Then, on Wednesday evening, Tony Lloyd had a question for debate during the dinner hour on the Supreme Court. The significance of this was enhanced by the fact, which I should have mentioned above, that Tony Blair left office as Prime Minister last week and Gordon Brown, taking over, had appointed a new Cabinet. Among other things, Charlie Falconer – who had started the project, after all – was sacked and replaced as Lord Chancellor by Jack Straw, sitting in the House of Commons. A junior Minister, Lord Hunt of King's Heath, was appointed at the start of the week to represent the Ministry of Justice in the House of Lords. I decided that I ought to contribute to the debate, mainly to make my presence known to the new Minister. Brendan Keith made disapproving noises, but I said that as this was not legislation and as it affected us there could be no sound objection. It being a timed debate we were allowed five minutes each, apart from Tony Lloyd and the Minister. I wrote my speech at 6pm. It contained tributes to colleagues including Brendan for all their help, and three points of importance to draw to the attention of the Minister: delay and the need to give the quality of the building priority over timetable; staff needs and probable unfairness for those who transferred; and finance. The other speakers were on party lines – reverting to old points for and against the project. I was the only speaker on practical issues. Lennie Hoffmann and Jonathan Mance attended too, which was good, but they did not speak. The next day Tom, rather to my surprise, came up to me and congratulated me on it, wondering whether he should have spoken too. So I did do the right thing. The staff were obviously delighted that I had spoken up for them. I felt that I was showing leadership where it was needed. It was all my own doing and my idea. The choice of President is, of course, an issue to be faced before much longer. But I was not trying to project myself more than necessary to do what was needed. The Minister seemed pleasant and receptive. So I hope that the President, whoever he or she is, can build on this and get the difficult issues addressed by him, as they need to be now that Charlie Falconer has gone.

Meantime I have been chairing a lengthy Scots appeal, with two days to come next week, and a two-day Scots appeal after that. It is a busy time.

28 July 2007

Almost at the end of the term. There are two days to do next week, then off to Craighead at last.

Somerville[264] and *Moncrieff v Jamieson*,[265] the two Scots cases referred to above, turned out to be very interesting and enjoyable. *Somerville* was about the segregation in isolation of prisoners from other prisoners and whether their claims, which were made on the ground of incompatibility with Convention rights, were time barred: there was no bar if made on the ground of lack of devolved competence under the Scotland Act, but there would be a bar if made on the ground of a breach of a Convention right under the Human Rights Act. Alan and I had indicated in an earlier case that these claims should, or at least could, be made under the Scotland Act. The First Division, for no very sound reasons, said that we were wrong. Aidan O'Neill, for the appellant, was not perhaps the best advocate to present an argument to support our view. The other side had Gerry Moynihan and the Advocate General. Alan and I saw more and more reasons why we were right. Unfortunately Richard Scott and Jonathan Mance,

---

264 *Somerville v Scottish Ministers* [2007] UKHL 44, 2008 SC (HL) 45.
265 [2007] UKHL 42, 2008 SC (HL) 1.

neither of whom seem to be as sensitive to the need to achieve unanimity and tend to dissent too readily, take the view on different grounds from the First Division that the Human Rights Act rules. So it is down to Robert Walker, who really does think things through and is more supportive of the need for consensus, in our direction I hope. The *Moncrieff* case was about a servitude right of way to an isolated seaside dwellinghouse in Shetland, the question being whether the owners' right of way extended to a right to park their car on the servient property. This is a difficult issue, and here again there was a split. Scott and Mance were with me, and Alan and David Neuberger the other way. But David has come round to supporting me, and probably Alan will too. That would be nice, as it would be a sensible result for a family who wish to park their cars beside their house, which is only accessible by car via a route through their neighbours' property and has no area of its own onto which cars can go when they get there.

Then we had a week in the Privy Council on a case from Brunei. Prince Jefri, the Sultan's brother, was being sued by the Government of Brunei, in effect by the Sultan himself as this is an absolute Monarchy, for breach of a settlement agreement. The result – against Prince Jefri, who seems to be the cause of all the trouble and was lucky to get such a generous settlement in the first place – was never really in doubt. Meantime, or rather in between, Mary came south for the Lord Mayor's Dinner for HM Judges and the Royal Garden Party. Once again, but this time as I was the Senior Law Lord attending (Bingham and Hoffmann never go, and Donald Nicholls has retired), I was seated next to the Lady Mayoress. On her other side, arriving late due to votes in the Commons (can it have come to this?) was the new Lord Chancellor, Jack Straw. Nicholas Phillips made a confident speech as Lord Chief Justice, Jack Straw a more diffident one, both trying to be conciliatory. We are already far away from Harry Woolf's 'concordat' with Charlie Falconer, which never did have a very secure or long-lasting foundation. There was little time for the Royal Garden Party, as we sat right up to 4pm on Thursday. But we got to the Royal Tea Tent, without any time to walk around, by 4.45pm and had fun speaking to the newly accredited diplomats – from North Korea and a group from West Africa. The Duke of Edinburgh spotted my Highlanders' tie and joked about the problems of keeping up with such things as the ties keep changing as regiments amalgamate. Then, after some lovely raspberries and iced coffee, it was time to go.

This week we had the annual dinner in the Cholmondeley room for the judicial assistants – an ever-increasing number of delightful young people now making good their careers in the outside world. After dinner we ended up on the terrace for after-dinner champagne provided by the Judicial Office. No one wanted to leave. Some did not do so until well after midnight.

That afternoon, between court and the dinner, there was a meeting of the Supreme Court sub-committee at Somerset House where the architects, Feilden & Mawson, have their offices. This was to discuss the art strategy and Brenda Hale was in charge. Thanks to her, we were addressed by a fascinating team of specialists from various fields, with a distinctly African flavour. Elsie Owusu, herself a very cultured, well-educated lady, obviously has many contacts with that community in London. There were people from other European countries with a fascinating range of ideas for our furniture. Colours, designs and materials had been well thought through, and much of what was on display was attractive and interesting. The only real disappointment was the design for an insignia or seal for the new Court. Yvonne Holton, the herald painter from Edinburgh, had produced some designs based on flowers and trees, but none were convincing. It is not easy. Brenda suggested that it would be good to get away from a badge based on the Royal Coat of Arms now that we are in the 21st century. Not everyone will agree with this, but the fact is that the Royal Coat of Arms produces problems for us, as each of our three jurisdictions has a different approach to it.[266] But where to go? The suggestion of a design based on lilies has to be discarded because lilies raise sectarian feelings in Northern Ireland. We will have to try to get consensus on such a sensitive issue. That will not be easy.[267]

On Thursday Charles McCall and his assistant Kylie Freeman, in charge of publicity, came to see me about the plans for the Royal Opening. This is odd to contemplate, as we are still two years away from that and we still do not know who is to be our President. But I was able to contribute some ideas, based on my experiences of an opening ceremony which I conducted with the Princess Royal in Parliament House in Edinburgh when I was Lord President. Given the increasingly ominous loom of problems in getting agreement on sensitive issues, it will be a welcome release if I was not to be invited to be President of the new Court. The uncertainty as to who this is to be continues to hover over me, nevertheless.

31 July 2007

The term ended today with a party for everyone in the Conference Room. Zoe, who has been such a success as an assistant to me in her quiet, thoughtful way, gave me a picture of the opening of the Middlesex Guildhall in 1913, showing the old building (rather more attractive than today's version, I think), and the new which is the one we will be required to occupy. I put it on my wall for everyone to admire. The day began with an oral hearing on a procedural matter – a rare event these days – with Brenda and Jonathan. We were being asked in effect to case-manage a petition by a child to intervene in his mother's asylum

---

266 The quartering differs as between England and Scotland, and the Royal Coat of Arms is no longer used in the courts in Northern Ireland.
267 Yvonne Holton came to see me in Edinburgh during the first week of the vacation to see if we could find a way out of this difficulty. She suggested that we should try a design based on a badge which had symbols for each of our three jurisdictions: England and Wales, Scotland and Northern Ireland. She proposed that she should use flowers for this, and within a few days came up with a design based on a rose, a thistle and a flax flower for Northern Ireland, which we were able to adopt after she had added the leek for Wales: see the entries for 27 August and 12 September 2007.

claim with a view to putting his own separate case for asylum. Brenda and Jonathan had made equally valid points for and against giving leave, so I decided that having this hearing was the best way out. Brenda protested by email at my taking this step. But in the event it was a thoroughly useful and helpful hearing, and after it was over she very graciously thanked me and said that she withdrew her protests. She is a formidable, vigorous person with a strong agenda of her own, but many of her ideas are valuable and thought-provoking. I try my best to satisfy her demands and she is quick to respond positively in return. She is a thoroughly useful member of the team. She is making a major contribution to our work in a way that one might not have thought was possible.

Lennie presided excellently over an interesting two-day hearing in an international arbitration case.[268] He is very much at home in this subject. I was delighted to see that one of the cases to which we were referred was one in which our son James had appeared as a solicitor advocate when he was with an American law firm, Skadden Arps, in London. It was a case in his special subject too. What a remarkable variety of cases we get to see in our job, including as they do such specialities.

So ends my eighteenth year as a judge and my eleventh in the House of Lords. It has been very busy indeed, and the coming year looks like being just as busy. The Supreme Court is eating more and more into my spare time. I do hope that I can live up to what is expected of me, and that as hard decisions loom before us we can all continue to be friends. Not every supreme court enjoys such happy relations between its members as we have done on the Law Lords' Corridor. That is something to hold onto.

2007 – August and September

18 August 2007

We had only two weeks at Craighead before it was time to return to Edinburgh to get ready for the CMJA's 2007 meeting, which this year is in Bermuda. It was unfortunate that the date was in mid-August and not later. But the other side of the coin is that we will be back in Scotland for the Lonach Ball in Strathdon and the Braemar Gathering, to which David and Elisabeth Stewart have very kindly invited us again this year.

So I am writing this on the BA2233 from Gatwick, somewhere in the mid-Atlantic. We are in a Boeing 777, a very comfortable aircraft. We left home at the reasonable hour of 9.45am, parting company with Poppy, Mary's delightful Maine Coon cat, who had been watching us pack during the previous 12 hours and wondering, no doubt, whether she was coming with us or going to be left

---

268 *Fiona Trust and Holding Corporation v Privalov* [2007] UKHL 40, [2007] Bus LR 17129.

behind. Our flight to Gatwick appeared at first to be on time but was delayed by a cello whose owner insisted that it had to be stored in the cabin somewhere instead of in the hold. So we missed our slot and were 55 minutes late on take-off. But we had more than enough time for our transfer once we arrived. As we entered the BA executive lounge we were greeted by the news that we had been upgraded from Club World, for which I had paid, to First Class. So here we are, in row 1 at the front of the aircraft, in spacious seats after an excellent lunch of asparagus, salmon and rhubarb tart with ice cream. We have not much idea of what to expect when we arrive. But we have already met Michael and Jane Lambert, Henry and Biddy Brooke, Helen and Douglas Allan, Bobby Dickson and several other CMJA members from the UK.

. . . The approach to Bermuda was very striking. There were lots of small, fluffy tropical clouds scattered over a calm sea. Then a fragment of land – the east end of the island, St Georges – appeared, and then an airfield close by. We glided in past a lighthouse and closely-packed, neat white-roofed houses, like paper cut-outs, to land on a spacious but largely deserted airfield. A steel band was playing in the arrivals hall. Amazingly all our baggage was already there when we entered it. Soon we were in a taxi with two others, driving along narrow roads at a leisurely pace in luxurious scenery to our hotel, the Fairmount Southampton situated towards the western end of the island, where the conference is to be held.

25 August 2007

Now at the start of the return journey, waiting for our flight home at Bermuda Airport.

The conference began in the usual way with an evening reception in the conference hotel so that we could meet old friends and spot new ones. Richard Ground, the Chief Justice of Bermuda, was our host – very brisk, efficient and genial. His enthusiasm for the conference was obvious all the way through. The main organisation was in the hands of one of his puisne judges, Norma Wade-Miller, who was supported by a very friendly team with our own Karen Brewer and Paul McDermott on hand to link in with Keith Hollis's educational programme. My successor as President of the CMJA, Siti Yakob from Malaysia, was absent without any adequate explanation or apology. Henry Brooke,[269] the Executive Vice-President, stood in for her quite excellently. We were in good hands.

Monday's opening ceremony was designed by Norma, with Clover Thompson Gordon from Jamaica in the foreground too as this was to a large extent her conference. There was a flag ceremony, with flags on placards, brought in procession by brownies, scouts, cadets, police and other officers. There was a prayer and there were a few not unnecessarily long speeches. Then we settled

269 Sir Henry Brooke, formerly Lord Justice Brooke.

into a three-day educational programme, punctuated by an evening reception at the Dockyard on the Monday; an evening cruise with dinner on board a ferry from Hamilton to the Dockyard and back on the Tuesday; and a Gala Dinner and Ball on the Wednesday. The plenary sessions were all well handled, well attended and thoughtful. The emphasis was on human rights issues, mainly with regard to children but also in regard to economic development in a session which I chaired. There were notable and very moving contributions on the tragic conditions facing orphans or war-beleaguered children in Africa, and by Judge Leona Theron of the High Court of South Africa on her struggle, as a woman and a mother, to make progress in the legal profession and on the Bench in that country. We were invited to join Richard Ground's table at the Gala Dinner.

Friday was the council meeting day, presided over with great charm by Henry Brooke. There was much concern over the absence of Siti Yakob who, on last year's showing, would not have made nearly such a good chairman. She has been almost uncontactable until very recently, and has given no written report or explanation or sought any help with her difficulties. When she was elected she was a judge and all the signs were that she would secure that our next triennial meeting would be held in Malaysia. Now all of that has fallen apart. She has lost her job as a judge. Her six-month appointment, it seems, was not renewed. Malaysia has withdrawn from the idea of hosting a conference and it has cancelled its membership of the CMJA. The Chief Justice of Malaysia has taken great exception to Siti's appointment as President, and all official communications with her have become impossible. She says that, official funding having been withdrawn, she cannot afford to attend. So reports Michael Lambert. But money could have been made available had she asked for it. I said that we had to look to the future. We must have an active President by the time of the next triennial conference and preferably by next year. There were suggestions that, as the immediate past President, I should fill the position. But that would not be easy for me with the creation of the Supreme Court on the horizon for 2009. But in the end the resolution, or at least the general view of the council, was that Henry should ask Siti to make her position clear within the next two months. She really has to resign if we are to get anywhere. If she does the council can then fill the vacancy. If she does not, we have no power to remove her. We will be stuck.

There was much discussion about money, as usual, and the need to take action to raise funds. Philip Bailhache of Jersey, who was an excellent addition to the council, suggested setting up an endowment fund. His idea of what individual members could contribute was rather extravagant – he comes from Jersey, after all. But we did decide to relax the fetter on outside sponsorship, provided that it was through charitable and not commercial links. Banks through their trust funds, for example, or law firms through *pro bono* programmes, would be acceptable. We may make progress here. There were also discussions on constitutional changes to give more of a place to associate or individual members. This is not an easy topic, as the committee in charge of the proposals is itself divided on how this should be done. David Armati, its Australian chairman, is in vigorous disagreement with the rest of his committee on almost everything. Time ran out as we discussed venues for future conferences. But Turks and Caicos has been agreed for the triennial in 2009, with South Africa, Malta or Northern Ireland in that order as possible venues for a meeting in 2008. It is not clear whether I will be able to attend either of them. This makes the state of the Presidency an anxious topic for me.

As dates begin to be mentioned for the next two council meetings and conferences I wondered more and more whether I will be able to participate. Next year's meeting, if in South Africa, as is being suggested, is likely to be in October or November, as Ramadan is in September. That is term time for me. Even more troublesome for me is the date suggested for Turks and Caicos in 2009: 28 September to 2 October. That covers the opening of the new Supreme Court on 1 October, which, whatever capacity I will be in then, I must attend. It is difficult for me to make my position clear, should Siti have to be replaced as President, as my own future is still so obscure.

27 August 2007

Returned to a modest amount of mail and a few days at home before five days more at Craighead and at Braemar. The most pressing issue is the Supreme Court seal. Jonathan Mance has raised the inevitable question of the Welsh. How can the three-flowered foliage pattern of rose, thistle and flax which Yvonne Holton has designed for us, be seen to accommodate them? We will have to sort this one out before the design is settled.[270] Brenda is still out of touch on holiday, so I do not know how she will react to the alternatives that are now on offer. Elsie Owusu phoned this morning putting forward various points on which a decision is needed by mid-September. Much will depend on how Yvonne Holton can resolve the Welsh problem as to whether we can achieve this. Elsie seemed surprised when I told her that not all the Law Lords were in favour of the project, and that some indeed were rubbishing anything put before them. Not an easy task.

12 September 2007

Yvonne Holton came up with a very clever solution – a leek from which, at the top, emerges the rose. The thistle and Northern Ireland's flax are set side by side below, the whole encased in a libra (a sign of the zodiac) or an omega (indicating finality) according to one's taste. Brenda Hale accepts this as a very lovely design and – with no real objection from Jonathan Mance – I authorised Elsie Owusu of the architects to proceed with the design on the basis of this format. There was no time to consult with the other Law Lords. So I have taken a risk. But I do not think that this design can be improved upon.

270 See fn 267.

There was a memorial service for Charles Jauncey at Comrie yesterday. He had asked me to deliver the address. Fortunately I had prepared it some time ago, so there was no last-minute pressure. Camilla asked me to lunch at Tullichettle with the family beforehand. It is a lovely, quite modest Georgian house with a spacious garden. There is a delightful walled garden, part of which was full of mouth-watering vegetables. The service itself was marked by tributes by Cressida, Charles' daughter by his third wife Camilla, and by Simon and Jamie, his sons by his first marriage to Jean. They were all very direct, touching and revealing about the happiness and humour of his whole life which we as his professional colleagues never saw. It was, as I expected, a real county occasion. There were many regimental ties: Scots Guards, Black Watch, Argylls, Highland Brigade and so on. Some old friends from the Court of Session were there: William Prosser, James Clyde, Alastair Cameron, Kenny Cameron, John Cameron and Patrick Hodge. William Berry was there too, and various people from the Cockburn Association such as Oliver Barrett, and from the National Trust such as Patrick Stirling-Aird. It was a fine turn-out for a very fine man.

I have been working on two big lectures, now both more or less in place. They are the W A Wilson Lecture for Edinburgh University in November – 'Strange Habits of the English', and the Neill Lecture for All-Souls, Oxford in February – 'From Clova to Godmanchester: Public Rights over Private Land'. I have put a great deal of time and effort into both of them. Neither has any depth academically, however. I am anxious that the audiences will have expected more of me. But it is not possible for me to be other than true to myself. That means that I am writing (or speaking) about a subject I have enjoyed looking at and writing about. The Wilson Lecture is really about Bill Wilson, his style of lecturing and his special interests. The Neill Lecture is really a kind of present to Pat Neill, after whom this year's lecture is named, as he is the Laird of Auchenleish in Glenisla on the edge of the Mounth over which the right of way exists whose origin is the subject of my lecture.

Our judgments in two Scottish cases[271] – *Moncrieff*, about the private right of way in Shetland, and *Somerville* about whether just satisfaction claims for infringement of Convention rights by a member of the Scottish Executive can be claimed under the Scotland Act without incurring a time-bar – are reaching their final stages. Alan Rodger, who is the last to deliver, has produced his drafts. Rather irritable ones, I think. He can never resist singling me out for criticism and has done so again in both, rather gratuitously I felt. But I am resisting the temptation to complain.

---

271 See fns 264 and 265.

2007 – October to December

14 October 2007

The Abbey service was presided over by Jack Straw, Charlie Falconer's successor as Lord Chancellor – wearing the robes of his office but no wig – together with the Lord Chief Justice. Two very fine lessons and an excellent sermon by the new Dean of Westminster, the Very Rev John Hall, made it more than unusually enjoyable. The breakfast was in the Royal Gallery instead of Westminster Hall, which is still occupied by an exhibition on slavery. There was a great deal of food, quite beyond the tiny morsels that were common about ten years ago.

On the Law Lords' Corridor the most significant event is Helen McMurdo's decision to retire at the end of this month. She broke the news to me in my room, as we were trying to sort out start of term problems with my computer. Her explanation was a wish to emigrate to Ireland, where her children and grandchildren now are. Her house sold more quickly than expected, and the rent for the house where they now live is very expensive. But it is hard not to think that the lack of a future for her in this building is part of it, probably a very important part. Christine Salmon, Brendan's second-in-command, is leaving too for another appointment in the House, as is Kate Lawrence from the Judicial Office. Oh dear, oh dear, we are being bled dry already, even before our start in the new building. Brendan's position, after so many attempts at negotiation, is not so secure either. We are on the verge of a collapse in our administration.

We had two sub-committee meetings this week, devoted to artwork, furnishings and the recruitment of a Chief Executive. The design of the seal is now settled, as there have been no protests to counteract general approval for Yvonne Holton's design. Artwork is going well under Brenda's art panel, as are furnishings. We had a bit of an argument about carpeting in our rooms. Brenda objects strongly to fitted carpets, while Jonathan and I want them. We compromised: four rooms to be unfitted, eight fitted. As for the Chief Executive, the post is now being advertised and we have worked out a timetable for meetings, shortlistings and interviews, to add to our other burdens this term. Rockpools, the recruitment agency, produced some very garbled and ungrammatical texts for the advertisement and job description. To my relief they did not argue with me about the changes which I proposed to put them into proper English. So we are on course for this very important appointment. I wish we knew who the President is to be. Latest timing suggests we may have to wait until June for this.

As for work, two quite simple cases last week have been followed by five and a half days on fox hunting on which we are now engaged.[272] The human rights issues have probably been worked through to exhaustion, and we will have

---

272 See fns 273 and 274.

nothing much to contribute. But there is an interesting issue on EU law which may require a reference. If it does that puts the cat among the pigeons.

We had dinner last night on board the Royal Yacht *Britannia*, now in her permanent mooring at Ocean Terminal in Leith, as guests of the Rotary Club of London. This was a speaking engagement for me, as I was to be the principal speaker. It was to an unknown audience of about 90 people, a bit of an ordeal. John and Mary Buchanan, ex-CMJA, collected Mary and myself from India Street, and we were welcomed aboard by a piper and shown into the spacious drawing-room, whose scale was reminiscent of government houses and British embassies everywhere. A rather daunting selection of elderly rotarians and their spouses arrived. We were given a tour of the ship, charming in its simple furnishings and touches of the practical. There was a garage for the Rolls Royce. We sat down to supper/dinner in the formal dining-room. An excellent dinner, beautifully served, created just the right atmosphere. I was between Doreen, Baroness Miller of Hendon, whom I of course recognised as a Tory peer, and the President, Hugh Kirk FCCA, a rather elderly and bumbling gentleman, but talkative nevertheless. I was supposed to speak at 10pm but it was nearly 11pm when we got round to this. The President caused great amusement as he said 'What's your name?' as he attempted to introduce me. 'That was deliberate', he added, *sotto voce*. He had asked me to insert some humour into a moderately serious address about the House of Lords and the Supreme Court. This I tried to do and the audience did indeed find something to laugh at which was a relief. The light-hearted atmosphere, in contrast to the rather grim faces on arrival, was aided by the announcement that, contrary to all expectations, England beat France in Paris by a narrow margin to get into the final of the Rugby World Cup. I felt that I had done my bit, and was rewarded by a fascinating visit to the lovely vessel. But it was a relief to get it over.

21 October 2007

England lost in the final to South Africa 6–15. It was a tight game, a creditable performance and a fine way to end the competition in which they had entered well below their best. Brenda Hale was there for the final in Paris, and for the play-off for third place which Argentina won over France. Scotland really ought to have been there instead of Argentina after a quarter-final which was within their grasp. But they would not have finished as well as Argentina. It was bad luck on the French.

We had our first meeting with the members of the Chief Executive selection panel on Thursday. With us were Elisabeth Arfon-Jones, who chairs tribunals, and Sir Ian Magee, a senior civil servant. It was a useful, lively discussion which alerted me to the void which will confront our appointee in the absence of a President to whom he or she will be responsible during the critical initial period in the job. The selection process for the President is being very badly done. Delays may be deliberate, however. Perhaps Tom does not want the selection made until he is about to go. This will make it much easier for Nicholas Phillips to step over from three years' service as Chief Justice. Lennie Hoffmann, predictably, shows no interest whatever in succeeding Tom for a few months in office until May 2009. But what are we to do? I have decided that it is my responsibility to put myself forward as the point of contact for the time being. Unless this is done much momentum will be lost, playing into the hands of the Ministry of Justice whose interest it is to sew up the Chief Executive as one of their own. So I shall send out a memo next week making the point that, while I have no wish to assert for myself a position that is not mine, there is a void that must be filled and asking for everyone's support and approval.

We finished a long hearing in conjoined cases from England on the Hunting Act 2004[273] and from Scotland on the Protection of Wild Animals (Scotland) Act 2002[274] in which attempts were made to challenge their validity. Among those who addressed us was a party litigant, Brian Friend, whose case had come to us from the Court of Session. He was very charming, sincere and resolute, yet restrained. He was clad, as he told us, in his country suit. Sadly I do not think that we can do anything for the hunting community, although there is much force in the contention that these measures were enacted by an ignorant majority against people they do not like.

4 November 2007

Helen McMurdo left us last Thursday. There was a party to see her off, with a nice speech from Lennie as Tom was at a lecture, and presents from all of us, for which she kissed each of us goodbye. What a gap she leaves behind her. My secretary Georgina Isaac will occupy her seat until we find a replacement. In her place for me comes a temp called Sara Shah, a strange very reticent person who is hard to make out and seems to be quite confused by her situation. It will be a difficult period.

I had a week out of court which was useful for various reasons. I took the opportunity to sit on the prorogation ceremony in the House, which for the first time had no Lord Chancellor as Jack Straw is not a member of the House of Lords. The Leader of the House, Baroness Ashton of Upholland, filled the vacancy very well but it is odd to see yet one more ancient tradition fall away. Then back to the usual early November weekend – a graduation day at Strathclyde, the Stair Society's annual general meeting and lecture, given by Sir Neil MacCormick, for me to chair, and then changing the plants in the tub at our front door from summer plants to wallflowers and bulbs for the winter.

---

273 *R (Countryside Alliance) v Attorney General* [2007] UKHL 52, [2008] AC 719, under the Human Rights Act 1998 on the ground that the Hunting Act was incompatible with the claimants' Convention rights.

274 *Whalley v Lord Advocate* [2007] UKHL 53, 2007 SC (HL) 107, under the Scotland Act 1998 on the ground that the Protection of Wild Animals (Scotland) Act 2002 was outside the legislative competence of the Scottish Parliament.

9 November 2007

We had an awkward devolution case in the Privy Council this week.[275] It arose from the conflict between *R v HM Advocate*,[276] in which the three Scots (myself, Clyde and Rodger) held that the Lord Advocate had no power to continue to prosecute a case after unreasonable delay within the meaning of Article 6 ECHR, and *Attorney General's Reference (No 2 of 2001)*[277] in which the two Scots (myself and Rodger) were outvoted by seven English judges as to the remedy for this which was available in England. As it happens, a series of cases in Strasbourg has clarified the law somewhat. It can now be said to be clear – as it was not before because these cases were not cited to us, or were not available, previously – that the continuation of a case after an unreasonable delay is not in itself a breach of Article 6. That is odd, but it is what the Strasbourg Court thinks. So we are all agreed that *R v HM Advocate* should be departed from. This was rather a gentle let-down, really.

All would have been well but for Alan Rodger and Jonathan Mance. Jonathan questioned the scope to be given to devolution issues for the purposes of the Privy Council's jurisdiction. As it happens, several previous cases have addressed this issue, and practice on the matter has been settled for the past eight years. This is no impediment to Jonathan, who seems determined to press the point. Tom wrote a few words in his judgment accommodating that point of view. But it is, so I think, quite wrong and potentially quite damaging. Tom, on being told so by Alan, suggested that I should write something which Alan could agree to so that he could adopt it. Alas, Alan, who has been behaving very oddly all week, refused to discuss this with me. Indeed he has quite pointedly refused to discuss the case with me at all. Why he has done this is difficult to understand, unless it is because he has taken to blaming me for what is being planned for the Supreme Court. He is wholly opposed to it and to anything to do with it, so I suppose I am a kind of traitor in his eyes. He is an odd character. He finds it hard to control his emotions, is very disorganised and yet strikingly clever: rather like his Oxford mentor David Daube, one imagines. It is not healthy for us to be at odds with each other. This is certainly not of my doing, as I am willing to meet him more than halfway. But he is not approachable when he is in this neurotic state of mind, and I do not know how to handle him without making things worse.

24 November 2007

Yesterday evening I gave the Wilson Lecture at Edinburgh University.[278] Mary came with me and to the dinner in the University afterwards. It seemed to be well received and was very well attended with many old friends with whom to share memories of such a marvellous man.

275 *Spiers v Ruddy* [2007] UKPC D2, 2009 SC (PC) 1.
276 See fn 189.
277 See fn 210.
278 Entitled 'The Strange Habits of the English', after the title that Professor Bill Wilson gave to one of his lectures.

7 December 2007

A large brown envelope appeared in my pigeon hole marked 'Restricted – Appointments'. It was a letter from Tom Bingham, starting the process for the appointment of the person who is to succeed him as Senior Law Lord/President of the Supreme Court as mandated by section 27 of the Constitutional Reform Act 2005. We were told – I say 'we', because this was a formal letter sent to all those who are required by the section to be consulted at this stage – that the Appointments Commission is to consist of Tom and Lennie, as Senior and Second Senior Law Lords *ex officio*, together with Baroness Prashar, Chair of the English Appointments Commission, and Sir Neil McIntosh and Sir Anthony Campbell from the equivalent bodies in Scotland and Northern Ireland. All the current Law Lords other than Tom and Lennie are on the list of consultees, as are the Lord Chief Justices of England and Wales and of Northern Ireland, the Lord President and the Lord Justice Clerk, and the heads of the Divisions in England and Wales. We are asked to state, with reasons, whom we consider best suited on merit for the appointment and to state also whether we are willing to allow our names to be considered – in which event we disqualify ourselves from being part of the consultation process.

It is a relief that the process has begun. We are urged to respond without delay, as there are a number of other appointments that will need to be made. Whatever this may mean for the others, it is time for a serious decision to be taken on my part. Am I willing to be considered, or am I not? I really have no alternative. So many of the people with whom I have been working on preparation for the Supreme Court look to me already as the leader of this initiative. They would be astonished if I were to withdraw now, so in the interests of continuity of progress I simply must stick to the task. It is a sense of duty, not a search for honour that drives me into this position. It is not nice to be forced to declare oneself in this way. Tom's letter says that all this will be treated in strict confidence, but I suspect that everyone on the Corridor is expecting me to be a candidate. Nicholas Phillips, of course, is the other obvious one.

A great deal will depend on what my colleagues will say in response to the consultation. Support from them will carry me a long way. Lack of support will mean the end of my candidature. I would not want this position without their support anyway. What people outside the Corridor will say goodness knows. Probably they will mostly go for Nicholas Phillips. My sense is that Tom wants to dispose of the issue on paper without interviews. He may not carry the lay members with him on this, but Lennie and Anthony Campbell will support him. An interview would be an ordeal I would rather avoid.

This is so reminiscent of standing for Dean of Faculty and of my agreeing to my name going forward for appointment as Lord President. Less agonising than the former and less momentous than the latter, for obvious reasons. I am assured of a place in the Supreme Court come what may, after all. But once again I am in the hands of views which others have of me and my abilities and my personality. Mary, as always, is my best support at these critical times in my career.

Otherwise a good and enjoyable week in the chair in the Privy Council, and on a one-day case about the European arrest warrant[279] in the House of Lords with Tom which ended with me having to write the judgment. Travelling is hazardous, however. Three weeks ago my BA flight south was cancelled and we were taken through to Glasgow. Two weeks ago my BA flight was three hours late, and this week my Bmi flight was cancelled due to high winds at Heathrow and I was very lucky indeed to be given a standby seat on their last flight of the day. The forecast is for high winds again this weekend. Fortunately, I am with Bmi, whose record is so much better than that of BA in such circumstances.

27 December 2007

Christmas has come and gone, and in between it and my last entry a lot has happened.

The week of 10 December saw the final stages in the appointment of the Chief Executive: see 21 October. Our shortlist had been reduced to five, whom we interviewed. There were two women and three men. Of these three, two men and one woman were eminently appointable. But we had to defer our final decision to enable all five to go through the civil service assessment process. The results were quite revealing and, although we were anxious not to give too much weight to them, it did alter our impressions following our 45-minute interviews. We met on Wednesday 12 December to reach our final decision. We had favoured a retired Admiral and, with a slight edge, a very nice man who offered a sound civil service and business background. But in the end we decided to recommend Jenny Rowe, who was legal assistant to James Mackay and Derry Irvine as Lord Chancellors, has long experience in the Department of Constitutional Affairs and is now with the Attorney General. She is a quiet but determined woman, and a safe pair of hands.

Also difficult is the process for selecting a replacement for Helen McMurdo as office manager. The HR Departments of the Ministry of Justice and the House of Lords came up with only two candidates worth appointing out of five applicants: Ayoola Onatade, who was Brenda Hale's clerk in the Court of Appeal and now works for Mark Potter, President of the Family Division, and James Bowyer, a comparatively young clerk who works in the Table Office of the House of Lords. On paper there seemed to be no contest, but I had a 15-minute interview with both of them and was much more impressed by James Bowyer. There are various complications. These interviews should have been conducted by Jonathan Mance, but he was not available as he had to go to a close friend's funeral. So I took his place. Then there is Brenda. She has put in a reference in favour of Ayoola and was not available to make a selection either for this reason. Doubts were expressed about Ayoola's keyboard skills. She had failed a test which was to be redone. So I was not able to make a final decision before having to leave London to get ready for the trip to The Bahamas (as to which

---

279 R (Hilali) v Governor of Whitemoor Prison [2008] UKHL 3, [2008] AC 805.

see below). I had a quiet word with Tom before I left, as a result of which I decided to ask for a further reference for Ayoola from Mark Potter. This – after our departure for The Bahamas – resulted in a further and more elaborate reference from Brenda, to whom Ayoola had evidently expressed her misgivings about what was going on. I discussed the situation with Jonathan in The Bahamas. We agreed that the situation was rather delicate in view of Brenda's lobbying and probable attitude if her candidate – about whom we both have doubts – were not to be appointed. At his suggestion I asked Alan Rodger and Robert Walker to conduct fresh interviews together with David Neuberger. But this has been, in effect, vetoed by the HR Departments. So we are in limbo until I can get to grips with the situation at the start of next term. It looks as though I shall have to take the decision myself, which will expose me to Brenda's displeasure as I believe that James Bowyer is the better candidate.

Later that day, with Mary who had come down to enjoy the annual Gray's Inn Miscellany with me the previous evening, I flew up to Edinburgh to pack for the Privy Council's visit to The Bahamas which I have been asked to lead this year. The team is myself, Alan Rodger, Robert Walker, Jonathan Mance and Sir Christopher Rose. Mary Macdonald of the Privy Council and Brendan Keith of the Judicial Office are also in the party. I returned to London the next evening with my two suitcases, was collected by the Government Car Service from Heathrow to get me to Gray's Inn, and was picked up by them at 6am the next morning to go to Terminal 4, collecting Brendan Keith on the way, for our 9.50am flight to Nassau.

I can only sketch in various details of what turned out to be a very happy and successful visit. Our plane was delayed in take-off by two hours, but this did not matter much for us – rather frustrating for the welcoming party in Nassau, however. On arrival there we were transferred via the VIP Lounge to a small plane with Pineapple Airlines – a chartered Beachcraft – to fly south-east to the island of San Salvador, on the Atlantic fringe of The Bahamas where Christopher Columbus was said to have landed in 1492. We were taken on arrival at the tiny San Salvador international airport to the Club Med resort nearby, which attracts the international business at the airport, for a day-and-a-half rest and recreation. This was very pleasant. It had a French-run restaurant, with good food and a relaxed atmosphere. There was time to do some useful pre-reading for the week to come, and Brendan joined me for a two-and-a-half-hour bicycle ride to the Dixon Hill lighthouse. This is a fine, though rather rundown, working lighthouse with a paraffin light and mechanical turning equipment made in Birmingham. Next day we left at midday to return to Nassau dressed in suits to start our official visit. We were met by an official party at the airport, who greeted us in order of seniority as we stepped down from our aircraft. We were each allocated a car and a driver – car no 7 for me, with Sergeant Devereaux as my security officer and Sergeant Murphy as my driver. Sergeant Bain, remembered as my security officer from my previous visit, was with Robert Walker. We set off on the first of many motorcades with two outriders in attendance, sirens calling and lights blazing, to the Sandals resort where we were to stay. I was in the same room looking out to sea as Mary and I were in for our visit in January 2005. It was lonely without her. Then, with no time to linger, we were off to the centre of Nassau for the Royal Bahamian Police Force Band's Annual Christmas Beat Retreat. We had seats in the front row in Rawson Square. It was a fine performance with a mix of Christmas carols and popular Christmas music, very well played and with excellent drill, all done entirely from memory, for one and a half hours. They had some amazing touches too. There were antics from the cymbal player and the drum major, and songs by members of the band. We all enjoyed it greatly before returning to the hotel for supper.

Next day our work began. We were provided by the police with a guard of honour, which was led onto parade by the band. It marched on to 'Oh come, all ye faithful', and marched off in slow time to 'Rudolph the red-nosed Reindeer'. As the most senior person I was called on to receive the salute on a dais and to inspect the guard of honour. I spoke to five of the smaller members of the very well-turned-out guard whom I could look in the eye as I did so. Then upstairs in the courtroom we had an opening ceremony, in which there were addresses by the Attorney General, the leader of the Inner Bar and the President of The Bahamas Bar, Wayne Munro, to which I replied. Then, after a short time in our separate rooms – I was allocated the room of Dame Joan Sawyer, the President of the Court of Appeal – we were back on the Bench to commence business.

Our programme was a criminal appeal, *Quincy Todd*, which I allocated to Christopher Rose; a dispute about the enforced sale of property over which a charge had been created by the non-payment of a debt, allocated to Robert Walker; a Cayman Islands case about the categorisation of drugs offences allocated to Alan Rodger; and a dispute about a licence to provide voice-over internet services in competition with Bahamas Telecom Company to which BT were objecting, allocated to myself and Jonathan Mance, but about which I decided to write as Jonathan was uncertain about his views and was going off to Cuba on holiday with his wife Mary to see his son who is working in Colombia. It was a good, varied programme which we completed in four days, leaving the Friday free for clearing up. We had English counsel in the first three cases, mostly with local juniors, and local counsel in the last. The cases were all well argued. The working conditions were perfectly adequate, although we were sitting not at a table but on a raised bench. We were provided with lunch each day by Chez Willie – excellently produced and served, if a little too much for comfort.

We returned each evening except on Friday to Sandals in our motorcade as darkness was falling. So there was little time to relax there, even if we had wanted to in rather indifferent, windy weather. But our evenings were well occupied: a reception at the Ocean Club on Monday; a dinner at the Wyford Cay Club on Tuesday; dinner at Sandals' restaurant, Gordon on the Pier, on the Wednesday; and a formal Inn of Court style dinner in Sandals on the Thursday, where I had to reply to speeches by the Prime Minister, Hubert Ingraham, and the Leader of the Opposition, Perry Christie. I had my speech written out on the back of seven envelopes. My reference to us as being like 'the Saxons' produced some cheers, as this is a much-favoured group at the Junkaroo event at New Year when the rival groups process on floats down the main street. There were a lot of people to thank too. On Friday afternoon there was just time for a 45-minute trip to an island a short distance offshore which is on Sandals' private estate, before it was time for us to set off back home, still under the watchful eye of my security man.

Indira Francis masterminded the whole expedition, as she has done for all the visits these past years. Whether they can continue without her must be open to doubt. She is looking for other employment, not surprisingly. She has asked about being given a position in the Supreme Court, but I think it is too late for that even if she could compete with the other candidates.

Our only complaint – for most of us there was almost nothing to complain about – was the tight security. We could not go or do anything outside Sandals or the courtroom without supervision, and all journeys to and from Sandals had to be in a full team in convoy. Jonathan found this hard to take and tried without success to elude the security network. That apart, we were relaxed, happy and very well looked after and enjoyed each other's company. I hope that I lived up to what was expected of me as leader. Nothing at least went wrong in that respect. I was fully prepared, able to say the right things at the right time and well supported by my colleagues.

At the end of my speech at the dinner I recalled that the Royal Bahamian Police Force Band had marched off to 'Auld lang syne' at the end of the Christmas Beat Retreat. There is another Scots saying that is used, as I said, when hosts say goodbye to their guests: 'Will ye no come back again?' I was bold enough to say, yes we would, if we were asked to do so. My emphasis had been on the purely voluntary nature of the service that we offer in the Privy Council. It seems likely that there will be another invitation next year. But Indira is really the key. Much will depend on her and what she decides to do, especially when Dame Joan retires from her office as President in the next two years or so.

2008 – January to April

9 January 2008

I completed by the start of the New Year my judgment from The Bahamas trip, and I have revisited my draft in a difficult value added tax case.[280] This is a carousel fraud case. A series of transactions was entered into, which had the effect that the VAT paid on the first transaction was reclaimable on the last.

---

280 *Total Network SL v Revenue and Customs Commissioners* [2008] UKHL 19, [2008] AC 1174. In the event I was not alone in my dissent, as Lord Neuberger agreed with me.

The Revenue and Customs Commissioners are seeking to recover the VAT on the ground that this was an unlawful means conspiracy, cheating the public revenue. I may be on my own in holding that there is no claim in tort for the Commissioners, as the legislation does not admit the use by the Commissioners of means for collecting VAT which are not provided for by the statute. So I am now well up-to-date. There is a lecture in October to prepare for, but lack of urgency does not encourage me to do much about it just now.

On the Supreme Court front there are two developments, both symptomatic of the problems we face. Only two candidates have come forward for the post of deputy to the Director of Court Administration – Brendan's number two. We will have to re-advertise to try to create a broader pool from which to choose. As for the office manager, the young man who impressed me so much – see the last entry – has withdrawn in favour of another post in the House of Lords which has become available and which he has secured on promotion. No surprise there, as I questioned him a lot about his future when we met and this must have sunk in. So we have no choice. This removes one worry, which was Brenda's reaction if Ayoola was not accepted. But there is still a doubt as to whether she is best suited to the job, which we must now work to overcome.

19 January 2008

I was not sitting on either Monday or Tuesday, so I was able to get to work on various Supreme Court details which needed early attention. I began the day on Monday with the usual weekly meetings with Brendan Keith and then with my sub-committee of Brenda Hale and Jonathan Mance. Then at 11am I had a meeting with the Ministry of Justice's project team, led by Stephen Foot, to discuss tactics for the first of what had been described as the Carnwath Seminars. This is a series of six seminars to discuss the practice and procedure of the Supreme Court initiated by Robert Carnwath of the Court of Appeal and Andrew Le Sueur of Queen Mary's College, London. This is a somewhat aggressive initiative, designed to tell the Law Lords how they should run their own business. On the other hand it would be unwise of us to allow them to proceed, as they will, without our involvement and some useful ideas may perhaps be generated. David Neuberger is acting as a go-between and has done useful work by getting all the Law Lords, other than Simon Brown, who will go forward to the Supreme Court interested and willing to contribute. My task will be to set the scene on our behalf and make it clear that, while we will listen, we cannot be dictated to. I suspect that Brenda is more enthusiastic about the programme than I am.

At 2pm, at short notice, I had a meeting with the newly-appointed Chief Executive of the Supreme Court, Jenny Rowe. I was particularly keen to meet her as early as possible following her appointment, to establish contact and introduce myself to her. The appointment has not yet been made public – it will be at the start of next week – but confirmation of it has just been received. So I was able to make contact and ask her to come to see me, which she readily agreed to do. It was a very useful meeting. She is very alert, well-informed and pleasant to deal with. It was clear from the start that she has grasped the essence of her role during the interim period, to work for the separate identity of the Supreme Court and its own terms, not on terms made out for us by the Ministry of Justice. She will not start with us until April, but I was able to get one or two dates into her diary for the meantime so that she can get a feel for her job as soon as possible. She will come to the first sub-committee of the year on Monday and the first Carnwath Seminar as well as the seminar which is to be held for the sub-committee next Friday on IT. We discussed the staffing problem, which is going to be a major item on her agenda. Email contact with her was established later in the afternoon.

On Tuesday I had two more significant meetings. The first was with Rowena Collins-Rice, the Chief Legal Officer in the Ministry of Justice, who has succeeded John Lyon as head of the Supreme Court project on his appointment as the Parliamentary Commissioner for Standards. She is really in charge of the overall policy and runs the meetings of the project board. Strategic issues such as what to do about Brendan Keith's transfer to the Supreme Court are in her province. I do not expect that she will need to be seen often, but she is an important point of contact. Then in the afternoon I met the officer in the House of Lords, Ian Denyer, who is in charge of protocol and to whom the Leader of the House has referred my query about what is to be done about the State Opening after the Law Lords have gone and the Supreme Court is established. He indicated that it was rather unlikely that the practice of inviting the English judges[281] to attend the State Opening by writs of attendance will cease. That being so, the logical next step would be to issue these writs to justices of the Supreme Court. Whether that is appropriate, in the case of those justices to whom as peers writs of summons have already been issued, is under discussion. But of particular interest was his comment that justices of the Supreme Court will need to be robed if they were to attend, and that some distinctive attire will be needed if they were to be recognisable for what they are. I have always favoured robes for special occasions. Simon Brown is implacably opposed, and it will be difficult to achieve anything in face of such opposition. But here at least is an argument that might carry weight with some people. I will have to think carefully how best to make progress on this one. At least there is a reason now for asking for some thought to be given to possible designs.

Of course there remains the question who is to be President. The steps which I have been taking had to be taken now, and no one else but me appreciates the need for this or how to go about it. So I am in the odd position still of acting as a kind of interim President until someone else comes along to displace me.

On Wednesday afternoon, quite unexpectedly after a day's sitting with Tom in the House of Lords in an extradition case, I was walking along the Corridor to

---

281 Judges from Scotland and Northern Ireland were not invited until the practice was changed in 2016 at the suggestion of the Lord Chief Justice, Lord Thomas of Cwmgiedd.

give some papers to my secretary when I met, coming in the opposite direction, the members of the Appointments Commission who were to select the President: Baroness Prashar of the English Commission, Sir Anthony Campbell of the Northern Irish Commission and Sir Neil McIntosh of the Scottish, all of whom are to work with Lennie and Tom in performing this task. They were obviously on their way to the Conference Room for their first meeting. Each of them recognised me and smiled at me, Neil McIntosh shaking my hand. There was genuine warmth in this greeting. I suppose that if they had come to vote against me they would have looked embarrassed. That was not the case. But I cannot read anything into this encounter. The meeting which followed went on for over an hour, so no doubt there was an intense discussion. At least the process is underway. In the meantime I must just carry on doing my best to hold the system together as, one by one, the various pieces come into place.

On Thursday I was in the chair in a building contract case.[282] It was about the right of the employer to rely on a certificate of non-completion despite the subsequent grant of an extension of time, and to withhold payment of damages to the contractor. The answer to the relationship between the two remedies depended on the proper construction of the standard form of building contract. There was a very poor performance by counsel and some very lengthy and tangential interventions by Richard Scott which made it an uncomfortable and unsatisfactory day. The afternoon was not made easier by the handing to me by Jacqui, one of our doorkeepers, of a note from my secretary saying that due to an incident at Heathrow flights there were being seriously disrupted and offering me an alternative flight home via Gatwick. It was obvious that I was going to be in difficulty in getting home from either airport, especially as the Gatwick flight at 6.05pm was too early for me to get safely there after a full day in court. Fortunately we finished a bit early, so I made a dash for Gatwick but, as I feared, I was just not in time. The flight closed just minutes before I reached the North Terminal after the obstacle race of the Underground to Victoria, the Gatwick Express and the train to the North Terminal – unfamiliar ground for me. However, a kindly BA stewardess put me on stand-by for the next flight to Glasgow and I was lucky enough to get a seat. The trip home from Glasgow involved three buses via Glasgow city centre and the Maybury roundabout, from where I went back to Edinburgh Airport to collect my car.

The incident at Heathrow was a remarkable one. A BA Boeing 777 flying from Beijing had lost power in both engines 600 feet above the ground while it was still one and a half miles from the runway. The pilot managed to keep it from stalling and to clear, by only a few feet, various obstacles and land the aircraft short of the runway where it lost its undercarriage, skidding over the grass to a halt just as it met the concrete. All the passengers disembarked by chutes within 90 seconds. There were only a few minor injuries and there was no fire. It was a remarkable escape from what might have been total disaster. The

---

282 *Reinwood Ltd v L Brown & Sons Ltd* [2008] UKHL 12, [2008] 1 WLR 696.

coolness and modesty of the crew have won much praise. It was a fine display of professionalism. But closure of one runway followed, and many flights have had to be cancelled as the other runway could not cope with all the traffic. Campaigners against the prospect of a third runway at Heathrow, so badly needed to avoid congestion, are having a field day. But the chances of such an incident happening again are minute in the extreme, and there is force in the arguments that the amount of open space at Heathrow at each end of the runway is a positive factor in favour of it. As a regular at Heathrow, I am, of course, on the side of those who want expansion. Increasing delays and incidents such as this, so much easier to cope with if there were a third runway, are not helpful. So I began this weekend in a state of disarray as I had so little time to clear up before darting off to Gatwick. All is well if things go smoothly. But more often than not, recently, that has not been the case. I am coming to look on my journey out to the airport with increasing anxiety as to the delays and disruption that will confront me.

2 February 2008

Alan Rodger sat beside me on the Bmi flight to Heathrow on Sunday evening. He usually travels by BA when he is at home in Edinburgh at weekends, but their decision to produce only sandwiches for their Sunday passengers instead of salad and pudding has discouraged him, as it has me. Fortunately Bmi is still providing a hot meal.

Rather to my surprise, he engaged me in conversation about the selection process for the President of the Supreme Court. I have deliberately not raised the subject with anybody, not even him. But he told me a bit about what is going on which, of course, I do not know and I told him some things that he was not aware of about the statutory procedure. There appears to have been quite a lot of talk in the Corridor, as one would expect. He did not give me details and I did not ask for any. But he said that when David Neuberger asked Tom whether he was being expected to suggest a variety of names Tom's reply was 'Don't be stupid – there are only two candidates'. David has also suggested to Alan that Nicholas Phillips was rather odd and not easy to communicate with. On the other hand, Simon Brown said that for Nicholas to be appointed would get the Court of Appeal out of a lot of trouble, as he is trying to promote reforms there that are very unpopular and had become becalmed. Alan protests that this is the last sort of person we want. He suggested that his letter to Tom was vigorously in support of me. There has been no further communication from Tom or his Commission to him or, indeed, to me.

Nobody else has given me any hint of what they are thinking. I have been carrying on as if nothing is happening, which is all I can do. Frances Gibb of *The Times* carried a story about the appointment a week ago in which she indicated that Nicholas would get it and did not mention me. Commenting on another article by her this week, Lennie observed to me when we were in the loo together that she always gets everything wrong. But the system is not under his control, even though he is a member of the Appointments Commission.

It has been a busy week. I had my usual Monday meetings with Brendan and then with Brenda and Jonathan. Brenda was in Washington in the second half of last week. In her absence I was asked by Stephen Foot of the Project Board to sanction the removal of her application to set up four standing stones, with suitable inscriptions, outside the front entrance of the building so that all the other components of the art strategy would go through the Planning Committee. He told me that if the standing stones were kept in the application would be refused. It was better – indeed essential – to take them out and try again later, he said. So I agreed. When I reported this to Brenda she exploded in anger at what I had done. The whole project is her special responsibility into which she has put much effort, so I understood how she felt. I told her to get onto Stephen Foot so that he could give her the explanation he had given me. 'It is all down to your trusting personality', she said. Later, having made inquiries, she sent an email apologising and saying that, having been told the position, she was less angry. That evening we had a meeting with Luke Hughes and his Japanese assistant to clarify some details about our court bookcases with the architects. The following afternoon David Neuberger and Matthew di Rienzo of the IT team came to see me to review progress on the IT seminars which began last Friday. It became clear that I will have to cover the seminar which is to be held next Friday – another day out of my weekend. Later that afternoon I joined with others for a tour of the Middlesex Guildhall building, now fully gutted and ready for more construction works to begin. The scale of the project becomes apparent as never before. It really is a major undertaking, even though most of the essential structure has been retained.

On Wednesday I attended the first of another series of seminars. As mentioned earlier, this lot which is to be held monthly is called the Carnwath Seminars, as Robert Carnwath played a large part in setting them up with Andrew Le Sueur and Kate Malleson of Queen Mary's College, London. Their focus is on the work of the Supreme Court with the aim, I think, of persuading us to alter some of our current practices. There is something to be said for going along with this exercise, so long as its limits from our point of view are clearly understood. Much of our planning work, including the preparation of our new rules, is now well advanced. And we must work by consensus, not be directed to. I was down as the Law Lords' speaker for the evening. Others will follow me. Brenda, Jonathan and David Neuberger all attended, and there were about 30 others drawn from academics, other judges and professionals. I was invited to make a ten-minute introduction, with Stephen Foot and David Pearson of the Treasury Solicitor's office to follow me. I had prepared a short address in writing to which I spoke, ending with 'Give us the arguments. We will listen to them. But do not expect miracles'. I hoped that this would not put down too much of a dampener on the proceedings, and it did not appear to do so. We three then found ourselves facing a kind of *Question Time* from our audience for the rest of the session about a variety of aspects of the plans for the Supreme Court. Very little of what was raised was new to us. Mostly we – mainly I, in fact – had good answers for what was already being planned for. Later seminars may be more testing.

On Thursday I had a one-hour meeting with Jenny Rowe, who had raised with me the question as to how our relationship with the Lord Chancellor was being organised. We cannot make progress with this until we have a President Designate, as is the case with so many of the more sensitive subjects. But I was able to let her have such details as I have about our financial arrangements generally, which she will now need to explore. She is really good to talk to – very quick to pick up points, constructive and well-organised. She has made many contacts in the course of her career which could prove useful in the times ahead. I am more and more certain as time goes on that we made the right choice when we selected her.

I took home with me a collection of papers about the new rules for the Supreme Court and for the Judicial Committee of the Privy Council. Robert Walker has done excellent work in preparing them. But the Ministry, having involved its legal department, have revealed a number of problems and inconsistencies. It was very hard to grapple with them on a casual glance at the papers. So I spent all yesterday, Friday, going over them and preparing various notes and other documents in readiness for a meeting which I am to have with Robert Walker, Mary Macdonald of the Privy Council and Charles McCall of the Ministry of Justice on Monday.

Last weekend I was in a fit of depression about the Presidency and the futility of my involvement in all of this work, probably for nothing. This week has been far too busy for thoughts of that kind. I told Alan Rodger that I was putting in about ten hours a week on the project. This week I have given about 18, including this Friday. There is a constant stream of email traffic, quite apart from all the meetings and two lots of seminars to contend with. I have to confess that, when I am so busy, I enjoy it. It is just the prospect of having to give it all up for someone else to reap all the benefits of my hard work that upsets me.

9 February 2008

Another fit of depression, for the same reason. I had recovered from the last, but it set in again when Alan Rodger told me that Lennie Hoffmann told an inquiring journalist at a reception they were attending that the Commission had decided nothing yet. The prospect of more endless delay is very demoralising and I feel trapped in an impossible situation. But I must carry on as if nothing is happening. We had a welcome reception for Jenny Rowe and for Ayoola, or Ayo as we can now call her as she is one of us, which went well, and I had an hour with the IT consultant about my personal requirements. Then I had to stay down for the IT working party on Friday morning held in Church House, Dean's Yard which was well handled and to which I felt I made a useful contribution. So progress continues, as of course it must.

It was an interesting week. We sat as nine to hear an appeal by the President of Equatorial Guinea in an action which he and the State had raised against six defendants, including Simon Mann,[283] in which they claim damages for the cost of defeating an attempted coup in which he is said to have been one of the conspirators. It raised two issues of interest and importance. One was whether the action was justiciable at all, given that the damages claimed were for acts of State within the foreign jurisdiction – although it was claimed that they were private acts. The whole flavour of the case was that they were done *ius imperii*. The other was whether an unlawful means conspiracy was actionable in tort – an issue which a committee of five chaired by me in *Total v Commissioners of Revenue and Customs* had considered and on which we were about to give judgment. We had three days of excellent argument, with the redoubtable Sir Sydney Kentridge QC (aged 85) leading for Equatorial Guinea. Then a crisis opened up, as Simon Mann's counsel explained that they had been denied access to their client who is imprisoned in Malabo, the State's capital, having been extradited there from Zimbabwe in rather suspicious circumstances. On Wednesday Tom Bingham on our behalf directed in no uncertain terms that access by telephone to Mann be made available 'forthwith'. When we were told by Sir Sydney on Thursday morning that access had still not been made available he was uncompromising. With no hesitation we decided to adjourn the hearing indefinitely. It will be resumed only if the State pays the wasted costs to date and we are satisfied that access has been made available. This was a dramatic end to the case which, in a way, we all regretted. The justiciability issue was so fascinating that it would have been good to have had the opportunity of giving judgment on it. Lennie suspects that the purpose of the action is not to get damages – Simon Mann, clearly, has no money. It is to get information about the conspirators and their contacts by the release of documents under discovery. How determined the State is to get hold of them will no doubt decide the question whether they are interested in having the hearing resumed. It will not be soon, as it is not easy to get nine of us together at any one time.

15 February 2008

The Appointments Commission met again this Tuesday. This time I did not meet them face-to-face. I saw them from behind as they went into the Conference Room. They were there for nearly two hours. When it was time for me to leave to go off to a concert in Gray's Inn where one of our judicial assistants, Corinna Ferguson, was playing her violin in very distinguished company, I thought they had left. But I came upon them as they were getting into the lift beside the secretaries' offices. Tom turned towards me as I tried to bolt for cover in the offices. He looked quite benign and spoke to me without any show of embarrassment. Lennie appeared from his room. He looked less willing to see me. I sensed that there might have been a disagreement, but about what and in

---

283 A British mercenary and former army officer, who was said to be an associate of Sir Mark Thatcher.

which direction I cannot of course begin to ask. It remains a curiously impersonal experience. The following evening at a lecture in Lincoln's Inn given by Aaron Barak, the former Chief Justice of Israel, I was looking for a seat. Seeing Baroness Prashar, one of the Commission, I tried to avoid her by sitting in the next row. But Simon Brown hailed me and insisted that I greet her and sit beside her. Of course he had no idea of what was going on. She was very pleasant and showed no embarrassment either then or at dinner afterwards where we were placed opposite each other. At least things are moving on, which is something to be thankful for.

The CMJA is in difficulty, as Siti Yakob has resigned and we need an interim President to preside over the next two annual meetings. Most people seem to want me to resume the Presidency, which is kind of them and I would be willing to do. But I am trapped until the issue of who is to preside over the Supreme Court is resolved. The dates of the next two meetings are in early October, which cannot be done if I am to be one or other of the two top members of the Court. So here again we must just wait.

We sat again this week as nine. This time it was to hear an appeal in an application by the mothers of two servicemen who were killed in Iraq after the 2003 invention – Trooper David Clarke of The Queen's Royal Lancers and Fusilier Gordon Gentle of the 1st Battalion The Royal Highland Fusiliers.[284] They were seeking an inquiry into the circumstances in which the Attorney General, Peter Goldsmith, came to change his mind about the legality of the invasion. The claim is made under the Human Rights Act. He had ended up by giving an unequivocal assurance to the Chief of the Defence Staff that it was legal, which persuaded him to deploy his troops. The circumstances in which he did so are very obscure. There are strong indications that Tony Blair's mind had been made up months ago, and that everything including the advice was tailored to make this possible. But the argument depends on finding this to be a breach of the Article 2 ECHR guarantee that everyone's right to life shall be protected by law, and this simply cannot be done. Rabinder Singh represented the mothers and Jonathan Sumption represented the Prime Minister, the Defence Secretary and the Attorney General. So the case was well argued. We finished comfortably within the allotted three days, and in our discussion afterwards we were unanimous in refusing the mothers' appeal.

23 February 2008

Tom came to see me in my room first thing on Tuesday morning to tell me that the Commission had decided to recommend Nicholas Phillips for the appointment of President. He said that he was sorry to have to tell me this, and that it had been a very difficult choice as there was so little to choose between us. 'Your ears would have burned at the things people had been saying about you', he said. 'We would not like to be in your position at having to choose between

---

284 R (*Gentle*) v *Prime Minister* [2008] UKHL 20, [2008] AC 1356.

them', someone had told them. Fortunately, I have been holding my expectations in check for so long that I was able to take this very calmly. But I took the chance to put to Tom the problem that has been worrying me all along – what does this mean for me? Is there now to be another competition for the post of Deputy President? He dismissed this out of hand, saying that there was no question to be considered. I was the only candidate, and there was no enthusiasm on the part of the Commission to go over the ground all over again. This was reassuring. I would inherit the post when Lennie goes if there is no contest, but I had thought that a competition might have been thought to be necessary. I asked him to confirm with both Lennie and Nicholas that they were content with this, and the next morning I asked him to secure Jack Straw's agreement too in order to avoid any misunderstandings. This he undertook to do.

It was a relief to have had the situation resolved in this way. I had been composing in my mind all sorts of letters I might have written had Tom not made the first move and had I not been confident that, once he grasped the situation, he would do for me what I need to reassure me that I should carry on with the work I had been doing in a position of some authority. What a good thing I never set pen to paper. In the event the whole thing was dealt with calmly and with dignity on both sides. I have never been sure what Tom really thinks of me, but at least I did nothing of which I could possibly be ashamed at any stage in this affair.

I had to stay in London on Friday for yet another IT seminar. This was good, as a letter arrived for me on Friday morning from Nicholas Phillips. He said some kind words, adding that he was fortunate to have me as his Deputy President and inviting me to dine with him at Brookes on 5 March for a *tour d'horizon*. It was good of him to break the ice so promptly in this way. As I said in my reply, any disappointment on my part was moderate only and his appointment made very obvious good sense. He said that it was entirely due to geography, and he is probably right. An Englishman in charge of the Supreme Court is really much more obviously credible than a Scot. James Mackay warned me of this some weeks ago, and a writer in *The Guardian*, Marcel Berlins, said the same thing shortly afterwards. On the whole an Englishman at No 1 and a Scotsman at No 2 is not a bad deal.

Meantime no one else in the Corridor knows of this result. They will have to wait until Jack Straw writes to them, as he is required to consult them by the statute before deciding whether to accept the recommendation (as he will).

1 March 2008

The letter of consultation from the Lord Chancellor was sent out this week. I did not see it, but Alan Rodger told me about it on Friday when I was in the Corridor that morning. There has been no obvious reaction one way or another. He thinks it is the wrong decision but agreed that not everyone will see it that way and that an awkward situation has been avoided. We must now make the best of it.

I paid two visits to Oxford. The first was on Wednesday. I had been invited to judge the final of the Oxford Law Society mooting competition. I have very little experience of this art and was rather reluctant to become involved. But no very convincing excuse presented itself, especially as I was not down to sit on Thursday. I had asked for a problem in tort or contract, pointing out that I was a Scots lawyer. In the event, the problem was, in part at least, one of English property law. But I had time to prepare and it was focused on one or two quite recent cases, on one of which I had sat in the House of Lords. So a solution to it was not hard to devise. I was asked to bring an assistant if I wished, so I asked Matthew Hancock, my judicial assistant, to accompany me. We went by train from Paddington, changed at Reading and arrived on time shortly after 6pm. We were taken by our hosts to University College where, after being conducted through a maze of staircases and corridors, we ended up in a modest lecture room equipped with trestle tables. Members of the Society fell upon a scratch meal of quiche, crisps and coke – ravenous, as if Oxford undergraduates are not properly fed. We were not offered any of this. An excellent dinner at a nearby restaurant called Quod was to come later. The competition itself was between four young men, divided into two teams each with 12 minutes. They were to be marked on various aspects of presentation, including response to interventions. So I intervened quite a lot – I hope not too much, but it is hard to tell. In the end, one very clear winner and one very clear loser emerged. It was hard to choose between the middle two, but I had to make my choice after giving a brief judgment. It was all a bit hit and miss, as there are so few hard and fast rules that one applies. I hoped that I had not been unkind or unfair. The dinner afterwards was most enjoyable. Our train got back to Paddington just after 11.30pm.

The second visit was on Friday, to give the Neill Lecture in honour of Lord Neill of Bladen, Patrick Neill QC, a former Warden of All-Souls. I had prepared the lecture last September – so little time since then to get to work on things of that kind. I called it 'From Clova to Godmanchester: Public Rights over Private Land'. It was, in a way, a personal tribute to Pat Neill whom I rather like, based on an idea which came to me when visiting him at his Angus home called Auchenleish in Glenisla. It was an account of a case which established a public right of way through the hills from Braemar to Glen Clova, now called Jock's Road. On reflection, it was not a very exciting topic. But I enjoyed researching it. We were taken to Oxford on Friday afternoon by government car, at Brendan Keith's insistence. Finding All-Souls College in the High – just opposite University College, as it happens – was a challenge for the driver as well as for us passengers, but we were in luck. Mary and I were shown to a rather nice set of rooms where we were to spend the night, and then taken to have tea with the Warden, Professor Davis, before the lecture. Pat and Caroline Neill appeared. She is rather severely disabled but was very bright and cheerful and was clearly intent on enjoying herself. The tea was a rather odd affair with a lot of cakes which no one really wanted. Then across the road to the Examination Schools where a large lecture room had been made available – far too large, as only about 40 people turned up to hear me. Neither I nor my subject was much of a draw. Some of my audience appeared to fall asleep almost as soon as I started, after a remarkably brief and rather inept introduction by the Sub-Warden, Professor Dan Segal. But Caroline remained alert throughout, as did David Pannick QC who had kindly come to hear me, as also had Professors Treitel, Honoré and Ashworth. After it was over we returned to All-Souls for what turned out to be a very pleasant evening in the remarkable monastic surroundings of the College. It was reminiscent, Mary said, of *The Golden Compass* by Philip Pullman, though slightly less eerie and ominous. There was a drinks reception, then dinner in the enormously high-ceilinged hall with the fellows in gowns, then dessert, then coffee in a small drawing-room. Jeremy Leaver, a non-academic fellow like David Pannick, then took us under his wing and gave us a tour of the magnificent libraries of which he is immensely proud. Then, at 10pm, it was time for us to retire to our rooms. The atmosphere is, of course, unique because there are no undergraduates in this College. It is for fellows only, and most of them are quite mature – if not elderly. The intellectual level is very high, and in some cases it was hard for me to detect any common ground. Mary, as ever on such occasions, was quite superb, sparkling, full of enthusiasm and conversation, a delightful companion, absolutely fascinated by it all. After a not particularly comfortable night and a pleasant leisurely breakfast we got a bus from just outside the college to Heathrow for our flight back by Bmi to Edinburgh. It will be a short weekend – only about 24 hours at home before I go south again to London.

16 March 2008

It is Palm Sunday today, and the start of Holy Week and our Easter holiday. This is remarkably early this year. I read somewhere that you would have had to be a hundred years old to have had the same experience.

I was in the chair in Committee Room 2 all last week. This is a lovely room with rich blue Pugin wallpaper and huge paintings of the Black Prince's exploits. On Monday we had a Scots appeal which raised a short point of no general importance at all about a buy-out contract, the question being whether time was of the essence for completion of the sale of the property.[285] The answer to it, that it was not, was obvious from the start. With the agreement of all my colleagues I did not call on counsel for the respondent, Jonathan Mitchell. Christopher Haddow for the appellant was unable to inspire us to feel that we should let the case run into a second day. The case for Wednesday and Thursday was very different. It raised a difficult issue about the interaction between a landlord's unqualified right to possession and the occupier's right to respect for

---

285 *Simmers v Innes* [2008] UKHL 24, 2008 SC (HL) 137.

his home under Article 8 ECHR.[286] The problem has been with us twice before, with the argument going the landlord's way on both occasions with my leading a rebellion against our seniors by the majority of junior members of the Committee. This time room has been found for an exception in favour of gypsies, in view of a decision by the European Court at Strasbourg. The problem is how to do this without opening up a chasm in the law as declared by the two previous cases. We were treated to excellent arguments by Messrs Jan Luba, Philip Sales and Nicholas Underhill. It is for me to prepare the first draft of a judgment, which I have just completed in the third day of a busy weekend. I hope that my colleagues will agree with it and that we will not have another split and overworked decision in this field.

I had dinner with Nicholas Phillips, as mentioned in my 24 February entry, on 5 March. I told him as much as I reasonably could about progress with the Supreme Court. He is receptive, but the fact is that he is far too busy as Chief Justice to get involved in any of our problems. He told me that he had 20 meetings a week and gets up each day at 5.30am. He also has to sit in court as Chief Justice to give the job credibility. I know all the problems, as I faced them for seven years as Lord President. I may have to put some very important issues to him for a decision. But for the time being it is for me to keep the show on the road on his behalf.

Tom Bingham wrote to me just before we broke for Easter saying that he has now established that Jack Straw will write to me confirming that I am to be the Second Senior Law Lord when Lennie retires, and Deputy President when the Supreme Court is set up. It was good of him. He has been true to his word. In my reply I said that I was grateful to him for the way in which the whole process has been conducted. As I said, I am under no illusions as to what it might have been like had he not stamped his authority on the process at the outset, and his successors will be very grateful to him for having done this.

A cloud of uncertainty is developing over the timing of the project. A defect has been found all round the parapet of the building, caused by rusting of the steel frame which in its turn is causing some bulging of the stonework. The state of the tower has still not been investigated. The estimate is that it may take between 40 and 60 weeks to put this right. It is hard to see how we can be sure of getting entry to the entire building in time for an opening on 1 October 2009 if it takes 60 weeks. We will know more about this in about one month's time.

21 March 2008

A letter from Jack Straw MP, the Lord Chancellor, was forwarded to me from London. In it he said that it was his intention that I should succeed Lennie as Second Senior Law Lord when he retires, and I should then become Deputy

---

286 *Doherty v Birmingham City Council* [2008] UKHL 57, [2009] AC 367.

President of the Supreme Court without further process. He asked whether I would be willing to undertake the duties of these offices. In my reply I thanked him for this reassurance and said that I would. So this prolonged affair is now settled. This is a relief, and it provides me with a secure platform that I need to carry on with the task.

13 April 2008

I had a meeting with Rowena Collins-Rice and Stephen Foot in a busy week of three Supreme Court meetings – the sub-committee, a session about IT proposals and this private meeting. It was agreed that publicity should be given to my appointment as Deputy President, of which most people in the Law Lords' Corridor still seem to be unaware. But more significant were concerns about the effect of the defect in the stonework. The cost of these repairs will take up almost all of the contingency fund which was built into the resources that were allocated to the project. Rowena was firm on the point that no more money will be forthcoming – one that Brenda and Jonathan will find hard to accept, especially Brenda, as this may result in even more curbs on her art panels work than those that are the result of Westminster City Council's obstructiveness over the planning process. I suspect that the position is that it is up to the Ministry of Justice to decide how to spend its money, which is not open to renegotiation with the Treasury, and that other demands on its budget will make more spending on the Supreme Court unacceptable. I see no prospect of achieving anything by huffing and puffing about this. Perhaps if a real crisis develops Tom Bingham will have some leverage with Jack Straw, but we may not know this until Nicholas Phillips has taken over. His ability to pull strings may not be as powerful.

I am engaged in a series of asylum cases, all raising issues about Article 3 of the ECHR. There are a number of important cases on their way up to us too. The Serious Fraud Office's decision to close down an inquiry on arms to Iraq is one. The decision that soldiers sent into combat have a right under Article 2 not to be ordered to do this with defective equipment is another. I said things to inject what I thought was a sensible element of reality into this idea in my opinion in *Gentle v The Prime Minister*,[287] in which we gave judgment in the House of Lords on Wednesday. Could we possibly have won the last war against Nazi Germany if our leaders had been playing safe for fear of claims under the Human Rights Act? I am not sure how my colleagues, almost none of whom have had military experience, will feel about this, however.

Zimbabwe causes great concern. President Mugabe refuses to accept an election result which went against him, and the country plunges into an even greater state of despair and incipient famine. Thabo Mbeki, the South African President, is a close friend of Mugabe. He says that there is no crisis and will do nothing to press Mugabe to accept the result and go. I am rather relieved that

---

287 See fn 284.

my commitments to the Supreme Court and to Nicholas Phillips's taking over in October prevent me from attending the CMJA's conference in October in South Africa. I do not admire that country's complacency, or worse – invoking antipathy against the long-past colonial era to preserve such a disastrous, undemocratic regime on its northern border.

20 April 2008

Donald Macfadyen, Lord Macfadyen of the Court of Session and an Inner House judge, has died aged 62. He contracted cancer about two years ago, and after a brave struggle has now gone. He will be very much missed. He was the best judge of his generation in the Court of Session. A gentle but determined, thoughtful and hard-working man. He really came into his own as an appellate judge. His judgments were outstandingly good and reliable. It is a great pity to lose someone of his calibre at such a young age. The Court will be much poorer without him.

26 April 2008

There were signs of the civil servants trying to backtrack on Tom Bingham's agreement with Jack Straw about my future. I was told that no announcement had yet been made because Jack Straw had said only that he was 'minded' that I should be the next Second Senior Law Lord, etc. I went to see Tom and asked whether he would at least let the position be known along the Corridor as the proposal had not yet been revealed to the Law Lords. He was as good as his word. Next day a circular went out to all the Law Lords explaining the position, saying that there was no point in a further contest as it was what everyone wanted anyway – and that it was no secret. Brenda very kindly said that she nearly sent out a reply with the words 'Hoorah' on it. But I must be careful not to get carried away.

That day *The Times* published a list of the top 100 in the legal profession in the UK. Tom Bingham, very deservedly, came top. Brenda Hale was sixth. After the top ten places had been allocated the remaining 90 were listed in alphabetical order. Lennie Hoffmann, myself and David Neuberger were listed. Lennie said, when I wondered whether I had been placed 97th, that we were all eleventh equal. No other Law Lords were on the list. I was there, I suppose, as a failed candidate to be President but also as playing a significant part in plans for the Supreme Court. There was a comment on a blog site declaring that it was 'a load of nonsense', written by someone calling himself 'Simon of London'. We teased Simon Brown as being the author of this splendid comment. Alan Rodger declared that Simon was a closet blogger, making use of someone else's computer – he proclaims himself as having no such skills. More teasing over lunch of Jonathan Mance, who has departed for a week's conference in the Democratic Republic of the Congo at the request of the United Nations. Alan said that this was his last lunch with us, and that arrangements were already in hand for the Mance memorial lecture in the event of his non-return. It was not entirely funny. The Congo is not a safe place to go to at all. He was warned not to go initially, but the FCO has changed its advice because there are definite advantages in trying to make an impact there. I am sure that Jonathan's enthusiasm will carry him through.

A case from Northern Ireland about adoption by an unmarried couple occupied us for the second half of the week.[288] Next week we will hear a Scots appeal about limitation of actions brought by people who claim to have been physically abused decades ago in care homes run by nuns.[289] Then two one-day cases, one of which is about charterparties. We are not short of variety.

2008 – May to July

11 May 2008

Last week was Strathclyde's University Day and the follow-on engagements which occupied the rest of the week. Three days' exposure to the University is most enjoyable, and everything went well. I managed to make a suitably amusing speech at the dinner at Ross Priory on the Tuesday evening, to get everything correct and in the right order during the ceremonies on University Day itself, to put on a suitably interested and encouraging form during the visits to various departments on the Thursday, and to do what was expected of me at the University Court and congregation meetings in the Collins Building on the Friday. As ever, it was an exhausting process. There is no room for relaxation or for taking the mind off the job. I ended the week feeling very tired, and it will require quite an effort to get back to work in London for the last two weeks of the Easter term.

Andrew Hamnett has announced that he is to retire as Principal and Vice-Chancellor. He and Suzanne are large people for whom moving around is a physical effort, and one cannot but applaud their decision to retire now so that they can enjoy a less demanding life. He has done wonders for the University, however. It is enjoying its higher standing, especially in research but in teaching too in most areas, than has been the case for many years. It will be difficult to find such a hugely intelligent and energetic replacement.

12 May 2008

Suma Chakrabarti, the Ministry of Justice's Permanent Secretary, paid a series of courtesy visits to the Law Lords and senior staff this week. He called to see me for 15 minutes on his round. He presents himself as a pleasant, understated sort of person – efficient, very able but not a showman. I went straight to the

---

288 *In re G (Adoption: Unmarried Couple)* [2009] AC 173.
289 *AS v Poor Sisters of Nazareth* 2008 SC (HL) 146.

point: three main points of immediate concern about the Supreme Court project – the critical importance of meeting the programme. I said that a failure to do this simply could not be contemplated and that somewhere the resources had to be found to meet the demands of the remedial works required to the parapet without delaying the main contract; the importance of working out the financial model, especially how income from court fees was to be channelled to the Court; and how cash flows are to be maintained if the product was erratic or short of what had been predicted – not points that had occurred to him. There was also the importance of ensuring that Jenny Rowe had a free hand over grading and conditions of service to ensure that as many people as possible move with us. I also mentioned the problem of what the Justices were to be called. I suggested that Her Majesty might be asked to permit them to be called Lords, on the model of the honorary title given to the Scottish judges. The point I asked him to consider about this was whether there might be a political objection. He said that he would discuss this later that day with Nicholas Phillips. I felt that I put on a quite convincing performance, of someone who was very clear-headed and on top of his job. I do feel so in these administrative areas – less so in my judicial work, where I sometimes struggle to keep pace with those around me.

Alan Rodger is becoming irksome again about the design of the seal which is required for the Court by the statute.[290] He will not let the issue drop. He is so implacably hostile to the Supreme Court that he worries like a dog with a bone over it. I spent much of Thursday and Friday morning preparing a note of the various steps we have taken over its design. We have not sought agreement from the politicians, as Alan thinks we should – rather absurdly suggesting that Alec Salmond's agreement is essential, as if such a thing were possible. The new Court will be a UK institution with which, as a vigorous promoter of the campaign for Scottish independence, he will want as little to do as he can. The decision is for us, not the politicians. But we have consulted widely within the devolved institutions. One or two minor quibbles have been raised. Wales suggests a daffodil not a leek, but a daffodil is not a heraldic symbol whereas the leek is.[291] Scotland raised the point which Alan deplores – the fact that the thistle lies below the rose. But attempts to rotate the design to meet this objection were not successful without destroying the whole design concept. The fact is that nobody else seriously objects, and most people rather like it. I have to deal with Alan myself, as his attack is against me personally. But I doubt whether I will be successful in persuading him. This is an unwanted burden.

There was a dinner in the Signet Library yesterday evening to celebrate Colin McEachran's retirement from practice after 40 years. He is a near contemporary of mine. I am two years' senior in call, and our paths crossed frequently. I succeeded him as an advocate depute and I presided as Lord President over one

---

290 Constitutional Reform Act 2005, section 55.
291 The leek is the badge of the Welsh Guards, for example.

of his great victories: *O'Brien v British Steel*.[292] Mary and I were placed at his top table, with Mary beside him which was a very nice gesture. He is a most charming, eternally cheerful man who really has enjoyed his practice, never as far as I know having sought judicial office. He was and is too much of a free-thinker, an individual with too many commendable outside interests to be tied down to life on the Bench. There was a very large gathering of friends, who regard him with real affection. A very happy evening.

15 June 2008

Last week was especially busy, largely because of my annual task of interviewing candidates for judicial assistant. The atmosphere has changed somewhat. Tom Bingham will be leaving us, so there is no place there to fill – the most demanding and rewarding one, I always felt. Nicholas Phillips is bringing his own part-time assistant, Penelope Gorman, wth him from the Court of Appeal. So we have only nine places to fill among the Law Lords, Hoffmann and Saville being absentees from the scheme, with only four appointees to fill them. The shortlist of 12 was fully stocked with good people and by the end of the first day two slots were certainly taken and there were two good people for the other two – an unusual luxury. This became an embarrassment when three of the next day's group fell into this category too. Louise di Mambro, who has been appointed Deputy Head of the Judicial Office with a view to her moving with us to the Supreme Court, and Simon Burton who has taken over as clerk in the House's Human Resources Department, were both helpful and constructive. In the end we all agreed on the top four, but it was sad to have to leave out the other three and I was full of concern that such narrow decisions might not have been the best ones. For myself I have a very able replacement for Matthew Hancock who has served me so well this year. Christopher Stephen is another Scottish solicitor, who will shoulder the burden of supporting my work for the Supreme Court very well. There is also an excellent chancery barrister, John Townsend, who will plainly go far and is absolutely right for Robert Walker and David Neuberger. The other two are women – Jacqueline Kingham and Elizabeth Prochaska. They will go to Alan Rodger and Brenda. Alan is so good to his assistants that I have no worry there. But Brenda is not quite as generous with her time as Alan, so I am taking a risk. But I would have been whoever I chose.

After all that I found myself in the chair for an appeal about housing benefit and the way this is approached by rent officers in Sheffield.[293] The two-day hearing ended in one day, just. We spent much of Thursday morning discussing it – an excellent meeting with Alan, Richard, Robert and David Neuberger. Then there were petitions for permission to appeal to deal with and much paperwork, which I just got on top of when it was time to leave for the flight home from Heathrow.

---

292 *O'Brien's Curator Bonis v British Steel plc* 1991 SC 315.
293 *R (Heffernan) v Rent Service* [2008] UKHL 58, [2008] 1 WLR 1702.

Unusually I have been leaving the flat shortly after 7am instead of 7.30am, to get to work even earlier. The early start for the interviews made this necessary, but once such a habit starts it is hard to break!

21 June 2008

My great and loyal friend Alan Johnston died suddenly while on a weekend visit to his cottage in the Borders last Sunday. He was sitting in a chair when Anthea left the room. When she returned he was dead. It was a great shock: a heart attack, when he was aged only 66. Alan Rodger broke the news to me first thing on Monday morning. Mary was in touch by lunchtime, asking Ayo Onatade, our new secretary in the Law Lords' office, to call her back. She had been contacted by Anthea in a very emotional conversation, with the request that I should deliver an address at his thanksgiving service just after the funeral next week – on a weekday. Mary would not take no for an answer, which had been my first reaction as we are all sitting next week and there is no slack whatever in the programme. But of course Mary was right, and Alan gave me his full support. I went to see Tom for his advice. He too was entirely supportive, so we then set about rearranging the week's programme to set me free to be at the service in Edinburgh. There was a delay until Thursday morning as there had to be a post-mortem and there was a delay in getting the death certificate. But on Thursday morning I was told that the service was to be on Monday, so we were able to make plans. A three-day case for Monday to Wednesday, which was already tight for that timetable, will be squeezed into Tuesday (with an early finish because of a Royal visit to the Temple Church to which Mary and I have been invited), Wednesday (which cannot sit late because of Jonathan Mance's European Union Sub-Committee E which he chairs) and Thursday (which cannot start until 2pm because we are sitting nine in the morning on the Equatorial Guinea case on a procedural matter). Fortunately Lennie Hoffmann is in charge, so it might just be possible. It is Robert Walker's absence on Tuesday and Wednesday for a long-running engagement that left no other room for manoeuvre. The lack of retired Law Lords and the absence of access to other replacements is a real problem in such situations. It is made more frequent by Brendan Keith's understandable wish to get as many House of Lords cases heard before we leave next summer.

We finished a case I was chairing at 3.45pm on Thursday as Jonathan Mance wanted to go off to Oxford. His rather cavalier attitude to his sitting obligations is a real hazard, but we have to live with it. The good thing was that I was able to get the 6.35pm Bmi flight home instead of the very late alternative of 9.35pm. Once home I set about researching my archives, these diaries and my scrapbooks for information about Alan Johnston. By bedtime I was well on the way to getting sufficient material.

Yesterday, Friday, I was able to start my text for the memorial service. But just in time I remembered that I had a meeting of the Judicial Council in Parliament

House to attend. This is an interesting body, drawing its membership from all ranks of the judiciary in Scotland. But it is depressing to see the senior judiciary, in particular, becoming so beset by administration. Hours spent on this work and visits to all sorts of places, plus an increasing emphasis on education to satisfy the politicians, undermines the judiciary's ability to concentrate on what it ought to be doing. The productivity in terms of man hours spent on each case must be far less than it was only 10 or 15 years ago. Closer involvement by the politicians may increase democratic accountability. But it comes at a heavy price for not much of any discernible benefit.

By bedtime on Friday I had more or less completed the text for my address, which is about the same as for Charles Jauncey's service last July in length and tone. Today I went to see Anthea first thing to go over some details. She was being very brave, but the sudden loss is really quite devastating. Her sons Charlie and Alex were there, which was a great help. I returned to my computer and by lunchtime I had completed my text and a 1,000-word obituary which *The Independent* newspaper had asked me to prepare for them.

Now, having worked myself out, I feel a very deep sense of sadness at the loss of Alan. He was immensely kind to me both as Dean and as Lord President. It was more difficult to keep in touch when I went south and as his health began to deteriorate with a series of hip operations which he had to endure. But I will miss him greatly – totally loyal and discreet and full of common sense. It will be a real privilege to speak on his behalf on Monday.

28 June 2008

We spent much of Monday with the Johnstons. We were invited with a number of other friends to the cremation service at Warriston for 11am. We felt rather out of our depth at first, as so few there were people we knew. But Gail and Anthony Campbell from Belfast were there, and it was a pleasure to meet them again. The service was conducted by the Rev Charlie Robertson, formerly Minister of the Canongate, with his usual charm. Anthea's three sons, Charlie, Nick and Alex, all read pieces that they had composed about their life with a man who had obviously been a marvellous father to them. It was very moving. Then we drove the Campbells to 34 India Street and walked from there the short distance to the New Club where all those at the cremation were guests for a buffet lunch in the Long Room. We left early to walk to the Canongate Church with the Campbells, as I wanted to check on the place I was to deliver my address from. We met the minister, the Rev Neil Gardiner who was formerly the Minister at Alyth, when we arrived. It was agreed that I should deliver my address from the pulpit, especially as that was what Anthea had asked for. The church was already filling up when we arrived. By 3pm when the service began it was already packed out, every seat taken and lots of people standing. There must have been 700 people or more there. I felt nervous at the responsibility I was facing on such a very public occasion, but I was confident in what I had prepared. Anthea and the boys and Alan's brother Brian arrived and sat in the

Royal pews in front of the place where Mary, Will and I were sitting, and the service began.

There was a fine hymn, 'Praise my Soul', some prayers from Neil Gardiner, three readings by the boys and a solo by Katy Thomson of Loretto, formerly a chorister at the Cathedral, and then I was on. It was a bit difficult to adjust to the unfamiliar space and sounds, but I soon settled down. My address was designed to go step by step through Alan's career as I had seen it. I embellished some bits a little for effect, and my audience was surprisingly – and happily – quick to spot the humour and to laugh with it. I must have had four really good laughs in the speech, especially at the end where I had timed perfectly Alan's and my appearances as thinly disguised models for characters in the book *Murmuring the Judges* by Quintin Jardine. Everyone thought I was referring to Alan when Jardine's hero visits the Lord President in Circus Gardens until I said that the Lord President was a diminutive bespectacled man, whereupon my audience dissolved into gales of laughter. It was obviously a success and hit exactly the right note. But I saw before me just before I spoke Anthea's face, deep with sadness: a lonely, still mask of grief. It was a stark reminder of the loss we all felt. At the end we went out with the family, said our goodbyes to them and to the two ministers, Neil and Charlie, and then walked back to India Street. Then Mary and I went south to London on the 19.20 BA flight to Terminal 5. A consequence of my absence in Edinburgh on Monday was the rescheduling of the three-day case about the rateability of the Mormon Temple in Preston: *Gallagher (Valuation Officer)*.[294] It was a scramble to get the case heard in the rest of the week. We had a short day on Tuesday, as there was what Lennie Hoffmann referred to as a State Occasion in the Temple Church – the presentation of a new warrant to the Inner and Middle Temples by the Queen.

Mary and I, with the other Law Lords, had been invited to the service and we were given fine seats in the front row with excellent views of the processions in which Her Majesty, the Duke of Edinburgh and the Archbishop of Canterbury took part. It was a fine service with music taken from the time of James VI and I, Tompkins, Dowland, etc, and a fine intellectual sermon from the Archbishop, Rowan Williams. Afterwards there was a garden party in the garden of the Inner Temple, and we ended the day by entertaining Richard and Rima Scott to dinner at Chez Gerrard in Chancery Lane.

It was difficult to catch up with the backlog which my day's absence had created, but by Thursday I was more or less back to normal. Fortunately our nine-judge hearing in the case about Equatorial Guinea[295] settled, so we were able to devote Thursday afternoon to finishing off the Mormon Temple case. When it was over I joined Nicholas Phillips and Jenny Rowe for a visit to the Middlesex Guildhall. It is still a building site, but it was pleasing to see that the stonework indoors has responded very well to cleaning. The progress is satisfactory, and

---

294 *Gallagher v Church of Jesus Christ of Latter Day Saints* [2008] UKHL 56, [2008] 1 WLR 1852.
295 See 9 February 2008.

Nicholas said that it was 'exciting' – a sentiment that would not have appealed to Alan Rodger.

Alan is being very difficult about *Doherty v Birmingham City Council*, in which he has still not written a draft opinion although we heard the case in March. He has a point, as it is not an easy case. But my attempts at getting it to judgment are being met by non-co-operation and a determination not to commit to writing. In effect he has us over a barrel, and I face the embarrassment of being unable to get a case over which I presided – now the longest running since its hearing in March – out for judgment before the term ends. He wants the case reheard by nine judges, but that could delay us for another six months or more. I find it hard to keep my temper, but it is no good losing one's temper with him. He can be very stubborn. Yet, as I repeat, he has a point when he says that we must be clear what we are saying before we pass judgment.

I returned home to celebrate my seventieth birthday with Mary, Will, Lucy, her husband Andrew Meakin and our grandsons Sam and Jamie at a tea-party on Friday afternoon. They very kindly gave me a Pentax digital camera. This is a very impressive hi-tech object which will take some time for me to understand and master. It was hard to treat reaching 70 as an achievement when so many of my colleagues in London are already over that age. I feel very fit and quite youthful despite the number of years that I have been around: still well away from retirement, anyway.

5 July 2008

The *Doherty* case caused me further anxiety this week. After a sleepless night I went to see Brendan to seek advice as to what to do, if, as seemed quite possible, we found ourselves without an opinion from Alan. He reassured me. There was really no hurry from his point of view, and in any case it simply would not do to put out a case for judgment with an opinion missing. We will just have to wait until the missing opinion turns up. I sent an email message to Alan commenting very briefly on a rather brusque note which he had circulated on Monday, adding that the case was driving me to thoughts of retirement. In response he sent me a retirement card with the word 'Not' in all the relevant places, showing that he had not lost his sense of humour and that he was not really all that hostile after all. I had a day out of court which I spent getting on top of some new points that in his latest draft were being made by Robert Walker. This was his fourth, to my sixth and Richard's third. Then Alan telephoned me in the evening when I was back at Gray's Inn, saying that he did not understand Robert's draft and asking what I made of it. Fortunately I was sufficiently in touch with the arguments to explain my position and share his doubts about Robert's, for reasons given. Alan then said that he was probably going to agree with me and circulate a brief opinion simply to that effect. This was a real surprise. It encouraged me to think that we were making progress at last.

Then on Thursday morning we had yet another meeting about the case. I explained my own position, and got general agreement that we ought not to send the case to be reheard by a committee of nine. Then Jonathan Mance, who has been more active in sending notes and updating his own opinion, pitched in with a complaint that we had not heard sufficient argument on one of the key points and that, in any event, he strongly disagreed with the line I was taking with which Alan now said he agreed. At this Robert Walker, who is so reticent and careful in all he says, pitched in with some extremely sharp words in criticism of Jonathan's whole attitude to the case. This took Jonathan by surprise, and he was obviously upset by this intervention. We ended the meeting in some disarray, but in a quite different stage from where we were when the week began. Now it is Jonathan who stands in the way of our giving judgment this summer, not Alan. I have arranged for the case to be listed as the last available this term in the hope that Jonathan's dissent will be forthcoming by then.

Alan's resistance I could understand. He wanted a clear, secure position which did not risk undermining the existing law. I believe that at last, with Robert's help, I have been able to give this. Jonathan has been calling for the same thing, but he has not been at all constructive in suggesting a solution. His call for further argument is not helpful as it comes so late, and his tendency to dissent is not helpful when one is trying to reach a consensus by discussion – which is what he was encouraging us to do. It has all been very wearing. But I circulated my final draft before setting off for home, and I hope that this will mean that we can put the case to rest at last.

On Friday I was in Glasgow for the first of my two Friday summer graduations. As I have so often said, I always feel rather ill with nerves as I set off for these ceremonies when so much depends on me as I have to run the whole show and speak 'off the cuff' at the start and make an address at the end. But once underway I get into the swing of the thing again and begin to appreciate what it means for all those who are graduating. Mary remarked, as did Andrew Hamnett when he very kindly gave a small party for me for my seventieth birthday in his office afterwards, how many of the young glamorous ladies who were coming across the platform towards me had such conspicuously low necklines which are made all the more revealing as they bend towards me to be capped. 'I always look them in the eye', I said, to general laughter. But it is true: I have to catch their eyes as they start moving to be sure that they stop in front of me to shake hands and allow me to cap them – not always successful! We had as our Honorary Graduate for the law degrees Dennis Canavan, formerly an MP and MSP, who came with his partner and six-year-old son, Adam. His three sons by his previous marriage have all died, and he has obviously lost all contact with his former wife and their daughter. However, Adam was a dear, lively little boy who delighted the photographers as they gathered for the usual crop of celebratory photographs, one of which was on the front page of today's *Herald*. Mary sat beside him at lunch and near the end, when he was getting bored, invented a game of pinging little balls made up of screwed-up chocolate wrappers through a tunnel made up of his and her place-name cards. This clever surreptitious game made all the difference – Mary at her best, of course, with just the right touch of invention and encouragement. By the end we were all cheering them on and adding to the length of the tunnel. It was, as always, a very hot and exhausting day, expending so much energy in shaking hands and making speeches.

20 July 2008

A busy week in London. I was not sitting as both cases were, quite unusually, taken out of the list. It would have been better if only one case had gone this week and one the next. As it is, next week will be four full days with many meetings, etc to cope with as well. Time out of court is often harder work than sitting in court listening to argument, as there are so many odds and ends to attend to and so many interruptions. There was time, however, for a meeting with Kate O'Regan of the South African Constitutional Court who is my opposite number in arranging an Exchange in Edinburgh next June. She is lively, engaging and highly intelligent. I had hoped to take her to see a Judicial Committee sitting, but none were taking place. So I took her and her husband to the 11am Questions in the Chamber of the House of Lords instead. This is always good value, with Lord Davies of Oldham and Lord West of Spithead responding for the Government on issues ranging from the current banking crisis to knife crime.

The main event of the week was the Lord Mayor's Mansion House Dinner for HM Judges. There was the usual anxiety about the car to take us there. On busy evenings the Government Car Service hires cars in from other suppliers who often get lost. This happened again this year, as our driver was particularly clueless. The car was 25 minutes late in reaching us as a result, and because he lost his way on the route to the Mansion House we were almost the last to arrive before the dinner was called. There was just time to congratulate Igor and Judith Judge on Igor's appointment as Lord Chief Justice – the only candidate in truth, as he has made a real success of his post as President of the Queen's Bench Division and is such an engaging, positive character. The speeches, and the dinner itself, were rather muted affairs. This was Nicholas Phillips' last dinner and speech as Lord Chief Justice. There was far more enthusiasm for Igor when his name was mentioned than there was for Nicholas. His attempts at reform, not well judged or supported, have led to a rather frosty relationship with the senior members of his court. I wonder what will be in store for us. He will have a hard act to follow when Tom leaves. I told Mary that I was glad not to be exposed to all the criticisms that are bound to come his way when we move over to the Middlesex Guildhall. To my relief I have no feelings of resentment at not having been offered the top job in the Supreme Court after all.

26 July 2008

It was an absurdly busy week. This time I was sitting on all four days. The first two were devoted to an immigration human rights case with Tom Bingham in the chair. The second two saw me in the chair in a case from Northern Ireland about the Accession Treaty of 2003 for ten new members of the EU, most of them from Eastern Europe. It concerned Polish workers and the conditions for their access to the UK labour market.[296] The first case was about a Lebanese woman who was on the run from Sharia law whose effect, if she were to be returned to the Lebanon, would be that she would immediately lose custody of her son. That is because there is an absolute rule under that law that the custody of a child passes to the father or other male relatives when the child reaches the age of seven.[297] There was a background of a violent husband, a divorce and a lack of contact with the father since birth. It was a compelling case for leave to remain on humanitarian grounds. Brenda, as might be expected, was all for allowing the appeal. Tom and Bob Carswell saw no problem either. But Simon Brown and I did. Sharia law, with its male domination theme and deeply-rooted discrimination against women, will create thousands of problems like these. How does one control the right of the UK to deny entry for aliens in the face of such dreadful cases where to return a mother and child will destroy their family relationship? I was uneasy, but there was no point in dissenting. It will all have to go into my judgment. The second case, by contrast, was interesting, well presented and lacking in the tension of personal tragedy. My team – Brenda, Bob, Simon and David Neuberger – was very good to deal with, and although we ended up after an hour's full discussion with a division of views it was all very good-natured. I felt on top of the case and really enjoyed myself.

Around these cases was a barrage of meetings and social engagements. Monday began with the usual trio of meetings: my judicial assistant Matthew at 8.30am, Brendan and Jenny at 8.45–9.15am, and Jonathan and Brenda at 9.30–10.15am, as there was so much to discuss. Then at 4.30pm there was the last Supreme Court sub-committee of the term with a packed agenda: the state of the building, approval of the seal, the state of the art programme, the choice of transfer date, approval of the consultation paper on fees and so on. We did not finish until well after 7pm. Then on Tuesday Mary and I went to the Royal Garden Party at Buckingham Palace. We had risen from court at 3pm, so we were able to walk round the gardens on a warm, dry day before entering the Royal Tea Tent – such a privilege. There seemed to be more people there than usual – a large gathering of newly-appointed High Commissioners and Ambassadors. We spent some time talking to Alan Rodger, who seemed rather lonely. But I suppose he is used to this on occasions such as this, although he is usually very gregarious at legal gatherings. We spoke to the Indian High Commissioner and his wife and a charming medical couple who had connections with the Wypers Centre in Glasgow where Mary takes her horse for veterinary treatment. The

---

296 *Zalewska v Department for Social Development* [2008] UKHL 67, [2008] 1 WLR 2602.
297 *EM (Lebanon) v Secretary of State for the Home Department* [2008] UKHL 64, [2009] AC 1198.

husband mentioned that he had the Order of Merit, so he must be a very distinguished doctor. The Royal Party concentrated on the diplomats. There was no opportunity for us to be introduced to them, to my relief. But Lady Airlie spotted us and was delightfully friendly. She pressed us to invite ourselves to visit her and Lord Airlie at home at Cortachy Castle when we are at Craighead. We walked back to the Palace of Westminster, savouring the privilege of having a place in that magnificent building. Then by Underground to Temple, the walk back up Chancery Lane and a quick change for dinner in our flat in Gray's Inn.

The dinner was in Lancaster House in honour of Tom Bingham's retirement. It was a select gathering of Law Lords, present and retired, Heads of Divisions including Nicholas Phillips and Igor Judge, his successor, and their wives and four Lords Chancellor: James Mackay, Derry Irvine, Charlie Falconer and Jack Straw, who presided. Mary and I were placed at the top table with Tom and Elizabeth, Jack Straw and his wife Alice Perkins, Igor and Judith Judge and Nicholas and Christylle Phillips. We felt very honoured, and it was a real pleasure for us to sit between the Judges and the Phillips, who will share so much of what lies ahead of us when Tom goes. There was a moderately acceptable speech from Jack Straw at the start, with a typically entertaining reply from Tom. But the occasion really came to life when, after coffee was served, a Welsh brass band marched in and song sheets were distributed. The leader of the band was dressed in rustic dress carrying a coloured umbrella, and all the others were much the same: hats and colourful costumes with trumpets, drums and clarinets. It was very amusing, as indeed were the songs which were sung to familiar tunes like 'All the Saints' – all with humorous references to Tom. It was a glorious way to end the evening.

On Wednesday I had to go to Russell Square to collect Avron Sherr of the Institute of Advanced Legal Studies for a meeting with the Vice-Chancellor Graeme Davies. Davies had asked for it, with no agenda or warning of what it was about. It turned out to be a discussion about accommodation for the Institute's library. The IALS, of whose Council I am chairman, has been trying to get support for expansion to a vacant site next door for ages. We were told that this was still on the table but were asked to consider a move to the north wing of the Senate House where we were assured there is ample space and we would be the sole occupiers. It is not for me to choose. Avron will have to discuss this with Jules Winterton, the librarian. But it was thought helpful to have me there – partly to keep the peace, as Avron can be very sharp when he is suspicious, as he often is, with good reason. After this, when I got back to the flat, I felt quite worn out.

Thursday was at last a less crowded day and I was able to get the 18.30 Bmi flight home instead of the 21.35 one, which is useful for late meetings but gets me home too late for supper.

This was Tom's last case in the House of Lords. He insisted on there being no ceremony, and it all passed off as if nothing unusual was happening. He will be in the Privy Council next week and on the Woolsack for a large number of judgments next Wednesday. But this really was his last time in Committee Room 1, where he has presided with such conspicuous good manners and authority. Jack Straw said in his speech that Tom was an outstanding jurist of his generation. He has certainly had a high profile and has worked very, very hard. I am not sure just how thoughtful and penetrating some of his judgments really are, however. As Alan has pointed out more than once, the drive has been to get them out as quickly as possible – usually by the following Monday (as I try to do too). Much effort goes into the masterly narrative and references to case law, and they are beautifully presented. But sometimes one is left wishing there was a little more time given to thought and self-criticism. Perhaps his supreme confidence in his own opinions gets in the way. All that said, his departure will leave a huge hole, and it is really sad to think that this was his last case.

31 July 2008

Tom finally left us this week.

We sat together on a Scottish devolution case in the Privy Council – an interesting, well-presented one-and-a-half-day case about the developing process of disclosure of witness statements to the defence in criminal cases by the Crown.[298] He conducted the proceedings with the tactful, light touch he has used in these cases which has done so much to settle this system down. Richard Scott beside him – not a criminal lawyer, of course – was his usual talkative self, scattering the conversation with bizarre ideas. Alan Rodger contributed massively as always, steeped as he is in the law of the Crown Office and the Scottish criminal process generally. David Neuberger, new to these cases, was reserved and thoughtful but very constructive nevertheless. We had lunch together in the sunshine on the terrace, aware that this was nearing the end of the affair. I have never found it easy to converse with Tom. He is so wrapped up in himself and his own ideas, and my voice does not easily get through to him. But these occasions were never dull.

On Tuesday evening we had a dinner in the Cholmondeley Room on the terrace for the judicial assistants. This is an annual event, increasing in size as the family of judicial assistants grows by four each year. This time all the Law Lords were invited and nine came (Lennie is in Singapore this week giving a lecture and on holiday, Bob Carswell was, as Romayne is unwell, in Northern Ireland, and Mark Saville is a permanent absentee due to his Bloody Sunday Inquiry). We were 40 in all. Twenty judicial assistants and various others – Jenny Rowe, Louise di Mambro, Brendan Keith and Christine Salmon and two taxing masters included. I steeled myself and broke the tradition by making a speech on this occasion. In Lennie's absence I felt that this was expected of me, although nobody actually suggested it. I played it with a soft bat – saying that one or two people deserved to be thanked and that there was no right of reply, any implied

---

298 *McDonald v HM Advocate* [2008] UKPC 46, 2008 SLT 993.

right to that effect in Article 6 of the European Convention being suspended. I thanked Christine for organising the dinner, Brendan for all he had done for the scheme and then Tom – expanding a bit saying that these last years had been for us immensely happy, rewarding and stimulating. There was some laughter as I spoke and people clapped in all the right places. Afterwards Tom thanked me, teasing me for saying 'I'm not going to make a speech, but . . .'. I was absolutely sure that I had done the right thing, that only I could have done it and that Tom was rather pleased despite his aversion to ceremony. On Wednesday there was a late afternoon party for lots of people in the Privy Council's chamber with no speeches, on Thursday morning we gathered in Committee Room 1 for a group photograph of the Law Lords. Then he was gone.

Later that day, after saving some of Tom's beautifully kept notebooks from the cases he has heard here from being discarded as waste paper, I went with Alan to look at the room Tom had occupied. It was empty of all his belongings: deserted – all very sad.

2008 – September to December

15 September 2008

It was overcast today, with a light south-west wind. Two family parties of swallows, about eight to ten in each group, were moving up Gloucester Lane, behind our house, at roof top height. They were obviously on their way south on migration. We have reached autumn, after all.

3 October 2008

Another legal year has begun.

With a small team, I started ten days early. I had been asked to lead a visit by the Judicial Committee of the Privy Council to Mauritius for a week's sitting there on the pattern now well established in The Bahamas. This was at the invitation of the Attorney General of Mauritius, who had persuaded his government that this example should be followed in his country. Mary Macdonald, the Privy Council's registrar, and Brendan Keith went on ahead a week early to check that everything was in order. They had a lot to do. The weather was dreadful – three days of unremitting torrential rain. Fortunately the weather had improved for our visit, and the work of the advance party had produced a habitable court for us in a building across the street from the Mauritius Supreme Court, smelling strongly of freshly applied varnish.

I took with me Alan Rodger, Bob Carswell and Jonathan Mance, together with Sir Paul Kennedy, a retired Court of Appeal judge. We met in the Upper Class lounge of Virgin Atlantic in terminal 3 in Heathrow on Friday afternoon 19 September. This airline had been chosen as less expensive than British Airways and more comfortable than Air Mauritius, as Virgin provides flat beds for the 12-hour night flight. The rather glamorous futuristic surroundings in the lounge were matched on the aircraft itself, an Airbus A340 four-engined plane. The flight attendants were charming and informal, and a good but not elaborate meal was served before it was time to settle down for what, for me, was a rather long and restless night. On arrival we found ourselves in a modern airport on the south-east corner of the island in sunshine, having passed over some of the strange volcanic outcrops that serve as mountains in the countryside. There was a party to meet us in the VIP lounge, consisting of Brendan, Mary and the Supreme Court's registrar. Jonathan Mance, hyperactive as ever, made a brief bid for freedom as he managed to bypass the welcoming party. But he was eventually retrieved and we set off in a convoy of cars with outriders across the island to the Hotel Maritime, north of Port Louis on the west coast. This was a journey of about an hour through sugar plantations and farmland to the urban heartland from Curepipe onwards to Port Louis. We had Saturday and Sunday to recover from our journey. We spent this at the hotel, a pleasant seaside resort with high standards of cleanliness and very good food. We had rooms of generous proportions, with balconies overlooking trees towards the beach and a lagoon inside the reef. Bob, Jonathan and Paul played several rounds on the nine-hole golf course. Alan confined himself to his room, reading and writing on some academic project. I walked around looking for birds and, with Mary Macdonald, paid a visit to the courtroom to see how things were. It was rather bare but adequate, as were our retiring rooms. The layout of the courtroom was modelled, successfully, on what we have in Downing Street. When a Union Jack was offered I insisted that a Mauritian flag be found to be put on display behind us instead. This was to make it clear that we were there to hear appeals under the Constitution of Mauritius, not as a court of the UK. A Mauritian coat-of-arms appeared there later in the week.

The week began without ceremonies or fuss. We were taken into town in a motorcade each day – a 20-minute trip. I decided to make an opening statement on the first day, setting the scene for our visit, as it was immediately clear that there was a great deal of press interest. Indeed about 20 press people complete with cameras and a TV video burst into my room when they were invited to do so by Brendan. We then settled into our diet of four one-day appeals. One was about the dismissal of a magistrate, Mr Panday, which attracted a great deal of interest. Another was about the dismissal of 60 health workers, which had some rather obvious political overtones. There was a commercial case about the interaction between the Code Civile and the Code de Commerce, which took us into an intriguing area of French law.[299] And there was a tax case.[300] I asked Bob, Jonathan and Alan to deal with the first three in that order, and I took on the tax case for myself. Fortunately we were all agreed, there being no dissents. So judgment writing worked out as planned.

---

299 *Société Alleck & Cie v The Indian Ocean International Bank* [2008] UKPC 64.
300 *Lutchumun v Director-General of the Mauritius Revenue Authority* [2008] UKPC 53, [2009] STC 444.

Paul had an interesting criminal permission case to deal with on the Friday. There was a pleasing mix of English and Mauritian counsel, and the courtroom was packed almost all the time with members of the profession, students and members of the public.

The extra-mural activities planned for us were light. But they increased as people realised that we were, as a press headline proclaimed, cheerful and friendly and approachable, not formidable and remote. I had quite a lot of interviews to give and a few speeches to make as well: at the High Commissioner's reception where the Prime Minister, who was present, declined to reply to our host's welcome, and I volunteered to do this in his place; a seminar with the Mauritian Bar; a dinner hosted by the Chief Justice in a Chinese restaurant; and a very pleasant one-hour meeting with the Magistrates in the building of the Intermediate Court. My remarks were closely modelled on what I had said in The Bahamas – which I had with me, in case they were needed. Overall the impression we had was that the local Bar and Bench were very pleased indeed to see us and to spend time with us. I made it clear repeatedly that we were there by invitation, not as of right, and as part of the Mauritian Constitution, not as a relic of Empire. This went down well. A few remarks were made suggesting that we were too close to the politicians, but I do not think that we made any mistakes in that direction – this small island is over-sensitive to it. But it is a point to bear in mind when we go back next time, as it was made clear to me that we are expected to do.

There was a day at home after my journey up to Edinburgh after a night in London on our return to the UK. Mary and I then drove down to Gray's Inn with various supplies for the coming year, including my usual bag of potatoes from Craighead. On Wednesday we attended the Abbey service. Lessons were read by Jack Straw, the Lord Chancellor, and Igor Judge, the new Lord Chief Justice, and there was a sermon. There were only two hymns, one of which – as Mary pointed out to me later – was plainly an Easter hymn and curiously out of place: 'Thine be the Glory'. At the end of the service we were allowed to leave the Law Lords' stalls after the Heads of Division and before the Court of Appeal and all the other judges, as Tom Bingham declared we should after last year's event. The effect was rather spoiled because the front row, which got out first, was composed of retired judges and two retired permanent secretaries, Hayden Phillips and Tom Legg. We must sort that out for next year, when we will be on parade for the first time as the Supreme Court.

I spent the rest of Wednesday organising papers, receiving a courtesy visit from Dame Joan Sawyer and Indira Francis from The Bahamas in which we discussed next spring's visit which I would not be on (Nicholas Phillips will be in charge), and getting my hair cut in the excellent House of Commons salon. Then on Thursday, after a visit to the British Museum where we were guests at an early morning private view, Mary and I drove back to Edinburgh.

Nicholas Phillips, whom Alan refers to as 'our leader', lead our procession out of the Abbey but he was not much in evidence otherwise. So for him it is a low-key start. I went to see him to confirm that I should continue to head the sub-committee on the Supreme Court as I had been doing under Tom. He has been given Georgina Isaac as his secretary, as he has declined Tom's part-timers Elaine and Gabriel who are very discreet and efficient. This is a curious decision, but rather to my benefit as I am to have them to look after me instead.

18 October 2008

A rather hectic start to the term, once we got down to business on Monday 6 October. I spent these last two weeks in the Privy Council. Early meetings with Jenny and Brendan on Mondays have resumed, as also have meetings with Brenda and Jonathan. There was an early start in the Privy Council to contend with, and engagements after work. One was to discuss the arrangements for the appointment of the three new Law Lords or Justices who are to replace Lenny Hoffmann, Bob Carswell and Richard Scott. We did not mention names, but Alan tells me that the Master of the Rolls, Tony Clarke, is expected to come to us to be replaced by David Neuberger – something that Nicholas Phillips has always favoured. There is to be a single round for these appointments, selecting all three names before the end of January. We will all be consulted. Then there was the first Supreme Court sub-committee meeting of the term which had to grapple, among other things, with Westminster City Council's obstruction of Brenda Hale's plans (yet again!) for the entrance to the Guildhall building to be placed in an appropriate setting with standing stones, a poem and lots of space. The arrangement proposed for security bollards is a problem. More meetings will be needed to resolve this.

Next day Brenda, Jonathan and Jenny Rowe met with Nicholas to look at the proposals for ceremonial robes. Things are moving in the right direction here. Brenda and Jonathan both appreciate that something is expected of us, and that we have to get our act together on the first day or not at all. Simplified Court of Appeal black and gold robes with a broad-brimmed hat with a gold tassel seems an ideal solution. Nicholas said that he wondered whether we ought not to have something simpler, but this was quickly pounced on by Brenda. She pointed out that we had to have something grand to distinguish us among so many others who were so equipped. He backed down and appears to have been won over. As he put it, we need only one other Law Lord with us to have a majority among those who will go to the new building. At lunch a day or so later Simon Brown seemed to indicate that his mind too was, at last, moving towards the idea of ceremonial robes at least for our successors, if not for him. Alan remained steadfastly opposed. He said that he could attend the State Opening in peers' robes.[301] But, of course, he could not sit with us if he did so – or join our procession into or from the Abbey at the Opening of the Legal Year. I do hope that even he may swallow his objections in the end.

---

301 This seemed unlikely, in view of the disqualification of judges of the Supreme Court from sitting in the House under section 137(3) of the Constitutional Reform Act 2005. Its effect was that he would not have been able to take a seat in the Chamber.

At the end of the first week Alan came into my room saying 'It's not the same'. This was a comment on our having Nicholas in place of Tom Bingham, one of whose many lectures that autumn I had attended in Gray's Inn, with dinner on the Monday evening. There is no sense that Nicholas had the grip of the case that Tom would have had. The following week we were all together in an appeal from The Bahamas in the Privy Council about a will, a neat but really quite simple problem.[302] The fact is that the interpretation of wills is not Nicholas's subject. Some things were said by him, and by counsel which he did not challenge, which led Alan, who does not mince his words when irritated, to exclaim later 'Does he know *any* law?' This was unfair. The answer, surely, is that he knows a great deal. But Nicholas has insisted on writing the judgment in this case. So we shall see.

A round of lectures for me started on Monday as I face another heavy week, in the Lords this time. My week in the Privy Council ended with me chairing an awkward oral hearing for special leave by Mrs Anne Schofield, the wife of Derek Schofield, the Chief Justice of Gibraltar, who has been suspended for an inquiry into his alleged misconduct. She is a Kenyan human rights lawyer. Her application was for leave to appeal against the decisions of two English judges sitting part-time in Gibraltar, Michael Turner and Murray Stuart Smith, not to recuse themselves when confronted by her with accusations of bias, or at least of apparent bias. I have an uneasy feeling that the judiciary on Gibraltar's Appeal Court, staffed from London, has all the characteristics of an old boy's network. But her allegations were extravagant and emotional, and they lacked any real substance. It was hard work preparing for the hearing in view of the volume of papers, and hard work keeping control of the hearing too. But I did manage to keep it within reasonable bounds, and she seemed to accept our decision to refuse leave without protest.

As for the lectures, I am to give the King James Lecture in the Middle Temple[303] at the request of Michael Blair QC, the Treasurer, in celebration of the part that King James VI and I played in the Inn's foundation. Mary is coming south with me this evening for this one. Two weeks later will be the Mann Lecture, which I have called 'The Judge's Dilemma', which she cannot attend but my two judicial assistants Matthew Hancock and Chris Stephen can. It will be in the Old Hall at Lincoln's Inn, probably with a large attendance. It is a good and interesting title. I am not so sure about the substance. Then two weeks after that I am to give a paper at a conference about the Supreme Court. That paper I have yet to write. The two lectures are now ready to give, however.

---

302 *Sammut v Manzi* [2008] UKPC 58.
303 Its title was 'The Best of any Law in the World'. The law that King James was referring to in this declaration was the law of England. His plan had been to unify the laws of England and Scotland on the model of English law. My theme was that, while Scotland was vulnerable to such a proposal in 1605, it had developed its own mature system by 1707 and was thus able then to insist that Scotland should retain its legal system in all time coming as part of the Treaty of Union.

26 October 2008

The week began with the arrival of the four US Temple Bar scholars on their annual visit from the United States to the Law Lords' Corridor. They had all just finished serving as clerks to US Justices in the Supreme Court or the Court of Appeals in the Federal system – the cream of their generation of lawyers. Alan Rodger, Robert Walker, Simon Brown and I acted as their hosts, with the help of our judicial assistants, with whom they spent most of their time. The four of us took them to dinner in the Barry Room on the Tuesday evening, which was a real pleasure. We could not help wondering whether this will be possible next year when we will be in the Supreme Court and whether, if it is, the dinner will still be funded, as it always has been so far by Brendan's ability to draw on funds at his disposal in the House of Lords. That evening, Monday, I did the King James Lecture in the Middle Temple with Mary and Tony and Kay Holland, who regularly invite me to their parties in the Barbican, as our special guests. I felt at ease with my lecture, and it seemed to have been well received with some interesting questions from the audience. Then we had a very pleasant dinner party – Mary between Scott Baker and Master Treasurer Blair, and me on his other side next to Simon Brown. Michael Blair is now in his third career, now at the Commercial Bar, leading a highly successful life. It was good to meet up with him again.

That night, and again on Wednesday night, my sleep was interrupted twice in the small hours by the defective car alarm of an elderly Lotus Elan in Gray's Inn Square. Much disturbed sleep left me ill-equipped to grapple with two cases this week. One was a complex one about enfranchisement in the context of the English law of tenancies and freehold tenure.[304] The other was the first day of a five-day/two-case appeal about the extradition of three men judged to be a risk to national security, including the notorious cleric Abu Qatada, to Algeria and Jordan.[305] The first appeal was presided over by Lennie, who was very opinionated from the start. It was a lively debate in which David Neuberger, who is in his special field, took an active part too. I found it hard to follow, and was suspicious of the position that Lennie was taking. It was some relief to discover at the end that David Neuberger did not entirely agree with him either. It was an enjoyable debate nevertheless, which Lennie conducted with his usual skill. What a contrast when we came to Thursday and Nicholas was in the chair on the first of the extradition cases. He was silent for much of the time, and such interventions as there were did not seem to be entirely on point. As a result it was a rather dull day, not helped by my lack of sleep beforehand. I also wonder what leadership he will show and how effective it will be. As Alan Rodger said to me – see the previous entry – it is not the same. Tom would have been so much sharper, pointing to the real issues. To be fair, his was of course a very hard act to follow. Lennie is on Nicholas's right, contributing a few very neat and accurate interventions. But he cannot run the debate.

---

304 *Earl Cadogan v Sportelli* [2008] UKHL 71, [2010] 1 AC 226.
305 *RB (Algeria) v Secretary of State for the Home Department* [2009] UKHL 10, [2010] 1 AC 110.

I spent much of the weekend tidying up a judgment which I did in *Zalewska*[306] in response to Brenda's dissent – always a useful spur to further thought – and my Mann Lecture, now only one week away and much more difficult and sensitive than the King James, and then preparing a paper for a 20-minute address I must give at our Supreme Court conference on 17 November in three weeks' time. My diaries and press cuttings in scrapbooks provided some useful facts and inspiration. On occasions like these it is helpful to go back to these contemporary records.

The Under-Treasurer at Gray's Inn, Brigadier Tony Faith, responded with commendable speed to an email I sent to him on Thursday morning about the Lotus Elan's car alarm. He observed to me that it had now been removed. I hope that it has not come back again when I return to London this evening.

1 November 2008

We sat early almost every day this week to complete our two extradition cases of *RB and U* and *Othman*[307] – RB and U to Algeria, with a risk of being subjected to torture there, and Othman (otherwise known as Abu Qatada) to Jordan, with the risk of being convicted there on the basis of evidence obtained by torture. These are not easy cases, and they are not helped by the massive amount of paper that was thrust upon us – 42 volumes of authority and huge written cases, one of which ran to 165 pages. It would take two and a half hours to read, at one minute per page, if one read every one – which I could not bring myself to do. And a lot of scattered notes came in too, day after day, adding to our quantity of paper. The advocates were on the whole very good: Robin Tam and Michael Beloff for the Secretary of State; Richard Drabble, Rabinder Singh and Edward Fitzgerald for the applicants/extraditees. But the material we were given was far too detailed to cope with in comfort. Nicholas came to life a bit near the end of the hearing, but he lacked the crispness and tension which Tom used to generate. Of course, I must not think that I could have done any better. I was cross with myself for presenting a rather muddled summing-up at the end, when I had all the material to do this in an organised way. But we were under pressure to get away home by that stage.

More awkward is the draft judgment that Nicholas has prepared in a case from The Bahamas on the interpretation of a will: see 18 October entry. I cannot bring myself to agree with it, as it is so wrong in several respects. He was, in fairness, playing in a field outside his experience as a commercial lawyer. As it is, he has no real understanding of what the phrase *per stirpes* means – elementary to any Scots lawyer who knows anything about testamentary interpretation. I spent yesterday, Friday, writing a piece of my own. It will be rather awkward if others desert his in favour of mine, which I presented as a dissent

---

306 See fn 296.
307 Reported as *RB (Algeria) v Secretary of State for the Home Department*: see fn 305.

from the reasoning of the majority. I do not want to be unfair to him. But I cannot allow a judgment which is badly researched and has some elementary mistakes in it to go unchallenged. Oh woe!

2 November 2008

I encountered a great-spotted woodpecker flying over Wemyss Place from Heriot Row Gardens to Moray Place this morning. It was calling its 'chip' call and bounding along in flight as these woodpeckers do. It was quite a surprise, as I have never seen this species in our town centre area before.

30 November 2008

The *Sammat* case was resolved by a generous concession on Nicholas's part, some changes to mine and an adoption of my reasons by the majority as part of their own. But another similar problem has arisen in a case called *ZT (Kosovo)*,[308] where I may not be so fortunate. It is a silly case really. Everyone has agreed that on the merits the claimant must fail. It is all about a confusion of procedure in cases where the Secretary of State certifies an asylum claim as clearly unfounded, with the result that the appeal if any must go out of country. The Court of Appeal confused this with an in-country rule about fresh claims. The Secretary of State came to the Lords to have this confusion sorted out. Unfortunately Nicholas has made things worse by, as I see it, misconstruing the rule and failing to explore and respect the context in which it is operated. The arguments were not easy for us to understand, but having spent some time looking into the details I saw how the thing works. But Nicholas has not changed his view. My contrary opinion is now on the table but Simon Brown, rather to my dismay, has brushed it aside. I cannot help suspecting that he has already been asked for his support by Nicholas. Unlike Tom, he seems to need and seek to enlist the support of others. I shall stick to my position of course. But I may find myself alone.

In the meantime much else has been going on. On 3 November I gave the Mann Lecture in the Old Hall at Lincoln's Inn, chaired by the delightful and admirable Sir Sydney Kentridge, which was a great honour. It was very well attended and there was an excellent dinner afterwards in 2 Temple Place. I asked my judicial assistants, Matthew Hancock of last year and Christopher Stephen of this, to join me. The following week I chaired a session at the Institute of Advanced Legal Studies on the *Pinochet* case[309] on a day off from sitting, which was made particularly lively by the attendance of one of the Spanish prosecutors and by relatives of the disappeared. Later that day I entertained Margaret Hastie, my very charming and dependable secretary as Chancellor of Strathclyde University, and her husband to tea in the House of

---

308 *ZT (Kosovo) v Secretary of State for the Home Department* [2009] UKHL 6, [2009] 1 WLR 348.
309 See fns 100, 106 and 113.

Lords. The previous Friday there had been a visit to Strathclyde for the degree ceremonies. Back home on Friday I went to join Douglas Cullen, Donald Ross, Brian Gill and Gerald Gordon at the Royal Society of Edinburgh to discuss a critical response to the Scottish Government's proposals for a sentencing commission. This meeting, said Gerald Gordon, was the closest he was ever likely to come to sitting on the Judicial Committee of the Privy Council – the rest of us being, of course, Privy Councillors.

The following week I was on my feet again, delivering another paper. This time it was the UK Supreme Court seminar, which we held at the request of the Ministry of Justice, to introduce the Supreme Court to a wider audience and follow up the seminars at Queen Mary College earlier in the year. About 200 attended from all three jurisdictions – a good turnout. Nicholas Phillips introduced it with a few neat remarks, and I spoke for about 20 minutes about the work of my sub-committee. Jenny Rowe then spoke for about 15 minutes about her own role. There was a very good hour-long session of a kind of question time, with Brenda Hale, David Pannick (now newly enobled as Lord Pannick – an excellent appointment), Tony Clarke MR and Professor Dawn Oliver. There were good questions from the floor – none raising unexpected issues, it has to be said – and the event did not drag at all. It was a good public relations exercise. There was then a well-attended IALS council meeting, which I had to chair, and the annual Law Lords dinner in Brookes for which Mary joined me on the two following days.

Then there was a Strathclyde residential weekend at Ross Priory. I am not on the University's Council although I am the Chancellor, so I feel a bit of an outsider. But people were nice to me, and it is a privilege to be there. The main point of interest – though not debated, as it had been decided – was Professor Jim McDonald's appointment to succeed Andrew Hamnett as Principal. He was the inside candidate of a shortlist of six, reduced to three. He is a hugely energetic man and seems to be much liked, so this is a popular choice. I confess to some slight misgivings, however. He does not have Andrew's steady and measured, but immensely careful, approach. He may rush into things, as he almost did when he said on explaining his vision for the future on the Saturday morning that he thought that we should proclaim ourselves as 'The Technological University'. It was an unhappy choice of words – images of 'the tec', a downmarket institution, for example. Gerry Wilson spotted this, and I ventured a question of my own to promote discussion – which it did, with Frances McMenamin making the contrary point on behalf of the Law School. I hope that this will encourage Jim to think again. But we do need his enthusiasm and his energy.

This week was eventful too. On Wednesday there was the visit to Westminster of the Moderator of the Church of Scotland, the Very Rev Dr David Lunan, with his wife Maggie. I was to receive him as Chairman of the Scottish Peers Association. At first it looked as though this would be difficult as, though I had asked to be kept free, I had been put down to sit but, fortunately, our three-day case, which I was chairing – *Austin*,[310] about an incident in Oxford Circus on May Day 2001 in which the police resorted to the tactic known as 'kettling' – ended in two days. So I was able to read the lesson in the crypt at Westminster Hall, attend a rowdy Prime Minister's Question Time, have lunch at Dover House, take the Moderator to meet the Lord Speaker and attend Questions in the House and have tea with him there. It all went well – a very nice, approachable man. He made a very good sermon and a perfectly judged short speech in Dover House. Then off to Gray's Inn where I was on the platform for a debating evening with Brenda Hale for us to be interviewed together by our fellow Bencher, Joshua Rozenberg. It was a lively occasion. We agreed on most things, but not everything. At least an hour was well occupied. There was another good dinner, this time with the Treasurer Michael Beloff and his guests.

The issue of 'names' has surfaced. Nicholas Phillips sent out a questionnaire: What should we be called? What are people to call us? What are we to be called in court and outside? Robert Walker favoured 'Justice' all through. I sent out a note recommending that we allow things to develop by usage rather than prescription but insisting that we must continue to be called outside by the names we already have. To my surprise Simon Brown agreed and Alan has too, of course. We should win this argument. It will be up to Nicholas Phillips to ask the Palace to allow newcomers to adopt honorary titles as Lord or Lady on the Scottish model.

Then back in Edinburgh I attended a Scottish Judicial Council meeting on the Friday afternoon. This ate greatly into the weekend's working time, and I had to spend the rest of it writing my opinion in the *Austin* case. Mary had a second eye operation this week and was at home recovering very bravely from it. It was a complete success. How wonderful that cataracts, so disabling, can be cured in this way.

17 December 2008

The last week of term. I was not sitting – some recompense for sitting out of term in September in Mauritius. So, after two days tidying things up, I left London today, Wednesday, on the 2.45pm BA flight from Terminal 5 at Heathrow. I had gone into work later than usual so that I could do some shopping around Gray's Inn, which my normal routine cannot accommodate. Leaving my room before lunchtime felt like playing truant, as five of us were away in Downing Street for a sitting of the Privy Council. It was a real treat to travel out to Heathrow by the District Line to Baron's Court and then by Piccadilly Line to Heathrow in an uncrowded train with seats all the way, and then enjoy a nice help-yourself lunch of soup, pasta and camembert cheese in the Executive Club lounge, with its spectacular view over Heathrow for a daytime flight north to Edinburgh. BA have at last got on top of things in Terminal 5 and their timekeeping is much improved. So I am using them

---

310 *Austin v Commissioner of Police of the Metropolis* [2009] UKHL 5, [2009] AC 564.

without the sense of dread of a year ago, when hours of delay were possible. Good weather helps, of course, but the operation does seem more efficient.

I leave London with a rather heavy heart, however. The *ZT (Kosovo)* case – see 30 November – has, as I feared, not resulted in a compromise. Nicholas Phillips has Simon implacably on his side and David Neuberger too. Bob Carswell is on the fence, but with a majority in his favour Nicholas Phillips will not examine the detail at all, nor will he or Simon bring themselves to study the system of rules and instructions that the Home Office is operating to understand it, and, having done so, appreciate what they are doing. I find this very irritating because, to me, the error is so very obvious. It is uncomfortable nevertheless to be seen to be adopting such a contrary position in what they regard as a wholly unimportant case. Diana Procter, who revises my judgments now that Tom is gone, has persuaded me to tone down my remarks somewhat. But it will still be very obvious, when the judgment is published, how critical I am of the stance they are taking. I wonder what the outside world will think of it? Fortunately I found myself in agreement with Nicholas in another case a week ago. He and I against the other three, who were open to persuasion. So I am not, I do hope, thought to be a habitual opponent.

There is another problem. We will have three vacancies to fill in 2009 to replace Lennie, Bob and Richard. A selection commission with Nicholas Phillips in the chair, with Lennie and the three jurisdictions' representatives, has convened and asked for views as to the possible candidates on merit. Nicholas Phillips has made it very clear for some time that he wants Tony Clarke, the Master of the Rolls, to come in and David Neuberger to take his place. So much so that David Neuberger has taken to sitting more and more with the Court of Appeal when he has days off. But this is certainly not Lennie's view – nor Brenda's, I think. The Northern Ireland place must be taken by Brian Kerr, the only candidate from there. He is very pleasant and will do the job well. When Lennie came to see me yesterday I did my best to persuade him that we simply cannot not have an Irishman on the team when the Supreme Court opens in October. So that leaves two places. The outstanding candidates on merit are Lawrence Collins LJ – who has had a fascinating career, from solicitor and academic to the Bench very late and late too to the Court of Appeal – and Jonathan Sumption QC, a person of quite remarkable intellect who has offered himself for appointment direct from the Bar. There are obvious problems with both. Collins is already 68 and will have to retire at 70. Sumption has never been a full-time judge, although he sits as a judge of the Courts of Appeal of Guernsey and Jersey. But there is reason to hope that Collins's appointment will prompt the Government to restore the retirement age for Supreme Court judges to 75 in time for him to remain for seven years, not two. And Sumption is such an interesting and exciting person that he would add real lustre to the Court – as would Collins – when it really does need an injection of people of that calibre. Robert Walker has already voted for Collins and Sumption, as now have I. But Nicholas Phillips has more or less told Tony that he will be the next Law Lord. It will be an uncomfortable committee meeting.

I am glad I shall not be there when the commission meets, although I will be next time, when Lennie goes.

These worries apart it has been a good term, with Chris Stephen my judicial assistant giving splendid support and some good interesting cases to write about. I have quite a lot of work to do over the holiday: a judgment in the *Abu Qatada* extradition case[311] on which Nicholas Phillips has written at very great length. A lecture to start on for Gerald Gordon's party in June, a foreword to write in a book about the Pitcairn case;[312] and a chapter about the Supreme Court to do for the *Court of Session Practice* volume. I will be busy over Christmas.

19 December 2008

An interesting conversation with Alan Rodger on his return to Edinburgh by train today, Friday. He had been in David Neuberger's room talking about something else when Lennie Hoffmann came in to discuss the vacancies. It was a rather poignant discussion in David's presence, for obvious reasons, but Lennie's mind has not changed. He has reluctantly agreed that Northern Ireland cannot be missed out despite his reservations about Brian Kerr. Alan reinforced the point I had already made. As for the other two places Lennie, not surprisingly, still favours Lawrence Collins and Jonathan Sumption and Alan firmly agrees. Tony Clark would not stand out from the rest if he were not Master of the Rolls, and the whole point of the new process is that it should be on merit only. Lennie let it slip that, in the contest for Senior Law Lord/President of the Supreme Court he had voted for me: see 15 February 2008. This explains the expression on his face when I came across the group after their meeting. I am nicely sheltered by Nicholas Phillips from my own enthusiasm, however, which might have got the better of me and led me to make enemies of my own. So I am not at all put out at what has happened.

26 December 2008

A lull between the rush to get things done for Christmas. There never seems to be enough time for the Christmas festivities before the arrivals for our New Year parties begin.

In the meantime I try to fit in time for work. I managed to complete my opinion in the extradition case before Christmas, and today I sent off to Dawn Oliver of UCL my foreword for the book about the Pitcairn judgment, in which I decided to be quite frank about what went wrong, producing such a disappointing result from the Judicial Committee. I did so by quoting from my diary of 21 July 2006, in which I refer to the way in which Lennie Hoffmann destroyed the case in half an hour. It is perhaps too revealing, but the event did take place in public

---

311 See fn 305.
312 See fn 253.

and was recorded on DVD, so I am not breaking any confidences. Dawn Oliver's response at what I have written is that it is 'utterly brilliant' which, coming from a much respected senior academic, is very touching. Now I am settling into the laborious work of editing my chapter in *Court of Session Practice*, in the hope that I can get this well underway before returning to London in 2009.

2009 – January to April

18 January 2009

Back to work. I spent the last week, as I was not sitting, in my room engaged on the very arduous task of updating my text in *Court of Session Practice* – a looseleaf publication – on the House of Lords and the Privy Council to reproduce it in a form for use in the Supreme Court. In place of the House of Lords Standing Orders and Practice Directions, we will now have the Supreme Court Rules and the Supreme Court Practice Directions. The Rules, for the drafting of which Robert Walker has borne the major responsibility, are delightfully clear and simple. But the Practice Directions, which Louise di Mambro has prepared, are complex and very numerous. It was hard work matching them up with each other and converting them into a workable text. But it was a valuable check on Louise's work, which is admirable but had produced a large number of questionable points which had escaped our notice, and some inconsistencies. I had a meeting on Thursday afternoon with Louise, Robert and Brendan Keith to work through these points which, I think, took them by surprise as there was so much to deal with. It was just as well that I had settled down to this task while there is still time before we have to issue this material to the public.

On Tuesday afternoon we had a meeting of those Law Lords who are to go to the Supreme Court to discuss several points that cannot be resolved by the sub-committee: code of conduct, disciplinary procedures, ceremonies and, above all, robes. There was no problem about the first three. Tom had drafted a brisk and simple procedure for dealing with disciplinary complaints about two years ago and, apart from some changes in terminology now that we have a Chief Executive, it was not worth tinkering with. I had prepared and circulated a draft guide to conduct based on the English model which, typically, most people had mislaid but which we will adopt without dissent. Ceremonies of introduction for new Justices along the Scottish model were agreed too, as was the draft Letter of Patent for the Justices. Robes, hats and badges were much more sensitive. Simon Brown was bent on rotting the whole thing up. He asked a series of absurd questions to ridicule each idea – in very good humour, it has to be said. Nicholas conducted the discussion admirably, with equal good humour and a very light touch. The atmosphere could have been tense and confrontational, but it was not – quite an achievement. In the end we agreed to have a ceremonial robe based on Ede & Ravenscroft's design, with epaulettes using our four nations symbol to be worn for the Abbey service, the State Opening and introduction ceremonies. Hats were vetoed by most except by Brenda.[313] We will get them, but wearing will be, at best, optional. Badges around our necks for regular sittings were vetoed completely, but we will have small ones for optional wearing or on special occasions – dinners and the like. Not a bad conclusion. Alan Rodger declared that he had resolved when he left school never to wear a hat again, but with good grace he did not refuse to have anything to do with robes. This was a good start to our future communal relationship. I hope that we can go on like this – with Simon's apt jokes to keep us going.

30 January 2009

I was presiding in Committee Room 1 all week, as I will be all next week too. My Committee for the three days Tuesday to Thursday included Igor Judge, the newly ennobled Lord Chief Justice, which was a real pleasure. He is a very alert, intelligent and well-adjusted man who clearly enjoyed being with us – a much more relaxed and, quite deliberately, more leisurely experience than the Court of Appeal (Criminal Division). Our case was a troublesome one about people sentenced to indeterminate sentences for public protection, a much under-resourced form of disposal which has resulted in their being kept in custody for much longer than they probably should have been due to lack of suitable programmes to justify the Parole Board.[314] Igor is fully up-to-speed on this and, with Simon Brown, Bob Carswell and Jonathan Mance, it was a good team. I asked Igor and Simon to do the leading speeches, though the rest of us will probably say something too.

On Monday our sub-committee made its final decision on design to authorise Jenny Rowe to go ahead and order the Supreme Court robes. Badges continue to incite controversy. But she has ordered them anyway, in the belief that it is better to lay them in now and plan for their use in the future once we have a clearer idea of our uniform for special occasions and what these are to be.[315]

On Wednesday I found myself on the Woolsack once again, presiding over the judgment in *Austin*.[316] The bishop was the Bishop of Carlisle. He told me that he was a recent arrival and that he will have to go all too soon in April. There is a waiting list except for the top six bishops, and he retires at 70. Nevertheless he is enjoying the privilege while it lasts. As for me, what a privilege it was once again to occupy the Woolsack, however briefly, to enjoy its sofa seat – firm but soft, though my feet hardly touch the ground – and to kneel for prayers on the

---

313 In the event none of us except Brenda Hale wore hats when we first appeared in our robes on the occasion of the opening of the Supreme Court.
314 *R (Walker) v Secretary of State for Justice (Parole Board intervening)* [2009] UKHL 22, [2010] 1 AC 553.
315 In the event the Justices decided not to wear the badges, but Jenny Rowe and Louise di Mambro decided to do so.
316 See fn 310.

enormous red cushion that was placed there for me and then whisked away by the doorkeeper when prayers were all over. Igor came to sit with us for the experience.

8 February 2009

We had a meeting last Wednesday to discuss what the routine should be for our annual visits to Mauritius and The Bahamas, as it is clear that these jurisdictions will want the Judicial Committee's hearings there to continue. Two factors were important. One was to avoid eating into recess periods, as happened last autumn in the case of Mauritius. The other was to avoid undue strain on the administration, which having them too close together would create. Climate also came into consideration. The result was visits to Mauritius in February during the half-term weekend when counsel in the UK want to take time off with their families, and to The Bahamas in early May just before the bank holiday weekend. We agreed that we could not accept an invitation to go to Mauritius this December, as we will still be settling into our new premises and our ability to travel then is in doubt.

After this discussion Nicholas announced, in strict confidence, that the *ad hoc* appointments commission had decided that the new Law Lords to replace Lennie, Bob and Richard should be Lawrence Collins LJ, Brian Kerr LJ of Northern Ireland and Tony Clarke MR in that order. He then said that David Neuberger was expected to replace Tony Clarke as Master of the Rolls and that Jonathan Sumption QC would take his place. There was no real surprise there. The promotion of Lawrence Collins will be widely welcomed. Brian Kerr's move is welcome too, as Northern Ireland must be represented in the Supreme Court.

Afterwards Jonathan Mance came to see me, in some distress. His wife Mary was, of course, one of those who had asked to be considered for promotion. He told me that he has always felt awkward at the fact that he, as her junior, came here first and that Tom had told him not to worry saying that her time would come. She is hugely conscientious, hard-working and well in touch with many other jurisdictions, as indeed is Jonathan. Both of them must have had high expectations that with two or three places on offer for England and Wales she would have got one of them. So Nicholas's announcement was a severe blow. How can Jonathan be expected to hold this news in strict confidence when his own wife is involved? I could not have withheld it from my own Mary – indeed she told me to tell Jonathan in no uncertain terms that he must tell her, and I said so a day later when Jonathan came to see me again. Tom was always very conscious of Jonathan's unusual position in these discussions and would not have broken the news in this way. Poor Jonathan – I felt very sorry for him. Of course I did not say that I doubted that Mary would have been selected in any event in place of Tony Clarke and Jonathan Sumption. But that is not the point.

I was in the chair for two very interesting and enjoyable cases this week. I took three cases home to write about as a result, adding to them a judgment from the Privy Council about the Order of Trinity in Trinidad and Tobago.[317] Objection had been taken to it on the ground that its symbolism discriminated against non-Christians. The question for us was whether its continued existence was protected by the Constitution. As a result of late submissions in writing, it has had to be largely rewritten. That was a day's work in itself.

Snow has been the talking point of the week as the country is in the grips of the coldest spell for 20 years. I was lucky to get to Gray's Inn on Sunday evening before the blizzard began in London. It resulted in 4 to 6 inches of snow and led to huge disruption on Monday. All the buses were off, for the first time ever it was said, and most trains and Tube lines were not operational either. I walked to work to find that none of the office staff were able to get in. All the Law Lords were in, however, some clad in climbing boots. So we were able to sit as usual, if a bit late. Frosty nights kept snow on the ground all week and further west further heavy snowfalls caused real problems, as happened in the north east of Scotland too. There are forecasts of more snow next week, but my trip to London with BA this evening ought not to be affected. Monday is our next snow day, they say.

20 February 2009

The snow did not reappear in London, though it did affect much of the country elsewhere during another very cold week. My journey home via BA and Terminal 5 seemed to be going well on Thursday evening when I boarded the 20:45hrs flight more or less on time. But de-icing was required and the equipment was slow to turn up. After it had done one wing and was moving to another it broke down. It took over 45 minutes for a repair to turn up, and then 45 minutes more for a replacement de-icer to appear. We were two and a quarter hours late for take-off, and I got home at 1.30am. The Sunday trip south with Bmi was, bizarrely, one of the quickest ever, door-to-door in four hours and five minutes. Everything worked in time with each other, no delays. The weather at last began to warm up a little.

Parliament was not sitting this week, as it was the half-term holiday. So we seized the opportunity and sat for three days in the Chamber. Brendan Keith, our clerk in the Judicial Office, was unwilling. It meant some extra expense and inconvenience – a bishop, the mace, extra doorkeepers and so on. But I felt that, as our time here is running out, we should do this, especially as many of our team had never had the opportunity. As it happened – and was only fair, as I sat there quite often before Tom Bingham put a stop to it – I was not on the list to sit. But on the Monday I went down into the Chamber with Brenda Hale (not sitting either) to inspect the layout, join the others for prayers and watch

---

317 *Sanatan Dharma Maha Sabha of Trinidad and Tobago Inc v Attorney General of Trinidad and Tobago* [2009] UKPC 17.

the first few minutes. The tables set out close to the Bar are small, but there is enough room with the support of bookcases and cushions. Those who were sitting – Alan Rodger, Bob Carswell, Simon Brown and Jonathan Mance with Nicholas Phillips – said that it was all remarkably comfortable. Not so good for the Bar, however. There were long wigs for silks, and juniors at the back found it hard to hear what was going on. But it looked very spectacular.

We gave judgment on Wednesday in the case about the compatibility with their Convention rights of the extradition of the notorious Muslim cleric, Abu Qatada, and other undesirable aliens to their home countries where they are at risk of torture but as to which assurances of safety had been given at the highest level.[318] The Securities and Immigration Appeal Tribunal which had heard all the evidence, quite a lot of it 'closed' and thus not available to them or to us as we declined to look at it, held that the assurances could be relied on. The Court of Appeal disagreed, but we restored the decisions which had been given by SIAC. Press reaction was mixed. It is easy to be critical, as Human Rights Watch, *The Guardian* and *The Independent* were. *The Times* and *The Daily Telegraph* and all the other tabloids were in favour, though everyone knows it will take three years or so before any extradition order can be put into effect as those affected are appealing to Strasbourg. I hope that our judgment is sufficiently well-reasoned to persuade them to agree. The other judgment was in an important Scottish reparation case: *Mitchell v Glasgow City Council*.[319] Alan Rodger and I were shown on BBC Scotland evening news giving judgment in the Chamber. This is the first time I can recall this having been done in a Scots appeal. As Alan said, perhaps they were short of news as the politicians are all on holiday. But it was good. I hope that we can produce something that can be used in the same way when we get to the Supreme Court. Brenda has suggested that our judgments should just be handed out by the officials. But that would be a pity, as it would deprive the judges of the publicity value of the authority that being seen to be delivering them personally and in public would give.

We had an interesting procedural hearing on Thursday: Nicholas, myself and Simon Brown. It was a preliminary to the main hearing by nine judges in two weeks' time in a case as to whether detainees in control order cases can have had a fair hearing when the evidence against them was for the most part not disclosed to them, as it was treated as closed material on grounds of national security under legislation introduced by the Prevention of Terrorism Act 2005.[320] We were being invited to look at the closed evidence at the main hearing. The purpose of this procedural hearing, as set up by Nicholas, was to discuss the practicalities. He was all for allowing it in. Simon, on the other hand, is vigorously opposed to this. I warned Nicholas that we could not possibly assume that the others – or even a majority of them – would agree to look at it. So the hearing changed in character. We told counsel, including the

---

318 See fn 305.
319 [2009] UKHL 11, 2009 SC 21.
320 *Secretary of State for the Home Department v AF (No 3)* [2009] UKHL 28, [2010] 2 AC 269.

special advocates who have access to the material but cannot discuss it with their clients, that a decision as to what to do will be held over until the end of the four-day 'open' argument. It is a very big issue. I am in the middle – less adamant than Simon, less compliant than Nicholas. But it is a very big step to take, and once taken we will have set the course for all future cases. We will have crossed the Rubicon. It creates huge practical problems. We would have to have separate closed and open judgments in the same case and the Strasbourg Court, which will certainly have to look at this case too if we decide against the detainees, would be given an incomplete picture as it will not be able to look at anything that is closed. My instinct is to join Simon and refuse to look at the closed material, on the ground that our job is to deal only with issues of principle.

Mary and I are off this evening to Strathclyde University, where there is to be a farewell party for the retiring Principal, Andrew Hamnett, over which as Chancellor I must preside. It is a 'hooley' so-called. 'A wild or noisy party', says the dictionary. About 250 people will be there to say thank you and goodbye to a really great and good Principal, whose warmth and genial exterior covered a strongly-ordered mind and a clear-sighted resolve to do what was best for the University. I must make a speech in his honour, impromptu style – always worrying. Trying to work out what to say has occupied much time and made other work today impossible.

28 February 2009

The hooley turned out to be rather enjoyable. The old Glasgow Fruit Market, full of atmosphere, was a good venue. There was a very good attendance – many old friends and familiar faces. An excellent jazz and traditional music concert performed by the University's Applied Music Department, with some graduates brought back to swell numbers, was followed by a reception and a buffet dinner. It was not easy to engage in substantial conversation because of the noise, but this did not matter. After the main part of the buffet was over I took Andrew up onto the stage for our speeches. It was a bit daunting being so high up and with lights shining in my face, but I got through my bit with some good laughs and no mishaps. Andrew replied, rather too long perhaps, but good-natured and a kindly audience. Jim McDonald was very friendly and said we would meet again soon. I agreed.

Back in London I presided over a case about equitable mortgages from the British Virgin Islands in the Privy Council.[321] It required a lot of thought and preparation as the subject is way out of my Scots law expertise, but I felt in control of it. Robert Walker will write the judgment and will make a superb job of it, as he always does.

---

321 Çukurova Finance International Ltd v Alfa Telecom Turkey [2009] UKPC 19, [2009] Bus LR 1613.

Lord McDonald of Tradeston set up a dinner break debate on public broadcasting in Scotland for the Wednesday evening. I decided to take advantage of the timing and uncontentious subject matter to put my name down for the debate. I was unsure of what to say. It was a piece of self-indulgence really, as so little time is left until my disqualification[322] as a Justice of the Supreme Court kicks in. I wrote out eight minutes' worth, and then had to prune it drastically when at 2pm the list of speakers said that we could have only four minutes each. It was a nice gathering: Lords Wallace, Fraser of Carmyllie, Gordon of Strathblane, Wilson of Tillyorn and Steel of Aikwood, and then me. There were a few other Scots in the Chamber, as Lord Maclennan of Rogart and the Duke of Montrose spoke from the front benches for the Liberal Democrats and the Conservatives before Lord Carter of Coles, the Minister, replied. The other speakers were very knowledgeable about the real problems about broadcasting in Scotland and made relaxed, largely unscripted, speeches which were good to listen to. I stuck to my script and, short though it was, had to hurry as my time ran out. I felt rather inadequate, but I got a good laugh with my story of the STV programme about a man who was on trial for stealing a bus.[323] It is good to keep some kind of contact with the Chamber and how it feels to speak there. So, inadequate though it was, it was worth doing.

7 March 2009

I was much saddened by the news that James Clyde has died. He had recovered remarkably well from the illness he contracted when he retired as a Law Lord seven and a half years ago. But recently his cancer seemed to have returned. Ann has always been very secretive about his illness. The details have not been made known, and he too had kept them hidden. But a week or so ago Alan Rodger heard that he was in the Murrayfield Hospital. There, it seems, he died aged 77.

His life, as it seemed to me, had frequently been beset by misfortune or, at least, what seemed to him to be such. He did not become Dean of Faculty or Lord Advocate or Lord President – in none of these cases not for the lack of trying. He retired from the Law Lords' Corridor while still under 70 on completing his 15-year period as a judge. He might have made a bit more of it, but he did not. Nevertheless he was a most attractive, cheerful, debonair person when things were going well. He was someone whom I very much liked and admired. But there was always a sense of restless disappointment about him, especially when he missed these great offices, which tinged his life with an element of sadness. His comparatively early death, so painful as it must have been, seems to have added to that feeling. I do not know quite how to express myself when I write to Ann, as I must do when the news is made public.

---

322 Under section 137(3) of the Constitutional Reform Act 2005.
323 This was the first of a number of documentaries which were shown on television following my decision as Lord President to allow the filming of criminal trials for that purpose.

In London we are in the middle of the nine-judge case about control orders for people suspected of terrorism.[324] It is an anxious case. The Government insists that these are dangerous people and must be controlled. But much of the case against them is withheld on grounds of national security, and a very recent case from Strasbourg says that this will not do. I fear that we cannot support the Government, despite the risks of relaxing the controls on these people.

13 March 2009

The nine-judge case finished on Monday of this week, and we were not required to sit in the remaining three days. So I came back to Edinburgh on the Wednesday afternoon to work at home.

We ended up in agreement that the line a majority had taken in an earlier control order case could not be supported in the light of the decision of the Grand Chamber in *A v United Kingdom*[325] where the Strasbourg Court had in effect gone Tom Bingham's way[326] although he was in the minority. It is hard to say that the Strasbourg Court were wrong, as there is so much earlier common law authority in favour of the view that a person accused must be told why so that he can defend himself. It is odd how the security services' line that the public interest lies in keeping things secret has seeped into our sub-consciousness so that we find it hard to stand up for the old values. We say that we are taking our decision with regret – and with resentment, added Lennie Hoffmann. But in truth, I believe, it is the right one.

There was another meeting of the sub-committee without the civil servants on Tuesday. We are getting down to the difficult issues. This time it was the form and delivery of judgments in the Supreme Court. Brenda has strong views about this, as she will have too about the system for selecting who is to sit on what cases. As always, she has a point, however. I would like to stick to the system of delivering judgments in open court, as this enables the Court to present its face in public. To deliver them under the counter, as it were, would be a lost opportunity for the Supreme Court to assert itself. Brenda has fastened on the fact that this is not how things are done in Canada, and Nicholas objects to the expense of counsel turning up to do nothing when judgments are delivered. On the other hand there is much to be said for having the option to deliver them through the Registry when the Court is not otherwise sitting – in the recess, especially. So Brenda has a toe in the door on this one. Her next battle, on the selection of panels, is motivated by her desire to sit in the cases that she wants to write about. Most of us are quite relaxed about what we are asked to sit on and would rather not interfere. But Brenda does have specialist skills which she

---

324 See fn 305.
325 (2009) 49 EHHR 625.
326 See his dissenting speech in *Secretary of State for the Home Department v MB* [2007] UKHL 46, [2008] AC 440.

is hugely energetic in promoting. One can understand her frustration if she is kept off a case if she thinks she can provide a lead on it.

James Clyde's obituary is in today's *Scotsman*. It was very well written, with contributions from Alan Rodger and David Edward and a charming photograph. I was not approached by anyone, for which I am rather grateful. It was my good fortune to hold two of the offices he so much wanted: Dean and Lord President. In comparison with him I seem a much less deserving figure. I wrote a letter to Ann last night, and this morning I tore it up and wrote a better letter on larger paper. I do hope that I have done the right thing.

15 March 2009

James Clyde's son Jamie telephoned this morning. He said that *The Times* had been in touch because they do not have an obituary on file and that the family wondered whether I would like to provide one. It is an unexpected honour that I could be trusted to do such a thing at the family's request. We had a long conversation, in the course of which he told me more about how James died. He had a month in hospital, after 12 months of investigations and chemotherapy which had all become too much for him, and he died in his sleep. Obviously his two boys are providing immense support to Ann, who is relieved now that all the pain and worry is over but faces a huge loss. Of course I shall do my best for them. The newspaper's deputy editor of obituaries, Angus Clarke, assured me that there is no time pressure. Jamie asked me to mention James's time from 2003 to 2006 as the Justice Oversight Commissioner in Northern Ireland. This is something of which I know very little, so it will require some research.

27 March 2009

The Middlesex Guildhall building was handed over by the contractors, Keir, to the Ministry of Justice last week. It was, we were told, a period of much activity to keep to the contractual handover date. Over 200 people were at work inside the building finishing things off. But the date was achieved, and the contractors' huts which had obscured the front of the building had gone by the start of this week. The full impact of the cleaning of the stonework is now there for all to see. It is a gleaming white building which commands attention, the entrance to which is decorated with elaborate images of robed and behatted figures which give it an ecclesiastic appearance in keeping with the great Abbey on the other side of the Broad Sanctuary.

Jenny Rowe, our Chief Executive, began the process of introducing us to our new quarters. The Law Lords were in first, in small groups, as the building is still under wraps inside while it is checked over and finished off with matters which lay outside the main contract. Room selection, in order of seniority, was the main object of these visits. Nicholas Phillips and I have no choice. Our rooms as President and Deputy President on the east front are already pre-determined. Mark Saville, rather to the dismay of those who have actually been working as

Law Lords – not lost in the morass of his Bloody Sunday Inquiry, as he still is – got the first choice and not surprisingly he chose the best room. This is the south-east corner with one window looking across to the Abbey with the other looking down to the Palace of Westminster. It has lots of light and fine rooms. Alan Rodger chose a room in the opposite corner on a level immediately below his and came away clearly highly delighted. I am so glad, as he cares so much at being moved out of the Law Lords' Corridor. Brenda has a good corner room at the north-east with views to Big Ben and the Treasury. Nicholas is much put out at his room which has lots of space but not much by way of windows although it looks east to the House of Commons. So does mine, but my view is even more obscured than his is by huge plane trees on Canning Green just outside. I dare say that we will get used to what we have got. But it feels like a real drop in standards from the handsome rooms in the Palace of Westminster which we will be leaving, with their huge windows, fresh air and superb views of Westminster Abbey.

We were taken on a tour of the rest of the building. Simon Brown was in my small group. He secured a room on the south front looking across to the Abbey, which is not a bad choice. But he will not be in the strategic position beside Ayo's room which he has just now – the centre of gossip, as Alan says. My room is in the best position from that point of view, so I shall make a point of keeping my door open as is my style anyway. The general impression is that a superb job has been made of cleaning and opening the place up to natural light wherever possible. The stained glass windows which look out to the light wells have come to life, and the entrance hall is full of light and interest. The carpets, based on the design that Yvonne Holton devised at my suggestion in August 2007 and carried forward with such enthusiasm by Brenda, are lively and colourful and add much to the overall sparkle that the building has now acquired. The courtrooms too are much more bearable than what we were shown when we first went into the building. Indeed, the new one, which we will call Court 2 and looks out to the Abbey, will be quite spectacular. It is hard to be sure until we get the furniture in, but it looks as though here too we have made significant improvements. The process of transfer to our new surroundings seems suddenly very much closer.

I was visited by the House's art committee chaired by Viscount Falkland to discuss a painting to be commissioned of the Law Lords at work. I suggested that it would be best to show us giving judgment in the Chamber, and that a good moment to choose would be our last judgments on 30 July when we all expect to be there. This is a rather nice and generous proposal. We can have some retired Law Lords from the back benches too – Lennie, Bob Carswell and perhaps some others who care to join in. This, together with a team of photographers at work in various places, will create quite a handsome historical record. I feel rather privileged to be in the centre of such attention.

James Clyde's obituary was published by *The Times* today. There was a very nice email of thanks from the obituaries editor to which I replied. Unfortunately it was accompanied by a rather unflattering photograph of him in Northern Ireland. This was due, no doubt, to the emphasis that I placed on that part of his career after his retirement when he did so much for the administration of justice in the Province. The family will be disappointed. But my research showed he did a wonderful job there, and it was right that it should be placed on the record.

3 April 2009

The Bahamas team under Nicholas, with Scott, Brown, Mance and Neuberger, will be travelling home as I write after a visit which, by all accounts, has been fairly useless. There were only about two and a half days work there, if that. The event was rather overdone with ceremonies and hand-shaking, as David Neuberger said to Lennie in an email. The impression he conveyed was that it was a waste of time. We may find that this event which the Registrar Indira Francis is so keen on for personal reasons, perhaps as it maintains her high profile in the local community, will be hard to support in future years if this is how the work that is assigned to it turns out to be. The next visit is at the end of November, when it will be my turn to preside.

Meantime the team left at home – Lennie, myself, Rodger, Walker and Hale – were engaged in much more substantial things. There was a one-day case about a pricing arrangement for the placing of photocopiers in shops,[327] and a really interesting three-day case about a contract between Charterbrook, a landowner, and Persimmon, a development company.[328] The latter was all the more important, as it was Lennie's last case. He has to retire this month, as he will be 75 in a few weeks' time. This is a huge loss to the Law Lords' Corridor. Unpredictable he may have been on occasions – really quite misguided sometimes. But his contribution has been immense. His intellectual brilliance and capacity to enjoy life and engage with others has given us an atmosphere of academic prowess, combined with an almost schoolboy lightheartedness which it will be impossible to recapture when he leaves. I suppose that it is because everything is so easy for him to grasp and understand that he can cope with our work with such apparent effortlessness – yet produce, when it is needed, some quite remarkable opinions.

Yesterday, at the end of our hearing which had been conducted with great skill by Christopher Nugee QC and Robert Miles QC – a credit to the Chancery Bar, as Lennie himself said – we had a little ceremony. George Lawrence, a former pupil of Lennie's, came forward and made a most amusing little speech, recalling former days. He was wearing a wig which Lennie had given him, still with the name L H Hoffmann inside it – an article which he could now sell for thousands of pounds, he said. Fortunately Alan Rodger had suggested to me that I really ought to say something too, as Nicholas had apparently not hit

---

327 *TRM Copy Centres (UK) Ltd v Lanwall Services Ltd* [2009] UKHL 35, [2009] 1 WLR 1375.
328 *Charterbrook Ltd v Persimmon Homes Ltd* [2009] UKHL 38, [2009] AC 1101.

anything like the right note at an office party which was given for Lennie last Thursday. So I had a piece ready of my own, mainly in my head, helped by a few notes. I said that age sadly had at last caught up with him, although anyone who had seen him running upstairs to the Committee Room as he always does, leaving the rest far behind, would find this hard to believe. I said that there could not have been a better case for him to end with. It had brought out all the qualities we so much admire – prodigious memory, clarity and speed of thought, grasp of the subject matter and all of it accompanied by a lightness of touch and generosity which facilitated discussion with counsel and among colleagues. It was absurd that he should have to retire when at the height of his powers. But 'rules is rules', I said, and not even he with all his ingenuity had found a way round the statute. To say that we would miss him was a gross understatement. It had been a real privilege for us all to work with him and, when we read his judgments later, to be able to say that we knew him and that we were there.

I think that Lennie was pleased and rather touched to have been made a bit of a fuss of. His wife Gillian had come to see him sitting on his last day, and several members of staff were there at the end too. He found it a bit difficult to say the usual words to end the hearing before the Bar was cleared, which was a sign that he was really quite emotional about it all. How very wise of Alan Rodger to spot what was needed and to give me time to think what I might say.

Now at last we have reached the start of Holy Week and the Easter Holiday. Spring weather during this last week has turned my thoughts to Craighead and the early daffodils there. In London a G20 Summit, which Gordon Brown presided over with considerable stature and was graced by President Obama and his wife – both calm, elegant, warm-hearted and superbly well mannered – has passed off without serious incident and with some measure of international agreement. The huge financial crisis still hangs over us, of course. But there is an atmosphere of optimism at last, as it does seem that world leaders are able to generate some kind of a consensus.

Judges' salaries are being given a 1.5% increase. This is less than the 2.6% recommended by the Senior Salaries Review Board. This is the first time that its recommendation has not been implemented in full. But we are secure in our jobs and quite well paid, which is more than can be said for many people. There can be no complaint.

12 April 2009

There have been two more significant deaths: Sir Neil MacCormick and Lord Slynn of Hadley, people who in very different ways commanded much respect in Europe as well as here, and much affection with it too.

Neil MacCormick, who died of cancer much too young at 67, was a remarkable man – immensely gifted intellectually and also politically very active. His political roots were in the Scottish National Party, in which his father too had been very active. He was the pursuer in the famous case in 1953 about the Royal

Cipher: *MacCormick v Lord Advocate*.[329] Unlike his father, however, Neil was an extremely friendly man who seemed to be on good terms with everyone. I came across him from time to time in his capacity as a renowned academic in public law, often when he was giving lectures in Edinburgh or in London. I last met him in November 2007 – it seems like yesterday – when he delivered the annual lecture to the Stair Society in his typically laid-back but absolutely absorbing style. He became seriously ill about six months ago, and had a slow but very cheerful period of decline when he was visited by his many friends. He was interviewed shortly before he died, emaciated but very relaxed and content with his life.

Gordon Slynn, of course, was a colleague of mine in the House of Lords where he was already very senior when I arrived in 1996. From the outset of my time with him he was seriously ill with cancer, but he made a series of quite remarkable recoveries and was only recently put out of action. He died aged 79, which was a pretty good track record given his state of health a decade ago. I last saw him about four months ago when he made a remarkably fine speech in the House of Lords about the European Court of Justice. He had lost his voice and found it hard to speak, but what he said was compelling and listened to with great respect. He had the knack of speaking logically and grammatically without notes at considerable length. He was a very good advocate and excellent at judicial education. He presided over moots with great skill, summing up in the way I have described. He was perhaps less successful as a judge and fell out with Lennie Hoffmann in a big way over Pinochet. I think it was due to some lobbying by Lennie that he was passed over when his turn arrived to become a Senior Law Lord. Tom Bingham was brought in instead. This was a far better result for all of us. Gordon had too many fingers in too many pies, and was too disorganised as a result, to lead us in the way Tom was able to do. I think that he was deeply hurt by this rejection, and he retired soon afterwards. But he still had many contacts and many admirers, particularly in the EU countries to the east where he had done much to promote an understanding of the rule of law and, rather surprisingly, in the Solomon Islands where he was President of the Court of Appeal – part-time, of course. With Tony Lloyd he was one of the few former Law Lords of my generation who took a real interest in the work of the House of Lords.

Some news from the Privy Council's last sitting in The Bahamas, via Alan Rodger's email. He remained in London on Friday of the week before Holy Week. Jenny Rowe came into his room to see him about something completely different, and then told him that Mary Macdonald had been suspended for getting drunk at a social function there. 'Our leader', as Alan calls Nicholas Phillips, had ordered that she be prohibited from making her next overseas trip to the Commonwealth Law Conference in Hong Kong this month. This is likely to be difficult, thought Jenny Rowe. But it is clear that she cannot be trusted to go overseas again on Privy Council business. She is a strange mixture,

329 1953 SC 396.

an able administrator but with a muddled personal life and an abrupt manner which does not go down well with everyone. I have not been told the details, but her tendency to over-indulgence was noted on the first visit with amusement and was barely perceptible during the second when I was in charge. Jenny Rowe is her line manager – since 1 April this year, as it happens – and it will be her responsibility to discipline her. I do not see how she can be allowed to continue. But getting rid of her may not be easy, and an upheaval of this kind is the last thing we need as we move everything over to the Supreme Court building.

2009 – May to July

3 May 2009

There was a memorial service for James Clyde this afternoon in St Mary's Cathedral. It was a very remarkable tribute to such a remarkable man. There were excellent addresses by Kenneth Cameron,[330] his contemporary and best man, and Judith McClure, former headmistress of St George's School of which he was Chairman of the Directors. There were moving tributes too by his two sons, Jamie and Tim. There was lovely music, chosen by him. He had time to express his thoughts while in hospital and was well equipped to do so: three fine hymns for us all to sing, two anthems sung by the choir of St Mary's and two pieces of music he particularly loved: a Bach cello sonata prelude – he was a cellist – and a Beethoven piano sonata which he had been learning before the very real promise of an LRCM. There were six members of the clergy, plus the Bishop of Edinburgh. James's remarkably active life beyond the law was celebrated as much, or even more so, than his legal achievements. Not many of us could have deserved such a tribute, certainly not I as I have not anything like his breadth of literacy and musical appreciation, nor have I made anything like such a contribution to public life. There was a reception in the Cathedral afterwards, with tea and cake and the pleasure of meeting again many friends. Then a walk home in chill air but lovely sunshine through the New Town which is full of flowering shrubs and trees and even the song of a song thrush in Moray Place Gardens. The world seems a poorer place without him.

10 May 2009

It was Strathclyde University Day last week so, after a very busy day of meetings and paperwork in London on the Tuesday, I went by BA to Glasgow on the 5.30pm flight to get to Ross Priory for the graduands' dinner. Rain and low cloud obscured the lovely views as we flew into Glasgow Airport from the north, and it was very wet at Ross Priory. But the dinner was fun, as ever, this time under Jim McDonald. The graduands were Andrew Hamnett, also to be

---

330 Lord Cameron of Lochbroom.

made a Fellow as our former Principal, Jeff Fergus and Frances McMenamin of the University Court, Derek Casey,[331] and Bill McArthur, an astronaut from NASA. McArthur was dressed for dinner in US Colonel's uniform, and he wore a kilt for the ceremony next day. He was proud to show off his many medals and was full of stories about his four trips into space, one of which had lasted for six months. This time, instead of being taken to University House, Mary and I were given a room in Ross Priory for the night, and we had a delightful walk in the early morning sunshine and an excellent breakfast. I had a lot to do: the dinner speech, a welcome speech to Jim McDonald at the ceremony, a presentation for Andrew Hamnett's DUniv, and a speech for the unveiling of his portrait by John Bayne later in the afternoon. Then home to rest, Wednesday's festivities over. On Thursday I visited the Business School and the Department of Engineering to discuss Malawi and the provision of solar panels there. Then an early start on Friday for the Court Conveners' nomination group, the Court meeting and the Convocation.

The meetings on Friday were held in unusual circumstances. There was a large demonstration going on. As I predicted in my entry of 30 November 2008, Jim's catchword of Strathclyde as an international technological university has not gone down well with the English Department. The Law School too is uneasy. The Business School less so, as it has its own very strong identity. There was quite a lot of noise audible from within the Council meeting room. There were said to be placards stating 'Sack the Principal'. The demonstrators were said to be equipped with eggs and flour. Jim seemed quite undismayed. Peter West and Fraser Livingston were less so. Fraser had expressed some concern to me that Jim was moving too fast: 'But what can you do if the Principal is doing what he wants to do?' he said. There was quite a discussion of this in the Court meeting. There seemed to be few doubters there, and feelings were reassured when the line was taken, which I had encouraged in private discussion with Frances McMenamin, that Strathclyde is already a technological university as technology informs all that it does and that the aspiration is to be one of the leading members in a group to which it already belongs. The situation is not a very happy one, however. There will be more redundancies as money is short. The concentration will be on the University's strong areas, not the weaker ones. I wrote to Jim with a mixture of congratulations for meetings well-handled and of concern at the words he is using to describe his project. But I do not think that he is really a listener, so I fear that we may have more demonstrations before the year is out.

16 May 2009

A turbulent week at Westminster. *The Daily Telegraph* has been running a series of exposures of MPs milking the system of expenses, especially for the purchase and upkeep of second homes. It has been going on for about ten days, and with

---

331 It was largely to his efforts, which were already bearing fruit, that the Commonwealth Games 2014 came to Glasgow.

each day more and more abuses are exposed. The Speaker has got himself into trouble by trying to defend the system in the face of the public outcry – he had been no slouch in the claiming of expenses either. The Labour Party's standing has never been lower in the polls. They are now only two points above the Liberal Democrats. Gordon Brown is struggling to maintain his authority. The Tories have not been free from exposure, but the worst cases seem to be Labour's. David Cameron seems to be more on top of the situation than the others, but all the politicians from whatever party are facing public condemnation and ridicule. The European Parliamentary elections are only two weeks away. A disastrous showing for Labour may end Gordon Brown's premiership, and there is to be a vote of no confidence in the Speaker next week. There seems to be general agreement that this situation of turmoil is unprecedented.

14 June 2009

There was a sustained attack on Gordon Brown, the Prime Minister, before and after the European Parliamentary elections on 4 June, as opinion polls showed the lowest ever support for the Labour Party. A 15% result in those elections, third in place below the Tories and UKIP, confirmed what the polls had suggested. Several members of the Cabinet resigned, and it looked as though there was to be a vote of confidence on his leadership. In the event, due partly to poor co-ordination and partly to self-interest as Labour MPs face certain defeat at the next election whenever it is and were in no mood to hasten their own removal from Parliament, the whole thing fizzled out. From our point of view on the Appellate Committee this is a relief, as Jack Straw remains Lord Chancellor and Minister for Justice. He is sound, is a lawyer and carries authority. Who knows who would have replaced him and with what qualities.

The last two or three weeks have been very busy, and it is not possible to narrate even most of it. There were visits by the family; a dinner at the Royal Hospital, Chelsea, the home of the Chelsea Pensioners, which was organised by Martin Drury for our Michell House at Rugby School group; an awards dinner given by The Times Higher Education people for University administrations held in the Hilton Hotel with 900 guests and a ceremony presided over by Rory Bremner and organised with impressive efficiency; a 48-hour Tube strike; a dinner at Gray's Inn for Lennie Hoffmann which Mary attended; flying back to Edinburgh with Mary by BA from Terminal 5 for the start of a UK/South African Judicial Exchange, for which I have been planning and acting as the UK co-ordinator for months.

The Exchange was a remarkable gathering – the first ever with South Africa, though we have had UK exchanges with other jurisdictions for many years. It was deliberately based in Edinburgh, in view of the 'mixed systems' connection as we both have aspects of the civil law and the common law in our legal systems. On the UK side we had Higgins LJ from Northern Ireland, although he was forced to pull out at the last moment due to pressure of work; Lord President Hamilton and Lord Hodge from Scotland; Igor Judge, the Lord Chief

Justice, and Mary Arden from the Court of Appeal and Linda Dobbs J for England and Wales; and Richard Scott and myself from the House of Lords. For the South Africans it was six from the Constitutional Court: Dikgang Moseneke DCJ, Bess Nkabinde, Kate O'Regan, Albie Sachs, Johann van der Westhuizen and Themibile Skweyiya; and five from the Supreme Court of Appeal: Louis Harms, the Deputy President, Fritz Brand, Tom Cloete, Carole Lewis and Ken Mthiyane JJ. We had five working sessions: two on Friday on judicial independence and relations with the press and government, and procedures for the recovery of proceeds of crime from drug dealers; and two on the Saturday on the influence of the Constitution and the European Convention on Human Rights on tort and delict and on access to housing and social problems connected with it. On Sunday we had a one-hour session on judgment preparation and writing judgments. The level of debate was excellent, and everyone had a chance to contribute in a very amicable and orderly manner. Dikgang Moseneke was particularly impressive in a quiet, thoughtful, well-organised way – authority worn with great charm. It was of course a privilege to have the much celebrated hero Albie Sachs with us, and also Kate O'Regan who had done so much of the organising at their end.

On the social side, which was very well put together by the Scottish Government, the delegates were accommodated in the Scotsman Hotel and we met in excellent rooms at the Balmoral Hotel with coffee, buffet lunch and tea provided. There were dinners at the Signet Library, Prestonfield House Hotel and Edinburgh Castle, and trips to Rosslyn Chapel and HMY *Britannia* for the spouses which Mary, Judith Judge and Rima Scott all supported. Our CMJA background was a great help, as was my experience of running exchanges with the Conseil d'Etat. This one was at the highest level in comparison. The common language helped, of course, but so too did the level of intellect and judicial experience of the judges we were dealing with. The two South African courts had not met with each other before, which gave our meeting an added significance. It was a busy weekend, into which I added a lecture on distress and corroboration in honour of Sir Gerald Gordon[332] on the Friday evening to which almost all the delegates came – welcome support, as my lecture was rather controversial. I was criticising a decision of Alan Rodger's[333] which overruled one of mine, me holding that distress could corroborate the victim of a sexual assault's evidence. He, with four others, held that it could not. I found this uncompromising overruling, shortly after I had left office as Lord President, distressing in itself. Further study showed that I should have worked harder to find authority for my argument. as it was not as lacking as Alan Rodger made it out to be. My position is in line with England and Wales and South Africa, so in that respect I had many friends.

---

332 'Corroboration and Distress: Some Crumbs from Under the Master's Table' published in *Essays in Criminal Law in Honour of Sir Gerald Gordon* (edited by James Chalmers and others, Edinburgh Studies in Law 2010), p 12.
333 See fn 37.

20 June 2009

Impossibly busy! After the UK/SA weekend we had a week on a seven-judge case in the Privy Council about the proposed removal from office of Derek Schofield, the Chief Justice of Gibraltar.[334] At first sight this looked to be a clear case for his removal, on the basis of a report by Douglas Cullen, Peter Gibson and Jonathan Parker. But the more we got into it the more uneasy I became. Some aspects of the report seemed to completely overlook the practicalities of the situation in which the Chief Justice found himself, the strength of the drive towards maintaining the independence of the judiciary, including by the CMJA of which he is a member, and the extent to which he quite reasonably felt himself to be under attack by the Government of Gibraltar. Alan Rodger and Brenda Hale shared my misgivings, but we were outnumbered by Nicholas Phillips, Simon Brown and Igor Judge and Tony Clarke whom Nicholas had invited to join us – a closely-knit body which it will be hard to split. I am uncertain what to do about this, whether to dissent or just to express my misgivings. I started to draft an opinion but had to spend a day at Craighead in lovely weather to sort the garden out for the summer and cut the grass.

Two cases in the Privy Council again this week with me in the chair. One is a devolution issue reference: *Murtagh*, in which I will have to write.[335] The first of two Strathclyde graduation days, a mixture of apprehension, enjoyment and exhaustion as usual, prevented me from getting to grips with my opinion which, as I leave for London, is still in a rather disorganised and incomplete state. The other case was in Lawrence Collins's territory, but it was significant as it was Bob Carswell's last case with us. I will miss him very much. He is very steady and reliable, full of biblical and classical quotations to enrich our conversation.

Mary came to London for a supper in the Barry Room with our old Canadian Bar friend Patrick Peacock and his wife Virginia. She took the opportunity of visiting the new Supreme Court building with Jenny Rowe and was very much impressed. So too was Sir Michael Peat, the Prince of Wales' Secretary, whom we took round the following day. The cool inside the building was in marked contrast to the heat and humidity in the Privy Council room in Downing Street as the midsummer heat begins to build up. This, at least, is something to look forward to.

12 July 2009

Still impossibly busy. In London we had the excitement of the Royal Garden Party, and then a dinner in the River Room of the House of Lords to say goodbye to the Law Lords which was hosted by the Lord Speaker.

The Garden Party was terminated prematurely by an enormous and violent thunderstorm which produced sudden torrential rain. It then turned to hail

---

334 *Hearing on the Report of the Chief Justice of Gibraltar* [2009] UKPC 43.
335 *HM Advocate v Murtagh* [2009] UKPC 35, 2010 SC (PC) 39.

and, after a rather treacherous lull, returned with renewed vigour to drench those outside yet again. We and the Royal Party were in the Royal Tea Tent when it broke out, so we were dry. But many, many others were exposed to the storm with unimaginable consequences. No one was injured despite dramatic thunderbolts. The noise in the tent was deafening. Her Majesty wandered about with a charming smile on her face, almost inaudible to her guests. We escaped at last in a dry spell and were lucky to get a lift back to the House with Nicholas Phillips.

Our dinner was a more peaceful, relaxed occasion. There was a nice mixture of guests, including Lord Strathclyde, Harry Woolf and Michael Pownall, the Clerk of Parliaments, at our table. A nice speech from Baroness Hayman, as Lord Speaker, all without notes, was followed by an amusing one from Nicholas who did use a pre-written speech. There is to be a more formal occasion in the House on 21 July at which a tribute will be paid to the Law Lords from the front benches to which I, as the senior of the Law Lords who have made their maiden speeches, must reply.

I had my last case in the Privy Council in Downing Street this week, and my last journeys to and fro in our ancient Daimler motorcar. The case was a rather messy one from The Bahamas, about a development on Abaco–Guana Cay, which lasted two and a half days. The last day was uncomfortable, as speeches went on too long and were not well directed. This was difficult to handle for me as chairman, with Alan Rodger expressing irritation beside me. The seating is not all that comfortable either, nor are the arrangements for laying out the authorities on trollies beside us. Despite the lovely room and the fun of those journeys in our old motorcar, it will be a relief to move to our new premises. Lawrence Collins summed up well, and Robert Walker agreed to write the judgment. I felt rather under-performing on both counts, as my summing-up was disorganised and I felt that I should have offered to do the judgment. Sometimes I feel rather inadequate in such excellent company.

19 July 2009

I spent virtually the whole weekend on a judgment in *R (L) v Commissioner of Police of the Metropolis*[336] – an important case about the disclosure of personal information from public records: 30 pages, 47 paragraphs, the longest of this term. It was important to get it out of the way before the term ends. Mark Saville (for once), Simon Brown, David Neuberger and Richard Scott were with me. There was another interesting case this week too, about the new system of local government on Sark.[337] We were very well served by Lord Pannick and Jonathan Crow as counsel, and there was a brief contribution by an incomer to the island, Dr Slivik from Slovenia, which I confess I found much more interesting than my colleagues who, city dwellers that they are,

---

336 [2009] UKSC 3, [2010] 1 AC 410.
337 *R (Barclay) v Lord Chancellor and Secretary of State for Justice* [2009] UKSC 3, [2010] 1 AC 464.

have no real interest in the social mores of those who live on small islands. I also chaired the last Appeal Committee hearing of the Law Lords' existence in the House of Lords in Committee Room 2 – an oral hearing in a petition for leave to appeal.

The week was also marked by the Lord Mayor's Banquet for the judges which, for the first time, Mary was unable to attend as there had been so many competing demands for her to come to London. It was as ever a fine occasion with excellent food and wine. Jack Straw made a typically uninspiring and disorganised speech as Lord Chancellor. But Igor Judge's speech as Lord Chief Justice which preceded it was the best of its kind I have ever heard.

The packing cases have arrived, in large quantities, to warn us – as if we needed any warning – that our move from the House of Lords is imminent. I shall ignore them for one more week.

24 July 2009

We had our last meeting of the Law Lords' Supreme Court sub-committee on Monday at 4.30pm in the Conference Room. There was little left to discuss – just one or two snagging details in the building, and some final arrangements on dealing with the handover. There was also a presentation of the exhibition which is to go into the new building designed by an enterprising firm called Easy Tiger. Brenda Hale and Jonathan Mance were there, as was Nicholas Phillips in an observer capacity. Charles McCall, Alan Sloan and Kylie Freeman were there for the Ministry of Justice, Stephen Foot having now left. Brendan Keith, Jenny Rowe and Jackie Lindsay were there for our administrators. These monthly meetings have been going on now for about five years, enormously worthwhile – essential indeed. We have got most of what we wanted, but I owe a huge debt to Brenda Hale. She is an uneasy companion, not the most tactful of individuals. But her eye for detail, persistence and sense of what needed to be done have been unrivalled. As I said to her as we were leaving, I do not know what we would have done without her. This event was followed by a reception in the River Room to launch a volume about the Law Lords in Parliament, *The Judicial House of Lords 1876–2009*,[338] to which I and many others have contributed.

Tuesday 21 July was the last sitting day for public business in the House of Lords as Parliament was going into recess. It was our last day of being able to sit in the Chamber in public business while still serving as Law Lords, so the first item of business after prayers was a motion of appreciation in honour of the Lords of Appeal in Ordinary. This was to be proposed by the Leader of the House, seconded by the front benches, the Convenor of the Crossbenchers, a Lord Spiritual and replied to by me. There was no question but that it was my job to reply, and I insisted on this without discussing it with anyone as this was so

---

[338] Edited by Louis Blom-Cooper, Brice Dickson and Gavin Drewry (Oxford, 2009).

obviously for me. Nicholas Phillips, like so many of the current team, has not yet made his maiden speech. This is rather regrettable and short-sighted, but I suppose that the Londoners among us see nothing special about being in the House. As for the idea of being able to speak there without engaging in legislation or politics, it does not seem to have occurred to them. Only I, Richard Scott, Simon Brown and Jonathan Mance (all chairmen of Sub-Committee E of the EU Committee) have spoken, plus Alan Rodger as Lord Advocate but who has remained silent as a Law Lord.

I had rather hoped that the event would go unnoticed by my colleagues and that, it being the last day, it would be thinly attended. The reverse was true. The word had passed around on Monday – most people do not read the Crossbench brief or the minutes. I was in the chair for the last sitting of the Appellate Committee in *A v Croydon and Others*,[339] so we sat at 10.00am instead of 10.30am and stopped at 10.45am so that we could go downstairs in time to get into the Chamber for seats before prayers at 11.00am. I sat between Richard Scott and David Neuberger (now to be Master of the Rolls) on the second bench back on the left side of the crossbenches. This was my usual place, the best for a view of the whole House. The place began to fill up and when people came in to add to the numbers after prayers it was absolutely full. There were staff and many others in the galleries and some MPs at the Bar, including Edward Garnier and Dominic Grieve, the two Opposition Shadow Law Officers, in the middle. It was packed – pure theatre. The Leader, Baroness Royall, started off with a pro-Government version of the event. She was followed by Tom Strathclyde for the Conservatives, full of regret, by Lord Wallace of Saltaire for the Liberal Democrats – 'We don't want to lose you but we think you ought to go' – and then Baroness D'Souza and then the Bishop of Portsmouth. There had been some inter-/cross-party reactions to these speeches, but the last two were listened to largely in silence. Then it was my turn. Strangely, and despite such an enormous audience, I did not feel nervous. I had taken a lot of trouble over my speech and had it in my hand – typed on A4 sheets and then cut in half, for easy reference. I had positioned myself under one of the microphones so that I could be heard right away. With familiar faces all around, I have spent a lot of time in the Chamber these past 13 years – I felt at home and among friends.

Though I say it myself, it was a triumph and immensely enjoyable. Their Lordships responded to me after listening to my carefully crafted first sentence 'What is really happening today is that the House is losing part of itself'.[340] 'Hear, hear', Hansard records Noble Lords as saying. I spoke for seven minutes – several splendid moments with laughter as when I said, 'If I may be so bold, your Lordships are on your own now' – this was broadcast in *Today in Parliament* that evening – and 'The cat's away, the mice will play', as I told them about our plans for the next week and how, unlike the Last Day of Judgment, this event

---

339 *R (A) v Croydon London Borough Council* [2009] UKSC 8, [2009] 1 WLR 2557.
340 See Hansard: HL Debates, vol 712, no 112, col 1514.

– 'Our last Judgment' – was something the timing of which we could predict with absolute certainty and that we would all be there. I sat down to loud 'hear, hears'. Then Earl Ferrers, the elder statesman on the Conservative benches, made an unplanned but very amusing, wistful speech to wind the whole thing up. We then had to leave the Chamber to return to our Committee Room. On the way out all sorts of people congratulated me, including Baroness O'Cathain, Harry Woolf and Lord Lawson of Blaby, the former Tory Chancellor of the Exchequer, who said, 'We have never met, but that was a marvellous speech', and held out his hand to add his congratulations. Alan Rodger, who, on his own admission had been skulking on the benches behind me, sent me an email. 'Terrific – just the right note. Elegant, etc, making it clear what they were losing.' David Wilson, among others, met me in the Corridor and said how much he had enjoyed it too. My own feeling was of huge relief that I had not let the side down. But it was a marvellous way for us all to say goodbye.

That evening, such a crowded programme of events. There was the annual dinner for our judicial assistants, past and present. The present ones were there as guests, all the others now pay. This was well attended. There were 48 present, one half of them judicial assistants and all years represented but one. This may be our last dinner, but it was such a good occasion that many would like us to try to keep it going as long as possible.

Next day I was sitting as usual in Committee Room 1 with my Committee: Scott, Walker, Hale and Neuberger. Then in the evening another farewell party, this time in Downing Street for us to say goodbye to the Privy Council chamber there – such an elegant, wooden-panelled room, designed by John Soane. What the Government will do with it, goodness knows. It was full of familiar faces, staff, and members of the Judicial Committee of all generations. I took them in small groups to the Retiring Room overlooking 10 Downing Street, which many of those present had never seen. Curiously none of my colleagues had thought of doing that.

Then on Thursday it was our last day as an Appellate Committee in the House of Lords. What a privilege to be in the chair on such an occasion, as successor to all those fine men in past generations who have sat there since 1948. We ended the case at lunchtime. I said a few words to mark the occasion, and John Howell QC did so on behalf of the Bar. He remarked that it was the last time that counsel would be confronted in that room by the baleful painting of the Burial of King Harold which hangs on the wall behind the Law Lords. I assured him, to general laughter, that King Harold would not be coming with us.[341] Then that was it. After a brief discussion about the case we left it to the doorkeepers, John and Jacqui, to clear up. Next week the dear old room will be gutted – as will Committee Room 2, to convert it into a modern committee room just like anywhere else.

---

341 It was moved to the opposite wall in Committee Room 1 to make room for a painting of the Law Lords by Sergei Pavlenko delivering their last judgments which had been commissioned by the House of Lords to mark the event.

2 August 2009

The final week was as busy as the last one, but the House had risen and the place was being pulled apart around us with increasing intrusion into our Corridor as time went on. Long lines of packing cases were in the corridors and as the week ended more and more workmen appeared – strange people who had no interest in us, only in getting us out and getting the place ready for those who were to move in.

I spent all of Monday clearing out cupboards and discarding years of accumulated unwanted papers. Three huge sack loads of junk had to be dragged down the Corridor to the rubbish collection point. Part of Tuesday was spent checking over my collection of books and getting rid of some – quite a lot – that were outdated or no longer relevant. This was hard, dusty work. It was not easy to prepare for the two cases I was to hear on the last two days, but fortunately I had read them up over the weekend. On Tuesday evening there was a reception at the Royal Courts of Justice for a conference that Mary Arden had arranged to coincide with our last two days of term, conveniently removing Nicholas Phillips from the judicial work of our Corridor, so leaving the way clear for me to preside. There were several old friends at the reception: Sian Elias from New Zealand, Kate O'Regan from South Africa, Terry Olsen from the Conseil d'Etat, Michael de la Bastide from the Caribbean Court. Igor Judge presided with his masterly charm and courtesy.

Wednesday and Thursday were occupied with two one-day appeals in the Chamber. As I was presiding I was on the Woolsack for prayers, with the Bishop of Chichester beside me. Counsel were called in while I was still there, and I was instructed by Brendan Keith to remain there until they had taken their places and then step two paces to the left and say 'My Lords, for the more convenient hearing of the Appeal, I shall move closer to the Bar of the House'. With that I went forward to take the chair in a central position between the desks of my four colleagues. I was in a very comfortable armchair, from which it was possible to converse with counsel very easily. Wednesday's case, about a European arrest warrant,[342] was simple and over by lunchtime. We entertained Chief Justice John Roberts of the US Supreme Court to dinner in Brooke's Club that evening, ten of us, with him as our guest – a very approachable and obviously very talented and self-assured young man, still in his late 50s. The case on the Thursday was more complicated, about asylum and the law about repeated or fresh claims.[343] Simon, Brenda, Alan and Richard Scott were with me. Alan, Jonathan Mance, Lawrence Collins and Brian Kerr were on the earlier case. We had a bit of a pantomime on Thursday as first counsel and then Richard asked to go to the loo in the course of the hearing, for which – as the House had to adjourn – I had to go to the Woolsack and put the motion that the House 'do adjourn during pleasure' to release them from the Chamber. At

---

342 *Louca v Public Prosecutor, Bielefeld, Germany* [2009] UKSC 4, [2009] 1 WLR 2550.
343 *R (BA (Nigeria)) v Secretary of State for the Home Department* [2009] UKSC 7, [2010] 1 AC 444.

4.15pm the last appeal ever to be heard by the Lords of Appeal in Ordinary in the Chamber came to an end. I thanked counsel, paid a tribute to Richard Scott who retires in September, and then said: 'The House will take time to consider its judgment, which will be issued in another place in due course'.

Then it was time for our last judgments. People had been gathering at the Bar and in the galleries as we concluded our last appeal. The conference delegates – we had met them again at a reception at 2 Carlton Gardens the previous evening, including the Chief Justices of the US Supreme Court and of Israel, Ghana and Namibia – had gathered in a gallery on the south side of the House looking down on us as we took our usual places for judgments and Nicholas, as our chairman, came into the Chamber. There were seven judgments, each delivered with the usual formality of speeches. There were inevitably some slight errors here and there, which gave a hint of frivolity to what was a sad and momentous occasion. We ended with Mrs Purdy's case against the DPP about the need to clarify that prosecutor's practice on assisted suicide,[344] for which I had written the leading judgment and had taken the lead – as Nicholas Phillips seemed not to be doing so – in getting everyone to see that it had to be delivered this term before we rose. It was a highly significant case, on an issue of intense current debate, on which to end. Mrs Purdy was there herself in her wheelchair, as were so many others. David Pannick QC, her leading counsel, was there at the end, very fittingly, to attend for the judgment. When it was over it was for me to move the adjournment. It was not the occasion for a speech, but I felt that a few words more than the simple motion were required. So I said:

> 'My Lords, we have delivered our last judgment in the name of the House of Lords. The clock above the Bar which has presided over our proceedings has beneath it an inscription: *Omnia tempus habent* – all things have their time. Sadly our time here has now come to an end. We could perhaps prolong these proceedings for a while if we wished, but the fact is that there is nothing left for us to do. So I make the only motion that it is open to make in the circumstances. I beg to move that the House do now adjourn.'

Nicholas Phillips should have simply said 'That the House do now adjourn', as that is the practice when the House rises. But to mark the occasion he put it to us as a motion, to which most of us said 'Content'. Not so Alan Rodger. 'Not content' he said, under his breath.

There it all ended. My team gathered in the Chamber to discuss our case after we had exchanged greetings with our various visitors. I then went back to my room to clear up, having said goodbye to Chris Stephen, my excellent judicial assistant, earlier. Mary came down from Edinburgh on the 5.00pm train. I met her at King's Cross later as the news of Debbie Purdy's 'victory' in her assisted suicide case was in full swing. We transferred some more fragile and sensitive belongings from my room to the Supreme Court next morning and then, after

---

344 *R (Purdy) v Director of Public Prosecutions* [2009] UKHL 45, [2010] 1 AC 345.

lunch and some more goodbyes, went to St John's College, Cambridge for a dinner for those who had been given the Sir Joseph Larmor Award – as I was in 1962, for no reason that was ever obvious to me: a very happy occasion nevertheless.

It was a very real privilege to be in such a central position in these last two weeks as a Lord of Appeal in Ordinary. I took some pride in the fact that it was a Scot in the chair, following the traditions of Lords Reid, Keith and Fraser. I am now at the end of my twentieth year as a judge, seven as Lord President and 13 as a Law Lord. It has been immensely rewarding and enjoyable, particularly during these last 13 years, with such fascinating and able colleagues and such a range of interesting work.

To leave the House of Lords is, of course, sad. But the turmoil of these last two weeks of farewells and all the effort of cleaning up amid increasing numbers of packing cases and workmen has brought about a strong belief that it is time to move on. I feel as someone who is all packed up and ready for the taxi to take me to the airport: time to go, the sooner the better. My new room in the Supreme Court is really quite attractive, and Mary has been encouraging me to think so. It is hard to know how we will all feel once we are in the new building. But we have, through my sub-committee, done our very best to make it fit for purpose. There will be a lot to do to make it work, but there is much to look forward to. Meantime we have ten days in Malawi, and then four weeks at Craighead for what I feel is a very well-deserved holiday.

Index of Cases

A v Scottish Ministers 2002 SC (PC) 63 91
A v Secretary of State for the Home Department
   [2005] 2 AC 68. . . . . 228, 230, 231, 261
A v Secretary of State for the Home Department (No 2) [2005]
   UKHL 71, [2006] 2 AC 221 258
A v United Kingdom (2009) 49 EHHR 625 369
AS v Poor Sisters of Nazareth 2008 SC (HL) 146 338
Abnett v British Airways plc, Sidhu v British Airways plc [1997]
   AC 430, 1997 SC (HL) 26. . . . . 7, 16
Advocate (HM) v Murtagh [2009] UKPC 35, 2010 SC (PC) 39 379
Archibald v Fife Council [2004] UKHL 32. 2004 SC (HL) 117. 219
Aston Cantlow Parochial Church Council v Wallbank [2003]
   UKHL 37, [2004] 1 AC 546 . . . . 175–76, 181
Attorney General's Reference (No 3 of 1994) [1998]
   AC 245. . . . . 16, 28, 31, 34
Attorney General's Reference (No 2 of 2001) [2003] UKHL 68,
   [2004] 2 AC 72 . . . . 194–95, 198, 205, 318
Attorney General's Reference (No 5 of 2002) [2004] UKHL 43,
   [2005] 1 AC 167. 223
Attorney General for Jersey v Holley [2005] UKHL 23, [2005] 2 AC 580   238
Austin v Commissioner of Police of the Metropolis [2009] UKHL 5,
   [2009] AC 564. 359

B (A Minor) (Adoption Order: Nationality), In re [1999] 2 AC 136. . . . 79
Beattie v HM Advocate 1995 JC 33 46
Beaufort Developments (NI) Ltd v Gilbert-Ash NI Ltd [1999]
   1 AC 266. 47
Beggs v The Scottish Ministers [2007] UKHL 3, 2007 SLT 235 289
Begum v Tower Hamlets London Borough Council [2003] UKHL 5,
   [2003] 2 AC 430. 171
Bellinger v Bellinger [2003] UKHL 21, [2003] 2 AC 467 172
Benedetto and Labrador v The Queen [2003] UKPC 27, [2003]
   1 WLR 1545 175
Berezovsky v Michaels [2000] 1 WLR 1004 105
Boodram v Baptiste [1999] 1 WLR 1709. 85
Boyce v The Queen [2004] UKPC 32, [2005] 1 AC 400 . . . . . 205, 213, 214
Bradford v McLeod 1986 SLT 244 72
Brown v Stott [2003] 1 AC 681, 2001 SC (PC) 43 118

Burke, In re [2000] 1 AC 422. 107
Burnett's Trustee v Grainger [2004] UKHL 8, 2004
    SC (HL) 19 . . . . 201–03, 207
C (A Minor) (Interim Care Order: Residential Assessment), In re
    [1997] AC 489. 11
Cadogan (Earl) v Sportelli [2008] UKHL 71, [2010] 1 AC 226 355
Campbell v HM Advocate 1998 JC 130 46
Canon Kabushka Kaisha v Green Cartridge Co [1997] AC 728. 23
Cape & Dalgleish v Fitzgerald [2002] UKHL 16 146
Carter Holt Harvey Building Products Ltd v The Commerce
    Commission (New Zealand) [2004] UKPC 37 218–19
Charterbrook Ltd v Persimmon Homes Ltd [2009] UKHL 38,
    [2009] AC 1101 372
Chester v Afshar [2004] UKHL 41, [2005] 1 AC 134 . . . 219, 223, 224, 229
Chief Adjudication Officer v Faulds [2000] 1 WLR 1035,
    2000 SC (HL) 116. . . . . 103, 105
Chief Justice of Gibraltar (Hearing on the Report of) [2009] UKPC 43 . . 379
Christian v The Queen [2007] 2 AC 400 274
Church v HM Advocate 1995 SLT 604 47
Clingham and McCann, see R (McCann) v Crown Court at Manchester
Cockburn v Chief Adjudicator [1997] 1 WLR 799. 16
Co-operative Retail Services Ltd v Taylor Young Partnership Ltd [2002]
    UKHL 17, [2002] 1 WLR 1419 146
Coventry and Solihull Waste Disposal Co Ltd v Russell [1999] 1
    WLR 2093 88
Çukurova Finance International Ltd v Alfa Telecom Turkey [2009]
    UKPC 19, [2009] Bus LR 1613 367
Dabas v High Court of Justice in Madrid, Spain [2007] UKHL 6, [2007]
    2 AC 31 297
Daley v The Queen [1998] 1 WLR 494. 42
Darmalingam v The State [2001] 1 WLR 2303 164
Davidson v Scottish Ministers [2005] UKHL 74, 2006 SC (HL) 41. . . . 263
Davidson v Scottish Ministers (No 3) 2005 SC (HL) 1 195
Designers Guild Ltd v Russell Williams (Textiles) Ltd [2000]
    1 WLR 2416 119
Deutsche Morgan Grenfell Group plc v Inland Revenue Comrs [2006]
    UKHL 48, [2007] 1 AC 558. 276
Dingley v Chief Constable of Strathclyde Police 2000 SC (HL) 77. . . . 104
Director General of Fair Trading v First National Bank [2001]
    UKHL 52, [2002] 1 AC 481. 135, 136
Director of Public Prosecutions v Jones [1999] 2 AC 240 63
Doherty v Birmingham City Council [2008] UKHL 57, [2009]
    AC 367. . . . . 335, 344–45
Dollar Land (Cumbernauld) Ltd v CIN Properties Ltd 1998
    SC (HL) 90 52

Index of Cases

DS v HM Advocate [2007] UKPC 36, 2007 SC (PC) 1 294
Dyer v Watson [2002] UKPC D1, 2002 SC (PC) 8, [2004] 1 AC 379 . . 138, 143
Edinburgh (City of) Council v Secretary of State for Scotland 1998
   SC (HL) 33 32
Elliott v HM Advocate 1995 JC 95. 47
EM (Lebanon) v Secretary of State for the Home Department [2008]
   UKHL 64, [2009] AC 1198 347
Fairchild v Glenhaven Funeral Services Ltd [2002] UKHL 22, [2003]
   1 AC 32 165
Fiona Trust and Holding Corporation v Privalov [2007] UKHL 40,
   [2007] Bus LR 17129. 310
Fisher v Minister of Public Safety and Immigration (No 2) [2000]
   AC 434. 58–59
Fletcher Estates (Harlescott) Ltd v Secretary of State for the
   Environment [2000] 2 AC 307 102
Follen v HM Advocate [2001] UKPC D2, 2001 SC (PC) 105. 121
Fornah v Secretary of State for the Home Department [2006] UKHL 46,
   [2007] 1 AC 412. 278
Foskett v McKeown [2001] 1 AC 102 278
Fox v HM Advocate 1998 JC 94. 45
G (Adoption: Unmarried Couple), In re [2009] AC 173 338
Gallagher v Church of Jesus Christ of Latter Day Saints [2008] UKHL
   56, [2008] 1 WLR 1852 343
Geddes v Geddes 1993 SLT 494 56
Gibbs v Rae [1998] AC 786. 42
Girvan v Inverness Farmers Dairy 1998 SC (HL) 1 33
Gray's (Lord) Motion [2002] 1 AC 124, 2000 SC (HL) 46 95
Gregg v Scott [2005] UKHL 2, [2005] 2 AC 176. . . . . 223, 229, 230
Hall (Arthur J S) & Co v Simons [2002] 1 AC 615 110
Hamilton v Al-Fayed [2001] 1 AC 395. 93
Harley v McDonald [2001] UKPC 18, [2001] 2 AC 678. 121
Heaton v AXA Equity and Law Life Assurance Society plc [2002]
   UKHL 15, [2002] 2 AC 329. 146
Herd v Clyde Helicopters Ltd [1997] AC 534, 1997 SC (HL) 86 19
Heritable Reversionary Co Ltd v Millar (1891) 18 R 1166 22
Hunter v Canary Wharf Ltd [1997] AC 655 8–9
Inland Revenue Comrs v William Grant & Sons Distillers Ltd [2007]
   UKHL 15, 2007 SC (HL) 105, [2007] 1 WLR 1448 293
Jameel v Wall Street Journal Europe [2006] UKHL 44, [2007]
   AC 359. 273
Jameson v CEGB [2000] 1 AC 455. 146–47
Jaroo v Attorney General of Trinidad and Tobago [2002] UKPC 5,
   [2002] 1 AC 871 141

K v Craig 1999 SC (HL) 1 63
Kearney v HM Advocate [2006] UKPC D1, 2006 SC (PC) 1 261
King v Bristow Helicopters Ltd, Morris v KLM Royal Dutch Airlines
 [2002] UKHL 7, 2002 SC (HL) 59, [2002] 2 AC 628. . . . . . . 142, 143
Kirin-Amgen Inc v Hoechst Marion Roussel Ltd [2004] UKHL 46,
 [2005] 1 All ER 667 221–22
Kleinwort Benson Ltd v Lincoln City Council [1999] 2 AC
 349 . . . . 48, 50, 52–53, 60, 65
Kuwait Airways Corporation v Iraqi Airways Co (Nos 4 and 5) [2003]
 UKHL 19, [2002] 2 AC 883 . . . . 142, 145

Lafarge Redland Aggregates Ltd v Shephard Hill Civil Engineering Ltd
 [2000] 1 WLR 1621 108
Leeds City Council v Price and Others [2006] UKHL 10, [2006]
 2 AC 465. 260
Little v Little 1990 SLT 784 56
Louca v Public Prosecutor, Bielefeld, Germany [2009] UKSC 4, [2009]
 1 WLR 2550 351
Lutchumun v Director-General of the Mauritius Revenue Authority
 [2008] UKPC 53, [2009] STC 444. 351

MacCormick v Lord Advocate 1953 SC 396 374
McDonald v HM Advocate [2008] UKPC 46, 2008 SLT 993 349
MacDonald v Ministry of Defence [2003] UKHL 34, [2003] ICR 937,
 2003 SC (HL) 35 (*sub nom* Advocate General v MacDonald) 172
McFarlane v MacFarlane, *see* Miller v Miller
McFarlane v Tayside Health Board [2000] 2 AC 59, 2000
 SC (HL) 1 . . . . 87, 88
McGhee v National Coal Board 1973 SC (HL) 37, [1973] 1 WLR 1 165
Mackie v HM Advocate 1994 JC 132 . . . . 45, 47
Mann v Secretary of State for Employment [1999] 1 ICR 898. 65
Matthew v State of Trinidad and Tobago [2004] UKPC 33, [2005]
 1 AC 433. . . . . 213, 214
Matthews v Kent and Medway Towns Fire Authority [2006] UKHL 8,
 [2006] ICR 365. 263
Matthews v Ministry of Defence [2003] UKHL 4, [2003] 1 AC 1163 . . . 171
Mayhew of Twysden's (Lord) Motion [2002] 1 AC 109 95
Melanesian Mission Trust Board v Australian Mutual Provident
 Society (New Zealand) [1996] UKPC 53 14
Melville Dundas Ltd v George Wimpey UK Ltd [2007] UKHL 18, 2007
 SC (HL) 116, [2007] 1 WLR 1136 293
Millar v Dickson [2001] UKPC D4, 2002 SC (PC) 30, [2002] 1 WLR
 1615 138
Miller v Miller, McFarlane v McFarlane [2006] UKHL 24, [2006]
 2 AC 618. 263
Mills v HM Advocate [2002] UKPC D2, 2003 SC (PC) 1, [2004]
 1 AC 441. 158

Index of Cases 391

Mills (No 2) v HM Advocate [2002] UKPC D2, 2003 SC (PC) 1,
    [2004] 1 AC 441. 164
Mitchell v Glasgow City Council [2009] UKHL 11, 2009 SC 21 366
Moncrieff v Jamieson [2007] UKHL 42, 2008 SC (HL) 1
    . . . . 307, 308, 314
Montgomery v HM Advocate [2003] 1 AC 641, 2001 SC (PC) 1. 110
Morgan Guaranty Trust Co of New York v Lothian Regional Council
    1995 SC 151. 48
Moses v The State [1997] AC 53. 58

O'Brien's Curator Bonis v British Steel plc 1991 SC 315 340
O'Hara v Chief Constable of the RUC [1997] AC 286 . . . . 4, 6, 16

Pantmaenog Timber Co Ltd, In re [2003] UKHL 49, [2004]
    1 AC 158. 185
Pearce v Governing Body of Mayfield Secondary School [2003]
    UKHL 34, [2003] ICR 937. 172
Percy v Board of National Mission of the Church of Scotland [2005]
    UKHL 73, 2006 SC (HL) 1 263
Pickford v Imperial Chemical Industries plc [1998] ICR 673 50
Pirelli Cable Holdings NV v Inland Revenue Comrs [2006] UKHL 4,
    [2006] 1 WLR 400. . . . . 259, 261
Porter v Magill [2001] UKHL 67, [2002] 2 AC 357 . . . . 73, 140
Pratt v Attorney-General for Jamaica [1994] 2 AC 1 59
Preston v Wolverhampton Healthcare NHS Trust (No 3) [2006]
    UKHL 134, [2006] ICR 606. 265

R v A (No 2) [2001] UKHL 25, [2002] 1 AC 45. . . . . 123, 127, 129
R v Bournewood Community and Mental Health NHS Trust, ex p L
    [1999] 1 AC 458. 53
R v Bow Street Metropolitan Stipendiary Magistrate, ex p Pinochet
    Ugarte [2000] 1 AC 61. 67
R v Bow Street Metropolitan Stipendiary Magistrate, ex p Pinochet
    Ugarte (No 2) [2000] 1 AC 119. . . . . 71, 141
R v Bow Street Metropolitan Stipendiary Magistrate, ex p Pinochet
    Ugarte (No 3) [2000] 1 AC 147. . . . . 76–77, 106
R v Burt & Adams Ltd [1999] AC 247. 47
R v Chief Constable of Sussex, ex p International Trader's Ferry Ltd
    [1999] 2 AC 418. 54
R v Director of Public Prosecutions, ex p Kebilene [2000]
    2 AC 326. 87
R v Gough [1993] AC 646 . . . . 72, 141
R v Governor of Belmarsh Prison, ex p Gilligan [2001] 1 AC 84 93
R v Governors of Brockhill Prison, ex p Evans (No 2) [2001]
    2 AC 19 105
R v HM Advocate [2002] UKPC D3, 2003 SC (PC) 21. . . . .
                164–64, 167–68, 194, 195, 205–06, 318

R v Immigration Appeal Tribunal, ex p Shah [1999] 2 AC 629 79
R v Kansal (No 2) [2001] UKHL 62, [2002] 2 AC 69 . . . . . . 137, 138, 141
R v Lambert [2001] UKHL 37, [2002] 2 AC
  545. . . . . .127, 128, 129, 137, 141
R v Manchester Stipendiary Magistrate, ex p Granada
  Television Ltd [2001] 1 AC 300. 102
R v Mills [1998] AC 382 25
R v Myers [1998] AC 124. 32
R v Sargent [2001] UKHL 54, [2003] 1 AC 347 136
R v Secretary of State for Scotland 1999 SC (HL) 17 63
R v Secretary of State for the Home Department, ex p Launder [1997]
  1 WLR 839. . . . . 28, 29
R v Secretary of State for the Home Department, ex p Pierson [1998]
  AC 539. . . . . 28, 30, 34
R v Secretary of State for the Home Department, ex p Venables [1998]
  AC 407. . . . . 21, 29
R v Secretary of State for Transport, ex p Factortame Ltd (No 5) [2000]
  1 AC 524. 87
R v Shayler [2002] UKHL 11, [2003] 1 AC 247 . . . . .144, 145
R (A) v Croydon London Borough Council [2009] UKSC 8, [2009]
  1 WLR 2557. 382
R (Amin) v Secretary of State for the Home Department [2003] UKHL
  51, [2004] 1 AC 653. 193
R (BA (Nigeria)) v Secretary of State for the Home Department [2009]
  UKSC 7, [2010] 1 AC 444. 384
R (Barclay) v Lord Chancellor and Secretary of State for Justice [2009]
  UKSC 3, [2010] 1 AC 464. 380
R (Countryside Alliance) v Attorney General [2007] UKHL 52, [2008]
  AC 719. 317
R (European Roma Rights Centre) v Immigration Officer at Prague
  Airport [2004] UKHL 55, [2005] 2 AC 1 229
R (Gentle) v Prime Minister [2008] UKHL 20, [2008] AC 1356 . . . . 331, 336
R (Gillan) v Commissioner of Police of the Metropolis [2006]
  UKHL 12, [2006] 2 AC 307. 263
R (Heffernan) v Rent Service [2008] UKHL 58, [2008]
  1 WLR 1702. 340
R (Hilali) v Governor of Whitemoor Prison [2008] UKHL 3, [2008]
  AC 805. 320
R (Jackson) v Attorney General [2005] UKHL 56, [2006]
  1 AC 262. . . . . 249, 250–52, 255
R (L) v Commissioner of Police of the Metropolis [2009] UKSC 3,
  [2010] 1 AC 410. 380
R (McCann) v Crown Court at Manchester [2002] UKHL 39, [2003]
  1 AC 787. 157
R (O'Byrne) v Secretary of State for the Environment, Transport and
  the Regions [2002] UKHL 45, [2002] 1 WLR 3250. 163

Index of Cases 393

R (Pretty) v Director of Public Prosecutions [2001] UKHL 61, [2002]
    1 AC 800. . . . . 138, 140
R (Purdy) v Director of Public Prosecutions [2009] UKHL 45, [2010]
    1 AC 345. 385
R (Quark Fishing Ltd) v Secretary of State for Foreign and
    Commonwealth Affairs [2005] UKHL 57, [2006] 1 AC 529 248
R (Rottman) v Commissioner of Police for the Metropolis [2002]
    UKHL 20, [2002] 2 AC 692 144
R (Walker) v Secretary of State for Justice (Parole Board intervening)
    [2009] UKHL 22, [2010] 1 AC 553 363
R (West) v Parole Board [2005] UKHL 1, [2005] 1 WLR 350. 229
R (Yogothas) v Secretary of State for the Home Department [2002]
    UKHL 36, [2003] 1 AC 920. 160
RB (Algeria) v Secretary of State for the Home Department [2009]
    UKHL 10, [2010] 1 AC 110 . . . . 355, 356, 366, 369
Real Honest Investment Ltd v Attorney General (Hong Kong) [1997]
    UKPC 34. 31
Redrow Homes Ltd v Bett Brothers plc 1998 SC (HL) 64. 41
Rees v Darlington Memorial Hospital NHS Trust [2003] UKHL 52,
    [2004] 1 AC 309 193
Reid v Secretary of State for Scotland 1999 SC (HL) 17 91
Reinwood Ltd v L Brown & Sons Ltd [2008] UKHL 12, [2008]
    1 WLR 696. 326
Rey v Government of Switzerland [1999] 1 AC 54 49
Reynolds v Times Newspapers Ltd [2001] 1 AC 127. . . . . 87, 88
Rhys-Harper v Relaxion Group plc [2003] UKHL 33, [2003] ICR 486. . . . 171
Ruddy and Others v Procurators Fiscal of Perth and Aberdeen [2006]
    UKPC D2, 2006 SC (PC) 22 261
Robertson v Fife Council [2002] UKHL 35, 2002 SC (HL) 145. 158
Rodney District Council v Attorney General (New Zealand) [2002]
    UKPC 47. 160
Roodal v The State [2003] UKPC 78, [2005] 1 AC 328 . . . . . 205, 213, 214
Royal Brompton Hospital NHS Trust v Hammond [2002] UKHL 14,
    [2002] 1 WLR 1397 146

Sammut v Manzi [2008] UKPC 58 . . . . 354, 357
Sanatan Dharma Maha Sabha of Trinidad and Tobago Inc v Attorney
    General of Trinidad and Tobago [2009] UKPC 17 365
Sanderson v McManus 1997 SC (HL) 55 16
Scott v HM Advocate, *see* DS v HM Advocate
Secretary of State for the Home Department v AF (No 3) [2009]
    UKHL 28, [2010] 2 AC 269 366–67
Secretary of State for the Home Department v MB [2007] UKHL 46,
    [2008] AC 440 369
Semco Salvage and Marine Pte Ltd v Lancer Navigation Co Ltd
    [1997] AC 455 . . . . 5, 31

Shamoon v Chief Constable of the RUC [2003] UKHL 11, [2003]
    ICR 337 . . . . 164, 169, 171, 174
Sharp v Thomson 1995 SC 455 22
Sharp v Thomson 1997 SC (HL) 66 . . . . 8, 22, 201–02, 203
Shimizu (UK) Ltd v Westminster City Council [1997]
    1 WLR 168. . . . . 10, 15
Simmers v Innes [2008] UKHL 24, 2008 SC (HL) 137 334
Smith v Bank of Scotland 1997 SC (HL) 111 31
Smith v Lees 1997 JC 73 . . . . 21, 31
Snell v Beadle [2001] UKPC 5, [2001] 2 AC 304 118
Société Alleck & Cie v The Indian Ocean International Bank [2008]
    UKPC 64. 351
Society of Lloyds v Robinson, on appeal from Lord Napier and Ettrick
    v R F Kershaw Ltd [1999] 1 WLR 756 79
Somerville v Scottish Ministers [2007] UKHL 44, 2008
    SC (HL) 45 . . . . 307–08, 314
Spiers v Ruddy [2007] UKPC D2, 2009 SC (PC) 1 . . . . 205, 318
Stack v Dowden [2007] UKHL 17, [2007] 2 AC 432 290
Stafford v The State [1999] 1 WLR 2026 58
Starrs v Procurator Fiscal, Linlithgow 2000 JC 208 98
Strathclyde Regional Council v Wallace 1998 SC (HL) 72 41

T, Petitioner 1997 SLT 724. 10
Three Rivers District Council v Bank of England (No 3) [2001]
    UKHL 16, [2003] 2 AC 1 . . . . 102–03, 121
Three Rivers District Council v Bank of England [2004] UKHL 48,
    [2005] 1 AC 610. 223
Total Gas Marketing Ltd v Arco British Ltd [1998] 2 Lloyds Rep 209. . . . 50
Total Network SL v Revenue and Customs Comrs [2008] UKHL 19,
    [2008] AC 1174 . . . . 323–24, 330
TRM Copy Centres (UK) Ltd v Lanwall Services Ltd [2009] UKHL
    35, [2009] 1 WLR 1375 372

Wallis v Wallis 1990 SLT 784 56
Watson v The Queen [2004] UKPC 34, [2005] 1 AC 472 . . . . . . .213, 214
Whalley v Lord Advocate [2007] UKHL 53, 2007 SC (HL) 107 317
Wilson v First Country Trust [2003] UKHL 40, [2004]
    1 AC 816. . . . . .175–76, 181

Zalewska v Department for Social Development [2008] UKHL 67, [2008]
    1 WLR 2602. . . . . 347, 356
ZT (Kosovo) v Secretary of State for the Home Department [2009]
    UKHL 6, [2009] 1 WLR 348. . . . . 357, 360

Index of Names

Abernethy, Lord (Alastair Cameron), 17, 314
Ackner, Lord, 20, 184–85
Adams, Edward, 63, 215
Adams, Gerry, MP, 178
Ahmad, Aysha (judicial assistant), 119, 131
Ailes, Victoria (judicial assistant), 303
Airlie, Lady, 155, 276, 348
Airlie, The Earl of, 120, 157
Alderson, Reevel (BBC Scotland), 189
Alexandra, HRH Princess, The Hon Lady Ogilvy, 276
Al-Fayed, Mohamed, 93
Al-Khalifa, Hamad, HRH King of Bahrain, 243
Allan, Alex, 237, 264, 266, 280, 288
Allan, Douglas, Sheriff, 91, 112–13, 311
Allan, Mrs Helen, 113, 311
Allanbridge, Lord (Ian Stewart), 45, 283
Ancram, Michael, MP, 238
Andenas, Dr Mads, 132
Andrew, HRH The Duke of York, 15, 149
Angiolini, Elish (Solicitor General for Scotland; Lord Advocate), 159, 227, 279, 299–300
Annand, David, 190
Anne, HRH The Princess Royal, 4, 92, 149–50, 175, 290–91, 309
Arbuthnott, John (Principal and Vice-Chancellor, Strathclyde University), 43, 45, 47, 51, 55, 57, 83, 92, 99, 227
Arbuthnott, Elinor, 51, 83, 99
Arden, Mary, Lady Justice, 251, 273, 284, 364, 378, 384
Arfon-Jones, Elisabeth, 316
Armati, David (CMJA President), 55, 112, 114, 313
Artemides, Christos (President, Supreme Court of Cyprus), 258
Artemis, Petros, 258
Arthur, Sir Gavyn (Lord Mayor of London), 191

Ashton of Upholland, Baroness, 246, 317
Ashworth, Andrew, Professor, 334
Auld, Robin, Lord Justice, 6, 30, 37, 54–55
Avery, Rachel (judicial assistant), 246, 263

Baglai, Marat (Chairman, Russian Constitutional Court), 49
Bailhache, Philip (Bailiff of Jersey), 312
Bain, Sergeant, 321
Baker, Scott, Lord Justice, 355
Ball, Kate, 159–60
Banda, Dr Hastings (President of Malawi), 93, 108, 175
Banda, Richard (Chief Justice of Malawi), 114
Banner, Charles (judicial assistant), 246, 263
Barak, Aaron (Chief Justice of Israel), 123–25, 331
Barak, Ehud (Prime Minister of Israel), 122, 124
Barrett, Oliver, 314
Bartole, Sergio, Professor, 297
Bates, Alan (judicial assistant), 226
Beale, Hugh, Professor, 132
Beaton, Peter, 200
Beckett, John (Solicitor General for Scotland), 279, 300
Beckham, David and Victoria, 198
Beinisch, Dorit (Justice, Supreme Court of Israel), 125
Beith, Alan, MP, 203
Beloff, Michael, 93, 95–96, 356, 359
Berlins, Marcel, 332
Berry, William, 314
Biabella, Dr Maria, 296
Bile, Franco (President, Italian Constitutional Court), 296–97
Bin Laden, Osama, 132
Bingham of Cornhill, Lady, 232
Bingham of Cornhill, Lord, 6, 13, 20, 30, 33, 41, 62–3, 68, 104, 106, 109–10, 117–19, 121, 125, 127–31, 135–36, 138, 140,

Bingham of Cornhill, Lord – *contd*
    142–45, 159–63, 165, 169, 171, 174,
    184–88, 190, 193–96, 198–99, 201–07, 209,
    211, 213–17, 219–20, 233, 227–32, 234–37,
    239, 241–42, 244–47, 250–51, 255–63,
    265–66, 274, 277–80, 283–84, 287, 289,
    292, 294, 296, 298–99, 301–03, 306–08,
    316–21, 325–27, 330–32, 335–37, 340–41,
    346–50, 352–57, 360, 362, 364–65, 369,
    374
Birks, Peter, Professor, 132
Black, Robert, Professor, 66
Blackadder, Elizabeth, 99
Blackmore, Sasha (judicial assistant), 277
Blair, Euan, 173
Blair, Michael, 354–55
Blair, Robin, 154–55
Blair, Tony, MP (Prime Minister), 26, 28, 73,
    126, 132, 152, 172–73, 176–77, 179, 192,
    209, 218, 222, 238–40, 248, 279, 284, 298,
    306, 331
Blake, Nicholas, 213
Bland, Sir Christopher, 11
Blatch, Lady, 20
Bledisloe, Viscount, 231
Blundell, David (judicial assistant), 197
Blunkett, David, MP, 185–86, 198, 228, 231
Boateng, Paul, MP, 238
Booth, Cherie, 26–27, 172, 179
Boothroyd, Betty (Speaker, House of
    Commons), 9, 150
Bottomley, Peter, MP, 203
Bovey, Mungo, 294
Bowen, Edward, Sheriff Principal, 103
Bowyer, James, 320–21
Boyd of Duncansby, Lord (Lord Advocate),
    28, 105, 126, 189–90, 208, 261, 273, 279
Bracadale, Lord (Alastair Campbell), 244
Bradley, Tony, Professor, 304
Brand, Fritz, J (Supreme Court of Appeal of
    South Africa), 378
Bremner, Rory, 377
Brennan, Lord, 211
Brewer, Dr Karen (Director General, CMJA),
    112, 114
Bridge of Harwich, Lord, 104
Brodie, Philip, Lord 272
Brooke, Henry, Lord Justice, 167, 311–12
Brooke, Lady, 311
Brooke of Sutton Mandeville, Lord, 167

Brown, Chester, 264
Brown, Craig, 99
Brown, Gerry, 217
Brown, Gordon, MP (Prime Minister), 284,
    306, 373, 377
Brown, Thomas (judicial assistant), 159
Brown of Eaton-under-Heywood, Lord, 193,
    206–08, 212, 221, 227, 232, 258–60,
    262–63, 265, 275, 284, 287, 294, 301–02,
    324–25, 327, 331, 337, 347, 353, 355, 357,
    359–60, 362–63, 366–7, 371–72, 379–80,
    382, 384
Browne, Sir Stephen, 55
Browne-Wilkinson, Lord, 7, 10, 15, 21–22,
    29–30, 41, 44, 48–49, 51–55, 62, 64–65,
    70–81, 84, 88, 93, 95, 102–04, 106, 108–11,
    117, 119, 141, 199, 203
Brownlie, Ian, Professor, 72, 76
Bryde, Brun-Otto, Professor, 304
Buchanan, John and Mary, 316
Buquicchio, Gianni (Venice Commission),
    243
Burne, Anna (judicial assistant), 197
Burton, Michael, Mr Justice, 198
Burton, Simon, 340
Bush, George W (US President), 122, 132,
    173, 176, 222, 240
Butler of Brockwell, Lord, 88, 222
Butler-Sloss, Elizabeth, Lady Justice, 200
Buxton, Richard, Lord Justice, 37
Byatt, Marilyn, 4, 6, 13, 20, 26, 55, 63, 76
Byron, Dennis (President, Caribbean Court of
    Justice), 114

Calvert-Smith, David, Mr Justice, 295
Cameron, David, MP, 377
Cameron of Lochbroom, Lord, 168, 283, 314,
    375
Callaghan of Cardiff, Lord, 152
Campbell, Alistair, 209
Campbell, Anthony, Lord Justice, 48, 273,
    319, 326, 342
Campbell, Anthony and Gail, 342
Campbell, Colin (Lord Malcolm), 138, 168, 293
Campbell, Glenn (BBC Scotland), 189
Campbell, Menzies, MP, and Elspeth, 116
Campbell, Niall, 91
Canavan, Dennis, MSP, 86, 345
Canivet, Guy (President, Cour de Cassation),
    199

Index of Names

Fergusson, Robert, 190
Ferrers, The Earl, 383
Finlay, Johan, 112
Fitzgerald, Edward, 75, 213, 356
Flood, Elizabeth, 94
Foley, Hugh (Principal Clerk, Court of Session), 17–18, 24, 43
Foot, Stephen, 324, 328, 336, 381
Forbes, Alan, 57
Ford, Anna (BBC TV presenter), 14
Forsyth, John, 40
Forsyth, Michael, MP (Secretary of State for Scotland), 3, 5, 9, 13n, 15, 26, 126, 154, 172
Forsyth, Susan, 9, 154
Forte, Angelo, Professor, 65
Francis, Indira (Registrar, Court of Appeal of The Bahamas), 233, 323, 352, 372
Franks, Tommy, General (US Army), 177
Fraser, Sandy (portrait painter), 168, 174
Fraser of Carmyllie, Lord, 69, 105, 108, 168, 257, 368, 386
Fraser of Tullybelton, Lord, 1
Freeman, Kylie, 309, 381
Friel, Edward, Professor, 183

Gale, Stuart, 202
Gallagher, Jim, 225
Gallie, Phil, MP, 12, 26
Gane, Christopher, Professor, 48
Ganpatsingh, J (Court of Appeal of The Bahamas), 233
Garden, Graeme, 112
Gardiner, Rev Neil (minister, Canongate Kirk), 342–43
Garnier, Edward, MP, 269, 382
Gault, Thomas, J (Court of Appeal of New Zealand), 42
Gerstenberg, Frank (Principal, George Watson's College), 113
Gibb, Frances, 187–88, 327
Gibson, Nicholas (judicial assistant), 303
Gibson, Peter, Lord Justice, 14, 33, 34, 379
Gibson of Market Rasen, Baroness, 217
Gill, Lord (Lord Justice Clerk), 17, 133, 135–36, 138, 140, 190, 242, 252–54, 256–59, 270–71, 283, 285, 291, 294, 358
Gilligan, Andrew (BBC reporter), 192, 209
Girvan, Paul, Lord Justice, 272
Gleeson, Murray (Chief Justice of Australia), 92

Glidewell, Sir Iain, 86
Gloucester, HRH The Duke and Duchess of, 166–67
Goff of Chieveley, Lord, 4–5, 8, 16, 21, 25, 29, 30, 33, 37, 41–43, 45, 47–49, 51–52, 54, 56, 58, 60, 65, 70, 72, 75–80, 84, 119, 132–33, 141
Golding, Baroness, 218
Goldsmith, Lord (Attorney General), 128, 176, 223, 228, 241, 250, 273, 331
Gönez, Arpád (President of Hungary), 85
Goodhart, Lord, 130, 185, 188, 211, 218
Goodwin Gill, Guy, 229
Gordon, Sir Gerald, 378
Gordon of Strathblane, Lord, 144, 358, 361, 368
Gorman, Penelope (judicial assistant), 340
Grant, David, 268–69
Gray, Lord, 96–97, 178
Greenwood, Christopher, Professor, 76, 165
Grenfell, Lord, 94
Grieve, Dominic, MP, 382
Griffiths, Lord, 15
Griffiths, Nigel, MSP, 259, 270
Grimmerson, Dr Tony, 291
Gross, Peter, Mr Justice, 295
Grossart, Sir Angus, 28, 44, 51, 120
Ground, Richard (Chief Justice of Bermuda), 311–12
Gubbay, Anthony (Chief Justice of Zimbabwe), 136
Guest, Lord, 1
Guigou, Elisabeth (La Garde des Sceaux; French Minister of Justice), 38, 40
Guthrie, James, 281
Guyomer, Mattias (Conseil d'Etat), 272
Gwynne-Jones, Peter (Garter King of Arms), 23

Haddow, Christopher, 334
Hague, William, MP, 69, 128
Hajducki, Andrew, 158
Hale of Richmond, Baroness, 159, 193, 201, 206–08, 213, 216, 219–20, 228, 230, 232, 235, 237, 239, 246, 253, 256, 260, 264, 277, 280, 287, 290, 294–95, 303, 308–10, 313, 315–16, 320–21, 324, 328, 336–37, 340, 347, 353, 356, 358–60, 363, 365–66, 369, 371–72, 379, 381, 383–84
Hall, Sir Burton (Chief Justice of The Bahamas), 233

Hall, Very Rev John (Dean of Westminster), 315
Hambledon, David, Professor, 183
Hamill, Hamish, 111
Hamilton, Lady, 268, 271
Hamilton, Lord (Lord President), 252–54, 256–59, 265–68, 270–71, 273, 283, 285, 294, 377
Hamilton, Neil, 93
Hamnett, Andrew (Principal and Vice-Chancellor, Strathclyde University), 182, 183, 245, 282, 290, 300, 338, 345, 358, 367, 376
Hamnett, Suzanne, 182, 291, 338
Hancock, Matthew (judicial assistant), 303, 333, 340, 347, 354, 357
Harcastle, Sally, 40
Hardie, Lord (Lord Advocate), 28, 48, 91, 97, 103–04, 133, 153–54
Harman, Harriet, MP, 283
Harms, Louis (Deputy President, Supreme Court of Appeal of South Africa), 378
Harries, Rt Rev Richard (Bishop of Oxford), 88, 292
Harry, HRH Prince, 100, 149
Hastie, Margaret, 191, 357
Hayter, Paul, 288, 298, 301–02
Heath, Sir Edward, 152
Higgins, Malachy, Lord Justice, 377
Higgins, Mr (Depute Clerk of Session), 285
Hillhouse, Russell, 10
Hills, Graham, Professor, 227
Hind, Rt Rev John (Bishop of Chichester), 384
Hobhouse of Woodborough, Lord, 54, 58, 64, 68, 74, 88, 108–10, 121, 136, 142–43, 172, 182, 195, 202, 206, 211, 238
Hodge, Patrick, Lord, 202, 224–25, 252, 270, 314, 377
Hoffmann, Lady, 68, 184, 373
Hoffmann, Lord, 8–9, 23, 30, 47–49, 52–53, 56, 59, 60n, 62, 64n, 65, 67–70, 72–77, 80, 88, 102, 105–06, 110–11, 119, 142, 144, 159, 163, 169, 171, 184–85, 194–95, 202, 205, 211–15, 221–22, 227–28, 230–31, 234, 236, 241, 255–56, 263, 266, 274–76, 278, 280, 284, 289–93, 299, 301–02, 307–08, 310, 317, 319, 326–27, 329–30, 332, 335, 337, 340–41, 343, 349, 355, 360–61, 364, 369, 371–74, 377
Hogg of Cumbernauld, Lord, 161
Holland, Sir Anthony and Kay, 355
Hollis, Keith, HHJ, 112, 311
Holloway, Rt Rev Richard (Bishop of Edinburgh), 14, 99, 287
Holmes, Kelly (athlete), 238
Holton, Yvonne (herald painter), 309, 313, 315, 371
Honoré, Tony, Professor, 334
Hood, Jimmy, MP, 94
Hood, Neil, Professor, 197
Hoon, Geoff, MP, 152, 283
Hope, Rt Rev Dr David (Archbishop of York), 34
Hope, James (son), 310
Hope, Mary (wife), 3, 5, 10–13, 15, 17, 19, 21, 23–25, 27, 32–33, 37–38, 41, 43–45, 47, 50–51, 53, 56–58, 61–63, 76, 82, 84–86, 95, 99, 102, 104–05, 107–08, 110, 112–14, 177, 122–26, 131, 133–34, 145–46, 153–54, 156–57, 159, 163, 165–68, 182, 184, 188, 191–93, 196, 198, 200, 211, 218–20, 223–27, 229, 232–33, 245, 248–50, 254, 258, 260, 268, 273, 275, 278, 284, 290–91, 302, 306, 308, 310, 316, 318–19, 321–22, 333–34, 340–41, 343–48, 352, 354–55, 358–59, 364, 367, 376–79, 381, 385–86
Hope, William (son), 13, 20, 50, 60, 76, 89, 147, 157, 343–44
Houston, John, 99
Howard, Michael, MP, 13n, 14, 26, 28, 201, 238
Howard, Wendy, 272
Howe of Aberavon, Lord, 215, 302–03
Howell, John, 229, 383
Howieson, Dr Stirling, 291
Hoyt, William, J (Bloody Sunday Inquiry), 178
Hughes, Luke, 328
Hunt of King's Heath, Lord, 306
Hunter, Archie (Convenor, Strathclyde University Court), 212, 282, 300
Hunter, John (judicial assistant), 226
Hurd of Westwell, Lord, 88
Hussein, Saddam (President of Iraq), 73, 132, 176–80, 192, 209
Hussey, Sir Marmaduke, 11
Hutton, Lady Mary, 33, 131
Hutton, Lady Lindy, 184, 219

Index of Names

Hutton, Lord, 6, 25, 33, 42, 49, 54–55, 59, 63–65, 70–72, 75–79, 84, 102–03, 109–10, 118, 127, 131, 137, 141, 143–44, 160, 169, 184, 192–94, 197, 206–07, 209, 218–19

Iglesias, Rodriguez (President, European Court of Justice), 62
Ingraham, Hubert (Prime Minister of The Bahamas), 322
Irons, Norman, 87
Irvine of Lairg, Lady, 219
Irvine of Lairg, Lord (Lord Chancellor), 28, 30, 33, 54, 56, 62–63, 67, 70, 72, 76, 84, 104, 106, 118, 125–26, 128, 131, 134, 142, 151–52, 159, 163, 185, 190, 198, 204, 219, 320, 348
Isaac, Georgina, 317, 353
Ivory, Brian, 53, 120

Jackson, Gordon, 45, 189
Jacobs, Francis (Advocate-General, European Court of Justice), 62, 159
Jamieson, Iain, 61
Janu, Dr Ivana, 297
Jauncey of Tullichettle, Lady, 314
Jauncey of Tullichettle, Lord, 1, 22, 52, 64–65, 76, 84, 119, 126, 151, 179, 201, 314, 342
Jay, Sir Michael (British Ambassador to France), 39
Jay of Paddington, Baroness, 96, 128, 152
Jefri, Prince of Bahrain 285–86, 308
John Paul II, Pope, 239–40
Johnson, Roy (Convenor, Strathclyde University Court), 51, 57, 159, 183
Johnston, Alan, Lord, 17, 100, 130, 168, 258, 283, 341, 343
Johnston, Lady Anthea, 341–43
Johnston, Brian, 342
Johnston, David, 52
Johnston, Laura (judicial assistant), 197
Jones, Alun, 72, 76
Jospin, Lionel (Prime Minister of France), 38, 40
Judge, Igor, Lord Justice, 20, 241, 247, 295, 346, 348, 363–64, 377, 379, 381, 384
Judge, Lady Judith, 348, 378

Kaufman, Gerald, MP, 88
Keen, Richard, 95–96
Keene, David, Lord Justice, 37, 39, 138, 199
Keith, Brendan (Clerk of the Judicial Office), 194, 236–37, 241, 244–45, 266, 280–81, 288, 290, 295–96, 298–99, 301–02, 304, 307, 315, 321, 324–25, 328, 333, 341, 344, 347, 349–51, 353, 362, 365, 381, 384
Keith, Hugo, 194
Keith of Kinkel, Lady, 8
Keith of Kinkel, Lord, 1, 4n, 8, 22, 65, 108, 126, 179, 386
Kelbie, David, Sheriff, 301
Kelly, Barbara, 78
Kelly, Dr David, 192, 209, 222
Kennedy, Paul, Lord Justice, 48, 62, 350
Kentridge, Sir Sydney, 14, 205, 250, 330, 357
Kerr, Andrew, 51, 112, 133
Kerr, Bruce, Sheriff Principal, 3, 103, 133
Kerr, Robin, 23
Kerr of Tonaghmore, Lord, 273, 284, 360–61, 364, 384
Kerse, Christopher, 76, 107
Kingham, Jacqueline (judicial assistant), 340
Kintore, Lord, 98, 178
Kirk, Hugh, 316
Kirkwood, Ian, Lord, 283
Kitchen, David, 221
Knox, Peter, 213, 281
Korner, Joanna, 295

Lacey, Very Rev Dr David (Moderator, Church of Scotland), 245, 269
Lamb, Robin (British Embassy, France), 242
Lambert, Jane, 311
Lambert, Michael (CMJA), 112–14, 162, 311–12
Lamont of Lerwick, Lord, 80
Lang of Monkton, Lord, 26, 154, 196
Larsson, Henrik (footballer), 244
Lawler, Mrs Pat, 101
Lawrence, Kate, 315
Lawrence, George, Lord Trevethin and Oaksey, 372
Laws, John, Lord Justice 62
Lawson of Blaby, Lord, 383
Le Quesne, Sir Godfray, 213
Le Sueur, Andrew, 324, 328
Leaver, Jeremy, 334
Lee, Kuan Yew (Prime Minister of Singapore), 92
Leeming, Dorothy, 286
Legg, Sir Thomas, 6, 30, 37, 227, 352

Leggatt, Andrew, Lord Justice, 117, 141
Lester of Herne Hill, Lord, 130, 211, 229
Levene, Lord (Lord Mayor of London), 85
Lewis, Carole, J (Supreme Court of Appeal of South Africa), 378
Leyden, Patrick, 190
L'Hereux-Dubé, Claire, J (Supreme Court of Canada), 59
Liddell, Helen, MP (Secretary of State for Scotland), 126, 177, 244
Lindsay, Jackie, 381
Linklater, Magnus, 86, 90, 99, 197
Linklater, Veronica, Baroness, 99, 133, 144, 161, 287
Livesay, Admiral Sir Michael, 9
Livingston, Fraser (Convenor, Strathclyde University Court), 376
Lloyd, Timothy, Mr Justice, 132
Lloyd of Berwick, Lady, 14
Lloyd of Berwick, Lord, 5–6, 8–11, 14–15, 29, 33, 47–49, 53–54, 56, 59, 63–64, 68, 74–76, 119, 137, 141, 147, 184–85, 206, 211–12, 231, 306–07, 374
Lloyd-Jones, David, 76
Lochhead, Liz, 57
Lockhart, Brian, Sheriff, 112–13, 115
Loudon, Euan, Brigadier, and Penny, 286
Lowry, Lord, 14
Luba, Jan, 335
Lunan, Very Rev Dr David (Moderator, Church of Scotland), 358
Lyne, Colin, 256
Lyon, John, 280, 301, 325

McAleese, Mary (President of Ireland), 291
McArthur, Bill (US astronaut), 376
McCall, Charles, 299, 301, 309, 329, 381
McCall Smith, Alexander, 286
McClure, Judith, 375
McCluskey, Lord, 3, 18, 46–47, 64, 97, 103, 230, 257
McConnell, Jack, MSP (First Minister of Scotland), 139, 162, 257–59, 300
McCormick, John (BBC Scotland), 83, 99
MacCormick, Sir Neil, 317, 373–74
McCoubray, Robin (judicial assistant), 159
McCulloch, Grant, 24
McDermott, Paul, 311
McDonald, Very Rev Dr Alan (Moderator, Church of Scotland), 292, 299

Macdonald, Very Rev Dr Finlay (Moderator, Church of Scotland), 159
McDonald, Jim, Professor (Principal and Vice-Chancellor, Strathclyde University), 358, 367, 375, 376
MacDonald, Margo, MSP, 189
Macdonald, Mary (Registrar, Judicial Committee of the Privy Council), 281, 321, 329, 350–51, 374
Macdonald, Roderick, 261
McDonald, Sheena (broadcaster), 10
McDonald of Tradeston, Lord, 368
McEachran, Colin, 7, 339
McEwan, Robin, Lord, 105
McFall, John, MP, 27, 269
Macfadyen, Donald, Lord, 133, 135, 337
McFarlane of Bearsden, Lord, 87
McGhie, James, Lord, 48
McGowan, Alan, Professor, 92, 191, 291
MacGregor, Neil, 44, 51, 272
McGuinness, Martin, MP, 178
McInnes, John, Sheriff Principal, 103
McIntosh, Sir Neil, 252, 254, 270, 319, 326
McIntosh of Haringey, Lord, 20, 27
Mackay of Ardbrecknish, Lord, 95, 122
Mackay of Clashfern, Lady, 204, 284, 306
Mackay of Clashfern, Lord (Lord Chancellor), 3, 5, 13, 19, 26, 43, 102–04, 109, 119–20, 126, 143, 150, 152–54, 158, 204, 245, 257, 271, 284, 306, 320, 332, 348
Mackay of Drumadoon, Lord (Lord Advocate), 13, 17, 26, 95, 97, 105, 126, 168, 258
McKendrick, Ewan, Professor, 65
Mackersie, Andrew, 160, 277
Mackie of Benshie, Lord, 144
McLachlin, Beverley (Chief Justice, Supreme Court of Canada), 117
MacLean, Ranald, Lord, 119, 283
McLeish, Henry, MSP (First Minister of Scotland), 66, 116, 120, 134, 138–40
McLellan, Rev Andrew, 287
Maclennan of Rogart, Lord, 368
McMenamin, Frances, 358, 376
Macmillan, Rt Rev Gilleasbuig (minister of St Giles), 15
McMurdo, Helen, 161, 266, 268, 296, 315, 317, 320
McNair, Charles, 56
McNicoll, Iain, Professor, 245

Index of Names

McPartland, Noel, Sheriff, 199
Macphail, Iain, Sheriff, and Rosslyn, 134, 225
MacQueen, Hector, Professor, 123, 189, 303
Magee, Sir Ian, 316
McSherry, Michael, 121–22
Machin, David, 10
Major, Sir John, 128, 152, 201
Malleson, Kate, 328
Mance, Lord, 198, 251, 253, 256, 263, 265, 272, 275, 279, 281, 284, 287, 290, 293, 295, 307–10, 313, 315, 318, 320–24, 328, 336–38, 341, 345, 350–51, 353, 363–64, 366, 372, 381–82, 384
Mandelson, Peter, 73
Mansfield, Michael, MP, 25
Manson, Colin (Faculty officer), 61, 114
Mar and Kellie, Earl of, 10, 98
Margaret, HRH Princess, Countess of Snowdon, 148
Marnoch, Lord (Michael Bruce), 78
Martin, John, 183
Martin, Michael, MP (Speaker, House of Commons), 151, 153, 292
Martin, Roy (Dean of Faculty), 273, 285
Martin, Roy and Mrs, 188
Mason, Anthony (Chief Justice of Australia), 92
Massot, Jean (Conseil d'Etat), 37
Maxwell, Alan, 284
Mayer, Josef (Rector, Lodz University), 51
Mayhew of Twysden, Lord, 23, 96
Mbeki, Thabo (President of South Africa), 336
Meakin, Andrew and Lucy (daughter), 344
Miles, Robert, 372
Mill, Douglas (Secretary, The Law Society of Scotland), 24, 112
Miller, James and Mrs, 99
Miller, Rt Rev Dr John (Moderator, Church of Scotland), 155
Miller, Kenny, Professor, 227
Miller of Hendon, Baroness, 316
Millett, Lord, 6, 54, 65, 68, 74–81, 102, 108, 110–11, 118, 132, 143, 160, 169, 185, 193–95, 198, 205–06, 211, 232, 238
Milligan, Eric (Lord Provost of Edinburgh), 99, 108
Mills, Alan, Professor, 85
Milosovic, Slobodan (President of Yugoslavia), 81–82

Mitchell, Andrew, 50
Mitchell, Jonathan, 334
Mkandawire, Charles, 114
Mohamed, Ismail (Chief Justice of South Africa), 41
Mohan, Tom, 94
Montgomery, Clare, 71–72, 76
Montrose, Duke of, 97, 292, 368
Morison, Thomas, Mr Justice, 62
Morris, Bill (General Secretary, TGWU), 88
Morritt, Sir Andrew (Chancellor), 284
Moseneke, Dikgang (Deputy Chief Justice, Constitutional Court of South Africa), 378
Mosson, Alex (Lord Provost of Glasgow), 175, 183
Moules, Richard (judicial assistant), 246, 263, 277
Moynihan, Gerry, 103, 307
Msaka, Bright and Primrose, 108
Mthiyane, Ken, J (Supreme Court of Appeal of South Africa), 378
Mugabe, Robert (President of Zimbabwe), 336
Mulholland, Frank (Solicitor General of Scotland), 300
Muluzi, Dr Bakili (President of Malawi), 107–08, 196, 218, 234
Muluzi, Patricia, 107
Mummery, John, Lord Justice, 284
Munden, Gail, 158, 168–69, 182, 230, 265–67, 288
Munro, Kenneth, 88
Munro, Wayne, 322
Murphy, Sean, 294
Murphy, Sergeant, 321
Murray, Andy (tennis player), 273
Murray, Duncan, 217
Murray, John (Chief Justice of Ireland), 286–87
Murray, Scott (rugby player), 267
Mustill, Lord, 5–6, 14, 16, 28, 30–31, 119

Napier of Magdala, Lord, 80, 97, 98, 178
Naughtie, Jim (BBC Today programme), 11
Neill of Bladen, Lady, 333–34
Neill of Bladen, Lord, 314, 333
Neuberger of Abbotsbury, Lord, 284, 287–88, 290, 293, 308, 321, 323n, 324, 327–28, 337, 340, 347, 349, 353, 355, 360–61, 364, 372, 380, 382–83
Newall, Lady, 167

Newbatt, Akash (judicial assistant), 131, 159
Newman, George, Mr Justice, 272
Nicoll, Alexander (Lord Mayor of Westminster), 295
Nicholls of Birkenhead, Lady, 14, 184
Nicholls of Birkenhead, Lord, 11, 14, 30, 33, 51, 68, 71, 76, 89, 94–96, 106, 111, 119, 142–45, 152, 169, 172–73, 182, 184, 193–95, 200, 203, 205, 208, 211, 213, 215–17, 227–28, 230–32, 234–37, 239, 241, 255, 259–63, 267, 274–75, 277, 283–84, 287–88, 290, 308
Nichols, Colin, 71
Nickson, Lord, 154
Nimmo Smith, William, Lord, 5
Nkabinde, Bess, J (Constitutional Court of South Africa), 378
Noble, Iain, 53
Nolan, Lord, 6, 52, 54, 56, 58, 70, 75, 141, 152
Norrie, Kenneth, Professor, 227
Nugee, Christopher, 372

Obama, Barak (US President), 373
O'Cathain, Baroness, 383
Oliver, Dawn, Professor, 88, 358, 362
Oliver, Michael (Lord Mayor of London), 166
Oliver of Aylmerton, Lord, 20
Olsen, Terry (Conseil d'Etat), 384
Omar, Dr Dullah (Minister of Justice, South Africa), 41
Onatade, Ayoola, 320–21, 324, 329, 341, 371
O'Neill, Aidan, 307
O'Regan, Kate, J (Constitutional Court of South Africa), 346, 378, 384
Osadebay, J (Court of Appeal of The Bahamas), 233
Osborne, Kenneth, Lord, 259, 271
O'Shea, Michael, 286
Otton, Philip, Lord Justice, 121
Owen, David (Registrar, Judicial Committee of the Privy Council), 27, 57
Owusu, Elsie, 309, 313
Oxfuird, Viscount, 178
Oxner, Sandra (CMJA), 114

Pannick, David, 228, 334, 358, 380, 385
Papadopoulos, Tassos (President of Cyprus), 258
Parker, Emma (judicial assistant), 159, 163, 207
Parker, Jonathan, Lord Justice, 198, 379
Parker-Bowles, Camilla, 100, 239–40
Paterson, Alan, Professor, 224, 227
Paton, Ann, Lady, 103
Patullo, Sir Bruce (Governor, Bank of Scotland), 44, 51
Peacock, Patrick and Virginia, 379
Pearson, David, 328
Peat, Sir Michael, 379
Penman, David (*Daily Record*), 57
Penrose, George, Lord, 158, 283
Perham, Richard, Professor, 264
Perkins, Alice, 348
Perry, David, 194, 274
Perthick, Jan (High Sheriff of Greater London), 295
Philip, HRH Prince, The Duke of Edinburgh, 9n, 151–54, 156–57, 238, 240, 250, 275, 308, 343
Phillips, Sir Hayden, 98, 163, 190–91, 208, 227, 352
Phillips, Peter, 149
Phillips of Worth Matravers, Lord, 6, 30, 54, 76–79, 84, 106, 118, 132, 159, 166, 236, 241–42, 247, 273, 275, 278, 284, 286–87, 289, 298, 302, 308, 316, 319, 327, 331–32, 335–37, 339–40, 343–44, 346, 348, 352–61, 362, 364, 366–67, 369–72, 374, 379–82, 384–85
Pinochet, Augusto, General, 64, 67–71, 74–79, 81–82, 210
Pochard, Marcel (Conseil d'Etat), 272
Pollock, Gordon, 223
Potter, Sir Mark (President, Family Division), 320–21
Porter, Dame Shirley, 140
Pownall, Michael, 380
Prashar, Baroness, 319, 326, 331
Pritchard, Kenneth, 20, 24, 44, 50
Prochaska, Elizabeth (judicial assistant), 340
Procter, Diana (Council of Law Reporting), 360
Prosser, William, Lord, 85, 122, 314

Quinn, Joyce, MP, 68

Ramsay of Cartvale, Lady, 154
Randall, Mr (Gray's Inn), 11, 19
Raulinga, Joe, 162
Reader, Eddi (Scottish singer-songwriter), 299

Index of Names

Reed, Robert, Lord, 60, 139, 199, 252
Rees-Mogg, William (*The Times*), 81, 140
Rehnquist, William (Chief Justice, US Supreme Court), 117
Reid, Kenneth, Professor, 22, 202
Reid, Lord, 1, 9, 80, 108, 205, 386
Renton of Mount Harry, Lord, 73
Rhee, Deok Joo (judicial assistant), 119, 131
Rice, Frances, 49, 75, 80, 87, 135–36, 154, 159, 161
Richardson, Sir Ivor (President, Court of Appeal of New Zealand), 118
Rider, Barry, Professor, 137, 167, 203
Rifkind, Malcolm, MP, 26, 28, 128, 196
Risk, Douglas, Sheriff Principal, 103
Ritchie, Iona, 112
Roberts, John (Chief Justice, US Supreme Court), 384
Robertson, Rev Charles, 10, 154, 342–43
Robertson, Sir Lewis, 87
Robertson of Port Ellen, Lord, 10, 197
Robinson, Geoffrey, MP, 73, 81
Robinson, Sir Ian, 57, 197
Robinson, Olivia, Professor, 282
Robinson, Patrick (judicial assistant), 119, 131
Roddick, Andy (tennis player), 273
Roddick, Graham, 183
Rodger, Christine, 144
Rodger of Earlsferry, Lord, 5, 8, 13, 17, 24, 32, 40, 43, 52, 60–61, 97–98, 104, 112, 114, 119, 126, 130, 133, 135–38, 143–44, 147, 150–51, 158, 162, 164–65, 168–70, 172, 179, 185–87, 189–80, 194–95, 198–99, 202–07, 212–14, 221, 223–24, 227–28, 230, 232, 234, 237, 239, 241–42, 246, 249–50, 252–59, 261–63, 275, 277, 279, 281, 283–85, 289, 291, 294, 300, 303, 307–08, 314, 318, 321–22, 327, 329, 332, 337, 339–41, 344–45, 347, 349–55, 359, 361, 363, 366, 368, 370–74, 378–80, 382–85
Rose, Sir Christopher, 54, 321
Ross, Lord (Lord Justice Clerk), 17–18, 22, 27, 41, 43, 46, 144, 283, 358
Rowallan, Lord, 178
Rowe, Jenny (Chief Executive, UK Supreme Court), 320, 324, 329, 339, 343, 347, 349, 353, 358, 363, 370, 374–75, 379, 381
Roy, Kenneth, 301
Royall of Blaisdon, Baroness, 382

Rozakis, Christos, Professor, 304
Rozenberg, Joshua, 125, 203, 230, 257, 359
Rudden, Bernard, Professor, 59
Rumsfelt, Donald, 177
Russell, The Earl, 185
Russell, Sir Muir, 116, 120, 161

Sabharwal, Y K (Chief Justice of India), 273
Sachs, Albie, J (Constitutional Court of South Africa), 291, 378
Saeed al-Sahhaf, Mohammed (Minister of Information, Iraq), 180
Sales, Philip, 335
Salmon, Christine, 315, 349–50
Salmond, Alec, MSP (First Minister of Scotland), 300, 339
Saltoun of Abernethy, Lady, 78, 97
Saunders, Cheryl, Professor, 305
Saunders, Ernest, 29
Saville of Newdigate, Lord, 6, 30, 51, 54, 76–79, 84, 118, 178, 220, 236–37, 283, 340, 349, 370, 380
Sawyer, Dame Joan (President, Court of Appeal of The Bahamas), 322–23, 352
Schiemann, Konrad, Lord Justice, 132, 138, 153
Schofield, Mrs Anne, 354
Schofield, Derek (Chief Justice of Gibraltar), 114, 354
Schulze, Reiner, Professor, 153
Scott, Joanne, Dr, 203
Scott of Foscote, Lady, 193, 198, 223, 284, 343, 378
Scott of Foscote, Lord, 54, 62, 64n, 106, 118–19, 121, 140, 142, 160, 164, 169, 172, 185, 193–95, 198, 208–09, 212–14, 218–19, 223, 227–28, 231, 235, 239, 256, 259–61, 266, 284–87, 289, 290, 302, 307–08, 326, 340, 343–44, 349, 353, 360, 364, 372, 378, 380, 382–85
Sedley, Stephen, Lord Justice, 138, 198, 272
Segal, Dan, Professor, 334
Seif, Ulrike, Professor, 153
Selby, Rt Rev Peter (Bishop of Worcester), 185
Sellar, David (Lord Lyon King of Arms), 154
Sen, Amartya, Professor, 107
Sen Gupta, Diya (judicial assistant), 159
Sewel, Lord, 20
Shah, Sara, 317

Sharon, Ariel (Prime Minister of Israel), 122, 124
Sheldon, Mark, 161
Sheridan, Tommy, MSP, 86
Sherr, Avron, Professor, 222, 348
Shields, Tom, 183
Singh, Rabinder, 331, 356
Sissons, Peter (BBC newsreader), 147
Skouris, Vassilios, Professor, 304
Skweyiya, Thembile (Constitutional Court of South Africa), 378
Slade, Christopher, Lord Justice, 141
Slater, Admiral Sir Jock, 23
Slater, Matthew (judicial assistant), 277
Slivik, Dr, 380
Sloan, Alan, 381
Slynn of Hadley, Lady, 61, 88, 166
Slynn of Hadley, Lord, 3–4, 6, 16, 25, 27, 32–33, 50, 54, 59, 62–64, 67–71, 84–85, 88–89, 94, 96, 104, 106, 109–11, 117–19, 117–19, 127, 129, 137, 141, 158–60, 166, 206, 229–30, 236, 254, 373–74
Small, Mrs Margaret, 17–18, 20, 24
Smillie, Carol (BBC presenter), 99
Smith, Anne, Lady, 56, 135, 136, 199, 252, 270
Smith, Elvind, Professor, 304
Smith, Irvine, Sheriff, 282
Smith, Janet, Lord Justice, 37
Smith, John, MP, 28
Smith, Sir Thomas Broun, Professor, 59
Soley, Clive, MP, 203
Sorabjee, Soli, 273
Southwell, Robert, 49
Starmer, Keir, 213
Steel of Aikwood, Lord, 87, 107, 134, 162, 196, 218, 368
Steel of Aikwood, Lord and Lady, 53
Stephen, Christopher (judicial assistant), 340, 354, 357, 361, 385
Stern, Baroness, 287
Stewart, Alan, MP, 26
Stewart, David (Scotland Office Justice Department), 112–14, 252, 270
Stewart, David and Elisabeth, 310
Steyn, Lord, 6, 22, 28, 29, 42, 49–50, 54, 62, 64, 68, 71, 74, 80, 93, 103, 106, 110, 118–19, 123, 125, 127, 129, 137, 141–43, 145, 147, 159, 164–65, 167–69, 172, 186, 188, 193–94, 198, 204–06, 209–11, 213–15,

Steyn, Lord – contd
219, 221, 227–28, 230, 232, 234, 236, 238, 241, 246, 251, 253, 262–63, 265, 274, 304
Stirling, Mrs Hannah, 183
Stirling-Aird, Patrick, 200
Stirn, Bernard (Conseil d'Etat), 272
Strathclyde, Lord, 69, 188, 212, 302, 380, 382
Straw, Jack, MP (Lord Chancellor), 69–70, 78, 81–82, 128, 196, 234, 283, 306, 308, 315, 317, 332, 335–37, 348–49, 352, 377, 381
Stuart, Moira (BBC newsreader), 14
Stuart Smith, Sir Murray, 354
Summers, John (judicial assistant), 277
Sumption, Jonathan, 223, 331, 360–61, 364
Sutherland, Ranald, Lord, 18, 31, 46, 52, 97, 283
Swinney, John, MSP, 162, 188

Tam, Robin, 356
Taylor, Claudia, 162
Taylor, Kay (judicial assistant), 131, 159, 244
Templeman, Lord, 151
Templeton, Lord and Lady, 34
Thatcher, Baroness, 128, 152, 166
Thatcher, Sir Denis, 166
Thatcher, Sir Mark, 330n
Theron, Leona, J (High Court of South Africa), 312
Thomas of Cwmgiedd, Lord, 325n
Thompson-Gordon, Clover, 311
Thomson, Joe, Professor, 47, 56, 227
Thomson, Katy, 343
Thorpe, Mathew, Lord Justice, 55
Tipping, Andrew, J (Court of Appeal of New Zealand), 152, 184
Tombs, Lord, 43, 51
Toohey, John, J (Bloody Sunday Inquiry), 178
Tordoff, Lord, 68, 89, 93–94
Townsend, John (judicial assistant), 340
Tracey, Catherine (judicial assistant), 246, 260, 263–64, 272, 303
Treitel, G H, Professor, 334
Tudor, Philippa, 245, 304
Tumim, Sir Stephen, 14
Turner, Sir Michael, 354
Tweedie, Melanie (judicial assistant), 226
Tyre, Colin, Lord, 293

Ullrich, Kay, MSP, 90
Ullswater, Lord, 178

Index of Names

Underhill, Nicholas, 335

Vallance White, James (Clerk of the Judicial Office), 15, 34, 69, 71, 100–01, 152, 158–61, 193, 277, 288
van der Westhuizen, Johann (Constitutional Court of South Africa), 378
van Gerven, Professor, 203
van Vught, Frans, Professor, 299
Vaz, Keith, MP, 203
von Bar, Dr Christian, Professor, 132

Wade-Miller, Norma, 311
Wagstaff, Norman, 291
Wakeham, Lord, 88
Walker, Bill, MP, 26
Walker, Michael, 12
Walker of Gestingthorpe, Lord, 159, 163–65, 174, 194, 205, 214, 221, 227–31, 239, 241, 256, 259–60, 284, 290, 293, 302, 308, 321–22, 329, 340–41, 344–45, 355, 359–60, 362, 367, 372, 380, 383
Wallace, Jim, MSP (Deputy First Minister) 10, 91, 97, 108, 269
Wallace of Saltaire, Lord, 382
Wallace of Tankerness, Lord, 368
Waller, Mark, Lord Justice, 7
Waring, Emma (judicial assistant), 226
Wark, Kirsty (BBC presenter), 11–12, 99–100
Warwick, Henry (judicial assistant), 119, 131
Watherstone, John (Registrar, Judicial Committee of the Privy Council), 57, 184
Watson, Alan, Professor, 137
Watson, Mike, MSP, 162
Weatherill, Lord, 69, 150
Weekes, Anesta, 281
Weir, Bruce, Lord, 178, 283–85
Wessex, Earl and Countess of, 149
West, Margaret, 191
West, Peter (Secretary, Strathclyde University), 47, 55, 92, 175, 183, 191, 245, 290, 300, 376

West of Spithead, Lord, 346
Wheatley, John, Lord, 103
Wheeler-Booth, Sir Michael, 34, 88
Widdecombe, Ann, MP, 201
Wilberforce, Lord, 7, 9, 108, 151, 250
Wild, Robin, 294
Wilford, Derek, Lieutenant Colonel, 178
Wilkinson, Wendy, 113
William, HRH Prince, 36, 100, 149
Williams, John, 55
Williams, Rt Rev Rowan (Archbishop of Canterbury), 240, 343
Williams of Mostyn, Lord, 95, 128,187–88, 197
Wilmot, Catherine, 295
Wilson, Gerry, 358
Wilson, Joe, 237
Wilson, W A (Bill), Professor, 314
Wilson of Tillyorn, Lord, 43, 90, 133, 144, 154, 368, 383
Winfield, Sir Percy, 264
Winterton, Jules, 203
Woolf, Lady, 106, 166, 191, 223
Woolf, Lord, 4, 6, 8, 20, 30, 39, 61, 72, 104, 106, 110, 117, 159, 116–67, 184–85, 191, 211–12, 222–23, 231, 241, 249, 254, 260, 274, 308, 383
Wright, John, 52
Wyrzykowski, Miroslaw, 296
Wyse, Morag, 56

Yakob, Siti (President, CMJA), 311–13, 331
Yong, Pung How (Chief Justice of Singapore), 92
Yudkin, Michael, Professor, 221

Zacca, Edward, J (President, Cayman Islands Court of Appeal), 213
Zellick, Graham (Vice Chancellor, University of London), 167
Zimmerman, Reinhard, Professor, 32

Index of Events

American College of Trial Lawyers—
  50th annual meeting (Washington 2000), 117
  Honorary Fellowship (Hawaii 2000), 104
Bahrain Constitutional Court opening (2005), 241–45
CMJA annual council meetings—
  Jersey (2004), 225
  London (2002), 162–63
  Singapore (1999), 92
CMJA triennial conferences—
  Bermuda (2007), 310–13
  Cape Town (1997), 41
  Edinburgh (2000), 111–15
  Malawi (2003), 196–97
Conseil Constitutionnel seminar (1997), 39–40
Cyprus Supreme Court inauguration (2005), 258
Diana, Princess of Wales, death (1997), 35–36, 38
Elizabeth, HM The Queen, Golden Jubilee (2002), 151–57
Elizabeth, HM The Queen Mother, death (2002), 147–50
EU COSAC meeting (Helsinki 1999), 93–95
General Election (May 1997), 24–26
General Election (June 2001), 128
General Election (May 2005), 239
House of Lords reform—
  Constitutional Reform Bill (2004–05), 211–12, 216–18, 222, 231
  hereditary peers removed (1999), 98
  House of Lords Bill (1998–99), 67, 69, 89, 95–98
  Royal Commission (1999), 88
  tributes in the House to the Law Lords (2009), 381–83
Hutton Inquiry, death of Dr David Kelly (2003), 192–93, 197, 209–10
Italian Constitutional Court seminar (2007), 296–98
JCPC sittings overseas—
  Mauritius (2008), 350–52
  The Bahamas (2006), 287
  The Bahamas (2007), 320–23
  The Bahamas (2009), 372
John Paul II, Pope, death (2005), 239–40
Judicial Exchanges—
  Conseil d'Etat (1997), 39–40
  Conseil d'Etat (2001), 138–39
  Conseil d'Etat (2006), 272
  Franco-British (2003), 199–200
  Spanish-British (2003), 197, 198–99
  UK-South African (2009), 377–78
Kosovo War (1999), 81–82
Lionel Cohen Lecture, Israel (2001), 122–25
Scottish Parliament—
  election (May 2007), 300
  first meeting (2001), 90
  official opening (2001), 86
  referendum (1997), 36
  Scotland Bill (1997–98), 59–61, 64–66
Second Gulf War (2003), 176–78, 179–81, 222
Seventh World Congress of Constitutional Law (Athens, 2007), 304–05
State Opening of Parliament (1996), 9
State Opening of Parliament (1998), 66–67
Stone of Destiny return to Scotland (1996), 15
Supreme Court—
  Crown Court leaves Middlesex Guildhall (2007), 294–96
  Middlesex Guildhall handed over to MoJ (2009), 370–71
  new court announced (2003), 186–90
Terrorist attacks—
  9/11 Twin Towers tragedy (2001), 131–33
  Glasgow Airport (2007), 305
  London (2005), 247–48, 251